Warfare in History

WAR CRUEL AND SHARP

ENGLISH STRATEGY UNDER EDWARD III, 1327–1360

Warfare in History

General Editor: Matthew Bennett
ISSN 1358–779X

Already published

The Battle of Hastings: Sources and Interpretations
edited and introduced by Stephen Morillo

Infantry Warfare in the Early Fourteenth Century:
Discipline, Tactics, and Technology
Kelly DeVries

The Art of Warfare in Western Europe during
the Middle Ages, from the Eighth Century to 1340 (second edition)
J. F. Verbruggen

Knights and Peasants:
The Hundred Years War in the French Countryside
Nicholas Wright

Society at War: The Experience of
England and France during the Hundred Years War
edited by Christopher Allmand

The Circle of War in the Middle Ages:
Essays on Medieval Military and Naval History
edited by Donald J. Kagay and L. J. Andrew Villalon

The Anglo-Scots Wars, 1513–1550: A Military History
Gervase Phillips

The Norwegian Invasion of England in 1066
Kelly DeVries

The Wars of Edward III: Sources and Interpretations
edited and introduced by Clifford J. Rogers

The Battle of Agincourt: Sources and Interpretations
Anne Curry

WAR CRUEL AND SHARP

ENGLISH STRATEGY UNDER EDWARD III, 1327–1360

Clifford J. Rogers

THE BOYDELL PRESS

First published 2000
The Boydell Press, Woodbridge

ISBN 0 85115 804 8

The Boydell Press is an imprint of Boydell and Brewer Ltd
PO Box 9, Woodbridge, Suffolk IP12 3DF, UK
and of Boydell and Brewer Inc.
PO Box 41026, Rochester, NY 14604–4126, USA
website: http://www.boydell.co.uk

A catalogue record for this book is available
from the British Library

Library of Congress Cataloging-in-Publication Data
Rogers, Clifford J.
    War cruel and sharp : English strategy under Edward III, 1327–1360 /
Clifford J. Rogers.
        p. cm. – (Warfare in history, ISSN 1358–779X)
    Includes bibliographical references (p.) and index.
    ISBN 0–85115–804–8 (alk. paper)
    1. Edward III, King of England, 1327–1377 – Military leadership.
2. Military art and science – England – History – Medieval, 500–1500.
3. Great Britain – History – Edward III, 1327–1377. 4. Great Britain –
History, Military – 1066–1485. I. Title. II. Series.
DA233.R64 2001
944'.025 – dc21   00–042922

This publication is printed on acid-free paper

Printed in Great Britain by
St Edmundsbury Press Ltd, Bury St Edmunds, Suffolk

CONTENTS

LIST OF MAPS

To my mother

GENERAL EDITOR'S PREFACE

Between 1337 and 1360 the kingdoms of England and France were engaged in a bitter war, out of which Edward III emerged victorious. Few historians would dispute this, although many have doubted the completeness of his victory as represented by the Treaty of Brétigny. Edward's 1359–60 campaign has been interpreted as a failure, a stalemate, which denied him the crown of France and left him merely to make the best of a situation which had been more favourable a few years earlier, immediately following the battle of Poitiers (1356). This Dr Rogers would refute. For him, 1360 was Edward's personal victory achieved as a result of his thorough knowledge of war (see pp. 421–22). He had learnt the lessons dealt him by the Scots in 1327, turned the tables on them in 1333, and then proceeded to teach them to the French in two long decades of warfare, after which he achieved his aims.

Edward's genius was the combination of the strategic offensive and the tactical defensive: in other words, keeping the enemy on the back foot by devastating *chevauchées* and punishing sieges, while at the same time seeking to draw him into battle, defeat him and bring about a 'political catastrophe' which enabled Edward to dictate peace terms. The author's viewpoint is summarised in the title for Chapter 15, a quote from the chronicler Geoffrey le Baker: 'Eager for battle because of the peace which usually comes with it'. In this interpretation Dr Rogers is truly radical, because he disputes a century's historiography, and current orthodoxy, that when the English conducted *chevauchées* (mounted raids), they sought only to damage the means and reputation of the French king, and indeed hoped to avoid battle. He argues his case strongly that Edward III (in 1346) and his son Edward, Prince of Wales (in 1356) manoeuvred to achieve a position in which they were the defenders and the French the attackers. This gave the English a substantial tactical advantage which they were able to convert into impressive victories and which led eventually to French submission. Edward did not achieve as much as Henry V, of course, who was accepted as heir to the French throne (little good though that did him in the short term, or England in the longer term). But Dr Rogers argues that Edward sought less: a return to the position enjoyed by twelfth-century Angevin monarchs, whose 'empire' included Normandy and most of western France. Certainly, this was the position identified by the 1359 London treaty (and which Brétigny delivered in a reduced form).

Whatever the virtues of the conflicting interpretations, Dr Rogers has invigorated the debate and presented a challenging and cogently-argued thesis. His presentation of medieval warfare should correct many of the misunderstandings still common to many military historians: that rulers and commanders had no concept of strategy; that they were driven solely by misplaced chivalric ideals;

that they thought of little except displaying their knightly skills and personal bravery in the mêlée. This not to say that the two latter influences were not significant – they were – but that rational analyses, just as much as mistakes, were as common as in any other historical period. Employing the models provided by Clausewitz and other theorists and practitioners of war, the author is able to draw out conclusions from his texts which may have been simply ignored by previous commentators. Perhaps this is not surprising for an academic who works for the contemporary military, nor that I, who share that role, should applaud it; but by doing so he enables students and historians of other periods to achieve a much richer understanding than might otherwise have been possible.

The depth and breadth of Dr Rogers' research is remarkable. In addition to a powerful narrative of events, he provides a detailed analysis of a wide variety of historical sources, ranging from unpublished chronicles and documents, to a thorough dissection of better-known materials, which enable us to understand properly the composition of the forces deployed in the campaigns which he describes. So, this book can be mined for information on many issues, from high level politics, diplomacy and strategy, down to the balance of men-at-arms and archers in the English armies (especially) and how they were deployed in the field. The work forms a fitting companion to the same author's *The Wars of Edward III* also published in this series. Together they form a compelling argument for the sheer professionalism at arms of Edward, his companions and his soldiers. It is a great achievement to bring both volumes to publication within a year of each other and so make such a substantial contribution to the understanding of medieval warfare – which is the purpose of this series.

Matthew Bennett
Royal Military Academy Sandhurst
July 2000

PREFACE

Like most works of history, this book started with a question: how was it that in 1360 Edward III, purportedly a bad strategist, and at his accession the ruler of a relatively small, poor, and militarily backward realm, persuaded Jean II, the dauphin, and the Estates of France to accept the Treaty of Brétigny – by which they were to surrender a third of their kingdom to his rule? This result was, as the contemporary Italian chronicler Matteo Villani observed, "as if Capalle had conquered Florence." I have spent the last eight years pursuing the answer to that question, and the results of my research and reflection are presented here.

Looking back on so many hours spent on this project, it is perhaps inevitable that at its close I must ask myself "was it worth it?" It seems to me that it was. For reasons set out in the Introduction, the question of how the English won the first phase of the Hundred Years War is an important one both for military history and for medieval history, and I think the answer I give here is better than any thus far available to historians. Even though I am reworking ground already covered by a number of fine scholars, this book does add some new material, particularly information and insights drawn from several unpublished chronicles. Thanks in part to those sources and in part to approaching the material with a fresh perspective, I have been able to improve the narrative of events in many places, both in the descriptions of campaigns and in the discussions of the strategic decision-making and the diplomacy which set the stage and provided the motives for military action.

This improved narrative is valuable, I think, not only in its own right but also in providing a whole series of case studies in the techniques of fourteenth-century warfare, as conducted by its foremost practitioners. All the tools in the medieval commander's strategic "kit bag" are displayed: battle, and the maneuverings necessary to prepare the situation for an offer of battle under favorable circumstances; devastation, whether to impede an enemy's foraging, to undermine his economy and political structure, or to provoke him to battle; and sieges, used as bait or as part of a program of conquest. Viewed as a whole, these case studies both refine and add weight to the growing scholarly consensus that medieval warfare was marked by quite sophisticated conceptions of strategy, ones firmly grounded in the Clausewitzian unity of politics and war. This should come as no surprise, for we are looking at a period when those who directed strategy also ruled, and also fought with sword in hand to implement their own designs.

This book is an expanded and revised version of my doctoral dissertation, and so I must acknowledge my debt to my dissertation committee: John F. Guilmartin, Jr., Williamson Murray, and Frank Pegues, of the Ohio State University. My colleagues at the United States Military Academy have shared their enthusiasm for history with me, and a number of them have read and commented on portions of the manuscript. Dr Richard Barber read the whole manuscript and offered a number of useful suggestions. Dr Mark Buck kindly provided me with a copy of his transcription of the *Historia Roffensis* so that I could check my own, and corrected my translation of it in places. Drs Geri Smith and Kim Kagan discussed some difficult passages of (respectively) French and Latin with me. The maps, except 7-1 and the map of Scotland, were prepared by Mr Frank Martini. I also owe thanks to the U.S.-U.K. Fulbright Commission and the Institute of Historical Research for the opportunity to spend a year doing research in London; to O.S.U. for a Presidential Fellowship; to Yale University and the John M. Olin Foundation for supporting a postdoctoral fellowship during which I spent some of my time working on this book; and to the Faculty Development and Research Fund of the United States Military Academy, which funded several short research trips in support of this project. The staff of the USMA library has been very helpful, and I am much indebted to Vassar College and the staff of its library for their courtesy in extending borrowing privileges to me. My wife, Shelley Reid, has patiently made many sacrifices for the sake of this book.

This book is dedicated to my mother, Jacqueline H. Rogers, who fostered my love of reading, provided for the superb undergraduate education I received at Rice University, and has always been my role model in many ways.

A Note on Money

In England, the basic monetary units were the silver penny (abbreviated "d.," from the Latin *denarius*), the shilling (abbreviated "s.," and worth 12d.), and the pound sterling (£), worth 20s., or 240 pence. A mark was worth ⅔ of a pound (i.e. 13s. 4d.). An idea of purchasing power can be gained by considering that the daily wage for a farm laborer in the 1330s was under 2d.

French money of account was based on *livres* (l.) worth 20 *sous*, each worth 12 *deniers*. The value of the *livre* varied depending on its origin and current economic conditions, but the normal exchange rate in the fourteenth century was 5–6 *livres tournois* (l.t.) per pound sterling.

The florin was a gold coin of varying weight and value depending on its place and time of minting; the florin of Florence (the original) was worth 36d. sterling in 1338. The *écu* was a similar French coin, worth 40d. sterling in 1360.

LIST OF ABBREVIATIONS

Manuscript Documentary sources

WBRF		Wardrobe Book of Robert Ferriby, 1334–1337. BL MS Cotton Nero C VIII
WBWF		Wardrobe Book of William Farley, 1359–1360. PRO, E101/393/11
PRO		Public Record Office, London
	C47	Chancery Miscellanea
	C49	Chancery and Exchequer: Parliamentary and Council Proceedings
	C61	Gascon Rolls
	C66	Patent Rolls
	C81	Warrants for the Great Seal
	E101	Exchequer, Accounts Various
	E372	Exchequer, Pipe Rolls
	E359	Exchequer, Lord Treasurer's Remembrancer, Enrolled Lay Subsidies
	PRO31	Roman Transcripts
	SC1	Ancient Correspondence

Printed Documentary Sources

"1339 Campaign Diary"	"Le commencement de la chivauchée de nostre seigneur le roy Edward en le réalme de Fraunce," in *KdL*, 84–93
BB	Letter of Bartholomew Burghersh to John Beauchamp, September 1356, in *KdL*, 385–387
BLF	*Benoit XII (1334–1342). Lettres closes, patentes et curiales se rapportant à la France*, ed. Georges Daumet (Paris: Bibliothèque des écoles française d'Athènes et de Rome, 1920)
CCR	*Calendar of the Close Rolls* (London: HMSO, 1892–1945)
CDS	*Calendar of Documents Relating to Scotland*, ed. Joseph Bain (Edinburgh: HMSO, 1887)
CEPR	*Calendar of Entries in the Papal Registers Relating to Great Britain and Ireland. Papal Letters. Vol. 2: 1305–1342*, ed. T. Bliss (London: PRO, 1895)
CPR	*Calendar of the Patent Rolls* (London: HMSO, 1891–1942)
DEB	F. Bock, *Das deutsch-englische Bündniss von 1335–1342: Quellen* (München: C. H. Beck'she Verlag, 1956)

EMDP	Pierre Chaplais, *English Medieval Diplomatic Practice. Part I, Documents and Interpretation* (London: HMSO, 1982)
ERS	*Exchequer Rolls of Scotland. Vol. 1: 1264–1359*, eds J. Stuart and G. Burnett (Edinburgh: HMSO, 1878)
GGG	I. A. Nijhoff (ed.), *Gedenkwaardigheden uit de Geschiedenis van Gelderland*, vol. I (Arnhem: P. Nijhoff, 1830)
KdL	Baron Kervyn de Lettenhove (ed.), *Oeuvres de Froissart, tome 18: Pièces justificatives*. Reprint edition (Osnabrück: Biblio Verlag, 1967)
PL	Letter of the Black Prince to the Mayor and citizens of London, 22 October 1356, in H. T. Riley, *Memorials of London Life in the XIIIth, XIVth, XVth Centuries* (London: 1868), 207
PW	Letter of the Black Prince to the Bishop of Worcester, 20 October 1356, in H. T. Riley, *Memorials of London Life in the XIIIth, XIVth, XVth Centuries* (London: 1868), 206–8
RFH	*Foedera, conventiones, litterae etc.*, ed. Thomas Rymer (The Hague, 1739–1745)
RFR	*Foedera, conventiones, litterae etc.*, ed. Thomas Rymer, revised edn by A. Clarke, F. Holbrooke and J. Coley (London: Record Commission, 1816–69)
RP	*Rotuli Parliamentorum*, vol. II, ed. J. Strachey *et al.* (Record Commission: London, 1783)
RS	*Rotuli Scotiae in Turri Londinensi et in Domo Capitulari Westmonasteriensi asservati, vol. I: Edward I–Edward III*, ed. David Macpherson (London: Record Commission, 1814)
RTC	*Registres du Trésor des Chartes*, ed. J. Viard and A. Vallée (Paris: Archives Nationales, 1979–84), t. III, par. 2
Tournai Bulletin	Clifford J. Rogers, "An Unknown News Bulletin from the Siege of Tournai in 1340," *War in History*, 5 (1998)
WBWN	*The Wardrobe Book of William de Norwell, 12 July 1338 to 27 May 1340*, eds Mary Lyon, Bruce Lyon, H. S. Lucas, and Jean de Sturler (Brussels: Commission Royale d'Histoire, 1983)

Printed Chronicles

Acta Bellicosa	"Acta Bellicosa Edwardi Tertii," in J. Moisant, *Le Prince Noir en Aquitaine 1355–6, 1362–70* (Paris: Alphonse Picard et Fils, 1894)
Acts of War	*The Acts of War of Edward III (1346)* in *The Life and Campaigns of the Black Prince*, ed. and tr. Richard Barber (London: Folio Society, 1979) [trans. of *Acta Bellicosa*]
Anonimalle	*Anonimalle Chronicle 1333–1381*, ed. V. H. Galbraith (Manchester: Manchester U.P., 1927)

Anonimalle Brut	*The Anonimalle Chronicle 1307–1334*, eds Wendy R. Childs and John Taylor (York: Yorkshire Archaeological Society [Record Series vol. CXLVII], 1991)
Avesbury	Robert of Avesbury, *De Gestis Mirabilibus Regis Edwardi Tertii*, ed. E. M Thompson (London: Rolls Series, 1889)
Barbour	John Barbour, *The Bruce*, ed. A. A. M. Duncan (Edinburgh: Cannongate Classics, 1997)
Bridlington	*Gesta Edwardi Tertii Auctore Canonico Bridlingtonensi* in *Chronicles of the Reigns of Edward I and Edward II, v. II*, ed. W. Stubbs (London: Rolls Series, 1883)
Chron. Anon. Cant.	*Chronica Johannis de Reading et anonymi Cantuariensis, 1346–1367*, ed. J. Tait (Manchester: Manchester U.P., 1914)
Chron. Com. Flandr.	*Chronicon comitum Flandrensium* in *Corpus Chronicorum Flandriae*, ed. J. J. de Smet (Brussels: Commission Royale d'Histoire, 1837), vol. I
Chron. des quat. prem. Valois	*Chronique des quatre premiers Valois (1327–1393)*, ed. Siméon Luce (Paris: Sociètè de l'histoire de France, 1862)
Chron. Jean II et Charles V	*Chronique des règnes de Jean II et Charles V, tome I (1350–1364)*, ed. R. Delachenal (Paris: Société de l'histoire de France, 1916)
Chron. Normande	*Chronique Normande du XIVe siècle*, eds A. and E. Molinier (Paris: Société de l'histoire de France, 1882)
Chronographia	*Chronographia regum Francorum*, ed. H. Moranvillé (Paris: Société de l'histoire de France, 1891–7)
Chron. Pays-Bas	*Chronique des Pays-Bays, de France, d'Angleterre et de Tournai* in *Corpus Chronicorum Flandriae*, ed. J. J. de Smet (Brussels: Commission Royale d'Histoire, 1856), vol. III
Cont. Manuel, 1328–39	Clifford J. Rogers, "A Continuation of the *Manuel d'histoire de Philippe VI* for the years 1328–39," *English Historical Review* CXIV (1999) [Note also *Cont. Manuel, 1339–46*, under Manuscript Chronicles, below]
Dynter	Edmond Dynter, *Chronique des Ducs de Brabant*, ed. P. F. X. de Ram (Brussels: Commission Royale d'Histoire, 1854–60), vol. II
English Brut	*The Brut or the Chronicle of England*, ed. F. W. Brie (London: Early English Text Soc., 1906–8)
Eulogium	*Eulogium historiarum*, ed. F. S. Haydon (London: Rolls Series, 1858–63), vol. III
Fordun	John of Fordun, *Chronica Gentis Scotorum* [Historians of Scotland, v. I], ed. William F. Skene (Edinburgh: Edmonston and Douglas, 1871)
Fr. Chron. London	*French Chronicle of London*, ed. G. J. Aungier. *Camden Series* XXVIII (1844)
Grandes chroniques	*Grandes chroniques de France*, ed. Jules Viard (Paris: Société de l'histoire de France, 1920–53)

Hemingburgh	*Chronicon Domini Walteri de Hemingburgh*, ed. H. C. Hamilton (London: English Historical Society, 1849), vol. II [Includes continuations of Guisborough's chronicle]
Knighton	Henry Knighton, *Chronicon*, ed. J. R. Lumby (London: Rolls Series, 1895)
Lanercost	*Chronicon de Lanercost, MCCI–MCCCXLVI*, ed. J. Stevenson (Edinburgh: The Bannatyne Club, 1839)
Le Baker	Galfridi le Baker de Swynebroke [Geoffrey le Baker], *Chronicon*, ed. E. M. Thompson (Oxford: Clarendon, 1889)
Le Bel	Jean le Bel, *Chronique de Jean le Bel*, eds Jules Viard and Eugène Déprez (Paris: Société de l'histoire de France, 1904)
Le Muisit	Gilles le Muisit, *Chronique et Annales*, ed. H. Lemaître (Paris: Société de l'histoire de France, 1906)
Lescot	Richard Lescot, *Chronique (1328–1344), suivie de la continuation de cette chronique (1344–1364)*, ed. J. Lemoine (Paris: Société de l'histoire de France, 1896)
Melsa	Thomas Burton, *Chronica Monasterii de Melsa*, ed. E. A. Bond (London: Rolls Series, 1866–8)
M. Villani, *Cronica*	Matteo Villani, *Cronica*, in Roberto Palmarocchi (ed.), *Cronisti del Trecento* (Milan: Rizzoli, 1935)
M. Villani (*Porta*)	Matteo Villani, *Cronica*, ed. G. Porta (Parma: Fondazione Pietro Bembo, 1995)
Murimuth	Adam Murimuth, *Adae Murimuth. Continuatio Chronicarum*, ed. E. M. Thompson (London: Rolls Series, 1889)
Nangis	Guillaume de Nangis *et al.*, *Chronique Latine de Guillaume de Nangis de 1113 à 1300, avec les continuations de cette chronique de 1300 à 1368*, ed. H. Géraud (Paris: Société de l'histoire de France, 1843), vol. II
Pluscardensis	*Liber Pluscardensis* [Historians of Scotland, vol. VII], ed. Felix J. H. Skene (Edinburgh: William Patterson, 1877)
Reading	Johannis de Reading, *Chronica Johannis de Reading et anonymi Cantuariensis, 1346–1367*, ed. J. Tait (Manchester: Manchester U.P., 1914)
Récits	*Récits d'un bourgeois de Valenciennes*, ed. Kervyn de Lettenhove (Louvain: Lefever, 1877)
Scalacronica	Sir Thomas Gray, *Scalacronica*, ed. Joseph Stevenson (Edinburgh: Maitland Club, 1836)
Scalacronica (Maxwell)	Sir Thomas Gray, *Scalacronica*, ed. and tr. Sir Herbert Maxwell (Edinburgh: Maclehose, 1907)
Tournai Chronicles	*Tournai Chronicles*, in Jean Froissart, *Oeuvres*, ed. Kervyn de Lettenhove (Bruxelles, 1870 etc. Reprint: Osnabrück: Biblio Verlag, 1967), vol. 25, 344–65
Venette	Jean de Venette, *The Chronicle of Jean de Venette*, tr. J. Birdsall, ed. R. A. Newhall (New York: Columbia U.P., 1953)

Vie du Prince Noir	Chandos Herald, *La Vie du Prince Noir*, ed. Diana B. Tyson (Tübingen: Max Niemeyer Verlag, 1975)
Villani, *Cronica*	Giovanni Villani, *Cronica*, in Roberto Palmarocchi (ed.), *Cronisti del Trecento* (Milan: Rizzoli, 1935) [Note also M. Villani, above]
Wyntoun	Andrew of Wyntoun, *Orygynale Cronykil of Scotland* [Historians of Scotland, vols II, III, IX], ed. David Laing (Edinburgh: Edmonston and Douglas, 1872–79)

Manuscript Chronicles

AM Brut	Fifteenth-century copy of an early redaction of the French *Brut* to Halidon Hill. British Library, London. Additional Manuscripts, 18462
Chron. CCCO	Unpublished independent *Brut* continuation, MS 78 of Corpus Christi College, Oxford
Chron. St. Omer	An anonymous chronicle related to the garrison of St. Omer, covering the years 1342–1347. Citations are to MS Fr. 693 of the Bibliothèque Nationale in Paris
Cleopatra Brut	Another French *Brut* manuscript, of a later redaction similar to the English version. British Library, Cottonian MSS, Cleopatra D III
Cont. Manuel, 1339–46	A second continuation, for 1339–1346, of the *Manuel d'histoire de Philippe VI*. Citations are to MS Fr. 693 of the Bibliothèque Nationale in Paris. [Note also *Cont. Manuel, 1328–39*, under Printed Chronicles, above.]
Historia Aurea	Bodleian Library, Oxford, MS 240
Historia Roffensis	William of Dene (?), *Historia Roffensis*. British Library, London: Cottonian MSS, Faustina B V
Pakington	Epitome of the chronicle of William de Pakington, Clerk and Treasurer of the Black Prince's Household in Gascony. British Library, London. Cottonian MSS, Tiberius A VI
Pipewell	*Chronica Monasterii de Pipwell*. British Library, Cottonian MSS, Caligula A XIII and Harleian MSS, 624. Citations are to the Caligula MS
Royal Brut	Long *Brut* continuation in French, 1307–1329. British Library, London. Royal MSS, 20 A XVIII

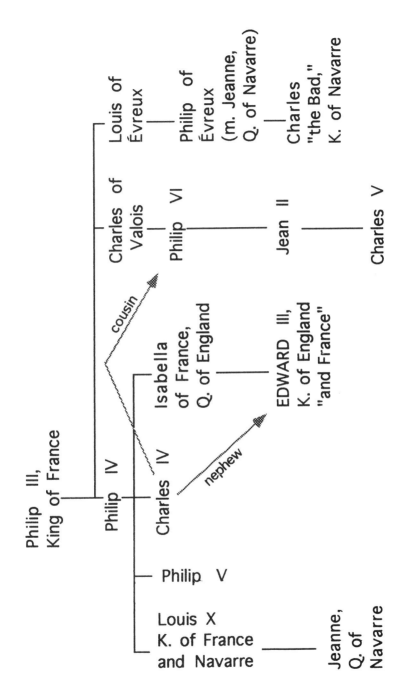

Genealogical table showing the French and English royal families.

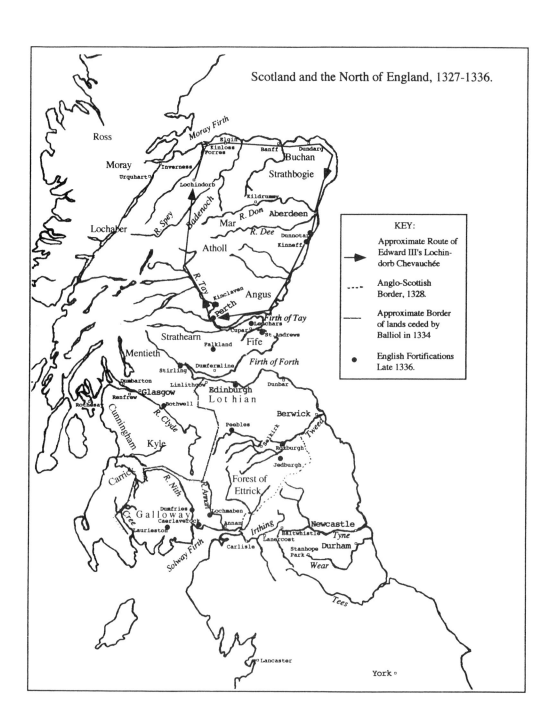

Scotland and the North of England, 1327-1336.

KEY:

→ Approximate Route of Edward III's Lochindorb Chevauchée

---- Anglo-Scottish Border, 1328.

— Approximate Border of lands ceded by Balliol in 1334

• English Fortifications Late 1336.

Ross

Moray Firth

Moray

Elgin
Kinloss
Forres
Banff
Dundarg
Buchan
Inverness
Strathbogie
Urquhart
Lochindorb
Kildrummy
Badenoch
R. Spey
Mar
R. Don
Aberdeen
Lochaber
R. Dee
Dunnottar
Kinneff
Atholl
R. Tay
Kinclaven
Angus
Perth
Firth of Tay
Leuchars
Cupar
St. Andrews
Strathearn
Falkland
Fife
Mentieth
Dunfermline
Firth of Forth
Stirling
Linlithgow
Dunbar
Dumbarton
Glasgow
Edinburgh
Renfrew
Lothian
Rothesay
Bothwell
Cunningham
R. Clyde
Berwick
Peebles
Kyle
Selkirk
Roxburgh
Tweed
Carrick
R. Nith
R. Annan
Jedburgh
Forest of Ettrick
Cree
Galloway
Dumfries
Lochmaben
Caerlaverock
Annan
Newcastle
Laurieston
Irthing
Haltwhistle
Tyne
Solway Firth
Lanercost
Durham
Carlisle
Stanhope Park
Wear
Tees
Lancaster
York

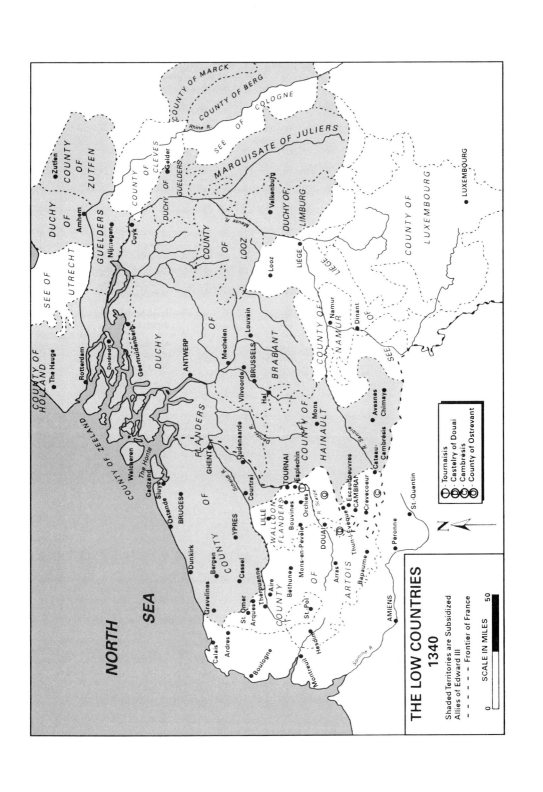

NORTH
SEA

COUNTY OF MARCK

COUNTY OF BERG

SEE OF COLOGNE

Rhine R.

SEE OF
UTRECHT

DUCHY
OF
GUELDERS

Zutfen

COUNTY
OF
ZUTFEN

Amhem

GUELDERS

Nijmegen

Cuyk

COUNTY
OF
CLEVES

DUCHY
OF
GUELDERS

Gelder

MARQUISATE OF JULIERS

Valkenburg

DUCHY OF
LIMBURG

Meuse R.

COUNTY
OF
LUXEMBOURG

LUXEMBOURG

COUNTY OF HOLLAND

The Hague

Rotterdam

Dordrecht

Geertruidenberg

COUNTY OF ZEELAND

Walcheren

The Honte

Cadzand

Sluys

Ostende

BRUGES

Dunkirk

Gravelines

Calais

Ardres

Boulogne

DUCHY
OF
BRABANT

ANTWERP

Mechelen

Vilvoorde

BRUSSELS

Hal

Louvain

COUNTY
OF
LOOZ

Looz

LIÈGE

SEE OF
LIÈGE

Dinant

Namur

COUNTY OF NAMUR

COUNTY
OF
HAINAULT

Mons

Avesnes

Chimay

Cambrésis

Cateau

FLANDERS

GHENT

Oudenaarde

Courtrai

YPRES

Cassel

Bergues

Schelde R.

Dendre R.

TOURNAI

Esplechin

Bouvines

Orchies

LILLE

WALLOON
FLANDERS

Mons-en-Pévèle

COUNTY
OF
FLANDERS

Bethune

Aire

Therouanne

St. Omer

Arques

St-Pol

Hesdin

Montreuil

COUNTY
OF
DOUAI

R. Scarpe

Thun-l'Evêque

Escaubœuvres

CAMBRAI

Crèvecoeur

R. Sambre

Peronne

Bapaume

Arras

ARTOIS

Somme R.

AMIENS

St.-Quentin

N

THE LOW COUNTRIES
1340

Shaded Territories are Subsidized
Allies of Edward III

- - - - Frontier of France

SCALE IN MILES

0   50

⊙ Tournaisis
⊙ Castelry of Douai
⊙ Cambrésis
⊙ County of Ostrevant

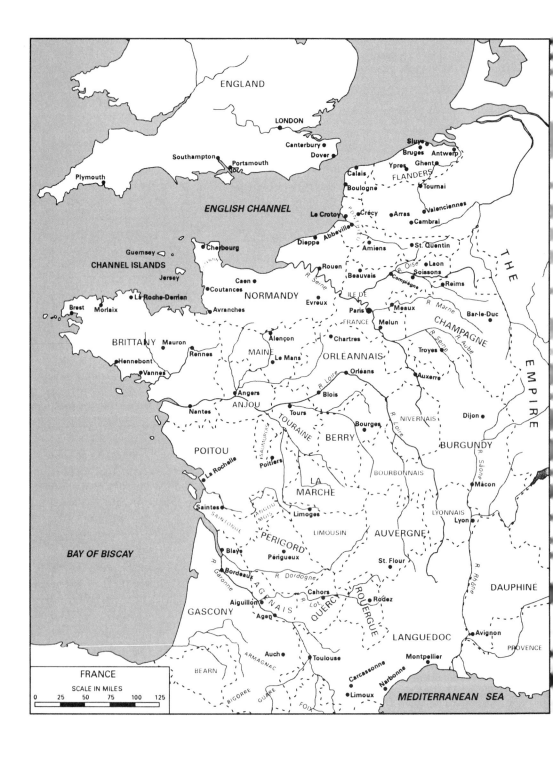

ENGLAND

LONDON

Canterbury
Dover

Southampton
Portsmouth

Plymouth

Sluys
Bruges Antwerp
Ypres Ghent
Calais FLANDERS
Boulogne Tournai

ENGLISH CHANNEL

Le Crotoy Crécy Arras
Valenciennes
Abbeville Cambrai
Dieppe Amiens St. Quentin

Guernsey
CHANNEL ISLANDS
Jersey

Cherbourg

Rouen Beauvais Laon
Soissons Reims
Compiègne

R Oise

THE

Caen
Coutances

La-Roche-Derrien

NORMANDY

Evreux

ILE DE

Paris

Meaux

Melun

R Marne

Bar-le-Duc

CHAMPAGNE

EMPIRE

Brest Morlaix
Avranches
FRANCE

R Seine

Mauron
BRITTANY

Rennes

MAINE
Alençon

Le Mans

Chartres

Troyes

R Aube
R Seine

Hennebont

ORLEANNAIS

Vannes

Angers
ANJOU

Nantes

TOURAINE
Tours

Blois

R Loire

Orléans

Auxerre

NIVERNAIS

Dijon

BERRY

Bourges

R Loire

BURGUNDY

POITOU

La Rochelle

Poitiers

LA
MARCHE

BOURBONNAIS

R Saône

Mâcon

Saintes

Limoges

LYONNAIS

Lyon

BAY OF BISCAY

PERIGORD

LIMOUSIN

AUVERGNE

Blaye
Périgueux

St. Flour

Bordeaux

R Dordogne

DAUPHINE

Aiguillon
Agen

GASCONY

Cahors
QUERC

Rodez

ROUERGUE

R Rhône

Auch

Toulouse

LANGUEDOC

Avignon

PROVENCE

BEARN

ARMAGNAC

Montpellier

FRANCE

SCALE IN MILES

0 25 50 75 100 125

BIGORRE GUARE FOIX

Carcassonne
Narbonne

Limoux

MEDITERRANEAN SEA

CHAPTER ONE

INTRODUCTION

*War is a matter of vital importance to the State; the province of
life or death; the road to survival or ruin. It is mandatory that
it be thoroughly studied.*   Sun Tzu, I.1[1]

THIS BOOK DEALS with English strategy in the wars of Edward III from
1327, the beginning of his reign, up through 1360, when the Treaty of Brétigny
closed the first stage of the Hundred Years War. Chapters II through V trace
Edward's military development from the complete failure of his first campaign,
which led to the "Shameful Peace" of 1328, through his triumphant victory at
Halidon Hill in 1333, and through his stubborn and quite successful efforts to
bring all of Scotland under his sway in the following years. The remaining
eleven chapters are devoted primarily to an examination of his war against the
Valois kingdom of France. Before we turn to the study of the individual
campaigns of our period, however, this chapter will provide some context to
explain why a thorough study of this topic is so important for medieval history
and military history in general.

The Hundred Years War, fought intermittently by France and England
between 1337 and 1453, was perhaps the most important war in European
history. Like the more recent contenders for that title – the Thirty Years War, the
Wars of the French Revolution, and the World Wars – it was at the center of a
period of genuinely revolutionary developments in military history. Indeed, I
have argued elsewhere that the military revolution which reached maturity
during the reign of Edward III sparked the processes of "punctuated equilibrium
evolution" through which European armies became, by the end of the early
modern period, the most powerful military forces the world had ever known.[2] As
with those other wars, however, the importance of the Hundred Years War
extended far beyond strictly military developments. It was, for example, the
midwife of the European "nation-state," which would eventually become the

---

[1] Sun Tzu, *Sun Tzu. The Art of War*, ed. and tr. Samuel B. Griffith (Oxford: Oxford U.P.,
1971), 62.
[2] Clifford J. Rogers, "The Military Revolutions of the Hundred Years War," *Journal of Military
History* 57 (1993), 241–78. Reprinted with revisions in C. J. Rogers (ed.), *The Military
Revolution Debate* (Boulder: Westview, 1995). References below are to the latter. Cf. Michael
Prestwich, *The Three Edwards* (London: Routledge, 1980), 181.

dominant form of political organization over the entire world. At the beginning
of the war, neither France nor England (nor any other realm in Europe) could
reasonably be considered an exemplar of that form of state. The domains of the
King of England, for example, also included the Duchy of Aquitaine and the
County of Ponthieu in France, which in peacetime could provide more than
twenty-five per cent of the royal revenues.[3] The consequent lack of geographic,
linguistic, or cultural unity in his realm makes it impossible to consider it even
an embryonic nation-state. Edward III and the four English kings after him, in
fact, ruled their substantial Continental possessions officially as "Kings of
England and France."[4] And, although I refer to the kingdom of Philip VI and
Jean II as "France" throughout this book, that designation is in some ways
misleading. Even before the outbreak of the war, the Valois king exercised only
the most limited control over many areas of what we now think of as France, and
by the 1360s he had no power at all in Gascony, Saintonge, Limousin, the
Agenais, Poitou, Quercy, Ponthieu, the Calais Pale, Périgord, Guare, Bigorre, or
Rouergue, while Brittany and Flanders had become virtually independent states.
For much of the first half of the fifteenth century, the Valois kings' writs did not
run in Normandy or the vast holdings of the dukes of Burgundy. By the end of
the war, however, Normandy and all the lands in the southwest had been reconquered, including even Gascony, which had not been really ruled by a French
king since the days of the Carolingians. Burgundy, Flanders, and Brittany again
recognized the authority of the French crown.[5] For the first time, the kings of
France truly ruled over a political entity essentially the same as the France of the
modern period. Before the war, it could be difficult to distinguish an
Englishman from a Frenchman – Francophone subjects of English kings often
being referred to as "English French," and easily described as having "turned
French" or "become English" when their political alignment changed – but after
1453 such a differentiation was not only practical, but emotionally charged. It
might be premature to argue that "nationalism" had been born, but it had
certainly at least been conceived.[6]

---

3   Ibid., 167; Sir James H. Ramsay, *Revenues of the Kings of England, 1066–1399* (Oxford:
Clarendon, 1925), Table 1 (facing p. 292), years 1328–31. At the beginning of Edward III's
reign, Bordeaux was perhaps the largest city in his realm. Margaret Wade Labarge, *Gascony:
England's First Colony, 1204–1453* (London: Hamish Hamilton, 1980), 78.
4   From 1340, except between the signing of the agreement at Brétigny in 1360 and the
renewal of the war in 1369. The monarchs of England officially maintained their claim to the
French royal title until the Treaty of Amiens in 1802.
5   These lands did remain at least semi-autonomous for a few decades after the end of the
Hundred Years War, though they were effectively integrated into France by the end of the
1480s; but by the end of the war their dukes recognized the King of France as their sovereign.
6   Cf. the opinion of Professor Edouard Perroy, *The Hundred Years War* (New York: Capricorn, 1965), xxviii: "Out of their [the people of England and France's] wounds, out of their
blood, the modern monarchies were born, and the transition from a feudal society to a State
bureaucracy was hastened, since it was imposed by the necessities of war and buttressed by
the nationalism that the war itself developed." The emergence of nascent nationalism had
become noticeable even by the beginning of the Lancastrian period. See John Barnie, *War in*

The process of "state-formation" has attracted a great deal of attention recently among historians and political scientists alike. Thanks in great part to the work of historians of early modern Europe, especially those studying what Michael Roberts dubbed the "Military Revolution," it is now widely accepted that war was the dominant force in creating and molding the early modern nation-state.[7] Brian Downing has made an interesting argument that the rapidly increasing demands of war in that period compelled many states to crush medieval traditions of representative government in order to gain the greater efficiency which came from more authoritarian (or "absolutist") forms.[8] What medieval historians have long since recognized is that the power of the greatest of the medieval representative institutions, the English parliament, was itself the product of the growing demands of war.[9] On the other hand, the trend towards more centralized administrative power in France with which Downing deals also had its origins in the period of the Hundred Years War. By 1453, melted down in the crucible of the war and recast in a new form, France had already gone a long way towards becoming "a monarchy of a new type, strongly centralized and omnipotent, claiming an absolute jurisdiction over all in the land."[10] It is a historical commonplace that the devastation of Prussia in the Thirty Years War put that state on a new course towards absolutist centralism. Fewer historians realize that the equally catastrophic devastation which the *chevauchées* of Edward III and his lieutenants inflicted on France[11] had a similar effect on that

---

Medieval English Society: Social Values in the Hundred Years War 1337–99 (Ithaca, NY: Cornell University Press, 1974).

[7] E.g. see Charles Tilly, *Coercion, Capital, and the European States, AD 990–1990* (Oxford: Blackwell, 1990), 191; John A. Lynn, "Clio in Arms: The Role of the Military Variable in Shaping History," *Journal of Military History* 55 (1991); Geoffrey Parker, *The Military Revolution* (Cambridge: Cambridge U.P., 1988); S. E. Finer, "State and Nation-Building in Europe: The Role of the Military," *The Formation of National States in Western Europe*, ed. C. Tilly (Princeton, NJ: Princeton University Press, 1975); Richard Bean, "War and the Birth of the Nation State," *Journal of Economic History* 33 (1973); Michael Roberts, "The Military Revolution, 1560–1660," and the other articles in *The Military Revolution Debate*, ed. Clifford J. Rogers (Boulder, Col.: Westview Press, 1995).

[8] Brian M. Downing, *The Military Revolution and Political Change: Origins of Democracy and Autocracy in Early Modern Europe* (Princeton, NJ: Princeton U.P., 1993).

[9] The literature on this subject includes: G. L. Harriss, *King, Parliament and Public Finance in Medieval England to 1369* (Oxford: Clarendon Press, 1975); Sir Goronwy Edwards, *The Second Century of English Parliament* (Oxford: Clarendon Press, 1979); G. L. Harriss, "The Formation of Parliament, 1272–1377," *The English Parliament in the Middle Ages*, ed. R. G. Davies (Manchester: Manchester U.P., 1981); Thomas N. Bisson, "The Military Origins of Medieval Representation," *American Historical Review* 71 (1966). For further references, see the bibliography to Harriss' book.

[10] David C. Douglas, in his introduction to the English translation of Perroy, *The Hundred Years War*, xxii.

[11] For an examination of the extent of the damage suffered by France due to these great "war-rides," see Clifford J. Rogers, "By Fire and Sword: *Bellum Hostile* and 'Civilians' in the Hundred Years War," *Civilians in the Path of War*, eds Mark Grimsley and Clifford J. Rogers (Lincoln: University of Nebraska Press, forthcoming).

realm almost three centuries earlier.[12] The ransom of £500,000[13] for King Jean II (captured on the Black Prince's 1356 *chevauchée*) did more than any other single event to establish regular, national taxation in France.[14] And, in a way, the virtual collapse of the Valois royal government in 1358–60 cleared the ground for the construction of a new, stronger monarchical state in the reign of Charles the Wise.

The pressures of the Hundred Years War had an opposite effect on the political development of Britain. The English parliament got its start largely because of the wars of Edward I, but it was only in the reign of Edward III that it became a truly powerful political body. The Commons, which met as a separate body for the first time at a parliament called to advise Edward III on how to respond to the battle of Dupplin Moor in 1332,[15] gained the most in this process. The great British constitutional historian Bishop Stubbs observed long ago that the proceedings of the parliament of January 1340, which was called to help Edward pay for his extraordinarily expensive campaigns in the Low Countries in 1339 and 1340 "very distinctly mark the acquisition by the third estate of its full share of parliamentary power," and this judgment has held up very well since he wrote.[16]

In 1351, redress of common grievances was for the first time listed among the causes of summoning a parliament. Between 1350 and 1360, while the English war effort was in full swing, parliament added a number of important privileges, including control over the granting of indirect taxation and feudal aids, and strong statutory controls of war purveyances, to its established right to grant direct taxes. "By 1369," writes the parliamentary historian G. L. Harriss, "the Commons . . . had secured all the powers they were to enjoy for the next

---

[12] Consider the observations of the English legal theorist Sir John Fortescue, writing just a few years after the end of the Hundred Years War: "You remember, most admirable prince, you have seen how rich in fruits are the villages and towns of the kingdom of France, whilst you were traveling there, but so burdened by the men-at-arms, and their horses, of the king of that land, that you could be entertained in scarcely any of them, except the great towns. There you learned from the inhabitants that those men, though they might be quartered in one village for a month or two, paid or wished to pay absolutely nothing for the expenses of themselves and their horses . . . This is done in every village and town that is unwalled in the whole of that country, so that there is not one small town which is free from this calamity, and which is not plundered by this abominable extortion once or twice a year." *De Laudibus Legum Anglie*, ed. and tr. S. B. Chrimes (Cambridge: Cambridge U.P., 1942), 81–3.

[13] By comparison, the total annual revenue of the English Crown in 1328–31 averaged only £37,297. (Ramsay, *Revenues of the Kings of England*, Table I, facing p. 292.) It is easy to see why a financial burden on this scale would have major implications for taxation. It should be noted, however, that a number of other forms of permanent royal taxation, including the infamous *gabelle*, had already been implemented by that point – though mainly also due to the pressures of Edward III's wars.

[14] J. B. Henneman, *Royal Taxation in Fourteenth Century France: The captivity and ransom of John II* (Philadelphia: University of Pennsylvania Press, 1976).

[15] *RP*, 67.

[16] Stubbs, *Constitutional History*, 2:401. Cf. Ibid., 400; Harriss, *King, Parliament and Public Finance*, 259.

200 years."[17] Part of the reason for the increasing power of the Commons was that it represented the county gentry and small landholders who provided most of the men-at-arms and archers (respectively) who served in Edward III's armies.[18] But the most important impetus for the development of parliament during this critical period was the great need of money in which the king stood because of the almost incomprehensibly vast cost of the alliance strategy he pursued between 1337 and 1340. At the January 1340 parliament mentioned above, for example, the Commons listened to a letter from Edward describing

> how our lord the king needed to be assisted with a great aid, or he would be dishonored forever, and his lands on both sides of the sea would be in great peril; for he would lose his allies, and he would have to return personally to Brussels, and remain imprisoned there until the sums for which he was obligated had been fully paid. But if he were granted an aid, all these difficulties would cease, and the emprise which he had begun would be brought, with the help of God, to a good conclusion, and peace and calm restored everywhere.[19]

They then granted him the tax he needed, but only on condition that he accede to a long and highly significant list of petitions, which included among other things the renunciation of the king's old right to levy arbitrary tallages on his demesne lands and the royal boroughs.[20] This is just one of many examples of how Edward III's conduct of the Hundred Years War propelled the evolution of parliament into the first really powerful national representative assembly since classical times.

All of this argues that the wars of Edward III merit an important place in the study of late medieval history, or even in the study of Western history as a whole. If we want to understand the initial rise to prominence of the House of Commons, we must understand the character of Edward III, and the reasons why he was so desperately in need of such immense sums of money in 1339 and 1340. To understand that, we must understand the alliance strategy with which he opened the war. Similarly, if we want to know why the Hundred Years War became one of the infamous "crises of the fourteenth century" for France, or to comprehend that kingdom's transformation into the first proto-absolutist national monarchy, we must carefully study the *chevauchée* strategy which Edward pursued between 1346 and the Treaty of Brétigny in 1360. The main purpose of this book is to facilitate the exploration of the grander ideas outlined above by providing a detailed analysis and explanation of those two strategic

---

[17] Harriss, *King, Parliament and Public Finance*, 513.
[18] Rogers, "Military Revolutions of the Hundred Years War," 61–2 and note 53. The fact that France, by contrast, continued to rely primarily on aristocratic men-at-arms for its soldiers also contributed to the failure of the French third estate to gain the kind of political power enjoyed by the commons of England.
[19] *RP*, 112.
[20] The tallages which he gave up were no small thing. In 1332, for example, he had ordered a tallage of 1/40 of the goods and 1/9 of the income of the men of his boroughs and domains. *RFR*, II:2:840, but cf. Stubbs, *Constitutional History*, 2:395 n.1.

approaches, which determined the course of the first stage of the Hundred Years
War – especially the latter, which, as we shall see, has often been misunderstood
by modern historians.

Edward III's conduct of the Anglo-French war, however, cannot be fully
appreciated without a careful examination of his earlier wars in Scotland. Of
course, his campaigns there from 1327 to 1336 were of very great importance in
their own right. The failed campaign of 1327, Edward's first military experience, led directly to the Shameful Peace of 1328, which ended the First War of
Scottish Independence by acknowledging Robert Bruce's sovereign rule over the
northern realm.[21] The new war which began after Edward Balliol's victory at
Dupplin Moor in 1332 nearly reversed that outcome. Edward III occupied eight
counties of southern lowland Scotland for most of the period from 1334 to 1337,
and twice (in 1333 and 1335) restored his vassal Edward Balliol to effective
control over nearly all the remainder of the kingdom.[22] If England had not
become involved in the war in France, as even the Scottish author of the *Book of
Pluscarden* admitted, Edward III would likely have made the annexation of the
eight counties to England permanent, and made the feudal subordination of
Scotland to the English crown a reality.[23] But even aside from their inherent
importance, Edward's Scottish wars are critical to an understanding of the
development of his strategy in the Hundred Years War. The English king's
prodigal expenditures in 1337–40 were to a great extent the result of his attempt
to imitate in France his victory over the Scots at Halidon Hill.[24]

If in the opening years of the Hundred Years War he was trying to do to the
French what he had done to the Scots in 1333, in his later campaigns (starting
1346) he was, instead, trying to do to the French what the Scots had done to *him*
in 1327. This proved a highly effective strategy. Much as the swift, devastating
raids of the Scots had left the north of England in smoldering ruins and
compelled the young Edward III to accept the Bruce's sovereignty over Scotland, so the *chevauchées* of the English reduced much of France to smoke and
cinders, and forced Jean II to cede an expanded Aquitaine to Edward III in full
sovereignty.

The magnitude of the events of Edward III's wars themselves, and their
implications for the development of France and England, provide more than
adequate justification for a study of the military strategy which guided their
prosecution. But I have chosen that topic for this book for other reasons as well,
ones more confined to strictly military history. There is a persistent perception
among military historians that strategy was "absolutely non-existent" in medieval warfare in general, and in the Hundred Years War in particular.[25] Historians

---

[21] See below, Chapter 2.
[22] See below, Chapters 3–5.
[23] *Pluscardensis*, 286.
[24] Below, Chapters 3 (Halidon Hill), 5–9 (1337–40).
[25] C. W. C. Oman, *The Art of War in the Middle Ages*, revised and ed. John Beeler (New
York: Cornell U.P., 1953), 61. Beeler commented that "this is still the generally accepted

in the first two-thirds of the twentieth century, men like Sir Charles Oman, J. M. Tourneur-Aumont, and Sir Basil Liddell Hart, concluded that the *chevauchées* of the fourteenth century were nothing but "purposeless parades," displaying an "absence of strategy, of policy, of any thought at all," and that "in the Hundred Years' War there is nothing to learn, save negatively," from the strategy of Edward III and the Black Prince.[26] A great number of historians have agreed with the assessment of the distinguished medievalists Brian Tierney and Sidney Painter that Edward III "had too little grasp of reality to be a competent strategist" – even though the Treaty of Brétigny, which ceded a third of France to be ruled by him in full sovereignty, was unquestionably one of the greatest strategic victories of the age.[27]

Such views continue to appear regularly in the works of military historians not specializing in the middle ages – even the very best of them.[28] Since the mid-1960s, however, historians of the period have begun to reassess medieval strategy. Following the lead of H. J. Hewitt, they have argued that war in the middle ages was primarily an affair of sieges and devastating raids like the *chevauchées* of Edward III, which were employed as a form of economic warfare, intended to destroy the resources with which the enemy supported his war effort.[29] This school of interpretation, which focusses on the fourteenth-century campaigns of the Hundred Years War, argues specifically that Edward III and his eldest son actively sought to avoid battle during their great *chevauchées*.[30] Indeed, it has become almost a truism that medieval

---

view of the medieval concept of war." Ibid., 61 n.2. Similarly, Professor Ferdinand Lot, another pioneering medieval military historian, concluded that "grand strategy was non-existent" in the middle ages. *L'art militaire et les armées au moyen âge* (Paris: Payot, 1946), 2:449.

26 J. M. Tourneur-Aumont, *La Bataille de Poitiers (1356) et la construction de la France* (Paris: Presses Universitaires de France, 1940), 404 (second quotation), 74–5, 78, 82, 88, 385, 388. Cf. Oman, *Art of War in the Middle Ages*, 62 n.3, and idem, *A History of the Art of War in the Middle Ages* (London: Methuen, 1924), 2:160. Cf. also J. F. C. Fuller, *The Decisive Battles of the Western World*, ed. John Terraine (London: Granada, 1970), 311.

27 Brian Tierney and Sidney Painter, *Western Europe in the Middle Ages, 300–1475* (New York: Knopf, 1983), 495. In *The Encyclopedia of Military History* (New York: Harper & Row, 1970), R. Ernest Dupuy and Trevor Dupuy describe him as a general of "scant strategical skill." Oman declared him to be "a very competent tactician, but a very unskilful strategist." *History of the Art of War in the Middle Ages*, 2:111. The article on him in *The Dictionary of National Biography*, 51, observes that "as a leader in war Edward could order a battle and inspire his army with his own confidence, but he could not plan a campaign." See also Tourneur-Aumont, *Bataille de Poitiers*, 77.

28 E.g. see John Keegan, *The Face of Battle* (New York: Penguin, 1984), 336: " 'generalship' and 'planning' are concepts one can doubtfully apply to medieval warfare." Cf. Geoffrey Parker, *The Dutch Revolt* (Revised edition. London: Peregrine, 1988), 228; Sir Michael Howard, *War in European History* (Oxford: Oxford University Press, 1977), 27.

29 H. J. Hewitt, *The Organization of War Under Edward III 1338–62* (Manchester: Manchester U.P., 1966), ch. 5; Kenneth Fowler, *The Age of Plantagenet and Valois* (New York: Putnam, 1967), 152. For a fuller discussion of the historiography of the *chevauchée*, and of Edward III's campaigns in particular, see Chapter 10, below.

30 C. T. Allmand, "The War and the Non-Combatant," *The Hundred Years War*, ed. Kenneth

commanders in general were extraordinarily anxious to avoid battle whenever possible.[31]

The emphasis these writers place on the strategic use of devastation, like the growing emphasis on siege operations in medieval warfare, is a valuable corrective.[32] There is no doubt that earlier historians of the medieval art of war, like military historians in general, perhaps, focussed too narrowly on the clash of armies in open battle.[33] More recent writers, however, seriously overreacted to this problem when they removed the quest for decisive battle from medieval strategy. It is my intention to show that Edward III saw the devastation inflicted by his *chevauchées* not as a way to avoid the risks of battle, but precisely as a provocation intended to force the Valois into attacking his army in the field. Indeed, even the major sieges of his reign were intended to accomplish this goal of bringing his enemies to battle, more than to capture strategic strongholds.[34] Neither Napoleon Bonaparte nor Ulysses S. Grant was more anxious for decisive battles than was Edward III, even though Edward (unlike those two commanders) usually had to fight his fights with forces greatly smaller than his adversary's. Furthermore, even though his enemies were often almost as eager to avoid a battle as he was to bring one about (provided he could do so on his own terms), the strategic situations which his campaigns created forced them to take the risk of attacking his army time and again: in 1333 at Halidon Hill, in 1346 at Crécy, and in 1356 at Poitiers, to list only the most brilliant of the many victories of his reign.

Of course, even in his prime, Edward had his military failures. The alliance strategy he followed from 1337 to 1340 was, in the end, a complete fiasco, and a very expensive one at that. Once he became involved in the war in France, his

Fowler (London: Macmillan, 1971), 166; idem, *The Hundred Years War* (Cambridge: Cambridge U.P., 1988), 54–5; cf. Hewitt, *Organization*, 99–100; Michael Prestwich, *The Three Edwards: War and the State in England, 1272–1377* (London: Routledge, 1990 [reprint ed.]) 177–8, 180, 186; Scott L. Waugh, *England in the Reign of Edward III* (Cambridge: C.U.P., 1991), 17.

31 John Gillingham, "Richard I and the Science of War in the Middle Ages," *War and Government in the Middle Ages*, eds J. Gillingham and J. C. Holt (Woodbridge: The Boydell Press, 1984), 82 et passim. Idem, "War and Chivalry in the *History of William the Marshal*," reprinted in *Anglo-Norman Warfare*, ed. M. Strickland (Woodbridge: The Boydell Press, 1992), 256. Matthew Strickland rightly observes that "the contention that the majority of commanders were anxious to avoid pitched battle whenever possible," which he himself accepts, "is now so commonplace that it may safely be said to have moved from revisionism to orthodoxy." *War and Chivalry* (Cambridge: Cambridge U.P., 1996), 43, 43n. Cf. also Malcolm Vale, *The Origins of the Hundred Years War. The Angevin Legacy, 1250–1340* (Oxford: Clarendon Paperbacks, 1996), 245.

32 For the growing recognition of the importance of siege warfare, see Jim Bradbury, *The Medieval Siege* (Woodbridge: The Boydell Press, 1992), and the other works considered in the review essay of Bernard Bachrach, "Medieval Siege Warfare: A Reconnaissance," *Journal of Military History* 58 (1994).

33 E.g. see Oman, *History of the Art of War in the Middle Ages*, 2:201.

34 This is true of the sieges of Berwick (1333), Cambrai (1339), Tournai (1340), and Calais (1346–7). See Chapters 4, 7, 9, and 12, below.

extensive conquests in Scotland gradually faded away until little more than Berwickshire and a narrow strip of borderlands remained. Still, on balance, Edward III was outstandingly successful in the conduct of his wars. The Treaty of Brétigny which he imposed on France in 1360 was the worst humiliation suffered by that country until 1940, with the possible exception of Henry V's Treaty of Troyes (1420). At the beginning of Edward's reign, the military reputation of England had been so low that people said that two Englishmen were hardly a match for one debilitated Scot.[35] By the 1350s, in contrast, some claimed that two Frenchmen (previously considered the most martial race of Christendom) were barely the equal of one Englishman.[36] Jean le Bel, a contemporary chronicler from Liège who had himself borne arms in the king's 1327 Weardale campaign, unhesitatingly gave the credit for this dramatic change to Edward III.[37] Although Edward's tactical ability and the skill and experience of his captains, archers, and men-at-arms contributed to this alteration in England's military reputation, his personal guidance of the war's strategy also made a major difference. Once we realize that the victories at Halidon Hill, Sluys, Crécy, and Poitiers, along with the consequent Treaty of Brétigny, were gained by design and not by "accident"[38] we must acknowledge him as a genuinely outstanding military commander, one who must indeed be ranked among the most successful of European history. If this book serves to re-establish Edward III's military reputation, and to restore the decisive battle to its proper place in the analysis of medieval strategy, it will have done enough.

[35] *Knighton*, 1:452: "duo Angli vix valebant debilem Scotum." Cf. the opinion of Francesco Petrarch, quoted in R. Boutruche, "The Devastation of Rural Areas", 26, and also Walter Bower, *Scottichronicon*, vol. 7, ed. A. B. Scott *et al.* (Aberdeen: Aberdeen U.P., 1996), 316.

[36] *Wyntoun*, 2:489. According to the *Anonimalle*, 43, "a hundred Frenchmen did not want or dare to meet twenty English in the field."

[37] *Le Bel*, 1:155–6.

[38] The verdict of the medieval military historian J. E. Morris on the battle of Crécy. John E. Morris, *The Welsh Wars of Edward I* (Oxford: Clarendon, 1901), 108.

CHAPTER TWO

"HE MIGHT COME AND AMEND IT":
THE WEARDALE CAMPAIGN OF 1327,
EDWARD III's MILITARY APPRENTICESHIP

Invulnerability lies in the defense; the possibility of victory in the attack.   Sun Tzu, IV.5.[1]

ON 15 JUNE 1327, a large Scottish army crossed into northern England, and "laid it waste by fire and sword,"[2] shattering the truce of 1323 nine years before it was due to expire. The Scottish invasion, led by James Douglas and the earls of Mar and Moray, posed a serious challenge to the new regime of Roger Mortimer and Queen Isabella, who had recently deposed Edward II and replaced him on the throne with the young Edward III.

The subsequent campaign, in which a massive English army strove to come to grips with the raiders who were ravaging England, was Edward III's introduction to war. Although only fourteen years old, he personally served as the nominal commander of the English host. The complete failure of his first expedition deeply affected the young monarch, and strongly influenced his future ideas about war – at the political level, the strategic level, even the tactical.

The strategy of the English in 1327 was essentially reactive, so before we turn to a more detailed examination of their conduct of the campaign it is necessary to consider the political aims of Robert Bruce and the military means which he employed to achieve his goals. The Scottish king's main objective in 1327 was the one which had been so forcefully enunciated in the Declaration of Arbroath in 1320: complete independence for Scotland from the crown of England.[3] His method, in a word, was extortion.

---

[1] Griffith (ed.), 85.
[2] *Fordun*, 351.
[3] *Pluscardensis*, 252–4. In the Declaration, the nobles of Scotland wrote to the Pope that they would support Robert Bruce to the death, "both because of his right and because of his personal merits, in order to maintain our independence. But, if he gave up his undertaking and wished anywise to put us or our kingdom under the English king, we would straightway drive him out, as our enemy . . . for, as long a hundred of us remain alive, we will in no wise be brought under the dominion of the English. We fight not for warlike glory, or for riches and honours, but only for our independence and the laws of our fathers." Translation from *The Book of Pluscarden* (tr. F. J. H. Skene) [Historians of Scotland, v. X] (Edinburgh: William Patterson, 1890), 165.

Ever since 1311 he had ravaged the north of England, making it a grazing-stock for Scottish plunderers.[4] To save themselves from the destruction inflicted by the Scottish raiders, the impoverished northerners were forced to pay large sums of protection money; during the reign of Edward II, "always lily-livered and luckless in war," there was little hope of meeting force with force.[5] In 1313, for example

> when the truce with the English ended, Robert Bruce threatened to "visit" England in his usual manner. Fearing this, and neither having nor hoping for any defense or help from their king – who was then busy in far-off parts of England, appearing forsooth not to care about them – the people of Northumberland, Westmorland and Cumberland, and the other Marches, offered no small sum of money, and indeed a very large one, to the said Robert, so that they might have a truce up until September 29 of the next year.[6]

The following year, the Scots devastated the northern three counties, and spared Durham only because it paid a substantial ransom.[7] Year after year, the state of the north was so miserable that Northumberland, Westmorland, and Cumberland could contribute nothing to the national lay subsidies (assessed as a proportion of total wealth) raised to finance defense efforts, and even the counties in the next tier southwards – Yorkshire and Lancashire – were so impoverished that their contributions fell to one-half or less of the peacetime levels.[8] Petitions like that of Thomas de Bekering, who complained that all of his lands in Northumberland had been burned and destroyed by the Scots, and his people "driven into exile," flooded in to the royal chancery.[9]

By 1323, the year after the city of Lancaster was put to the torch, the situa-

---

4 *Pluscardensis*, 236.
5 *Lanercost*, 247–8: "qui semper fuerat cordis pavidi et infortunatus in bellis." For the devastation and the protection payments paid by northern counties in the earlier fourteenth century see: ibid., 222; *Fordun*, 338–342; *CDS*, nos. 463, 529, 543, 707, 715, etc.; and the other sources cited below.
6 *Lanercost*, 222. When the English failed to pay, the Scots launched a punitive raid and secured their money. Ibid., 224.
7 Ibid., 228–9. The "comunalté" of the bishopric of Durham had negotiated a similar truce with Bruce in 1312, for which they agreed to pay 450 marks; the agreement is printed in E. L. G. Stones, *Anglo-Scottish Relations, 1174–1328: Some Selected Documents* (London: Nelson, 1965), 144–5. For more on the payment of ransoms by northern communities, see Jean Scammell, "Robert I and the North of England," *English Historical Review* [hereafter *EHR*] 73 (1958), 385–403.
8 PRO E359/14, mm. 13, 13d; J. F. Willard, "The Scotch Raids and the Fourteenth-Century Taxation of Northern England," *University of Colorado Studies* 5, no. 4 (1908). Cf. the case of the parishes of Norham, Holy Island and Ellingham, in Richard A. Lomas, *North-East England in the Middle Ages* (Edinburgh: John Donald, 1992), 59. In general, see also J. A. Tuck, "War and Society in the Medieval North," *Northern History* 21 (1985).
9 *CDS*, no. 899 ["exillez"]; Cf. numbers 891, 892, 896; C. M. Fraser, *Northern Petitions Illustrative of Life in Berwick, Cumbria and Durham in the Fourteenth Century* (Gateshead, Northumberland: Surtees Society, 1981), 141; *CCR, 1318–23*, 27; *Historical Papers and Letters from Northern Registers*, ed. J. Raine (London: Rolls Series, 1873), 203–6.

tion was so bad that even Andrew Harcla, Earl of Carlisle – one of Edward II's most loyal supporters (and, incidentally, the commander whose innovative tactics had proved so effective at Boroughbridge the preceding year) – had concluded that

> the King of England neither knew how to govern his realm nor was able to defend it against the Scots, who devastated it more and more each year . . . and decided that it would be better for the community of each realm if each king should possess his own kingdom freely and peacefully without any homage, instead of so much killing, burning, taking of prisoners, devastation and plundering happening each year.[10]

Harcla's secret negotiations with the Scots led him to promise to work for a settlement by which the English king would give up his claim to sovereignty over Scotland in exchange for peace in the north.[11] The fact that Robert Bruce was willing to agree to this shows that his raids were more than mere booty- and ransom-collecting expeditions: they had an underlying strategic rationale.[12] He wanted the English to drop their claims to suzerainty over Scotland, and he was prepared to make them suffer for their obstinacy until they did so.[13]

The negotiations came to nothing, however: when Harcla's agreement was discovered, he was condemned as a traitor and executed. This did not, however, mean that Edward II and his councilors were unaware of the pain the Scottish raids inflicted on northern England, nor that they were opposed to a truce. Edward, like Harcla, wanted peace; he simply was not prepared to pay so high a price for it. In the king's mind, and the minds of most Englishmen, officially accepting the loss of English suzerainty over Scotland would have been a high price indeed.[14] As it turned out, even the Scots were not willing to fight indefinitely for English acknowledgment of an independence that was already de facto theirs, so in 1323 they agreed to a truce without insisting on that concession by their southern enemies.

The truce of 1323 was very definitely only a truce, accepted by both sides out of exhaustion, and not a peace based on agreement. The underlying political reason for the conflict had not been resolved: the English still wanted the Scot-

[10] *Lanercost*, 248.
[11] The agreement, which is printed in Stones, *Anglo-Scottish Relations*, 154–7, also stipulates that Bruce would pay 40,000 marks to Edward; marry his heir male to one of Edward's relatives; and endow an abbey with 500 marks per annum to pray for the souls of those lost during the war.
[12] Tuck, "War and Society in the Medieval North," 35, believes that "[t]heir purpose was to compel the inhabitants of the northern counties to buy truces," but it should be emphasized that the impoverishment of the north, whether by extortion or direct plunder, was meant to put political pressure on the English, not just to seek financial profit, as Bruce's willingness to make peace shows.
[13] This was no new development, either: cf. Ronald McNair Scott, *Robert the Bruce, King of Scots* (New York: Peter Bedrick, 1989), 194–5.
[14] Witness the charge leveled against Edward II at his deposition, that he had "lost" Scotland. See the document printed in *KdL*, 17.

tish crown to be subordinate to their own, and the Scots still insisted on the independence of their nation. A secondary, but still very important issue – the restoration of the confiscated lands of "disinherited" lords from both sides of the border[15] – also remained unresolved. The aggressive Robert Bruce remained on the Scottish throne, and the weak Edward II still wore the English crown. The Scots' destructive raids continued to pose a threat for which the English had no effective counter. The truce, as a result, was shaky from the start,[16] and collapsed completely in 1327, after events in England destroyed the balance of disadvantage which had made both sides willing to accept a temporary end to hostilities.

Although Robert Bruce was already seriously ill in 1327, when his countrymen launched their invasion, he knew that the situation of the English leadership was even worse than his own. Edward II had just been deposed by an army led by his own wife Isabella (later known to history as the "She-wolf of France") and her lover, Sir Roger Mortimer. At a parliament in January of 1327, the teenaged Prince Edward had received the crown in his father's stead, but the new king remained under the tutelage of Mortimer and Isabella. The elder Edward, imprisoned under harsh conditions, remained a focus for opposition to the new regime, and plots to restore him to the throne further weakened the unity of the English. Among the plotters was the Earl of Mar, a Scottish-born nobleman raised at the English court who had fled north on Edward's deposition.[17] The young Edward III was personally popular,[18] but the real rulers of the country, Mortimer and Isabella, had risen to power more because of opposition to Edward II than due to any real support of their own. Bruce seems to have believed that Edward II, for all his weaknesses, had been in a better position to resist Scottish attacks than were the pair responsible for his deposition.

So, with England distracted by the domestic political crisis which culminated in the deposition and eventually the gruesome murder of Edward II, the time seemed right for Robert to try to extort a much greater prize than the cash and cattle he had earlier taken from the north: the end of English claims to feudal sovereignty over Scotland. The articles of deposition read at the parliament of January 1327 had accused Edward II of "losing" Scotland; certainly his repeated failures in the Scottish wars contributed greatly to his downfall.[19] The first duty of a good lord was to defend his vassals, which Edward II had failed to do. If they wanted to hold on to power (as they most definitely did) Mortimer and Isabella would have to do better on that score. They would have to put an

---

[15] Englishmen who claimed Scottish lands by right of inheritance (or vice versa), but could not take possession of their territories because of the wars.
[16] Ranald Nicholson, *Edward III and the Scots* (Oxford: Oxford University Press, 1965), 13–14.
[17] *CDS*, no. 919; cf. no. 925.
[18] *Scalacronica*, 152–3.
[19] In *KdL*, 17.

end to the massive Scottish raids which left whole counties burned out,[20] either by crushing the Scots in open battle, or by buying them off with the political concessions which Bruce sought. The Scottish king was betting that he could avoid a battlefield defeat, leaving only the latter option open to the new English regime. He would, in the end, win his wager.

We are fortunate to have an excellent eyewitness account of the English side of the 1327 campaign, from the pen of the Liègeois chronicler Jean le Bel. His chronicle provides the best picture of the military means which Robert Bruce was able to deploy in carrying out his strategy of extortion:

> When they want to pass into England, they are all mounted, except for the camp followers [*ribaudaille*], who are on foot; the knights and esquires are mounted on good, large rouncies, and the other Scots on little hackneys. They bring no carts because of the mountainous terrain, nor do they carry any supplies of bread or wine. They are so little addicted to luxury that,[21] in time of war, they can subsist well enough for a long time on half-cooked meat, without bread, and good river-water, uncut with wine. They do without pots and kettles, since they cook their meat inside the hides of the animals which they have skinned, and they well know that they will find a great abundance of cattle in the country they are raiding. So they carry no other supplies, except that each one carries a large flat stone in his saddle-bags, and ties behind him a sack of oatmeal. When they have eaten so much of this badly-cooked meat that their stomachs feel weak, they throw this stone in the fire, and mix a bit of their oatmeal with water. When the stone is hot, they make a sort of biscuit on it, which they eat to restore their stomachs. So it is no marvel that they make longer marches than other people. . . . They enter into England, and burn and devastate the country, and find so many cattle that they don't know what to do with them all. They have a good 3,000 men-at-arms, knights and esquires, mounted on good large rouncies and coursers, and fully 20,000 men armed in the local way,[22] crafty and tough, mounted on their little hackneys.[23]

---

20 PRO E359/14/m. 13; Cf. Willard, "Scotch Raids"; Fraser, *Northern Petitions*, 141, etc.
21 "leur sobriété [est] si grande . . ."
22 These numbers, incidentally, though somewhat exaggerated, are not as fanciful as they may seem. Even after the losses suffered at Dupplin Moor in 1332, the Scots were able to produce about 15,000 men for the battle of Halidon Hill in 1333. See below, ch. 4. This is comparable to the size of the armies Edward III was able to put into the field, even though his realm was vastly richer and his administrative bureaucracy infinitely more developed: but the Scottish army, unlike the English, did not have to be paid. Furthermore, it usually served for short periods, and on raids like the one described by le Bel there was relatively little danger, and a great deal of opportunity for profitable plundering.
23 *Le Bel*, 1:51–2. Le Bel's remarks are fascinatingly close to those of one royalist peer in 1746: "the slowness of the motions of so heavy a body as our army gives [the Scots] opportunities of assembling, separating upon expeditions, and assembling again when they please, hardy people who can sleep sound on the ground, and wet through without catching cold; who can live upon a little oatmeal made into a cake upon a flat stone before a fire in the open air, or mixed with hot water." Quoted in Jeremy Black, *A Military Revolution? Military change and European Society, 1550–1800* (Atlantic Highlands, NJ: Humanities Press, 1991), 45–6.

Obviously, le Bel was very impressed by the great mobility which the Scottish raiders were able to achieve, thanks to their practices of mounting all their soldiers, living off the land, and doing without any significant baggage train. By the end of this campaign, the English had developed an equal appreciation of the advantages this mobility brought to their enemies, and of how a similar capability might be turned to their own profit.

Another noteworthy characteristic of the Scottish methods was the wide dispersion of their forces over the countryside, with troops spread out over as much as thirty miles' radius.[24] Contemporary military thought normally stressed the importance of keeping an army on the march in a tight formation to ensure that it would be ready in the event of a sudden attack, so this dispersal of force may seem surprising.[25] The explanation is that the Scots derived substantial operational and strategic advantages from such dispersion to compensate for the purely tactical advantages of a tighter march order. They could plunder and devastate much more area when spread out than when concentrated, thus increasing both their own profit and the harm they inflicted on their enemy. Equally important, by spreading out over such a distance they were able to forage more effectively for the supplies which they could only get from the land, since they brought no carts with them, and received nothing from Scotland. Considering their superior mobility, there was little risk that they would be overtaken and attacked without an opportunity to form up into their battle schiltrons. The breadth of their advance also, paradoxically, made their movements more difficult to track. The English headquarters would receive reports of sightings of the Scots at various places, often many leagues apart, and would have to decide which if any of them corresponded to the center and main line of the Scottish advance. As a result, the English were often reduced to tracking the raiders by following the smoke from the burning villages of the Border.[26]

It was in just such a loose order of march that the Scottish army of some ten thousand men, led by Mar, Moray and Douglas, re-entered England in July of

---

[24] Thomas Gray's *Scalacronica* reports, for example, that a portion of the Scottish army defeated at Darlington a contingent of Englishmen who were marching to join King Edward. Darlington is twenty-nine modern miles as the crow flies from Stanhope, where the main body of the Scottish army was then positioned. This indicates a ten-league radius of action, equivalent to a full breadth of twenty leagues. *Scalacronica*, 154. It may possibly be to this dispersion, rather than to the length of their forward advances, that le Bel refers when he says "ilz mainnent bien leur ost XX ou XXXII liewes loing."

[25] Vegetius (Flavius Vegetius Renatus), *The Earliest English Translation of Vegetius' De Re Militari*, ed. Geoffrey Lester (Heidelberg: Carl Winter Universitätsverlag, 1988), I.8, p. 57: "there nys no thyng that oughthe so wel to be keped in iourneyeng of the oos as that knightes kepe wel her ordre of goyng and rydinge" [there is nothing that ought to be so well kept in the journeying of the army as that knights keep well their order of going and riding]; cf. I.26 (p. 72), III.6 (p. 115). Vegetius' treatise was very widely read in the middle ages, often in translations and abridgements. Whether or not their inspiration came from his work, the English in 1327 were very serious about keeping good, tight order on the march, as le Bel's account of the campaign (passim) makes clear.

[26] *Le Bel*, 1:53.

1327 "and brent and destroiede al the North contre through-out."[27] Their coming was no surprise: Mortimer and Isabella had been preparing for a Scottish invasion at least since April, and the mid-June incursion had served definite notice of the breakdown of the truce.[28] By the time the Scots crossed the border, the two had gathered a substantial army at York, with the teenaged Edward III in nominal command. They knew that it would have been political suicide to allow Bruce's attack to go unchallenged: the first duty of a good lord, after all, was to defend his vassals from attack.[29] Furthermore, even a troubled England could muster a larger and better-equipped army than Bruce's – especially since the force under Edward was supplemented by a strong contingent of Hainaulters under Jean d'Hainault, whose services had been so valuable to Isabella the preceding year.[30] Edward II had been a handicap to the morale of the Englishmen, but Edward III, a promising youth of clearly martial disposition, had the potential to improve the fighting spirit of his subjects as much as his father had sapped it. Thus, if Edward III's army could bring the invading army to bay, it would stand a good chance of defeating the Scots, erasing the stain which Bannockburn had left on the national escutcheon, and securing the new regime's hold on power.

Such, in fine, was the admirably simple English strategy for 1327: come to grips with the enemy and defeat him. Unfortunately for Edward, however, in war even the simplest thing is difficult.[31] This maxim of Clausewitz's would likely have brought a grimace of agreement from a member of the English army which experienced so much difficulty in bringing the Scots to battle in 1327.

That army was already beginning to assemble at York and Newcastle in late May.[32] Although the gathering English army suffered from maladept planning,[33] and a violent conflict between the English archers and Jean d'Hainault's contingent of 780 men-at-arms,[34] it nonetheless was a force to be reckoned with by the

---

27 *English Brut*, 1:250. Numbers: *Barbour*, 713.
28 Writs of summons were sent out on 5 April. *RFR*, II:2:702. On 20 April, the commissioners of array were warned that the king had "definite knowledge" that the Scots were ready to invade. *RS*, 206.
29 As the powerful Count of Foix expressed it, "all landed lords are duty-bound to guard their people; it is for that that they hold their lordships." Jean Froissart, *Oeuvres*, ed. Kervyn de Lettenhove (Brussels, 1870 etc.), 12:109. Or, as the great legist Sir John Fortescue put it late in the 15th century, "All the power of a king ought to be applied to the good of his realm, which in effect consists in the defence of it against invasions by foreigners, and in the protection of the inhabitants of the realm and their goods from injury and rapine by natives." Fortescue, *De Laudibus Legum Anglie*, 89.
30 Jean d'Hainault had knighted the young Edward III in conjunction with the coronation, according to William of Dene's *Historia Roffensis*, fo. 50, and *Bridlington*, 95.
31 Carl von Clausewitz, *Vom Kriege* I.7, p. 159.
32 Nicholson, *Edward III and the Scots*, 19–20.
33 Nicholson, *Edward III and the Scots*, 18–22.
34 *Le Bel*, 1:42–5; *Récits*, 146. *Le Bel*, 1:41, like the *English Brut*, 1:249, sets the number at only 500, but in this case the higher number is more credible, considering the very large amount of wages and *restor* paid to the Hainaulters at the end of the campaign. PRO, Exch., Q.R.: E101/18/4.

time the Scots crossed the border. News of the invasion reached the Edward at York on 17 June, and all fencible men of the northern counties were ordered to assemble immediately.[35] By 5 July, after the Scottish army had made its way as far south as Appleby-in-Westmorland,[36] Edward's forces were at last in motion. Their movement from York, though, was not northwest towards Appleby, but rather almost directly north towards Durham on the river Wear.

To the north of the main body at Durham were positioned two substantial detachments of Edward's forces: a "great plenty" of Welsh at Carlisle to defend the passage of the Irthing, and a large number of men-at-arms at Newcastle to cover the Tyne.[37] Since there is only a five-mile gap (backed by hilly forests) between the two rivers, the English apparently felt that these two covering forces would be able to prevent the raiders from retreating back into Scotland, or at least delay them until the main body could be notified and brought to bear.[38] The task facing these covering forces was made more manageable by the fact that there was only one substantial bridge (at Corbridge) between Newcastle and Carlisle.[39] Carlisle and Newcastle were of course too well fortified and garrisoned for the Scots to pass there. Fords were few and far between, and the rivers were too fast and rocky to be passed elsewhere.[40]

With the Scots' retreat thus cut off, the main English host could devote itself to tracking and closing with the enemy. The royal headquarters had had no news of the Scots since the sighting at Appleby, though it was feared that they might have passed south of the host on their way to attack York where Queen Isabella was staying.[41] As soon as Edward's forces reached Durham on 15 July, however, they could see the smoke from the hamlets and villages which the Scots had burned, so they knew that the enemy was nearby.[42] On the 16th, Edward's army formed into three great "battles" on foot, each flanked by two small wings of men-at-arms who remained mounted. The host then set off southwards in search

[35] *RS*, 214–215 (incl. Lancashire and Yorkshire).

[36] *Lanercost*, Illustrative Documents, LI, shows that by 4 July Edward had received a report that the Scots had been sighted near Appleby. The date of the sighting is indicated in the document by the day of the week rather than of the month, so it cannot be determined with certainty, but it must have been either 2 July or 25 June. Considering the distance between Appleby and Edward's headquarters at York, it was more likely the latter.

[37] *Le Bel*, 1:49. The *Scalacronica*, 155, sets the number of men-at-arms in the Newcastle force as 1,000.

[38] *Le Bel*, 1:49, who mistakes the Irthing and the Tyne for a single river, remarks that "The Scots could not leave the realm of England without passing this river." Cf. ibid., 55.

[39] For Corbridge, see *CDS*, no. 891, p. 162.

[40] There nearest ford to Haydon Bridge, for example, was at Haltwhistle, some nine miles upstream. Even at the fords, the crossing could only be made "with great difficulty [*malaise*] and peril." *Le Bel*, 1:62.

[41] *RS*, 218 and *RFH*, 2:2:192. The council's worries about the queen may have had something to do with the memory of 1319, when the Scots had broken the siege of Berwick partly by a threat to Queen Isabella in Carlisle. Cf. Scott, *Robert the Bruce*, 192–3.

[42] PRO E101/382/9, m.42 (date); *Le Bel*, 1:50, 53.

of the Scots, tracking them by following the smoke of the burning villages until late in the evening. Even though the Scots were burning the land within five leagues of the host, the English could not locate the enemy army. At dawn the next day, they set slowly off again, still in battle formation, through woods and moors, over "savage wastes and toilsome mountains and valleys," never drawing nearer to the fast-moving raiders.[43] At this point the king's advisers realized that, if they continued this pursuit, they would never catch the Scots – unless the latter, having taken a strong position on a hilltop or in a pass, decided to wait for their enemies where they could fight at an advantage. So a great council of the lords in attendance met to devise a new strategy. The result was a decision that, rather than try to outmarch the invaders, they would try to outmaneuver them. To return into Scotland, the raiders would probably have to cross the Tyne. If the English were to rise before midnight, and make a swift march northwards to cross the river first, then they could control the river passage and force the Scots to either fight at a disadvantage, or else remain in England, caught in a trap.[44] So it was agreed.

The next day, beginning before dawn, the men-at-arms of the English host formed up and set off in great haste across the rugged terrain of the north, leaving the infantry to follow as best it could. The baggage train was simply abandoned, for battle was expected within a day. Between the sunrise and evening of the 20th, when the cavalry reached the Tyne, they had covered some twenty-eight miles cross-country "without stopping," says le Bel, "except to piss, or to regirth a horse."[45] The English barely had time to cross the ford at Haydon before darkness fell. They spent the night on the north bank of the Tyne, fully armed, each man holding his horse's reins in his hand, since there was nothing there to tie them to. Neither was there wood to burn, nor food to cook, nor wine to drink, nor shelter to be had. To add to the army's misery, the morning brought with it a heavy downpour, which lasted for days, causing the Tyne to swell up until it could not be crossed. Messengers were sent to encourage the locals to bring supplies for sale to the camp, and enough did arrive to sustain the troops, but the suppliers charged outrageous prices for their low-quality wares. There at Haydon the host remained for a week, each day expecting the appearance of the Scots.[46] As late as the 26th, one member of the

---

43 Edward was at Trudhoe, just five miles south of Durham, on the 17th. PRO E101/382/9, m.42. *Le Bel*, 1:54 (quotation).

44 *Le Bel*, 1:55: "conviendroit qu'ilz se combattissent à meschief, ou ilz demourroient tous en Angleterre pris à la trape." The *Scalacronica* says that the decision to march to the Tyne was based on a scout's mistaken report that the Scots had been sighted that day retreating northward. *Scalacronica*, 154.

45 *Le Bel*, 1:55–8, at 58. The king was at Auckland on the 19th, "Bagrowe" [Billy Row?] on the 20th (apparently the day of the long ride), and at Heyden [Haydon Bridge] on the 21st. PRO E101/382/9, m.42. The distance is actually about 25 miles in a straight line; the figure of 28 "English leagues" is from le Bel.

46 *Le Bel*, 1:60–61. A week: i.e. 21 July–27 July, though by the last day the king had moved to "Rattonrowe" on the way to Haltwhistle, slightly ahead of the bulk of the army. The chro-

army still believed that they had succeeded in blocking the Scots from re-entering their own country.[47] Others were less pleased with the results of their new strategy, and a rumor circulated that those who advised the march to the Tyne had meant to betray the king.[48]

Under this pressure, and tired of the "discomfort and poverty" of their camp at Haydon, Edward's advisers decided to change their strategy again.[49] A large reward was offered to anyone who could guide the king to the enemy, leading fifteen or sixteen English men-at-arms to ford the Tyne and split up in search of the Scots. Meanwhile the main army marched some nine miles up the river to the easier ford at Haltwhistle. After crossing on 28 July, they marched south on the 29th and 30th, not hearing anything of the Scots until they met one of the esquires who had gone scouting, Thomas Rokesby.[50] He had been captured by the Scots, who, when they learned his mission, set him free on the condition that he not rest until he had informed the English of their whereabouts. The Scottish leaders had been as ignorant of the location of the English as the English had been of theirs. Furthermore, Rokesby was instructed to tell Edward that "they have as much desire to fight with you as you have to fight with them."[51] After hearing mass and giving confession, the English host followed the esquire south, over the Wear, and then east to where the Scots had taken him prisoner, not far from Stanhope Park.

On their arrival, the English were dismayed to observe that the Scots had crossed to the northern bank and taken up a truly formidable defensive position in a place "hard and bare."[52] The river Wear, strong and swift though not very broad, separated the two hosts. As the English approached along the south bank, the Scots formed into three well-ordered schiltrons (hedgehog-like formations of spearmen) on the slope of a large hill. The two foremost divisions were situ-

---

nology of the king's itinerary is very difficult to untangle, but Jean le Bel is very helpful once one realizes that he seems to have kept, or later created, a sort of campaign journal, with day 1 of the expedition being the day of the long ride after the carts were abandoned (20 July), and day 22, the last day, when the baggage was rediscovered at Durham on 10 August. Thus when he says they stayed eight days at Haydon, he really means "until day 8" (27 July), and when he says the army was opposite the Scots on the Wear for 18 or 22 days, he really means "until day 18" (6 August) [the day the Scots departed for Scotland] or "until day 22" [the day the army reached Durham]. Because of the difficulty of establishing the dates in this campaign, and because my conclusions differ from those of earlier historians, I have provided rather long footnotes on the subject, which I hope are justified.

47 *CDS*, no. 926, p. 168.
48 *Le Bel*, 1:61.
49 *Le Bel*, 1:61.
50 Dates: PRO E101/382/9, m.42 (Haltwhistle on the 28th, "Alwenton" [Allendale Town?] on the 29th, Stanhope on the 30th]; *CDS*, nos. 926, 927, p. 168. *Le Bel*, 1:62; *RFH*, 2:2:198.
51 *Le Bel*, 1:62–3, at 63: "ilz dient que aussy grand desir ont ilz de combatre à vous comme vous avez à eulx, et là les trouverrez." R. A. Lomas apparently doubts this, but I see no reason to. Lomas, *North-East England in the Middle Ages*, 46.
52 *CDS*, no. 936, p. 169; *RFH*, 2:2:198. *Barbour*, 715, specifies that the Scots occupied the "north halff Wer towart Scotland" (*contra* Nicholson, *Edward III*, 31–2, 34, and Colm McNamee, *The Wars of the Bruces* (East Linton: Tuckwell Press, 1997), 242.

ated on craggy outcroppings of rock,[53] where they could not easily be attacked, and from where they could hurl stones or other missile weapons down on the English with deadly effect. Furthermore, the Scottish schiltrons were positioned close enough to the river that there was insufficient space for the English to form up their own battles, even if they succeeded in crossing. This was precisely the situation that the earlier forced march to Haydon had been intended to avoid – but even worse than the English leaders had imagined.[54]

The initial responses of Edward's counselors to this situation seem to have been dictated more by wishful thinking than anything else. The English forces were formed up into three battles; the order was given that no one was to advance before the banners on pain of death; Edward himself was brought out to encourage the troops, and spoke "very graciously;" then the battles began to march slowly forward while scouts watched to see if the Scots would come down from their crags.[55] Following Douglas' advice that "fecht on na maner sall we / Bot it be at our avantage," however, the Scots remained in their positions.[56]

Consulting quickly to come up with a new plan, the king's advisers sent a few good men-at-arms on coursers to cross the river, skirmish with the Scots, and observe their position. A body of archers crossed the river and began shooting into the Scottish formations at range, hoping to provoke the Scots into abandoning their position, but the bowmen were driven off by the enemy cavalry.[57] Stymied, the English sent heralds to the Scottish leaders with an offer: they would gladly retire from the river, allowing the Scots to cross over so that they could have a battle; or, if the Scots would move off, the English would ford the river to the north. The Scots delivered a response which, considering their numerical inferiority,[58] was as sensible as it was trenchant:

> When they heard this, they took counsel and [then] responded that they would do neither the one nor the other. The king and all his council could well see that they were in his realm and had burned and devastated it; if this troubled him, he might come and amend it, for they would tarry there as long as they liked.[59]

---

[53] *Le Bel*, 1:65.

[54] The decision to march to Haydon, as noted above, had been taken when the English realized that they would not be able to overtake the Scots unless the latter "wanted to wait for them, if they had positioned themselves well on a mountain or in a pass in such a way that the English couldn't fight with them without very great disadvantage." *Le Bel*, 1:54. The Scots' position on the Wear was so strong that the English "thocht foly and outrage/To gang up till thaim till assaill/Thaim at thar strenth in plane battaill." *Barbour*, 721.

[55] *Le Bel*, 1:65; *Barbour*, 715–17.

[56] I.e., "we shall by no means fight, unless it be at an advantage." Douglas went on to justify this seemingly unchivalrous attitude by saying "For methink it war na outrage/To fewar folk aganys ma/Avantage quhen thai ma to ta" (I think it would be no outrage, for fewer folk against more, to take advantages when they may). *Barbour*, 715.

[57] *Barbour*, 717.

[58] *Scalacronica*, 154; *Barbour*, 715; *Murimuth*, 53 (3 to 1).

[59] *Le Bel*, 1:66.

This left the English in a lose-lose situation. To attack would be to invite a repetition of Bannockburn, which is clearly what the Scots hoped for. On the other hand, not to attack would be to allow the enemy to escape unpunished, the massive effort and expense put into mounting the English expedition dissipated without result, and the royal government's prestige once again sent to rock bottom. The English, opting for the lesser of two evils, declined the Scottish invitation and instead went about setting up their camp, still on the south side of the Wear. The two armies remained in this standoff for three days, inactive except for a few chivalrous skirmishers fighting in the no-man's land between them.[60]

As Jean le Bel makes clear, the plan of the English lords was to "besiege" the Scots in their camp, and starve them out. No supplies could reach the Scots this deep in English territory, and Edward's men knew from prisoners that the raiders had no supplies of bread, salt or wine – only a large number of stolen cattle.[61]

There was, however, a flaw in this plan. Although later documents claimed that the Scots were "encircled and besieged" on the Wear,[62] in point of fact they were *not* entirely encircled; their escape route north was blocked by a wide and treacherous swamp, but they could go some distance east or west along the river bank without great difficulty. This point was brought home on the morning of the fourth day of the standoff, 3 August, when Jean le Bel and his companions arose to discover that the Scots had decamped during the night.[63] Edward's surprised and worried counselors immediately dispatched their scouts in an attempt to discover what had happened to the Scots. Within a few hours, the scouts returned, reporting that the enemy had simply moved a short distance along the river to a new, even stronger defensive position within the walled confines of Stanhope Park proper, where the cover provided by the forest made it possible for them to come and go without being observed.[64]

The English did not take this opportunity to cross the river and position themselves between the enemy and Scotland, probably because the Scots were still close enough that they might fall upon the English in the midst of a crossing.

---

[60] As noted above, Edward reached Stanhope on 30 July, and the many sources that say the English and Scots faced off in the Weardale for eight days are counting that day, and also 7 August, the day when the Scots started for home before dawn. It seems, however, that some of the army did not catch up with the king until the following day, 31 July, the vigil of the Feast of St. Peter (Jean le Bel employs the unusual form "la *nuit* Saint Pierre d'aoust"), which seems to be when le Bel starts enumerating the days of the standoff. *Le Bel*, 1:67. Thomas Gray does the same for the days, but counts the nights in the Weardale from 30 July.

[61] *Le Bel*, 1:68; *Royal Brut*, f. 330v; *AM Brut*, f. 90v.

[62] *CDS*, no. 957, p. 173: "circumdati et obsessi." Similarly, the *Royal Brut*, f. 330v, has: "od son hoste [Edward] assegea le dit park issint qe les escots ne savoient ou isser sinon a lour damage."

[63] Le Bel, as noted, gives his first day facing the Scots as 31 July, and says the Scots were found to be missing on the morning of the fourth day, i.e. 3 August. The *Scalacronica*, 154, confirms that the Scots moved "in the fourth night" (the first night for Gray being 30 July).

[64] *Le Bel*, 1:68–9; *Barbour*, 723–5.

Instead, Edward's men followed the south bank of the Wear and posted themselves on a mountain opposite the Scots. The result was a continuation of the
previous situation: the English would not make a suicidal attack on the powerfully positioned Scots, and the outnumbered Scots would not fight otherwise –
though James Douglas did launch a daring night raid into the midst of the
English army on its first night in the new camp, reaching all the way to King
Edward's tent before being forced to retreat.[65] The leaders of the English army
were convinced that this attack was a probe which heralded an all-out attack;
they believed that the Scots, low on supplies and trapped by the swamp behind
them, would soon have no choice but to make some desperate attempt to cut
their way through the English army. Thus, on the nights of 4 and 5 August they
maintained careful watches, though no attack came.[66] On the 6th, they captured
a prisoner who seemed to confirm their expectations, for he said that all the
raiders had been ordered to prepare to move out that night, and follow James
Douglas' banner to an unknown location. Not wanting to be caught by surprise,
the English lords ordered the construction of three great bonfires, and had every
man-at-arms sleep fully armed in his battle position outside the camp, under his
banner.[67] That night, however, Douglas, Randolph, Mar and their men, who were
indeed low on supplies, again showed that the English "siege" of their position
was incomplete. Once more they decamped secretly at midnight, then carefully
made their way on foot, leading their horses, through the dangerous swamp
north of the river valley, which Edward's counselors had presumed impassable
for an army. Once out of the moss, the raiders sped all the way back to Scotland
with "gret gladschip."[68] The young King Edward, learning of their escape the
next morning, "was wonder' sory, and ful hertly wepte with his yonge eyne."[69]

65 *Le Bel*, 1:70, specifies that the raid was on the first night in the new position, which
matches Thomas Gray's statement that the Scots departed on the third night after the raid (the
night of 6/7 August). *Scalacronica*, 155. For Douglas' raid, see also *Barbour*, 727–31; *Anonimalle Brut*, 139. The *Royal Brut*, fo. 331, adds Mar and Randolph to the raiding party, but
probably incorrectly.
66 *Le Bel*, 1:71 (dates by calculation).
67 Ibid., 71–2. Le Bel says this was on the last of the 18 days ("Le desrain de XVIII jours"), a
reference to his earlier statement (p. 69) that "Ainsy logeasmes nous là encontre eulx, et
demourasmes XVIII jours, tous accomplis, sur celle seconde montaigne." This appears to say
that the army was eighteen days in its second camp, the one opposite Stanhope park, but actually le Bel is referring to the fact that this happened on their last ("desrain") day in that
position, which was the 18th day of the expedition, i.e. the 18th day after the baggage was
abandoned, viz. 6 August. This was the 8th day after Edward III reached Stanhope (counting
the 30th); hence the statement of Barbour and many other sources that the two armies were
opposite each other for eight days. Barbour confirms that on the eighth day of the standoff,
the Scots were packing up their goods and preparing to depart, and the *Scalacronica* agrees
that it was the third night after Douglas' raid when the Scots left. *Barbour*, 735; *Scalacronica*,
155.
68 *Barbour*, 735–7.
69 *English Brut*, 251. Cf. *Scalacronica*, 155: "The king, an innocent, wept." *Lanercost*, 260,
also supports the story. Edward reached Durham on 7 August. E101/832/9, m.42. The Scots
reached Scotland on the following day. Bower, *Scottichronicon*, 7:34 ("in previgilia Sancti

Douglas, Moray, Mar and their troops had gone where they pleased in England, ravaging, burning, and plundering. The damage they inflicted was so great that for the lay subsidy of 1327, collected after the campaign, the three northernmost counties were deemed unable to pay a single shilling, and even more southerly Yorkshire and Lancashire contributed only about forty per cent of their peacetime levels.[70] Though the English troops had marched long and hard, and borne with poor provisions and lack of shelter during inclement weather, they had been unable to catch up to the raiders except when the Scots wanted them to. Even then, after the two armies came face to face, there was no battle; the only significant action was Douglas' embarrassingly successful raid. The Scots had easily escaped the English "siege" – twice – and then escaped to their homeland . . . scot-free, as it were. Little wonder that young King Edward made his return to York "in great desolation and sorrow because things hadn't gone better for him at the beginning of his reign; and, severely stricken with shame, he grieved much."[71] Murimuth describes him as "sorrowing and without honor."[72] Public opinion considered it "to the great shame, dishonor, and scorn of all England" that the Scots had been allowed to escape from a place where, it was believed, they could have been held, defeated, and killed.[73]

In the aftermath of the Weardale campaign, the military situation only grew worse for the English. Jean d'Hainault took his men-at-arms home, leaving behind in their place a massive bill for wages and other compensation due. The campaign had been very expensive – the wages, expenses, and *restor* (compensation for lost or surrendered horses) of the Hainault contingent alone amounted to over £41,000[74] – and the treasury was empty. The Scots, their army even larger after a reinforcement by the Earl of March,[75] continued to ravage the countryside of Northumberland, while one force under Robert Bruce besieged

Laurencii," which is 8 August, not 9 August). Jean le Bel, along with the bulk of the army, followed King Edward much more slowly. On the 7th, when it was discovered the Scots were gone, the army made a short journey, then encamped in the field. On the 8th, riding slowly because of the poor condition of their horses, the troops reached an abbey two leagues outside of Durham, where they rested on the 9th. Then, on the 10th, in Durham, they were reunited with the wagons they had abandoned "22 days earlier in a woods at midnight," which the citizens had recovered for them and stored in empty granges, each cart marked with its little pennon. *Le Bel*, 1:73–5.

70 Willard, "Scotch Raids," 238–40. Cf. *RP*, 176.

71 *Knighton*, 1:445.

72 *Murimuth*, 53. Cf. *Royal Brut*, fo. 331.

73 *Anonimalle Brut*, 136.

74 PRO E101/18/4, m.2. As the *English Brut*, 252, observed, "the Kyng had despended miche of his tresour', and wasted." Note that the £21,0482 for restoring warhorses represented over £27 for every man-at-arms in John's contingent, which is a princely sum considering that few English men-at-arms owned warhorses worth over £20. Even the mount of the great northern magnate Henry Percy was evaluated at that amount in 1336. PRO E101/19/36; cf. E101/5/27. The extremely large amount of *restor* paid to Hainault thus suggests that the money was, in this case, more a general reward than an actual payment for lost horses.

75 *Barbour*, 739, 743.

Norham (near Berwick), and another under James Douglas and the Earl of
Moray kept the English forces under Henry Percy (the Warden of the East
March) bottled up in Alnwick.[76] Once again, as in the dark days of Edward II,
the Borderers were constrained to pay large sums to the Scots in exchange for
brief truces.[77] To ratchet the pressure on Mortimer and Isabella's government up
another step, Bruce even began to hand out titles to Northumbrian lands, as if
the county were his possession by right of conquest.[78]

Worst of all, there was nothing to prevent a repetition of the 1327 campaign
in the following year. Mortimer and Isabella had to have peace if they wanted to
maintain their hold on power. They had made their play for peace through
victory, and failed, so they sent envoys to Robert Bruce to discover what he
would require for an end to hostilities. They learned that his key demand was the
same one it had been all along: that Edward abandon his claim to suzerainty over
Scotland.

In 1323, the Earl of Carlisle's agreement to work for a peace based on that
concession was deemed a treason punishable by death. In 1328, Mortimer and
Isabella accepted terms even less favorable than the ones to which Harcla had
agreed. The treaty they made with Bruce is usually referred to as the Treaty of
Northampton, after the parliament where it was confirmed, but was more often
known to contemporary Englishmen as the *turpis pax* or "shameful peace."[79]
While most Englishmen were dismayed by the treaty, the Scots rejoiced: "how
much pride and exultation there was in Scotland, after so much hardship, tongue
cannot utter nor pen describe."[80]

The quitclaim sealed by Edward in fulfillment of the agreement both met
Bruce's main requirement – that the English abandon their claim to suzerainty –
and also made it abundantly clear *why* they agreed to abandon the diplomatic
position they had so long maintained:

> We, and certain of our predecessors as Kings of England, have tried to assert
> rights of rule, dominion, or superiority over the realm of Scotland, and in con-
> sequence a grievous burden of wars has long afflicted the realms of England

---

[76] *Lanercost*, 260; *Scalacronica*, 155; *Bridlington*, 97.

[77] *Lanercost*, 260.

[78] *Barbour*, 743 and 742n; *Historical Papers and Letters from Northern Registers*, 344–6.
Nicholson, *Edward III and the Scots*, 44–5, argues that the Bruce had in fact launched a new
strategy, one based on conquest rather than devastation. I would suggest, however, that when
he provided charters giving title to Northumbrian lands to his men, his action was more
intended to scare the English government than to reflect a serious policy option. Considering
his own ill health, the youth of his heir, and the disparity in resources between his kingdom
and England, he could hardly have seen a permanent conquest of Northumberland as a practical possibility.

[79] *Murimuth*, 56; *Barbour*, 743–5; *Le Baker*, 40; *Avesbury*, 283. The *English Brut*, 257 (like
Royal Brut, fo. 333), refers to the treaty as "the cowardise pees."

[80] *Pluscardensis*, 257; translation from *The Book of Pluscarden*, 191. For more on the
English response to the treaty, and on Edward's personal opposition to it, see Nicholson,
Edward III and the Scots, 51–6, and PRO 31/9/16/p. 19.

and Scotland; therefore, considering the killings, slaughters, crimes, destructions of churches, and ills innumerable which so often befell the inhabitants of each realm . . . we wish, and grant by the present letter . . . that the realm of Scotland . . . shall remain for ever to the eminent prince Lord Robert, by the grace of God illustrious King of Scots, our ally and dearest friend, and to his heirs and successors, divided in all things from the realm of England, entire, free, and quit, and without any subjection, servitude, claim or demand.[81]

To make sure that this concession would by fully implemented, the Scots required the English to give up all the documents from their archives which could be used to support their case for feudal superiority over the northern realm. Furthermore, Edward's young sister, Joan of the Tower, was married to David, Robert Bruce's son and heir. Edward, who personally objected to the treaty though he did not have the power to block it, expressed his disapproval by refusing to attend the wedding ceremony.[82]

Edward was also required by the treaty to ask the Pope to lift the excommunication which had been pronounced on the Bruce. Another provision of the agreement established the principle that Englishmen who had been disinherited of lands in Scotland would not be able to secure the return of their lands, and vice-versa. A few great northern magnates were excepted; no decision was reached as to whether or not they would get their Scottish lands back. This clause later proved a major bone of contention between the two kingdoms.

Bruce's negotiators agreed to only two major concessions (aside from peace itself): Edward was to receive a payment of £20,000, and Robert Bruce was to provide Joan's dowry of land worth £2,000 per year from his own resources.[83] These concessions were relatively small ones when viewed in perspective with the wealth of England: the £20,000 did not even come close to paying the nearly £70,000 of expenses the royal government had incurred for the campaign of 1327 alone, much less the damage inflicted by the Scots on the north or the cost of earlier campaigns against Scotland. It was, however, large enough to be an influential bribe for Isabella personally, and at least half the money eventually found its way to her private purse.[84]

The "killings, slaughters, crimes, destructions of churches, and ills innumerable" to which the king referred – inflicted by a fast-moving army which was

---

[81] Stones, *Anglo-Scottish Relations*, 162.

[82] *Pluscardensis*, 257. Cf. *Royal Brut*, fo. 332v: the marriage was "a grant abassement del noble sank roial dount ele nadquist, allas." See ibid., fo. 333, for widespread disapproval of the treaty.

[83] Stones, *Anglo-Scottish Relations*, 159, 165. Since Joan was, thus, well provided for by the terms of the treaty, the failure of the English royal government to allot any additional dowry to her was not, as Nicholson makes it out to be, an insult to Bruce and to Edward's own sister. Nicholson, *Edward III and the Scots*, 52.

[84] *CDS*, nos. 997, 1002. Scammell, "Robert I and the North of England," 402–3, argues that the £20,000 may have been meant as repayment of the "blackmail" (what in France would be called *appatis*, *patis*, or *suffrances de guerre*) paid by the people of the north to the Scots during the war.

dominated by mounted infantry who relied on the strength of the tactical defensive when faced with the immediate prospect of battle, but otherwise spread out across the countryside to inflict as much damage as possible by fire and theft – had been the levers which Robert Bruce used to put pressure on the English government. With them, Bruce secured his political objectives over the opposition of a larger, more populous, richer kingdom with a bigger and better-equipped army. In the process, he provided Edward III with an introduction to warfare and to strategy. The lessons the young Plantagenet king took from this campaign would later serve him very well in his wars against France.

CHAPTER THREE

"ONELICHE TO CONQUER [T]HAM IN BATAILE":[1]
THE DUPPLIN MOOR CAMPAIGN, 1332

*Throw the troops into a position from which there is no escape
and even when faced with death they will not flee. For if
prepared to die, what can they not achieve? Then officers and
men together put forth their utmost efforts. In a desperate
situation they fear nothing; when there is no way out they stand
firm.*   Sun Tzu, XI.33[2]

IN THE SUMMER OF 1415, Edward III's great-grandson Henry V met with
his advisers to set a strategy for the war with France, which he was about to
reopen. War with France would mean renewed war with Scotland, and the main
issue before the council was whether to direct the primary English military
effort northwards against the Scots, or across the Channel against the Valois.
The Earl of Westmorland argued at length that the proper course would be to
take on the weaker enemy first. He supported his case with historical examples,
with reminders of the dangers of leaving an unbeaten enemy in the rear and of
the advantages of direct supply lines, and finally with "the old auncient
proverbe used by our forfathers, whiche saieth, he that will fraunce wynne, must
with Scotland first beginne."[3]

That "old auncient proverbe" was certainly a legacy of the reign of Edward
III, who had himself begun with Scotland before making his bid to defeat
France.[4] The implication, however – that the Scottish wars of 1330s were
consciously planned to clear the way for Edward's Continental ambitions – is

---

1   *English Brut*, 277–8; see note 90, below.
2   Griffith (ed.), 134.
3   Edward Halle, *The Union of the Two Noble Families of Lancaster and York* (Menston:
Scolar Press, 1970) [Facsimile of 1550 edition], fo. vii. verso, sub Henry V. The Duke of Exe-
ter's counter-argument, that defeating France would also solve the Scottish problem, since
Scotland "is of it selfe, litle able to defende and lesse able to invade lyke a noune adjective
that cannot stand without a substantive," (ibid., viii) eventually carried the day. On Halle's
book, see Benedicta J. H. Rowe, "A Contemporary Account of the Hundred Years War," *EHR*
41 (1926).
4   Joshua Barnes, indeed, states that Robert of Artois used this argument with Edward III,
but his source is unclear. Barnes, *History of Edward III*, 72.

misleading.[5] Edward Balliol and the barons who invaded Scotland in 1332 did have Edward III's covert blessing, as this chapter will show, but the English monarch played no open role in the campaign which led to the battle of Dupplin Moor. The king's more active interventions in 1333, 1334, 1335, and 1336 were aimed at reversing the political and military humiliations of 1328, and regaining the suzerainty over Scotland which his grandfather had for a few years maintained, not at clearing the way for an attack on France. Edward was still looking backward more than forward.

And yet the campaigns of 1332–1336 strongly influenced the English king and his advisors when the war with France broke out in 1337. The alliance strategy of 1337–1340 can only be understood properly in reference to Edward's Scottish successes five years earlier. Although Edward did not personally participate in the Dupplin Moor campaign, he paid close attention to it. Thanks to the events of 1332, he found himself fighting in Scotland regularly until and beyond the outbreak of the war with the Valois – an event which itself can be considered a consequence of the events of the Dupplin Moor campaign, as we shall see. If the Weardale campaign had been Edward III's military apprenticeship, the invasions of 1333 and 1335 were his journeyman works. From the Scottish wars (including the campaign of 1332) he learned lessons which would serve him in good stead in his future wars, and also developed strong ideas about how wars were won – ideas which to a certain extent led him astray when they were applied to his greater enemy, France.

The political situation in England in 1332 was very different from what it had been in 1328. The main change had come in 1330, when the 17-year-old Edward III staged a dramatic coup against his mother and Mortimer, and took effective power over the kingdom into his own hands. The young king was well liked, especially in comparison with his mother and her lover, whose popularity, never great, had suffered severely from their much-criticized "cowardise pees."[6] Thus his rise to real power immediately strengthened the realm.

This new strength was particularly evident when contrasted with the situation in Scotland. Robert Bruce, as cagey a warrior as ever reigned in the north, had died in June of 1329. David II, Robert's heir, was only five years old at the time of his father's death. The Scots suffered another important loss the next year, when their best soldier, Sir James Douglas, that "brave hammerer of the English," fell in battle against Saracens in Spain.[7] In July of 1332, Thomas

---

[5]   Sumption seems to fall into this error when he writes that one of the defects of the Treaty of Northampton was that, since it failed to break or override the Franco-Scottish alliance of 1295, "any English king who envisaged a violent quarrel with France would wish to deal firmly with Scotland first in order to protect his rear." *Trial By Battle*, 124.

[6]   *English Brut*, 257; *Royal Brut*, fo. 333. Cf. Nicholson, *Edward III and the Scots*, 54.

[7]   *Fordun*, 354. He was seeking to fulfill his vow to carry the Bruce's preserved heart to Jerusalem. It seems likely, incidentally, that Bruce sent Douglas on this last mission in part to give the warden, Thomas Randolph, a chance to stabilize his new government while his only potential rival was out of the kingdom.

Randolph – Earl of Moray, Warden of Scotland, and the last experienced and effective military leader among the Scottish magnates – followed Douglas into the grave.[8] Thus, by midsummer of 1332 the situation of 1327 had been neatly reversed: now it was Scotland which labored under the burden of a royal minority and the resultant "dissensions and disputes,"[9] and England which was united in support of a popular and aggressive warrior-king.

Other factors exacerbated the instability of the situation on England's northern border. First among these was Edward III's proclamation that he had taken power into his own hands because "up to now the affairs of the realm have been conducted to our damage and dishonor and that of our realm" – which suggested a possible repudiation of the Shameful Peace of 1328, especially considering Edward's well-known disapproval of the treaty.[10] Relations between France and England added to the uncertainty. In the summer of 1330, before Edward launched his coup, Philip VI had declared him to be in breach of his feudal obligations respecting the Duchy of Aquitaine, because he had not yet done liege homage for the fief. Early in 1331, Philip's brother Charles of Alençon had led an army into the duchy and sacked Saintes, the chief town of Saintonge. This situation was enough to keep Edward's attention focussed to the south until the late spring, when he capitulated to Philip's demands, issuing a letter stating that his homage of 1329 should be considered as liege.[11] Philip did not press the matter further, and indeed after the two monarchs met in France in April, they parted as friends.[12] With the French situation resolved – or at least

8 As William Stewart, *The Buik of the Croniclis of Scotland*, 3:291, puts it: "The gouernour of Scotland, erle Thomas, / And his colleg schir James of Douglas, / Departit war out of this present ly[v]e; / Nane vther wes agane him [Balliol] that mycht stry[v]e." Froissart, *Oeuvres*, 2:277, makes a similar remark. Moray, who had commanded one of the Scottish schiltrons at Bannockburn, died on 20 July after a long illness. *Pluscardensis*, 264 (date). Among his other military feats were the capture of Edinburgh castle in 1313 and the leadership of the raids against northern England in 1318, 1319, and 1321. For his key role at Bannockburn, see *Barbour*, 457, 475–9.

   Ranald Nicholson, *Scotland in the Later Middle Ages* (Edinburgh: Oliver & Boyd, 1974), 125, points out that a number of other Scottish leaders, including Walter the Steward and the bishops of Moray and St. Andrews, also died at around this time.

9 *Wyntoun*, 2:384; *Fordun*, 354. The most immediate cause of the internal divisions in Scotland in 1332 was the election of the Earl of Mar as Warden of Scotland (following the death of the Earl of Moray); but resentments also lingered from the Black Parliament of 1320, when Robert Bruce had condemned for treason the Countess of Strathearn, the lords David Brechin and William Soulis and the corpse of Roger Mowbray. The conspirators had probably been involved in a plot to put Balliol on the throne. McNamee, *Wars of the Bruces*, 235–6; A. A. M. Duncan, "The War of the Scots, 1306–1323," *Transactions of the Royal Historical Society* [hereafter *TRHS*] 6th ser., 2 (1992), 129–31. Cf. also *Pluscardensis*, 263; Bower, *Scottichronicon*, 66.

10 *RFR*, II:2:799. For Edward's disapproval of the treaty in 1328, see *Scalacronica*, 156 ("The king was not in agreement with all this; but because of his young age the queen and Mortimer did all of it") and Nicholson, *Edward III and the Scots*, 55.

11 *RFR*, II:2:813.

12 *Grandes chroniques*, 9:121 ("furent amis ensemble"). For the concessions made by Philip

defused – Edward's position vis-à-vis Scotland became much stronger. Further-more, in the summer of 1331 the Scots made the last payment of the 30,000-mark "contribution for peace" to which they had agreed in the Treaty of North-ampton.[13] This eliminated one more factor which had encouraged Edward to maintain the truce. Last, Edward's rise to real power meant the restoration to favor of a number of powerful lords who had opposed the regime of Mortimer and Isabella. Henry Beaumont, Thomas Wake, and David Strathbogie – all of whom had good reason to press for war with Scotland, as we shall see – were among the foremost of this group.

None of these pressures, however, sufficed to make Edward openly violate the terms of the Treaty of Northampton, in which he had sworn on his soul to be a "good friend and loyal ally" to his young brother-in-law. Edward was a chival-rous monarch, and he took his honor very seriously. He could, and later did, argue that the treaty, ratified against his will while he was a minor, did not bind him.[14] As it happened, when Edward did invade Scotland in 1333, his reputation did not suffer for it, the glory of Halidon Hill obscuring the reproach of a broken oath.[15] Yet he could not, in advance, have been entirely sure that this would be the case. Furthermore, even given the settlement of 1331, there was a real possi-bility that an attack on Scotland could lead to a resumption of hostilities in France, since the French were bound by the terms of the recently renewed "auld alliance" to aid the Scots against the English "to the best of their power as loyal allies."[16] The English were by no means prepared for this eventuality.

Even if Edward III himself had wanted to renew hostilities with Scotland at this point, he would have found it very difficult to do so. After thirty years of failed military expeditions against the Scots, most of his subjects had little confidence in England's ability to prevail over Bruce's kingdom. Even after the

on this occasion (including offering reparations of 30,000 l.t. for the damage done to Saintes, and permission to leave standing four English-held castles of which the treaty ending the war of St.-Sardos had called for the demolition) see *RFR*, II:2:815–17.

13 Cf. *RFR*, II:2:804–5.

14 *RP*, 67. This was based on the same principle that allowed him to disavow the homage he did to Philip VI, that a minor cannot legally alienate his heritage.

15 This was the case in England and generally on the Continent, at least, but by some in Scot-land he was considered "a base, faithless perjurer, breaking through the ties of the treaty of alliance and peace . . . regardless of his own promise ratified by his seal and his oath." *Book of Pluscarden*, 201. Cf. *Wyntoun*, 2:395.

16 Nicholson, *Scotland in the Later Middle Ages*, 117. The terms of the alliance, however, were unequal, in that the French were not required to go to war if their ally were attacked, while the Scots were so obligated.

The fact that in October 1331, just six months after the settlement with France consequent on Edward's recognition of his homage as liege homage, Edward felt the need to ask the Pope to write to Philip in favor of peace indicates how serious was the possibility of war. At the same time, Edward was laying the groundwork for an alliance with Hainault, Guelders, Juliers and Brabant (the same Netherlandish princes who would join his alliance against France in 1337) in case war did break out. *RFR*, II:2:826–7.

battle of Dupplin Moor, which shattered any myth of Scottish invincibility, parliament showed little enthusiasm for war with Scotland, as we shall see. All of this combined to ensure that Edward would break the 1328 treaty only if spurred by an extraordinary provocation or opportunity. Such an opportunity did arise, in 1332, as the result of a lacuna in the Northampton agreement itself.

One of the issues discussed in the negotiations for the "final peace," as we have seen, was the restoration of confiscated lands to disinherited lords from both sides of the border. The two sides agreed in principle that Englishmen who had lost lands in Scotland, and Scots who had lost heritages in England, should be barred from pursuing their inheritances. The lords Wake, Beaumont, Percy, and la Zouche, however, were specifically exempted from this clause; they were given the chance to sue for their hereditary lands and titles in Scottish courts.[17] The end results of this arrangement were closely related to the political connections of the nobles in question: Percy received a partial settlement of his claims, and so he stood by Mortimer and Isabella in the political crisis of the winter of 1328–29, while Wake and Beaumont, both members of the opposing Lancastrian affinity, got nothing.[18]

Henry Beaumont, who claimed the titles of Earl of Buchan and Constable of Scotland in right of his wife Alice Comyn,[19] was a man of remarkable military experience. He had fought in Flanders in 1297 and at Bannockburn, and distinguished himself at Falkirk in 1298. Under his leadership, a group of soldiers led and financed[20] by the disinherited lords began to prepare an invasion force which could restore them to their rights by force. Among their number was the son of John Balliol, who in the time of Edward I had been "disinherited" from the crown of Scotland itself.[21] This son, Edward Balliol, had grown up as a hostage in England and then a minor nobleman in France. According to the *Brut*, a dispute with Philip VI had landed Balliol in prison until Beaumont bailed him out in 1331.[22]

David Bruce's claim to the Scottish crown was not entirely secure, given that it was only a generation old and that he himself was a young child. By supporting Balliol as a pretender to the throne, the Disinherited[23] gained several important advantages. First, they made it possible for individuals or factions

17 *Scalacronica*, 156; Stones, *Anglo-Scottish Relations*, doc. 42; *RFR*, II:2:804.
18 See Nicholson, *Edward III*, 58–62.
19 He was also the guardian and father-in-law of David of Strathbogie, dispossessed heir to the earldom of Atholl.
20 With the help of Edward III. See below.
21 John actually described Edward's intent in 1296 as "ad exheredandum nos." Stones, *Anglo-Scottish Relations*, doc. 23, p. 71.
22 *English Brut*, 1:273; *AM Brut*, 97v; Cazelles, *Société politique*, 136n. John Barneby, the esquire who is said to be the cause of Balliol's problems, did exist; before 1335 he received a land grant from Balliol, and at Perth in 1336 he sold Edward III a courser for his banner. R. C. Reid, "Edward de Balliol," 59; *WBRF*, fo. 214v.
23 This ("exheredati") is the name given to Beaumont's group by William Dene's *Historia Roffensis* (e.g. fo. 62), and also used by modern historians.

unhappy with the current political situation to support the invaders without committing manifest treason. In other words, Balliol's participation raised the possibility of transforming their war from a simple foreign invasion into a civil war – a civil war in which Balliol's faction expected to get substantial backing. They were encouraged in this belief by Donald, Earl of Mar, the ranking nobleman of Scotland after the Earl of Moray, who (according to the *Brut*) secretly attended Balliol at Sandhall in Yorkshire, did homage to him, and promised that all the magnates of Scotland would serve him and hold him for the true King of Scotland.[24] While this did not prove terribly important at first, since as things developed Mar switched to David's side shortly before the beginning of the Dupplin Moor campaign, and in general the Bruce's support turned out to be stronger than the English expected,[25] Balliol's claim to the throne did greatly strengthen the Disinherited's position in the aftermath of their battlefield victory.[26] Second, according to contemporary legal theory, Balliol could argue that his attempt to claim the throne qualified as a *bellum hostile* – a war waged by a sovereign prince[27] to secure the restoration of a wrongfully withheld heritage or right. Such a war was by definition "just," and so the men who fought in it gained the right, if captured, to be treated as prisoners of war rather than marauding criminals. Third, the prospect of a Balliol on the Scottish throne greatly increased the likelihood of gaining support from Edward III. John Balliol, Edward's father, had received the Scottish crown in 1292 as the result of a judgment by Edward I, whom John and the other claimants had recognized as "soverayn seignor" of Scotland. John had, furthermore, done liege homage to Edward for the realm.[28] Later, the Scottish king defied Edward I and was driven out of his kingdom by an English army. Shortly thereafter, Balliol formally surrendered the realm of Scotland to the English king.[29] Thus, a resurrection of the Balliol claim to the throne implicitly meant a revival of the English claim to suzerainty. This was true in practical reality as well as legal theory, since all concerned must have realized that Balliol would not be able to make his hold on power secure, even if the invasion were successful in the first instance, without strong support from south of the border.

24 *AM Brut*, fo. 98: "promist que toutz lez grauntz descoce serreyent a luy entendantz et luy tiendroient a Roy com dreyt heir descoce"; cf. the *Cleopatra Brut*, fo. 177v, which changes the verbs ("attendantz . . . tiendrent") and adds "et tant ferroient ils qe il serroit coronee Roi de la terre." The *AM Brut* on fo. 99 also describes the earl as "Donebald Counte de Marre cil qi fist a luy [Balliol] homage a Sandhall el countee Deuerwyk." Cf. *English Brut*, 274, 278.
25 *Scalacronica*, 159. On Mar, see notes 36 and 37, below.
26 An English document in *RFR*, II:2:849, states that after Balliol's coronation, many Scots who earlier had been supporters of his father entered into his peace and aided him with men. Cf. *Pluscardensis*, 266.
27 A position which he did not actually hold, but which he did claim. Since there was no terrestrial superior acknowledged by both David Bruce and Edward Balliol, the processes of "normal" law offered no remedy, which justified resort to the judgement of God. See Maurice Keen, *The Laws of War in the Middle Ages* (London: Routledge & Kegan Paul, 1965), passim.
28 Stones, *Anglo-Scottish Relations*, docs 17, 19, 20.
29 Stones, *Anglo-Scottish Relations*, doc. 24.

With that in mind, Balliol, Beaumont, and their cohorts sought to involve the king in their plans. According to the credible account in the *Brut*, they met with Edward III before launching their invasion to ask for his support – or, at least, for permission to launch an overland invasion from his territory. The king declined, explaining that if he let the invaders cross his lands, then people would say that he had assented to the attack, and so broken the Northampton treaty. Beaumont countered with an offer which virtually guaranteed that Edward would benefit, regardless of the turn of events. If the invasion were successful, Edward would stand to reverse the Turpis Pax, and regain suzerainty over Scotland – a suzerainty which would be much strengthened by the fact that his loyal subjects would number among the great magnates of Scotland (Beaumont as Earl of Buchan, Strathbogie as Earl of Atholl, etc.). If, on the other hand, the Disinherited were defeated in battle by the Scots, Edward could deny any connection with them and, as proof of his goodwill towards David, could confiscate the substantial English fiefs of the invaders.[30]

Balliol almost certainly did homage to Edward III at this time, receiving Scotland as a fief.[31] This act, as part of the deal proffered by Beaumont, sufficed to convince Edward to give the Disinherited as much support as he could without losing the ability to make a plausible denial of his involvement. On 27 March, for example, Edward made a gift of £500 (exactly enough to pay the wages of a thousand foot archers for two months) to Henry Beaumont, the leader of the gathering invasion force.[32] Edward must have been fully aware of the purpose to which Beaumont would put this money acquired by the alienation of his lands; yet less than a week earlier a royal warrant had been sent to the sheriffs of the northern counties, ordering them to arrest any men-at-arms gathering for an invasion of Scotland.[33] The king also assisted the Disinherited by granting numerous licenses for the Beaumonts and their ward, David of Strathbogie,[34] as well as lesser players like Richard Talbot and Thomas Wake,[35] to alienate or lease lands in order to raise capital for the expedition. This demonstrates pretty clearly that he was not really interested in blocking the plans of the Disinherited. If further proof of this were needed, it could be found in the presence of Walter Mauny, one of Edward's favorite household knights, among Balliol's army.[36]

---

30 *AM Brut*, fo. 98; *English Brut*, 275. Cf. *Melsa*, 2:362–3; *Murimuth*, 66.
31 Stewart, *Buik of the Croniclis*, 3:292; *Nangis*, 139; *Grandes chroniques*, 9:137–8. See also *RFR*, II:2:847, and below, pp. 51–55.
32 *CPR, 1330–4*, 270. At 2d. per day, the going rate; the calculation is mine. In accordance with the "deniability" principle, the gift was described as compensation for losses incurred when Beaumont was banished by Isabella and Mortimer. For Beaumont as the real leader of the force see *Historia Roffensis*, fo. 62.
33 *RFR*, II:2:833.
34 *CPR, 1330–4*, 283, 305–6, 326, 385, 397, 461.
35 CPR, *1330–4*, 260, 308, 367.
36 *Avesbury*, 296; see also *CDS*, no. 1086, p. 196. As Nicholson points out (*Edward III and the Scots*, 80), Mauny "would scarcely have engaged in the enterprise without the king's consent."

Thanks to the king's covert support, Balliol's army was able to assemble in Yorkshire and prepare for its daring enterprise without interference, despite publicly pronounced royal orders forbidding any such activity.[37] The invasion force was absurdly small – about five hundred men-at-arms and a thousand archers and other foot[38] – for a task which had for a generation proved beyond the capability even of full royal armies an order of magnitude larger. The reason that the Disinherited were willing to undertake such a great task with such a small army was that they expected to find many backers in Scotland.[39] Foremost among these, they thought, would be the Earl of Mar, "who had always incited Edward Balliol to come into Scotland and, through his [Mar's] help, gain his kingdom."[40]

---

[37] *RFR*, II:2:833, 843–4. Note that the latter prohibition, directed specifically against Henry Beaumont and the others planning to invade Scotland, was issued on 9 August, after they had already departed for Scotland. This was doubtless intentional. Indeed, since they left on 31 July, it seems quite possible that the king issued this proclamation immediately upon receiving word that the Disinherited had sailed. After his coronation, Balliol acknowledged that his success was due to the sufferance of Edward III and the great help provided by his people. *RFR*, II:2:848; see Chapter 4, below, for a full treatment.

[38] *Bridlington*, 102–3, 106; *Scalacronica*, 159; *Pluscardensis*, 265; *Lanercost*, 267; *Wyntoun*, 2:383; *Melsa*, 2:362. According to the *Anonimalle Brut*, 150, which is followed by Knighton, the Disinherited's force was somewhat larger, 2,500 men in total; the *Historia Aurea*, 560, gives the total as 2,400. The *Historia Roffensis* (c.1350) gives the total as only 1,400 (fo. 61v.), while the Pipewell chronicle says 1,600 (*Pipewell*, fo. 13), and *Chron. CCCO*, fo. 171v, says 2,000.

[39] *Scalacronica*, 159, has the soldiers of the army, on seeing the size of the Scottish host arrayed against them, complain that Beaumont "had led them to understand that they would have great support in Scotland"; this echoes Wyntoun's remark (*Orygynale Cronykil*, 2:383) that, when the Scots learned how small the English army was, "Folk wondered then how they dared take in hand such a weighty task, unless by connivance from within the country." Furthermore, Wyntoun, 2:391, reports that when Balliol's army was briefly besieged in Perth, after the victory at Dupplin, Beaumont said to his men "Luk that yhe be / Mery and glayd, and ha[v]ys na dowt; / For we have frendis in yhone rowt [army]."

[40] *Lanercost*, 267, says that before his election as warden, Mar "semper . . . excitaverat dominum Edwardum de Balliolo, ut veniret in Scotiam et haberet per suum adjutorium regnum suum, sed postquam vidit se electum in custodem regni adhaesit parti David, Edwardo relicto." Similarly, *Bridlington*, 104, refers to "Marr, qui per litteras et internuntios consilium et auxilium eisdem dominis multipliciter promiserat" [Mar, who by letters and messengers had many times promised counsel and aid to these [Disinherited] lords]; see also 105: "de suis [Mar's] consilio et auxilio confidentes, cum hujus regni recto herede domino Edwardo de Balliolo hucusque advenimus." The *Historia Roffensis*, fo. 62, fully supports this, stating that Beaumont came to Scotland by the counsel and assent of Scots who had promised to aid them, particularly Donald of Mar. See also the *English Brut*, 274, 278, *AM Brut*, fos 98, 99. This is made more credible by Mar's pro-English background, and by the mercy which he apparently wanted to show to the Balliol army when it was trapped before Dupplin Moor. Cf. *Wyntoun*, 2:383, 391.

According to the confession forced from the Earl of Kent in March of 1330, Mar had participated in a plot against Mortimer and Isabella that year which also involved Henry Beaumont, Beaumont's sister the Lady Vesci, Fulk Fitzwarin, and William de la Zouche – all of whom were active members of the group which sought to put Balliol on the Scottish throne in

Beaumont's strategy seems to have been quite simple. Since he would be coming by sea rather than land, the Scots would have to anticipate his attack at many points: he might land south of the Firth of Forth and threaten Edinburgh, or at its mouth to attack Stirling, or he might land on one of the banks of the Firth of Tay and move directly on Perth.[41] Given the small size of Balliol's army, the Scots could be expected to divide their forces into at least two parts. If the pretender expected malcontent Scots to flock to his standards, David's adherents could not afford to ignore the possibility that Balliol was right. Thus, they would want to strike quickly against the invaders, before the latter could attract supporters. This would require at least two forces, one to the north of the Firth of Forth, the other to the south. Beaumont clearly intended to meet one of these forces in battle.[42] The English had apparently made arrangements for that force to be the one led by the Earl of Mar, with the understanding that the earl would defect to Balliol's side at the crucial moment – which explains why Beaumont was willing to take such a large risk with such a small force.[43] The defeat of one Scottish force could be expected to strengthen Balliol's position at the expense of David Bruce's, as the latter's lukewarm adherents trimmed their sails to the wind.[44] This would leave the pretender a clear run at the throne, though the exact path would have to be determined by the course of events.

The Disinherited were well aware of the Earl of Moray's illness – later, in Scotland, they were widely believed to have caused it by poisoning.[45] When he died on 20 July, the news was broadcast throughout Scotland, along with summonses to a meeting where a new warden could be chosen. Word quickly reached England. On 31 July, Balliol's army took to the sea in some eighty-eight vessels, and set course for the Firth of Forth, hoping to strike while the Scottish leadership was still in turmoil.[46]

The men on board were not numerous, but they included an impressive roll-call of military potential. Henry Beaumont, the de facto commander of the

---

1332. The 1330 plot, intended to restore Edward II (who was falsely rumored to be still alive), was to involve a landing by Beaumont "towards Scotland, by the aid of Donald of Mar, who would aid them to carry out those matters, and as much as he could." The text of Kent's confession is printed in *Murimuth*, 253–5. One additional piece of circumstantial evidence is *CDS*, no. 1040, a safe-conduct for Mar and twelve followers to enter England in October 1331 "on his affairs" – making the meeting between him and Balliol reported by the *Brut* more credible.

[41] As Jomini argues, this is in general the great strength of the strategic offensive.

[42] This is suggested both by the general logic of the situation and by his earlier discussion with Edward III, where he referred to the possibility that the invaders might "be defeated in battle by the Scots." *AM Brut*, 98; *English Brut*, 275.

[43] See notes 38–9, above.

[44] Cf. *AM Brut*, 98v ["sils soient travaillez par vostre hardesce les autres Escots que a eux viegnont en aide countre nous les meyns oisont seur nous combattre"], 99; *English Brut*, 276.

[45] *Pluscardensis*, 264; *Wyntoun*, 2:383; *Barbour*, 773.

[46] Scots: Nicholson, *Edward III and the Scots*, 79. Balliol: *Pipewell*, fo. 13; *Bridlington*, 104; *Melsa*, 2:362.

expedition,[47] had been an active soldier for over thirty years already. Fulk Fitz-warin possessed comparably wide-ranging experience of war. Richard Talbot, who would later be Steward of the King's Household on the Crécy *chevauchée*, had already earned a reputation as a "famous young warrior."[48] Ralph Stafford, Henry Ferrers, Gilbert d'Umfraville, Thomas Ughtred and Walter Mauny would all become famous martial names. Of their coming military triumphs, however, few would shine brighter than the campaign of 1332.

While the Disinherited were still under sail, the parliament of Scotland met at Perth and, "efftyr gret and lang dyssentyown," chose Donald, Earl of Mar, to replace Thomas Randolph as warden.[49] Mar, as the lone survivor of the three Scottish commanders of 1327 and a close relative of the king, was the obvious choice.[50] The only real alternative candidate was Robert Bruce, King Robert's bastard son, but the manifest lack of wisdom of making an ambitious, illegitimate son the guardian for his younger legitimate brother must have ruled him out.[51] The "dissension" probably related to the rumors that Mar was in league with the English; certainly these rumors later led to the catastrophic argument between Mar and Bruce just before the battle of Dupplin Moor.

Mar took command of the Scottish forces to the north of the Forth; Patrick of Dunbar, the Earl of March, was made warden for the land to the south. Knowing that the Disinherited were on the way, they began to make appropriate preparations. Four days after Mar's appointment, on 6 August, Balliol's army landed at Kinghorn on the northern coast of the Firth of Forth.[52] Their landing was opposed by a number of Scots under the banners of Robert Bruce, Alexander Seton the younger, and Duncan, Earl of Fife. The Scots – who outnumbered the entire English army[53] – made a fierce attack before Balliol's men-at-arms had landed, but were driven off by the archers and a few other footmen.[54] Seton and

---

[47] As *Wyntoun*, 2:382, says: "Henry Beaumont was the one who carried the most weight in their councils, for he was a wise and worthy man."

[48] Barnes, *Edward III*, 59.

[49] *Wyntoun*, 2:384.

[50] Nicholson, *Edward III and the Scots*, 81.

[51] The Earl of March, though well respected, was not so closely related to David.

[52] *Bridlington*, 104; *Melsa*, 2:362; *Anonimalle Brut*, 148; *Pipewell*, fo. 13. Wyntoun seems to be confusing the date of the invaders' arrival at Kinghorn with the date of their departure.

[53] *Lanercost*, 267, gives their number at 4,000; the *Anonimalle Brut* and the *Brut* set the number at 10,000, as do *Knighton*, 1:462; *Hemingburgh*, 2:304; and the *Historia Aurea*, 560. *Melsa*, 2:363, says they had 14,000 and that 900 were killed; the *Historia Aurea*, the *Anonimalle Brut*, and *Chron. CCCO* (fo. 171v) repeat this casualty figure. *Bridlington*, 104, claims that the Scots numbered 24,000. The Scottish chroniclers give a much different story. *Pluscardensis*, 265, says the attack was made by a "few men," led by Alexander Seton who fell "with four or five nobles." Cf. *Fordun*, 354 and *Wyntoun*, 2:384. Considering the presence of Bruce and the Earl of Fife, the Lanercost chronicler's figure is probably closest to the truth; this would match well with the statement of the chronicle ascribed to William Pakington that the Scottish force had "twice as many people as the English had, or more." [avoit le double les gentz que lez gentz dengleterre avoient ou plus.] *Pakington*, fo. 184v.

[54] *Historia Aurea*, 560; *Melsa*, 2:363; *Murimuth*, 66; *Le Baker*, 49; *Knighton*, 1:462; cf. *Pipewell*, fo. 13: "Anglici ad terram exilentes de navibus sine equis istos [Scotos] animose

four or five other nobles were among the slain.[55] The English, much encouraged by this "great victory," marched fifteen miles west, to the abbey of Dunfermline.[56] The fleet, meanwhile, sailed for the Firth of Tay.[57] At the abbey the invaders found, among other supplies, more than five hundred newly made Scottish-style pikes of fine oak; Beaumont had these distributed to the strongest men of the company.[58]

When Mar and Dunbar learned of these events, they made a "generale gadryng" of armed men to repulse the invaders.[59] Mar's forces – which included the survivors of the action at Kinghorn – waited at the capital, Perth. Earl Patrick presumably moved first to Stirling, from where he could block any move by the enemy to the west. As the Scots gathered their forces, the Disinherited rested at Dunfermline for two days.[60] From there they struck out directly due north, heading for Perth. They clearly had this objective in mind from the first, as the dispatch of the fleet to the Tay shows. This leads to the question of why the expedition landed at Kinghorn rather than closer to its objective.

The answer is, it seems, mainly one of careful timing. Beaumont expected an encounter with one of the two major Scottish forces shortly after landing, but he did not want it to come either too soon or too late. The Englishmen would need at least a day or two to restore themselves to full fighting form after their six days and nights at sea.[61] And, if the Disinherited still expected help from Mar, or the arrival of other supporters, they would need to leave them a little time to maneuver. On the other hand, the longer the interval between the landing and the battle, the more strength the Scots could gather. The chance of striking while the Scottish leadership remained unsettled after the death of Moray might be lost. The plan to hit the northern division of the Scottish forces before it could join with the southern army would certainly become impossible if they delayed too long. A landing at Kinghorn would avoid an immediate encounter with either of the main Scottish forces – the warden could not anticipate a landing there – while leaving the army within striking distance of Perth, which the Scots could be expected to fight to defend.[62] The initial march to Dunfermline may have been partly for logistic reasons (to secure the food supplies which could be

---

invadebant"; *Historia Roffensis* fo. 62: "ad terram applicantes. Statim sine quiete contra Scotes congredientes, plures de Scochis occidentes."; *Chron. CCCO*, fo. 171v: "entra Escoce a Kynkorne et sodeignement lez archers tant soulement venquerent le count de Fiff."

55 *Pluscardensis*, 265.

56 Stewart, *Buik of the Croniclis*, 3:292; *AM Brut*, fo. 98v; *English Brut*, 276; *Scalacronica*, 159.

57 *Pluscardensis*, 265; cf. *English Brut*, 275; *AM Brut*, fo. 98.

58 *English Brut*, 276; *AM Brut*, fo. 98v; *Scalacronica*, 159.

59 *Wyntoun*, 2:384–5.

60 *Bridlington*, 104.

61 Ibid.

62 Note that the fact that the warden's army was not present at Kinghorn to oppose the English does not eliminate the possibility that Mar had been in collusion with the English. Informing Mar of their intended landing site (assuming that they even had a specific one picked in advance) would have gained the Disinherited nothing, but added an additional

expected to be found there), but was probably equally for navigational ones. One march directly west, followed by another directly north, would take them straight to Perth with a minimal chance of getting lost.

Much the same might have been accomplished by first marching north from Kinghorn to the monastery of Lindores on the Firth of Tay, then advancing west along the coast. That course might have allowed the Disinherited to rendezvous with their fleet before facing a major Scottish army, and would have had the advantage of keeping the invaders farther away from the Earl of March's division. Beaumont and Balliol, however, seem to have viewed the potential for an early meeting with the fleet to be more a disadvantage than an advantage. By taking the Dunfermline route, they ensured that their fellow adventurers would have to conquer or die: there would be no escape by sea.[63] In the eyes of contemporaries, this move gave the Englishmen a critical advantage when the battle came, for "dispare gyvys hardyment."[64] Indeed, if the invaders had taken the route via Lindores, the battle of Dupplin Moor would likely never have taken place: as the anticipated Scottish supporters failed to appear, many in Balliol's army would have been glad of a chance to escape before fighting.[65]

In the event, though, the English reached the Earn river, only a couple of miles from their destination, on 10 August. Dunbar's force paralleled their advance, encamping at Auchterarder some eight miles west of Balliol's position at Forteviot.[66] Mar's army had already come out of Perth, and was waiting for the invaders on the north bank of the Earn. The English spent the remainder of the 10th "eye to eye" with the Scots,[67] each side waiting to see what the other would do. The Scots had no motive to hasten their attack, since (as Balliol observed) "the power of Scotland may euery day wax and encresce, and we may nought so."[68] The English, heavily outnumbered, would have been foolhardy indeed to try to make an assault over the water. So neither side made a move.

The situation looked grim for the outnumbered Englishmen.[69] If they were still expecting Earl Donald to defect to their side, they were disappointed.[70] With Mar's forces before them and Dunbar's behind, they seemed like fish in a net, or

element of risk should he choose to double-cross them, or be discovered as their collaborator by the other Scots, so they probably did not do so.

[63] *English Brut*, 275; *AM Brut*, fo. 98. Cf. R. Muntaner, *The Chronicle of Muntaner*, tr. Lady Goodenough (London: Hakluyt Society, 1920–1), 2:520 for a parallel.

[64] *Wyntoun*, 2:386–7, who supports his opinion with reference to "Scypio, that wes wys," showing that he had drawn this lesson from Vegetius' *De Re Militari*, III.21.

[65] Ibid.; *Melsa*, 2:364; *Scalacronica*, 159.

[66] *Wyntoun*, 2:385–6.

[67] *Knighton*, 1:463; *Anonimalle Brut*, 148; *Pipewell*, fo. 13.

[68] *English Brut*, 276; *AM Brut*, fo. 98v: "Qar le poair de Escotes se multeplye et nous ne sumes que poy de gent vers eux."

[69] *Anonimalle Brut*, 148; *Historia Roffensis*, fo. 62 ["pauci anglici erant non valentes resistere viribus multitudinis totia scotorum in propria terra"]; citations in note 65, above.

[70] This is the story given by *Bridlington*, 104–5.

a hare chased into its warren.[71] The Scots planned to send a large force to surround Balliol on the next day, so that they could attack from all sides.[72]

It may seem odd that the leadership of the Disinherited made no offer of surrender to the Scots once they discovered that their supposed ally, Earl Donald, did not intend to come to their aid. Their last experience of battle, after all, had been the disastrous English defeat at Bannockburn. In the intervening eighteen years the English had proved unable to recoup from that catastrophe; as far away as Italy they were seen as "inferior to the wretched Scot."[73] It should be remembered, however, that Beaumont had also fought with distinction at Falkirk in 1298, where an English army destroyed a large Scottish host under William Wallace. In the years after Bannockburn, moreover, the English may not have won any major fights, but they did not lose any regular battles either. The lesson of those years, as exemplified in the outcome of the Weardale campaign – and reinforced by Beaumont's own experiences in 1314[74] – was that attacking a body of pike-armed men, well-disciplined and in a good defensive position, was likely to lead to defeat.[75] Beaumont knew that, given the circumstances, his men could be counted on to stand their ground. They would also benefit from the fire of their archers, who had made an important contribution to the victory at Falkirk.[76] Thus the leaders of the Disinherited still preferred to stand the test of battle, despite their small numbers and their perilous position.[77]

The position of the English looked so hopeless, though, that the Scots "took no account" of them, but sent to Perth for wine and ale, then spent the night dancing, singing and drinking.[78] Considering their overwhelming strength and the difficulty of crossing the Earn, they felt no need to set a general watch, although the best-armed of Mar's host were delegated to "besiege" the broken bridge over the river.[79] Despite this precaution, they thought it more likely that the English would flee in the darkness than that they would make a night attack.

---

[71] The latter simile, "regettez com vn leuer," (*Scalacronica*, 159), is difficult to interpret; I take it to be the equivalent of "regîtez comme un lièvre." Maxwell interprets it as "ensnared like a hare" (*Scalacronica*, ed. Maxwell, 89). The first simile is used by *Wyntoun*, 2:386.

[72] *Scalacronica*, 159.

[73] See the quotation from one of Petrarch's letters, in R. Boutruche, "The Devastation of Rural Areas during the Hundred Years War and the Agricultural Recovery of France," *The Recovery of France in the Fifteenth Century*, ed. P. S. Lewis (New York: Harper & Row, 1972), 26.

[74] Cf. *Scalacronica*, 141–2.

[75] Cf. my "Offensive/Defensive in Medieval Strategy," 158–61.

[76] *Hemingburgh*, 180.

[77] In addition to these calculations, according to the *Historia Roffensis*, were the justice of their cause; the fact that God can easily deliver a multitude into the hands of a few; that men's quality is more important than quantity in determining victory; and (somewhat contradictorily) that it is better to die fighting for a just cause than to flee. *Historia Roffensis*, fo. 62.

[78] *Wyntoun*, 2:386; cf. ibid., 387, and Stewart, *Buik of the Croniclis*, 3:293.

[79] *Bridlington*, 106; *Melsa*, 2:363 [obsidebant]; according to the *AM Brut*, fo. 98v, the burghers of Perth had earlier broken the bridge (which was made of planks) to hamper Balliol's advance.

But the Disinherited knew that they were doomed unless they could take the initiative. As the Scots "made myrthis swa," the English discovered an unguarded ford by which they could secretly cross the river.[80] Near midnight, when all the Scots had gone to sleep, Balliol's troops picked their way across the dangerous ford, making the crossing almost unscathed and without alerting their enemies.[81] When they came upon a detached encampment of sleeping Scots at Dupplin Moor, they attacked fiercely, killing or capturing all who did not flee. At first they thought they had routed the main body of the Scots, but when morning came, they discovered that they had done no such thing.[82] The lords Vesci and Stafford, who had been sent to scout the area, returned bearing word that the Scots, well arrayed in two large schiltrons, were at that moment advancing against them, with helms and shields gleaming.[83]

In the absence of pay records or similar documents, it is impossible to determine the size of Mar's army accurately. The narrative sources are, however, surprisingly consistent: English writers number the host at forty thousand,[84]

---

[80] *Wyntoun*, 2:387; Bower, *Scottichronicon*, 77, 82. These sources claim that the English were shown the ford by a Scottish traitor – presumably someone involved in the earlier plot with Mar. William of Dene agrees that they were led by a Scot. *Historia Roffensis*, fo. 62v. However, the *Anonimalle Brut*, 148, says the crossing was made at a ford "with which Sir Alexander Mowbray was familiar." Cf. also *Bridlington*, 105.

[81] One of the men-at-arms, Roger de Swinnerton junior, drowned in the crossing. *Scalacronica*, 160; *English Brut*, 277; *AM Brut*, fo. 98v. William of Dene (*Historia Roffensis*, fo. 62 v) says that the English killed all the Scots "deputed to guard the crossing at the ford" [ad custodiendum transitum vadi deputatos]; but since Dene does not break the battle into the two phases described below, this is probably a reference the defeat of the first encampment of Scots encountered, before the battle proper.

[82] *Bridlington*, 105; *Scalacronica*, 160; *English Brut*, 277; *Knighton*, 1:463. Exactly whom they *had* defeated is open to question: the *Scalacronica*, says it was only the "garsouns et cheuaux de lour enemys," [servants and horses of their enemies] while different versions of the *Brut* make different claims: "mich peple of men of armes ful wel arraiede," says the *English Brut*, 277; "ces furrent les plus vaillantz gentz" says the *Cleopatra Brut*, fo. 178v; "ces fusrent gentz paisantz" says the (earlier) *AM Brut*, fo. 99. Most likely the English actually hit neither men-at-arms (no noblemen were mentioned as slain in this action, and the men-at-arms were apparently guarding the bridge) nor grooms (even the *Scalacronica* agrees that the Disinherited at first thought they had struck "le poar del ost lours enemys" [the power of the enemy army], a mistake they would not likely have made if they were fighting only boys and servants), but rather a group of the Scots' common infantry. Cf. also *Bridlington*, 106, *Melsa*, 2:363. The statement of the *Chronica Monasterii de Pipwell*, fo. 13v, that the English killed "more than fifty Scots" in this encounter is hard to reconcile with the Englishmen's apparent belief that they had secured a major victory: perhaps the scribe erroneously substituted "quinquagintos" (50) for "quingentos" (500)?

[83] *AM Brut*, fo. 99; *Cleopatra Brut*, fo. 178v; *English Brut*, 277. All the versions of the *Brut* have the Scots approach in three battles, as does the *Historia Roffensis* (fo. 62v), but other sources (e.g. *Wyntoun*, 2:388; *Lanercost*, 268) make it clear that the Scots were in two battles.

[84] *Anonimalle Brut*, 148; *Bridlington*, 106; *Melsa*, 2:363–4; *Knighton*, 1:462; *Murimuth*, 66; *Le Baker*, 49; *Hemingburgh*, 304; *Pipewell*, fo. 13v.; *Chron. CCCO*, fo. 171v. *Lanercost*, 267,

while Scottish chronicles say thirty thousand.[85] At first glance, these figures may seem wildly exaggerated, considering that there was another Scottish force under the Earl of March which is not included in this total, and that Edward III's field armies probably never reached thirty thousand, though England was far more populous and wealthy than Scotland, and possessed a much more developed military administration.[86] On the other hand, the martial culture of Scotland, where every adult man was expected to be a warrior, made it possible to raise remarkably large numbers of troops relative to the population.[87] In the situation of 1332 – a brief general gathering on home ground to repel an invader – questions of military or financial organization were almost irrelevant, since the troops were not paid, and barely organized. The prospect of an easy victory over a vastly outnumbered enemy (along with the possibility of lucrative ransoms) would also have helped to swell Mar's army. Taking all of that into account, my conservative guess (and it is only a guess) would be that Earl Donald's force exceeded fifteen thousand men. The English would, then, have been outnumbered by some ten to one. In any case, there can be no question that Edward Balliol was correct in observing that his army comprised "ful litel peple" compared to the Scots.[88]

The soldiers in the army of the Disinherited suffered a moment of despair as their illusion of triumph evaporated before the reality of their unvanquished enemies advancing "*in multitudine maxima.*"[89] Lord Fulk Fitzwarin then spoke up, saying that though he had been in many tactical formations (*eschiels*), he had never yet seen even the fifth part of one actually fight. Therefore, if the English would stand steady, be of bold heart, and think neither upon their wives nor their children, but concentrate only on defeating the enemy, then there would be enough of them to win the battle.[90] Whether this would have sufficed to fill the

---

gives the number of Scots as 30,000. Neither the *Brut* nor the *Scalacronica* gives a number for the Scots.

[85] *Wyntoun*, 2:385; *Fordun*, 355; *Pluscardensis*, 265.

[86] Some 32,000 soldiers served on the Crécy-Calais campaign, but not all at the same time. It should be noted, however that England was able to put another force into the field at the same time, one strong enough to defeat a major Scottish invasion at Neville's Cross – probably about 10,000 men. See my "Scottish Invasion of 1346" for details. Furthermore, the Black Death, which struck England in 1348–49, made the armies of the later fourteenth and the fifteenth centuries smaller, but in 1332 was not yet a factor.

[87] Cf. Contamine, *War in the Middle Ages*, 164: "It is true that the *Italian Relation* of 1500 considered the Scots could provide their king in an emergency with 50,000 or 60,000 men serving at their own expense for thirty days."

[88] *English Brut*, 276; cf. *Pipewell*, fo. 13v: "exercitus scotorum fortis et quasi innumerabilis respectum eorum," and *AM Brut*, fo. 99.

[89] The quote is from *Bridlington*, 106; for the English reaction, see the sources in note 65, above.

[90] This remarkable passage is worth quoting in full, for the light it casts on the chivalric warrior's *mentalité*: I will give it here from the *AM Brut*, fo. 99, but note that there are significant variations in the *English Brut* (pp. 277–8), which changes "quinte part" to a fourth part, and

Englishmen with resolve had they been offered a chance to surrender cannot be said; but in the event the issue did not come up, since the first division of the Scots was already bearing down upon them at full speed.

The English had taken up their position at the base of a declivity at the edge of the moor, in a narrow passage where the hills protected their flanks.[91] In order to match the frontage of the Scottish schiltrons, the men-at-arms deployed, on foot, in a thin line spread across some six hundred feet. Most likely this formation was only four ranks deep – three of men-at-arms backed by one of spear-carrying infantry. On each flank of this line the archers formed up, probably on the slopes of the hills.[92] A troop of forty "German" men-at-arms, still mounted, took position behind the main battle-line to act as a mobile reserve; the horses of the other men-at-arms were sent to the rear.[93]

in the *Cleopatra Brut*, fo. 178–78v which changes "el mounde et" to "sibien envers sarsyeny come envers gents Descoce mais."

    Donqes disoit sire Fouk filtz Garyn un baroun renomez d'armes: "Sachez, seigneurs, que j'ay este en diverses eschieles el mounde et unqes unqore ne vy jeo la quinte parte de nul eschiele combatre. Pur quey sy nous volons combatre et countre ester noz enemys nous y sumes assetz arester lour force et de combatre od eux, mez sy nous ne soions de bone volunte a ceo faire certes nous sumes trop petitz a ceste assemble. Et purceo p[re]nons nous bon cuer, vigour, et hardiesce et ne pensons rien de femmes d'enfauntz ne de parentz forsqe soulement de conquerre la bataille et nous venquerons noz enemys ou l'eide dieu."

[91] *AM Brut*, fo. 99: "a un pendant del bout del more en un estrait passage." "Bout" may possibly refer to a sheep-fold, rather than simply the "end" of the moor; cf. *English Brut*, 278, and *Cleopatra Brut*, fo. 179: "a un dependant al bught' de la more."

[92] The length of their front is given by *Avesbury*, 297. Given that the number of men-at-arms was around 500, a three-line formation would mean one soldier would have just over a 3.6 feet to occupy, which seems about right. (Four lines of men-at-arms in 600 feet would require each man to cover 4.8 feet, which is probably too much for a medieval pike fight (though 17th-century drill did call for such loose formations), while a two-line formation would leave each man-at-arms only 2.4 feet, which is probably too tight – especially considering that the English began the battle with their chests, rather than their shoulders, turned to the enemy. *Scalacronica*, 268. Furthermore, a three-deep line was dangerously thin; two-deep would be even more so. I posit the fourth line of common infantry because the sources make it clear that the 1,000 English infantry included both archers and other "pedites," but only the archers (and the small cavalry troop) are described as being positioned to attack the flanks of the enemy formation. *Bridlington*, 107; *Melsa*, 2:364. Cf. J. R. Hale, *War and Society in Renaissance Europe* (London: Fontana, 1985), 59, for a fifteenth-century example of lines three ranks deep. Presumably, then, the spearmen were in the center, strengthening a perilously thin line. That these men were at the rear rather than the front is suggested by the fact that 35 of the English men-at-arms were killed, but none of the archers or *pedites*, and by the logic of putting the best armored in front. It is possible, however, that the spearmen were interspersed with the archers instead. *Melsa*, 2:364–5; *Knighton*, 1:463.

[93] This is the conclusion I draw from the *Anonimalle Brut*'s statement that "les parties sassemblerent coraiousement sauve xl hommes darmes Dalemaine" (pp. 148–50), a reading which is supported by another version of the shorter *Brut* continuation (cited by the editors of the *Anonimalle Brut*, p. 54), and by the *Historia Aurea*, 560. Cf. *Knighton*, 1:463, and *Bridlington*, 106, for a slightly different version. I put "German" in quotation marks because it is

Meanwhile, a dispute broke out between the Scottish leaders. The Earl of Mar suggested that the English be given a chance to surrender; this would be an act of mercy towards fellow Christians as well as an opportunity to extract "grievous ransoms" from them.[94] Under other circumstances this proposal might have found favor among the Scots, but not while the cries of the men wounded in the English surprise attack still echoed in their ears.[95] Coming when it did, this proposal was enough to revitalize the rumor that Mar was secretly allied to Balliol. Robert Bruce, who commanded the first schiltron, accused Earl Donald of being a traitor to Scotland. Mar denied any connection with Balliol's faction, and proclaimed that he would prove the accusation false by being the first to strike the invaders' army. Bruce, replying that he would strike the enemy before Mar, spurred forward at the head of his schiltron.[96] Since he had command of the vanguard,[97] his followers (including the earls of Menteith and Moray) did indeed win the race to the English lines, but in their haste they became disordered and dispersed, leaving behind all but eight hundred men.[98]

They smashed straight into the English center, driving it back some twenty or thirty feet.[99] When Lord Stafford called out that the Englishmen should turn their shoulders to the pikes, rather than standing with their chests to the enemy, the English did better and were able to hold their ground.[100] The short retreat of the English men-at-arms actually would have worked to their advantage, for it would have left the archers on the wings in an even better position to fire into

---

very possible that they in fact came from the Imperial portion of the Low Countries, where the English were better connected, rather than from Germany proper.

94 *AM Brut*, fo. 99; *Cleopatra Brut*, fo. 179; *English Brut*, 276.

95 The main body of the Scots became aware of the English attack "be the noyis, and the cry off men, that slayne and stekyd [stabbed] ware, that thai herd heyly cry and rare." *Wyntoun*, 2:387.

96 *AM Brut*, fo. 99: ["Certes, Donebald," feat le dit sieur Robert, "ore say jeo bien qe vous estes enemy et traitre descoce depuys qe vous vuyllez salver noz enemys mortlex. Ore piert ceo bien qe vous estez de lour assent." "Certes, Robert," fait sr Donebald, "vous y mentez. Jeo ne suy pas de lour covyne et ceo verrez vous en haste car jeo me combateray a eux eynz qe nul aultre de ceste host ne ferra." "Certes," fait sr Robert, "jeo lez assaileray devant vous maugre le vostre teste."]; *Cleopatra Brut*, fo. 179. The translation in the *English Brut*, 276, is much less clear.

97 At least, the account in the *Scalacronica*, 160 (which was based partly on Scottish sources, since it was written when the author was imprisoned in Scotland) refers to the first unit to strike the English line (which was Bruce's) as the "auauntgard," and the second as the "areirgard." *Wyntoun*, 2:388, similarly, calls Bruce's unit "the fyrst rowt."

98 Number: *Wyntoun*, 2:387. Disorder: Bower, *Scottichronicon*, 7:76 [preter ordinem]; *Cleopatra Brut*, fo. 179, "ove ceo le graunt host de les Escotz espernelment viendrent encontre le Baillol"; *AM Brut*, 99: "lour escheles lez suyeront a randoun." Note that the *Cleopatra Brut* (fo. 179) and the *English Brut*, 276, wrongly change "followed at random" to "followed in a rank."

99 Not, as one historian writes, "twenty or thirty paces." See *Lanercost*, 268: "quasi per viginti pedes vel triginta." (A pace ["gradus" or "passus"] is five Roman feet.) See also *Bridlington*, 106.

100 Ibid., *Wyntoun*, 2:388.

the flanks and rear of the Scotsmen – a sort of "Cannae effect." On the Scottish side, the momentum of the men in the rear, charging downhill against a steady enemy, caused great difficulties for the men to the fore: "so hastily did they come against them," says the *Brut*, "that they piled into a heap of thousands, each on top of others."[101] While the two centers remained deadlocked, Balliol's archers rained their fire into the Scottish flanks at point-blank range.[102] Many of the Scots were wounded by the arrows – especially, according to the Lanercost chronicler, in the face – leaving them helpless.[103] Those on the outside of the Scottish formation naturally tended to press away from the incoming arrows. Especially in the center, one man was crammed against another into a solid mass, until they could no longer move, or even breathe.[104] The Lanercost chronicler's source was so impressed by the importance of this factor that he said the battle was won "primarily by the English archers."[105]

The Earl of Mar, seeing that the first schiltron had failed,[106] led his much larger force forward with such haste that it became disordered "out of burning desire to fight."[107] Whether he meant to rescue his compatriots, or simply to outdo them, in fact he sealed their doom as well as his own. His men slammed into the back of the first schiltron, bearing to the ground all who stood before them. The crush at the center of Bruce's formation had been bad when it was under pressure from three sides; with the impact of another unit ("friendly" or

[101] *Cleopatra Brut*, fo. 179: "tant ils lour hastirent envers eux qe ils ahepirent millers chescun sur altri." The *AM Brut*, fo. 99–99v, conveys the same idea somewhat less clearly: "et taunt sey hastierent vers le Baillol quils recuylleront a plusours Ml chescun seur aultre." Cf. *English Brut*, 278–9.

[102] *Historia Roffensis*, fo. 62v; cf. *Bridlington*, 106.

[103] Or, possibly, leaving them unable to help each other. The Latin, "victi sunt Scotti maxime per sagittarios Anglicorum, qui primam aciem Scottorum ita excaecaverunt et vulneraverunt in facie continuis ictibus sagittarum quod non poterant se juvare," is somewhat ambiguous. The first reading is more probable, since "each other" would usually be "inter se" rather than "se" alone. *Lanercost*, 268. The same phenomenon was observed at Halidon Hill the next year, where the English archers "shot so fast and sore that the Scottis myght not helpe hamself." *English Brut*, 285; cf. the *Lanercost*, 274, and the *Historia Roffensis*, fo. 100.

[104] *Bridlington*, 106: "hostium vero minores turmae per sagittarios plurimum lacerati, adhaerere magno exercitui compelluntur, et in brevi conglobati, alius ab alio premebatur; ita a suis suffocati"; *Pipewell*, fo. 13v: "Scoti autem per sagittarios graviter vulnerati in unum globum convientes se ipsos compresserunt"; *Historia Roffensis*, fo. 62v: "Tanta fuit pressura inter scotos ut nullus valuit contra anglicos manum levare sed omnes in unam massam conglobati"; Bower, *Scottichronicon*, 76. This phenomenon was surprisingly common in medieval warfare (especially in battles where the English archers were involved). See my "The Offensive-Defensive in Medieval Strategy," 160.

[105] *Lanercost*, 268.

[106] Wyntoun's remark (*Wyntoun*, 2:388) that "Syndry men trowyd rycht fermly, that had thai [Bruce's schiltron] hade to feycht laysare, thai had noucht bene dyscumfyt thare," smacks of old veterans passing the blame; considering the Lanercost chronicle's account, it seems that the archers' fire had them in desperate straits even before the impact of Mar's schiltron.

[107] *Pluscardensis*, 266.

not) on its rear, the situation went from critical to horribly lethal. Whoever fell was trampled, never to rise again.[108] Mar, and the others with him at the front of the second schiltron, found themselves unable to come to grips with their enemy in the confusion, as the survivors of the vanguard struggled to escape the press. Yet the weight of the deep Scottish formation continued to push forward. Over a thousand men, according to Wyntoun, were smothered there, without a drop of blood being spilled. The combat became a butchery as the English, climbing on top of the corpses in front of them, stabbed with swords and lances into the mass of their enemies until they were ready to drop from exhaustion.[109] The earls of Mar, Moray, and Menteith fell in the mêlée, along with the lords Robert Bruce and Alexander Fraser, thirteen other barons, 160 knights, and "numberless" men of lower rank. The number of Scots killed, in total, far exceeded the size of the entire invasion force.[110] The Earl of Fife fled the scene, and the other surviving Scots saved themselves as best they could.[111] The dead lay in heaps, the highest pile as tall as a spear.[112] The English, over the course of the six-hour fight, suffered the loss of only two knights and thirty-three esquires; the bowmen and other *pedites* were reported to have avoided a single death.[113]

Once the Scottish defeat had become a rout, the victorious men-at-arms mounted their horses and began to pursue the fugitives, killing most of the ones

---

[108] *Wyntoun*, 2:388; Cf. *Brut*, 278–9.

[109] "Le Baillol et ses gentz fortement esturent envers eux et lour tuerent et naufrerent si longement qe ils esturent sur eux et leur poignerent ove lour espieez et launces parmy lour corps et taunt ovrerent ils sur eux que ils deviendrent si lassez q'ils ne savoient qe feare." *Cleopatra Brut*, fo. 179.

[110] *Wyntoun*, 2:388; *Bridlington*, 106–7; *Scalacronica*, 160 are the best accounts; all, along with the *Historia Aurea*, 560, the *Historia Roffensis* (fo. 62v), and *Chron. CCCO* (fo. 171v) agree with *Fordun*, 355, that "from the bruising of their bodies squeezing against one another, more fell, though unwounded, than were slain by shaft or sword." (Translation from Fordun, *Chronicle*, 347). For the Scottish casualties, see also *Anonimalle Brut*, 150; *Pipewell*, fo. 13v; *Knighton*, 1:463; *Melsa*, 2:365. *Hemingburgh*, 2:304, lowers the number of knights to 80, and (like the *Anonimalle Brut*) specifies 2,000 men-at-arms and 13,300 infantrymen killed; the *Historia Aurea*, 560, gives the same numbers, except that it cites 800 knights (a number also given by *Chron. CCCO*, fo. 171v). The Scottish chroniclers claim that only two or three thousand were killed, in total. *Wyntoun*, 2:388; *Fordun*, 355; *Pluscardensis*, 266, says over three thousand. Stewart, *Buik of Croniclis*, 3:295, however, who gives a more detailed accounting of Scottish casualties than the other Scottish sources though his account of the battle is very poor overall, says that 3,000 "nobillis" died, "of other men out of nummer vntald." Bridlington gives the number of Scottish casualties as 18 bannerets, 58 knights [milites], 800 esquires [equites], 1200 armored troops [armati], and "many common foot [pedites]."

[111] *Bridlington*, 106; *English Brut*, 270. *Fordun*, 355, and Bower, *Scottichronicon*, 78 say that 360 of his men-at-arms had fallen under Fife's banner before he decided to flee.

[112] *Lanercost*, 268; *Historia Aurea*, 560; *English Brut*, 279; *Chron. CCCO*, fo. 171v; *Hemingburgh*, 2:304; *Scalacronica*, 160; Bower, *Scottichronicon*, 78. *Avesbury*, 297, has the mound of the dead being 200 yards long, reaching in places a height of 6 cubits (about 9 feet) or more. *Melsa*, 364, says 20 feet. *Bridlington*, 107, gives the height of the mound as 15 feet.

[113] *Chron. CCCO*, fo. 171v; see also *Hemingburgh*, 304; *Anonimalle Brut*, 150; *Knighton*, 1:463; *Historia Aurea*, 560.

they could catch. The Earl of Fife, the only survivor of comital rank, was captured.[114] Once the setting sun brought an end to the pursuit, Balliol's army made its way to Perth.[115] The citizens, deprived of their defenders by the battle, surrendered the unwalled town without a struggle.[116] Balliol's men made merry with the ample supplies they found there, then began to repair the town's old defenses (a broad ditch and a wooden palisade) in preparation for an anticipated siege by Dunbar's army.[117]

It took somewhat over a week for the earl to raise the largest possible army and move against the English.[118] The Scots, however, soon realized that there was little they could do with their great host. If attacking the invaders on open ground had led to disaster, then assaulting them in a prepared position would be suicide. Dunbar did not order an assault. Starving out the invaders was impossible: Balliol had captured plenty of supplies in Perth, and had in any case far fewer mouths to feed than did his besiegers. Whatever chance of implementing such a strategy there might have been was destroyed when the English fleet defeated the ships sent by the Scots to complete the siege from the sea side.[119] When the Scots began to run out of forage, their army broke up.[120]

As news of the battle of Dupplin Moor and the failed siege spread through the realm, a large number of noble Scots hastened to Perth to yield themselves to Balliol, and do him homage and fealty.[121] Among those turning to his side were the recently captured Earl of Fife and thirteen knights of his following.[122] Support was even more forthcoming from the ecclesiastical magnates of the realm. At Dupplin Moor, so few had triumphed over so many that it was universally seen as "Goddis deide;" accomplished "not by their virtue, but by the

---

[114] *AM Brut*, fo. 99v; *English Brut*, 279; *Fordun*, 355.

[115] *Cleopatra Brut*, fo. 179v (night). The *Historia Roffensis*, fo. 62v, notes that in this advance they encountered and dispatched a number of Scots who came up to meet them, assuming that Balliol's men were the victorious Scottish host.

[116] *AM Brut*, fo. 99v; *Anonimalle Brut*, 150; *Pluscardensis*, 266; Stewart, *Buik of the Croniclis*, 296.

[117] *Anonimalle Brut*, 150; *Knighton*, 1:464; *English Brut*, 279; *Scalacronica*, 160; *Bridlington*, 107.

[118] *Scalacronica*, 160. Fifteen days according to the *Historia Roffensis*, fo. 62v.; three days according to *Pipewell*, fo. 13v (though this may mean three days after the defenses were completed).

[119] *Anonimalle Brut*, 150–2; *English Brut*, 280; *Knighton*, 1:464–5; *Historia Aurea*, 560; *Pipewell*, fo. 13v.

[120] *Scalacronica*, 161; *Historia Roffensis*, fo. 62v, which notes that the English sallied out and killed many of the retreating Scots.

[121] Stewart, *Buik of the Croniclis*, 3:297; *English Brut*, 280; *Wyntoun*, 2:392, says that they were primarily from Fife, Fothrif, Gowrie, and Strathearn. Cf. also *Fordun*, 355, and *Pluscardensis*, 266. Stewart (ibid.) says that they "come richt glaidlie with thair hart," which accords with Beaumont's remark, concerning the Earl of Dunbar's army, that "we have frendis in yhone rowt." *Wyntoun*, 391. See also *RFR*, II:2:849, which indicates that many of John Balliol's adherents rallied to his son after the coronation.

[122] *Lanercost*, 269.

grace of God."[123] By going to war, Balliol had (according to contemporary just war theory) brought his claim to the throne before the court of the Lord, and the case had clearly been decided in his favor.[124] Faced with what appeared to be divine judgment, all the bishops of the realm except James Ben of St. Andrew's entered into Balliol's peace. The abbots of Dunfermline, Coupar, Inchaffray, Arbroath and Scone did likewise.[125]

On 24 September, in the presence of some of these prelates and nobles gathered at Scone, the Bishop of Dunkeld solemnly crowned Edward Balliol as King of Scots. Duncan, Earl of Fife, assisted with the ceremony.[126] Many of Balliol's men came fully armed to the coronation: a fitting comment on the basis of the new monarch's rule.[127]

The immediate results of the battle of Dupplin Moor, which one Scottish chronicler described as being "no less astounding than unfortunate,"[128] could hardly have been more decisive. Within a year, Balliol went from a French prison to the Scottish throne. Beaumont gained the earldom of Buchan; Strathbogie got Atholl; Umfraville became Earl of Angus. The other Disinherited were restored to the fiefs their ancestors had lost. They held the capital, Perth, and basked in martial glory. Every day, more Scots entered into Balliol's peace.[129] There was still opposition to face, but without doubt these few men had already done more to subdue Scotland than the kings of England had managed in the past generation. They had done so partly by supporting a pretender with a credible hereditary claim to the crown, but mainly by standing against the power of their enemy in the open field, and conquering.

123 *Wyntoun*, 2:389; *Murimuth*, 67. Other statements of the "miraculous" nature of the victory can be found in *Fordun*, 355; *Bridlington*, 106–7; *Lanercost*, 269; *Hemingburgh*, 2:304; *Scalacronica*, 160; *Avesbury*, 296–7. *Pluscardensis*, 266, is one of the only exceptions. It attributes the Scots' defeat to their pride and rashness. The *Historia Roffensis* combines the two explanations (fo. 62v).
124 See Clifford J. Rogers, "By Fire and Sword: *Bellum Hostile* and 'Civilians' in the Hundred Years War," *Civilians in the Path of War*, eds M. Grimsley and C. J. Rogers (Lincoln: University of Nebraska Press, forthcoming), for a concise treatment of the medieval view of war as a resort to God's judgement.
125 *Lanercost*, 269. *Wyntoun*, simply says that the Bishop of Dunkeld crowned Balliol at Scone, in the presence of "othir ma prelatis," but the presence of seven Scottish bishops at Balliol's 1334 Holyrood Parliament (*RFR*, II:2:876) makes the Lanercost chronicler's claim credible. Ben resigned his see.
126 *Fordun*, 355.
127 *Bridlington*, 108–9.
128 *Fordun*, 355.
129 *RFR*, II:2:849.

CHAPTER FOUR

"TO KINDEL YOW CARE, AND CRAK YOWRE CROWNE":[1]
THE SIEGE OF BERWICK AND
BATTLE OF HALIDON HILL, 1333

When I wish to give battle, my enemy, even though protected by high walls and deep moats, cannot help but engage me, for I attack a position he must succor.   Sun Tzu, VI.11[2]

THE CORONATION AT SCONE was a triumph, but Edward Balliol had not yet won his war. Though many of David II's most powerful supporters had fallen at Dupplin,[3] and others had deserted his cause in the aftermath of the defeat, the Bruce cause still had many adherents. King David could also hope for help from one of his treaty allies – Philip VI of France, or possibly even Edward III. The English king had not officially repudiated the Treaty of Northampton, and his sister Joan was the young David's queen. Though the Scots presumably realized that the Plantagenet had allowed his vassals to take part in the invasion, the fact that he had refused to give them any overt support, and required them to enter Scotland by sea rather than across the border, gave the Bruce party some grounds for hoping that the English might lend them some aid, or at least remain neutral in the conflict. For the time being, Edward III did nothing to dispel these hopes.

Balliol, too, had his supporters. Every day more of them arrived to do him homage as their new king. Many, presumably, were half-hearted at best, trimming their sails to the wind "more through fear than love."[4] Others, apparently, joined his party out of anti-Bruce sentiments dating back to the Black Parliament of 1320.[5] Some hoped to gain their fortune in the new king's service.[6] Still others, especially in Galloway, where his ancestors had long held lands, rose in support of the Balliol name.[7]

---

[1]   See page 75, below.
[2]   Griffith (ed.), 97.
[3]   Froissart, *Oeuvres*, 2:277, comments that after the deaths of Robert Bruce, Thomas Randolph, James Douglas, and the leaders who fell at Dupplin, the Scots had no good commanders or wise warriors such as they had had in times past.
[4]   *Pluscardensis*, 266.
[5]   See note 9, Chapter 3, above.
[6]   Stewart, *Buik of the Croniclis*, 3:302.
[7]   *Lanercost*, 269; see also *RFR*, II:2:889.

As the new king consolidated his hold on Perth, a miniature civil war erupted between that last group, led by Lord Eustace Maxwell, and the remainder of the Scottish army which had abandoned the siege of Perth.[8] Historians have not put much emphasis on this, but to Balliol it must have been very important indeed. He had so far seen little of the spontaneous support which Beaumont had led him to expect, and so the Gallwegians' loyalty to their "special lord"[9] must have warmed his heart, especially since the current Lord of Galloway was Alexander Bruce, the Earl of Carrick. Even aside from Edward's personal feelings, events in Galloway held substantial strategic importance. The first duty of any lord – and of a king especially – was the protection of his subjects.[10] The course of events in Galloway would signal to all Scots which claimant to the throne could fulfill that duty, and which one could not. If Balliol failed to defend even his most active supporters in his family's traditional base of support, then who would rally to him?

Balliol responded energetically to the situation. Having established a small garrison under the Earl of Fife to protect Perth, he rode out to the southwest at the head of his army, prepared to bring the Scots to battle again. They reached the coast at Cunninghamhead near Irvine, then continued south to Galloway via Coylton.[11] Cowed by the presence of Balliol's victorious army, his enemies either fled[12] or submitted to his rule. Even Alexander Bruce entered into the new king's peace.[13] The operation was so successful that the army hardly had to slow down before sweeping back towards Jedburgh.

Near that key border fortress, the Bruce party made its first attempt to directly oppose the army of the Disinherited since the break-up of the siege of Perth. One of the leaders of the resistance, Archibald Douglas, tried to ambush Balliol's army on its march. The ambush was detected, however, and the Englishmen handily defeated the Scots. Sir Robert Lauder the younger, whose father was a prominent supporter of the Bruce cause,[14] fell into Balliol's hands

---

8 *Lanercost*, 269; *Anonimalle Brut*, 152.

9 *Lanercost*, 269: "Galwithienses, quorum rex [Edward Balliol] erat dominus specialis"; cf. *Anonimalle Brut*, 152.

10 John Fortescue, *De Laudibus Legum Anglie*, 33, 35, 38; Froissart, *Oeuvres*, 12:109; F. H. Russell, *The Just War in the Middle Ages* (Cambridge: Cambridge U.P., 1975), 262.

11 *Scalacronica*, 162; *Wyntoun*, 2:393. Battle: *Anonimalle Brut*, 152. The *Historia Roffensis*, fo. 62v, is probably exaggerating when it says that in this transit, the English "decapitated whatever Scots they could get their hands on" [Quotquot scotorum apprehendere capita amputarunt].

12 Some into England – see *CDS*, nos. 1067–9, p. 193.

13 *Wyntoun*, 2:393–4; *Pluscardensis*, 267.

14 The elder Robert Lauder was Sheriff of Berwick-upon-Tweed and Justiciar of Lothian in 1331, and one of two representatives sent by the Warden of Scotland to treat with the Edward III in late October of 1333, while he was serving as Chamberlain of Scotland. *CDS*, nos. 1034, 1035; *RFR*, II:2:847; *Handbook of British Chronology*, 185; other references in *CDS*, passim.

along with several others.[15] By 3 October, the victors of this skirmish reached the large ruined fortress of Roxburgh, which they occupied without a struggle.[16] While the army encamped there, Balliol himself took up residence at the abbey of Kelso, just across the river Tweed.[17] In just over two weeks, they had come over two hundred miles, traversing most of Scotland below the Forth without meeting any significant resistance.

The Scots may have been unwilling to stand up to the army of the victor of Dupplin Moor, but they were willing to oppose him wherever he was not. On 7 October, the Bruce party scored its first major success since the landing of the Disinherited, when Simon Fraser and Robert Keith managed to recapture Perth, taking prisoner the Earl of Fife (who subsequently went over to their side) and casting down the new-built walls.[18] But this victory was offset by a defeat at Kelso Bridge on 14 October.[19] Andrew Murray, the warden, "who was always following the king and his men at a distance to harass them,"[20] planned to break the bridge over the Tweed while the river was in flood and so isolate Balliol from his army. A group of men-at-arms from Roxburgh, alerted to the Scots' action, swam their horses across the river and rescued their king. This defeat turned into a minor disaster for the Scots when Murray was captured – the third warden lost within a year![21] Almost as serious a loss to the Bruce cause was the capture of John Crabbe, a Flemish pirate and military engineer who had been in Scottish service for many years. The loss of one of their few remaining experienced captains was serious enough; it was made twice as bad when Edward III won him over to English service.[22] Crabbe's skill with siege engines and his detailed knowledge of the defenses of Berwick were well worth the 1,000 marks which Edward spent to buy his ransom from Walter Mauny.[23] The loss of these men was such a blow that the remaining leaders of the Bruce party – Archibald Douglas, who succeeded Murray as warden, and Earl Patrick of Dunbar – felt compelled to arrange an armistice. Balliol agreed to cease hostilities until the Purification (2 February), when a parliament would be held to treat of full peace

---

[15] *Scalacronica*, 161.

[16] *Lanercost*, 270, says he reached Roxburgh on the 14th, but a grant by Balliol recorded in the *CDS* (no. 1480, p. 269) is dated at Roxburgh on 3 October.

[17] *Lanercost*, 270.

[18] *Fordun*, 355–6; *Wyntoun*, 2:394; *Pluscardensis*, 267.

[19] *Lanercost*, 270, and *Scalacronica*, 161; *Melsa*, 2:366. *Pipewell*, fo. 13v, has "in crastino Sancti Martini," which would probably be the 11th but could be the 12th, depending on which St. Martin was meant; see Cheney, *Handbook of Dates*, p. 55. *Wyntoun*, 2:396, and Fordun have this event take place at some undetermined point *after* the attack at Annan (see below), but this is clearly incorrect.

[20] *Lanercost*, 270: "qui semper sequebantur regem et suos a longe ad gravandum eos."

[21] *Lanercost*, 270. The same source claims that many Scots were killed or captured in an eight-mile pursuit. Cf. the rather confused account in the *Anonimalle Brut*, 152–4.

[22] According to the Lanercost chronicler (p. 270), Crabbe defected because of the ingratitude of the Scots, who refused to ransom him, and indeed killed his son for some unstated reason.

[23] *CDS*, no. 1086, p. 196.

and reunification between the two sides. Meanwhile, he dismissed his army, and most of his English followers departed for their homes.[24]

Balliol sent Murray to Edward III – who, by accepting David II's captured warden, made the first open indication that he would side with the new king rather than with his own brother-in-law.[25] Edward III was still, however, far from making a full commitment to the Balliol cause. About the same time Murray reached him, Edward III sent out writs summoning a parliament to meet at York on 4 December.[26] On 26 October, he sent deputies to treat with King David's representatives.[27] As we shall see in the discussion of the December parliament, Edward was keeping all his options open.

Some word of the English king's apparent equivocation must have reached Edward Balliol. On 23 November, apparently in a bid to discourage Edward III from deserting his cause, he published what appears to be the secret agreement made between the two Edwards prior to the beginning of the Dupplin campaign.[28] Balliol's letters patent opened with a historical summary of the Great Cause, when Edward I had been acknowledged as "sovereign lord" of Scotland,[29] and a statement that Scotland "should be, and for all times past should have been, held of the Kings of England by liege homage and fealty." The document then explained that Balliol had regained his heritage by the sufferance of King Edward and the aid of his men.

> We [the letter continued,] knowing the ancient right by which the realm of Scotland, and the Isles appertaining thereto, is, and has been, held of the Kings of England, as from a sovereign lord, have entered into the liege homage and fealty of the King of England, our very dear lord and cousin, by the following words, the said king holding our hands between his:
>
>> I, Edward, by the grace of God King of Scotland and of the Isles belonging thereto, become your liegeman [for] the said realm and isles, against all people who may live and die.

---

[24] Although the truce is reported only in certain English chronicles – *Historia Roffensis*, fo. 64; *Anonimalle Brut*, 152; *Hemingburgh*, 306; *Melsa*, 2:366–7; and *Knighton*, 1:465 – these are generally reliable sources for northern affairs in the period. Furthermore, the ease with which Balliol was taken by surprise at Annan on 17 December (see below), and the fact that he had dismissed many of his most important supporters to return to England, only make sense if he thought himself to be protected by the truce.

[25] As late as 25 October, he still officially considered the peace to be in place. *CDS*, no. 1062, p. 193.

[26] The writs were dated 20 October. Before summoning parliament, Edward tried to get advice on the situation from an ad hoc council of those he could bring together easily; they said that the matters at hand were so important that a full parliament should be summoned to address them. *RP*, 69.

[27] *RFR*, II:2:847. *Le Bel*, 1:106–7, suggests that these messengers may have asked David for the return of Berwick and acknowledgement of England's sovereignty over Scotland (the two main concessions offered by Balliol) in exchange for Edward III's support – an offer which Bruce's councilors indignantly refused. Cf. Froissart, *Oeuvres*, 2:261.

[28] *RFR*, II:2:847–8; cf. *RS*, 262–3.

[29] For a concise and well-considered summary, see Prestwich, *The Three Edwards*, 43–7.

And the said King of England, as sovereign lord of the said realm of Scotland and the Isles, received our homage in the form said below: [blank.]

And then, next, we entered into fealty of the said King of England, sovereign lord of the said realm of Scotland and the Isles, touching the Holy Bible, by the following words:

> We will be faithful and loyal, and bear ourself faithfully and loyally towards you, our very dear lord King of England, and to your heirs, as to the sovereign lords of the said realm of Scotland and the Isles, against all people who may live and die.

The rest of the document set out the terms of the agreement more fully. Balliol's heirs were obliged to repeat the homage at each change of lordship on either side. Out of gratitude for the great honors and profits he had gained due to the sufferance of the King of England and the great aid of his men, Balliol promised to grant to his liege-lord £2,000 worth of border land, including the castle, town and county of Berwick.[30] This land would be permanently severed from the realm of Scotland, and joined to England. Balliol also promised to serve in Edward's overseas wars with two hundred men-at-arms (at his own cost for up to one year; afterwards at the King of England's cost).[31] To assuage Edward III's conscience, Balliol agreed to make such provision for David Bruce as the English king should advise, and also to take Joan as his own queen if – as she had the right to do, since she was still just short of the age of consent – she repudiated her espousal to David.[32] Other clauses offered guarantees for the fulfillment of the main provisions, including one that under certain circumstances

---

[30] The precise lands to be included in the 2,000 librates, aside from Berwick, were to be of "reasonable extent" as determined by a joint committee. They were to be handed over by the next Michaelmas. Later, after Edward III had made a second intervention, defeated the Scots at Halidon Hill, and restored Balliol's control of Scotland, a huge block of land encompassing nearly all of southern English-speaking Scotland was transferred to English sovereignty under the 2,000 librates provision. This land was far in excess of any reasonable evaluation of 2,000 librates, however, and is certainly not what Balliol intended at first. Given the revenues of the city of Berwick (cf. note 83, below), it seems likely that Balliol expected Berwickshire to cover most of this commitment. In other words, despite what one recent writer has said, this agreement of 1332 did not envision "the permanent cession of the southern counties of Scotland." Nicholson, *Edward III and the Scots*, 98. Balliol also granted, at one time or another, 2,000 marcates to Henry Percy, and offered more than another 2,000 librates as a dowry for Joan of the Tower. If they had all been assessed at the same rate as Edward III's 2,000 librates, there would have been nothing left of Scotland after those three commitments alone were met.

[31] For his heirs this requirement would be reduced to 100 men-at-arms. Balliol was to have six months' notice [*garnissement*] before the beginning of his service each time it was called for. It is not clear if this called for Balliol to bear the cost of service for a total of one year over his lifetime, or for up to a year each time he was summoned, but (*contra* Sumption, *Trial by Battle*, 127), it definitely does not call for service of six months per year.

[32] On Joan's legal position, see Nicholson, *Edward III and the Scots*, 99 n.1. If Joan declined, Balliol offered to marry another one of Edward III's relatives instead.

would give the King of England the right to occupy Scotland until the northern monarch's obligations were met.[33]

A separate letter patent essentially embodied the terms of a mutual defense alliance between the two monarchs. Balliol promised to come in person, with all his power, to the aid of the King of England, within England, Wales and Ireland, against anyone who would make war against him or by force deprive him of his rights in those lands. This promise was made, the letter stated, because of Edward III's past help, and because the English king had already obligated himself and his heirs to maintain Balliol on the throne of Scotland against any who would try to deprive him of his rights.[34]

These letters were apparently delivered to Edward III by Henry Beaumont and David of Strathbogie before the beginning of his parliament at York on 8 December.[35] The events of that parliament indicate that someone – either Balliol or Edward III – was acting rather dishonorably. Geoffrey le Scrope, the king's prolocutor, opened the assembly by asking for advice on the king's behalf.[36] There were, as he explained, three courses of action available as a result of the civil war in Scotland. Edward could support Balliol, support David Bruce, or discard both their claims and seek to reimpose the direct lordship over Scotland which his grandfather had briefly exercised after the expulsion of John Balliol.[37] Scrope reminded his audience that Edward III did not consider himself bound by the Treaty of Northampton, since it had been made against his will while he was a minor; and also that the elder Balliol had surrendered his rights in Scotland to Edward I.[38] Since Scrope (so far as the Rolls of Parliament indicate) made no mention of the concessions Balliol had offered, and gave no hint that Edward III had already received Balliol's homage for Scotland, the king was implicitly making it known that he would prefer to be advised to assert his direct lordship.[39]

---

[33] According to the epitome of the chronicle ascribed to William Pakington (*Pakington*, fo. 84v), there was also an agreement that if Balliol died without heir of his body, the realm of Scotland would revert to Edward III and his heirs. This is not contained in Balliol's letter per se, but it could be seen as a natural consequence of the acknowledgement of English suzerainty.

[34] *RFR*, II:2:848; see also *Lanercost*, 280–1.

[35] *Lanercost*, 270, carries this implication.

[36] The details of the parliament may be found in *RP*, 67–8.

[37] *RP*, 67. For a concise summary of the expulsion of John Balliol, see Prestwich, *The Three Edwards*, 43–7.

[38] *RP*, 67. A damaged document in the British Library gives an argument which was prepared by a royal clerk assigned during this parliament to consider the various rights of Edward III, Edward Balliol and David Bruce. The clerk concluded that, since Edward I's wars in Scotland had been given papal approval, a war by Edward III to recover his own lost rights in Scotland, and the rights of his vassals, would be a just war. The Franco-Scottish alliance, supposedly aimed at the "universal disinheritance and destruction of the said King of England and the English nation," was also cited as a justification for the conquest of Scotland. BL, Cottonian MSS, Vespasian F VII, fos 5–9.

[39] This conclusion is also drawn by Nicholson, *Edward III and the Scots*, 101.

The omission of any mention of Balliol's homage is particularly interesting. If Edward did indeed intend to ignore Balliol's offer and attempt an outright conquest of Scotland, it indicates ambition bordering on foolhardiness. To take on a war in Scotland, even with the support of a claimant to the throne whose victory in battle had won him much support, was a serious matter enough. After all, the last time an English army had enjoyed any considerable success against the Scots had been before Edward III's birth. Not counting Balliol's invasion, the last major battle fought against them, Bannockburn, had been one of the worst disasters in English military history; the last campaign against them, in 1327, had been a complete fiasco. The battle of Dupplin Moor suggested – to those who were anxious to see such a suggestion, at least – that the situation had changed; but the more naturally cautious, including most of the men at the York parliament, were less sanguine. Balliol's victory at Dupplin was far more often ascribed to divine intervention than to English military superiority; and if God favored Balliol's claim to the Scottish crown, that was all the more reason for Edward to avoid getting into a war against him. Even if divine intervention were discounted, a single victory could not reassure men who had, for most of their lives, been on the losing side in every struggle against the Scots. Besides, the wars of Edward I and Edward II in Scotland had greatly strengthened national sentiment in that realm, and the feeling of enmity to England as well. If the Scots had been willing to fight so hard to rid themselves of English domination in the days of Edward I, they could now be expected to at least approach the level of determination they had expressed in the Declaration of Arbroath.[40] "Of Ingland had my hert grete care," wrote the poet Laurence Minot, "when Edward founded first to were."[41] He was not alone in his worries.

If Edward III was indeed planning to ignore the homage and fealty he had received from Edward Balliol and strive to conquer Scotland in his own right, however, then he was not merely rashly over-ambitious: he was also a felon. To accept a vassal's homage, then pretend it had never happened and make war to capture his fief: it would be hard to imagine a more unchivalrous act. Indeed, such an action seems so uncharacteristic of Edward III – who, though he was not above ignoring the letter of the law when he felt he was morally in the right, did generally act honorably in his diplomatic dealings[42] – that we should consider the possibility that the act of homage described by Balliol's letters never, in fact,

---

[40] See note 3, Chapter 2, above.
[41] Minot, "Songs on King Edward's Wars," 59.
[42] The king's covert support of the Disinherited might be cited to dispute this assertion, but it should be noted that (a) Edward considered the Treaty of Northampton an illegitimate peace imposed on him by coercion while he was a minor and (b) before authorizing the Disinherited's action, if the *Scalacronica* is correct, Edward was asked by them "either to restore the heritages which for his sake they had lost, or allow them to make their own arrangements [ou les lesser couenyr]," upon which he forwarded the requests to the Earl of Moray, the Warden of Scotland, who "responded honorably by letter, asking that he allow them to carry out their plans, and let the ball roll" [requeraunt qil lour lessoit couenyr et le pellot aler]. *Scalacronica*, 159; see also Nicholson, *Edward III*, 77.

took place. A few pieces of evidence point to this conclusion. First is the fact that Balliol's letters left blank the form of words by which Edward III received his homage, and gave no indication as to just where and when the ceremony had taken place. Second is the lack of any English documentary record of the event. Considering the tenacity with which English chancery clerks maintained the records relating to English suzerainty over Scotland, the absence of any such document – along with the fact that Balliol's letters make no reference to letters prepared at the time of the homage – is a significant datum, though admittedly these lacunae could be due to the secret nature of the arrangement, and Edward III's desire to be able to deny any involvement with Balliol's invasion in case it failed.

On the other hand, the continuator of Guillaume de Nangis and Walter Stewart's metrical chronicle (neither, it should be noted, a very reliable source) agree that Edward Balliol did his homage to Edward III before leaving England for Scotland.[43] This seems inherently credible: it is unlikely that Edward III would have neglected to demand Balliol's homage before granting the Disinherited the substantial, if covert, support which he did. Furthermore, the elaborate guarantee clauses contained in the letter sound much more like something that would have emerged from a process of negotiation than like concessions decided upon unilaterally as an attempt to "bribe" Edward into supporting Balliol rather than David.[44] Also, it is hard to see how Balliol would have gained enough by inventing a fictitious homage ceremony to make up for the anger which doing so would be likely to generate in Edward III.[45] Last, it should be noted that when the Plantagenet eventually agreed to the terms set out above, he did so simply by referring to Balliol's previous letters, rather than producing a new document incorporating the same provisions but deleting the material concerning the earlier ceremony of homage.[46] Similarly, when Balliol (again?) did homage and fealty to Edward III for Scotland in 1334, he used precisely the same words as given in the 1333 letter.[47] These actions by Edward III implicitly confirmed the prologue of Balliol's letter, which described the pre-Dupplin homage.

Any conclusion as to the veracity of Balliol's claims must remain speculative, but on balance it appears that they were accurate. It is possible that Edward's decision not to mention his acceptance of Balliol's homage at the York parliament of December 1333 was an expression of his anger at the new King of Scots for having published a potentially embarrassing document that was supposed to

---

[43] *Buik of the Croniclis of Scotland*, 3:292 (not very reliable in general); *Nangis*, 139 (followed by *Grandes chroniques*, 9:137–8) – not reliable on Scottish affairs.
[44] Cf. Nicholson, *Edward III and the Scots*, 98–9, for a contrary view.
[45] The fact that Edward did not have Scrope explicitly deny the information contained in Balliol's letters, which he might have been expected to do if they were pure fabrication, also adds some credibility to them.
[46] *RFR*, II:2:875–8. But cf. the interpretation of Nicholson, *Edward III and the Scots*, 153.
[47] The form of homage and fealty in 1334 is given (without reference to Balliol's 1333 letter) in *Pipewell*, fos 13v–14.

have remained secret. It may perhaps even have been the case that he implied a preference for the strategy of asserting direct control over Scotland as a bargaining chip, realizing that parliament would be very unlikely to agree to that option. The more restrained plan of aiding Balliol – which still may have seemed overly dangerous to some elements of the assembly – would look sober and reasonable by comparison.[48]

Whatever answer the king hoped to elicit from his parliament, he did not get it. On 11 December, those present for the assembly complained that they were too small a body to decide such a weighty matter, since only a few magnates and prelates were in attendance. There was little to be done in any case this late in the season, so Edward agreed to reopen the parliament late in the following January, after taking measures to ensure that the baronial and ecclesiastical attendance would be improved.[49] In the interim, he actively pursued his diplomacy with both parties in Scotland. The day after the parliament's close, he granted safe-conduct for six Scotsmen and their retinues, presumably David Bruce's representatives, to come into England to meet with him.[50] Two days later he sent Sir Ralph Basset and an experienced diplomat, William Denholme, north to treat with the warden and nobles of Scotland.[51] This did not represent a shift of his policy in favor of the Bruce side, however: on 17 December, he also appointed Henry Beaumont to treat amicably with the Scottish prelates and magnates (i.e. the Balliol faction) on his behalf.[52] Perhaps Edward III, like Edward Balliol, believed that the two sides would meet in parliament and make peace after the truce expired.

---

[48] This possibility is all the more credible when we consider that (as we shall see) Edward III later decided to launch his invasions of Scotland nominally as an ally of Balliol, without trying to assert his own direct rule, even after Balliol had been driven out of his realm. If he wanted Balliol's help and legitimizing presence enough to leave the crown in his hands at that stage, it is hard to believe that he would have been unwilling to make the same arrangement in early December of 1332, when Balliol's legitimacy as King of Scots was far greater, and his position much stronger.

It is also possible that Edward was seeking an affirmation of his right to direct lordship to set a precedent for the long term, but planning, once he had received it, to give up that right to Edward Balliol in exchange for homage; cf. *RS*, 263, where Edward suggests that Balliol's homage gave the English king the *right* to demand the Scottish king's attendance at parliament and to hear appeals against judgments in Scottish courts, but then releases and quit-claims those rights to avoid future friction. Edward was later to use a somewhat similar logic in pursuing sovereignty over his French lands: he argued that he had the right to sovereignty over all of France, but for the sake of peace was willing to accept less than his full rights, i.e. sovereignty over just part of it.

[49] *RP*, 67.

[50] *RFR*, II:2:849.

[51] Ibid. Denholme, or Deanham (Denum in contemporary documents), a royal justice high in the king's regard, had been involved with Anglo-Scottish diplomacy since Edward II's day. *RFR*, II:2:847; *CDS*, nos. 861, 948, 1062; Stones, *Anglo-Scottish Relations*, 144, 160. He was later appointed a member of the council of six "wise men" who were to advise the king after the closure of the January 1333 parliament.

[52] *CDS*, no. 1071.

Beaumont, however, probably turned back well before reaching the border. Only a day before he received his commission from the English king, a large group of Scotsmen led by Archibald Douglas attacked Balliol, who had retired to Annan in Galloway for the Christmas season.[53] Assisted by traitors among those who had come to do homage to Balliol,[54] Douglas' men achieved complete surprise in a dawn attack. Thinking himself protected by the truce, and lulled by the large number of Scotsmen entering his obedience, Balliol was completely unprepared. About a hundred of his followers, including his only brother, were killed in their beds, and he himself only escaped by breaking through the wall of his chamber and fleeing south, half naked and wearing only one boot.[55] Among those killed were John Mowbray and Walter Comyn, both prominent members of the Disinherited.[56] The fugitive king reached Carlisle in safety some days later; the inhabitants, whose appreciation for the victor of Dupplin Moor matched their hatred for the Scots, gave him a royal welcome despite his bedraggled state.[57] For the moment at least, the Balliol position in Scotland had been completely destroyed by a single coup.[58] Many of the Scots who had supported him up until then promptly abandoned his faction.[59]

Unfortunately, we have no records, narrative or documentary, to indicate Edward III's immediate reaction to this turn of events. Even the accounts of the parliament which opened on 21 January do not make the king's position clear. None of his options looked as good as before the events of 16 December. The Bruce party, triumphant for the moment, would be far less likely to make the kinds of concessions he was demanding as the price of his support.[60] Balliol, though willing to make great concessions to Edward, was now little able to help make those concessions a reality. The uprising against Balliol also served as a reminder of how difficult it would be to hold Scotland in direct rule, even if it could be conquered in the first place.

Parliament, which had not been anxious for war even before, now was positively averse to the idea. It is unusual to find an example of a medieval parliament offering direct opposition to a popular king's foreign policy, but this one came close. First the Bishop of Winchester (speaking for the whole body) explained that the various groups of the parliament had discussed the issue with great diligence, but failed to reach any full agreement as the proper course to

---

[53] *Lanercost*, 270–1. Note that the chronicle's reference to the Earl of Mar as one of the attackers is probably an error for the Earl of Moray; Donald of Mar's son and heir was an infant.

[54] *English Brut*, 281; Cf. *Historia Roffensis*, fo. 64; *RFH*, 3:2:120 (proditionaliter).

[55] *Lanercost*, 271; *English Brut*, 281; *Pluscardensis*, 267.

[56] *Lanercost*, 271; *Knighton*, 1:465.

[57] *Lanercost*, 271.

[58] *Scalacronica*, 161: "All his people chased out of Scotland to begin their conquests again from scratch."

[59] *Lanercost*, 272.

[60] *RP*, 67, viz. "to have [the King of Scots] in his service, as his ancestors had, or the equivalent [*Valu*]." Cf. Froissart, *Oeuvres*, 2:261.

take.[61] Then he suggested that Edward seek the advice of the Pope and the King of France on the matter.[62] Since Philip VI remained David II's staunch ally, and the Pope was known to be malleable to French pressure, this practically amounted to a recommendation that the king do nothing, but allow the Treaty of Northampton once again to define Anglo-Scottish relations. This Edward was of no mind to do. "The king [was] eager for arms and honors, and his council enterprising and anxious for war . . . desiring to recover their prestige [*pris*] from those to whom they had lost it."[63] If he had ever planned to try to conquer Scotland and rule it directly, however, then the unsupportive response of the community of the realm dissuaded him from taking that course. Instead, he agreed to back Edward Balliol fully and restore him to the Scottish throne. Although the new king had shown himself unable to rule Scotland without substantial English support, he had also demonstrated that he was not entirely without partisans there. The substantial number of Scots who had submitted to his rule indicated that he was at least potentially acceptable to the inhabitants of the realm, if circumstances thrust him upon them. And his military prestige, as the victor of Dupplin, could still be a valuable asset to the English war effort.

Still, Balliol's bargaining position was by no means as strong as it had been in November. It was apparently at this stage that Edward III made a major new demand in exchange for his help: he wanted not merely Berwickshire and a few additional lands, but the entire counties of Roxburgh, Selkirk, Edinburgh, Peebles, and Dumfries, along with the constabularies of Haddington and Linlithgow.[64] Together, these lands comprised the richest, most populated, and most anglicized areas of Scotland. Edward had, in effect, found a compromise between full support of Balliol and the assertion of direct lordship: he would take the parts of Scotland he most wanted (and would be most likely to be able to hold), and leave the remainder to be held by his vassal.

No public disclosure of these terms was made, but soon enough the king's bellicose intentions became evident. On 30 January, just three days after the close of parliament, he began issuing writs to raise troops.[65] One letter of 7 February mentioned "the great and difficult business in which we are involved

---

61 *RP*, 69.

62 *RP*, 69, "le Roi voleit prendre l'avis du Pape, & auxint du Roi de Fraunce, lequel lui avoit mande ses Lettres sur ascunes choses tochantes meisme les busoignes; Et outre par l'avis de eux et d'autres faire ce qu'il deveroit, a son honur, a l'eide de Dieu." The phrase "prendre l'avis" in modern French means to *ask* advice, rather than to "take" (i.e. follow) it, and that is how I have interpreted it here, but the context suggests the alternate could be meant.

63 *Scalacronica*, 162. Froissart, *Oeuvres*, 2:250, says almost precisely the same thing. The council "wanted war with the Scots and to avenge the death of those close to them who were killed before Stirling [i.e. at Bannockburn] and in the chase [after the battle], which was quite damaging and shameful for the English."

64 *Scalacronica*, 162; *Lanercost*, 275; *Anonimalle*, 1. These lands were eventually granted by Balliol to Edward III (nominally as making up the 2,000 librates agreed to in 1332 and confirmed by the Holyrood parliament in 1334) in June of 1334. *RFR*, II:2:888.

65 *CPR, 1330–34*, 400–1.

these days by reason of our war in Scotland."[66] Other writs began the process of gathering enough supplies for a major expedition.[67] One of the most dramatic proofs of the seriousness of Edward III's commitment to this war was his order, on 20 February, that the bulk of the royal administration move north from Westminster to York for the indefinite future.[68]

On 12 February, Balliol confirmed his letters of 23 November, and empowered two representatives to swear on his soul that he would abide by their terms. About the same time, Edward III gave him official permission to recruit English volunteers for his army, and to invade Scotland overland.[69] By the beginning of March, the Disinherited had once again put together a substantial army for an assault on Scotland. Most of the money to pay their troops had come from the English exchequer in the form of royal gifts to prominent members of the invasion force – Mowbray, Felton, Beaumont, Strathbogie, Umfraville and Ferrers.[70] Balliol's new army also included a number of important English magnates, including Henry of Lancaster, Henry Percy, Ralph Neville, William Montague, and Richard FitzAlan, Earl of Arundel.[71] Except for young Lancaster, these men too received subsidies directly from Edward III.[72] Balliol's forces also included many Scots, "manly, brave and stout," who supported his claims.[73]

Although it had been assembled primarily of the King of England's men and paid, if indirectly, with his money, still the army which Balliol led across the border around the start of March 1333, was nominally his own, gathered for the prosecution of his own right.[74] The chroniclers' estimates of its size – the round

---

[66] Nicholson, *Edward III and the Scots*, 109.

[67] Ibid., 109–10; *RFR*, II:2:855.

[68] *CCR, 1333–37*, 18–19; Nicholson, *Edward III and the Scots*, 109.

[69] *Melsa*, 2:367; *Murimuth*, 67. Or, as *Bridlington*, 111, describes them, "stipendiariis" (mercenaries or paid soldiers).

[70] *CCR, 1333–37*, 7–8.

[71] *Anonimalle Brut*, 154; *Knighton*, 1:486. The *Scalacronica*, 162, describes the men who went with Balliol as dome of the king's closest counselors.

[72] *CCR, 1333–37*, 7–8.

[73] *Wyntoun*, 2:398 [manlyk, wycht, and stowt]; *Pluscardensis*, 268; *Lanercost*, 272.

[74] The *Anonimalle Brut* has Balliol and the army of the English lords enter Scotland on 20 February. This matches reasonably well with the *Scalacronica*, 162, which has them open the siege in the second week of Lent (24 February–2 March). Knighton (*Chronicon*, 1:466) has the entry into Scotland that same week. Two good chronicles, however, have the entry into Scotland take place on 9 March, and the 10th or 11th, and another good source has Balliol arrive at Berwick on the 12th: (respectively) *Hemingburgh*, 306; *Lanercost*, 272 [which says on the 10th, namely on the morrow of the Feast of the Forty Holy Martyrs, which is confusing since the morrow of that feast is actually the 11th]; *Melsa*, 2:367. The *Historia Roffensis*, fo. 65, has the siege opened on the 17th. The likely explanation is that several separate contingents are referred to, one of which entered Scotland, perhaps from Carlisle, around 28 February and reached Berwick by 6 March, then another which entered Scotland on 9 or 10 March and reached Berwick two or three days later, and finally the contingent under the English magnates which captured Oxnam, and reached Berwick on the 17th. See below.

figures of ten or twenty thousand men – are far too large.[75] It was, however, almost certainly much larger than his first invasion force. With the memory of Dupplin Moor and their setbacks at Jedburgh and Kelso Bridge fresh in their minds, the Scots did not dare to oppose the invading army directly.[76] Having apparently gained some information as to their enemies' intentions, they did take vigorous steps to put Berwick in a state of defense, repairing its fortifications and supplying it with a substantial garrison.[77]

As the invasion army swept north from Carlisle, small detachments spread out from the main body, burning and killing in good Border style. As the host passed Roxburgh and proceeded to Berwick, a division under the last-named English magnates[78] captured the small fortress of Oxnam, taking prisoner Robert Colville along with ten men-at-arms and a large number of men and women of the countryside, as well as a great quantity of supplies.[79] They brought both the prisoners and the supplies to Balliol's main army, which by the 13th had opened the siege of Berwick.[80] The soldiers quickly dug siege entrenchments and an earthen rampart to cut off the town and to protect their camp from a relief army's attack.[81] An English fleet completed the operation, sealing the town off from the sea and supplying the besiegers with plentiful victuals.[82] Edward III, meanwhile, remained in England, completing his slow and methodical preparations for a larger invasion later in the spring.

To understand fully the reasons for the campaign strategy adopted by the two Edwards, and the subsequent events leading to the battle of Halidon Hill, it is necessary to have some idea of the importance of the city of Berwick to the Scottish economy. The city held pride of place among the towns of Scotland as the largest and most prosperous in the realm. The royal customs revenues from Berwick alone accounted for about one-third of the total amount paid by the ten leading royal burghs.[83] Indeed, Berwick was of such great importance that later in 1332, William Keith was later able to convince the warden that, unless the

---

[75] *Bridlington*, 111, gives 20,000 horse and picked foot. *Melsa*, 2:267, makes the total 10,000.
[76] *Lanercost*, 272.
[77] *Wyntoun*, 2:395; Nicholson, *Edward III and the Scots*, 111.
[78] Viz. Montague, Percy, Neville, Henry of Lancaster, and Arundel. *Anonimalle Brut*, 154; *Knighton*, 1:486.
[79] This is mentioned by *Hemingburgh*, 306–7, and by *Knighton*, 1:486. Cf. *Historia Roffensis*, fo. 65 ("unum piel plenum Scotis armatis"). The identity of the fortress involved is deduced by Nicholson, *Edward III and the Scots*, 110.
[80] But possibly well earlier; cf. note 74, above.
[81] *Historia Roffensis*, fo. 65; *English Brut*, 281; *Melsa*, 2:378.
[82] *Lanercost*, 272; *Historia Roffensis*, fo. 65.
[83] Nicholson, *Scotland*, 108. Even in 1333–34, after the city was cut off from the Scottish economy and still recovering from a long siege, Edward III was able to get over £650 in receipts for royal rents, burgage, the wine tax, fish, etc., in less than ten months. PRO E 372/180/ 54d. Cf. also Campbell, "England, Scotland and the Hundred Years' War," 185.

siege were broken, "the desolation, nay rather the destruction, of the realm of Scotland would follow."[84]

The basic strategy followed by the Scots in their wars with England was to avoid battle and major sieges (except under very favorable circumstances), relying instead on raids of devastation as the main military means to gain their political ends. Since the Scottish armies were very mobile, avoiding battle was easy for them, as the description of the 1327 campaign in Chapter 2 above, illustrates. Of course, an unwillingness to fight their enemies on an even field meant that they could not prevent the desolation of their countryside[85] – but they *could* avenge it by reciprocal raiding. This response was particularly effective because the Scots could generally inflict more damage than they suffered, since England was richer and more densely populated. Though they would sometimes besiege English castles (usually abandoning the effort if a substantial relief army drew near), or try to take them by surprise, they in general saw castles as more a danger than a shield, and would tear down the ones they captured to prevent their use by English garrisons.[86] This fitted their strategy because a castle, unlike an army, could not simply avoid an attacking English force. But Berwick, because of its economic and symbolic importance, was a key exception to this rule. Defending it gave a hostage to fate (or at least an immobile target for English armies), but abandoning it was almost unthinkable.

Even after the siege had begun, however, the new warden, Archibald Douglas, stuck as close as possible to Robert Bruce's Fabian strategy. In doing so, he missed his best opportunity for victory. The Scots still had the capability to put together a very substantial army – one which might conceivably have succeeded against Balliol alone, even though it was soon to fail against the combined armies of the two Edwards. Victory in such an attack, however, would still have been far from certain, given that Balliol's forces in 1333 were larger and (once they had established their fortified camp outside Berwick) even more strongly positioned than the ones he had commanded at Dupplin.

So Douglas, instead of moving directly against the besiegers, did his best to draw them away from the beleaguered city. As soon as Balliol marched for Berwick, the Scots launched raids into Northumberland, killing, burning, gathering booty, and then returning to Scotland.[87] Then, with a substantial raiding force of about three to four thousand men, Douglas crossed into England on 23 March and laid waste the territory of Gilsland in Cumberland, devastating an

---

84 *Bridlington*, 114: "desolatio immo destructio regni Scotiae sequeretur."
85 Cf. Froissart, *Oeuvres*, 2:288–9, 318–19, and Robert's "Testament," quoted Oman, *History of the Art of War*, 2:99.
86 *Melsa*, 2:375: "Robert Bruce had razed nearly all the castles below the Firth of Forth, so that the King of England and his men should have no places in those areas where they would be safe from the Scots"; *Lanercost*, 223; *Scalacronica*, 144; *CDS*, nos. 681, 738, 739.
87 *Lanercost*, 272. The date is not given, but it is after Balliol's entry into Scotland and before Douglas' larger raid on 23 March. It was presumably also before 20 March, when Edward III issued writs which mentioned that the Scots had already many times made hostile raids into England. *RFR*, II:2:855.

area sixteen leagues in length and six in breadth and burning many villages. He then escaped into Scotland with much booty and many captives.[88] Balliol's army refused to rise to the bait, however; instead, an English force of eight hundred men under Anthony Lucy and William of Lochmaben rode twenty miles into Scotland from Carlisle during the night, then on their return "in retaliation burned and killed, and a captured a great booty in cattle."[89] William Douglas led an attack on this raiding party, but was defeated and captured, along with a hundred others.[90] One hundred and sixty Scots, including twenty-six men-at-arms, perished in the conflict.[91] Then, on the 25th, the English scored victories in two more skirmishes – one in Northumberland, the other just outside Berwick.[92] The warden was back to square one.

While the Scots collected their resources for another effort, Edward III squeezed every possible drop of propaganda value out of the raids. In a letter to Philip VI, for example, Edward recounted how

> the Warden of Scotland, and the magnates of the country, with all the power of the land, have entered into our realm of England many times, and have committed there arsons and robberies, and killed men, women and children, taken booty and prisoners, and led off and ransomed [them] by armed force [*a foer de guerre*].
>
> And so they have openly broken the peace which was made not long ago between us and sire Robert Bruce; wherefore we can suffer no more without applying such a remedy as we are able.[93]

A similar letter was sent to the Count of Flanders, who was requested not to aid the Scots.[94] Perhaps more importantly, a large number of letters and writs distributed within England rehearsed the same arguments. As far as Edward's council was concerned, the Scots had broken the peace which had brought an end to the last war (while the English government had not yet *directly* engaged

---

[88] *Bridlington*, 111; *Hemingburgh*, 307; *Anonimalle Brut*, 156; cf. *Melsa*, 2:367–8. *Bridlington* gives the date and specifically states the Scots' intentions ("reckoning that the English would desert the siege and pursue them, as usual"). *Hemingburgh* gives the date of the raid as the 21st; *Lanercost* says the 23rd. Knighton (*Chronicon*, 1:465–6) notes that Gilsland was the territory of Ranulph Dacre, who had aided Balliol after his flight from Annan. Knighton also adds that this raid lasted four days, but says that the territory devastated was fifteen by sixteen leagues, and that the plunder was small.

[89] *Anonimalle Brut*, 156–8; *Hemingburgh*, 307; *Melsa*, 2:368; *Lanercost*, 272–3.

[90] Ibid. Douglas and another noble prisoner, William Bard, were taken to Carlisle. Edward III ordered that they be kept in irons. *RFR*, II:2:865; cf. 857.

[91] *Hemingburgh*, 307; *Lanercost*, 275; *Melsa*, 2:368; Cf. *Bridlington*, 111; *Anonimalle Brut*, 158, and *Knighton*, 1:466–7. The Lanercost chronicler states that only two English esquires were killed.

[92] *Lanercost*, 273. These must have been minor victories, as they are not mentioned in any other source.

[93] *RFR*, II:2:860.

[94] Ibid.; cf. 862.

in warfare against David Bruce), and so justified any action the English might take.[95]

Whether or not they found the king's fig leaf of justification for setting aside the Shameful Peace convincing,[96] the people of England were infuriated by the Scottish raids on the north. The parliament of March 1333 showed none of the hesitancy which had marked the last two. The Scots had crossed the line, and Edward "could no longer with honor put up with the wrongs and injuries daily done to him and his subjects."[97] The Lords and Commons readily assented to the king's plan to assist Balliol in reducing Berwick, promising to aid him with their persons and their purses.

Edward had earlier sent out writs summoning his vassals to come with all their forces to Newcastle on 30 May.[98] The young king's patience did not extend so far, not when deeds of war were being done just miles away. By 9 May he had gathered together what forces were already available and marched to Tweed-mouth opposite Berwick.[99] His haste may have had something to do with intelligence that the French were planning to send a fleet of ten ships loaded with supplies and soldiers to aid the besieged garrison.[100] At his arrival, he publicly declared that he would never depart until he had the town at his will, unless the Scots came to give battle and raise the siege by force.[101] On 18 May the besiegers made a major assault on the town which failed because of the "extremely high" walls of the town. On the 20th, as the guns and other siege engines continuously fired large stones deep inside the town,[102] this was

---

[95] *RFR*, II:2:855–7. Typical of these are the writs summoning the barons of the realm for service against the Scots, which state in the preface that "The Scots have now entered our realm many times, with a great number of soldiers, with banners displayed, as enemies in war, and committed homicides, depredations, burnings, and innumerable other crimes, notoriously breaking the peace not long ago initiated between us and them, and made war on us." (Ibid., II:2:855.) For examples of the acceptance of Edward's perspective, see *Lanercost*, 273; *Le Baker*, 50; *Anonimalle Brut*, 158; *Pipewell*, fo. 13v.

[96] The Scots certainly did not: the *Book of Pluscarden*, 201, says that Edward acted "like a base, faithless perjurer, breaking through the ties of the treaty of alliance and peace, and like a palterer with his oath and a breaker of his word, unmindful of his salvation and regardless of his own promise ratified by his seal and oath" in aiding Balliol.

[97] *Parliamentary or Constitutional History of England*, 1:238.

[98] *RFR*, II:2:855; dated 21 March. He had also requested the Archbishop of Canterbury to organize masses, prayers and processions on behalf of his expedition. *Chartulary of Winchester Cathedral*, ed. and tr. A. W. Goodman (Winchester: Warren & Son, 1927), no.170.

[99] *Melsa*, 2:368, says the 9th, and this is confirmed by Edward's household accounts: PRO, E101/386/8. *Pipewell*, fo. 13v, and the *Anonimalle Brut*, 158, say the 16th; the *Historia Roffensis*, fo. 65, says the 18th, and links the move to the failed assault that day. The various dates probably reflect a piecemeal advance of Edward's army to Berwick.

[100] The expedition, which came to nothing because of unfavorable winds, is described briefly in *Nangis*, 139–40, and (somewhat differently) by Lawrence Minot, in his song of Halidon Hill. Its existence is confirmed by *Clos des galées*, vol. 3, no. 29. See also Stewart, *Buik of the Croniclis*, 3:303.

[101] Froissart, *Oeuvres*, 2:273.

[102] *Historia Roffensis*, fo. 65 [altissimis]; *Anonimalle Brut*, 158–60; *Lanercost*, 273; *English*

followed by an even greater attack on the town and the castle, by land and by sea, though again without success.[103] Meanwhile the four conduits bringing fresh water to the defenders were discovered and destroyed.[104] The inhabitants and garrison of Berwick had by then already suffered through two exhausting months of siege. They were running out of food,[105] and their situation was deteriorating rapidly.

Regular assaults[106] and constant bombardment by the besiegers were complemented by regular communications with the defenders, doubtless offering favorable terms if they surrendered and making fearsome threats concerning their fate if they allowed the town to be taken by storm.[107] These threats must have been taken very seriously, since within living memory the town's burghers had fallen "like autumn leaves" to Edward I's soldiers after a successful assault.[108] So, as Wyntoun says, those within the town "ware dredand rycht grettumly: Syne off yheldyng tretyd thai."[109]

Such a combination of attacks "by words and arms" was entirely typical of medieval siege warfare.[110] Indeed, the great number of strongholds which fell to negotiation rather than by assault led one later medieval chronicler to report the *bon mot* that "a castelle that spekythe, and a womane that wille here, thei wille be gotene bothe."[111] Very often, as was to be the case at Berwick, the two sides would agree on a temporary truce, at the end of which the besieged place would surrender if not relieved in the interim. Such arrangements benefited both sides. The besieged usually agreed to a deal of this sort only when they thought that, barring relief, their fall was inevitable; so by making an arrangement with the besiegers, they were not giving up anything they had a hope of permanently retaining. During the truce, they were spared the losses suffered in beating off regular assaults, and the damage done by the guns and other engines of the besiegers. More importantly, they avoided the risk of seeing the town taken by storm, and ensured that if and when they did surrender, their lives and goods

---

Brut, 281–2; Froissart, *Oeuvres*, 2:262. For the construction of some of these siege engines, see *RFR*, II:2:856 and Nicholson, *Edward III and the Scots*, 121. The use of guns, noted by the *English Brut* and the *Cleopatra Brut*, is omitted by the *AM Brut*, which is probably an earlier redaction. Even so, the evidence for gunpowder weapons in 1327 makes it likely that guns were also used for this siege five years later.

103 This particular assault is mentioned in several chronicles. *Lanercost*, 273, gives the date.

104 *Melsa*, 2:368.

105 *English Brut*, 282; Froissart, *Oeuvres*, 2:272; *Le Bel*, 1:117.

106 *Le Bel*, 1:117; cf. Froissart, *Oeuvres*, 2:274.

107 *Scalacronica*, 162: the two Edwards "assaulted the town, but did not take it; but went back to work to improve their entrenchments in order to attack the town again. *Meanwhile*, those within the town spoke of conditions." Emphasis added. See also *Le Bel*, 1:117; *Historia Roffensis*, fo. 65; *Murimuth*, 67.

108 Prestwich, *Three Edwards*, 47, quoting William Rishanger's chronicle.

109 *Wyntoun*, 2:398. (They were in great dread, and soon treated of yielding.)

110 The phrase is Froissart's (from another context). I intend to publish an article developing this theme fully.

111 Warkworth, *Three Chronicles*, 49.

would be spared. A city taken by storm could legally be – and usually was – severely sacked. The garrison in that case could expect to be put to death, quite possibly along with large numbers of the burghers.

Compacts of this sort also provided major advantages to the besiegers. First, they reduced the uncertainties of the siege: the attackers knew that, unless the defenders were relieved successfully, the stronghold *would* fall, and they knew precisely when. Meanwhile, they too avoided the losses associated with regular assaults on the walls, and could also relax somewhat their guard against sallies. Furthermore, though soldiers generally looked forward to the possibility of a sack (which could make them rich with plunder), the leaders of a besieging army often preferred to avoid one. A besieged castle or town was a valuable prize, and its value was all the greater the less it was damaged by assault or bombardment. In the case of a town or city one hoped to conquer, much the same could be said for its inhabitants: they were a valuable economic resource, and not to be wasted unnecessarily. Furthermore, if the besieging army hoped to fight a battle with its enemy, the surrender compact could provide a powerful incentive for a chary opposing commander to fight.

Thus, when on 26 June a Scottish attempt to burn the English fleet backfired, and much of the town was set alight, the English (under the impression that the Scots were ready to negotiate for a final surrender) were willing to grant the inhabitants a truce while they put it out.[112] But when the next day came, Alexander Seton, the captain of the city, showed no inclination to surrender. Seeing this, the English made a new assault on the town; this made a sufficient enough impression on the defenders for him to petition Edward III for a fifteen-day truce. On the evening of the fifteenth day, they agreed, if the town had not been relieved, they would hand over the town and castle, their lives and goods being spared. Twelve hostages from important families within the town put their lives on the line as security for the fulfillment of the agreement.[113]

On 11 July, the last day of the truce period, Archibald Douglas made his bid to rescue the city. Having gathered a very large army, he crossed the Tweed at the Yair ford,[114] then marched along the English side of the river until he was positioned opposite the army of the two Edwards. The Scots made a great display of their numbers, burned Tweedmouth, and sent messengers to declare that they would put all of England, from Berwick to London, to the torch unless the besiegers were prepared to break off the siege and do something about it. Edward also faced a more specific threat: Queen Philippa was not far south in

---

112 *Bridlington*, 111–12; the date is obtained by counting backwards from the date the 15-day truce was to expire.

113 *Bridlington*, 112. The *Brut* says that the truce period was to be eight days, which would put the date of the fire up a week.

114 *Scalacronica*, 162, has them cross at "Yarford"; Sir Herbert Maxwell, in his edition of the same chronicle (Thomas Gray, *Scalacronica*, ed. and trans. H. Maxwell [Glasgow: James Maclehose & Sons, 1907], 94), identifies this as Yair ford, a place I cannot find on maps of the area.

Bamburgh castle, and the Scots were ready to march against her.[115] They doubt-less remembered 1319, when Edward II's siege of Berwick had been broken by the same means: a threat to his queen in Carlisle, and the systematic devastation of the north country.[116] Edward, however, remained unmoved, declaring that he would not for any reason give up the siege until Berwick was in his hands.[117]

Some hours later, in the evening, about two hundred Scottish men-at-arms crossed the river by a ford where there had once been a bridge and made for the town. William Montague, at the head of two hundred English cavalry, inter-cepted the Scottish troopers before they had all passed through the gate: some were captured, some killed, and others, forced to flee back across the ford, fell into the river and drowned.[118] William Keith, one of the knights who did succeed in entering Berwick, took over as warden of the town,[119] symbolizing the fact that the Scots considered the relief operation to have succeeded, despite the losses they had suffered.[120]

Edward III was of another mind. In the morning, he demanded the surrender of the castle and the town, since Keith's force had entered from the English side of the river, while the truce agreement specified that they must approach on the Scottish side. The Scots answered "that the toune was rescuede wel ynow," and that they would not surrender.[121] Edward, infuriated by what he perceived as a broken treaty, ordered the hanging of one of the hostages – Thomas, son of Alexander Seton, the recent warden of the town (who had already lost a son at Kinghorn the previous year). The king commanded that every day two of the hostages be dealt with so, unless the defenders would yield the town; "and so he would teach them to break their covenants."[122]

This quickly brought the defenders back to the bargaining table.[123] By 15

---

[115] *Melsa*, 2:369: "They sent to the King of England that, if he would not raise the siege, they would destroy the greater part of England. To which Edward King of England answered that he would never lift the siege before the town had surrendered to him, or it had been cap-tured by his men [aut saltem viribus caperetur] . . . Finally they besieged the castle of Bam-burgh, where Philippa, Queen of England, was then staying, so that they might be able to end the siege of Berwick." Similarly, *AM Brut*, fo. 100v: "passeront lez Escotz . . . pur destruire le North pur resoun qe le Roy remua soun host et la seoge, et manancenont de mettre sa terre a flambe a Berwyk desqe al citee de Loundrez."
Thus, there is no specific statement that the Scots mentioned Philippa while they were at Tweedmouth, but it seems likely. For an idea of the extent of damage inflicted by the Scots in their raids while the Edwards were at Berwick, see *CDS*, no. 1085, p. 196.
[116] Scott, *Robert the Bruce*, 192–3.
[117] *Melsa*, 2:369 (see note 115, above).
[118] *Bridlington*, 113.
[119] *Scalacronica*, 163; *RFR*, II:2:865.
[120] *English Brut*, 282; *Bridlington*, 113.
[121] *English Brut*, 282; *AM Brut*, fo. 101v; *Bridlington*, 113.
[122] *AM Brut*, fo. 100v ("et issint enseigneront ils a freindre lour covenaunt"), clarifies the text which is corrupted in the *English Brut*, 283.
[123] *Scalacronica*, 163.

July, a new agreement had been reached, so detailed and carefully constructed that there was no room for further misunderstanding or fraud. This time the English insisted that the agreement be in writing, and verified with the seals of Dunbar and Keith.[124] An additional group of hostages was given to the English to ensure the Scots' compliance.[125] The indenture provided that another truce would obtain until sunrise on the following Tuesday, 20 July. The English promised that, during the truce, they would in no way harm the defenders; the latter promised not to make any improvements in their defenses, or resupply the castle. On the 20th, if they had not been rescued, the town and castle would be rendered to Edward III. All those within would be guaranteed life and limb, as well as all their lands, offices, rents, and so on.[126] The laws and customs of Berwick would continue to be in place. Those who chose to remain in Berwick under Edward III's obedience were to receive the king's protection without paying a fee; all others were to get free letters of safe-conduct after having forty days to dispose of their property.

William Keith was promised free passage to go to the Warden of Scotland, inform him of the agreement, and return. This would give the leaders of the Bruce party a chance to rescue the city before its fall; if they failed to do so, then the defenders could not really be blamed for surrendering. To avoid a repetition of the disputes following the events of the 11th, the conditions under which the town would be considered "rescued" were carefully spelled out. Any reinforcement of the garrison from the sea, or across the Tweed by ship or boat, would not count. The Scottish forces could approach and give battle by crossing the Tweed at the fishery known as "Berewyk Streme" to the west, or they could come over the land between the Tweed and the sea, on the Scottish side. If that were done, or if a battalion of two hundred men-at-arms managed to fight its way into the

---

124 The full text of the two indentures can be found in *RFR*, II:2:864–5. On the English side, the document was verified by the seals of Edward III and a group of twenty-five important magnates, including eight earls. Interestingly, Edward Balliol's seal is not appended, though he and his adherents were to be bound by its terms.

125 This is not stated in the written agreement, but it is mentioned in a number of chronicles. There were twelve new hostages according to the *English Brut*, 283, and six according to *Melsa*, 2:369.

126 This clause is worth giving in full as an example of how tightly defined the whole document is: "And that the said Earl [of March], and all the aforesaid people, shall have their lives and limbs, and they shall have heritably all their lands, tenements, rents, fisheries, offices, fiefs, and possessions, whether purchased or inherited, of which they had seisin the day that this accord was made, inside and outside of the said castle and town of Berwick, without other right being denied, according to the processes of the laws of Scotland; and that they will not be cast out in any way, except only by process of the Common Law of Scotland; nor denied any seisin or possession held, before the said day, by anyone whomsoever, in the time of any King of England or Scotland, with all their goods, castles, chalices, money, clothes, horses, armor, prisoners, and all other manner of goods, movables and otherwise, spiritual as well as temporal, in England as well as in Scotland, and with all their franchises, usages, laws, and customs, as held and practiced in the time of King Alexander, entirely, quit, and freely, without being imprisoned or otherwise troubled." *RFR*, II:2:863; a partial translation can be found in *The Wars of Edward III*, ed. C. J. Rogers (Woodbridge: Boydell & Brewer, 1999).

city during daylight without losing more than thirty men captured or killed, then the town would be held to have been rescued, and the hostages returned without delay.

Since William Keith's copy of the indenture was not written and sealed until the 16th, Edward III was in effect insisting that the Scots give battle immediately, or lose the town. He thus minimized the damage which the raiders in England would have time to inflict, and also left the Scots very little room to maneuver or plan. Moreover, since the burden of action rested solidly on the Scots, Edward could expect a *defensive* battle, where the tactics Balliol had used so successfully at Dupplin could once again be employed.

Even if Keith received his copy of the indenture early on the 16th, he could hardly have reached the warden, who was some forty miles to the south at Morpeth, much before midday on the 17th.[127] In a remarkable demonstration of the mobility for which the Scots were famous, Douglas managed to gather his troops from their scattered ravaging, march north, cross the Tweed,[128] and reach the park at Duns by nightfall on the 18th. The Scots had thus covered a good fifty miles in about a day and a half, and were now only about thirteen miles west of Berwick.[129]

The next morning, expecting the imminent arrival of his enemies and "joyous and happy" at that "most longed-for" prospect, Edward III readied his forces for battle.[130] A detachment of five hundred men-at-arms, with archers and spearmen in proportion, stood ready to guard against a sally by the defenders of Berwick. Another picked body of two hundred men-at-arms prepared to block the two hundred Scots who were expected to try to fight their way into the town.[131] The rest of the troops marched up onto Halidon Hill, a lone patch of high ground about two miles from the city, covering the approaches either along the Tweed or the coast. The men-at-arms, dismounted, were divided into three battles:[132] the first commanded by Henry Beaumont and the disinherited earls of Angus and Atholl, along with John of Eltham and Edward Bohun;[133] the second by Edward III; and the last by Edward Balliol. The archers deployed separately,

---

127 The warden's location is given in *Bridlington*, 113–14; cf. *Scalacronica*, 163 (the parish of Witton is near Morpeth).

128 Probably near Coldstream.

129 *Wyntoun*, 2:399; *Pakington*, fo. 184.

130 The *Anonimalle Brut*, 162, describes him as "joious et lee" at the news the Scots would come to give battle to raise the siege. The *Historia Roffensis*, fo. 79, refers to the "dies desideratissimus" when the rebellion and pride of the Scots were punished.

131 *Melsa*, 2:370.

132 The Bridlington chronicle describes them as "cuneos," or "wedges," but this term was often used in the middle ages as a synonym for the French "bataille," and does not necessarily imply a wedge-shaped formation; this is confirmed in this case by the *AM Brut*'s use of "escheles" (fo. 101v).

133 Eltham, Edward III's brother, was Earl of Cornwall; Bohun was Constable of England.

with a wing of them flanking each battle of men-at-arms, so that neither group would impede the other.[134]

About noon, scouts reported the approach of the enemy. Douglas had assembled a mighty force. According to the detailed and probably reliable account of the continuator of Walter of Guisborough, which appears to have been based on some record source now lost, the army included no fewer than seven earls (aside from the warden and the steward), seventy nobles of name, 1,100 *armatorum*,[135] and 13,500 of the commons, "lightly armed."[136] This does not include the men and soldiers within Berwick, who by a clause in the indentures of 15–16 July were expressly permitted to aid in the battle without prejudice to their hostages.

The size of the English army is impossible to determine. Though we can safely discard the claim of the *Brut* that it was outnumbered by five to one,[137] even the Scottish sources agree that it was substantially smaller than the Scottish host.[138] Given the very substantial group of warlike magnates present with the two Edwards,[139] it would be a reasonable guess that their forces at some point

[134] *Bridlington*, 114; *AM Brut*, 101v: "chescun dez escheles a lez ditz Roys dengleterre et descoce avoient denceles de bons archiers"; cf. *Cleopatra Brut*, fo. 182v; *English Brut*, 285.

[135] This would normally mean "men-at-arms," but in the case of Scotland likely includes soldiers from the £10 landholder class, who were merely required, by Robert Bruce's statute of 1318, to possess padded leather armor, a steel helmet, and gauntlets. They were thus much more lightly armed than English "men-at-arms." The light-armed infantry referred to by *Hemingburgh* would then be the "small folk having in goods the value of a cow" who were merely required to own a good bow or spear. Scott, *Robert the Bruce*, 190.

[136] *Hemingburgh*, 308–9. The close correspondence between the lists of notables in the various Scottish divisions in *Hemingburgh* and the *Brut* suggests that they both drew on the same source – though there are enough differences to indicate that the author of the *Brut* did not simply rely on *Hemingburgh*, or vice versa. The *Brut* gives improbably high numbers of soldiers, however, as do the other chroniclers (e.g. 90,000 in *Melsa*, 2:370; 60,000 in *Wyntoun*, 2:369, and *Bridlington*, 115; 80,000 in the *Anonimalle Brut*, 162) and the brief newsletter written within days of the battle, which gives the Scots 60,000 men. BL, Add. MS 43405, pp. 22–3. *Knighton*, 1:468–70, evidently draws on the same list, and indeed gives a somewhat fuller version than *Hemingburgh*'s. He is probably mistaken, however, in changing to 200 the 2,000 common soldiers reported by *Hemingburgh* to be in the second schiltron. Interestingly, the *Chronicle of the Kings of Scotland*, 66 (the relevant section of which was written in the sixteenth century) agrees that the Scottish army at Halidon comprised 15,000 men. The earls were Moray, Atholl, Carrick, Lennox, Ross, Sutherland, and Strathearn.

[137] *Cleopatra Brut*, fo. 182v; *English Brut*, 285, 288; also *Historia Roffensis*, fo. 66. This ratio is not found in the *AM Brut*, which implies a 4:1 ratio. *Melsa*, 2:370, has the English outnumbered three to one (90,000 to 30,000), but even this proportion is probably too high.

[138] *Wyntoun*, 2:399. *Hemingburgh*, 308 says the Scots "were confident in the great number of their people, for, compared to the Scots, the English army seemed exceedingly small." [confidebant enim in multitudine populi sui, quia, respectu Scotorum, exiguus valde videbatur exercitus Anglicorum.] *Lanercost*, 273–4, has the Scots approach "in gravi multitudine," and gives the number of Scottish casualties (36,320) as greater than the entire English army (30,000).

[139] As shown by the list of witnesses to the Berwick agreement: the earls of Cornwall, Norfolk, Warenne (Surrey), Warwick, Atholl, Oxford, Angus and Buchan [as Henry Beaumont]; Henry of Lancaster, Edward de Bohun, Henry Percy, William Montague, Thomas Wake, William de Ros, William Clinton, Ebulo Lestrange, Ralph Neville, John Mowbray,

passed thirteen thousand – as they certainly did during the major offensive of 1335, when roughly the same group of barons mustered troops.[140] But that high point would have been around mid-May, and in the two months between then and the battle, the English forces declined seriously due to desertion and the expiration of service terms. At one point in early June, Edward ordered the array of reinforcements, complaining that "a large proportion of our men-at-arms and foot soldiers have left us and returned [to England] without our leave, so that we are at present much alone."[141] By the day of Halidon Hill, the English host probably contained well fewer than ten thousand men. The claim of the *Chronicon de Lanercost* that the Scots were twice as numerous as the English is not improbable.[142]

Of course, though the English were seriously outnumbered, they were far less so than they had been the previous year at Dupplin. Furthermore, this time they had their choice of ground, and had picked a site "Quhare a man mycht dyscumffyte thre."[143] Under these circumstances, it may seem surprising that the Scots were willing to risk a battle, even given the need to relieve Berwick. Even a town with economic and military importance as great as Berwick's, after all, was hardly worth facing a certain defeat, especially since in the event of a battlefield defeat the town would be lost anyway.

But the Scots did not view defeat as a certainty – quite the opposite. They believed William Keith when he told them "That thai mycht fecht, for thai war ma/ and semyd fayrare folk alsua."[144] Indeed, he said, "they would undoubtedly

Richard Talbot, Ralph Basset, Robert Ufford, Thomas Berkeley, and Roger Swinnerton. *RFR*, II:2:865. Maurice Berkeley, Henry Ferrers and Hugh Audley apparently also served on the campaign, and William de Bohun, Reginald Cobham, William Fitzwarin, and Thomas Ughtred probably did as well. Cf. Nicholson, *Edward III*, 108, 110n, 145n; BL, Add. MS 35181, m. 10.

[140] See p. 97, below.

[141] *Lanercost*, Illustrative Documents, LII: "grant partie de noz gentz aussi bien darmes come de pie sont alez de nous et retournez sans nostre congie par qoi nous sumes molt sengle-ment en le cas que nous fumes en present." Dated 2 June. The letter also states that the king was expecting to be attacked by the Scots before 24 June. Nicholson, *Edward III and the Scots*, 131, gives additional details on the problem of desertion.

[142] *Lanercost*, 274. This chronicler states that his account came from a young Scottish knight who was captured in the battle. *Pipewell*, fo. 13v, gives the same ratio, though with obviously inflated totals: 80,000 Scots to 40,000 English.

If A. E. Prince is correct that only £5,629 was spent on the wages of soldiers and sailors for the 1333 campaign, the army may have been even smaller than that. Prince, "Army and Navy," 350. If the various classes of troops were present in the same proportion as those serving in the 1335 campaign, then that sum of money would only have supported an army averaging about 3,500 men for the period from 9 May to 24 July (and even that would leave nothing for the sailors, or for the pay of the soldiers who, under Balliol, arrived at the siege much earlier than Edward III.) This figure is intended only to give some idea of the order of magnitude of the Plantagenet's forces at Halidon Hill, and to reinforce the conclusion that his army was much smaller than that of the Scots.

[143] *Wyntoun*, 2:401 [Where a man might defeat three]; *Pluscardensis*, 269, says the same.

[144] *Wyntoun*, 2:399 [that they might fight, for they were more (*sc.* numerous than the English), and seemed better troops as well.]. Cf. *Scalacronica*, 163: the knights who had

prevail if they would return and array themselves to fight with the two kings."[145] As to the terrain, the Scottish leaders actually saw it as advantageous. Since they were approaching from the north, they would have the English trapped with nowhere to flee but into the waters of the Tweed (then at flood tide) or the sea, where they would be drowned.[146] After three decades of Scottish military superiority Bannockburn, rather than Dupplin, was the precedent on their minds. Furthermore, they had failed (or been unable) to scout the ground properly, and did not realize just how strong the English position was until it was too late.[147]

Shortly after noon, the schiltrons drew near to Halidon Hill, "covering the ground like locusts." The Scottish war-cries filled the air with a horrible din, which the minstrels accompanying the English army met with blaring horns, pounding drums, and skirling pipes.[148] The English soldiers, despite this encouragement, were "greatly cast down" when they saw the great size of the enemy force;[149] but, as at Dupplin before and Crécy and Poitiers after, they were steadied by the fact that they had nowhere to run.

To reach their enemies, the Scots had to traverse a marshy hollow, down one steep slope and then up another.[150] They had to cover the ground as quickly as possible, so as to minimize the time for which they were exposed to English arrows; yet they also had to advance in a controlled manner so as not to break their formation. By the time they reached the top of the 500-foot high hill,[151] the Scottish soldiers – who had already covered over sixty miles in the past three

entered the town "estoit auys qe lour poair Descoce surmountoit le ost le roy Dengleterre." [were advised that their Scottish forces surpassed the army of the King of England.]
[145] *Hemingburgh*, 308: "si redirent, et ad pugnandum cum duobus regibus se disponerent, indubitanter praevalerent."
[146] *Pakington*, fo. 184: "lour purpos fuist que nul Engleis devoit eschaper pur ceo que la ville de Berewyke et la terre d'escoce fuist d'un part et le mer d'une autre part et lewe de Twede de la tierce part et l'ost d'escoce vient de la quatre." *Bridlington*, 115; *English Brut*, 283, 287, 289; cf. *Hemingburgh*, 309. The *Anonimalle Brut*, 166, says that the Scots waited to advance against the English until the Tweed was in flood tide.
[147] *Wyntoun*, 2:401.
[148] BL, Add. MS 43,405, pp. 22–3 (noon); *Hemingburgh*, 309 (locusts); *Cleopatra Brut*, fo. 182v ("les Engleis minstrals amesnerent lour tabours lour trumpes et lour pipes; et escrierent les Escotz hidousement.")
[149] *Anonimalle Brut*, 162 (grantement abaiz). On the feelings of medieval soldiers when battle approached, cf. the view expressed by Jean d'Hainault's speech in the closely contemporary *The Vows of the Heron*: "When we are in taverns, drinking strong wines,/ at our sides the ladies we desire, looking on,/ with their smooth throats and heavy necklaces/ their grey eyes shining back with smiling beauty,/ Nature calls on us to have hearts desiring,/ to struggle, awaiting [their] thanks at the end;/ Then we could conquer Yaumont and Aguilant,/ and the others conquer Oliver and Roland./ But when were are in the field, on our galloping chargers / our shields 'round our necks and lances lowered,/ and the great cold is turning us entirely to ice,/ and our limbs rebelling [?*effendent*] both behind and before,/ and our enemies are approaching towards us/ then we would rather be in so deep a cave/ that we should never make a vow of how much [we will do in war] or when." In Wright, *Political Poems and Songs*, 21.
[150] *Pluscardensis*, 269; Bower, *Scottichronicon*, 92.
[151] Nicholson, *Edward III and the Scots*, 131.

days – were out of breath.[152] Their ranks had already been severely thinned by the fire of the English archers, who shot so fiercely – their arrows coming "thick as rays in the sunlight" – that the Scots were rendered helpless.[153] According to the *Brut*, the archers' arrows took thousands out of the fight.[154]

The Scots' first schiltron, led by the Earl of Moray,[155] avoided the first battle of the English army and boldly charged instead against rearward battle, which was commanded by Edward Balliol. Another schiltron collided with the English king's division.[156] The ensuing hand-to-hand combat at the top of the hill ended very quickly.[157] Unable to endure the flights of arrows or the blows of the English men-at-arms, the schiltrons began to dissolve as individual Scots in the rear took to their heels, casting away their weapons to speed their flight.[158] The lead schiltron was the first to collapse, but the one fighting Edward III did not last much longer.[159] Soon the English men-at-arms mounted their chargers and sped off in pursuit of the flying enemy; a great slaughter followed.[160]

Meanwhile, the Scottish schiltron containing the two hundred elite men-at-arms who had been deputed to try to break into Berwick continued to fight against Henry Beaumont's battle "with the ferocity of lions." In the end, though,

---

152 *Pluscardensis*, 269.
153 *Cleopatra Brut*, 182v: "treerent seetz si espessement come sount rays en la solaie"; *English Brut*, 285 [shot so fast and sore that the Scots could not help themselves]. Similarly, *Lanercost*, 274: "prima acie venientes ita fuerunt a multitudine sagittariorum Angliae vulnerati in facie et excaecati in hoc bello, sicut in priori apud Gledenmore, quod se ipsos adjuvare non poterant, et ideo cito faciem sagittarum ictibus avertere et cadere inceperunt." [The first battle, coming there, were wounded in the face and blinded in great numbers by the archers of England, as before at Dupplin Moor, so that they could not help themselves, and averted their faces from the striking arrows, and began to fall.] Also note the *Anonimalle Brut*, 166: "les archers Dengleterre les desbaretta et greva, ainsi qils estoient en petite hure auxi come estuffez et envoegles, et tost perdirent lour contenance" [The archers of England took them out of the fight and injured them, so that they were in a short time as if smothered and blinded, and soon lost their steadfastness] and the *Historia Roffensis*, fo. 66: "ceciderunt Scoti percussi a sagitariis Anglicorum et fugam capientes." [The Scots fell, hit by the English archers, and took flight.]
154 *Cleopatra Brut*, fo. 182v "ensi ferrerent ilz [i.e. les archiers] les escotz qe ils lour mistrent avale par plousours millers"; *English Brut*, 285; cf. *Knighton*, 1:468.
155 *English Brut*, 283.
156 *Bridlington*, 113–14; *Lanercost*, 273–4.
157 The *AM Brut*, fo. 101v; *Melsa*, 2:370; the *Anonimalle Brut*, 166; and *Wyntoun*, 2:401, are among the sources that mention the brevity of the battle. A poem on the battle contained in one version of the *English Brut*, 287, says "Alle thus the Skottes discomfite were/ in litell tyme with Grete feere."
158 *Bridlington*, 115–16; *Anonimalle Brut*, 166; *Historia Roffensis*, fo. 66 (see above, note 153).
159 The *Lanercost* chronicler, 274, states that the first schiltron was defeated by Balliol before the other two even began to fight; then they too were promptly defeated in the same way by the English army. *Melsa*, 2:370, says that the second two schiltrons were awaiting the outcome of the first one's fight before acting, and that, seeing the first schiltron defeated, they immediately began to flee.
160 *Bridlington*, 116; *Cleopatra Brut*, 182v.

they too were overcome. The earls of Sutherland and Ross, along with five hundred of the best soldiers of all Scotland, perished there.[161] So far as can be determined from the chronicles, Beaumont, Eltham, and the Disinherited earls were left to win this victory alone, as the battles of the two kings carried on their pursuit. It is likely, however, that the archers and other infantry attached to the kings' divisions were dispatched to help defeat the third Scottish schiltron, since none of the accounts mentions the participation of footmen in the pursuit.

The casualties inflicted on the Scots during the chase, which lasted for eight miles, were very severe.[162] More, indeed, were killed during this phase than during the actual battle.[163] The Scots who had participated in the battle were easy to recognize, for they had put on shirts over their armor to distinguish themselves from the English.[164] Though many of the Scottish soldiers had ridden to the battlefield, they had to try to escape on foot because their terrified grooms had ridden off with the horses when the defeat became obvious.[165] "And there might men see meny a Scottisshe-man caste doun vnto the earthe dede, and hir baneres displaiede, & hackede into pices, and meny a gode habrigoun of stele in hir blode bathede."[166] Small groups of fleeing men repeatedly gathered together to make desperate last stands, but were easily overcome.[167]

No reliable figures for the total number of men killed can be determined,[168] but some idea of the Scottish losses can be gained by the fate of their leaders. Of

---

[161] *Bridlington*, 116. The schiltron containing Sutherland and Ross (as well as Strathearn, who escaped) can be identified as the one which fought so bravely at "Hevyside" by the fact that it was the only one containing just 200 men-at-arms (*Hemingburgh*, 309), and by the fact that Wyntoun, though he says the Scottish army as a whole "rycht suddanly dyscumfyte ware," adds that "Bot Hw the Erle off Ros, thai say,/ That assemblyd in the way,/ Made stalwart and rycht lang fychtyng,/ That ser[v]yd bot off lytill thyng;/ For he wes dede, and all his men/ Ware nere-hand slayne abowt hym then." *Wyntoun*, 2:401. For further confirmation, Wyntoun later (2:402) says that Sutherland was "wyth thame [the Earl of Ross and his men] bwndyn in specyall band."

[162] *Melsa*, 2:370.

[163] Stewart, *Croniclis*, 3:310, specifies this, and given the brevity of the battle it is not surprising.

[164] *Melsa*, 2:370.

[165] *AM Brut*, fo. 101v; *Cleopatra Brut*, fo. 182v; cf. the incorrectly emended *English Brut*, 285.

[166] *English Brut*, 285 [And there might men see many a Scotsman cast down to the ground, dead; and their banners displayed, and hacked into pieces, and many a good steel shirt of mail bathed in their blood]; *Cleopatra Brut*, 182v.

[167] Ibid.

[168] *Melsa*, 2:370, says that, in addition to Douglas, the dead included 7 earls, 18 barons, 120 knights, and 38,600 others. The *Brut* (*Cleopatra Brut*, fo. 182 v; *English Brut*, 286) sets the number of Scots killed at 35,712. These figures are obviously greatly inflated. *Pluscardensis*, 270, says that the total number of men slain in the battle exceeded 10,000 men, "by the estimate of heralds worthy of belief." *Wyntoun*, 2:402, agrees. *Knighton*, 1:486, says that the Scots lost 1,100 men with armor, and 1,800 of the unarmored commons. (He also says that the total number killed was 40,000, but this can be discarded – who would there be aside from the armored and unarmored troops to make up the total?) The sum of 2,900 may be the best figure available for the number of Scots killed.

the nine Scots of comital rank (seven earls, the warden and the steward) who fought, six perished.[169] According to one Scottish witness, only five of the 203 knights dubbed on the field survived.[170] So many nobles were killed that, says the *Book of Pluscarden*, it would be tedious to give all their names, "and more saddening than useful."[171] Losses on the English side were very light.[172]

In contrast to many medieval battles, few prisoners were taken at Halidon Hill.[173] Of those few whose surrender was accepted, one hundred – all those who were not hidden away by their captors – were put to death the following morning at Edward III's order.[174] The reason for this action is nowhere recorded, but a clue can be found in the words of the contemporary author of the *Annales Paulini*: "it was commonly said that the Scottish war would finally be over, for there remained no one of that nation who had the ability, knowledge, or will to gather men together for a battle, or to lead them if they did assemble."[175] Having been defeated at Dupplin Moor, and suffered the loss of three consecutive wardens,[176] the Scots had simply chosen a fourth one, gathered another army, and mounted a new challenge to the claims of the two Edwards. Edward III did not want them to be able to do it again – though, as it turned out, even after the loss of Douglas, Ross, and so many other magnates and men, the fight was not out of the Scots.

For a full year, however, this was by no means evident. Balliol's supporters quickly overran the entire country, until only four castles – Dumbarton, Lochleven, Kildrummy and Urquhart – held out for the Bruce cause. The Earl of March joined the English side, receiving substantial gifts from Edward III in return. Balliol distributed comital titles and the lands that went with them to his

---

169 Viz. Atholl, Carrick, Douglas, Lennox, Ross and Sutherland.

170 *Lanercost*, 274. This was probably exaggerated: according to the *English Brut*, 283–5, the total of newly dubbed knights was only 140.

171 *Pluscardensis*, 270.

172 One knight and 10 archers according to *Chron. CCCO*, fo. 172; only seven infantrymen according to the *AM Brut*, fo. 101v; etc.

173 But cf. *Knighton*, 1:486. The Scots, according to the Bridlington chronicler, 115, were ordered to take no prisoners, and there may well have been a similar ordinance made for the English army. If so, it would make Edward III's order to execute the prisoners the following day much more understandable (see below). Such sanguinary battles became typical of the European battlefield after the advent of the "Infantry Revolution," in which Halidon Hill was a landmark event. See Rogers, "The Military Revolutions of the Hundred Years War."

174 *Melsa*, 2:370; *Pluscardensis*, 270; *Wyntoun*, 2:401.

175 *Annales Paulini*, 358: "Dicebatur tunc publice guerram Scotiae tunc fore finaliter terminatum, quia nullus remansit de natione illa, qui posset, sciret aut vellet, homines ad praelium congregare aut regere congregatos." Cf. *Murimuth*, 68. The execution of the Scottish prisoners may have been intended to punish those who had earlier done homage to Edward Balliol; cf. *Pakington*, fo. 197. Or, perhaps it already seemed to Edward III that (as Balliol later remarked) "to ransom the prisoners is nothing other than to prolong the war." PRO C49/6/29.

176 Thomas Randolph (of natural causes, before Dupplin), Donald of Mar (at Dupplin), and then Andrew Murray (at Kelso Bridge). Archibald Douglas, who fell at Halidon, was thus the fourth warden to die or be captured within less than one year.

main supporters. His and Edward III's men took over castles and royal offices all over the realm.[177]

Meanwhile Edward III himself, "loved and honored by great and small alike for the great *noblesse* of his deeds and words,"[178] returned to England "with myche ioye & worship."[179] A more different homecoming than that of 1327, when he had entered York "sorrowing and without honor" after the debacle of the Weardale campaign, would be hard to imagine. Thanksgiving masses and processions were held throughout England, Wales and Guienne.[180] A giant parade of all the clergy and citizens of London carried the city's relics from St. Paul's to Trinity Church and back, praising God and their king, and rejoicing greatly at the victory.[181] Especially in the north, people felt that they were finally released from "the misery in which the English had been held for thirty-five years" (i.e. since the uprising led by William Wallace and Andrew Murray in 1297.)[182] "Everyone," according to the chronicler Jean le Bel, "said he was a second King Arthur."[183] Jubilant songs were written in his honor, proclaiming that he had at long last avenged the English defeat at Bannockburn:

> Skottes out of Berwick and of Abirdene
> At the Bannok burn war ye to kene;
> Thare slough ye many sakles, as it was sene;
> And now has king Edward wroken it, I wene . . .
>
> Whare er ye, Skottes of Saint Johnes toune?
> The bost of yowre baner es betin all doune;
> When ye bosting will bede, sir Edward es boune
> For to kindel yow care, and crak yowre crowne.[184]

Edward had taken the first steps down a path which would soon lead him to such martial glory that, even in France, he would be acknowledged as "the most valiant man in Christendom."[185] A soldier-king in the midst of a society of chiv-

---

177 *Pluscardensis*, 270; *Wyntoun*, 2:404.

178 *Le Bel*, 1:119. Note that, although le Bel's chronology is rather confused when it comes to the Scottish wars, it is fairly clear that he is referring here to Edward's return from the siege of Berwick in 1333.

179 *English Brut*, 291 [with much joy and honor].

180 *RFR*, II:2:86; *Historia Roffensis*, fo. 66.

181 *Annales Paulini*, 358–9.

182 *Historia Roffensis*, fo. 65.

183 *Le Bel*, 1:118; cf. 119.

184 Minot, in Wright, *Political Poems and Songs*, 61–2. [Scots out of Berwick and Aberdeen, at the Bannockburn you were too keen; there you slew many innocents {or "many without cause"; see O. F. Emerson, *A Middle English Reader* (New York: Macmillan, 1924), 428}, as was seen; and now has King Edward avenged it, I think. . . . Where are ye, Scots of Perth? The boast of your banner is beaten all down; when you boasting will bede, Sir Edward [III] is bound, for to kindle you care, and crack your crown.] Cf. the poem in the *English Brut*, 287–9.

185 "le plus vaillant homme des crestiens." This opinion was expressed by Guillaume Brouart, one of Philip VI's men-at-arms, some time between 1340 and 1346. J. Viard and A.

alric warriors, he was tasting the sweetness of military success for the first time – but not for the last. Indeed, his future triumphs in France owed much to his experiences in 1333. He now had in his service a group of soldiers and officers accustomed to battle, and prepared to expect victory against the odds.[186] He had experienced the political benefits which winning a battle could bring – even to deciding the control of a kingdom – and gained the confidence to seek out such decisive conflicts, whether by using a besieged city as "bait" or otherwise. He had observed first hand the efficacy of the yew longbow in the hands of good archers, especially when they were combined with a strong defensive position and a solid core of steadfast men-at-arms. These lessons, along with the different but equally significant ones he had gained during the 1327 campaign, powerfully influenced his strategy in the opening years of the Hundred Years War, which was soon to start.

Vallée, *Registre du Trésor des Chartes* (Paris: Archives Nationales, 1979–84), no. 6706. Cf. *Chron. CCCO*, fo. 171.

[186] At least five earls (Arundel, Oxford, Suffolk, Huntingdon, and Warwick) and four key barons who rode on the Crécy *chevauchée*, for example, also served with Edward in 1333.

CHAPTER FIVE

"APON THAYME TYTE, FOR THAI AR WELLE NERE DYSCUMFFYTE": FROM SCOTLAND TO FRANCE, 1334–1337

To win victory is easy; to preserve its fruits, difficult.
Wu Ch'i, I.4.i[1]

FOR THREE YEARS after the battle of Halidon Hill, Edward III found ample outlet for his martial energy in Scotland. Over that period, his armies campaigned there during the winter of 1334–35, the summer and autumn of 1335, and the spring and summer of 1336. As late as July of 1336, Edward himself led a *chevauchée* into the far north of the kingdom, relieving the castle of Lochindorb and burning Aberdeen, Elgin and Forres – over two hundred miles past the English border.[2] Even then, Scotland was far from fully pacified, and Edward would probably have led another major campaign there in 1337 had he not been distracted by a new war with a much greater enemy: France. As we shall see in this chapter, the outbreak of the Hundred Years War in 1337 was not primarily a sudden outburst of hostility over the simmering disputes in Gascony or the increasing influence of Robert of Artois at Edward's court; on all of these issues, compromises acceptable to both sides could be and were found. War between England and France was, rather, a natural consequence of the two realms' irreconcilable interests in Scotland. King Philip felt honor-bound to use military force to aid his ally, David II, and Edward III was equally willing to fight for the claims of his vassal Edward Balliol.

Considering the magnitude of the victory outside Berwick, it may seem surprising that the war in Scotland lasted long enough to draw the Valois and Plantagenet kings into direct confrontation. Indeed, in the immediate aftermath of the battle, it seemed that there would be no need for further military activity on the English king's part.[3] Only a few hundred soldiers, if that many, were retained to garrison the reconquered lands.[4] The war in Scotland was officially

---

[1] In Sun Tzu, *Art of War*, ed. Griffith, 152.
[2] That is, from the traditional border, not the new one created by Balliol's cessions.
[3] *Wyntoun*, 2:403: "The Inglis men efftyre this fycht/ Persay[v]yd the Scottis off lytill mycht/ Agayne thare mekill mycht to stand." [The Englishmen after this fight/ perceived the Scots of little might/ against their great might to stand.]
[4] Ferriby's Wardrobe Book in fact does not show any payments for a garrison at Berwick

considered to be over.[5] As Edward III made provisions for the government of
Berwickshire, which was transferred to him immediately after the battle,[6]
Balliol worked to establish control over the rest of Scotland. The once-
disinherited lords fanned out to take possession of their ancient family lands,
and of new ones forfeited by Bruce adherents as well. David Strathbogie
received the title of Steward of Scotland, along with all the lands of Robert
Stewart, in addition to his earldom of Atholl.[7] Henry Percy (who became one of
Balliol's most active supporters after Dupplin) gained Annandale and other
Moray possessions as part payment of the 2,000 marcates earlier granted to him;
Richard Talbot became "Lord of Mar," and acquired title to the castle of
Kildrummy, along with substantial Comyn lands, in right of his wife Elizabeth.
Balliol, at Perth, ensured that the other offices, castles, and towns of the realm
were in the hands of men willing to submit to his rule.[8] A parliament was
summoned for the following February, an assembly which Balliol clearly hoped
would effect a national reconciliation and reunification under his leadership.

The Bruce party could not mount any significant opposition; only five scattered strongholds held out for Good King Robert's son.[9] Elsewhere, no one in
the kingdom except children too innocent to understand the consequences dared
to profess loyalty to David.[10] In May, the young king's guardians thought it
necessary to send him to safety in France. An embassy led by John Randolph,
the young Earl of Moray, persuaded Philip VI to provide a small fleet for the
operation, which sailed to Dumbarton and brought David to France. He and his
court-in-exile were graciously received and established in Château Gaillard.[11]

Things began to change after the Holyrood parliament of February, 1334.
There, with the assent of a group of prelates, representatives of the commons,
and magnates – mostly men who had come with him from England – Balliol
affirmed the agreement spelled out in the Roxburgh letters patent of 23 March

---

until September of 1334, when a force of 18 "homini armatorum" and 140 hobelars and
watchmen began to receive wages. In the same month the new Warden of the Marches, Ralph
Neville, came into service with a force of 60 men-at-arms and 60 mounted archers. *WBRF,* fos
248, 233, 252v. It is likely that some garrison forces were in place earlier, but not paid on the
Wardrobe accounts.

5   *CCR, 1333–37,* 129, 158.

6   See the extensive details in Nicholson, *Edward III and the Scots,* 142–5.

7   *Wyntoun,* 2:407, 413 (lands and lordship); BL Harleian MS 299 fo. 183 for the title (comes
Athol et senescallus Scocie).

8   See Nicholson, *Edward III and the Scots,* 147–9, 65–7; *Wyntoun,* 2:404, 407–8. The Percy
claim to Annandale and Mofattdale was later transferred to the Bohuns in exchange for Jedburgh and a pension from Edward III. J. M. W. Bean, "The Percies and their Estates in Scotland," *Archaeologia Aeliana,* 4th ser., 35 (1957), 97–8.

9   *Pluscardensis,* 270; *Wyntoun,* 2:404; *Scalacronica,* 164.

10 *Wyntoun,* 2:413.

11 *ERS,* 464 (note expense of greater than £2,000 sterling), 449; *Chronographia,* 2:31–2;
Scalacronica, 164; *Grandes chroniques,* 9:141.

1333, and promised to do public homage to Edward in the future.[12] Balliol may have tried to convince the Scottish parliament to ratify the cession of the eight southeastern counties which had been agreed before the Halidon campaign, but if so he was unsuccessful.[13] The extent of the two thousand librates was left unspecified. The first official acknowledgment of the scope of the transfer envisioned came only in June, when Balliol and a group of his key supporters met with Edward III at Newcastle. Edward pressed his new vassal to hand over the eight counties immediately, but Balliol resisted. Only after the English king distributed over £1,000 in cash bribes to Balliol, Beaumont and Strathbogie could the matter go forward.[14] On 12 June, Balliol sealed a letter patent authorizing the transfer of the eight counties to English sovereignty. The document was witnessed by all the Disinherited lords present, along with the Earl of March, Robert Lauder, and three English prelates.[15] Then, on the 19th, the affair was brought to closure when Balliol publicly performed the ceremony of homage and fealty to Edward III.[16] Patrick of Dunbar, Earl of March, did his homage at the same time, promising in addition to make all the lords of Scotland enter the obedience of the two Edwards. The earls of Fife and Menteith then joined Patrick in doing homage to Edward Balliol, and also swearing to Edward III that they would maintain his "tenant" [Balliol] as King of Scots.[17]

In July, the Earl of Moray returned to Scotland from France and joined up

---

12 *RFR*, II:2:876–8. See *RS*, 1:261–3; *Lanercost*, 280–1, for the ratification of the agreement by the English parliament at York shortly thereafter.

13 For this agreement, see p. 58, above.

14 Nicholson, *Edward III and the Scots*, 159. The payments – totaling 666 marks to Strathbogie, 500 to Balliol, 400 to Beaumont, and 100 to Richard Talbot – were ordered between 12 and 16 June. In a writ issued on the 18th, Edward stated that his business with Scotland "cannot be successfully completed" [ne se purront exploiter] without delivery to him of 1,000 marks; certainly this was the same 1,000 marks which his writ of 16 June had promised to Balliol, Beaumont and Talbot. The former writ is transcribed ibid., 241. The payment of 960 marks to Robert Keith for delivery of the lands of Keith was probably also related to these transactions. Reid, "Edward de Balliol," 60.

15 *RFR*, II:2:888; cf. *RS*, 271. The date of the letter, coming a few days before most of the writs for payments to Balliol's party, is somewhat odd; the most likely explanation is that the bribes were agreed just before the letter of cession was drawn up, but the documents providing for the cash payments were simply not prepared until a few days later. Then, when they had been completed and arrangements for the shipment of the silver made, the whole arrangement was finalized the next day by Balliol's homage.

16 Some chronicles – e.g. *Hemingburgh*, 309; Walsingham, *Historia Anglicana*, 1:196 – give the date as the 18th, and the *Anonimalle Brut*, 168, has it on the 21st; but Nicholson, *Edward III and the Scots*, 162, clearly establishes that the others (e.g. *Lanercost*, 277; *Bridlington*, 118; *Pipewell*, fo. 14) which give the date as the 19th are correct. Cf. also *Avesbury*, 299, which indicates the Earl of Atholl and Alexander Mowbray also did homage to Edward III at this time.

17 *Anonimalle Brut*, 170; *Pakington*, fo. 197: "lesditz Countz [Metieth and Fife] attornerunt au dit sire Edward Roi Descoce de lour homage come a celui qi fuist droit heire Descoce et tenant le Roi Dengleterre et puis furunt jurez au Roi Dengleterre de maynteigner soun tenant et soun estat en le roialme Descoce." As the same source notes, violation of this oath was the main reason Menteith was drawn and quartered after he was captured at Neville's Cross.

with the teenaged Robert Stewart – the future Robert II of Scotland – in the area of Renfrew. The region, which had long been closely associated with the Bruce and Stewart families, had already risen in Robert's favor. With a force of some four hundred men, the steward captured the castle of Dunoon. Hearing this, the inhabitants of Bute killed Balliol's sheriff and handed over Rothesay castle to the steward as well. Then in late July, Randolph and Stewart, who jointly assumed the office of warden, quickly gained control over most of nether Clydesdale, Renfrew, Carrick, Kyle, and Cunningham. Meanwhile, with the aid of a former Balliol supporter, Moray and William Douglas even managed to renew the internecine strife in Galloway that had broken out in 1332 while Balliol was besieged in Perth.[18] Guerrilla bands stalked through English-held areas like hunters, collecting "tribute" from the inhabitants. The royal officials appointed by Edward III for the recently annexed counties dared not leave Berwickshire, because the rest of the countryside was "in a state of war."[19] Resentment at Balliol's surrender of so much of the realm to England gained support for the rebels, as did rumors of support from France.[20] Their resources were small, however, and most Scots were unready to go up against the Disinherited and Edward III for yet another time.

Balliol might well have been able to gradually wear down or win over the Bruce partisans had it not been for a quarrel that broke out among his foremost vassals over the lands of John Mowbray, who had been killed at Annan. Alexander Mowbray, John's brother, claimed the lands, but so did John's daughters. Since the latter had the strong support of Henry Beaumont, David Strathbogie, and Richard Talbot, this was very awkward for Balliol. When he chose to back Alexander over John's daughters, Beaumont, Strathbogie and Talbot angrily abandoned him and retired to their own lands. About 24 August, Beaumont left for Dundarg, and Strathbogie set out for his northern castle of Lochindorb.[21] Talbot and some companions, sensing the hostility of the Scots all around them,

---

[18] *Wyntoun*, 2:414–16; *Pluscardensis*, 276–7; *Lanercost*, 278.

[19] *Wyntoun*, 2:415 ("as schawaldowris war wa[l]kand"); *Lanercost*, 278 (tribute); PRO E372/180/ 54d: "quia vicecomites ibid nec aliqui ministri R. in com' illis seu forestis audebant intrare eo quod tota patria illa extitit de guerra per totium tempore predictam," viz. 21 June 1334–15 October 1335.

[20] *Hemingburgh*, 309–10, and *Melsa*, 2:372, state that the rebellion was caused by Balliol's homage, but that had been no secret per se, and had even been approved at the Holyrood parliament. Furthermore, Edward III had made two major concessions concerning the homage to avoid just such an anti-Balliol rising. First, he had granted that Balliol would not be required to attend parliaments in England; second, he had granted that his position as Suzerain of Scotland would not entitle him to hear appeals from Scottish courts, thus ensuring that Scotland would (aside from the eight counties annexed to England and the military service Balliol owed) retain real independence. *RS*, 262. The cession of the southern counties, in contrast, could well have been seen as a surprising betrayal of the realm. *Lanercost*, 278, for the impact of rumors from France.

[21] *Bridlington*, 119 (date); *Wyntoun*, 2:406–7; *Pluscardensis*, 271. A number of sources state that Balliol departed for Berwick at this time, but Wyntoun, who places him at Perth, is more likely correct. Balliol's position was not yet so weak that he would flee his capital.

decided to hasten back to England.[22] On their way, they were ambushed and captured in Lothian by some recent Balliol converts, who were willing enough to abandon their new lord even though he had given them positions of honor.[23]

Balliol quickly realized how precarious his position was without the support of Beaumont and Strathbogie, and abandoned Alexander Mowbray. This only made things worse, however: Mowbray joined forces with the "rebel" Scots, taking with him Balliol's horses and treasury to ensure his welcome.[24] Spared the need to divide, Moray and Stewart could turn directly to conquering. Such forces as they and Mowbray could gather moved against each of their isolated enemies in turn. The Earl of Moray chased down David of Strathbogie, undisputed Earl of Atholl since his Scottish rival had been killed at Halidon. Strathbogie, "who had before all others loved Edward Balliol, and helped him and maintained him in his rule," escaped with his life only by switching to the Bruce side, swearing homage and fealty to King David.[25] Once he had done so, he was allowed to take a leading place in the rebellion against Balliol, "so that, having himself been converted, he might more easily win the others over to King David's side."[26] To make things worse for Balliol, two of his few remaining powerful supporters, Henry Percy and Edward Bohun, were embroiled in another, entirely separate, quarrel over the division of conquered lands in Scotland.[27] As the change of the political tide became unmistakable, Balliol fled to Berwick and appealed to his suzerain for help. By the end of September 1334, he had once again been almost entirely expelled from his kingdom, only Galloway east of the Cree and parts of Buchan (Henry Beaumont's earldom) remaining loyal to him.[28] Even in Buchan, Balliol's support did not extend much beyond the half-repaired citadel of Dundarg, where Beaumont was under siege by Mowbray and the recently-ransomed Andrew Murray.[29]

By the time Balliol reached Berwick, Edward III was already making prepa-

---

[22] *Bridlington*, 119; *Melsa*, 2:372.

[23] *Bridlington*, 119; *Scalacronica*, 164; *Fordun*, 357; Nicholson, *Edward III and the Scots*, 169. Talbot, John Felton, and John Stirling were held for ransom; their companions were killed. This was the event which stuck in the minds of many English chroniclers as marking the beginning of the revolt against Balliol.

[24] *Wyntoun*, 2:407; *Pluscardensis*, 271; *Bridlington*, 119; and *Melsa*, 2:372. Specifically, he linked up with Andrew Murray.

[25] *Anonimalle*, 2: "qe principalment amast le roi Descocez et lui eidoit et mayntenoit en soun regne"; cf. *Lanercost*, 278; *Scalacronica*, 164; *Wyntoun*, 2:417. According to *Fordun*, 358, his capitulation came on 27 September. *Pluscardensis*, 277, gives the place as near Lochaber.

[26] *Pluscardensis*, 281.

[27] See Nicholson, *Edward III and the Scots*, 147, 170–1; cf. PRO C49/6/29.

[28] *Lanercost*, 278; *Anonimalle*, 2; *Bridlington*, 120–1. He was chased to Berwick before 29 September.

[29] *Fordun*, 357; *Bridlington*, 120–2. *Bridlington*, 120, has Beaumont realize too late that "if the King of Scots and the various lords aforementioned had not dispersed, they would not have fallen into the hands of their enemies so; for, as the Philosopher says, every capacity is stronger if united than dispersed."

rations for another expedition into Scotland. He had been aware of trouble in Scotland since 3 August, and already by 1 September he had begun making arrangements to send ships and a large quantity of supplies (over 6,500 quarters of various grains) to the north. Three weeks later, he had begun the process of raising an army for a campaign in Scotland.[30] Other preparations for a renewed offensive were made on the diplomatic front: in October, Edward dispatched John Stratford, Chancellor of England and Archbishop of Canterbury, on an embassy to the French court. Stratford's primary mission was to confirm a deal which he had sketched out with Philip VI during another embassy earlier in the year, whereby the French king would, in return for Edward's participation in the crusade he was planning, restore the lands in Aquitaine which had been sequestered after the War of St. Sardos. According to Geoffrey le Baker, however, the archbishop had also, for this new embassy, been instructed to ensure that the French would halt their support of Edward's enemies in Scotland.[31]

While Edward was in Newcastle, preparing to set out into Scotland with the painfully small army he had gathered, the first frost of what was to be an unusually cold and stormy winter set in.[32] Of all the arrayed contingents Edward had summoned, only the a reduced levy of Yorkshire troops, 241 Welshmen from Radnor and Merioneth, and 143 men from the Forest of Dean had arrived by mid-November. Nevertheless, on the 14th the impatient king and his 4,000-odd troops (the majority of them from his household and the retinues of the magnates) set out on a slow march to Roxburgh, where they arrived around the 23rd.[33] A workforce of over two hundred laborers, masons, carpenters, pavil-

---

30 *RS*, 276–9; see also Nicholson, *Edward III and the Scots*, 173 et seq.
31 See below, pp. 91–93.
32 Weather: *Bridlington*, 120; *Melsa*, 2:373; Cf. *Brut*, 2:292; *Scalacronica*, 165.
33 Departure: *WBRF*, fos 233v (Warwick), 234. Impatience: *RS*, 1:294 (et passim). The king reached Bolton on the 17th, and Doddington on the 20th (*WBRF*, fos 201v, 268v). The *CPR, 1334–8*, 48, contains a document dated "Roxburgh, by the K." on the 23rd.
Number of troops (as of 11/14): 1,073 men-at-arms, 821 horse archers, 40 foot archers (under Northwell), and 73 household crossbowmen (not "valets" as Nicholson has them) accompanied by 65 "garcionem" (probably paviseurs) in various retinues and the royal household. 202 holders of charters of pardon, 2 serving as centenars, 40 as mounted archers, and 160 as foot. An arrayed contingent from the forest of Dean (20 mounted archers, 99 foot archers, and 24 miners). 100 *homini armatorum* (paid as hobelars) from the city of York; 1 knight, eighteen esquires, 103 "hobel' saggitar' ad equos" and vintenars, and 359 foot archers from Westriding; one knight, 27 esquires, 82 horse archers, and 258 foot archers from Eastriding; 12 esquires, 32 horse archers and 177 foot archers from Northriding – entering royal pay on 11/4, 10/30, 11/9, 11/14, respectively. For the Eastriding men, it is specified that this was at York. [Nicholson, *Edward III*, presumes that the Northriding troops had not joined the king by the 14th (the day they entered pay), but I think they must have, since if they had not but were expected shortly the king would probably have waited a day or two for them to unite with the army, and since the *RS* contain no angry writ on the 15th complaining of their non-arrival.] 114 men arrayed by Hugh Tyrel in Radnor on 21 October, and 127 arrayed by Walter Mauny who departed Merioneth on 29 October. [I have assumed the Welshmen and the Dean contingent arrived by the 14th, based on their muster date and standard march rates of about 20 miles per day, but this cannot be determined with certainty.] Total of above: 3,836. In addi-

lioners, overseers and smiths, which had accompanied the army from Newcastle, immediately set to work repairing the fortifications, which (along with many others) had been cast down twenty years earlier by Robert Bruce "so that the English could never in the future dominate the country by holding castles."[34] Since that last was just what Edward III intended to do, it is no surprise that he felt the need to rebuild what Bruce had destroyed; this continued to be a key element of English strategy on the Border for a very long time.

But Edward's ambitions for this late campaign extended far beyond the reconstruction of a single fortress. Over 250 road-miles to the north, Henry Beaumont, the Earl of Buchan, sat surrounded by enemies in Dundarg castle.[35] The area had the potential to be a strong center of support for Balliol's regime: Buchan, Strathbogie, Mar, Atholl and Angus (all names associated with the Disinherited) made a chain from Perth all the way to the northern coast beside the Moray Firth.[36] All of these areas, moreover, were in the English-speaking lowlands, which could be presumed to be more amenable to English influence, and which were certainly richer and less difficult to control, than the Gaelic highlands. The extensive coastline of the region could also be an aid to maintaining control over it, given the seapower England could deploy.

If Edward could march a powerful army all the way to Dundarg, he would have taken a great step towards realizing that potential. Though the border lands had often felt the pain of English armies' devastation, the far north had been largely immune. The sight of the English host arriving to rescue the Earl of Buchan – especially in winter, when the Scots traditionally expected to have a chance to recover in peace from the summer's fighting[37] – would bring home the

tion, there were craftsmen and laborers, a few pages, various clerks, messengers, grooms, etc., not included in the total above. *WBRF,* fos 233–5, 252–54v; cf. Hewitt, *Organization of War,* 41–2. There is no retinue listed in the Wardrobe accounts for Edward Balliol, who was not technically under Edward's pay, but the gift to him of £300 on 7 November may possibly have been a de facto payment for a force of 90 men-at-arms (assuming he would get 100 marks per twenty men per quarter, as Umfraville did). Balliol was certainly with the army at Roxburgh, as the gift of a further 200 marks on 27 November shows. *WBRF,* fo. 268.

34 Workforce: 106 laborers, 51 masons, 35 carpenters, 11 pavillioners, 4 overseers, 3 smiths. *WBRF,* fo. 254v. An idea of the scale of the work is given by the purchase of 7,000 nails (among many other supplies) for the construction of a new palisade. Ibid., fo. 212. Demolition by Robert Bruce: *Lanercost,* 223 [totum pulchrum castrum [of Roxburgh], sicut et alia castra quae adquirere potuerunt, in terram fundituus postraverunt, ne Anglici unquam postea per retentionem castrorum possent dominari in terra]. Cf. *Melsa,* 2:375.

35 The distance is slightly over 260 miles by modern roads; it is rather unlikely that the fourteenth-century route would have been more direct.

36 As noted above, Gilbert d'Umfraville claimed the earldom of Angus; David of Strathbogie was Earl of Atholl; Richard Talbot, husband of Elisabeth Comyn, had been granted the lordship of Mar. David of Strathbogie had, of course, just gone over to the Scots, but his loyalty to the Bruce cause seemed unlikely to be particularly strong, given his background.

37 *Lanercost,* 214, states that "The English do not freely invade Scotland before summer, mainly because earlier they cannot find fodder for their horses." The same chronicle adds that Edward III was at one point advised that Scotland could not be conquered except in winter (ibid., 287); cf. Edward Balliol's advice to Edward III that continuing the war through the

overwhelming might Edward could apply to the support of his protégés. To relieve Dundarg, however, would be no easy thing. Edward would need enough men to withstand battle should the Scots choose to fight to maintain their siege. Ideally, he should have so many men that he could afford to leave substantial garrisons behind him as he went to secure his lines of communication, and his vassals' Scottish fiefs with them.

The greatest dangers would not be the Scots, though, but rather hunger and cold. English rulers had long understood the difficulty of finding supplies for an army in Scotland in winter, and rarely surmounted it. Still, Edward was prepared to try. First, however, he needed to increase the size of the force at his command. On 15 November, just after leaving Newcastle, he sent writs to fifty-eight individual knights who had not responded to his previous summons. They were ordered to report to him with their men by the 27th. Another writ, on the 20th, required the soldiers arrayed in North Wales to join him by the 30th; other writs ordered some additional troops from Yorkshire to be arrayed at York, ready to set out in his service, on the 22nd. A whole series of writs provided for the collection of grain and other victuals all over the country, and for their shipment to Kingston-upon-Hull, Berwick, and other northern ports.[38] The king was evidently planning to launch his drive into Scotland in early December.

The middle of December, however, found Edward still at Roxburgh. His army had grown to over 5,300 men with the addition of a few tardy retinue archers and contingents of arrayed troops from Richmondshire, Derbyshire, and Wales, but it was still far from satisfactory.[39] Potential recruits were put off by the extraordinarily harsh and bitter winter, which was so "immeasurably cold" that it caused many deaths among the men who had joined the king at Roxburgh.[40]

winter would be greatly to their advantage and would much harm their enemies: PRO C49/6/29.

[38] *RS*, 290–6. In fact, the men of North Wales were not arrayed in Conwy until 27 November, when 319 of them set out for Roxburgh. *WBRF*, fo. 254. A flurry of other writs castigated the arrayers in Lancashire and Nottinghamshire for their delays, but without much effect – not until 1 January did the Nottinghamshire array enter royal pay, and Lancashire did not provide any troops until 15 January . . . and then it was only 30 archers! Ibid.

[39] The Richmond levy, which began to receive pay on 11/17, comprised 15 mounted and 158 foot archers. The Derbyshire array, which entered royal pay on 12/8, contained 354 men, but was quickly reduced to 216. The Welsh contingents comprised 319 troops raised in North Wales, and 457 from South Wales. Also, 120 hobelars from the bishopric of Durham entered royal pay on 1 December, but they had departed within three weeks. The only magnate listed as having joined the king at this stage is the Scottish baron Eustace Maxwell of Caerlaverock, who arrived with 20 men-at-arms and 20 mounted archers on 4 December. *WBRF*, fos 239, 253–54v. The tardy archers were William Bohun's 60 (16 November), Gilbert d'Umfraville's 80 (22 November), Thomas Ughtred's 34 (15 November), William Tynedale's 40 (24 November), William Pressen's 22 (20 November), Richard Denton's 14 (1 December) and four others who arrived on 3 December, as well as 60 Cheshire archers who began to receive pay on 20 November. Ibid., fos 253–53v.

[40] *Knighton*, 1:472; *Historia Roffensis*, fo. 76

"None of them would have willingly borne the hardship and the harshness [of the weather]," says William of Dene, "had he himself not labored so greatly. But he much comforted his army the whole time by words, deeds and gifts, saying that everyone was drinking out of the same cup."[41] To those who had declined to drink of that cup, Edward was less gracious. He sent smoldering letters to twenty-five individual men who had not yet brought their assigned contingents:

> The king to Nicholas de Meynil, greetings. We have been with our army in our lands in the march of Scotland for the safety and defense of the same [lands], and also of the marches of our realm [of England] and of our people of the said areas, against our enemies the Scots, who have risen against us in war and often entered as enemies into our said realm and lands, and have committed arsons and destructions, and still make themselves stronger [*s'affor-cent*] from day to day, gathering to them all the forces they can to harm us and our faithful subjects who are with us, and our said people. Yet, although we have often sent to you by our letters that you should come to us provided with horses and arms, to help our said faithful subjects to repulse the malice of our said enemies, you, nevertheless . . . willfully disobey our said orders, to our peril and in contempt of our commands, and to the detriment of the success of our said business, to your great dishonor and shame. We marvel at this, and are very annoyed, as well we should be. So we order you once again, on pain of forfeiture of all that you can forfeit to us, making no excuses, to come to us with horses and arms and as strong a force as you possibly can [*si afforciement come vous unques purretz*] so that you shall reach us at Roxburgh, well arrayed and equipped, on New Year's Day at the latest, with supplies for fifteen days . . . And we tell you that if you do not come to us on the said day in the aforesaid manner – considering the said disobedience, and the dangers which may come due to [your] default, and considering also the others of the country who take your example to hold back from our said service – we shall inflict on you such punishment that others will be taught a lesson by your example.
>
> Given at Roxburgh, the fifteenth day of December.
> By the king himself.[42]

Similar letters went to the men who had been assigned in early November to array hobelars and foot soldiers in Yorkshire. They were informed that the king was anxious to quickly gather a stronger force than he currently had. Therefore, considering the importance of the matters at hand, they were ordered to select a certain number of hobelars and archers from the strongest and most vigorous of the men previously arrayed. The footmen were all to be archers, well equipped with armor [*armeures*], bows, arrows and knives, as well as food for fifteen

---

41 Ibid.: "Nullus eo libentius dura et aspera sustinuit neque tam laboravit. Sed omni tempore exercitum suum verbis donis et factis multum confortavit, dicens quod omnes de uno cipho potarent." It is interesting to note that Queen Philippa joined the army for some time during December and shared the hardships of midwinter with her husband. *WBRF,* fo. 284v. In November and December the king lost a fair amount of money in gambling games; perhaps this was one of his methods for keeping morale up. Ibid., fo. 210.
42 *RS*, 302; cf. 292–3 for the previous summons.

days. This select group was to be led to the king immediately. Any delays, or substitutions of inferior men, would be punished severely. In total, these writs called for the selection of just 180 hobelars and 1,180 archers out of the 1,030 hobelars and 5,250 footmen previously arrayed.[43] Also ordered to be at Roxburgh on 1 January with fifteen days' worth of supplies were a contingent of 720 men arrayed in Lancashire, and all the men-at-arms of the counties of York, Lincoln, Derby and Nottingham who had not already come to the king's service.[44]

By the time the new year rolled around, it was too late. Just before Christmas, failing provisions and despairing of relief, Beaumont had surrendered Dundarg on being promised a safe-conduct to England for his household. In exchange, aside from paying a sizable ransom, he had to promise to work for peace.[45] Edward now had no one to rescue in the frozen north. The response to the latest rounds of summons had in any case been extremely poor,[46] so Edward gave up his plan of a winter *chevauchée* to Buchan.

Before breaking up his forces, however, he used them to sweep through Lothian and the forest of Ettrick, where Scottish guerrillas were known to be operating. The latter did not dare do battle with him, but wisely remained hidden and dispersed.[47] Edward's failure to relieve Dundarg apparently also contributed to the weathercock Earl of March's decision to abandon the English obedience, despite the lands and favors bestowed upon him by Edward III. This was a powerful blow to English control of the region.[48]

---

[43] *RS*, 302–4. The relationship between the number to be selected and the number originally called for was not consistent. The Wapentake of Herthull in the East Riding, for example, had its contingent cut by more than 90%, from 100 hobelars and 600 foot to just 10 hobelars and 40 archers.

[44] Ibid., 301–2.

[45] This was on 23 December. *Fordun*, 357; *Bridlington*, 121–2.

[46] It appears from the Wardrobe accounts that, although Nottingham provided a force of 163 men which served from 1 January to 15 February, the all-mounted Lincoln contingent of 209 men did not arrive until 19 February (departing five days later), and the Lancashire contingent proved to be a mere 30 archers, who did not arrive until 15 January. No increase to the Yorkshire or Derbyshire contingents is shown. *WBRF*, fos 253v–54.

[47] This is the inference to be drawn from *Lanercost*, 279, *Anonimalle*, 3, and *Scalacronica*, 164–5, which mention Edward's *chevauchées* through Ettrick and Lothian beginning 29 December, though they do not connect them with the fall of Dundarg or the imminent break-up of Edward's host. Note that, in view of *Scalacronica*, 165, and *WBRF*, 269v [showing a payment to a guide "in equitatura [Regis] per Foresta de Etrick et per partes de Louthean"] the editor's suggestion that in *Anonimalle*, 3, "Edynburgh" should be replaced with "Ettrick" should not be accepted. Most likely the original chronicle on which both *Lanercost* and the *Anonimalle* are based for this period had "forests of Ettrick and Edinbugh," which the former conflated to Ettrick and the latter to Edinburgh.

[48] *Scalacronica*, 164–5, however, states that Earl Patrick's departure was because Edward III refused to prosecute some men who had robbed him. See also *Anonimalle*, 2; *Hemingburgh*, 310; and *Melsa*, 2:375. For some of the rewards which Patrick had previously received, see *WBRF*, fo. 268v, for a gift of 100 marks, and *CDS*, p. 207, which deals with about twenty knights' fees (a very substantial amount of land) in Northumberland forfeited by the earl.

Now that the northern expedition had been canceled, there was no reason to keep such a large army concentrated in one place. A force under Balliol and the earls of Oxford and Warwick departed for Carlisle to guard the western marches; along their way, they took a detour through Peebles, having heard that Moray was in the area. Failing to encounter the Scots, Balliol's army burned and destroyed everything in its path, and so made its way to Carlisle. This was followed up by another destructive raid, in which the troops who had been arrayed from the northern counties participated, starting 6 January.[49]

At this point, there was nothing for the troops to do which could justify the substantial cost of retaining them – especially when their supplies had to be brought from England at great expense. They were gradually allowed to return home over the following month. In mid-February, Edward III, having gained a valuable lesson in the limitations of medieval kingship, dismissed most of his remaining troops and returned to England.[50] Over six hundred border-guard and garrison soldiers did remain in the north, in addition to the Anglo-Scottish troops under John Stirling (then Balliol's sheriff of Perth) besieging Lochleven castle.[51]

Although the Roxburgh campaign had been far from a success, it had demonstrated that the Scots were no longer able to mount any direct opposition even to a fraction of England's might. Edward had every reason to be confident that the campaign he was already arranging for the summer of 1335 would be able to overrun Scotland without difficulty, and that the northern kingdom would eventually be reduced to obedience, just as Wales and (to a lesser extent) Ireland had been. It would take money and patience. A system of fortifications similar to the one his grandfather had built in Wales would have to be completed. But it could be done. There was one more obstacle to be overcome first, however: Philip VI's moral and material support for the "rebel" Scots.

*

As noted above, the English government had made its first major effort to address that problem in October of 1334, when an embassy headed by the Archbishop of Canterbury was dispatched to France. Up until then, the decade's Anglo-French negotiations had revolved around two different issues: the Duchy of Aquitaine, and Philip VI's plan to lead a crusade to the Levant. The issue of Aquitaine was a thorny one, and the story of the diplomacy regarding it is very

---

[49] *Lanercost*, 279. Cf. *Melsa*, 2:373. The Scots were meanwhile raiding into England, though without much success. *Bridlington*, 121; *Melsa*, 2:374. The Yorkshire levies (and others) were mostly kept in pay until mid-February. *WBRF*, fos 253v–54.

[50] *Lanercost*, 279; *Bridlington*, 121; *WBRF*, fos 252v–54v, 233–4.

[51] Lochleven: *Pluscardensis*, 272–3. Stirling as Sheriff of Perth: Nicholson, *Edward III*, 225. 163 men-at-arms and 48 archers and Welsh foot under the Earl of Cornwall and Henry Percy guarded the marches until late March (44 men-at-arms remaining on pay until 3 April). In addition, there remained garrisons of 60 men-at-arms and 224 hobelars and watchmen in Berwick and 60 men-at-arms and 80 hobelars at Roxburgh. *WBRF*, fos 233, 235, 252v, 248, 248v.

complex, but it can be summed up as follows. Edward III had come to the throne in the wake of a significant Anglo-French conflict, the War of St. Sardos, during which an army under Charles of Valois had occupied the Agenais, the Bazadais, and part of Saintonge (all parts of the duchy) in retaliation for Edward II's efforts to evade doing homage for his Continental possessions, and for his officials' efforts to oppose the Capetian government's practices of undermining the near-sovereignty the Plantagenets had formerly enjoyed there. The war ended when Edward realized that he did not have the strength to oppose Charles IV's demands by force, and that while it was highly disagreeable to accept the French claims to personal and legal superiority over Aquitaine (that is, to do homage and to acknowledge Capetian sovereignty) it was far more disagreeable still to lose Aquitaine, which provided a very large portion of the English royal revenues, as well as the prestige and military service which came with lordship over such a rich territory.[52] For his part, King Charles, like his predecessors since St. Louis, recognized that there was no better use for Aquitaine than to keep it as a sword of Damocles suspended over the foreign policy of the English monarchy.[53]

It took a whole series of negotiations, maneuvers, and treaties between 1325 and 1331 before the two crowns came to any real understanding on how to implement these general principles, but in the latter year Edward III and Philip VI finally found a modus vivendi. Edward, though reluctantly, conceded that he held his French lands from the Valois king by liege homage, an admission which theoretically bound him to support King Philip against any and all enemies. He also acknowledged himself to be indebted to the French crown to the total of some £42,333, a very large amount of money, most of which represented a war indemnity to cover Charles IV's losses and expenses in the conflict of 1324–25.[54] For his part, Philip VI lifted the threat of confiscation under which the duchy had been placed, offered pardons for certain Anglo-Gascon officials who had acted against the French crown in the St. Sardos affair, and reined in the lawyers and administrators who had been encroaching on Edward's rights in the duchy largely (though not entirely) as a way of putting pressure on the English king to resolve the dispute over homage on Philip's terms. The Valois king also indicated (at least by implication) his willingness to restore the

---

[52] Even in 1324, Gascon revenues were estimated as a clear £13,000. Ireland, by contrast, was expected to bring in only £1,424. Harriss, *King, Parliament, and Public Finance*, 523–4.

[53] Vale, *Origins*, ch. 7, and Déprez, *Préliminaires*, chs 1–4, cover the topic, but should be read in conjunction with the documents (the most important of which are printed in Rymer's *Foedera* and Chaplais, *War of St. Sardos*). Note also Cuttino, "Process of Agen," esp. pp. 161–2.

[54] He owed 60,000 l.p. for Charles IV's permission to transfer the fief from Edward II to Prince Edward in 1325, and 50,000 marks sterling for the indemnity, less 30,000 l.t. for the damage done by Charles of Alençon when he sacked Saintes just before the Anglo-French accords were reached in 1331.

remaining occupied territories – the recovery of which was the most important goal of Edward's French policy – once the money due him had been paid.[55]

There was one major flaw with this arrangement, however: Edward was determined to recover the Agenais and the other lands seized from his father, but he did not have the wherewithal to pay the massive amount of cash needed to redeem them. It seems that he had ratified the agreement of 1331 thinking that he would be able to offset the war indemnity with a similar sum owed to him because Louis IX had never fulfilled a certain debt to Henry III; unfortunately, however, this turned out to be an illusion based on poor record-keeping, and when French ambassadors presented the relevant quittances, Edward had to acknowledge that he still owed the full amount.[56] There were still ways for this issue to be resolved, for example by betrothing one of King Philip's daughters to Prince Edward and using her nominal dowry to offset the indemnity debt, but any such plan would have to overcome the French king's reluctance to give up the valuable and strategically important areas he had thus far been able to retain (and which he could continue to keep without losing his prized lord-vassal relationship with the Plantagenet). Fortunately for Anglo-French relations, at this same time another issue arose, because of which Philip needed Edward's goodwill as much as Edward needed Philip's.

This new subject for diplomacy was a French plan to lead a crusade to reconquer the Holy Land.[57] The last five Capetians, from Philip IV to Charles IV, had each made an effort to organize a crusade (though none successfully); if the first Valois king managed to succeed where they had failed, it would be the strongest possible affirmation of the legitimacy of his new dynasty, as well as a chance to fulfill a long-standing personal ambition.[58] It was in the fall of 1331, a few months after the ratification of the Anglo-French entente outlined above, that King Philip, inspired by the preaching of the Patriarch of Jerusalem, began to focus on the Levant as the target for his *sainte voyage*.[59] This was a much more ambitious undertaking than his earlier plans to attack the Moors of Granada, and one which it would be impossible to attempt if on embarkation he left a hostile England behind him.

As early as October of that same year, Edward expressed plans to discuss the expedition to the Holy Land with the Valois, and shortly thereafter Philip VI requested Pope John XXII to order the bishops of France to begin preaching the

---

55 See *RFH*, 2:2:137–8; 2:3:27, 26, 46, 61, 63–5. The treaty of 1325 stipulated that the war indemnity would be owed only if the disputed lands were to be returned; later agreements promised to fulfill earlier treaties and held the money was due (implying that the lands were to be restored on payment).

56 *RFH*, 2:3:66.

57 C. J. Tyerman, "Philip VI and the Recovery of the Holy Land," *EHR* 100 (1985), gives a detailed and valuable treatment from the French perspective, though I think he is overly skeptical regarding Edward III.

58 Ibid., 26–7.

59 Tyerman, "Philip VI," 27.

crusade and collecting donations for it.[60] A whole series of embassies was
dispatched to France to pursue negotiations concerning English participation in
the effort, and Philip, anxious not to jeopardize these developing plans, made a
clear effort to keep Anglo-French relations in Aquitaine amicable, even after
Edward III's intervention against France's ally, Scotland, in the summer of 1333.
Edward, for his part, made it more and more clear that he expected a favorable
settlement of the remaining disputes over Aquitaine as a quid pro quo for his
participation in the reconquest of the Holy Land.[61]

It was on that basis that Archbishop Stratford's embassy of April–July 1334
negotiated over those two issues, and with substantial success. By the time the
chancellor returned to England, Philip had promised to guard the peace in
Aquitaine, and had agreed to a compromise proposed jointly by the English and
French members of the "Process of Agen," a commission which had been
working quite effectively for the past several years to effect mutual restitutions
of lands illegally seized by partisans of one side or the other in Aquitaine.[62] A
marriage alliance was negotiated between John of Eltham and a French noble-
woman; Philip agreed to pay a substantial dowry of 30,000 l.t.[63] Although David
Bruce had been granted sanctuary in Normandy, Philip declined to press his
vassal Edward on the Scottish king's behalf. The English ambassadors likewise
simply avoided the topic of Scotland, confident that their lord had settled affairs
there to his own liking and willing to let that sleeping dog lie. (At this time, it
must be remembered, Scotland was still largely under Balliol's control.) Immediately on Stratford's return to England, a parliament was called to discuss the
outcome of these discussions. The assembly looked favorably on the deal which
had been sketched out, and the king was assured that his realm would provide
him with the aid necessary to undertake the expedition to the Holy Land.[64] It is
no wonder, then, that in late 1334 the Plantagenet confidently expected that the
next round of negotiations would close the deal, amicably settle the disputes in

---

60 Ibid., 28; *RFH*, 2:2:71.
61 *Grandes chroniques*, 9:134; note also that when the chancery initially drew up the cre-
dences for the embassy of fall 1333 to address only the crusade and an interview between the
two kings, Edward insisted that the documents be revised to include powers to resolve disputes in Aquitaine. See Edward III's privy seal letters in Déprez, *Préliminaires*, 93 n.4, 96
n.1.
62 Cuttino, "Process of Agen," 166 (effectiveness), 167–9 (compromise). See also Déprez,
Préliminaires, 97–8, 110–11; *RFH*, 2:3:111–12, 117–19. Note that the letter of John Stratford
printed in Déprez, 110–11n, cannot date to March of 1334/5 as he gives it, because at that
time Stratford was neither chancellor nor in France. It must date to May of 1334; the document itself (PRO Anc. Cor., SC 1/39/57) is damaged at the date clause, and not clearly legible
on microfilm, but to my eye could well read May rather than March.
63 *RFH*, 2:3:118–19.
64 *Le Baker*, 53–4 (and cf. 56); *Murimuth*, 72–3 ("rex concessit quod iret in Terram Sanctam
propriis sumptibus" probably means his own costs as opposed to Philip's, not his own costs as
opposed to the community of the realm's; his own resources, without taxation, could hardly
have sufficed).

Aquitaine in accordance with what he saw as justice, and thus remove the remaining impediments to the crusade.[65]

All these factors gave Edward good reason to hope for a successful outcome for the embassy which Archbishop Stratford led to France at the end of October 1334, not long before the start of the Roxburgh campaign. Stratford came ready to make a number of concessions to the French, but also intending to ask for much in return. He brought letters ratifying the arrangements for the marriage of Edward's only brother to Marie d'Espagne, a less-than-favorable match for the Earl of Cornwall. It is likely that the ambassadors were also authorized to renew an earlier offer of the payment of a moderate cash indemnity ("as much as he [Philip] could reasonably ask for," Edward later claimed) to pay off a portion of the debts arising out of the events of 1324–25.[66] Most importantly, thanks to the support offered by parliament, Stratford could now pledge not only that Edward would participate in the crusade, but that he would do so at his own cost – an extremely significant point, since Philip was in dire financial straits due to the expenses of preparing for the expedition. Finally, the ambassadors were empowered to arrange a personal meeting between the two kings to finalize the arrangements over Aquitaine and the crusade.[67] This was something Philip had eagerly sought, for it would offer him an opportunity to publicly display the position of feudal superiority he enjoyed relative to Edward III, and to gain face by portraying whatever concessions he might make to the English as instances of his own liberality and good lordship.[68]

In return for all this, the archbishop was to seek agreement from the King of

---

65 See his letter of 15 November: Déprez, *Préliminaires*, 102, 407. Note also *RFH*, 2:3:114.

Jonathan Sumption and Eugène Déprez have, based on a misinterpretation of the sketchy chronicle evidence, given quite different assessments of the results of this embassy than the one presented above. In their version of events, it was this embassy of Stratford's which culminated in an abortive Anglo-French agreement which was wrecked when Philip suddenly chose to insist that the Scots be included within the peace. Sumption, *Trial by Battle*, 135–7, Déprez, *Préliminaires*, 96–7; similarly Nicholson, *Edward III*, 158. That scene actually took place January 1335, at the end of Stratford's *second* embassy, rather than in the spring of 1334 (and the *bon mot* Sumption discusses probably belongs to 1336). See below, notes 71 (1335) and 203 (1336).

66 Schedule of offers in *KdL*, 47–8 (the Latin version in *Bridlington* is a translation from the French, and wrongly omits mention of the indemnity, which is confirmed by *EMDP*, 287, and *RFR*, 2:4:194); *EMDP*, 435–6; *RFH*, 2:3:118–19 (marriage); ibid., 119–20 (powers; no mention of Scots presumably because the ambassadors were on that subject not to make any concessions). The indemnity was probably offered by Stratford in his first, rather than his second embassy of 1334 (given the explicit sequentiality of the list of offers), but since Edward was seeking even more than previously in Aquitaine (the full restitution of the occupied territories), the offer likely remained on the table for the second embassy.

On the marriage match with Marie, which both kings professed would make a major contribution to peace and the resolution of the discords between England and France, see also *DEB*, 175. She was the daughter of the Lord of Lara.

67 *RFH*, 2:3:119–20; *Le Baker*, 55–6. Philip's financial straits: Tyerman, "Philip VI," 40.

68 Cf. Froissart, *Oeuvres*, 2:523–4: at the March 1334 parliament, the English ambassadors affirmed that Philip had declared "that if it pleased the King of England to come to him per-

France to three proposals: first, continued friendship and goodwill (which in practical terms meant French forebearance from using appeals to *parlement* to undermine Plantagenet authority in Gascony); second, full restitution of the lands seized by Charles of Valois in 1324, including the Agenais, the Bazadais, and the occupied portion of Saintonge; and, third, an end to French support of the Bruce cause.[69] The first of these proposals had already been agreed, the second had at least been discussed, but the third was new.

The results of this diplomatic initiative were much less favorable than the English had hoped, probably because they had underestimated the seriousness of Philip's commitment to his Scottish alliance.[70] That commitment had clearly been strengthened by the military events which took place between the end of Stratford's first embassy in 1334 and the start of his second one. As we have seen above, when the archbishop set out on the earlier mission to France in the spring, the Bruce cause looked so hopeless that there was no point in Philip's staking his crusade policy on a favorable resolution of the Scottish conflict. It was just as Stratford was returning to England in early July, however, that Moray and Stewart revitalized the resistance to Balliol, and between then and October that Balliol's supporters broke down into disarray. The Earl of Atholl's submission to the Bruce partisans had come on 27 September, just three days before Stratford's letters of credence for the second embassy were sealed. All this, of course, was why the English government now felt the need to raise the Scottish issue in the negotiations, but the same considerations left Philip much less inclined to sacrifice an ally who now could realistically hope to benefit from a French diplomatic intervention. As late as June, to help his ally significantly Philip would have had to persuade Edward III to surrender what he and his vassal Balliol had laboriously conquered (a clear impossibility); in October, by contrast, Philip needed only to get the English to agree to a truce, for a truce would leave most of Scotland under Bruce control.

From the standpoint of the Valois court, then, Edward was asking the French to make one-sided concessions in Aquitaine, wanted to have things all his own

---

sonally, he would treat him more generously than any other" [il feroit plus de grâce à luy qu'à nul autre].

[69] See *Le Baker*, 55–6, which appears to be based on the text of letters now lost; *RFH*, 2:3:119–20. The request for the restitution of the occupied lands was probably the anticipated petition concerning the *res occupata* which Edward's negotiators at the Process of Agen had been concerned not to prejudice. Cf. Cuttino, "Process of Agen," 167–9.

[70] Even later, in retrospect, Edward could not accept Philip's straightforward statement that he could not in honor abandon David Bruce (even though Edward himself probably felt much the same about his commitment to support Balliol), and instead blamed the Valois king's unwillingness to sacrifice his ally to a covert desire to prevent Edward from regaining his rights in France. *Bridlington*, 125; schedule in *KdL*, 48–9. This is most unlikely, however; Philip's commitment to the crusade was undoubtedly genuine, and he must have realized that an expedition to the Holy Land would not be possible unless he could reach some accommodation with Edward. Furthermore, it is difficult to think that Philip's statement was anything but genuine, given that he made it on 7 July 1335, the same day he made a pilgrimage to St. Denis to give thanks for the near-miraculous recovery of his only son. See below, pp. 96–7.

way in Scotland, and was offering in return only to do what he professed to be eager to do anyway (to participate in the expedition to the Holy Land). If the Plantagenet truly desired Philip's goodwill, wanted highly favorable terms for the restitution of the detained territories, and was anxious for the crusade to proceed, then he should be willing to make some compromises of his own in Scotland. The French monarch, in other words, was making the same mistake his cousin had made: each underestimated the other's commitment to his candidate in the Scottish civil war.

Thus, when the English ambassadors reached Paris in late October, they received a very cool welcome.[71] Eventually, however, Philip assigned a group of his closest advisers to treat with Stratford's party, and once underway the negotiations progressed quite well, for, as noted above, the archbishop had been authorized to make substantial new concessions to the French in return for the restitution of the Agenais. Having already gained a sense of how much support for the Bruce cause had grown in Paris, the English ambassadors wisely decided not to bring up Edward's new request that the French halt their aid to the Scots, sticking instead to the issues of Aquitaine and the crusade.[72] As things now stood, French interference was making it substantially more difficult and costly to suppress the Bruce resistance movement, but without a major scaling-up of the Valois' commitment, it seemed safe to assume that the rebellion ultimately would be put down. If the current negotiations could restore goodwill between the crowns of England and France, and if the problems in Scotland could simply be pushed to the side and an escalation of the conflict there avoided, Edward III still could hope ultimately to have his way regarding Aquitaine, Scotland and the crusade alike.

---

[71] My description of this episode in the next paragraphs is based on the narrations of the *Grandes chroniques*, 9:142–2, and the closely related *Chronographia*, 2:22–3. In neither of those sources is it clearly dated, but although previous historians have universally associated it with Stratford's first embassy of 1334, it is fairly clear that it actually belongs to this second embassy of 1334–35. To fully rehearse the justifications for this conclusion would take us too far afield from the topic at hand, so I hope to address them in the future in a separate study. Here it must suffice to say my conclusion is based on (1) the course of Anglo-French diplomacy between July and November, which does not fit well with a blow-up at the end of Stratford's first embassy; (2) *Le Baker*, 55 ("post festum sancti Dionisii [9 October]"; cf. Déprez, *Préliminaires*, 97); (3) Philip's presence near Paris (at Vincennes) before the departure of the English ambassadors in December, but not in June (Viard, *Itin. Phil. VI*; Mirot et Déprez, "Ambassades," nos. XLVI, LII); (4) *Chronographia*, 2:22 (incorrect but understandable linkage between embassy and chronologically proximate death of John XII in December 1334); (5) the greater likelihood that the Scots would want to be "included" in a "peace" in late 1334 (when the military status quo favored them) than in early 1334 (when it did not).
The chill in Anglo-French relations at this stage could possibly also owe something to Philip VI's learning that Robert of Artois had taken refuge in England (cf. Cazelles, *Société politique*, 101–2), but on the other hand there is some reason to believe that Edward's provision of sanctuary for the exile was not known in Paris until after August 1336: see Philip's letter, printed in Déprez, *Préliminaires*, 414–15, and note 216, below.
[72] *Grandes chroniques*, 9:143 ("onques des Escos n'avoit esté mencion faite"); *Chronographia*, 2:23.

Even with the Scottish problem left aside, the English had to engage in some hard bargaining. At first Stratford sought to get the Valois king to agree to restore the occupied territories before the departure of the crusading forces, but it appears that when that offer was refused by the French, he went on to propose a half or partial restitution in advance; when that too was declined, he went so far as to proffer English participation in the expedition (at Edward's own expense) in exchange merely for Philip's promise to restore the occupied territories on the crusaders' return![73] This surprising concession was enough to win over the Valois negotiators. The two sides worked out the details of an agreement, and in late December they brought it before the king in his chambers in Paris. Philip heard them out and then approved their arrangements. Peace was made! Criers were sent to proclaim it throughout the capital city, and the jubilant English ambassadors were escorted back towards their lodgings by a happy crowd containing the chief councilors of the realm.[74]

Their rejoicing did not last long, however: before they had even reached their rooms, they were overtaken by messengers who summoned them back into the royal presence. Then the king announced that it was his intention that David Bruce and all the Scots should be included in the peace treaty.[75] The Englishmen were stunned. No mention had been made of the Scots during the negotiations, they protested. They did not dare accede to the French demand, even to salvage a laboriously negotiated settlement, for they had not been given the powers which would have been necessary to grant the Scots a truce, and indeed could well predict that their king would have no interest in an agreement which left Balliol locked out of Scotland.[76] Edward III was at that very time, after all, suffering through the bitter Roxburgh winter and struggling to organize the relief of Henry Beaumont in Dundarg. When Stratford and his colleagues refused to back down on this point, the negotiations over the crusade and Gascony were broken off in disarray. At the turn of the year, the Englishmen returned to England to recount the course of events to their lord, accompanied by French ambassadors who bore the French king's written response to Edward's overtures.

Philip's letter was strongly worded. Not only did he demand full payment in cash of the sums due to him before he would return the Agenais and the other occupied lands, and refuse to halt his aid to the Scots, he went so far as to reject

---

[73] This sequence of offers was certainly made, but they could possibly belong to William Aymerine's embassy of summer 1335. The relative duration of the talks, and congruity of offers, however, suggests that they belong to the earlier rather than the later embassy. *KdL*, 48.

[74] *Chronographia*, 2:23; *Grandes chroniques*, 9:143.

[75] What led to this apparent reversal? Probably, after he had given his approval to the agreement on which he had been briefed, either he found out that it did not cover the Scots, as he had assumed it did; or else, if he knew when he made the ratification that the Scots had not been included, then the Scottish representatives at court, on hearing the proclamations of peace, must have confronted him with this stab in the back, and persuaded him to reverse course.

[76] *Chronographia*, 2:23; *Grandes chroniques*, 9:143.

even Edward's request for continued friendship, saying that the Plantagenet was unworthy of his affection so long as he persecuted the Scots, who were just men, so unmercifully.[77] What the last of these refusals meant in practice had already been brought home by the intransigence of the French commissioners who had just recently begun to meet with their English counterparts at Langon in order to implement the compromise settlement for restitutions in Guienne which had come out of the Process of Agen, and which had been ratified by the two monarchs in June. In October, the French even threatened to confiscate Edward's county of Ponthieu in the north of France because the English (in accordance with their understanding of the compromise of the preceding summer) refused to hand over two castles near Bordeaux.[78]

Anglo-French relations in Gascony were on the verge of a crisis as Philip tried to use the duchy as a lever to force Edward to give up his Scottish policy, but it seems that neither player realized the difficulty of the impasse they had reached, for each overestimated the value of the cards in his own hand. Edward knew that David Bruce was Philip's ally, but he himself was Philip's vassal and his cousin, as well as being a potential crusading partner.[79] Furthermore, though the French king might threaten and bluster, the facts of geography and the weakness of the Scots (when matched against Edward III rather than Edward Balliol) meant that there was little he could do about it, short of invading Gascony, if Edward refused to cooperate in the north, and an invasion of Gascony would have virtually guaranteed the collapse of the crusading movement, as well as depriving the Valois king of his single most powerful vassal. (Remember the famous response of Louis IX when he was criticized for allowing Henry III to retain Aquitaine as a fief: "I think I have put the lands to good use, for Henry was not my man before, and now he has done homage to me.") Surely, if he were forced to make a choice, Philip would pick the renowned soldier Edward III, the best possible partner for his crusade, over the exiled, 10-year-old David Bruce? From the French standpoint, a similar logic applied: it must have been hard to conceive that the Plantagenet would be willing to risk the fruits of years of diplomacy, the success of the holy crusade, and the goodwill of his liege-lord, the richest and most powerful ruler in Europe, all for the sake of Edward Balliol, who in their eyes was little more than a pirate king. Would the Plantagenet really give up his hope of regaining Agen – much less risk losing Bordeaux, a city far larger than any other under his rule save London – for the comparatively primitive villages of Edinburgh and Roxburgh? Could even the two thousand librates of land ceded to him on the Scottish March really be put in the balance against

---

[77] *Le Baker*, 55–6 for the content. Le Baker's final tag ("Non enim," etc.) is, however, exaggerated and chronologically misplaced; cf. *EMDP*, 436, and below, page 121. Date: Stratford's account for his embassy shows it ending 15 January and the French ambassadors had reached the king at Berwick before the end of January. Lucas, "Machinery," 319; *WBRF*, 211v.

[78] Cuttino, "Process of Agen," 169–70.

[79] This had been one of the points of emphasis in Stratford's proposals and likewise in Philip's rejections.

the £13,000 or more in net annual revenues from Gascony?[80] The problem with these calculations, however, is that they are based on balances of interest, and fail to take into account fully the inflexibility of honor – a common cause of unwanted wars throughout history.

Edward, rather than backing down in the face of the French *démarche*, decided to play for time and to prepare a truly massive invasion of Scotland for the summer. Once this new "rebellion" in Scotland had been put down, he would present Philip with a fait accompli, and one way or another use the crusade to smooth things over with the Valois and regain the full extent of his inheritance in France. He doubtless realized that the military successes of Stewart and Moray were a major reason why the deal with France sketched out in the summer had been rejected in the fall, so it was not entirely unreasonable to hope that if he could restore the situation in Scotland to what it had been in June of 1334, he would also be able to restore Anglo-French relations to what they had been at that same time. Messengers were sent to the French court to promise that an embassy would be dispatched to discuss the resolution of the Scottish problem, though in fact no ambassador was sent until August, after the invasion was well underway.[81] Meanwhile, Edward blithely continued to make the preparations necessary so that he could lead an unusually powerful army into Scotland to re-establish his and Balliol's dominion there.[82] At the insistence of the French, he promised to the Scots a truce from Easter until midsummer, but this cost him little since the invasion force could not in any case be ready to go much before then.[83] The Scottish leadership – rent by quarrels between, on the one hand, Stewart and Atholl, and on the other, Moray, Mowbray, and Douglas – prepared to evacuate their people to the highlands. They had no resources to mount a more effective opposition.[84] Their only real hope was French intervention.

As the deadline for the end of the truce approached, however, King Philip was distracted by a grave family crisis. He had only one son, Duke Jean of Normandy; since 1328 he had lost six others, stillborn or perished within days of their birth.[85] In June of 1335, Jean was struck down by an illness so severe, and a fever which continued so long without breaking, that about midsummer's eve the doctors gave up hope for his life. Rather than despair, the king and queen turned to their religious faith. Everywhere there were public prayers for the heir-apparent's recovery; all the monks of St. Denis spent three solid days in barefoot procession. Jean's bed was surrounded with holy relics, including a finger of St. Louis. "I have so much faith in the mercy of God and in the merits of the saints and the prayers of the people," Philip was heard to proclaim, "that

[80] Harriss, *King, Parliament and Public Finance*, 523.
[81] *Bridlington*, 125 ("rescripsisti nobis," etc.).
[82] The details of Edward III's preparations for the summer offensive of 1335 are set out in Nicholson, *Edward III and the Scots*, ch. 13.
[83] *RFH*, 2:3:124.
[84] *Fordun*, 358.
[85] Sumption, *Trial by Battle*, 145.

if he were to die, he would be resurrected by the prayers which are sent to God on his behalf; so, if he dies, don't bury the body too fast, for I have great faith in the mercy of God."[86] In early July, the fever finally broke, and the young duke made a rapid recovery.

On 7 July, King Philip and his son made a pilgrimage on foot from Taverni, the site of Jean's sickbed, to the church of St. Denis, where for two nights and a day they gave thanks for the young man's life.[87] Before setting out that morning, however, the French king took the time to prepare a letter to Edward III concerning the situation in Scotland. Given the circumstances under which it was written, there can be little question of its sincerity. Its tone was conciliatory, but its message was uncompromising. The Valois king reiterated how much he desired Edward's company on his passage to the Holy Land, but implicitly reminded his cousin that any offers concerning that expedition were of no value so long as the Anglo-Scottish conflict continued, since the crusade could not go forward until the major participants were at peace. He observed that the ambassadors whom Edward had promised to dispatch to explain his reasons for declining peace with the Scots had not yet reached the French court (though the Anglo-Scottish truce had expired a fortnight earlier), and that the people of Scotland had been, and still were, making urgent requests for his assistance under the terms of the Treaty of Corbeil. He could not in honor fail to fulfill his obligation, nor, given the importance of the matter, could he postpone doing so any longer. Thus, he had promised to give them support and assistance. (The letter did not say, but Edward was probably made aware, that Philip was preparing to send a fleet with a thousand men-at-arms and five thousand foot to succor his Scottish allies.)[88]

Philip, however, still hoped to avoid what would be a costly and difficult war, and to salvage the expedition to the Holy Land, so he did not end his letter with that threat. Instead, he proposed that he and the Pope serve as mediators between Edward III and David II. This way of peace, he concluded, would advance the crusade, and be beneficial and honorable for Edward and for his realm, and he begged the English king to accept it.

The earliest this ultimatum could possibly have reached the council at York was 12 July – too late, for on that day some 13,500 English troops crossed the border into Scotland, launching one of the largest military operations of Edward's reign.[89] The army which had assembled at Newcastle starting in late

---

86 *Grandes chroniques*, 9:149. (Midsummer: counting backwards for twelve days of fever and about three of recovery before 7 July.)

87 Ibid.

88 The letter is printed in *Bridlington*, 125–6. For the fleet, see the "Chronique parisienne anonyme de 1316 à 1339, précédée d'additions à la chronique française dite de Guillaume de Nangis," ed. A. Hellot, in *Mémoires de la Société de l'histoire de Paris et de l'Ile-de-France* XI (1884), 164–5.

89 *Bridlington*, 122; *Anonimalle*, 4/ *Lanercost*, 281. *Knighton*, 1:472, notes that Edward only unfurled his banners – the sign of open warfare – after crossing the Annan on the 13th; this indicates that the Border land to the east of the river was still more or less under English

June seemed to William of Dene to be the best ordered and supplied army that
any King of England had ever led, so numerous and glorious that no one dared
to resist it.[90] The host was so large, in fact, that Edward decided to divide his
forces in two[91] – an action he would later often take in his wars in France. His
reasoning is not recorded, but can easily be surmised. Once the armies entered
Scotland, they inflicted widespread devastation intended to punish the Scots for
their "rebellion." Two separate armies, operating in entirely separate areas,
could lay waste far more ground than could a single, larger force.[92] Equally, they
would find it easier to live off the land with only half as many troops to feed
from a given region.[93] Edward may even have hoped that the Scots would be
tempted to risk a battle against an army of 6,500 though they would avoid one of
twice that size.[94]

So Edward III, along with his brother-in-law the Count of Juliers, the earls of
Cornwall, Warwick, and Hereford, and Henry of Lancaster, marched west to
Carlisle on 3 July, where they were joined by the Earl of Buchan on the 7th.
Balliol moved north to Berwick with the earls of Arundel, Surrey, Oxford and
Angus, as well as Ralph Neville and Henry Percy.[95] On the prearranged day, 12
July, both armies entered Scotland.[96] Meeting no resistance, they passed through
most of Scotland below the Forth, "burning and destroying and taking much

control. See also *Hemingburgh*, 310. For the timing, cf. *EMDP*, 779–89. Numbers: *WBRF*, fos
236–39v, 255–58v.

[90] *Historia Roffensis*, fo. 77.

[91] *Bridlington*, 122.

[92] The "radius of devastation" of medieval armies was reasonably constant, varying much
less than the size of the force, because of limitations on how far pillagers could safely go from
the main force and still be able to return to it at night. See Rogers, "By Fire and Sword,"
passim.

[93] This factor was far less important when the armies were positioned where they could
receive supplies by ship (as later in the campaign when they were at Perth), but during the
initial invasion they were operating well inland.

[94] This is perhaps suggested by *Anonimalle*, 4: "both the kings with their whole force
entered Scotland in separate places [but] they found no Scots who dared to encounter them or
give battle." Given that the Scots had been willing to fight in 1332 and 1333, it was not unreasonable to hope that they might do so again.

[95] *Anonimalle*, 4/ *Lanercost*, 281; *Scalacronica*, 165; *WBRF*, fos 239v, 237v. The mention of
the earls of Lancaster and Lincoln in the former two chronicles are probably both references
to Henry of Lancaster (heir of the elderly Earl of Lancaster, and heir through his wife of the
deceased Earl of Lincoln), who appears in the Wardrobe pay records. Juliers' retinue, incidentally, included two other unnamed counts from the Continent. One of them was very likely
Adolph, Count of Berg from 1308 to 1348, who had been an ally of Guelders and Juliers in
1324–26 and one of the guarantors of a treaty for the former in 1333; he had joined Jean
d'Hainault in escorting Philippa to England in December 1327 (Lucas, *Low Countries*, 166,
70, 126), and was among the first of the Continental princes to sign on with Edward III in
1337 (see below). The other was Heinrich von Vianden. Trautz, *Könige*, 212.

[96] *Lanercost*, 281; according to *Knighton*, 1:473, Edward III crossed the Annan and unfurled
his banners on the 13th.

booty."[97] Only the areas of Galloway which had remained loyal to Balliol were spared. The two forces closed into supporting distance along the Clyde, with Balliol occupying Glasgow, and from there advanced to Perth, meeting resistance only at the castle of Cumbernauld, which Balliol's division took by assault.[98] The armies of the two kings then united at Perth, where they remained for about a month thereafter, sweeping through the neighboring highlands and devastating the land all around.[99] All the Scots could do in response was snipe at the English supply lines.[100]

The French ambassadors, meanwhile, were kept firmly in England, for Edward, who doubtless knew at least the gist of the letter they carried, had no desire to receive it until after matters in Scotland had been settled to his own liking.[101] The council, however, was presumably able to maintain at least intermittent contact with the king, and its members rapidly took steps to ward off the threatened French intervention until it would be too late to do the Scots any good. On 18 July, powers were prepared for the Bishop of Norwich (along with Lord Wake, the Abbot of Dore, and Richard Bintworth) to conduct negotiations with the French court relative to the crusade and Aquitaine – but not, it should be noted, the Scots.[102] The ambassadors, however, did not complete their preparations and the journey to Dover until mid-August; there they encountered a further delay, since safe-conducts from the French had not arrived, so it was only on the 20th that they crossed the Channel.[103] In case diplomacy failed, steps were also taken to impede any invasion fleet, and to prepare the defense of England's coasts against French raids, but Edward's main attention remained focussed on his own offensive. French and Scottish sailors did indeed harry English shipping, and even burn a few fishing villages near Southampton, but this did little other than to boost public support for King Edward.[104]

---

97   *Anonimalle*, 4/ *Lanercost*, 282. *Melsa*, 2:373, probably is describing this campaign, though purporting to describe the earlier Roxburgh campaign; compare to *Lanercost*.
98   *Bridlington*, 122–3; *Scalacronica*, 165; *Knighton*, 1:473. Knighton gives credit for the capture of Cumbernauld to Earl Warrenne as well as Balliol; he adds that the captives included Lord David Marshal, his wife, and the wives of Archibald Douglas and Philip Mowbray. The castle fell either on 23 July (Knighton) or 28 July (Bridlington).
99   *Melsa*, 2:376; see also Nicholson, *Edward III and the Scots*, 222–3. Edward III was at Perth on 7 August, and still on the 23rd, having come by way of "Irewyn" [Inveravon near Falkirk?] (where he stayed on 15 July), Stirling (at the beginning of August) and Dunfermline. *WBRF*, fos 272, 202v, 239v. *Knighton* (1:473) says that in this period Balliol and Eltham occupied and strengthened the castle of "Donbretane" [Dumbarton], but this is unlikely; cf. *Fordun*, 360.
100 *Melsa*, 2:375.
101 He did not officially "receive" their letter until 20 August. *Bridlington*, 125.
102 The documents were dated at Carlisle; since the king was not there on that day, they were probably prepared by chancery at York, with the authorization of the council. *RFH*, 2:3:130–1.
103 Déprez, *Préliminaires*, 115.
104 *Lanercost*, 283; *Anonimalle*, 5; note that the chronicler wrongly believed that David II had done homage to Philip VI for Scotland (a claim also found in *Pakington*, fo. 184) and that

In Scotland, meanwhile, the Bruce position quickly crumpled in the face of the overwhelming power brought to bear by the two Edwards.[105] The Earl of Moray was captured, and William Douglas' brother James killed, in a skirmish early in August.[106] On the 7th, the Earl of Fife surrendered himself and the castle of Cupar, and on the same day two Dominican friars sent by the Earl of Atholl to see if Edward was interested in making peace arrived at Perth.[107] Shortly thereafter, Alexander and Geoffrey Mowbray came to the king to negotiate terms of surrender for themselves, the Earl of Atholl, Robert Stewart, and several others. On 18 August it was agreed that they would all return to the obedience of the two Edwards in return for a series of concessions.[108] Most of these were personal guarantees, but the Edwards also granted that the laws and customs of Scotland were to be maintained as in the days of King Alexander, that the Scottish church would retain its liberties, and that royal offices in Scotland should generally be held by Scots.[109] Balliol's wholesale replacement of Scottish office-holders with Englishmen had caused a great deal of resentment, and this was probably a sincere gesture of reconciliation.

After being appointed Balliol's lieutenant for the lands beyond the Forth,[110] Atholl undertook to reduce the Scottish holdouts to obedience. He pursued this

the French monarch had sent no fewer than 715 ships "to destroy the south country." Edward probably received word of Philip's threat shortly before 22 July, when he ordered the arrest of all ships over 40 tons in English ports in order to resist an invasion fleet. *RS*, 1:364–7. Edward's letter of 26 July in *RFR*, II:2:915, shows that the king anticipated a landing of soldiers in Scotland, not an invasion of England. The letter carefully avoids mentioning Philip or France, saying only that "some men from foreign lands, at the instigation of the Scots" [nonnulli homines de partibus exteris, ad procurationem Scotorum] intended to ship soldiers and arms to invade Balliol's kingdom. Cf. Déprez, *Préliminaires*, 111 n.3, and *RS*, 1:364.

[105] As the *Anonimalle*, 4, says: "The Scots felt themselves to be confounded and powerless to resist the two kings."

[106] *Bridlington*, 123–4; *Pluscardensis*, 279; *Wyntoun*, 2:420–1 (details); the name of his captor, William de Pressen, is given by *Scalacronica*, 166, and confirmed by *RFR*, II:2:923. On 8 August, Edward ordered the captive to be sent to York. *RS*, 371.

[107] *WBRF*, fos 239 (Cupar), 272 (friars); cf. *Melsa*, 2:376.

[108] The text of the agreement is printed in *Avesbury*, 298–300. For a list of 22 Scots entering the two kings' peace under these terms, see *RS*, 381. Cf. *Pluscardensis*, 279; *Wyntoun*, 2:421; *Knighton*, 1:473. The conditions were apparently considered excessively generous by many of the English magnates: "Modus vero reconciliationis fere omnibus magnatibus Angliae displicuit." *Bridlington*, 124.

[109] Nicholson, *Edward III and the Scots*, 216, comments on the accord that "Although it had been negotiated by emissaries who claimed to represent the steward as well as Strathbogie, no provision was made for the former, and nothing was said of his ancestral lands." Although it is true that none of the specific clauses deal with the steward, the preamble does state that he is a party to the agreement (or, more precisely, that it was agreed between the councils of the two Edwards and men empowered to treat for Atholl and Stewart), and the first clause states that Atholl, "the magnates [grauntz], and all others of the commons of Scotland" who accept the conditions of the agreement should have their lands, tenements, possessions and offices. Clearly, given the context, Stewart was included among these "grauntz."

[110] *Hemingburgh*, 311; *Scalacronica*, 166.

goal with notable harshness, reportedly having Bruce partisans who would not convert flogged, dispossessed, or killed.[111] Meanwhile English engineers were busy adding Perth and Edinburgh to their growing network of fortifications in southern Scotland. At Edinburgh, for example (where not long earlier Edward's ally the Count of Namur, while on his way to join Edward's army, had been captured by the Scots for want of a refuge), 116 masons, carpenters and other workers labored to rebuild the fortress, including eventually setting up a wind-mill so that the garrison of sixty men-at-arms and fifty-seven archers would not lack for flour. Other garrisons were stationed at Lochmaben in Annandale, Caerlaverock in Dumfriesshire, Cupar in Fife, and Roxburgh, Berwick, and Jedburgh in the southeast.[112] A few magnates – notably Andrew Murray, William Douglas, and the earls of March and Ross – kept the Bruce cause alive, but they could do little more than "lurk in hiding and live in weariness, awaiting the coming of better days."[113] Edward III seemed fully justified when, on 22 August, he wrote to tell Philip VI that the war in Scotland was over, and peace established.[114]

This was in response to the French king's letter of 7 July, discussed above, which King Edward did not officially "receive" until 20 August. On the day this formal response to Philip's ultimatum was sealed, an English embassy including the Bishop of Norwich and the Abbot of Dore (an experienced diplomat) had just crossed the Channel and begun the land journey towards the French court. Very likely, however, they had before their departure from England on the 20th received a report of the events in Scotland in early August, including the capture of Moray, the submission of Fife, and the arrival of the messengers seeking surrender terms for Atholl, Stewart, and the Mowbrays. They were probably instructed, then, simply to prevent the French from making any decisive action

---

111 *Pluscardensis*, 279.

112 *Avesbury*, 298; *Melsa*, 2:376 (Perth). Note, however, that the Wardrobe accounts for the Perth garrison do not begin until October of 1336 (*WBRF*, fos 250–1). *Melsa*, 2:375; *Scala-cronica*, 166; accounts in *CDS*, pp. 347 ff.; *RS*, 386–7; *WBRF*, fo. 249 (Edinburgh). *Pluscardensis*, 279, states more generally that "the dismantled castles were repaired and fortified."

113 *Pluscardensis*, 280; trans. from *Book of Pluscarden*, 211. To this list could be added William Keith, and Robert Lauder. The *Anonimalle*, 5, however, portrays them as somewhat less helpless: "They did much harm to those who had entered the [two kings'] peace."

114 The text in full is printed in *Bridlington*, 124–6; Cf. *Melsa*, 2:376; *Knighton*, 1:476. Signs of how thoroughly under control the situation seemed came on 30 August, when 4,000 marks in treasure were sent from York to Perth with an escort of only 30 men, and 31 August, when Edward III handed Cupar over to Balliol. *WBRF*, fos 212v, 239. One area which had not been subdued quite yet was the area around Dumbarton and Rothesay, but, as Edward knew, an army of some 1,500 of his men were about to set out from Ireland to subdue that region. In this they were moderately successful, having by 15 September overrun Bute (except for Rothesay castle) and Arran. Nicholson, *Edward III*, 219–21. They also apparently persuaded John, Earl of the Isles, to definitively join the Balliol side. Earlier he had been on friendly terms with the Earl of Moray, who tried to convert him to the Bruce cause, as well as with Balliol. *Pluscardensis*, 278. But by 12 September, three days before the departure of the Irish forces, he had formally done homage to Balliol for the Isles. He remained loyal to Balliol's cause at least until October of 1336. *RFR*, II:2:947; PRO C49/6/29.

by promising that Edward too desired peace in Scotland, and would very soon be sending a formal response to the French proposal.

The English king's letter of 22 August would have reached the Valois court around the end of the first week in September. To Philip's proposal for joint Franco-papal mediation of the Scottish conflict, so that continued fighting in the north would not impede the expedition to the Holy Land, Edward answered, in polite but very firm language, that the crusade would not be imperiled: he had already, through great labors and difficulties, established peace between himself and the Scots. As to the Franco-Scottish alliance, Edward claimed to believe that Philip ought to support him, rather than David, considering the ancient links of friendship, homage and blood between the kings of France and England. The relations between England and Scotland were in any case no business of Philip or the Pope; but Edward affirmed that he would always be ready to do what he reasonably should regarding any matters affecting Philip (which, by implication, did not include Scottish affairs).[115] This was a stinging rebuff, but to soften the blow the English ambassadors made it clear that the last clause of the letter was meant seriously, and that Edward would offer yet another major concession regarding the settlement of disputes concerning Aquitaine. Up until this point, Edward had insisted on some specific agreement for the restitution of the territories occupied in 1324 as recompense for his participation in the crusade. Now, the Bishop of Norwich announced, the English king had agreed to accept a simple promise that, at the end of the crusade, Philip VI would "do him justice" concerning Guienne.[116]

This was indeed a more than reasonable offer regarding Aquitaine, but (as the end of the last embassy had shown), it was not on that subject that English concessions were needed, for the representatives of the two realms had already

---

[115] *Bridlington*, 124–6. The 21-day trip of John de Monceaux on "secret business of the king" to France, Flanders and Normandy in August may have been related to these transactions. *WBRF*, fo. 209. Around the same time, there were messengers of the King of France, the counts of Hainault and Guelders, and the Duke of Brittany, in Perth – another sign of intensive diplomatic activity. Ibid., fo. 211v.

At the time Philip wrote his bellicose ultimatum to Edward III (in July), the childless Duke of Brittany was still planning to leave his duchy to Philip VI in order to head off a civil war among his heirs. At the end of July, however, a meeting of the Breton estates demonstrated strong opposition to this proposal. De la Broderie, *Histoire de Bretagne*, 243; Cazelles, *Société politique*, 140–1. By the end of the year Edward was sending ambassadors to Brittany to explore the prospects of a marriage between John of Eltham and the duke's favored heir, Jeanne de Penthièvre. *RFH*, 2:3:141. This possibility would have strengthened Edward III's diplomatic hand quite substantially, since on the one hand it gave Philip greater incentive to come to an arrangement with the English whereby he might be able to regain the Earl of Cornwall for one of his own relatives, thus preventing his marriage to Jeanne and possibly rescuscitating the prospect of Brittany's transfer to the French royal domain, and on the other hand, it threatened Philip with an Anglo-Breton alliance if war did come.

[116] Schedule of offers in *KdL*, 48; eighth proposition. This offer must have been made during this embassy because the list is explicitly in chronological sequence and offer eight is the last one before the events mentioned in the first full paragraph on p. 49, which took place in the fall of 1335, before the next embassy to France.

been able to hammer out a compromise regarding Guienne and the crusade. Where Philip had sought new concessions was regarding Scotland, and on that matter Edward was offering none whatsoever. The English, it seems, still did not understand that the Valois had made it a principal plank of his policy to support his Scottish ally (especially now that he had publicly proclaimed his intention to do so by force if necessary); they continued to believe that the main French concerns were the *sainte voyage* and the southwest of France. Had this been true, their new offer might have received favorably, but since it was not true, it was rejected out of hand.[117] Philip continued to insist on a settlement of Scottish affairs acceptable to David II.

In August and early September, Edward had been quite worried by the reports he was receiving that the French were preparing to send a major fleet to aid the Scots, either directly or indirectly by attacking the south coast of England. Preparations were even made to defend Gascony should that prove necessary. Still, given (from his perspective) the generosity of the proposals he had sent with his ambassadors, King Edward remained hopeful that he could avoid a war with his cousin, and so the writs he sent warning of an imminent invasion were diplomatic in their language, referring only to "certain foreigners" who were preparing to aid the Scots, never mentioning Philip VI or the French specifically. This left open the possibility of smoothing over attacks by a French fleet by portraying them as "Scottish" forces (in the same way that the armies which Balliol had led into Scotland in 1332 and 1333 had been "his" forces, not "English" ones) should that prove desirable. By the time the Bishop of Norwich and the other ambassadors returned to Edward's presence at Berwick in mid-October, however, attacks by a fleet from France had become unlikely due to the lateness of the season – especially since French ships were mostly designed in a way which made them less able than their English counterparts to weather the rough seas of the northern Atlantic in winter.[118] That provided a breathing space for diplomacy to seek a way out of the dangerous impasse to which Scottish affairs had brought France and England. That there was still a good chance that some negotiated settlement might be reached was due primarily to the vigorous intervention of Pope Benedict XII, who had succeeded John XXII the preceding January. Benedict, a man of both wisdom and intelligence who sincerely desired peace between England and France and maintained a respectable neutrality between the two kings, had already written

---

117 As noted above, Edward's letter, sent on 22 August from Perth, should have reached Philip VI between around 4 September (when he left Paris for Artois) and the middle of the month (when he was at Abbeville, the capital of Edward's county of Ponthieu). The English ambassadors were dismissed from court without receiving a formal answer, but having reached the port of Boulogne on their way home they were given one by 18 September (possibly on 12 September, when Philip VI was there). On the 18th, they returned to England, arriving at Berwick by 10 October. Déprez, *Préliminaires*, 115–16; Viard, *Itin. Phil. VI*.

118 *Cont. Manuel, 1339–46*, fo. 155, re 1339: "vraiment il [Edward] a plus de grans nefs que n'a le roy de france; pource peut il mieulx et moins s[ou]s[?] peril aler par mer en l'iver que galees et petitz vaissels. Et pource en yver le Roy d'angleterre a l'avantage de la mer."

to Philip VI in strong terms to urge him to avoid getting involved in a war in Scotland which would ruin the prospects for the crusade, and might even prove disastrous for France and for the Valois king's own reign. In early September, the Pope's ambassadors also wrote to Edward III to request safe-conducts so that they could deliver certain messages from the pontiff, adding that they carried with them a proposal for peace which, they said, they believed Edward would find agreeable.[119]

As early as 16 September, probably even before receiving the papal ambassadors' letter, the Plantagenet granted safe-conducts for a French embassy coming to England, and on the 28th he did likewise for the papal representatives. On 17 October, probably immediately after the arrival of the French ambassadors, he issued powers for Alexander Mowbray and William Bullock to treat with Andrew Murray (who was once again serving as Warden of Scotland) concerning a truce, and the next day issued a safe-conduct for Robert Lauder. By the 29th, a truce had been granted to the Scots, and a safe-conduct issued for Murray himself to join the English, French, and papal representatives for negotiations.[120] Before then, however, to ensure that his negotiators would have every possible advantage, Edward III hurriedly organized a substantial *chevauchée* into the far highlands [*ultra montes Scocie*] to show the Balliol flag there.[121] The forces for this brief expedition, which began on 23 September and ended in Berwick on 15 October, included nine bannerets, 93 knights, 403 esquires, and at least 197 archers, led by the nominal King of Scots himself, along with Henry of Lancaster, Ralph Neville, Robert Ufford, William Clinton, and the earls of

---

[119] Déprez, *Préliminaires*, 118n. Earlier warning: *BLF*, no. 60.

[120] *RS*, 384–5.

[121] This expedition began on 23 September and probably returned to "friendly" territory on 6 October (when William Clinton's archers were discharged), though most of the men-at-arms continued receiving pay through the 15th, when they reached Berwick. Nicholson (*Edward III and the Scots*, 218, 220) has the expedition start on 31 August, presumably based on the entries in *WBRF*, fo. 237, for William Latimer, William Clinton, and John of Norwich, which have these men and part of their retinues "existent' in comitiva Regis Scocie in equitatura sua ultra montes Scocie ab ultimo die Augustu anno X usque XVm die Octobr'." These entries, however, probably only establish the date on which these reduced retinues became part of Balliol's field force, as with the entry for the 10 archers of Ludlow who are listed as serving from 27 June to 7 October "quia ultra montes cum Rege Scocie," though the expedition certainly did not start in June. Ibid., fo. 256v. The pay given to the reduced group of Hereford's men "existent' in comitiva Regis Scocie in quadam equitatura facta per ipsum ultra montes Scocie per ordinacionem dominum Regis et consilium suum a XXIIJ die Sept. anno IX predicto usque XI diem October proxima sequenti utroque compotus per XIX dies" strongly suggests the later starting date, since it is much easier to imagine that the retinues of Clinton, Latimer and Norwich were reduced before the campaign than that Latimer's was cut in the middle of it. Furthermore, Nicholson takes the earlier date for the expedition because he links it with the Irish incursion into Bute; but his conclusion that Balliol was "intending probably to establish contact with the Irishmen" (p. 222) does not fit well with the description of the expedition as "ultra montes Scocie," since the route from Perth to Dumbarton or Rothesay rarely rises even to 400 feet above sea-level. Cf. the usage in *Fordun*, 360.

Warwick, Buchan and Angus.[122] As soon as the raiders had returned to friendly territory, Edward III was ready to start talking.[123]

This was less than two months after Edward (in his letter of 22 August) had brusquely rejected any possibility of Franco-papal mediation in the Scottish conflict. Why had he so completely backed down? The most likely explanation is that the hard line taken in the August letter had been something of a bluff. Edward recognized that he was dependent on Philip VI's goodwill even to be able to rule his Gascon territories effectively, much less to regain the Agenais, and while he was clearly not ready to simply throw Balliol to the wolves without a fight, he had every reason to cooperate if an honorable compromise could be found – and such a compromise did in fact exist, as later events would show clearly, and as the French ambassadors had probably already hinted. Besides, the war in Scotland was expensive and troublesome, and even though he was currently in a strong position, past events had shown how transitory military triumph there could be.[124] If all that were not enough to persuade him to go along with new negotiations, there was one more fact to consider. Philip VI had

---

[122] Totals are exclusive of the individuals named above. William Latimer and John of Norwich also led retinues in this *chevauchée*. It is unusual for this period to have fewer archers than men-at-arms, and there are no archers listed in the Wardrobe accounts for Lancaster, Neville, Ufford, Clinton, Buchan (Beaumont), Latimer or Norwich. I have not included John Ward and his 162 mounted Chester archers, who served through 12 October, in the total of 197 archers, since they are listed as having been recruited for service as a royal bodyguard and are not specifically noted as having participated in the expedition in question. However, they may well have done so, considering their release date. The only contingent of archers which *was* specifically noted as having joined the *chevauchée* "ultra montes" is a band of 10 men from the town of Ludlow; it is fairly clear, however, that the archers whose service dates ended on 7 October (including the Ludlow men and the archers of the earls of Angus and Warwick) or on 6 October (Clinton's archers) participated in this expedition. It seems likely that the magnates who did not receive Wardrobe pay for their archers (for whatever reason) nonetheless had them, in which case the total number of archers participating would also be higher than the 197 indicated above. It is also possible, however, that for those retinues numbers of archers were lumped together to form nominal men-at-arms for pay purposes, to simplify wage calculations, since three mounted archers received the same pay as one esquire. Thus, for example, it is conceivable that Lancaster's retinue, reported at 2 bannerets (including Henry himself), 19 knights, and 92 other men-at-arms, actually included only 64 esquires, along with 84 mounted archers (giving a balance of archers and men-at-arms). For examples of this practice around this period, see Andrew Ayton, *Knights and Warhorses*, 152–3. This would indicate a rather top-heavy retinue, however (too many knights per esquire), so it is probable that, if these magnates' retinues did in fact include any archers, they were listed in some other account instead of being paid from Wardrobe funds.

[123] It is a noteworthy coincidence that 15 October, when Balliol's expedition returned to Berwick, was the last day of the period during which one of Edward's officials had described the Scottish countryside as being in a state of war. See note 19, above.

[124] Between 31 July 1334 and 31 August 1337 alone, the Wardrobe's expenditures on "wages of war" (including field forces and also garrison and naval expenditures) amounted to no less than £84,083. *WBRF*, fo. 267. In a letter of June 1336, Edward complained to the Pope that he had been "ruined" by the need to assemble a great army for the Scottish war. Déprez, *Préliminaires*, 131 n.5. Indeed, already by May of 1334 he was complaining how the Scottish

already accused Edward of hindering the crusade by making unjust war on the
Scots. If Edward remained obdurate in refusing to accept a papal intervention on
behalf of peace – if he refused even to discuss a proposal which the Pope considered favorable for England – the Church could turn against him. The English
government's concern at this prospect is demonstrated by a document prepared
about this time, which compared John XXII's bull appointing the French king as
captain of the crusade with a bull issued by Innocent IV in 1252 putting those
who took the cross under papal protection.[125] Indeed, Edward's own chancery
later emphasized this factor in explaining why the English had gone the extra
distance to seek peace with Philip VI.[126]

This is not to say that the Plantagenet was merely putting up a show of
moderation for the sake of propaganda. The names of the three carefully chosen
negotiators he appointed to treat with Murray – William Montague, Robert
Ufford, and Ralph Neville – show how serious he was.[127] Montague, soon to be
created Earl of Salisbury, had been one of Edward's closest confidants since
childhood, and had helped engineer the coup of 1330.[128] He was also, like
Ufford (the future Earl of Suffolk), a banneret of the royal household. Ralph
Neville, a great border magnate (head of the family that would produce the
"Kingmaker" in the next century), had been Warden of the Marches in 1334,
and had served in most or all of Edward's Scottish campaigns as Steward of the
Household. He had also been one of Edward III's deputies at Balliol's Holyrood
parliament. It is not a coincidence that none of these men (unlike, say, Percy or
Beaumont) had received lands or offices from Edward Balliol. Neville and
Montague, however, had substantial personal interests in maintaining Edward
III's control over the annexed counties. Neville, with his wide territories in the
north, would benefit greatly from having an English-controlled buffer zone in
the lowlands. He had also recently acquired baronial holdings in Berwickshire.[129] Montague had as large a stake in the English lands in Scotland as any
man. Edward III had granted him the Isle of Man (which under the Treaty of
Northampton had been surrendered to Scottish rule), and then – only three
weeks before he was assigned to the negotiations – Montague had also received
control over the forests of Selkirk and Ettrick; the town and shrivealty of
Selkirk; and the town and county of Peebles.[130] The Scots seemed equally
earnest. Their negotiators included four of the six leaders of the resistance:

wars had exhausted his treasury. *RFH*, 2:3:125. *Lanercost*, 287, also comments on the
expense of the Scottish wars, where Edward had to support Balliol's army as well as his own.
[125] Tyerman, *England and the Crusades*, 250.
[126] *KdL*, 48: "pour estancher la malice le roy de France qui s'efforcea de surmettre l'em-
peschement dudit véage sur le roy d'Engleterre."
[127] *RS*, 385–6; *RFR*, II:2:921, 923, 925.
[128] An idea of the confidence in which Edward III held him can be gained from the fact that
he had been paired with the Archbishop of Canterbury in the last embassy to France. Ibid.,
II:2:894. Childhood: *GGG*, 390 ("quest nostre nurry"), though Montague was ten years older.
[129] Nicholson, *Edward III and the Scots*, 145 n.2.
[130] BL, MS Add. 38462; *RFR*, II:2:924.

Andrew Murray (the warden), William Keith, Robert Lauder, and William Douglas.[131]

The first brief meeting of the negotiators, at Bathgate near Edinburgh, probably took place in the first week of November.[132] It seems to have gone well: on 8 November, Edward extended the truce which had been granted to Murray and his supporters, and on the 16th he added one of his diplomatic right-hand men, Geoffrey le Scrope (Chief Justice of the King's Bench), along with Nicholas Beche, and Richard Bintworth (a professor of civil law who had recently served on embassies to France and Avignon), to his negotiating team. Arrangements were made for the two sides to meet again, this time at Newcastle-on-Tyne.[133]

Before Murray came to England for the new round of discussions, however, he took care of some business in the north. David Strathbogie, who had been charged by Edward Balliol to subdue the remaining Bruce supporters north of the Forth, was besieging Murray's wife, Lady Christian Bruce, in the castle of Kildrummy. This could be seen as a violation of the truce granted by Edward III, in which the king had declared none of his men should in any way harm Murray or his adherents. However, since Strathbogie was acting on behalf of Balliol rather than Edward III, it was not entirely clear that he was bound by the truce. In any case, Murray certainly did not consider Strathbogie to be protected by the truce, since the Earl of Atholl was not observing it himself. According to John of Fordun, William Montague gave his agreement that the truce should not prevent Murray from going to relieve his castle.[134]

Andrew therefore gathered together all the forces the Bruce party could muster – eight hundred men, including the Earl of March, Sir William Douglas, Sir Alexander Ramsay and probably William of Ross[135] – and swiftly marched against the besiegers. Having gained some intelligence of their approach, Strathbogie arrayed his men on a high hill at Culblean, some ten miles south of Kildrummy.[136] From there he controlled the road northwards as it approached

---

131 *RFR*, II:2:926; *RS*, 385–7. By the end of the negotiations, it appears that Alexander, Bishop of Aberdeen, and John, Abbot of Coupar, were also in English territory on the negotiating team. *RFR*, II:2:930.

132 A truce was granted to Murray and his adherents from 29 October to 12 November, during which time it was planned for him to meet with representatives of the king's council at Bathgate. *RS*, 385. Montague did in fact go to meet with Murray there [at "Basket"] at some point in November, taking six days including travel time to and from Doddington in Northumberland (which would have left very little time for discussions). *WBRF*, fo. 237. The king heard mass at Doddington on 1 November. Ibid., fo. 203.

133 *RS*, 385, 388; cf. 391. The safe-conducts for the last-mentioned negotiations were issued on 23 November.

134 *Fordun*, 360.

135 *Wyntoun*, 2:424; *Lanercost*, 284 (Ross); Ross, however, was young and not in fact invested with the earldom of Ross until the following year (*Handbook of British Chronology*, 518).

136 *Wyntoun*, 2:422, sets the size of his force at 3,000 men, but this seems too large to be within Atholl's resources, as Wyntoun himself suggests by adding "men sayd."

Boultenstone Pass. It seemed that the stage was being set for a repetition of Halidon Hill.[137]

Perhaps Murray thought so as well, for, instead of making an open attack on the Earl of Atholl's position, he attempted a surprise rear attack on the auspicious dawn of 30 November: the feast of St. Andrew, Scotland's patron saint.[138] This was done on the advice of John of the Crag, who had come to Murray's assistance with three hundred men from Kildrummy. Strathbogie's scouts detected their enemies' approach, however, and the earl had time to array his men across the path before Murray came in striking distance. When he saw this, Sir William Douglas (who commanded the elite vanguard of Murray's force) ordered his men to halt. Strathbogie took this hesitation as a sign of breaking morale. "Hey! apone thame tyte," he cried to his men, "for thai ar welle nere dyscumffyte."[139] His upbringing in England had evidently not taken the Scotsman out of the earl, for breaking his array he led his men in a wild highland charge at his enemies.

Between the two armies was a ford over the Burn of the Vat. Strathbogie had probably intended to attack Murray as he was in the midst of crossing it, with his men divided by the water. But now Douglas, seeing Atholl's men approach the ford in disorder, ordered a counter-charge: "Now we," he said simply. The two forces collided at the ford, and a sharp but brief combat ensued. The onset of the second division of Scots, under Sir Andrew Murray himself, was so rapid and fierce that none could withstand it. Most of Strathbogie's army took flight immediately, but Earl David's most loyal followers, including Sir Walter Comyn and three or four other knights, stood by him until he and they were killed.[140] Casualties were light, for the fugitives could easily escape their pursuers in the heavily wooded terrain, and Murray was in any case disposed to show mercy to those who had been compelled to serve Atholl.[141]

The battle made a substantial impact on Scottish opinion. After two catastrophic defeats, this small victory provided an important boost to the morale of David Bruce's supporters. Indeed, they were sufficiently revitalized that they were able, on a small scale, to go onto the offensive in Scotland, besieging Atholl's widow in Lochindorb and also Balliol's garrison in the castle of Cupar. Still, however, the battle of Culblean was by no means "the turning-point in the second war of Scottish Independence."[142] The force defeated by Murray and

---

[137] For the location, see Nicholson, *Edward III and the Scots*, 231–3.

[138] *Wyntoun*, 2:427. St. Andrew was presumably Andrew Murray's patron saint as well.

[139] *Wyntoun*, 2:426. [Hey! Upon them tightly, for they are well near defeated.]

[140] Ibid.; *Fordun*, 360. Edward III granted £10 each to several knights who lost their horses and arms in escaping from this fight. *WBRF*, fo. 268v.

[141] *Fordun*, 360; *Wyntoun*, 2:426–7.

[142] As claimed by W. Douglas Simpson and Ranald Nicholson. Nicholson, *Edward III and the Scots*, 236. It may even be too much to say, as Sumption, *Trial by Battle*, 149, does, that it was "a major reverse for the English cause." After all, it was *after* this fight that the Scottish negotiators agreed to make peace on terms that met all of Edward's important war-aims, with Balliol keeping the throne and the subordination of Scotland to England affirmed (see below).

Douglas had not been the full strength of Edward Balliol, much less Edward III. As the events of the following summer showed, the English were still capable of going where they willed in Scotland, even to the far north, and destroying everything in their path. Between them, the two Edwards retained control over most of the southeastern quadrant of Scotland, including many of the largest towns and strongest castles of the realm – Berwick, Edinburgh, Perth, Peebles, Stirling, Cupar, Roxburgh, Caerlaverock, Lochmaben, Lochindorb, Jedburgh, Selkirk, and others. The army which had been victorious at Culblean, the greatest the Bruce cause could assemble, had been less than one-quarter the size of even the small force the English deployed for the 1334 Roxburgh campaign, and under one-tenth the size of the invasion force of the summer of 1335. Under the circumstances, David Bruce's negotiators continued to seek a diplomatic solution, for a military one still seemed far out of reach.

Unfortunately, aside from periodic renewals of the truce granted by Edward III, we have very little information about the course of the discussions.[143] On or just before 25 January, however, the negotiators reached agreement.[144] Based on three chroniclers' accounts, it seems that with this draft "Treaty of Newcastle" the two sides had arrived at a solution which had a very real chance of working. Balliol, who was in his forties[145] and still unmarried, had no direct heir. David Bruce, on the other hand, was easily young enough to be Balliol's son. David was also Edward III's brother-in-law, and Edward doubtless was the more willing to make some concessions to him for that reason. Thus, it was tentatively agreed that Balliol should rule during his life, adopting David as his heir.[146] While Balliol lived, David would remain at Edward III's court, supported by the lands which his father had held in England, and his adherents would accept the suzerainty of the English king. Once David came to the throne, he would hold the realm of Scotland from the King of England, on the terms to which Balliol had agreed.[147] Messengers would immediately be sent to David II

The real "turning-point" in the Anglo-Scottish war was the outbreak of war on the Continent, as the Scottish author of the *Pluscardensis*, 286, clearly realized: "news came to the King of England that the deadly war between him and the King of France had been revived; this was indeed lucky for the kingdom of Scotland: for, if the King of England had gone on with that war which he had started, he would without doubt have subjected all of Scotland to his rule."

143 *RFR*, II:2:926, 928, 930, 933, 938. The English dispatch of ambassadors to Brittany at the end of December probably served to give the French extra incentive to support a general *entente*; see note 115, above.

144 *Bridlington*, 127, for the date. A few days earlier, on 22 January, messengers had been sent into Scotland with letters from Edward III and the French and papal mediators; very likely these contained the offer that the Scots agreed to on the 25th. *RS*, 395; *RFR*, II:2:930. Cf. also *Anonimalle*, 6, and Delpit, *Collection générale*, 66.

145 He was already old enough in 1295 to be considered for marriage alliances, and succeeded to his French estates in 1314. Nicholson, *Scotland*, 47.

146 However, according to the *Anonimalle/Lanercost* account, David would only succeed to the throne if Balliol had no heir of his own body. See the following note.

147 See *Knighton*, 1:477 [Scoti ... fecerunt securitatem per juramentum quod omnes magnates Scotiae venirent et David Bruz cum uxore venire facerent ad festum Michaelis apud

to secure his assent to the treaty, and in the interim the truce would be extended to include all of Scotland – including Balliol's besieged garrisons of Lochindorb and Cupar.[148]

Edward III had high hopes for this arrangement. It seemed that everyone would gain: he himself would secure the fruits of his years of hard campaigning, and with luck might eventually see a nephew raised at his court succeed to the throne of Scotland; Balliol would be able to rule his realm in peace; David (and with him Queen Joan) would eventually be restored to the throne from which he had been driven and the kingdom he seemed to have lost. The commons of both realms would gain the benefits of peace – which the people of Scotland, ravaged by the armies of both sides, particularly needed.[149] A major source of Anglo-French tension would be removed, and the path cleared for the crusade which was so dear to the hearts of Philip VI and Benedict XII (and, indeed, to Edward III himself).[150] The way would also be reopened for the restitution of Edward's lost lands in Aquitaine, on the terms so briefly agreed in December of 1334.

The English were expecting to receive David's response to these proposals at the Westminster parliament of 11–20 March 1336. The answer brought by the

---

Londonias ad parliamentum regis Angliae et stare ordinatione regis Angliae et concilii ejus, ita quod idem David et uxor ejus demorarentur in Anglia usque mortem Edwardi Baliol; et medio tempore Scoti facerent debitam subjectionem regi Angliae] and William of Dene's *Historia Roffensis* (fo. 77v): "David de Brus omnes terras quas pater suis in Anglia habuit habuisset et ipse moram quae in Anglia traxisset. Et Edwardus de Baillol regnum Scocie ad vitam tenuisset et post eius mortem predictus David et eius heredes et successores de Rege Anglie in capite tenerent." It is also partially supported by the account of the *Lanercost*, 284/ *Anonimalle*, 6, which states that around 2 February a "trewe et acorde" was made between the Scots and the two Edwards. The accord began with a petition on the Scots' part that a new discussion should be made by wise men neutral in the discord between the two realms, as to who had the better right to the crown of Scotland, Balliol or David Bruce. The same group should determine whether David should succeed to the throne after Edward if the latter engendered no heirs of his body. At the London parliament of 11–20 March (the account appears to say) these proposals were to be put forward: if they could be agreed, peace would be made; and if not, the war would proceed. See also *Bridlington*, 127.

[148] Safe-conducts for David's ambassadors to come from France to England were granted on the 26th, along with others for a group of Scotsmen to go to France and return (by 15 April); and on the same day the truce was extended for two and a half months, a much longer interval than in previous extensions. *RFR*, II:2:930; *RS*, 397–8.

[149] Cf. Bower, *Scottichronicon*, 124, 126, 130, 142–4.

[150] Despite Tyerman's strong views to the contrary, I think there is good reason to accept this sentiment as genuine. Edward III admired and emulated his grandfather Edward I, who had been a famous crusader; as W. M. Ormrod has observed, Edward's religious sentiments have every appearance of having been sincere and utterly conventional; certainly his devotion to chivalry cannot be questioned; and going on crusade was the ultimate expression of conventional religious and chivalric aspirations. Note also Edward's message to the Pope in November 1340, when he had his ambassadors rehearse the "magno zelo, quem semper habuit et habet ad sanctum passagium assumendum." *EMDP*, 436. Consider also Edward's offer to delay restitution of the Agenais until after he and Philip returned from the crusade; surely this cannot be reconciled with the proposition that Edward had "little intention of honouring his crusade promises." Tyerman, *England and the Crusades*, 249.

Scottish messengers, however, was not the one they wanted to hear: David rejected the draft peace agreement entirely. Knighton attributes this outcome to the malice of King Philip, who persuaded the Scots to continue the war.[151] The *Anonimalle* and Bridlington chroniclers, however, blame "the pride of the Scots."[152] The latter seems more likely: had the treaty been approved, Philip would, without loss of honor, and without ruining his crusade projects, have been freed from the troublesome (and potentially, given his plans for an invasion of Scotland, very expensive) duty of supporting his Scottish ally.[153] David, on the other hand, might well have objected to terms which required Scotland to give up the national freedom which his father had won with so much difficulty, and may also have been worried by the possibility that Balliol might yet have an heir of his body, who might supercede the Bruce's claim. Of course, King David was still only twelve years old, and must have been guided in this by his advisors – more particularly, those among his counselors who were not attached to the magnates (including Stewart and Atholl) who had recently made their submission to Balliol. This, indeed, was probably the key factor in the rejection of the compromise peace, as we can see if we consider who these men were. There were at this time only fourteen active earldoms (counting the Isles and the steward's lands) in Scotland, of which only eight were claimed by Bruce partisans who had not submitted to the English.[154] Of those eight, five – Ross, Menteith, Lennox, Sutherland and Dunbar – belonged to men (or boys) who could easily have been included in the treaty and restored to their lands after their submission. Of the remaining three, one, Angus, was claimed on behalf of Thomas Stewart (contesting the title of Gilbert d'Umfraville); since he was an infant,

---

[151] *Knighton*, 1:477. Cf. *Historia Roffensis*, fo. 79, and King Edward's own opinion, in Delpit, *Collection générale*, 66.

[152] *Anonimalle*, 6; *Bridlington*, 128. The latter describes the Scots as returning to their old malice and prideful spirit "like dogs returning to vomit."

[153] See above, p. 95.

[154] The earldoms were Angus, Atholl, Buchan, Strathearn (subsuming Caithness and Orkney), Sutherland, Dunbar, Fife, the Isles (not an "official" earldom, though John was often styled "Earl of the Isles"), Lennox, Mar, Menteith, Moray, Ross, and the Stewardlands (also not officially an earldom). Buchan was held by Beaumont; Fife and Robert Stewart had submitted to the English, as had Geoffrey Mowbray and his wife the Countess of Mar. John of the Isles had done homage to Balliol. The title to Strathearn was considered by the Bruce party to be in abeyance because of Malise's submission to the English, but had been granted by Balliol to the Earl of Surrey, who however did not use the title. The eight claimed by Bruce partisans were Angus and Atholl (both contested), Sutherland, Dunbar, Lennox, Menteith, Moray (effectively contested), and Ross.

The first was claimed by Gilbert d'Umfraville (and the infant Thomas Stewart); Atholl was claimed by the infant David IV of Strathbogie, in English care, and by William Douglas. Patrick of Dunbar continued in the resistance. Donald of Lennox, son of the earl killed at Halidon, was a minor, as was Thomas of Mar (whose mother had submitted to the Edwards). John Graham, who had recently married the heiress of Menteith, was probably in the resistance at this time, though he had sworn fealty to Edward III in November 1334. John Randolph, the young Earl of Moray, was a leader of the resistance; Henry Beaumont may have disputed his title, and many of his lands were claimed by Englishmen.

however, he could not have blocked the settlement, though his guardians would doubtless have opposed it. The remaining two earls – John Randolph, Earl of Moray, and William Douglas, who after Culblean had laid claim to Atholl – posed the real problem. (Randolph had recently been taken prisoner by the English, but since it was he who had arranged to bring David II and his entourage to shelter in France, it can be presumed that even during his captivity his interests were carefully looked after in the exiled court.) Aside from Murray, Randolph and Douglas were now the senior leaders of the resistance, and this fact is the key to the failure of the Treaty of Newcastle, for they were almost the only ones whose personal interests could *not* be reconciled with the compromise peace, for the Scottish lands they claimed could not be given back to them without disinheriting Edward III's ward, the infant David Strathbogie IV of Atholl (which would also mean taking away lands granted during Strathbogie's minority to John of the Isles, Balliol's most powerful Scottish supporter), and – even more consequentially – William Montague, Henry Percy and the Bohun family (who had been granted extensive Moray and Douglas lands).[155] These comrades-in-arms were men the two Edwards would not abandon, just as David II would not abandon Douglas or Moray.

Thus was lost the best chance for a negotiated peace between David and the Edwards. With it was lost the crusade. In early March, Philip VI arrived at Avignon to discuss the voyage to the Holy Land, and the Franco-Scottish alliance, with the Pope.[156] The two held a private meeting around 8 March,[157] at which Philip apparently informed the Pope that the proposed Anglo-Scottish

---

[155] The Isle of Man, which Edward III had given to Montague, had previously been a property of Thomas Randolph, Earl of Moray. *Handbook of British Chronology*, 65. Balliol had granted the peel of Lochmaben, Annandale, and Moffatdale, also Moray lands, to Henry Percy; but since these were also claimed by Edward Bohun, whom Edward III supported, Percy was in exchange given the castle, constabulary and forest of Jedburgh (which was also claimed by the Douglases, the fact at the root of the long Percy-Douglas feud thereafter). *RS*, 280–1. Edward Bohun had died before this treaty came up for ratification, but title to Annandale passed from him to his elder brother John, Earl of Hereford, and then (on the latter's death in January 1336, just days before the agreement in question was reached) to William Bohun, soon to be Earl of Northampton. *RS*, 399; cf. A. A. M. Duncan, "*Honi soit qui mal y pense:* David II and Edward III, 1346–52," *Scottish Historical Review* LXVII (1988), 128. Even the earldom of Moray itself may have been granted away, to Henry Beaumont. Nicholson, *Edward III*, 160.

Balliol had granted John of the Isles custody of Colonsay, Mully, Skye, Kintyre, Knapdale and other lands during the minority of David Strathbogie IV. Reid, "Balliol," 59–61; Bean, "The Percies and their Estates in Scotland," 97–9; *Lanercost*, 284. To this list of problematic cases could be added Sir Thomas Ughtred, whom Balliol had given Thomas Stewart's barony of Bunkle in Berwickshire. *RS*, 261.

[156] *Grandes chroniques*, 9:152.

[157] Ellis, *Original Letters*, 3rd. ser., 1:30. "In medio Quadragesimae" here probably means in the middle of Quadragesima *week*, rather than in the middle of the 40-day period. See also Déprez, *Préliminaires*, 410–13, esp. 411, and "Itin. Phil. VI," 120.

peace had collapsed. While Scottish participation was hardly necessary for the crusade to proceed, friendly relations between France and England were. As Benedict explained in a long letter to the French king dated the 13th, the continuing war between England and Scotland – along with tense situations in Germany, Tuscany and Lombardy, and Apulia and Sicily – made the crusade too dangerous to undertake.[158]

Benedict, a far-sighted man who considered Philip VI to be rather naive,[159] felt the need to warn the French king not to rush into a dangerous situation in Scotland. "Before getting involved," he wrote in another letter, "it is necessary to reflect maturely. It is not difficult at all to *begin* an enterprise; the key is to know in advance, through an effort of wisdom and reflection, how one will carry it through, and to what end."[160]

Philip was not deterred. Over Easter week, in Lyon, he had held discussions with the Scots, and promised to use all his power to restore David to the Scottish throne. Meanwhile, he had built up a very substantial invasion force in Normandy, including (according to an intelligence report received later by Edward III) thirty galleys strengthened with iron "so that no ship can resist them," and another five hundred more conventional vessels.[161] Philip planned to have half of this armada arrive in Scotland on 3 May, three days before the scheduled expiration of the truce,[162] rendezvous with Alexander Seton at Kinghorn, and then advance on northern England along with the Scottish army. The rest of the French invasion force would land at Portsmouth.[163]

At the same time, as Edward was well aware, Philip also kept one eye directed towards Gascony. Since around 1333, Edward had been receiving memoranda from chancery clerks arguing that the French royal government was using Gascon lawsuits to make trouble for Edward's ducal administration, with the intention of hindering his efforts against the Scots.[164] (Note how this makes Scottish affairs the *cause*, and Gascon problems the *effect* – a judgement which

---

158 Printed in Déprez, *Préliminaires*, 410–13.

159 As he wrote in a private letter at this time. Déprez, *Préliminaires*, 128.

160 Déprez, *Préliminaires*, 128; *BLF*, no. 184 (25 March 1336).

161 Ellis, *Original Letters*, 30–1: "in Pascha, Rex stetit Lugduni, et ibidem habuit tractatum cum Scotis, et promisit eis totum posse suum ad conducendum David de Bruys in Scotia," etc. Easter came on 31 March that year, and in fact Philip was in Lyon at least from 28 March to 31 March. Viard, "Itin. Phil. VI," 120–1. It was almost certainly in early December of 1335 that Philip VI decided to have his constable, Raoul de Brienne, take command of this expedition. See *RTC*, no. 4892; Émile Molinier, *Étude sur la vie d'Arnoul d'Audrehem*, *Mémoires présentés par divers savants à l'Académie des Inscriptions et Belles-lettres*, 2nd ser., VI (1883), 8n, and Viard, "Itin. Phil. VI," 116–28, 525–30 (only one stay at Châtell-erault).

162 The truce had been extended through "the Sunday immediately before the next feast of the Ascension of the Lord" – i.e., through 5 May expiring on 6 May. *RFR*, II:2:933.

163 Ellis, *Original Letters*, 30 (Kinghorn is the "loco ubi Balliolf applicuit"; see Chapter 3, above).

164 PRO C47[Chancery Miscellanea]/30/1/25–6. The reference to the Scots suggests that the document is later than the tentative dating of 4 Edward III (1330) given in the PRO catalog.

the chronicler Henry Knighton shared.[165]) So long as Edward held the diplomatic card of the crusade to play, however, he could expect that Philip would keep the situation in Guienne under control.[166] As discussed above, ever since 1331, Edward had been pressing for the restoration of Agen and other lands seized by the French during the 1320s, and Philip had been willing to listen.[167] Now that the two kingdoms teetered on the edge of war over Scotland, Philip was less accommodating. In 1336, Edward's clerks were writing up strong warnings about individual cases which could lead to war. The Sire de Navailles was prosecuting a claim for 31,000 l.t. against Edward, and in another case the seaports of England faced fines of no less than 600,000 l.t.[168] Another case involving an order to restore some lands near Bordeaux to the Count of Armagnac led Edward's officers to openly disobey a French royal writ; on 11 April, Edward wrote to ask Philip not to take further action on the matter until English ambassadors could arrive to discuss it.[169] He was well aware that the two-front war his diplomacy had been striving to avoid might now be imminent. Indeed, it is possible in retrospect to see that with the Scottish rejection of the proposed peace settlement in March, war had become inevitable. Edward would not abandon Balliol (or the lands and rights Balliol had ceded to him) especially not when his position in Scotland was so strong; Philip was ready to fight to restore David to the Scottish throne, especially since war would give him the opportunity and the justification to seize Gascony from a vassal who had shown himself to be obstinate and prideful; the only practicable compromise had been rejected. With war over Scotland clearly approaching, each side was more willing to take steps to improve its position in the coming conflict, even when such steps further reduced the already small possibility of avoiding a final rupture: before the end of the year, the French pushed matters to the breaking point in Gascony, and Edward openly gave sanctuary to Philip's mortal enemy, Robert of Artois.[170]

Even so, throughout the spring and early summer, Edward tried to stave off

---

[165] Knighton, *Chronicle* (ed. Martin), 2: "the French king seized the Gascon lands of the English king . . . and all because King Edward had so much labored to humble the Scots." It should be noted, however, that Edward III also accused Philip of supporting the Scots in order to prevent him from seeking his rights in France, e.g. in the letter in *Bridlington*, 132. Cf. note 70, above.

[166] E.g. see *Lescot*, appendix II; *RFR*, II:2:874.

[167] Déprez, *Préliminaires*, 90 n.2 (1333); cf. 92, 95, and above, n.54.

[168] Navailles: PRO C47/10/5/1. Seaports: C47/30/5/23: C47/28/1 (46). Both: C47/30/5/1. General: C47/30/5/3. See also Vale, *Origins*, 259.

[169] *RFR*, II:2:936; see also Cuttino, "Process of Agen," 169–70; *RTC*, nos. 3178–9, 3272.

[170] Philip's letter of 26 December 1336 suggests that he was first informed of Robert of Artois' presence at the English court by the ambassadors he sent to England *after* the confrontation in August 1336. Printed in Déprez, *Préliminaires*, 414–15; this is consistent with the Pope's mention of Artois in November 1336, discussed ibid., 135–6. Artois first began receiving generous subsidies from Edward III in November 1336, and was not formally and publicly received into Edward's court until January 1337. Thus, it seems clear that Edward's willingness to shelter Artois was a symptom, and not the cause, of the rupture in Anglo-French relations. See also below, notes 215, 216, 219, but cf. also *CEPR*, 561–2.

the outbreak of direct war with France, even though he knew the French were again planning to send troops to assist the Scots.[171] At the same time, in addition to preparing for yet another major invasion of Scotland, he took steps to defend against a possible landing of French troops on English soil.[172] His most important preparations were aimed at building up a war-chest. He called for a convocation of the clergy, to grant him an aid, to assemble before 4 June.[173] They would grant him a subsidy of a tenth of their goods; the laymen of the realm had already, in March, offered a tenth from the boroughs and a fifteenth from the counties.[174]

As the king attended to matters in the south, his vassals resumed hostilities in Scotland. As soon as the truce expired, the earls of March and Sutherland – along with the Earl of Fife, who had apparently once again left Balliol's obedience when David II rejected the peace arrangement – besieged Cupar castle in Fife. John Stirling, the commander of Edinburgh castle, responded to the situation with the characteristic boldness that would win so much praise for English arms over the following decades. Hiring thirty-two small boats, he secretly sailed across the Firth of Forth with his entire garrison of forty men-at-arms and 160 foot, mostly archers. Drawing near the besieged castle, his men set fire to two villages, then made a swift attack on the Scots. The garrison, alerted by the smoke from the burning villages, launched a simultaneous sally. The besiegers, thinking that Stirling's men were the advance forces of the main English army, panicked and fled, leaving behind them their siege engines, tents, and armor. The Englishmen pursued their routed enemies vigorously, killing all they could get their hands on. Then, after burning the abandoned siege engines, Sir John returned to Edinburgh four days after he had left it.[175]

Around 19 May, the English army of Scotland was divided into two parts. One, probably led by Henry of Lancaster, rode through the forests and the highland areas where William Douglas' band of guerrillas was operating. The English put the Scots to flight whenever they encountered them, cutting down as many as they could, and seized a good quantity of cattle and other supplies. Meanwhile the other division, under Edward Balliol, covered the lowlands. In the area of Stirling, Balliol's troops fought some skirmishes with Andrew Murray's men, again (according to an English report) victoriously.[176] When they

---

[171] See the preambles of his February writs for guarding the coasts (*RS*, 404) and his April appointment of Henry of Lancaster to command his army against the Scots (*RFR*, II:2:936). Cf. p. 113, above.

[172] Scotland: *RFR*, II:2:395–6. Defense: Edward ordered, for example, that Corfe, Tintagel, Launceston, Restormel, Bristol, Carisbrook, Portchester, Pevensey, Hastings, Dover, Rochester, Arundel and Lewes castles be put into a state of defense, and the Tower of London likewise. *RFR*, II:2:940 (4 June). See also *RS*, 404–5, 420–33.

[173] *RFR*, II:2:935 (26 March).

[174] *Murimuth*, 77.

[175] *Anonimalle*, 6; *CDS*, p. 354 (Account of John Stirling for works at Edinburgh).

[176] This information is from an anonymous letter of 19 June, printed in Ellis, *Original Letters*, 32–3; the date is from *Bridlington*, 128.

reached Perth, they found it deserted and in ashes, having been destroyed by the Scots. Balliol's men, joined by Lancaster and his forces, stolidly rebuilt the fortifications yet again.[177]

While he was still there, Balliol received a surprise visitor. Edward III had received word that the French were sending many soldiers to Scotland, and thought that with their aid Murray might attack the English forces in Perth. If so, Edward III wanted to be there.[178] So, appointing his brother the Earl of Cornwall, John, Archbishop of Canterbury (the chancellor), and Henry, Bishop of Lincoln (the treasurer) to open the parliament at Northampton in his stead, he sped north. By the 26 June he had reached Berwick, accompanied about fifty men-at-arms. With only twice that number, he rode the rest of the way to Perth "in the greatest danger," arriving two days later. His bravery inspired wonder and even tears of joy among the soldiers who welcomed him.[179] It was perhaps foolish to have ventured into hostile territory with such a small escort,[180] especially when the enemy was believed to be gathering in the area – but the adventurous, courageous nature the king had demonstrated won him much admiration in chivalric circles. His example spurred the martial nobility of England to try to equal his daring ideal; in the process, over the years, they won many striking victories on his behalf.

The *chevauchée* he launched from Perth two weeks later, after the looked-for Scottish attack failed to materialize, displayed even greater boldness. With only four hundred men-at-arms, and a like number of mounted archers and hobelars, he set out to the rescue the Countess of Atholl – Catherine Beaumont, widow of David of Strathbogie, daughter of Henry Beaumont.[181] Countess Catherine and

[177] Ibid.; *Anonimalle*, 7; *Scalacronica*, 166. They provided the city with a good wall of earth and a deep ditch.
[178] *Knighton*, 1:477. *Scalacronica*, 166; cf. *Bridlington*, 128; *Lanercost*, 286. Knighton specifies that the king was glad of this news, because he hoped that the Scots might now be willing to give battle: "Ex qua re rex Edwardus multum laetus effectus, credebat ipsos velle in bellum contra se procedere." It may have been the return of the Count of Eu's homages which provided this information. Cf. *RTC*, no. 4298.
[179] *Historia Roffensis*, fo. 78 (danger, wonder, tears); *RFR*, II:2:940–41 (date); *Scalacronica*, 166 (wonder, 100 men).
[180] The English had greatly criticized the Count of Namur for his "presumption" when, a year earlier, he had been captured while attempting roughly the same thing. *Lanercost*, 283.
[181] The number of his troops, along with most of the information in the following paragraphs, comes from a detailed newsletter printed in Ellis, *Original Letters*, 34–9. The letter, written by an unknown author just days after the close of the campaign, appears to be basically a copy of one (now lost) that the king sent to Queen Philippa at York. Just who accompanied Edward on this *chevauchée*, I cannot determine; but on the day he left Perth, the following men joined him in witnessing a charter: Henry of Lancaster, the earls of Warwick and Angus, Henry Percy, Ralph Neville, William Montague, and Robert Ufford. *CDS*, no. 1209. A *restor* roll dated the following 8 September shows that by then Henry Beaumont, Hugh Despenser, Thomas Ponynges, William Lucy, and John Hardreshull were also at Perth, among many others. PRO E101/19/36. Edward's small army for the ride to Lochindorb was

"othir ladyis, that ware luvely" had been besieged in the strong castle of Lochindorb by Andrew Murray since the day of the battle of Culblean.[182] Presumably the siege had been interrupted some time in February, for when Edward III extended the truce with Murray on 26 January, he specified that the inhabitants of Lochindorb should be included.[183] When the truce expired on 12 May, the siege apparently resumed. By mid-July, the defenders were running low on food.

Beautiful damsels trapped in a far-away wilderness castle, "en[v]yrownd wyth thaire innymyis": how could Edward resist?[184] Yet this was no mere romantic adventure; it was a superbly conceived and executed strategic maneuver.[185] With the small force he led, Edward could move quickly, find adequate supplies,[186] and still retain some hope of catching his enemies by surprise. Among the most frustrating aspects of his years of campaigning in Scotland were his enemies' ability to avoid a fight, and the difficulty of even finding out where they were. Well, in July of 1336, he at least knew where they were: at Lochindorb.

To catch them, he would have to move extraordinarily fast. He did. After a relatively relaxed ride of eight miles on Friday 12 July, he covered the twenty miles more to Blair castle on the second day.[187] On Sunday he climbed into the highlands, covered thirty miles, and reached Fythewyn in Badenoch by nightfall. Just after dawn the next day, he received word that Murray's army was congregated at the church of Kynkardyn in Stronkaltere wood, sixteen miles away. Leaving his baggage-train behind, Edward immediately set out in haste to come to grips with his troublesome adversary.[188]

Murray's scouts detected the English soldiers well before their arrival, but none of his men dared to interrupt him while he was hearing mass. Even when he was informed, he made a maddening show of being relaxed and in control.

---

doubtless drawn largely from the retinues of some combination of men from these groups; and indeed Andrew Ayton, using the same document, has managed to show that men-at-arms from at least the retinues of Henry Percy and John Tibetot were definitely involved. *Knights and Warhorses*, 72–3.

The information on the number of King Edward's troops given in the letter in Ellis, incidentally, is an excellent illustration of the unreliability of chroniclers' numbers. A number of chronicles (e.g. *Wyntoun*, 428) set the size of Edward's army at 20,000 men. Ironically, the newsletter, which gives the far smaller actual number of the English forces, gives that same figure – 20,000 – for the number of Scots under Andrew Murray. While Murray probably had more men available than did Edward III, his army was certainly nowhere near 20,000.

182 *Wyntoun*, 2:428; *CDS*, no. 1221.

183 *RFR*, II:2:930.

184 *Wyntoun*, 2:428.

185 As pointed out by Sumption, *Trial by Battle*, 160–1.

186 This would have been difficult or impossible with a larger contingent: even as it was, by the time they left Lochindorb his soldiers were suffering from a "great deficiency of supplies." *Scalacronica*, 166; Ellis, *Original Letters*, 36.

187 These are the distances given in the newsletter in Ellis, *Original Letters*, 35. They correspond almost exactly to the actual distance on the modern A9 highway.

188 Ellis, *Original Letters*, 35; *Wyntoun*, 2:429. This appears to be where the Scots were encamped.

His men "wald fayne have bene away," but Sir Andrew absolutely refused to be hurried. By the time he had his men in battle formation, the English were almost upon them. Perhaps Murray hoped that Edward's troops would break their array, as Atholl's men had done at Culblean, but these men were of another caliber. The English maintained their formation, and still came on so fast that the retreating Scots were almost overtaken. Fortunately for the latter, one of their number led them down a side path which passed through two rocky crags. When the king saw this, he realized it would be unsafe to pursue them farther.[189]

Sorry to have seen his enemies escape, Edward pressed on to Lochindorb.[190] When the garrison recognized the king's banners – the first news they had had of his coming – the countess hurried out to thank her sovereign for coming to their assistance. He had arrived just in time: the defenders were down to their last four bushels of grain.[191] Having fulfilled one of his objectives (the rescue of Countess Catherine) and failed in another (bringing Murray to battle), Edward turned to the third element of his strategy for this *chevauchée*: devastation. Since the death of the Earl of Atholl, virtually the entire north of Scotland had returned to David Bruce's obedience.[192] Earlier *chevauchées* by Balliol and Edward III had succeeded – more or less – in beating southern Scotland into submission. While a single expedition could not do as much to the north, Edward could at least serve notice that refusal to accept Balliol's rule could exact a heavy price, and remind the Scots that their defeat of David of Strathbogie did not equate to a defeat of the King of England.

The destruction of northern Scotland also served an even more important strategic function: the area was not rich to begin with, and once the English riders had put everything within view to the torch, there would be nothing left with which to support a Scottish army, much less a French invasion force. So, over the next week, Edward laid waste virtually the entire east coast of Scotland between the firths of Moray and Tay. First the town of Forres, with all the surrounding countryside, was set alight. Then the abbey of Kinloss was emptied of its food stores, which were shipped off to supply the garrison remaining at Lochindorb. The town of Elgin was spared out of reverence for the Holy Trinity church there, but all the land around – "the best and most fertile of all of Scotland"[193] – was devastated and burned. The large port of Aberdeen, a possible landing point for a French fleet (there were Flemish ships there when Edward arrived), was left in ashes, with its environs.[194] The king strengthened and garrisoned the castles of Dunnottar and Kinneff, on the coast just south of Aberdeen,

---

189 *Wyntoun*, 2:429–30.
190 *Wyntoun*, 2:430; Ellis, *Original Letters*, 35–6.
191 Ellis, *Original Letters*, 35–6.
192 *Wyntoun*, 2:428.
193 Ellis, *Original Letters*, 37.
194 Ellis, *Original Letters*, 36–8; note also *ERS*, 1:449. This was partly in revenge for the death of a famous English knight, Thomas Roscelyn, previously Edward III's Warden of Edinburgh and Sheriff of Lothian (*CDS*, no. 1186), who had been killed by the men of Aberdeen at Dunnottar not long before. *Wyntoun*, 2:430.

then returned to Perth. The Scottish author of the *Book of Pluscarden* considered that Edward had, for the moment at least, "subdued all beyond the highlands by fire and sword."[195]

Although Edward's *chevauchée* had eliminated any chance of a major French landing or Scottish offensive in the near future, the English king knew that only a network of secure fortifications on the model of Edward I's Welsh castles would enable him and Balliol to really control the country. New, elaborate fortifications for Perth, including a stone wall to replace the wooden peel, were begun, paid for by a special levy on six Scottish abbeys. Nearly 150 carpenters, masons, and ditch diggers were put to work strengthening the works at Stirling. The castles of Leuchars and St. Andrews and the tower of Falkland were rebuilt and garrisoned to secure Fife. A fortification at Kinclaven guarded the northern approach to Perth.[196] Perth, Stirling, and St. Andrews were put under men with personal stakes in the English dominion in Scotland: Thomas Ughtred, William Montague, and Henry Beaumont, respectively. In addition, a rather large field force under John of Eltham and Henry of Lancaster continued to operate in the southwest, wreaking havoc in areas which had not yet returned to Balliol's obedience. A new outpost of English control was established in Galloway at Laurieston, over fifty miles west of Lochmaben.[197] Once these arrangements were completed, King Edward returned to England, justifiably "considering himself secure about Scotland."[198]

Edward would probably have liked to stay in the north to oversee the consolidation of the defensive system he was setting up, but business even more important called him to Nottingham. In July of 1336, following the advice of the parliament which Edward had abandoned for the rescue of Lochindorb, the English government had sent a group of distinguished ambassadors to Philip VI to make another attempt to find some solution for the disagreements concerning Guienne and Scotland. The need to resolve outstanding issues in Gascony was made particularly acute when, on 11 July, the *parlement* of Paris finally declared Edward III to be in default of his 31,000 *livre* obligation to the Sire de Navailles. The embassy included the bishops of Durham and Winchester as well as Sir William Trussel and Richard Bintworth (the professor of civil law who had been on the negotiating team which came up with the draft Treaty of Newcastle, and future Bishop of London). They were empowered to arrange a personal meeting between the two kings in France; to treat concerning a joint crusade to the Holy Land, and even to agree to its timing, route, etc.; to make agreements on all current and future issues, cases, appeals, petitions, processes, etc., involving

---

195 *Pluscardensis*, 281.

196 *WBRF*, fo. 214 (stone wall); 215 (Stirling); *Pluscardensis*, 281–2. Kinclaven and Falkland may have been established slightly later or earlier. The work at Stirling lasted from 25 August to 19 October.

197 Ibid.; *Pluscardensis*, 281. For an idea of the extent of English control in the Dumfriesshire area, see *RFR*, II:2:960.

198 *Pluscardensis*, 282.

Gascony; and even to treat with David Bruce for a final peace between his adherents and Edward's. The grant of such broad powers – Edward promised to fulfill any agreement made by the ambassadors, or any three of them – indicates that this was a sincere effort on Edward's part to head off war with France.[199] In order to sidestep the impasse which had been reached in April, the English proposed, if a comprehensive peace including Scotland could not be worked out, to defer that thorny issue until later. Provided that the Scots would restore the lands which they had seized during the previous truce (i.e. in the aftermath of their victory at Culblean), Edward would grant them a truce of four or five years.[200] Meanwhile the crusade could proceed; goodwill among the Planta-genets and the Valois could build as they fought together against the infidels; and, at the end of the expedition to the Levant, Edward could receive justice and grace from Philip VI concerning the disputed lands in France. Then, in a spirit of friendship rather than hostility, they could try again to hammer smooth the remaining rough spots in the agreement they had negotiated over the Scottish succession.

Although these proposals seemed to the English to be more than reasonable (or so they said), from the standpoint of the Valois court they were less appealing. If the Scots handed back the lands they had captured after Culblean, they would be restoring Balliol's control over the majority of the country. In that case, a truce of four or five years would only give him time to consolidate his power in peace, and (with English financial help) build castles to further solidify his position. Such an agreement would also leave Moray and Douglas locked out of any chance of recovering or ruling the lands they claimed.

King Philip may have concluded that the course of negotiations thus far showed that Edward III had no stomach for a war with France, despite his bluster, for he had been willing to make concession after concession in the quest for peace. Once again the French king's negotiators took a hard line. The discussions went nowhere. On 20 August, the ambassadors were summoned to an audience with the king. Philip delivered his ultimatum. There would be no agreement unless the English agreed to restore *all* the Scots to the lands which they or their predecessors had held during his reign.[201] This meant at least that Montague, Bohun, Strathbogie and Percy would have to make way for Moray and Douglas; it might also mean, depending on how it was meant in relation to the Treaty of Newcastle, that Balliol would immediately have to step down in favor of David Bruce.

The Bishop of Durham and his colleagues would have none of this. They im-mediately objected that they were not authorized to make any such agreement, and that they doubted King Edward would have any interest in such peace terms anyway. Philip replied that he would, then, use all means at his disposal to aid

---

[199] *RFR*, II:2:941–2. Note also Déprez and Mirot, "Ambassades Anglais," no. LXVI ("cuj-usdam pacis reformande"), XVIII. The Gascony expert Henry of Canterbury also went.
[200] *KdL*, 49.
[201] *EMDP*, 436.

the Scots. His fleets and men-at-arms would shortly be dispatched to Scotland and to England to enforce the restoration of David Bruce's fortunes. After this shockingly blunt *démarche*, the French king closed the meeting with an observation which struck the ambassadors with chilling force: "It seems that all will not be well between the realms of England and France," he said, "until the same man is king of both."[202] As Jonathan Sumption wryly observes, this "made a firmer impression on the English than perhaps was intended."[203]

The English bishops instantly dispatched one of their clerks, William de Tikehill, to carry an oral report of Philip's "final answer" to King Edward and the council; they did not dare commit the French king's bellicose words to writing.[204] The incredible speed at which Tikehill traveled confirms that the news he bore was as urgent as the subsequent summaries of his report issued by the chancery claimed it was. Leaving Paris on 20 August, the clerk reached Dover late on the 23rd, and traveled that night all the way to London, via Canterbury, Rochester, and Dartford. From there, he rode post-haste to Northampton, where Archbishop Stratford, the chancellor, then was, arriving in the night of the 24th.

At that time Edward was thought to be in Perth, and the news was clearly too pressing to delay action until he could be contacted. The chancery sprang into action despite the late hour, preparing writs to the archbishops and bishops of the realm, thirty-one abbots and priors, the Sheriff of London, six earls, and thirty-five other magnates, summoning them to attend another Great Council to be held at Nottingham in thirty days (the practical minimum). The preamble to the writs explained that the king had received definite information that Philip, having rejected all proposals for peace, was gathering many men-at-arms, galleys, and sailing ships. The French king, the writs stated, intended to send them against England to aid the Scots in overthrowing English dominion in Scotland.[205]

---

202 Ibid., and writ in Delpit, *Collection générale*, 66; see also *Le Baker*, 58.

203 Sumption, *Trial by Battle*, 136. Sumption, like Déprez (*Préliminaires*, 97), has this episode take place earlier (apparently based on the somewhat chronologically confused account in *Le Baker*, 55–6), but it probably belongs to 1336 instead. It is clear from the accounts of William de Tikehill (*EMDP*, 779) and from the writs issued around the same time (see note 205) that it was not until late August of 1336 that Edward's ambassadors received the "final response" of Philip VI and his council which amounted to a declaration of war. From the credence provided by Edward III to his messengers to Pope Benedict XII in 1340, it is also clear that the insistence on total restitution for all the Scots and the remark about the two realms both were part of the final answer of the French king which led Edward to summon the parliament at which he broached his claim to the French throne, in early 1337. ("Audiens hoc"). Ibid., 436.

204 Tikehill's account, the foundation of the next three paragraphs, is published in *EMDP*, 778–81.

205 *RFR*, II:2:944; Delpit, *Collection générale*, 66. The comments of the *Grandes chroniques*, 9:158, are worth quoting for the light they cast on the relationship between the Scottish situation and the outbreak of war between England and France: "At this time, when Edward saw that King Philip of France would sustain the Scottish party due to the alliance

William got a little rest while the council prepared letters to inform the king of the steps they were taking to address the situation, then sped north to find his sovereign. Averaging over seventy miles a day, he reached Berwick on the 30th. He was somewhat delayed thereafter by lack of shipping and by the unwillingness of any soldiers to escort him through Lothian because of the proximity of William Douglas' guerillas. Eventually he did make it to Edinburgh, and from there to Perth, where he found the king. Edward returned to Berwick by 14 September, then hurried south to prepare for the meeting of the Great Council which his able chancellor had summoned in his name.[206]

Meanwhile there had been plenty of confirmation of the dire warnings carried by Tikehill. French ships raided the ports of Orton and Walford Roads and the Isle of Wight. English merchants and travelers in France were arrested and imprisoned.[207] The ambassadors themselves returned to England to describe their dramatic final encounter with Philip, and the Archbishop of Canterbury conveyed the story to the crowds from his pulpit.[208] To the extent that a state of war between the realms did not already exist, it seemed inevitable that it soon would. The council, although it was not a full parliament, nonetheless granted Edward III a substantial subsidy (a fifteenth from the counties, a tenth from the burgesses, and a tenth from the clergy, plus a heavy increase in the wool export tax) to finance "his wars in Scotland and Gascony."[209] The king, meanwhile, wrote to the seneschal of Aquitaine ordering him to put the castles of the duchy into a state of defense, and to redouble his activity and zeal in preparing for war.[210] John Thrandeston, Edward's agent in the Empire, traveled to the Continent to sound out the counts of Hainault and Guelders, the Marquis of Juliers, and the Duke of Brabant as potential allies against France.[211]

---

which Philip the Fair his uncle had made with the said Scots, he [Edward] prepared a great navy on the sea, and then made a great alliance with Louis of Bavaria [the Emperor] . . . who promised to aid him. Then there were very great commotions of battle between the two kings." Similarly, in the *Cont. Manuel, 1328–1339*, 1262, the heading "Of the War of France and England" is immediately followed by "In the year 1336 [1337 n.s.], because King Philip of France, formerly son of Count Charles of Valois, wanted to aid the Scots . . ."

206 *EMDP*, 779–80.
207 Sumption, *Trial by Battle*, 166.
208 *EMDP*, 436.
209 *Parliamentary History*, 241; *Knighton*, 1:477.
210 Déprez, *Préliminaires*, 134 (30 September); *RFR*, II:2:949 (20 October).
211 Thrandeston departed from the council at Nottingham on 14 September. For his accounts, see *KdL*, 154–4; *DEB*, 79–80 (Latin version with some additional information); note the dating by exchequer year, discussed ibid., p. 11, correcting Mirot and Déprez. William, Count of Hainault, was Edward's father-in-law. The Count of Guelders and Marquis of Juliers were his brothers-in-law (the former married to Edward's sister Eleanor, the latter married to Queen Philippa's sister). The Marquis of Juliers (in 1340 made Earl of Cambridge) had, furthermore, served in Edward's Scottish wars. All of them, as princes of the Imperial Low Countries, had reason to be hostile towards France. See Sumption, *Trial by Battle*, 192 ff., Lucas, *Low Countries*, passim, and below, Chapter 6. Cf. *RFR*, II:2:949–950. Other messengers were sent to Brittany, Germany, and Avignon. Ibid., 950; Mirot and Déprez, "Ambassades Anglaises," 563.

By late October, the threat of an immediate French invasion was effectively over: a major winter campaign in Scotland, especially after the devastation inflicted by Edward III's armies in the summer, was impossible, even if the French had been willing to risk transports full of soldiers in the rough seas of the season. The defensive fleet which the English government had assembled from impressed ships was allowed to turn to the more profitable business of bringing the year's wine production from Gascony to England. The king himself returned to Scotland to try to stabilize the English position there.

Andrew Murray had taken advantage of Edward III's absence to regain the initiative in Scotland. All three of the most remote English bases – Laurieston, Dunnottar and Kinneff – were captured and demolished in October. These losses were partly offset when, in the same month, Edward ordered the reconstruction of Bothwell castle in the middle of the western lowlands. There he remained through mid-December, supervising the work.[212] Then, leaving the defense of English Scotland to what local forces were available, he turned his attention to preparing for the upcoming war with France.

Before leaving Bothwell, the king had ordered preparations for the defense of England's coasts and the Duchy of Aquitaine.[213] He had also aggressively stepped up his diplomacy in the Low Countries. Various messengers were given letters of credence to move forward the negotiations with Hainault, Guelders, Juliers, and Namur, and to treat with the leaders of Flanders, the Archbishop of Cologne, and the Bishop of Liège. Powers were also prepared for the count of Hainault and Marquis of Juliers, in conjunction with two of Edward's men, to treat with any nobles or other persons about entering Edward's service.[214] The results of their diplomacy will be dealt with in the next chapter.

As Edward's men continued their work of recruiting allies in the Low Countries, Philip VI again moved the two realms closer to war. In November, a Franco-Scottish fleet raided the Channel Islands. On the day after Christmas, Philip sent a letter to the seneschal of Gascony demanding that Edward III extradite Robert of Artois, Philip's bitter enemy, who was under the English king's protection (perhaps in retaliation for the French king's harboring of David Bruce).[215] By addressing the demand to the seneschal of Gascony, Philip was making it known that this was an order of liege-lord to vassal, not a request of king to king, and reminding Edward of the duchy's vulnerability. The action was symbolic of much of the trouble over Gascony, for Artois was with Edward's court in England, not residing in Guienne. Thus, Edward was sheltering him as

---

212 Bothwell: *WBRF,* fos 206, 213v, 214, 215. The king's clerk in charge of the work at Stirling and Bothwell was Thomas Hatfield, the future Bishop of Durham, who later fought at Crécy.
213 *RFR*, II:2:951, 953.
214 *RFR*, II:2:952, 955 (William wrongly styled Count of Juliers); *KdL*, 155.
215 Demand: printed in Déprez, *Préliminaires*, 414–15. Edward's response: *KdL*, 31–3 (suggests link between sanctuary for Robert of Artois and David II).

King of England, not as Duke of Aquitaine: to surrender Artois would be a full admission that the consequences of Edward's homage to Philip extended even into his own realm, a principle that Edward could by no means afford to concede.[216]

The English government was now fully persuaded that war could not be prevented. In late January 1337, King Edward met with an assembly of magnates and prelates in the Tower of London. The royal prolocutor outlined once again the familiar points about the efforts Edward had made for peace, and about the lands in Aquitaine which Philip had steadfastly refused to return to Plantagenet rule. Then came the surprise: Edward was strongly considering the possibility of reasserting his claim to the French throne, which had been raised but quickly dropped on the death of Charles IV in 1328. The magnates and prelates were reminded that the king was then in his twenty-fifth year, and that by civil law (which allowed a plea of minority to contest alienation of inheritances made before that age) he was thus required either to lay claim to his heritage or to lose it. (The issue of Edward's claim to the French throne will be discussed in Chapter 8.) He concluded by asking whether the king should create a confederation of overseas allies in order to resist the French. The introduction of the dynastic issue implied a dramatic raising of the stakes: the lords were "stunned and astonished." After drawing apart to consider the matter, the council advised the king that to seek the crown of France would be extremely difficult, indeed almost impossible, and that he should send one more solemn embassy to seek peace before it was too late – but they also said that if Philip refused peace, then the construction of the Continental confederation should proceed.[217]

In February, a French official made the first serious attempt to impose the sentence passed on Edward III by the *parlement* as a consequence of the judgment in favor of the Sire de Navailles. The judgment had authorized the King of France to seize the revenues of the Duke of Aquitaine until the 31,000 *livre* debt was paid. The Master of Crossbowmen of France decided to start with the strategic border town of St. Macaire, which he attempted to capture by surprise. The effort failed, and there was no further military activity in the duchy over the winter, but all now knew that Philip's spring offensive would not be limited to coastal raiding or an expedition to Scotland.[218]

---

[216] Cf. the statement of principle in *EMDP*, 188. It is worth noting that it was only *after* this demand was made that Artois' presence became widely known in England, though Robert had been receiving substantial subsidies from Edward at least since November 1336 (by which date the king referred to him as "dilectis et fidelibus nostris"). *Historia Roffensis*, fo. 79v; *RFH*, 2:3:165; *DEB*, 47.

From Philip's perspective, on the other hand, what he was asking of Edward (the extradition of Robert of Artois) was only what he would have expected to be granted by *any* king or prince, "however foreign"; if he could not even get so much from the Plantagenet, then what was the point of receiving Edward's homage and fealty? Letter in Déprez, *Préliminaires*, 415.

[217] *Historia Roffensis*, fos 79–79v, and below, pp. 175–6.

[218] See Sumption, *Trial by Battle*, 173.

War was in the air at the parliament which met at Westminster on 3–16 March 1337. The Lords and Commons approved the decisions made at the January council, and granted Edward yet another subsidy without quibbling, a sign that they appreciated the full gravity of the situation. In accordance with parliament's advice, a last-ditch attempt was made to make an honorable peace with Philip before it was too late, but it is unlikely that anyone expected it to succeed.[219] The event which made the biggest impact on contemporary opinion, however, was a magnificent ceremony at which King Edward's eldest son was made Duke of Cornwall – the first time the title of duke was granted in England – and six other men were created earls. The new earls were a notably martial group, all among Edward's close circle of friends: William Montague, William Clinton, William Bohun, Robert Ufford, Henry of Lancaster, and Hugh Audley. All six had served in at least two of Edward's Scottish campaigns; all except perhaps Bohun had fought at Halidon Hill.[220] Except for Audley none could have been considered a great magnate (though Lancaster was the heir of one) were it not for personal grants received from Edward III.[221] The message to

---

[219] According to Edward, the ambassadors were to offer anything necessary for peace, short of surrendering his rightful inheritance (in which he presumably included suzerainty over Scotland and the full duchy of Guienne as Edward I had held it), but Philip refused even to meet with them. *KdL*, 49. The English were even were prepared to expel Robert of Artois from England if he were the last obstacle to peace. Ibid., 31–3. Indeed, if we can trust the testimony of the Bishop of Lincoln on the subject, Artois actually *was* expelled from England before December 1337, and not given support or protection by Edward at that time. *GGG*, 368–9. It was not until late March of 1338 that Edward granted Robert a large annuity, so this could well be true. *RFH*, 2:4:10.

[220] Montague, the new Earl of Salisbury, had served in Scotland in 1327, 1333, 1335, and 1336. Clinton, created Earl of Huntingdon, served in the Halidon Hill, 1335, and 1336 campaigns. Ufford, made Earl of Suffolk, had served in 1333, 1335, and 1336. Lancaster had participated in every campaign in Scotland from 1333 to 1336. Bohun (the new Earl of Northampton) had been on the Roxburgh campaign and the 1335 summer campaign, and in 1336 had served in Scotland and been given the castle and peel of Lochmaben in Annandale (*RFH*, 2:3:146, *RS*, 399); furthermore, although there is no definite evidence for his participation in the 1333 campaign, his brother Edward had served as Constable of England at Halidon and jointly commanded the vanguard (a fact which could have obscured William's presence), before dying while serving in Scotland in 1334. William, furthermore, was in receipt of robes as a household knight in the winter of 1333–34, which strongly hints at his presence at Halidon. BL, Add. MS 35181, m. 10. Hugh Audley (created Earl of Gloucester), who through his wife was one of the heirs of the Clare lineage, served on the 1333 campaign, and brought the princely retinue of 110 men-at-arms and 56 mounted archers on the 1335 offensive. (*WBRF*, fos 236v, 255v.) Most or all of these men had also served Edward III as ambassadors, negotiators, or in other administrative capacities, and several of them had been participants in the coup of 1330.
In addition to the creation of the new earls, a number of lesser men – including the Mayor of London – were knighted by the king at this time. *Annales Paulini*, 366.

[221] Bohun came from a great family (as a grandson of Edward I he was Edward III's first cousin), but his elder brother, the Earl of Hereford, had the lands.
As Andrew Ayton points out, these promotions served not only to reward past service, but to provide a much-needed group of senior captains for the army, with resources sufficient to fill that role, yet young enough for active campaigning. "Edward III and the English Aristoc-

ambitious young men-at-arms was clear: the road to prestige and wealth lay in military service to Edward III.[222] In the coming years, there would be no shortage of opportunities to travel down that road.

racy," *Armies, Chivalry and Warfare in Medieval Britain and France*, ed. M. Strickland (Stamford: Paul Watkins Publishing, 1998), 188–90.
[222] As in Napoleon's army where, it was said, every soldier felt as if he had a marshal's baton in his pack.

CHAPTER SIX

"GREAT EXPENSES AND LITTLE SUCCESS IN WAR": STRATEGY AND EDWARD III'S DIPLOMACY IN THE LOW COUNTRIES, 1337–1338[1]

Striving for the destruction of the enemy armed forces has a positive aim, and leads to positive successes, the ultimate object of which being the complete defeat of the adversary. The preservation of one's own armed forces has a negative aim, and so leads to the blocking of the adversary's designs, i.e. to pure resistance, the ultimate goal of which can only be to prolong the duration of the affair for so long that the opponent exhausts himself in it. Clausewitz, *Vom Kriege*, II.i.[2]

AS EDWARD III began to make plans for beginning his war in France, he was bombarded with historically based advice from a host of precedent-minded advisors. Unsurprisingly enough, most of this advice looked back to the reign of Edward I: though his invasion of France in 1297 had been beset with difficulties, it had at least succeeded in preventing the loss of Guienne.[3] The more distant and less successful campaigns of John Lackland were also brought to the young king's attention. Even the military principles recommended by the illustrious Ancients were cited.[4] These all had their influence on Edward, but probably none of them had as much impact on his approach to the upcoming war as did his own personal history. Since his childhood, he had witnessed a remarkable series of successful invasions: Mortimer and Isabella's in 1326; the Scots' in 1327; Edward Balliol's in 1332; his own in 1333; and also (to a somewhat lesser

---

[1] *Anonimalle*, 13: "illoeques demurra pur un an et pluis a costages graunde et poi a sa guerre esploitaunt." Cf. *Scalacronica*, 167: the alliances "cost very greatly of treasure, but profitted nothing."

[2] Carl von Clausewitz, *Vom Kriege*, II.i, p. 126.

[3] One memorandum, for example, argued that it was impossible for peace to be made between England and France except by returning to the principles agreed upon by Edward I and the French in 1303. PRO C47/30/6/14. Benedict XII, with his usual good sense, warned Edward III to read the annals and chronicles of the time of his grandfather. There, said the Pope, Edward could see how dangerous it would be to trust in German alliances. Quoted in Déprez, *Préliminaires*, 150. See also *Calendar of Entries in the Papal Registers Relating to Great Britain and Ireland*, 2:563.

[4] In Edward III's letter justifying his resort to war in 1339 (Walsingham, *Historia Anglicana*, 1:205); but despite the date the letter was justifying decisions made in 1337.

extent) the English campaigns in Scotland in 1335 and 1336. It is thus little wonder that he was willing to accept the "lessons of the theory of war, that he better avoids the dangers of war's commotions who distances it from the border of his own lands" and to conclude that his best course would be to engage his enemy with the aid of powerful allies, rather than alone.[5]

Like his grandfather Edward I in the 1290s, Edward III faced a whole array of threats and opportunities. No one doubted that there would be active campaigning in Scotland and Gascony at the least. Both sides of the Channel could also expect to suffer from the fires of war: the English were anxiously awaiting an invasion from France (one which was in fact being planned), and, in the tradition of Edward I and John, Edward III was seriously considering an attack on northern France.

Where, then, should the king focus his efforts? After the batterings the Scots had received at Dupplin Moor and Halidon Hill, not to mention in the invasions of 1335 and 1336, it seemed that a small force based around the retinues of the northern magnates would suffice to contain them. It was clear enough that even if Edward used 1337 to mount another major campaign in the north, the Scots would simply avoid him again, as they had done for the past two years. The armed force of their nation had already been broken. If the support they continued to receive from France could be stopped, then their will to resist could be expected to break as well. As an English privy councilor was to put it early in the next century, Scotland "is of it selfe, litle able to defende and lesse able to invade lyke a noune adjective that cannot stand without a substantive."[6]

France, in other words, was the wellspring of support for the Bruce cause, and if Edward wanted to finally secure his suzerainty over the northern realm, he would have to do so in France. The obvious way to win a favorable peace from Philip VI – one which would at least secure the official restoration of Guienne (as Edward I had held it) and Ponthieu, halt French support for David Bruce, and end or at least control the threat posed by the Gascon lawsuits before the *parlement*[7] – would be to advance into French territory, meet the royal army in battle, and defeat it. Set-piece battles, in Edward's experience, brought decisive political results.[8] True, in Scotland, those results had proved distressingly fleeting; but the Scots were able to persevere both because they were receiving external support and because they were fighting for their national life. France could hardly expect succor from foreign sources if defeated. Indeed, Benedict

---

5   Ibid., 207.
6   Halle, *Union of Lancaster and York*, fo. viii.
7   The minimum Edward was willing to accept before the outbreak of war, as indicated in *EMDP*, 435: "pro sola recuperatione ducatus predicti et ut a subsidio Scotorum se [Philippo] totaliter ammoveret." Cf. also *KdL*, 48, 31–3. After campaigning began in earnest, however, the minimum terms for an acceptable peace always included the provision that Edward's French lands be held in full sovereignty.
8   Dupplin Moor had put Balliol on the Scottish throne; Halidon Hill had restored him to it and won the eight counties of southeastern Scotland for England; even the much smaller fight at Culblean had meant the destruction of Balliol's power north of the Tay.

XII warned Philip that he could expect nothing but aggression from Imperial enemies and rebellion from discontented subjects if his military power were overthrown.[9] And the stakes were much lower for the Valois monarchy than for David Bruce's men, for the dynastic element which would later pose such an impediment to peace had not as yet come to the fore in the French war.

There was another major reason for the Plantagenet to seek a quick, decisive battle. England was, in relation to France, small, underpopulated, and not wealthy.[10] The French population was about triple England's, and Philip's regular revenues exceeded Edward's very substantially.[11] Ever since the days of Edward I, however, the English monarchy had been developing a solid working relationship with great Italian banking companies like the Bardi and Peruzzi. That relationship, combined with the consistent and substantial cash income provided by the export duties on English wool and Gascon wine, gave the kings of England an access to credit that probably surpassed that available to any other European rulers. Between May and October of 1337, for example, Edward borrowed about £100,000 (the equivalent of well over two years' worth of peace-time royal revenues) from the Bardi and Peruzzi alone, aside from the sums supplied by other lenders.[12] Certainly the French monarchy could not match his ability to anticipate future revenues through borrowing.[13] Furthermore, through the agency of parliament, Edward had the ability to mobilize the resources of his kingdom in support of his war efforts – so long as he could win the assent of the community of the realm – far more efficiently than was possible in Philip's het-erogeneous and parochial *royaume*. Of course, neither heavy taxation nor heavy borrowing could continue indefinitely, but in the short term Edward could not only match, but actually outspend, his Continental rival. With those expendi-

---

9 See Benedict's letter to Philip (*BLF,* no. 90); discussed in Déprez, *Préliminaires*, 114–15.

10 At the beginning of Edward III's reign, it had also been notably backward in military matters. See *Le Bel*, 1:155–6: "When the noble King Edward first reconquered England in his youth, one generally did not think much of the English: no one spoke at all of their prowess or their boldness."

11 English royal revenues before the beginning of Edward III's Scottish wars (excluding special subsidies and aids, which in some years could equal or exceed the regular revenues, but in most years of peace provided no income) were only about £37–40,000. Ramsay, *History of the Revenues of the Kings of England, 1066–1399*, 2: table facing p. 92, years 1329–31. Charles IV's revenues from 1322 to 1325, by contrast, averaged over 550,000 l.p. (about £137,500). Elizabeth Hallam, *Capetian France, 987–1328* (Harlow: Longman Group, 1980), 293.

12 *CPR, 1334–38*, 517, 541–2. Cf. Déprez, *Préliminaires*, 159 n.2, but note that the second loan he mentions was actually just part of the first. Paul de Monte Florum, the king's clerk, raised additional loans of £21,229 and £12,212, probably also secured from a group of bankers. Additional loans of approximately £7,750 came from Richard de la Pole and others. *CPR, 1334–38*, 518, 526, 538, 541–2, 545.

13 Richard W. Kaeuper, *War, Justice and Public Order. England and France in the Later Middle Ages* (Oxford: Clarendon Press, 1988), 5, 32–3, 52–4; cf. the expedients to which Philip VI was reduced, as described in the *Cont. Manuel, 1328–39*, 1263–4.

tures, he could afford to assemble and pay an army large and powerful enough to go head-to-head with the intimidating might of the French royal host.[14]

The key, then, was to win the war quickly.[15] Two obvious paths to the decisive battle he sought presented themselves to Edward: an advance into France from Gascony (where a French invasion army was expected to arrive in the near future, and where royal assistance seemed desperately needed), or, in the tradition of Edward I, a full-blown cross-Channel attack on northern France. At first, Edward favored the Gascon approach.[16] The retention or loss of Guienne was, after all, the main fighting-point of the war on the Continent. The members of his council, however, did not approve. The excellent English intelligence service had already provided them with extensive information on the French plans and preparations for an invasion of Britain – information which Edward's clerks had used to the fullest in royal propaganda.[17] The royal councilors were worried that, if the king sailed off for his distant Duchy of Aquitaine, Philip might simply fight a holding action in the south while concentrating his main power for a cross-Channel strike to England's heart. Primarily for that reason, they favored operations in the north of France.[18]

The deteriorating relationship between Valois France and the princes of the Imperial Low Countries also helped make this latter approach attractive. Edward was well aware of the situation there, for his agents and ambassadors had been active in the region at least since April of 1335.[19] Furthermore, his marriage to Philippa of Hainault gave him extensive kinship relations with the greatest nobles of the area. Between them, his brothers-in-law and his father-in-law controlled the counties of Hainault, Holland, Zeeland, Guelders, and Zutphen and the Marquisate of Juliers; the emperor too was his brother-in-law. Doubtless Robert of Artois also provided the English king with insight into Low Countries affairs.

Although the County of Flanders was a fief of the French crown, most of the rest of the Low Countries was held by vassals of the Holy Roman Emperor,

---

[14] As Pierre Dubois pointed out around 1300, the royal army of France had become *so* strong that the king's enemies no longer dared face it, leading to a new set of strategic problems. *Summaria Brevis et Compendiosa*, 2.

[15] Cf. G. L. Harriss, *King, Parliament, and Public Finance in Medieval England to 1369* (Oxford: Clarendon Press, 1975), 231–3.

[16] As late as 12 June 1337 he still planned to embark for Gascony with his main force, leaving his Imperial allies in the north to draw away at least some of the French royal forces. *RFR*, II:2:974; cf. ibid., 964. There is some evidence that Edward may initially have intended to send an army under the earls of Northampton and Salisbury to Gascony, while himself staying in England to guard the realm. See *Lanercost*, 289; *Anonimalle*, 9. An invasion of Normandy was also considered. *KdL*, 38.

[17] Ellis, *Original Letters*, 30–2; *RFR*, II:2:946, 950, 951, 953, etc.

[18] Sumption, *Trial by Battle*, 205. This was a reasonable fear; cf. the French plan of 1339 (n.s.), printed in *Avesbury*, 205–8.

[19] Mirot and Déprez, "Ambassades Anglais," no. LIV. In the summer, *WBRF*, fos 209, 211v; *RFR*, II:2:928. Furthermore, he must have received information on the state of affairs there from the counts of Namur and Juliers, who attended him in Scotland in 1335.

Ludwig of Bavaria. In this period, the Empire was little more than a confederation of practically sovereign principalities, and men like the Duke of Brabant or the counts of Guelders, Namur and Hainault ran their own affairs. Philip VI's policy was to take advantage of their disunity to extend his power into lands that were nominally Imperial fiefs, despite a long-standing convention forbidding the kings of France from acquiring lands within the Empire.[20] It was in pursuit of this policy that, early in 1337, the Valois king unwisely arranged to buy extensive lands in five areas of the Cambrésis from Béatrix de Saint-Pol, the Dame de Nesle, for Prince Jean.[21] This was a direct encroachment on the ambitions of William, Count of Hainault, Holland and Zeeland and nominal Lord of Friesland, Philip's own brother-in-law, who had already arranged to buy two of these fortresses, Crèvecoeur-sur-l'Escaut and Arleux, and had even partially paid for them.[22]

William, a very influential man who numbered both Edward III and the emperor among his sons-in-law,[23] had in the past been a strong supporter of Philip VI. But the French king had greatly angered William in 1332. The count had contracted a marriage alliance between his daughter and the eldest son of John, Duke of Brabant. But Philip, fearing that all these marriage alliances were making William dangerously strong in the Low Countries, convinced John to break off the wedding, and have his son marry one of Philip's own daughters instead. This seemed a poor return for William's past support of the Valois king.[24] He had therefore drawn closer to his sons-in-law, Edward III and the emperor, neither of whom was on the best terms with France. The count had been negotiating with the English at least since December of 1335, and a year later he had even received a commission to treat with other nobles about entering into Edward's service.[25] William might never have made use of the document, however, had Philip's underhanded purchase of the lands in the Cambrésis not pushed the count into open support for the English.[26] He began to take the lead in the construction of a powerful coalition of Philip's enemies.[27]

This proved easy enough to do, for Edward III's ambassadors had already laid much of the groundwork. Reginald, Count of Guelders and Zutphen, and

---

20 *Le Bel*, 1:141.

21 Lucas, *Low Countries*, 195–6, Trautz, *Könige*, 227, and *Le Bel*, 1:141 n.2.

22 See the younger William of Hainault's letter in *KdL*, 137.

23 The Marquis of Juliers was also his son-in-law; his son (also William) was married to the Duke of Brabant's daughter. *Récits*, 160.

24 *Grandes chroniques*, 9:127–8.

25 *RFR*, II:2:928, 955. This latter was in the aftermath of John Thrandeston's first embassy, on which see *KdL*, 154–5; *DEB*, 79–80; Trautz, *Könige*, 226–9.

26 Philip had made his first attempt to acquire the lands back in 1335, but only succeeded (despite the protests of the Emperor) in 1337, after William had been given the commission by Edward III, apparently in response to a favorable answer given by the count to the king's envoy on 3 November 1336. *RFR*, II:2:955; *KdL*, 155; Trautz, *Könige*, 227.

27 See the defiance sent by his son (also William, Count of Hainault, etc.) to Philip VI in 1340, printed in *KdL*, 136–40, esp. pp. 136–7.

William, Marquis of Juliers, Edward's brothers-in-law, were solidly in the English camp.[28] The emperor, who like William of Juliers was Edward's brother-in-law and William of Hainault's son-in-law, was also glad to see the opportunity to oppose Philip's ambitions on Imperial territory. This was especially true because, aside from his border encroachments, Philip actively supported the Luxembourg faction in their anti-Hapsburg and anti-Bavarian activities within the Empire.[29]

As part of his plan to expand this circle, William of Hainault called for a major conference on Franco-Imperial (and Anglo-French) relations to convene in his capital, Valenciennes. Philip and his Low Countries allies, notably the prince-bishops of Cambrai and Liège, were invited, along with Edward's partisans and the lords who as yet remained uncommitted. But by the time the conference opened in early May, there remained little hope of peace between France and England. Edward had already received a subsidy from parliament for the conduct of his wars in France and Scotland, and Philip had refused to receive a last-ditch peace embassy from England.[30] Both sides had begun raising troops and funds for the upcoming campaigning season in Gascony. Less than a week before the opening of the Valenciennes conference, the *arrière-ban* had been proclaimed throughout France.[31]

The magnates who attended the conference were, thus, well aware that any alliance with England would probably equate to war with France. The prospect was worrisome: their territories, unlike England, were not protected from French invasion armies by the Channel. Most of them held at least some property in France, which could be subject to confiscation in the event of war. Their confidence in protection from England can hardly have been strengthened by the memory of 1297, when Edward I had abandoned his Imperial allies once promised the restitution of Aquitaine. But even so, the distinguished representa-

---

[28] Reginald was married to Edward's sister Eleanor; William, who had served Edward in 1327 and 1335 and received a pension from him, was the husband of Queen Philippa's sister. As noted above, in 1335 Juliers' retinue had included two additional counts (one of whom was likely Adolph of Berg), and in 1336 Thierry, Lord of Heinsberg, another veteran of the Stanhope Park campaign, had become Count of Looz.

[29] John of Luxembourg, King of Bohemia – the son of one Holy Roman Emperor and the father of another – had long been a close ally of Philip VI; one of his first battles was Cassel in 1328, and his last was Crécy, where he died fighting for Philip. He was also the father-in-law of the future Jean II. On his position in 1336, see Lucas, *Low Countries*, 192.

[30] Letter of Edward III in *Bridlington*, 132, and *KdL*, 49 (embassy); *Chronographia*, 2:32 (conference date). See also *Le Bel*, 1:119–28. Furthermore, according to the *Historia Roffensis* (fo. 80), Philip sent messengers to the Hainault conference who bluntly asserted that he did not wish for peace with the King of England. See also *EMDP*, 287. It is worth noting that the English ambassadors were willing to make a reasonable compromise, one acceptable to Philip, concerning Robert of Artois: provided that the other grounds for war were dealt with (particularly regarding Scottish affairs), they offered to expel him from England if he could not satisfactorily clear himself. *KdL*, 31–3; Sumption, *Trial by Battle*, 196.

[31] Sumption, *Trial by Battle*, 184. The calling up of the *arrière-ban* was probably more an expedient to raise funds by taxing those who did not participate than a sign of actual military activity: cf. *Cont. Manuel, 1328–39*, 1263.

tives sent by Edward III to the conference – Henry Burghersh, Bishop of Lincoln, and the newly created earls of Salisbury and Huntingdon – managed to overcome these fears. Their main tool to that end was the promise of cash subsidies from England.

These were extraordinarily generous: the Count of Berg, for example, was granted £1,800 in subsidies, a pension of £180 per year, and an additional £225 per month in wages for the service of a mere hundred men-at-arms.[32] With just the £225, at the standard rates for service in England, Edward could instead have paid a hundred English men-at-arms *and* a hundred mounted archers; the count's £180 pension would have sufficed to pay more than two hundred additional Welsh foot archers for a three-month campaigning season.[33] The £1,800 subsidy far exceeded the total value of the three fighting ships in the royal navy, and matched the total of just £1,824 5d. sent from England in support of the Guienne war effort in the 1338–39 fiscal year.[34] Yet the Count of Berg was among the least powerful of the Imperial magnates retained by Edward III, and his subsidy among the smallest awarded.

More typical of the deals cut by the greater princes of the Low Countries is the arrangement the English ambassadors made with William, Count of Hainault, Holland and Zeeland.[35] William was promised a subsidy of no less

---

[32] *RFR*, II:2:970, 971 (Adolph "de Monte"). For the exchange rate between florins (in which most of the transactions with Imperial vassals are figured) and sterling, which is 100 fl. = £15 (i.e. 1 fl. = 3s.) see ibid., 984.

[33] The standard wage rates for service in Britain were 1 shilling per day for men-at-arms, 6d. or less for mounted archers (who were often actually paid *less* for service in Scotland than in England – 4d. instead of 6d. – on the theory that they could draw part of their "wages" in enemy territory from plunder), and 2d. for Welsh foot. *WBRF*, fo. 252v. In 1338–40, Edward paid his English men-at-arms double wages for service on the Continent. Horsed archers still received 6d., but foot troops, including Welshmen, received 3d. *WBWN*, 326, 356, 360. At these inflated rates, the local men-at-arms were actually 25% cheaper than English men-at-arms, if only their base wage is considered. Still, even at the inflated wage rate, for the cost of Adpolph's service (subsidy and pension) and the wages of his 100 men-at-arms for three months, Edward could instead have paid the wages of (for example) an English earl with a retinue of 4 bannerets, 13 knights, 150 men-at-arms *and* 250 mounted archers *and* 250 foot archers for the same period!

[34] Gascony subsidy – £9,120 and 2 sous of Bordeaux, in the form of 196 sacks of wool (not, as Sumption, *Trial by Battle*, 234, says, 196 sacks of wool *and* £1,824 cash): PRO E101/166/11, m. 7 (cf. m. 10 for £/l.b. conversion). Ships: Sumption, *Trial by Battle*, 175.

[35] *RFR*, II:2:970–2, 984. Sumption, *Trial by Battle*, 198, gives the subsidies to Hainault, Juliers and Guelders as £15,000, but the treaties actually call for *two* payments of £15,000 each, in addition to the advance wage payment: "nous lui ferons deliverer, par dela le mer, en liu seur & certain, cent mille florins de Florence, ou quinze mille libres d'estrelings, pour le sommes des florins dessusditz, dedens le jour Saint Pere, entrant Aoust procheinement venant.

Et encore, outre chou, autres cent mille florins de Florence . . . dedens le jour dou quaremme prendant prochainement ensuivant, ou dedens les octaves du dit jour, sanz mal enghien." *RFR*, II:2:984–5, here at 984; also in *Treaty Rolls* with no significant differences. The total of 200,000 florins in two payments is confirmed by the Bishop of Lincoln's letter in *GGG*, 367.

It is interesting to compare these treaties with the one made among the counts of Hainault

than £30,000 in exchange for raising a thousand men-at-arms for Edward's wars. In addition, when he joined Edward's army in the field, he was to receive two months' wages for his men (£4,500) in advance. If he or any of his men were captured while in English service, they were to be ransomed or exchanged by Edward; in return, all the prisoners the Hainaulters captured would be turned over to the king. The men-at-arms were also to receive full *restor* (compensation) for any horses, other than baggage horses, lost in war.

There were territorial elements to William's agreement as well as these fiscal ones. If his lands in France were confiscated by Philip (as seemed nearly certain), he would be compensated with lands in England worth 6,000 l.t. (£1,200) per year. If the allies captured the towns of Crèvecouer-sur-l'Escaut, Arleux, or St. Sulpice (some of the disputed lands in the Cambrésis purchased by Philip from the Dame de Nesle), these would immediately be transferred to him. And, if Philip threatened to conquer William's counties within the Empire, the count could raise a thousand men-at-arms for their defense at English expense, or even two thousand if necessary, and retain them until Edward arrived or (for the first thousand) for up to one year. This last clause alone represented a potential financial commitment of well over £30,000.[36]

The Count of Guelders and the Marquis of Juliers received terms essentially identical to Hainault's.[37] John, Duke of Brabant, Lotharingia and Limburg, who was less inclined to oppose Philip, procured the promise of the whopping sum of £60,000, and also got potentially very lucrative licenses for his subjects to buy wool in England for their textile mills. He even secured marginally more favorable terms of service for the twelve hundred men he was to raise for Edward's service: they were not required to hand over prisoners they took, but they would still themselves be ransomed by Edward if captured.[38] Emperor Ludwig, who had his own axe to grind with Philip of Valois, did not have to be bribed quite so extravagantly. He promised to bring two thousand men-at-arms for a subsidy of £60,000, plus wages, a sum exactly proportional to the amounts promised to

and Flanders and the Duke of Brabant in 1336. See H. Laurent, *Actes et documents anciens intéressant la Belgique conservés aux archives de l'état à Vienne, 1196–1356* (Brussels: Lamertin, 1933), no. 76. This treaty included mutual defense provisions requiring each signatory to raise 500 men-at-arms and 10,000 armed infantry when needed to aid the others.

[36] The wages for 1,000 men-at-arms for one year would be £27,000, so if the second 1,000 men were retained even for as little as two months, the total bill would reach £31,500. This agreement was made jointly with Hainault, Guelders and Juliers and applied to any of them, but apparently not to each of them separately – i.e. it could not be used to require Edward to pay for the wages of 6,000 men-at-arms, only for 2,000.

[37] *RFR*, II:2:985, 972. The only differences were that Juliers received an extra gift of £5,000 and was promised £200 more of lands within England to compensate for confiscated lands in France; also, obviously, neither Juliers nor Guelders was promised title to the three towns.

[38] *RFR*, II:2:971–2, 981. It is possible that in theory the £60,000 represented a subsidy of £50,000 and the favorable settlement of an unspecified claim for £10,000 he had against Edward (*RFR*, II:2:974), but in practical terms it was all money paid to Brabant to secure his alliance and military service. On Brabant's attitude towards the English and the French see Lucas, *Low Countries*, 210–11, 214–16.

Hainault, Guelders and Juliers.[39] In a separate document, the emperor also promised that if he himself were unable to take part in an invasion of France within six weeks after the first £45,000 of his subsidy were paid, he would make Edward his vicar-general.[40] The counts of Looz and Marck, the Count Palatine of the Rhine, the emperor's son the Margrave of Brandenburg, and the Lord of Valkenburg were offered a total of about £15,000 in subsidies, plus wages, *restor*, and ransom for their 750 men-at-arms.[41]

Edward's total obligation for cash subsidies – not including wages, *restor*, ransoms, compensation for lost lands, defense expenditures while awaiting the arrival of the English, or pensions – thus amounted to over £225,000, in return for which his allies were to provide more than seven thousand men-at-arms.[42]

---

[39] *RFR*, II:2:991–2. Note that this agreement was ratified by Edward III much later than the other major treaties, on 26 August. Rymer's heading for this document states that the payment due to the emperor was 300,000 florins (£45,000), a reading which has been accepted by subsequent historians (Déprez, *Préliminaires*, 152; Lucas, *Low Countries*, 219; McKisack, *Fourteenth Century*, 122; and Sumption, *Trial by Battle*, 198), but actually the agreement promises a payment of 300,000 florins on 29 September 1337 *and* another 100,000 florins on 2 February 1338: "vobis . . . in festo Sancti Michaelis proximò, tribus vicibus, centum milia florenorum auri de Florentiâ, et centum milia, consimilium florenum in festo Purificationis Beatae Mariae Virginis subsequenti . . . solvi et praesentari" [to pay and present to you . . . on next September 29, three times 100,000 gold florins of Florence, and 100,000 of the same florins on February 2 following.] The total of 400,000 rather than 300,000 florins is confirmed by the document discussed in Lucas, *Low Countries*, 292, and the one printed in *DEB*, 120. The reading of "tribus vicibus, centum milia" as calling for 300,000 on Michaelmas 1337, as opposed to three installments of 100,000 on successive Michaelmases, is somewhat unclear (though the singular "festo" indicates the former reading), but other documents clarify that 300,000 in 1337 is indeed what is meant. See the size of the king's anticipated debt for the spring of 1338 (below) and the letter of 20 July 1337 in *GGG*, 361, which refers to a payment of 300,000 ("tercentum milia") florins to be made prior to Edward's exercising his powers as vicar or the start of the expedition against Philip. Although the treaty with the emperor was ratified a good deal later than the other major treaties, some agreement between the ambassadors and the emperor had probably been reached before the last day of June, when an agreement reached with the count palatine specified that, after two months, his men should receive the same pay as Ludwig's. *RFR*, II:2:980. Before 20 July, Edward had asked the Pope for permission to make an alliance with Ludwig, despite the sentence of excommunication which had much earlier been passed on the latter. Lucas, *Low Countries*, 237.

[40] *GGG*, 361

[41] *RFR*, II:2:979–80, 982–3, 992, 970–1, 973. I have counted the Lord of Valkenburg as providing 200 men-at-arms, though the documents are not clear on this. Different letters were prepared for him; the first offered him £180 in pension and £1,800 in subsidy for the service of 100 men-at-arms; the others, which were not fully transcribed in the records, offered double the pension and subsidy – and so I presume called for double the military service, even though this is not specified. It is fairly clear from *DEB*, no. 316, that he took the larger subsidy.

[42] Above, notes 33–41, counting the gift of £5,000 to Juliers, and figuring the subsidy of the Duke of Brabant at £60,000. The main allies noted above were to provide 7,050 troops, and there were a number of smaller contractors such as John de Quatremars, who received a subsidy of £180, a pension of £18 and wages for 10 men-at-arms. *RFR*, II:2:985. (And see also *DEB*, nos. 197, 208, 212, 219, 313, 314, 316, 358, 372, 401, 404, 408, 432, 433, 522.)

Some £32,000 more would be due at the start of the campaign for their first two months' pay; thereafter each month's campaigning would cost the English king around £16,000 more for just these men – unless, that is, these wages were deemed insufficient, in which case Edward had provided for them to increase by a third after the first two months. The costs of ransom and *restor*, which could be very substantial (especially if the war went badly) would be in addition to these sums.[43]

To put these figures into perspective, bear in mind that £16,000 was greater than the total spent on the wages of men-at-arms and archers for the field armies in Scotland in 1336, and more than double the annual "old revenues" of the English crown (county and borough farms, quitrents, forest receipts, wardships, marriages, escheats, etc.).[44] The £225,000 in subsidies matched the income generated by the lay subsidies of 1326–27, 1331–32, 1333–34, the double grant of 1335–36, and the 1336–37 lay subsidy *combined*. It was more than nine times the total wage bill for Edward's armies in 1335, the year of the "great offensive" in Scotland.[45]

Despite the almost incomprehensible scale of the expenditures promised by his ambassadors, Edward was quite happy to approve their arrangements. The treaty with Ludwig of Bavaria was ratified in late August, over three months after the agreement with the Count of Berg. Though the deal with the latter was on a much smaller scale than the arrangement with the emperor, it was roughly in the same proportions.[46] Edward had made no attempt to rein in his representatives' extravagance in the interim; indeed, it seems that he must have actively supported it.

This does not include the contingents of Jean d'Hainault (which may have been subsumed in the count's) or Otto of Cuyk (who, like Jean, was already Edward's retainer), nor of Everhard of Limburg, who together could probably provide more than 500 men-at-arms. Note that these figures also do not include the 500 men-at-arms to be provided by the Archbishop of Trier, or the 100,000 florins (£15,000) of subsidy he was to receive, since his alliance was not purchased until September of 1338, and was never implemented. *DEB*, 112–15, 147.

[43] Consider that at the end of the 1339 campaign, Edward III owed the Marquis of Juliers 20,000 florins for the loss of horses and other damages suffered in his service, compared to only 7,000 florins for the wages for his men's "second month" of service (which may actually have only been about half a month). *RFH*, 2:4:58; cf. also 2:4:96. It was more typical, however, for this benefit to cost about 10% as much as wages: Ayton, *Knights and Warhorses*, 121.

[44] 1336: *WBRF*, fos 244, 260. The "old revenues" for the 1345–46 fiscal year, for example, amounted to only £7,360. Ramsay, *Revenues of the Kings of England*, 293. For one more comparison, consider that the annual land income of Thomas of Lancaster, the greatest magnate of the realm, was under £7,000. Fowler, *King's Lieutenant*, 226.

[45] Parliamentary subsidies: Ramsay, *Revenues of the Kings of England*, 295. 1335: the Wardrobe paid £25,402 in wages of men-at-arms and archers for the year, a figure which also includes Balliol's ultramontane *chevauchée* and some costs for warding the march. *WBRF*, fos 239v, 258v. Compare also the summary of Walter Wetwang's account book, printed in Grose, *Military Antiquities*, 278.

[46] The Count of Berg agreed to provide 5% as many men as Emperor Ludwig, on the same wage terms, and was promised 3% as great a subsidy, but also a life pension.

Edward III, like both his grandfathers (Edward I and Philip the Fair), had a tendency to push his resources to the limit and beyond in pursuit of his military ambitions.[47] We have already seen something of this tendency in him during the Roxburgh campaign in 1334–35, when he seemed unable to comprehend why he could not gather the large army he wanted for a winter campaign in Scotland. Never in his reign, however, did the gap between his plans and their results yawn so wide as here, in the construction of his Low Countries alliances.

Edward may have had an exaggerated idea of what his realm could do, and an even more exaggerated idea of what it *would* do, but still he was by no means a stupid man. He did not ratify the subsidy treaties until he had at least the outlines of a plan of how to meet the commitments he had incurred. This plan was finalized at a meeting of the council and some leading representatives of England's merchant community at Westminster around 26 July, but its basic provisions had been worked out at least a month earlier.[48] In essence, it was a simple idea, even an elegant one.[49] The price of wool on the Continent had risen steeply when the supply from England was cut to a trickle by Edward's export prohibition.[50] If most of the wool in England[51] were purchased by the crown at the usual prices, then sold on the Continent at the inflated prices, a huge profit would be made. Furthermore, since the wool could be purchased in England on credit (partly because the sellers had no other market because of the export restraints, and partly because of royal compulsion through the right of purveyance[52]), the merchants handling the transaction for the king would be able to

---

[47] Throughout the late medieval and early modern periods, it was almost always the demands of military expenditures which stretched royal resources to and beyond their old limits. The efforts to meet those demands, by a process of Lamarckian evolution, propelled the growth of the state. This is perhaps a consequence of the nature of war, which inherently tends to push combatants to the outer edge of the possible. Cf. Clausewitz, *Vom Kriege*, I.1.5 ("Äußerste Anstrengung der Kräfte"), 93.

[48] *CPR, 1334–38*, 480–2; Fryde, *William de la Pole*, 62–3.

[49] Fryde agrees that it was "practicable" and essentially sound. *William de la Pole*, 54, 56.

[50] Lucas, *Low Countries*, 244, argues that the £200,000 to be loaned by the merchants was just an advance on the king's share of the *profit*, which would indicate that the wool was expected to sell at about £18–£20 per sack. This seems inordinately high, even though, as Lucas points out, *Knighton* (2:2) does (wrongly) state that the king's wool was sold in Brabant for £20 per sack. Cf. also *Bridlington*, 133. However, since (1) the merchants evaluated their own wool at only about £10 per sack in the spring of 1338 (after another half-year of embargo since July) (2) the government got only about 14 marks per sack for wool sold in Bordeaux in 1339, and (3) the Florentine chronicler Giovanni Villani estimated the value of the wool and treasure aboard the first fleet only at around £90,000, it seems unlikely that the merchants ever expected to get much more than £10 per sack. Fryde, *William*, 85–6 (merchants); PRO E101/166/11 m. 7 (Bordeaux); Villani, *Cronica*, 368. In 1340, and again in 1341, the king's advisers only expected to get 10 marks per sack sold. PRO C47/2/233; *RFR*, II:2:1173.

[51] The plan called for the purchase of 30,000 sacks, while the total annual growth of wool was estimated at somewhere between 30,000 and 50,000. Lucas, *Low Countries*, 5, 279. In 1338, the wool crop was expected to total 40,000 sacks. See p. 150, below.

[52] It seems that the king did not expect great resistance from the sellers, for the writs to those

provide him with a loan of £200,000 – roughly three-quarters of which would in effect be an interest-free loan from the sheep owners of England to the king.[53] This loan was officially expected to be paid back in two semi-annual install-ments, but Edward doubtless had it in his mind that the repayment could be delayed if necessary. The net profits from the sale (which could perhaps have neared £100,000) would be split equally between the royal government and a syndicate of ninety-six merchants headed by a London alderman, Reginald Conduit, and the unscrupulous but highly capable northern merchant, William de la Pole. The £200,000 loan, combined with the income from the subsidies granted by parliament, the export duties on the wool, and Edward's share of the net profits of the wool sale, would just make it possible to meet the obligations he had incurred in the Netherlands, so long as the war did not continue too long.[54]

Edward seems to have been operating under the assumption that, in the event, he would not need to retain his Imperial allies' men-at-arms for more than a couple of months.[55] Philip had repeatedly declared that, if Edward invaded France, he would be met in battle before the day was out.[56] Edward had little reason to doubt this: after all, even the Scots – whose traditional national strategy centered on the avoidance of battle – had been willing to risk their armies at Dupplin Moor and Halidon Hill. Could the French, noted for their "ancient martial glory"[57] and the power of their army, be expected to do any less?

Battle was always a gamble, but Edward believed he had inside information as to who would win the bet. With his own forces and those of his Imperial allies, he would be able to match the number of men-at-arms in any army Philip

charged with buying the wool specified only a price for the best-quality wool, the rest was to be bought "at such lower price as the vendors will agree to." *CPR, 1334–38*, 480.

53 Technically, the members of the merchant syndicate, as the king's purveyors, were buying the wool from the owners on their own credit. The £200,000 loan to the king was officially from the merchants, and was secured on the king's customs revenues, on which they were to have first claim until they were fully repaid. But, if the wool were purchased for an average of £5 on credit, £150,000 of that sum would ultimately have come from the sheep owners.

54 For this whole transaction, see *RFR*, II:2:989, 988; *EMDP*, 1:294; *CPR, 1334–38*, 480; Fryde, *William de la Pole*, chs 6–7. Profits: If the 30,000 sacks had been sold at £10 (above, note 50), the net profit from the sale (allowing £1 per sack for expenses and £5 for the pur-chase of the wool, and deducting £1 for the customs duty) would have been in the area £90,000, of which half was to go to the crown. Edward would also receive an additional £1 per sack, or £30,000, as the customs duties (at a slight discount), for a total of £75,000. The £30,000 in duties were to be set off against the debt to the merchants, and this may also have been the plan for the profits, so that Edward would receive a loan of £200,000, of which he would have to pay back only around £125,000.

55 This is indicated by the course of the 1339 campaign. See Chapter 7, below.

56 At least, this is what Edward III claimed in a letter to his eldest son in 1339: "nostre cosyn Phelip de Valoys avoit tous jours jurez a ceo que nous avoioms nouelx que nous ne ferroms jammes demeore une jour od nostre host en Fraunce q'il ne nous durroit bataille." *RFR*, II:2:1094. See also *Knighton*, 2:11–12; *Bridlington*, 138–9.

57 Petrarch, quoted by Boutruche, "The Devastation of Rural Areas," 26.

seemed likely to be able to assemble.[58] Then his longbowmen, whose value he fully appreciated after Dupplin Moor and Halidon Hill, though likely Philip did not, would tip the balance in his favor, for the French had nothing to match them.[59] It was reasonable, furthermore, to think that winning a single battle would be enough to win the war, given that Edward's war aims at this stage (before the dynastic issue was brought into play in 1340) were relatively modest.

So, though Edward's diplomacy in the spring of 1337 was certainly prodigal, it was not completely beyond the limits of the practicable. Still, there were serious flaws in the king's plan, both strategically and administratively. The strategic error – the assumption that Philip would cooperate by quickly coming to give battle to the invaders – will become apparent in the discussion of the 1339 campaign in the next chapter. The administrative failures were typical of the young Edward III: he consistently underestimated the difficulty of using royal power to coerce his subjects into doing what they had no desire to do. Surrendering their wool for credit tallies – and at relatively low prices at that – definitely fell into that category.[60] The king's administrators found collecting even a fraction of the requisite thirty thousand sacks to be far more difficult than they had ever imagined.[61] As we shall see, Edward equally overestimated his officers' ability to manage such a complex transaction effectively, and underestimated the participants' drive to earn corrupt profits by abusing the system at his expense.

This analysis has carried us away from our narrative. Let us return to the eventful month of June, 1337. On 7 June, William of Hainault, the man who had organized the conference at Valenciennes, died. His eldest son (also William) succeeded him as Count of Hainault, Holland and Zeeland, and also, by prearrangement, took his father's place in all the treaties with England.[62] Six days later and many miles away, Oliver Ingham, Edward's seneschal of Aquitaine, received formal notification from French royal officials that the duchy had been declared confiscated. Ingham tried to stall the inevitable start of military action by making an appeal of the sentence to the court of the Peers of France (of whom Edward, as Duke of Aquitaine, was one), but without success. Ingham

---

58 In fact the French king proved in 1340 that he could under the right circumstances muster a phenomenal number of men-at-arms, so many that even with his allies Edward could not hope to match them, but in 1337 Edward's advisors clearly did not anticipate this; they probably expected to face something more like the substantial French army at Crécy, which included about 8,000 knights and esquires (as did also the French royal host at Breteuil in 1356). Edward III, letter to Thomas Lucy, in Chandos Herald, *The Black Prince*, 353–4; *Avesbury*, 463. If that had been the case, and his allies had met their quotas, Edward would have had to bring only about 2,000 English men-at-arms to surpass the French forces in this area, a figure not too difficult to meet.

59 As was fully demonstrated at Crécy. See below, Chapter 11.

60 *Murimuth*, 80. Part of the reason for the owners' unwillingness to part with the wool was that it was commonly believed that each sack, which Edward was purchasing for about £5–£6, was then being sold in Brabant for £20. *Knighton*, 2:2.

61 Lucas, *Low Countries*, 237–8. *CPR, 1334–38*, 516.

62 *RFR*, II:2:971; *GGG*, 370.

was informed that it was too late for that: an army was already on the way.[63] Just one day earlier, Edward had ordered the marshal of his household to direct the preparations at Portsmouth, where the king intended to embark with his magnates and men for an expedition to Guienne.[64]

The last week of June was a time of decisions for the king. Over a period of a few days, messengers arrived from Oliver Ingham, from King Alfonso of Castile, and apparently also from the English ambassadors in the Netherlands.[65] All of the information they brought pushed the king into abandoning his plan to sail for Gascony, and committing himself to operations from the Low Countries instead. According to Ingham, support for the king-duke remained strong in Aquitaine, despite French threats and blandishments. English chancery clerks worked feverishly on the 25th and 27th, turning out over 150 letters to various individuals and groups in Gascony, thanking them for their fidelity and urging them to continue to defend the king-duke's rights against the French. Perhaps more significant than what these letters said is what they did *not* say: they made no mention of the expedition which Edward had been planning to lead to Bordeaux.[66] This suggests that Edward had decided to leave the inhabitants of the duchy to fight a holding action in the south while he himself won the war in the north.

The letters which reached him from the King of Castile contributed to this decision. Edward's representatives had been negotiating with King Alfonso since the summer of 1335, and by March of 1337 (just as the final decision to go to war with France was being made) Edward received word that a treaty had nearly been arranged.[67] Around 27 June, however, Alfonso informed the English king that he would be unable to assist Edward in the war against France, because Castile had become involved in a conflict elsewhere.[68] What Edward did not know was that the double-dealing King of Castile had already concluded a treaty with France the previous February.[69] Still, the notice that he could not expect to

---

[63] Sumption, *Trial by Battle*, 206. The confiscation was issued 24 May 1337; it is printed in *KdL*, 34–6.

[64] *RFR*, II:2:974.

[65] *RFR*, II:2:975–7 (Ingham), 977 (Castile); these messengers apparently arrived around 25 June and 27 June, respectively. In addition, it was around this time that Nicholas Beche returned from an embassy to Germany (his account ends on 22 June). Mirot and Déprez, "Ambassades Anglaises," 564. On 1 July, the king authorized the subsidy of £60,000 to the Duke of Brabant (*RFR*, II:2:981); he had probably received the details of his ambassadors' arrangements with the duke somewhat earlier, brought by the messenger who had evidently arrived by 20 June to arrange for a naval escort for the ambassadors' return to England. *RFH*, 3:3:172.

[66] *RFR*, II:2:976–8.

[67] *RFR*, II:2:910, 932, 961. Among the issues discussed was the possibility of Edward's eldest daughter, Isabel, marrying the eldest son of King of Castile.

[68] *RFR*, II:2:977; *Grandes chroniques*, 9:157.

[69] Printed in Georges Daumet, *Étude sur l'alliance de la France et de la Castille au XIVe et XVe siècle* [118e fasc. de la Bibliothèque de l'École des Chartes] (Paris: E. Bouillon, 1898), p.j. 1, pp. 125–30; see also *Registres du trésor des chartes*, no. 3342. Philip and Alfonso had

combine his forces with a Castilian army in Gascony, as he had hoped,[70] was another factor which helped confirm the Plantagenet's decision to make his main effort in the north.

So, during the first two weeks of July, just after the wool scheme was informally worked out, Edward ratified the agreements with the Duke of Brabant, the Marquis of Juliers, and the counts of Hainault and Guelders discussed above.[71] The Gascony expeditionary force was scaled back to a few hundred men.[72] Edward was now fully committed to a large-scale invasion of France from the Low Countries.[73] Its timing and even the basic operational plan had already been determined. Edward promised to arrive on the marches of "Low Germany" with his men at the beginning of August – just over two weeks away! By 17 September, he said, he would unite with the armies of his allies between Cambrai and Cateau-Cambrésis – on French-controlled territory, but still technically just within the borders of the Empire.[74]

This impractical schedule had probably been agreed by Edward's ambassadors some time earlier, based on the assembly date of 28 July which had been set for the Gascony expedition. According to his treaties, Edward was required to bring with him the first installment on the various subsidies he had promised, and two months' advance wages, for the beginning of the campaign. The main source of money for these expenditures, the wool monopoly scheme, was not even formally authorized until 26 July, and it was obvious that it would take at least several months to carry through. Therefore, no serious effort was made to keep the late-July departure date.

A more realistic schedule was worked out at a council meeting between 16 and 26 August. At this meeting, the Bishop of Lincoln and the earls of Salisbury and Huntingdon, who had just returned from the Continent, presented the draft alliance with the emperor.[75] According to the *Scalacronica*, the Earl of Salisbury, perceiving the greed of the Imperial princes, argued that "the entry into alliance with the Imperials did not appear to be drawing to a favorable conclu-

been negotiating at least since the early autumn of 1336 (ibid.). Cf. *Grandes chroniques*, 9:158. In a letter of 17 March, Philip reminded Alfonso of their alliance, and that so far as he knew they were still "touz uns," and urged him not to listen to Edward's blandishments. Miret y Sans, "Lettres Closes," 62–3. (The letter, considering the references to "notre enemi" and to Edward's excessive promises to potential allies, clearly does not date to 1332, as Miret y Sans supposes. Cf. also "Itin. Philippe VI," 124.) Even so, in June Alfonso was still promising to send ambassadors to England in August to ratify an Anglo-Castillian treaty. *RFR*, II:2:977.
[70] Ibid.
[71] *RFR*, II:2:981, 984–5.
[72] Sumption, *Trial by Battle*, 206, 209.
[73] This had apparently been assumed by Burghersh and his colleagues at least since 24 May, when an agreement made with the Low Countries allies indicated that Edward's arrival was expected by 17 September. *RFH*, 3:1:169. Edward himself, however, was probably still unaware of this, given his expressed intent on 12 June to go to Gascony. The Channel was infested by French ships, which made communications difficult.
[74] *RFR*, II:2:984.
[75] For the business of this council, see ibid., 989–93.

sion, and that the king would not be able to bear the costs of the conditions which they demanded of him."[76] Others, however, thought that the alliances would enable Edward to win the war quickly and easily, if not cheaply: "whoever hindered the passage of the king and the fulfillment of the treaties should be held as traitors," they said, "and that he would not [need to] take anyone but his chamber-servant with him, as his allies over there would make him strong enough to conquer his heritage of France."[77] Some went even further, saying (according to William of Dene) that "they had developed such a confederation of great men to fight the King of France that, without doubt [Edward] would not need to fear even triple the power of the King of France."[78]

Edward inclined to the latter view. On 26 August, he ratified the agreement with the emperor, and also a group of relatively minor treaties which had not yet received his personal approval.[79] Indeed, Edward was so pleased with the alliances that, on 1 September, he granted Burghersh 1,000 marks of free gift, on top of the bishop's extraordinarily high £5 per diem.[80] The king still hoped to have an army and a transport fleet ready to sail by the beginning of October, but the rendezvous with the emperor in the Cambrésis was postponed until the end of November.[81]

The following month was one of frustrations, as the royal government scrambled to gather the cash, supplies, troops and ships that would be required to keep that appointment. To try to boost public support for the war, great pains were taken to explain the reasons for Edward's decisions to the people of England.[82] The response was lukewarm. Recruiting targets continued to be difficult to

---

[76] *Scalacronica*, 168. According to the same source, the earl then resigned his commission (as part of the council?) and departed to serve in Scotland in order to disassociate himself with a policy he believed to be in error. Since Salisbury had been fully involved in the negotiations (if we can believe the texts of the treaties referred to above), there is no obvious reason why he would have had a change of heart at this point. In any case, however, some of the king's advisers doubtless made these points.
[77] Ibid.: "ascuns disoient, com fust dit, as ceaux qui estoint entour le roy adonqes, qe qy endestourbast le passage le roy en acomplicement de lour tretice qils serrount vnqor tenuz traiters, et qe il ne amenoit oue ly fors Giliot de la Chaumbre, qil serroit asseitz fort de sez alyez depar dela pur conquer soun heritage de Franz."
[78] "Nunciis ad regem dixerunt se fecisse talem partem et tantam confederacionem magnorum ad debellandum Regem Francie quod proculdubio non foret dubitandum de potestate Regis Francie etsi triplicaretur." *Historia Roffensis*, fo. 80v.
[79] *RFR*, II:2:991–3. Note that, as a cross-check of the dates confirms, these ratifications did not involve the principal agreements with the Duke of Brabant, the counts of Hainault and Guelders, or the Marquis of Juliers. Those had previously (12–13 July) been approved by the king. Edward thus did not still have the freedom to reject the agreements with them implied by Lucas, *Low Countries*, 235.
[80] Déprez, *Préliminaires*, 152n.
[81] *RFR*, II:2:993 (1,000 Welshmen, due at Canterbury on 29 September, to be provided with uniform clothes); Déprez, *Préliminaires*, 160 n.1; *RFR*, II:2:991 (emperor). To be precise, the agreement with the emperor did not specify the meeting place, but it can be assumed that it had not changed since the agreements with Hainault, Juliers and Guelders were made.
[82] *RFR*, II:2:989–90, 994–5; *Historia Roffensis*, fo. 80v; Sumption, *Trial by Battle*, 220–1.

meet, and the wool scheme met surprisingly effective resistance. On 1 September, for example, Edward complained that "some men not regarding the safety of the realm are scheming to remove and conceal their wools." He ordered that any wools in the counties around London found to have been so concealed or removed be confiscated without payment, and that he be informed periodically of the names of those who were obstructing the wool collection, so that they might be punished in exemplary fashion.[83] Ships and mariners in diverse places deserted the king's service.[84] Further difficulties were presented by the fact that some of the scarce wool crop had been already purchased by merchants of Antwerp under the earlier agreement with Duke John of Brabant, and these sacks could not be requisitioned without aggravating an already difficult diplomatic situation.[85] On top of all this were problems arising from rampant corruption among the merchants involved, who not only abused their powers in their transactions with the wool producers, but themselves engaged in smuggling on an astounding scale. The results were that August, September, and October passed without any large shipments of the king's wool to the Continent, and even by the end of the year only 8,879 sacks had been legally exported.[86]

By 24 September, the unhappy king had to face the fact that he would not be leading his host to the Cambrésis that year, though he did still hope to cross the sea with at least a small force.[87] The expedition was officially put off until some indefinite date in the future. Previous orders to lead newly arrayed troops to London were canceled. If the men had not yet been arrayed, chosen and equipped, however, that was to be done immediately. In any case, the soldiers were to be held ready to come to London on twelve days' notice or less.[88]

This last note of continued optimism soon proved unwarranted. A force of English soldiers led by Sir Walter Mauny (the Admiral of the North) did cross the Channel in November, escorting the first wool fleet, and scored an impressive if rather useless victory against the French garrison of Cadzand in Flanders (one in which the English longbowmen played a key role), but Edward could not produce the men or the money to follow them up with a real army.[89] News from the north and from the south also helped convince the king that he neither should nor needed to cross the Channel immediately. The Scots had recovered much of the ground they lost during 1336, and were even conducting major raids into England. The situation was serious enough that Edward sent the earls of Salisbury, Arundel and Gloucester to the border area, where they later joined the

---

83 *CPR, 1334–38*, 516.

84 *CPR, 1334–38*, 580, 525.

85 Lucas, *Low Countries*, 251.

86 Fryde, *William de la Pole*, 68–9, 80n.

87 *CPR, 1334–38*, 527, 529, 530–4, 537, 539–40. Note particularly the protections to John Montgomery on 15 October, John Tibetot on 3 October, and William Lengleys on 1 October (ibid., 539, 531, 534).

88 *RFR*, II:2:997.

89 For the most detailed description of the attack on Cadzand, see Froissart, *Oeuvres*, 2:429–37; note also Fryde, *William de la Pole*, 73n.

lords Neville and Percy in besieging the Earl of March's castle at Dunbar.[90] The news from Gascony also reduced the pressure on Edward to begin military operations in northern France immediately: the French offensive, which had begun in July, fizzled out when Philip ordered many of the troops in that theater north to face the invasion from England he expected. Anglo-Gascon troops were beginning to recover much of the ground they had lost.[91] So, on 20 November, Edward finally gave official notice that the invasion plans would be put off indefinitely.[92]

Shortly thereafter, two cardinals arrived as legates from the Pope, hoping to put out the spark of war before it grew into an unquenchable flame.[93] The two, Bertrand de Montfavez and Pedro Gómez de Barroso, reported that Philip had agreed to a short truce to allow for peace negotiations, if Edward would consent. Although the Church hoped that a last-minute settlement could still be reached, the two kings probably had few illusions on that score. Neither side had been able to organize the kind of military effort it felt was needed, and so both monarchs were willing to agree to a truce in order to have time to prepare better for the next campaigning season. Edward's only major reservation concerning granting the truce was that doing so would put his Continental allies in a difficult position. This was especially true of those who were trying to stave off an open break with Philip VI as long as possible, since they would either have to declare themselves (to be included in the truce) or else risk being attacked when Edward (because of the truce) would be unable to aid them.[94] Considering that his treaties with them required that he not make a truce without their assent, the king wanted to send ambassadors to get their agreement, and also wanted to get approval from parliament, before agreeing to a truce. The cardinals were angry that the king refused to act without his allies' consent, and confided to him that they "knew for certain" that the Duke of Brabant and Count of Hainault only wanted his money and would fail him when the moment of truth came. Edward was not convinced: "he did not think it would be thus with the duke and the count," he responded, "and even if it were, he would rather that the default be found in them than in him."[95]

The cardinals were not mollified. The next day, they summoned the Archbishop of Canterbury and the other prelates in the area to a meeting where they brandished papal letters authorizing them deploy excommunication, interdict, and (in some cases) deprivation of benefices against anyone who refused to support a truce which might head off a war. Furthermore, they declared

---

[90] *Scalacronica*, 168; *Lanercost*, 295. Cf. also *EMDP*, 289.

[91] Sumption, *Trial by Battle*, 237; cf. also Vale, *Origins*, 260–2.

[92] *RFR*, II:2:1007.

[93] *BLF*, no. 370; *CEPR*, 2:563–5; *Murimuth*, 81; Villani, *Cronica*, 368 (arrived around 30 November); *EMDP*, 287–9. They had already visited the court of France: *Chronographia*, 2:55–6; *BLF*, nos. 368–369.

[94] *EMDP*, 288, 290.

[95] Ibid., 288: "le roi lour fist respondre . . . qil nentent qil soit ensi du duc ne du counte, et sil feut, si vorroit il mieux que la defaute soit trove en eux que en lui."

expressly that if Edward refused to treat for peace in accordance with the Pope's advice, "the Church would be entirely against him." Scotland and France were enemies enough: the king could not afford to add the Holy See to his list of adversaries.[96] He backed down.

He agreed to press his allies to assent to a formal truce, and promised to have an answer on the matter for the cardinals during the upcoming February parliament. To persuade them to wait that long without taking drastic measures, he agreed on 24 December to an informal truce – a "cessation" – until 1 March 1338.[97] Not long thereafter, he sent a letter to Nijmegen, where his chief advisor the Bishop of Lincoln then was, explaining what had happened, and asking Burghersh and the other ambassadors to

> talk it over with the allies, so that they will give such advice to the king at [the upcoming] parliament that he will not lose the Pope, nor have the Church opposed to him . . . And if the said bishop etc. and the allies, who understand and know fully the state of affairs on the Continent, are aware of such great profit for the king in the pursuit of his business over there that it would be more valuable than granting the truce, having regard to the danger of offending the Pope and the Church, then the king wishes to be certified of it at his said parliament . . . Also, in the case of some truce or treaty being made, the bishop etc. should make clear to the allies that the king does not wish to lose them in any way.[98]

He very nearly did lose them. When the news of the "cessation" reached the Continent, as Burghersh and his colleagues reported in February of 1338, "all the king's allies and well-wishers were very upset, and were on the point of giving up the whole business." Had it not been for the king's firm promises that he still intended to cross over and begin campaigning as soon as possible, they would have done so. If a formal truce were made without their assent, the ambassadors warned, or if matters were not vigorously carried forward, "then they will be lost."[99] This sobering message did not prevent the king from extending the cessation until 24 June 1338.[100]

*

As things turned out, the English king was not ready to begin his campaign even then. Indeed, all of 1338 was occupied by the same kind of financial and organizational frustrations which had led to the failure of the 1337 invasion plans. Meanwhile, during the spring and early summer, Edward tried to balance the wars in Scotland and Gascony with the difficult task of keeping his Imperial alliances from collapsing. Another claim on his attention came from Flanders,

96 Ibid.; *CEPR*, 537
97 *EMDP*, 288, 291; *RFR*, II:2:1014.
98 *EMDP*, 288.
99 Ibid., 290–1. The council abroad added that a truce would not so much allow for peace negotiations as predetermine their outcome, since it would mean a victory for the French.
100 The warning was sent to him, apparently from Nijmegen, on 4 February; he extended the cessation on 24 February, from Westminster. *RFH*, 2:4:3–4.

where a veritable political revolution had occurred, creating the potential for a reprise of the Anglo-Flemish alliance of 1297. Discussion of that last issue, however, will be reserved for a later chapter.

The most intractable problem for the English government was money. As noted above, the wool scheme had yielded disappointing results in the fall of 1337. The first of the three scheduled wool fleets had sailed only in November, rather than in August as Edward had hoped, and even despite the delay only 8,879 sacks of wool were legally exported for sale by the syndicate, well short of the ten thousand sacks planned. The shortfalls and delays were largely due to the merchants' corruption, for they seem to have spent more time and effort figuring out how to take advantage of the unusual circumstances with their own smuggled wool (which would have yielded well more than double the profit) than working to fulfill their obligations to the king. The evidence suggests that at least one sack of wool was smuggled overseas for every two sacks legitimately exported.[101]

This exacerbated a problem already inherent in the situation, which was doubtless the result of the wool contract and the foreign alliances having been negotiated simultaneously and separately: the payment schedules for the two were out of synch, as the following chart shows. [Table 6–1]

Thus, even if all had gone as originally planned, the allies would almost certainly have had to accept delays in their payments. Although this was doubtless annoying for them, it was not of great significance; the key was that they receive their subsidies before the opening of the campaigning season in the spring, and – if the planned wool schedules had been met – by the spring of 1338 Edward's cash-flow position would have been surprisingly good (though he would have been indebted to the merchant syndicate and others for huge sums). The Count of Guelders, who had already once agreed to a postponement of his subsidies, again proved willing to shift his two payments of £15,000 back, to 22 March and 31 May. The same schedule was very likely adopted for Hainault, Juliers, and the minor allies. It seems probable that the emperor and the Duke of Brabant, whose loyalty could less be taken for granted, were promised their initial installments by Christmas, and that they would have their arrears fully paid up by 22 March.[102] If this guess is correct, then Edward owed the allies for their subsidies something like £75,000 around Christmas, £75,000 more in March, another £45,000 in May, as well as around £32,000 in advance wage

---

[101] Fryde, *William de la Pole*, 80 (8,879 vs. 4,400). Note that the total of legal and smuggled wool falls neatly between the estimates given by Giovanni Villani and the Lanercost chronicler for the total amount of wool shipped – 12,000 and 14,000 sacks, respectively. Villani, *Cronica*, 368; *Lanercost*, 294.

[102] Guelders: *GGG*, 367. The first postponement, implied in the same document, had moved the payments to Michaelmas 1337 and 25 February 1338. (On "jour de my quaresme" and "quaresme prenant," see Mas Latrie, *Trésor*, 629, 650.) Christmas: Fryde, *William de la Pole*, 76n. Arrears for the emperor and Brabant: Ibid., 76 (£276,000, a sum so large it must include these).

Table 6-1: The Wool Scheme and the Subsidy Payments

Round £ Due	On											
To	6/30/37	8/1	9/29	11/1	11/21	12/25	2/2/38	4/12	5/21	12/25/38	12/25/39	12/25/40
Rhenish Palatinate			4650									
Juliers	1666	1666		1666								
Juliers		15000						15000				
Hainault		15000						15000				
Guelders		15000						15000				
Loos			2250		2250							
Brabant		15000				5000				13333	13333	13333
Valkenburgh			1800				1800					
Emperor			45000				15000					
Total	1666	61666	53700	1666	2250	5000	16800	45000		13333	13333	13333
Cumulative total:	1666	63332	117032	118698	120948	125948	142748	187748	187748	201081	214414	227747
Wool loans						(66666)		(66666)	(66666)			
Subsidies net of wool loans	1666	63332	117032	118698	120948	59282	76082	54416	(12250)	1083	14416	27749

payments due at the start of the campaign.[103] This was closer to matching his anticipated income stream from the wool loan, but to make it work there would be a tight squeeze at Christmas; the second fleet would have to sail early and the wool aboard would have to be disposed of rapidly; even then there would be difficulties.

Burghersh and his colleagues had some reasons, however, to think that these problems would not be insurmountable. There is some evidence to suggest that the few sacks of smuggled English wool (presumably of the best quality) which were being sold on the black market were going for as much as £15–£20, and the merchant syndicate valued its own wool at an average of over £10 per sack.[104] At that rate, even the 8,879 sacks on record as having been shipped with the first wool fleet could suffice cover the sums due at Christmas (with enough left over for the shipping expenses for the second fleet), and the ambassadors were probably aware that a good deal of "unofficial" wool had also made its way to Brabant as well. Thus, when they called in the representatives of the syndicate for a meeting at Geertruidenberg on 19 December, it was not unreasonable for them to ask for an increase of the 100,000-mark loan due the following week.

The results of their request, however, were incredibly bad. The merchants not only refused to offer any additional loans, they also said that, because of deterioration suffered by the wool and the ban on sales to Flemish and French-allied buyers, they would not be able to promise payment of the first installment of 100,000 marks until Easter (12 April) – when the government was expecting to receive the *second* installment! Only if Edward would allow them to sell to the Flemings, and block any further shipments of any wool but theirs to the Netherlands, could they do any better, and even then they might not be able to provide the first installment until 25 February.[105]

Burghersh was staring disaster in the face. On the schedule the merchants were proposing, Edward would not even come close to being able to meet his engagements on time, and if the second and third installments were delayed

---

[103] Assuming that the emperor was to receive 15,000 of his 60,000 on Christmas or St. Thomas' day, another 15,000 on the Purification (as originally scheduled), and the remainder by 22 March. That would still leave £40,000 due to the Duke of Brabant, as originally scheduled, in three annual payments on Christmas 1338, 1339 and 1340.

[104] £15–£20: Probably the source of the misunderstanding of *Knighton*, 2:2, and *Bridlington*, 133; note also the £200 penalty assessed on John Goldbeter for the illicit sale of just under 10 sacks, cited in Fryde, *William de la Pole*, 75. £10: above, note 50.

[105] E. B. Fryde, I think, misses the mark slightly when he says (*William de la Pole*, 75) that the merchants insisted that they should be allowed to sell to Flanders and "declared that, provided they could sell to whom they liked, and that no other wool save their own would be allowed to reach the Netherlands, they would be willing to advance 100,000 marks . . . [and] were vague about the time of payment, but promised to make it by the beginning of Lent (25 February) or, if not by then, by Easter (12 April) at the latest." Consider the text of the document: "ils respounderent que, *sils* puissent franchement vendre a tout manere de gent[z] . . . [et] nules autres leines forque les leines le rey ne veignent en le meen temps, que *adonques* ils purront servir le roy de c mille mars entre cy [20 December] et le comencement de Quaresme [25 February], et *si ce noun, adonques* entre cy et la Pasche." Emphasis added. *EMDP*, 293.

similarly, the money would not even be fully in his hands in time for the summer campaigning season. It probably seemed to the bishop and to Edward's other councilors that the merchants were being deliberately provocative: if they had nearly nine thousand sacks of wool on hand, which certainly were worth more than 100,000 marks, and quite possibly £100,000 or more – not to mention the smuggled wool, however much there might be of that – then how could they say they would not be able to pay the agreed £66,667 on time?

Burghersh then returned the volley with a bombshell of his own: unless the king received loans of £276,000 between then and 22 March, he announced, "the realm of England, and all the other lands of the king, were in peril of being lost."[106] It is hard to imagine how the royal debts could have mounted quite so high as that, unless Edward was paying interest to the allies on the delayed subsidies (which does not appear to have been the case). On the other hand, he was spending heavily to maintain his own household abroad, often using money borrowed at high rates, and was probably also paying interest on money he had borrowed to pay fragments of the overdue subsidies. In any case, this was much more than the merchants could reasonably be expected to provide that early; £276,000 was well over the total the merchants had agreed in their indenture to raise for the full thirty thousand sacks. Although the arrival of a new crop of wool in the spring and early summer might make it possible to complete the collection of thirty thousand sacks, or even more if that were authorized, there was no way it could all be collected by 22 March, much less shipped to the Continent and sold. This was particularly true since, in order to keep prices high, the wool had to be sold gradually. It may be that the bishop thought the merchants had overstated their case to establish a bargaining position, and was following suit by including in his total all the money needed before the upcoming campaign, including the wage advances and the subsidies which had been put off until May. If so, the tactic was not very successful. The representatives of the syndicate may have backed down slightly and offered to put up the money due at Christmas on time (the document is not entirely clear on that point),[107] but they absolutely refused to pay any more than that.

At the time of the sailing of the wool fleet in November 1337, it had already been clear to Burghersh that, given the delays already experienced, the merchants might need to be prodded to sell the first shipment faster than they would prefer. He therefore had secured a verbal agreement from William de la

---

106 Fryde, *William*, 76n. The money was needed "parentre la feste de Seintz Thomas [21 December] et le Noel [25 December] et la Purification de nostre dame [2 February] et la mi quaresme [22 March]." The references to intermediate dates suggest that the English had promised to meet the payments of £5,000 due to Brabant at Christmas and £18,500 to the emperor and the Lord of Valkenburgh on the Purification; on 22 March Guelders was owed his £15,000, and probably the same goes for Hainault and Juliers.
107 They said they would willingly fulfill the terms of their indenture and provide the 100,000 marks, but it is not clear if this meant by Christmas (as intended in the original agreement, but not actually specified in the indenture) or if this was simply a reiteration of their initial position.

Pole and Reginald Conduit that, contrary to the initial indenture with the wool syndicate, the royal ambassadors should have the right to direct the disposal of the first ten thousand sacks of wool if necessary. The merchants had agreed, saying that Edward's representatives could throw the wool into the Thames, for all they cared, provided that they were left enough cash to allow the second shipment to be carried through.[108] Since the merchants at Geertruidenberg refused to offer more than 100,000 marks, and that amount was simply insufficient to meet the needs of the crown, the Bishop of Lincoln decided to exercise that agreement. He evidently calculated that the wool on hand was worth a good deal more than the merchants were offering, and, as noted above, he did have some legitimate grounds to think so. What he did not appreciate was the extent to which the price of the wool would depreciate if it were all dumped on the market rapidly. The merchants doubtless cautioned him on that score, but by this point he was convinced that they were interested only in their own profit, not in the interests of the king, and indeed that they had been guilty of gross malfeasance to the detriment of the royal business, so their warning would not have carried much weight with him.[109] The results of his miscalculation, however, proved disastrous. Although the sale of the wool taken into the king's hand eventually yielded £68,139, slightly more than the advance the merchants had offered, the money was not all in hand until July, and none of it was available much before the Easter deadline the syndicate had proposed. Furthermore, since the wool was acquired by the administration at much higher prices than had been paid in England, Edward's debts were still further increased.[110] Worse yet, the wool merchants were enraged by the whole affair, and by February the syndicate had broken up, and the government was left without a means for implementing the remaining two-thirds of the wool scheme. The financial arrangements which underlay Edward's military strategy for 1338 had collapsed, and the alliances threatened to collapse with them.

Fortunately for Edward, he was able to secure a loan[111] of half the wool in England (set at twenty thousand sacks, doubtless as a match for the second and third shipments of wool under the old scheme which had never taken place) in support of his wars from the Westminster parliament of February 1338. Since this time the wool prices had parliamentary approval, there was reason to expect that the collection would be more successful, even without the participation of the merchant group. Considering the revenues which were expected to come from that wool, as well as tallages, the tenth and fifteenth also granted by parliament, and the regular royal revenues, the Bardi and Peruzzi soon stepped in to

---

108   *EMDP,* 291.
109   *EMDP,* 293.
110   He owed the merchants £92,662 for the wool which brought him £68,139. For all this, see Fryde, *William,* 76–86.
111   *Murimuth,* 82, states that this was a grant rather than a loan, and this has been accepted by Ramsay, *History of Revenues,* 173; even Edward III himself refers to it as a grant (letter in Déprez, *Préliminaires,* 418); but *CPR, 1338–40,* 167, 288–98, show that the king was to pay for the wool at a price set by county, as in the previous wool scheme.

help fill the gap caused by the collapse of the wool merchants' syndicate. Between the spring and fall of 1338, they provided the king with advances of some £85,000.[112] This was, however, not enough to keep the alliance intact, and further loans were sought from any source that could be found. Edward's desperation for cash was so great that he even agreed to sign over to William de la Pole the great manor of Burstwick, possibly the most valuable of all the royal estates, for somewhat over £20,000 in ready money.[113]

These funds and the proceeds from the wool loan (which, however, produced very disappointing results) made it possible to keep Edward's allies on the Continent from deserting him entirely, but they were still very displeased at the king's failure to honor his financial commitments fully. Edward, nonetheless, was still planning to lead an army to the Continent around 12 May, almost six weeks before the expiration of the truce.[114] This helped to reassure the allies that at least they would not be left to face King Philip's wrath alone. Meanwhile, the English did all they could to make up for the delay of the subsidy payments, and promised that the new provision of wool would enable them to make large payments to the allies at the time of Edward's arrival.[115]

Still, Edward's financial and diplomatic situation remained very delicate. What military action there was did not go well for the English either. A sizable English army under Salisbury and Arundel was tied up at the siege of Dunbar for months on end, without making any impression on a garrison led by the Countess of March, the valiant "Black Agnes."[116] In the month of March, French fleets burned much of Jersey, and sacked the substantial town of Portsmouth. In April, the French besieged two major English fortresses in Aquitaine, Penne and Blaye. Though Edward temporarily boosted the morale of his Gascon subjects by promising a relief force, it never materialized.[117]

When May came around, little had changed, except that the payments to the allies had fallen further in arrears. Neither Edward's army nor his fleet was ready, and the trip to the Continent had to be postponed until July. This time the king managed to put together an army of about 1,350 men-at-arms, two thousand English archers, and eight hundred Welsh troops – a smaller force than he had hoped for, but still stronger than even the one the emperor was due to bring – and sailed for Antwerp.[118] To assemble even this reduced contingent, however,

---

[112] Fryde, *William*, 89–90.
[113] Ibid., 94, 108–14 (partly sold, partly leased).
[114] *RFR*, II:2:1015, 1016, 1018.
[115] *RFR*, II:245–8; letter in Déprez, *Préliminaires*, 418.
[116] *Pluscardensis*, 284–6; *Wyntoun*, 2:431–5.
[117] Sumption, *Trial by Battle*, 324–37.
[118] The men-at-arms began to receive double pay after arriving on the Continent on 22 July. The largest retinues of men-at-arms were, respectively, those of the Earl of Salisbury (124), the Earl of Northampton (89), Henry Burghersh , Bishop of Lincoln (76), Henry of Lancaster (71), the Earl of Suffolk (56), Henry Ferrers (50), Walter Mauny (44), Reginald Cobham (30), John Beaumont (29), John Darcy (28), and John Moleyns (27). The archers, by my count, amounted to 1,031 mounted archers (about two-thirds of whom were in retinues and the rest

he had had to call off the siege of Dunbar and cancel the Gascon expedition.[119] For ready cash to tide him over until the parliamentary grants came through, he had confiscated all the tin in Cornwall and even pressured the bishops, priors, abbots and other clergy of the realm into lending him hundreds or thousands of pounds worth of precious vestments, gold and silver chalices, jeweled crosses, and other plate.[120]

Though the arrival of the English was quite a bit later than originally intended, it was by no means too late to begin a campaign. The loan of twenty thousand sacks of wool granted by the February parliament would not even come close to filling all of Edward's obligations, but the approximately £150,000 they represented would be enough to placate the allies temporarily and cover the wage bills for a short campaign. Once the campaign was over, assuming that Edward's forces had won the battle he expected them to, the king would gain some breathing room. If he were lucky (and Edward, forever an optimist, doubtless planned on being lucky) he might even be able to pay off his allies with the proceeds from ransoming prisoners or perhaps with a peace indemnity from Philip. Such, it seems likely, were Edward's hopes.

But hope, as Thucydides observed, is a thing by nature profligate and unreliable.[121] When Edward arrived in Brabant, he discovered to his dismay that barely the eighth part of his wool was on hand.[122] This, as he explained in an angry letter of 4 August, was far from the "treasure, food supplies, and all other necessary things in sufficient quantity for our affairs, for us and our men as well as for the sums we owe to our allies over here" which he had expected to find waiting for him. The treasurer and his colleagues were therefore ordered to send him cash, supplies, and wool without delay. An emergency loan obtained with great difficulty from a friend, Edward added, had made it possible to pay a part

---

arrayed), as well as 974 foot archers, nearly all from county arrays. The Welshmen included 51 from Chester, 424 from North Wales, and 307 from South Wales; the 89 troops from West Wales may also have sailed with the king. *WBWN*, 325–62; cf. *Bridlington*, 147, which suggests the Welsh troops were spearmen rather than archers. Sumption, *Trial by Battle*, 239, calculates nearly three thousand archers, but he includes the contingent of 445 volunteers under Henry Flamvill and Robert Moreux, which did not begin to receive pay until almost a month after the king sailed. *WBWN*, 360.

[119] The severe curtailment of operations in Scotland was particularly painful because the Scots had already recaptured Bothwell, raided into England, recovered the allegiance of Eustace Maxwell, and attempted sieges of Stirling and Edinburgh. *Anonimalle*, 10–13.

[120] *RFR*, II:1039–41, 1045–6 for £700-worth secured from 11 clergymen. This probably represents only a fraction of the money raised by this method, as, according to William of Dene, the king sought to get such valuables from all the churches, cathedrals, abbeys, convents, and priories of the realm. *Historia Roffensis*, fo. 81v.

[121] *Peloponnesian War*, V.103.

[122] Edward's letter of 24 July, in Déprez, *Préliminaires*, 418, says that there were barely 2,500 sacks – though E. B. Fryde, whose knowledge of these transactions is extraordinary, says that "A mere 1,846 sacks reached the Netherlands by the time of Edward's arrival at Antwerp." Fryde, *William*, 86. The discrepancy may be wool "left over" from the previous wool scheme.

of the money he owed to some of his allies. Otherwise, he would have been perpetually dishonored, and his people of England imperiled.[123]

Nor, as he soon found out, was this simply a shipping problem. The taxation, purveyance, wool prests, and forced loans already imposed had severely disrupted the English economy, making it very difficult to purchase wool or wheat at any price, so that it seemed that "the realm was on the brink of inescapable poverty."[124] Popular discontent was at dangerous levels.[125] Edward's officers had only been able to collect some 2,800 of the wool sacks due.[126] A hasty meeting with the main Low Countries allies revealed that there was no real hope of convincing them to go ahead with the campaign before they were paid at least a substantial portion of their arrears.[127] According to Jean le Bel, they had hardly begun to prepare for the campaign, even though Edward was expecting them to be ready to go. Furthermore, even the most pro-English of them were reluctant to act without the Duke of Brabant, the strongest of their group, who was not enthusiastic about the campaign.[128] Brabant, when pressed, stalled. He called for another meeting of all the allies to take place at Hal on the Hainault-Brabant border on 15 August. Edward, complaining of the costs he incurred with every passing day but seeing that he had little choice, agreed, provided that by then Brabant would be adequately prepared for action.[129]

The discussions did not turn out as the king had hoped. After a long and stormy meeting, Edward's allies claimed that they could not move against Philip until they were openly commanded to do so by the emperor or his lieutenant, since the nominal motive for the war was the defense of the Empire against French encroachment. This, it should be said, was what had been envisioned all along, and the allies' demand was fully consistent with the terms they had specified in their treaties.[130] Even so, Edward was furious at their lack of flexibility, perhaps because he thought the emperor's earlier action making Guelders and Juliers jointly his vicar in the diocese of Cambrai – where the invasion was to

---

[123] Printed in *KdL*, 64–5; cf. the slightly calmer letter of 24 July in Déprez, *Préliminaires*, 418–19. The friend was doubtless William de la Pole. See Fryde, *William*, chs 8–9.

[124] *Historia Roffensis*, fo. 81v: "vergebat Regnum ad paupertatem irrecuperabile." Similarly, *Pakington*, fo. 184: "pour les gages de ses ditz allies . . . la terre fuist graundement empovere et abbesse."

[125] Knighton, *Chronicle* (ed. Martin), 6.

[126] *CPR, 1338–40*, 245; Fryde, *William*, 86.

[127] The *Anonimalle*, 13, reflecting the general view of this situation in England, comments that Edward "found none of the faith or loyalty in them that they had recently promised to his ambassadors."

[128] *Le Bel*, 1:138–9. Lucas, *Low Countries*, 286, 289.

[129] *Le Bel*, 1:139–40: "au jour de la Nostre Dame enmy aoust," not 5 August as stated in Lucas, *Low Countries*, 289 n.34.

[130] E.g. *RFR*, II:2:984: "mesir Guilliames, contes de Haynun . . . nous a promis . . . ke en cas ke treshaus princes & poissans, li Empereres des Romains, voisit entreprendre come principals chievetains, par lui, ou par son vicaire . . . aians plein pooir de somonre les princes," etc.

begin – should have sufficed to fulfill that clause.[131] Since he had not even fulfilled the letter of his own end of the treaties, however, there was little he could do. Putting on his most diplomatic face, he told them that he wished he had been informed of this problem earlier. He hoped that his allies would better advise him in the future. Meanwhile, he said, he would take up the matter with the emperor immediately.[132]

The king was likely less confident of gaining Ludwig's support than he appeared. The emperor's subsidies, after all, were as far in arrears as those of the other allies, and his anticipated arrival at Antwerp had been postponed at the last minute several times.[133] After so many delays and improvisations, so much effort and pain, the chance of an invasion of France in 1338 was slipping through the king's fingers.

This period shows us King Edward at his worst, but also at his best. His will was strong, and he expected the universe – or at the very least his own subjects and allies – to bend to its demands. Though necessity often compelled him to break his own promises, he never anticipated the frequency with which his supporters would fail to fulfill their promises to him. He was all too willing to let hopes become expectations. But, on the other hand, he hardly showed a moment's hesitation in responding to the crisis once he had become fully aware of it. After a series of failures and embarrassments that might have caused a lesser man (or perhaps a wiser one) to simply give up and go home, Edward III acted quickly and decisively to salvage what could be salvaged.

Within four days of the king's arrival on the Continent, under the lash of his letters, a council meeting had opened back in England to address the wool problem. A new collection method, one which would eventually prove quite successful, was rapidly hammered out. The people of each county and burgh would be required to come up with a share of the total amount of wool due, in the same proportion as they contributed money to the regular lay subsidies. If they did not have the wool, they would have to buy it or pay its cash value.[134]

Meanwhile, Edward's men were scrambling to raise as much money as possible, at whatever price. After the meeting at Hal, Edward returned briefly to Antwerp,[135] then on the 18th departed for Coblenz, where the emperor was

---

[131] *GGG*, 359–60 (7 July 1337). Guelders and Juliers' commission also gave them the power to appoint someone else (presumably Edward) as vicar in their place. As noted above, the agreement made with the emperor in July 1337 had also envisioned making Edward Ludwig's vicar-general if the emperor himself were unable to lead the invasion of France, but since this was to happen only after Edward paid him the first £45,000 of his subsidy, this clause had never been activated.

[132] *Le Bel*, 1:139–42.

[133] Jan de Klerk (tr. Octave Delpierre), *Edouard III, roi d'Angleterre, en Flandre*, in *Miscellanies of the Philobiblon Society*, X (1867), 5 (postponements); Lucas, *Low Countries*, 292 (subsidies).

[134] *CPR, 1338–40*, 244–5; Schuyler B. Terry, *The Financing of the Hundred Years War, 1337–60* (London: LSE, 1914), 23–4.

[135] *RFR*, II:2:1055–7.

about to open an Imperial diet. There, after Edward paid him some £7,000 in cash[136] and promised to pay the remaining £48,000 of his debt by 21 March 1339, the emperor agreed to make the English king his vicar for all Germany, with all the same powers as possessed by the emperor himself.[137] The diet agreed that if the emperor or his vicar should undertake a campaign "to defend and recover the rights of the Empire, and repair the wrongs done to it, each person should be required to follow as far as the emperor or his vicar shall judge necessary." Any Imperial feudatory who failed to do so would forfeit all holdings within the Empire into Ludwig's hands.[138] With the consent of the electors who were present, the ceremony was performed on 5 September 1338.

With this coup, Edward had fulfilled the requirement imposed on him at the Hal meeting. All of the emperor's vassals (including all of the Plantagenet's allies in the Low Countries) were now legally bound to serve him in his war to protect the rights of the Empire against France. For the moment, at least, the English position had been snatched back from the brink of disaster. It is clear, however, that Edward realized how close he had come to seeing the complete failure of his plans. On 10 November he sealed a remarkable document in which he essentially, if circumspectly, admitted to having been too headstrong in the past, and promised henceforth to follow the advice of his council – Juliers, Guelders, the Bishop of Lincoln, Derby, Salisbury, Henry Ferrers, Bartholomew Burghersh, John Darcy, William van Duivenvoorde, Geoffrey le Scrope, and William Kildesby – without varying from it.[139]

Edward's appointment as vicar left the Duke of Brabant little room to maneuver.[140] In September and October the king convened two assemblies of his

---

136 Sumption, *Trial by Battle*, 243–4.

137 Payment promised: Lucas, *Low Countries*, 290–2. Title: Laurent, *Actes et documents*, n.84: "sacri romani Imperii, per totam Alemaniam et Germaniam ac universas et singulas earum provincias sive partes, vicarius generalis"; "qu'un véritable vicaire de l'empire possède pour agir et pour faire droit, tous les pouvoirs qui appartiennent à un véritable empereur," letter of the Reginald of Guelders printed in the notes to Froissart, *Oeuvres*, 2:548. For the appointment itself (dated 15 September), see *DEB*, 120–2. Ludwig also, on the next day, promised to bring his force of 2,000 men-at-arms to the Cambrésis on 8 May 1339, provided he received the promised gold. Ibid., 116.

138 Froissart, *Oeuvres*, 2:548.

139 *GGG*, 389–91: "nous bien le veons, coment noz dites emprises sont molt hautes et chargeantes, et plus pres chaces a mettre en oeu[v]re, et plus grant trauail, p[ar]emblece et entier counseil demandent, que auant ces heures faire ne soleient . . . nous vousissoins nomer auscunes certeins persons . . . qui feussent charge de par nous de nous conseiller et auiser, ceo qui mieltz serreit affaire, pour mesner noz dites emprises a bon exploit, *et que nous ne varias-soins mie de lour conseilx*." [Emphasis added.] For Duivenvoorde's identity, cf. *RFH*, 2:4:25. This document, with Lincoln included among those whose counsel he promised to follow, tends to reverse the usual understanding of Knighton's comment that the king "told the bishop of Lincoln and others close to him that he had not been well advised." Knighton, *Chronicle* (ed. Martin), 9.

140 Jan de Klerk, *Edouard III*, 9; cf. Edward's summons of the Duke of Brabant, threatening confiscation of the duke's Imperial holdings, in Laurent, *Actes et documents*, no. 83. Note, however, that Brabant had also received a more limited title as Imperial vicar. *DEB*, 118.

confederates, and secured their promises to fulfill their agreements.[141] It was now rather late in the year to begin a campaign, however, and in any case the wool collection in England had so far yielded little result. The rendezvous date for the Cambrésis campaign was therefore postponed until the following July.[142] This rather late date suggests that Edward was finally beginning to understand that "everything takes longer and costs more," and to allow for that principle in his plans. The execution of those plans in 1339, and the second invasion of France in 1340, will be the subject of the three next chapters.

---

[141] *GGG*, 383–4; *DEB*, 123–4; Knighton, *Chronicle* (ed. Martin), 10; Lucas, *Low Countries*, 292–3.

[142] *DEB*, no. 538, dated 20 November 1338, summons the Duke of Brabant and the other allies to join Edward's army between Mons and Binche on the Friday before the feast of the apostle Thomas in order to advance against Philip of Valois. It seems this must refer to the feast of the translation (3 July, making the rendezvous 2 July), since starting the campaign in the second half of December would be impractical. Furthermore, Edward had already, on 6 September, put off his rendezvous with the emperor until May of 1339 (*DEB*, 116), and it makes little sense that he would summon the other allies to begin a campaign before then.

CHAPTER SEVEN

"TO SHAC HIM BY THE BERD":
THE CAMBRAI-THIÉRACHE CAMPAIGN, 1339[1]

Invincibility depends on one's self; the enemy's vulnerability on him. It follows that those skilled in war can make themselves invincible but cannot cause an enemy to be certainly vulnerable. Therefore it is said that one may know how to win, but cannot necessarily do so.   Sun Tzu, IV.2–4[2]

AS SUCCESSFUL AS THEY had been, Edward's manoeuverings in the late summer and early fall of 1338 had served more to defer his problems than to solve them. He had planned an invasion for the summer of 1337 which had never happened, and another in 1338 which had fizzled. If he failed again in 1339, as was certainly possible, there was little chance of his being able to rally the Imperial princes for yet another attempt the following year. Over the winter of 1338 and the spring of 1339, Edward therefore took all possible pains to ensure that he and his allies would actually be ready to implement his two-year-old strategy in the summer. Despite the great need in which the king found himself, despite the fact that this time the wool scheme had parliamentary approval and that a new, more effective collection plan had been worked out, still the preparations for the summer encountered a host of problems, delays and failures of the type which had become so familiar. Royal orders, even when directed to specific individuals and accompanied by dire threats in case of noncompliance, were regularly ignored. Ships which had been ordered to serve in the king's transport fleet took on freight for Gascony instead.[3] John Irp, Constable of the Peace of the port of Ipswich, used force to prevent the Earl of Northampton from arresting ships for the king's use.[4] Smuggling and theft of wool were prevalent.[5] Some tax collectors in five counties refused to hand over the

---

[1]   The quotation ("To shake him by the beard"), from Laurence Minot's contemporary "Songs on King Edward's Wars," refers to Edward's intention in launching an invasion from the Low Countries into the Cambrésis and France: to provoke Philip into a fight. Wright, *Political Poems and Songs*, 67.
[2]   Griffith (ed.), 84.
[3]   *CPR (1338–40)*, 149.
[4]   Ibid., 184.
[5]   Ibid., 175, 179, 180, 184, 187, 191, etc.

money they had gathered; others found it impossible to make their collections.[6] A shortage of canvas for sacks prevented the shipment of wool already collected in Cambridge and Middlesex. Only with the greatest difficulty were Edward's agents able to borrow new money to make some payments to earlier lenders.[7]

Throughout this period, Edward continued to borrow prodigiously, spend prodigally, and complain perpetually at the inadequacy of the revenues reaching him from England.[8] "Since his first arrival across the Channel," complained a long list of articles sent by Edward to the council in England around March of 1339, "the king has never had anything of the issues of his realm for the aid and sustenance of him or his men, at which he marvels greatly, as do all those around him." Few of the twenty thousand sacks of wool granted for the war effort had been collected, and the Bardi, Peruzzi, and others who had advanced loans to the crown were not receiving the wool assigned for their repayment. The few fells which had found their ways to the Continent were of such poor quality and uneven color that they were virtually unsaleable. "The king cannot endure much longer," said one article, "and his affairs are on the point of being ruined." His servants in England were to be informed that the king had set a certain date to pay his allies the subsidies they were owed, and to ride against his enemies to recover his rights. The whole plan would collapse if he did not make his payments, and he could not make the payments without help from England. They should act with all diligence to send him all the treasure, wool and food supplies they could, as quickly as possible.[9]

The king also sent a covert order to repeal most previous assignments on revenues until he re-certified them (which would have been virtually a declaration of bankruptcy) along with other equally desperate steps, such as sending him the money from the subsidies of the northern counties, which had been

---

[6] Ibid., 273.

[7] Lucas, *Low Countries*, 293–6. Despite the limited effectiveness of the tax collections, they succeeded in taking enough money so that "the land was greatly impoverished and abased." *Pakington*, fo. 184v.

[8] It is interesting to note that Edward's great debts did not lead him to economize on his personal spending: to take just one small example, he paid the huge (perhaps record-breaking) sum of £168 15s for a destrier on 31 August 1339. This and many other details of his expenditures can be found in *WBWN*, here at p. 216. By comparison, the mean value of all assessed warhorses lost in Scotland 1336–38 was under £9. Ayton, *Knights and Warhorses*, 241.

[9] PRO C49/ file 7/7: "le Roi puis sa primere venue devers les parties de decea unqes riens navoit des issues de son Roaiume en eide ou sustenanie de lui ne de ses gentz de qoi il se merveille grauntement et touz ceux qi sont entour lui . . . le Roi ne peut plus longement endurer et que tot sa busoigne si est en point de perdre." . . . "Item ils dovient dire coment le Roi ad pris certaine iournee de avaler lempereur et des paiments a lui faire et a ses autres alliez et du lieu ou ils assembleront pur chivaucher [contre ses] enemys a ses droites conquere queu chose est tut perdue sil faille de ses paiementz et les queux paiementz ne se poont faire sanz confort et eide de son roialme pour quoi . . . [document damaged] . . . exciter et mestre la diligence qils purront que tresor, laines, et vitailles lui viegnent ove tote la haste quils poont." Cf. PRO 31/ 7/157, for part of the council's response. Neither of these documents is dated, but March seems likely given the timing of the visits of various people mentioned in it to England, as revealed in *WBWN*, 221 (Molyns), 223 (Donington), 228 (Askeby).

reserved for the Scottish war, and even the cancellation of the fees due to the officers of the crown. The council refused to implement any of these proposals, noting that if the assignments were cancelled, the king would not be able to raise more such loans; that the small revenues which could be gleaned from the north would not be worth the damage and shame which would result from taking them; and that the clerks said that if their fees were withdrawn, they would withdraw their service. Besides, they added, they *had* provided the king with a great deal of money indirectly, by paying monies he had assigned to the Bardi and Peruzzi, to Queen Isabella and Queen Philippa, to Robert of Artois, to wages for the sailors of the fleet and the soldiers on guard in Scotland and Gascony, etc.[10]

But the amount that came from England, even including such indirect payments, was not nearly enough. Before the beginning of the summer, Edward had incurred debts of well over £165,000 *over and above* what he still owed to the Bardi and Peruzzi and to his allies.[11]

Along with the unsatisfactory remittances from England came bad news from Scotland and Aquitaine. Oliver Ingham and the Gascons had been remarkably successful in defending the southern duchy against the French in 1337, but when the reinforcements promised by Edward failed to arrive, morale suffered. Furthermore, Philip was more willing to divert resources to the southern theater after the collapse of Edward's efforts in the north. French troops captured Caumont in February, but that was only the beginning. In April, inside of two weeks, Castelgaillard, Penne castle, Puyguilhem and the strategically key fortresses of Bourg and Blaye all fell. To make matters worse, two of Edward's most capable and important Gascon vassals, Bérard d'Albret and the Sire de Caumont, were captured in the fall of Blaye.[12] Meanwhile, the Scots renounced the truce with England. With French support, they mounted a siege of Perth in May. The same month, a galley fleet in French service burned Hastings after raiding several other places on the southern coast of England.[13]

Against this grim background, Edward remained in Antwerp, helpless to do anything but keep up appearances and stave off his creditors. The invasion of France for which he had borne so much travail and indignity was almost in reach, yet it seemed to hover constantly just beyond his grasp.[14] He desperately

---

10 PRO C49/ file 7/7 and PRO 31/7/157 ["il apparra bien qe il est servi dune grande somme des +issues+ profits de sa dite terre."]

11 These included 451,000 florins (!) owed to Rufus Vivelin, 140,000 florins owed to Nicholas Bartholomei of Lucca, and £76,180 owed to William de la Pole. Lucas, *Low Countries*, 302, 305–6; *RFR*, II:2:1081. For more loans, see *CPR (1338–40)*, 191, 202; Cf. 194, 196. On 6 July he issued a letter of obligation for a further 54,000 florins borrowed from three merchants of Mechelen. *RFR*, II:2:1085. Some of this money doubtless went to pay down previous debts.

12 *Nangis*, 163.

13 Hastings: *CPR (1338–41)*, 287, 258. *Historia Roffensis*, fos 83–83v. For the beginning of the truce, see *Anonimalle*, 13; *Bridlington*, 137.

14 To people back in England, it seemed that their king had been left destitute of advice and good counsel, and that all his friends and confederates had withdrawn from him, so that he

wanted the campaign to begin on schedule, so as to divert French resources to the north and take the pressure off his liegemen in Gascony, but it was not to be. In late June, he made camp in the fields of Vilvoorde to wait for his allies, but it soon became clear that they would not be ready to march on the previously set day of 15 July – not unless the English could find the cash to pay their subsidies, or at least the advance wages they had been promised.[15] As so many times before, Edward had to admit that his previous promises of payment would not be met, and still make new ones for the future.

The situation did not improve in July or August. In July, for the first time in longer than anyone could remember, a French army advanced all the way to Bordeaux. The soldiers even briefly entered the town before Ingham rallied enough men to drive them out in a desperate street fight. Fortunately for the English cause, the French did not have the supplies to maintain the siege for more than a couple of weeks, but the good news of the end of the French offensive in Gascony was more than counterbalanced by word of the fall of Cupar and Perth – the last Balliol holdings north of the Firth of Forth – in July and early August.[16]

Just days after the fall of these places, Edward had to admit to his allies that his latest round of promises for payment would not be kept. Indeed, he imposed on the majority of them to serve as guarantors for his huge debt (207,000 florins) to the Duke of Brabant, the due date for which was now put off until the following Easter. A truly remarkable roster of great men – the Archbishop of Canterbury, two bishops, the Duke of Guelders, the Marquis of Juliers, Jean d'Hainault, no fewer than twelve earls, and fourteen more lords ranging from Henry Percy to Thomas Ughtred – appended their seals to Edward's letter, pledging to meet the debt themselves if the king defaulted, or else to render themselves prisoners of the Duke of Brabant in Brussels until he was satisfied.[17] The extremely strict and elaborate terms imposed on the guarantors show how reluctant the Duke of Brabant was to continue in the alliance in the absence of the money due him; yet the willingness of Guelders, Juliers, and Jean d'Hainault to put their all on the line, though their subsidies were doubtless in arrears as well, shows that the charismatic King of England still had moral resources greater than his financial ones.

No money had come to the king from across the Channel for some time, and

---

was, along with a few supporters, "abandoned, alone, desperate and desolate" [*solum cum paucis desperatum et desolatum derelicquerent*]. *Historia Roffensis*, fo. 83v.

[15] Cf. Sumption, *Trial by Battle*, 273–4; Fryde, *William*, 127. The author of the *Cont. Manuel, 1328–39*, probably a monk of St.-Denis, noted (p. 1264) that it was no surprise that Edward did not get the help he wanted from his German allies, since he didn't pay them the money he had promised; "for as the proverb says, 'no money, no servants.' "

[16] Sumption, *Trial by Battle*, 275–6; Walsingham, *Historia Anglicana*, 1:225 (Bordeaux); *Fordun*, 355; *Pluscardensis*, 287–8; *Anonimalle*, 14.

[17] Laurent, *Actes et documents*, no. 84. The earls were: Lancaster, Warrenne [i.e. Surrey], Derby, Northampton, Salisbury, Arundel, Warwick, Devon, Gloucester, Suffolk, Huntingdon, and Buchan [Henry Beaumont].

his own men were in great distress.[18] It seemed that the nobility and the common people back in England had become "tepid" and unwilling to offer additional support.[19] Furthermore, the emperor let Edward know that, his subsidies being far in arrears, he no longer considered himself bound by their treaty. The king did his best to cover up his disappointment at this news, declaring that it was for the better – if the emperor had joined the expedition, and the combined army had won the victory, the glory of it would have gone to him. Furthermore, this way Edward would avoid the impropriety of campaigning with an excommunicate (as Ludwig then was).[20] This little speech, with its hint of St. Crispin's Day, was well received, but it did not fool anyone. On the verge of desperation, the king took a dramatic step.

"Trusting as always in God and our right," he later explained in a letter to his eldest son and his council in England, "we had our allies come before us and let them know for certain that we would not wait any longer for any reason, but would go forward in pursuit of our right, accepting whatever grace God should grant us."[21] As Vicar of the Empire, he summoned the allies to be ready to go with him on the appointed day.[22] He was going, in other words, with or without them: and if the army of France should attack him, he would conquer or die honorably in battle.[23] The allies, especially Brabant and the Count of Hainault, were not happy about beginning the campaign before they had been paid, but the vision of Edward's lonely host of 4,600 men[24] being wiped out because of their default was more than they could bear – especially since four of the five major allies were the Plantagenet's brothers-in-law, and the fifth was his cousin.[25] So (with the exception of the emperor) they agreed to follow him, "unable for very

---

18 Fryde, *William*, 127–8.
19 *Historia Roffensis*, fo. 83.
20 Jan de Klerk, *Edouard III*, 7–8; *Dynter*, 812.
21 Letter of 1 November, in *RFR*, II:2:1094 (also printed in Avesbury and Froissart, and translated in Rogers, *Wars of Edward III*, 71–74).
22 *Scalacronica*, 169.
23 *Murimuth*, 91.
24 His forces had increased moderately from what they had been in July of 1338. He now had approximately 1,800 men-at-arms, 1,100 mounted archers (mostly in retinues), and 1,700 foot archers (mostly arrayed from the counties) in the pay of his household, not including German troops paid by the wardrobe. *WBWN*, 325–62. These calculations involve some guesswork, among other reasons because the precise dates of service are not usually given; cf. Prince, "Strength of English Armies," 361 for somewhat different results. This provides an interesting counterpoint to those who assume chroniclers' numbers are always exaggerated, for the Bridlington chronicler gives the size of Edward's force as only 800 men-at-arms, 1,200 *hominibus armatis*, and 2,000 archers. *Bridlington*, 147.
25 Viz. the Marquis of Juliers and the emperor, who were married to his wife's sisters; the Duke of Guelders who was married to Edward's own sister; and the Count of Hainault, who was his wife's brother. The Duke of Brabant was Edward's cousin. Judging by later events and by Jan de Klerk, *Edouard III*, 7–8, the emperor was probably not at this meeting, and probably did not commit to join the allied army in person (as the earlier treaty required him to do); but, in the event, he still sent his son with a contingent of his men.

shame to hold back."[26] The Count of Hainault, for the sake of his sister Queen Philippa and her children who were "so close to him," even agreed to serve at his own costs within the borders of the Empire.[27]

Once this resolution had been taken, there were no further delays. On 20 September, the king and his confederates rode out of Valenciennes on their way to Cambrai.[28] [Map 7–1] They halted at Haspres to meet with a delegation of the episcopal city's bourgeois, who were ordered to evict the French garrison from the city and return to the Imperial obedience, or suffer the consequences. When the citizens failed to take this opportunity to surrender, the Duke of Brabant, his sense of propriety satisfied, agreed to proceed.[29] The army advanced to Cambrai.

The Bishop of Cambrai – who was solidly King Philip's man even though his territory was technically within the Empire – was fully braced to resist them.[30] He could do little more than hold the fortifications of his city, however, since Philip's army was not at hand. From 20 September to 8 October, the Anglo-German army systematically devastated the entire Cambrésis, "so that the country is quite completely destroyed, including the wheat, cattle, and other goods."[31] Three castles in the vicinity of Cambrai, including Thun-l'Éveque, rapidly fell into English hands, but Cambrai proved fully capable of resisting any attacks the besiegers could launch.[32]

Perceiving himself environed with enemies, the bishop wrote to Paris to ask for the French king's assistance.[33] Philip sent the unhelpful response that he was certain that the King of England was still in Antwerp, and would not move from there until the first of October.[34] Only after Philip received the report of the sole

---

[26] *Scalacronica*, 169: "qi ne sez purroit detenir pur hount"; cf. *RFR*, II:2:1094, and *Historia Roffensis*, fo. 83v, to the same effect.

[27] *RFR*, II:2:1089.

[28] *RFR*, II:2:1094. There is evidence to suggest that Guelders brought 1,200 men-at-arms rather than his treaty quota of 1,000: *GGG*, 413.

[29] *Dynter*, 812.

[30] It should also be remembered that in this the bishop was following the dictates of the Pope, who did not acknowledge Ludwig the Bavarian as the legitimate emperor. *BLF*, no. 464.

[31] *RFR*, II:2:1094. Cf. *Le Bel*, 1:157–8; *Chronographia*, 2:73.

[32] This information, and much of the material in the following paragraphs, is taken from a contemporary record of the campaign, obviously based on a campaign diary, printed in *KdL*, 84–96, here at 84–5. Hereafter this will be cited as "1339 Campaign Diary." There is a Latin version of the same account in *Hemingburgh*, 340–8, with some slight variations. The French appears to be the original, as the Latin version incorrectly changes the French "lieues" to "milliaria" and has omitted the name of the Earl of Derby in the fourth sentence on p. 346. However, the Latin version adds some information to the list of those in the English army at Flamengrie, pp. 346–7, and specifies the time at which the prisoner released to the French gave his report to Philip (p. 347). Perhaps both the "1339 Campaign Diary" and the Heming-burgh account are based on an earlier version, probably in French. The other two castles were probably Escaudoeuvres and "Relengues" (?). *Chron. Normande*, 41; *Chronographia*, 2:71–2.

[33] *Chronographia*, 2:72.

[34] *Chronographia*, 2:72, 73.

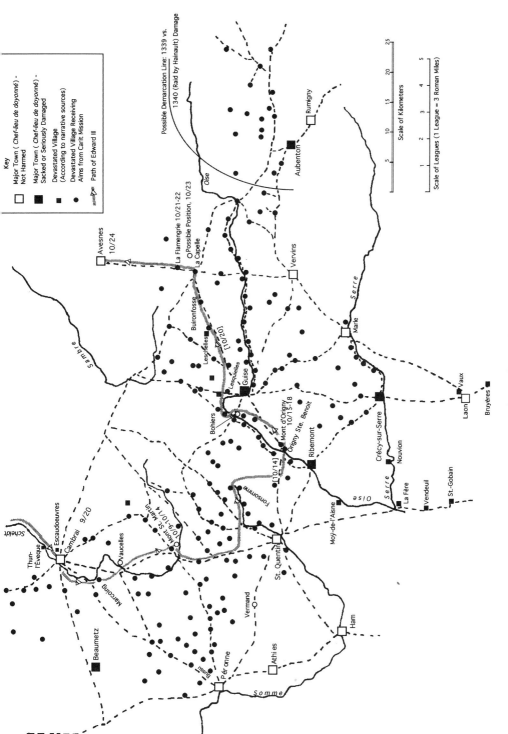

Key

Major Town (*Chef-lieu de doyonné*) - Not Harmed

Major Town (*Chef-lieu de doyonné*) - Sacked or Seriously Damaged

Devastated Village (According to narrative sources)

Devastated Village Receiving Alms from Carit Mission

Path of Edward III

Possible Demarcation Line: 1339 vs. 1340 (Raid by Hainault) Damage

Scale of Kilometers

Scale of Leagues (1 League = 3 Roman Miles)

Avesnes 10/24

La Flamengrie 10/21-22

Possible Position, 10/23

La Capelle

Buironfosse

Lesdrelles

[10/20]

Lesquielles

Guise

Bohiers

Mont d'Origny 10/15-18

Origny Ste. Benoît

Ribemont

[10/14]

Fonsomme

Vervins

Serre

Marle

Vaux

Laon

Bruyères

Crécy-sur-Serre

Nouvion

La Fère

Vendeuil

St-Gobain

Moy-de-l'Aisne

Oise

Serre

Oise

Rumigny

Aubenton

Sambre

Escaudoeuvres

Cambrai 9/20

Thun- l'Eveque

Vaucelles

Marcoing

Mont St. Martin [10/9-10/14]

St. Quentin

Vermand

Beaumetz

Ham

Athies

Péronne

Somme

Scheldt

Oise

Map 7-1. The Cambrai-Thiérache Campaign, 1339

survivor of a convoy which had been captured by the English while trying to deliver a pay shipment to the garrison of Cambrai did he grasp the situation and promise to come to the city's aid.[35]

During this period, Edward was still technically acting fully within his Imperial mandate. His main army remained inside the Imperial border (though some of his troops were already raiding into French territory by the 25th, and on the 28th the Earl of Suffolk sacked Beaumetz, just over the border into French Artois),[36] and the city his army besieged was an Imperial fief, the tenant of which had refused to acknowledge his authority as Imperial vicar. Still, there was no doubt in anyone's mind that this siege was intended to "shake [King Philip] by the beard."[37] The French king's full involvement was signaled by the presence of two of his main military commanders, the Count of Armagnac and the Lord of Beaujeu, in the garrison.[38] At first it seemed that the siege of Cambrai might serve Edward's purpose as well as had the siege of Berwick in 1333. The allies received reports that Philip was drawing towards them, coming from Noyon to Péronne.[39]

These turned out to be premature, however. Edward remained at Marcoign just south of Cambrai for a fortnight, through 8 October, but Philip did not reach Péronne, much less advance from there towards the Anglo-German army. The French king's delay arose in part from the frequent summonses and dismissals of troops he had made over the past two years (which left people skeptical as to the seriousness of this summons) and in part to the relative lateness of the season.[40] While the English awaited him in their camp at Marcoign, they were joined by the Duke of Brabant and his full twelve hundred men-at-arms on 30 September. The last of the allied princes, Emperor Ludwig's son the Margrave of Brandenburg, arrived on 3 October.[41] Despite these reinforcements, Edward's position was far from ideal. Winter was approaching, and his allies, who like the English had expected Philip to come and give battle immediately, were down to less than three weeks' supplies. Cambrai seemed too strong to capture.[42] In the

---

[35] Ibid. Cf. Villani, *Cronica*, 372.

[36] *RFR*, II:2:1094; campaign diary in *KdL*, 85. Cf. *RFR*, II:2:1091.

[37] See note 1, above; cf. *Le Bel*, 1:154.

[38] "1339 Campaign Diary," 85. Beaujeu would become a Marshal of France in 1347; Armagnac had been one of the leaders of the French army in the southern theater since 1337. Cf. Froissart, *Oeuvres*, 2:494–4 for other major French magnates reported to be in the city.

[39] *RFR*, II:2:1094. The timing of these reports is not entirely clear from the context, but it appears to have been around the 25th. In England and Germany, people also expected that Philip would do battle. Knighton, *Chronicle* (ed. Martin), 12.

[40] *Cont. Manuel, 1328–39*, 1265.

[41] "1339 Campaign Diary," 85; *Le Bel*, 1:159. Brandenburg arrived with no carts, so four of them and twelve horses were given to him by Edward. The margrave did, however, bring along some excellent musicians. *WBWN*, 216, 263. The emperor himself did not participate in the campaign.

[42] Froissart, *Oeuvres*, 3:12–13; "1339 Campaign Diary," 86; *Chronographia*, 2:76; *Dynter*, 812; winter: *Cont. Manuel, 1328–39*, 1265; cf. p. 1264, and Knighton, *Chronicle* (ed. Martin), 12, for the previous winter, which in Paris was the longest and harshest in living memory.

limited time available, there was no hope of forcing the bishop into making the kind of surrender treaty that had led to the battle of Halidon Hill. Philip was unwilling to bring his army onto Imperial territory and so give his enemies the moral high ground.[43] Furthermore, Philip generally speaking was inclined towards the teachings of Vegetius (a fourth-century Roman military writer whose *De re militari* was extremely well known in the middle ages), who held that it is better to defeat one's enemies with hunger than with the sword, because the result of battles is always uncertain.[44]

Stronger provocation was therefore needed.[45] As soon as Brabant and Brandenburg arrived, Edward pressed his allies to take the decisive step of leading their troops into France proper. Count William of Hainault, after consulting his advisers, refused outright. Falling back on rather old-fashioned (but legally correct) feudal logic, he argued that he had fulfilled his duty as an Imperial vassal by assisting in the attack on Cambrai, within the bounds of the Empire. But he was also the vassal of Philip VI for lands held in France, and he would not assist in an attack on his feudal lord's own territory. Indeed, if the allies crossed the Imperial border, William proposed to take his men to Philip's army to help defend France.[46] His brother Jean d'Hainault, Edward's long-time friend and the marshal of the Anglo-German host, was of a different mind, as were the majority of the Hainault men-at-arms. Even when Count William did as he said and abandoned Edward, about half of them stayed behind with the English king.[47] The other allies, too, were willing to go along with Edward's plan.[48]

Even the Duke of Brabant, perhaps calculating that he had better keep the

---

[43] *Grandes chroniques*, 9:172, but cf. *Nangis*, 163–4.

[44] Flavius Vegetius Renatus, *De Re Militari*, III.28. Jean de Hocsem says that Philip, in this campaign, prudently avoided battle, reckoning that the English could be defeated as well by lack of supplies as by direct attack. Jean de Hocsem [Joannes Hochsemius], *La Chronique de Jean de Hocsem*, ed. Godefroid Kurth (Brussels: Commission Royale d'Histoire, 1927), 290; Jan de Klerk, another local and contemporary chronicler, makes a similar observation (*Edouard III*, 11), emphasizing the approach of winter. See also *Cont. Manuel, 1328–39*, 1266: "Perhaps this was the best and most suitable counsel, and the healthiest; for the King of England, who had come to conquer the realm of France . . . departed, and defeated himself, without doing anything to his profit, and little to his honor . . . And this the counselors . . . could well have seen, for the weather was very cold and so rainy that neither men nor horses could remain longer in the field. So it seems that it would have been tempting fate [Dieu] to put so many good knights in danger without great necessity."

[45] Cf. *Chronographia*, 2:77.

[46] See his letter in *KdL*, 137–8; *Chronographia*, 2:76, 80; *Le Bel*, 1:157.

[47] *Le Bel*, ibid., states that William brought Philip 500 men-at-arms. (Confirmed by the *Récits*, 168.) This was half the contingent of 1,000 men-at-arms he had contracted to provide Edward. Cf. "1339 Campaign Diary," 91. *Hemingburgh*, 347. All of this, of course, may well have been in accordance with the count's plans, as a way for his family to play it safe, retaining influence on each side of the conflict.

[48] It doubtless helped that Edward had managed, on 3 October, to pay 3,000 florins to the Marquis of Juliers, and another 3,000 to the Duke of Guelders. *WBWN*, 418, 420 (where the year is given incorrectly).

friendship of at least one of the two protagonists in the war, agreed. Unlike the other allies, he had not yet sent his formal defiance to King Philip, but now he did so.[49] Once that was done, the allies were ready to move into the Vermandois in France. To add insult to injury, they chose to do so on 9 October – the feast of St. Denis, the patron saint of the French monarchy.[50] To further highlight the significance of the occasion, on the first day in France Edward created the young Laurence Hastings Earl of Pembroke, and knighted a number of other men.[51]

From the evening of the 9th until the 14th, the king remained based at the small abbey of Mont-St.-Martin near the source of the Scheldt.[52] He was only eighteen road-miles from Péronne, where Philip VI had just arrived, with the kings of Navarre and Bohemia and the dukes of Normandy, Brittany, Burgundy, Athens, Bourbon and Lorraine in tow.[53] As these notables approached from Noyon, they could see from far off the smoke of about two dozen burning villages which bands of English and German soldiers had put to the torch between their base and Péronne. As they drew nearer, burning cinders, flying messengers from the English, fell around the king's head.[54] Even the little village of Bussu, less than two miles from where Philip was staying, was devastated.[55]

Edward's position was such that his army could use the Scheldt as part of its defenses if Philip came out to attack them. Even though this would give the allies a tremendous tactical advantage, they thought that the sight of an enemy army burning and devastating his realm might force Philip to cross the river to attack them.[56] They were wrong: neither he nor his army budged out of Péronne.[57]

---

[49] *Le Bel*, 1:159; cf. *Dynter*, 812.

[50] "1339 Campaign Diary," 85.

[51] Ibid. At least 15 esquires from the English contingent received knighthood on the 9th. *WBWN*, 325–55. Hastings, interestingly, appears in Norwell's account books with the small retinue of three men-at-arms, and continued to receive a banneret's pay (rather than an earl's). Ibid., 331–2.

[52] "1339 Campaign Diary," 85; *RFR*, II:2:1093; *WBWN*, 454; *Lescot*, app. VI, p. 226; not in the nearby abbey of Vaucelles as stated by *Chronographia*, 2:76, and Lucas, *Low Countries*, 334. Edward himself was in the abbey of Mont-St.-Martin, but his army may well have been encamped in the fields on the opposite side of the Scheldt, where the river would serve as a perimeter against any French raids.

[53] *Chronographia*, 2:79.

[54] *Chronographia*, 2:79 (smoke); L. Carolus-Barré, "Benoit XII et la mission charitable de Bertrand Carit dans les pays devastés du nord de la France. Cambrésis, Vermandois, Thiérarche. 1340," *Mélanges d'archéologie et d'histoire publiés par l'école française de Rome* LXII (1950), passim (villages); *Historia Roffensis*, fo. 83v (cinders). Cf. also *Cont. Manuel, 1328–39*, fo. 177v: "le roy . . . moult estoit doulans des arseures que l'en lui compta, et desquelles il pot veoir aucunes."

[55] Carolus-Barré, "Mission charitable," map.

[56] *Le Bel*, 1:159–60: "Le noble roy Edowart et les aultres seigneurs attendirent là lendemain, et pensoient que le roy de France qui veoit ardre et gaster son royaume, ce que onques on n'avoit veu, deust passer par deça la riviere pour les combatre."

[57] Though, according to the *Chronographia*, 2:80–1, Philip had planned to move against

Two cardinals sent by the Pope to make a last-second effort to make peace had been with Edward since he entered France. The king was not much interested in their proposals. "I put a great deal of money and effort into seeking peace with the King of France," he is said to have replied to their entreaties, "but could not have it. Now I have switched to the path of war."[58] The royal counselor Geoffrey le Scrope was more acerbic in his remarks to Cardinal Montfavez, who was not well liked by the English: "My lord, you said in England that the King of England would never set foot in France. Well, now he can offer you a hundred feet."[59] On the 11th, seeing that Philip was not going to risk crossing the Scheldt to reach him, Edward sent the legates back to the French. It was probably through these cardinals that the allies warned Philip that unless he came to fight with them, "he would see such things as he had never seen before."[60] On the 14th, the French having failed to show, the allies fulfilled their promise and moved to a position on the road between St. Quentin and Origny, laying waste to the area of Noyon with great thoroughness as they went. To give Philip another reminder of the possible consequences of failing to oppose an invader, Edward also had it proclaimed that he would protect the lives, lands and goods of anyone who would come into his peace.[61] This was particularly telling because Philip, by contrast, had ordered as part of a scorched-earth policy that any of his subjects' goods which had not been carried to safety in the fortresses should be abandoned to anyone who wanted to take them, "because of which order, many were robbed and despoiled by their own neighbors."[62]

Edward the same day that the English moved off from Mont-St.-Martin. Philip's suspicion that Edward had decamped after receiving word that the French were ready to attack, however, is almost certainly incorrect, considering that (as the same source says on p. 77) Edward's whole purpose in approaching Péronne was "in order to have a battle with [Philip]" [ad finem habendi bellum contra eum].

[58] *Historia Roffensis*, fo. 84v; cf. *EMDP*, 287.

[59] *Historia Roffensis*, fo. 84v: "Domine, dixistis in Anglia quod Rex Anglie nunquam haberet pedem in Francia. Nunc dare vobis potest centum pedes." Cf. the related (and more familiar) story in *Le Baker*, 65. Cardinal Montfavez had in fact been in England on a last-minute papal peace mission in November of 1337. He and his colleague, Cardinal Pedro Gómez de Barroso, had claimed that they "knew for certain" that the Duke of Brabant and Count of Hainault would never aid Edward against Philip, and had threatened the hostility of the Church and excommunication against Edward III, the Archbishop of Canterbury, and anyone else who opposed the granting of a truce to the King of France, conduct which helps explain le Scrope's acidity. See above, p. 144.

[60] Cardinals: "1339 Campaign Diary," 85. Message: *Le Bel*, 1:160 [ilz luy feirent sçavoir que s'il ne venoit combatre à eulx par deça la riviere, il verroit encore chose laquelle n'avoit veu].

[61] "1339 Campaign Diary," 85–6. Noyon: Carrolus-Barré, "Mission charitable." In preparation for this symbolically significant move, twenty-three esquires were knighted. *WBWN*, 325–55.

[62] *Cont. Manuel, 1328–39*, 1265: "Et fut crie partout le pais de par le connestable que quiconques avroit aucunes bestes, biens, blesz, et autres grains es villes que dedens VIIJ jours ilz les eussent vuidez et appourtez aux forteresses, ou ce non ilz estoient habandonnez a tous ceulx qui prendre les vouldroyent; pour le quel ban mains furent robes et depredez par leurs propres voisins."

Philip's strategy of declining battle and letting winter and hunger defeat the Anglo-German army may have been wise, but it was not what the French people expected from their king. Even the most loyal Frenchmen could not understand why, after coming to oppose the invasion, Philip remained shut up in Péronne.[63] He was openly criticized throughout France, and particularly in his own army.[64] The English did their best to encourage this sentiment, using arrows to send scurrilous poems, which accused the Valois of acting more like a rabbit than a lion, into the walled cities where the French army was quartered.[65] When the French king heard what was being said about him, he finally moved out in pursuit of the invaders.

By then, Edward had crossed the Oise at Origny. He remained there waiting for Philip through the 17th, while raiding detachments pillaged and burned villages up to Crécy-sur-Serre, sixteen miles away.[66] Despite the plentiful supplies of cattle and other goods discovered by the foragers, the Anglo-German troops were suffering from a serious lack of bread and wine; heavy rainfall and the growing cold added to their discomfort.[67] As noted above, Edward's allies had expected Philip to give battle almost immediately, so they had not brought much with them. On the 17th, the Duke of Brabant came before Edward to argue that this problem, and the onset of winter, made continuing the campaign pointless. If Philip had so far refused battle, why should he change his tack at this point?[68] Edward remained confident that, if they could stay in the field a little longer, they would have their battle. "I have food enough," he replied to Brabant, "and I will give it to you and your men to sustain them. We will abandon our carts and the great burden of carriages we have, and put our footmen on horseback, and ride forward from day to day until we meet our enemies; that way we will find plenty of supplies."[69] The allies were not convinced, however. They still intended to return home.[70]

Early the next morning, however, they changed their minds. Letters had just arrived from Etienne le Galois de la Baume, the Master of Crossbowmen of France. He promised on behalf of King Philip that if the English would wait until the 20th, then the French king would delay no longer, but give battle on the 21st or 22nd. The offer was conditional on the English picking an appropriate place, where the action would not be affected by rivers, fortifications, or other

---

[63] *Grandes chroniques*, 9:172; cf. *Cont. Manuel, 1328–39*, 1265–6.

[64] Ibid.; *Le Baker*, 65; cf. *Nangis*, 164; *Lescot*, 49; Jean de Noyal, "Fragments inédits," 251. Philip's Vegetian strategy was, however, praised by Jean de Hocsem, *Chronique*, 290.

[65] *Le Baker*, 65; the last phrase, "lepus et linx, non leo, pares" is a clever pun, "leo pares" for "leopard," the heraldic symbol of England.

[66] Road distance. "1339 Campaign Diary," 86.

[67] *Le Bel*, 1:160–1; Villani, *Cronica*, 373. For the weather, see Jan de Klerk, *Edouard III*, 11.

[68] "1339 Campaign Diary," 86; *RFR*, II:2:1094; *Knighton*, 2:11; Jan de Klerk, *Edouard III*, 11 (French unwillingness to do battle).

[69] "1339 Campaign Diary," 86; *RFR*, II:2:1094.

[70] Ibid.

obstructions.[71] Edward was ecstatic.[72] Under the circumstances, the allies could hardly maintain their intention of departing. They acceded to Edward's plan, and the king sent a reply to Philip, saying that though he had already been waiting three weeks, still he would willingly wait until the assigned day and beyond, if Philip would come and give battle.[73]

With their supply problems, though, the Anglo-German soldiers could not easily remain stationary. Their foragers had so pillaged and robbed the neighboring areas that food had to be brought to the army over great distances and with large escorts.[74] Over the next few days they advanced slowly through Thiérache in order to secure enough food and also to cause all the destruction they could.[75] On the 21st, the first day Philip was due to give battle, the allies marched from near Autreppes to la Flamengrie, but the French army was still nowhere in sight. They waited there all day on the 22nd, hoping for some sign of the French army's arrival, but none came.[76] In the evening the king's council decided to move on the next day – presumably to the Count of Hainault's town of Avesnes, which was only about seven miles away along the road they had been following. This would have meant the end of the campaign. Once again, however, letters arrived from the King of France at the last moment, promising that if the allies would take up their position the next day, they would certainly have a battle.[77] This was confirmed by three captured enemy scouts who, interviewed separately, agreed that Philip was only a league and a half distant, and that he planned to fight the next day.[78] Edward rejoiced at this further reprieve for his strategy, and immediately summoned his allies. They once again agreed to await the French.[79] Over the following night, the Hainaulters Walter Mauny and Wulfard de Ghistelles led some daring troops in raids on the French encampments, which they discovered a few miles away around the village of Buironfosse. They attacked the sentries, captured some prisoners, and made enough noise that the French got little rest.

The next day, well before dawn, the allied host moved to a suitable battlefield, on some land belonging to the abbey of Clairfontaine, about one league from la Flamengrie.[80] The English, who took the front lines, formed up much as

71 "1339 Campaign Diary," 87–8; *RFR*, II:2:1093.
72 Cf. "1339 Campaign Diary," 90–1.
73 *RFR*, II:2:1093.
74 Villani, *Cronica*, 373: "lo re d'Inghilterra e' suoi allegati richiesono di battaglia il re di Francia, perocché la stanza non facea piú per loro perché aveano guasto e rubato tutto il paese, e la vittuaglia venía alla loro oste molto da lungi con grande scorta."
75 *RFR*, II:2:1094; "1339 Campaign Diary," 89–90.
76 "1339 Campaign Diary," 90; *RFR*, II:2:1094.
77 "1339 Campaign Diary," 90.
78 *RFR*, II:2:1094; *Dynter*, 812.
79 "1339 Campaign Diary," 90; cf. *Knighton*, 2:12: "De quo nuncio multum laeti facti sunt Anglici, et inmensa voluntate ad pugnandum exhilarati."
80 "1339 Campaign Diary," 90. The place has not been determined with certainty, but the fact that the reference points given in the two contemporary English sources ("1339 Campaign Diary," 90, and *RFR*, II:2:1094; cf. also Minot in Wright, *Poems and Songs*, 69) are

they had done at Dupplin Moor, with a central body of dismounted men-at-arms flanked by wings of archers. Small groups of Welsh spearmen seem to have been placed beside the archers, anchoring the flanks of the line.[81] The allies marveled greatly at this novel array, but saw that it was "good and profitable." Behind the English line formed a second division comprising the men of the dukes of Guelders and Juliers, the Margrave of Brandenburg, Jean d'Hainault, and all the other Imperials except the Brabançons. The Duke of Brabant with his men alone formed the third division.[82]

The allies were reassured to see that the king and all his men were full of confidence, and ready to do battle to the death.[83] Edward, for his part, was glad to see that his allies were also ready and willing to fight, despite their sometime lack of enthusiasm and the much larger size of the French host.[84] Captured enemy scouts again confirmed that Philip was already on his way. In an echo of the 1327 campaign, Edward freed one of these prisoners, presented him with a good horse and a large sum of money, and enjoined him to hasten directly to the King of France. The man was instructed to give a taunting message to Philip, and inform him that Edward would eagerly await him in the field.[85] The arrival of the French was expected at any minute, so well over fifty men received the

---

Clairfontaine and la Flamengrie, with no mention being made of la Capelle, makes the site given in Sumption's sketch-map (*Trial by Battle*, 287) unlikely, especially since it would be hard to describe the position he depicts as a league away from la Flamengrie. Furthermore, it would be dangerously open to outflanking maneuvers by the French. As an alternative site, I suggest that Edward's army may perhaps have been drawn up between the two woodlets in front of the abbey, about a league southwest of la Flamengrie, so that the woods (and the nearby creeks) secured his flanks. This position (unlike Sumption's suggestion) would also match very well with Jean le Bel's statement that the English waited "just two short leagues away from [Philip], in a flat place, without a river or the impediment of fortifications," since the position before Clairfontaine is just under 10 km from Buironfosse. *Le Bel*, 1:164. The "dangerous passage" which many sources say worried Philip would then be the passage between the two woodlets, from which Edward's archers could provide enfilading fire.

[81] By far the most reliable description of the English array, in "1339 Campaign Diary," 90, is unfortunately not entirely clear: "le roy . . . myst ses gents en arraie, les archiers à l'encoste des gentes d'armes, et les Galoys ove lour launces encouste eux." It seems from William Norwell's Wardrobe accounts that there were only 80 Welshmen still in the king's army at this stage, the great majority of them having departed for home on 20 February 1339. *WBWN*, 360–1. For the small troops of spearmen at the far flanks, cf. Jean de Bueil, *Le Jouvencel*, 1:152–3.

[82] "1339 Campaign Diary," 91–2.

[83] "1339 Campaign Diary," 90–2.

[84] *RFR*, II:2:1092; *Cont. Manuel, 1328–39*, 1266 (size).

[85] *Dynter*, 812–3. The scout was to say that Philip and his men were most discourteous and undutiful so to delay men who were daily striving to fulfill the requests (for battle) which the French king had made in his letters ["qu'il, ne sa gent, ne furent mie cortoises et ne feirent mye lour deveir par ensy targer la gent qui furent travaillés de jour en autre et de ceo qu'il avoient requis par lour lettres"]. "1339 Campaign Diary," 91; cf. *Hemingburgh*, 346. This not only resembles the message which Thomas Rokesby brought to Edward from the Scots in 1327, it also (as we shall see) reflects the message sent by Edward to Jean II via Marshal Boucicaut in 1355.

order of knighthood, many at the hands of King Edward himself, and at least thirteen knights raised banners for the first time.[86] Supplies of wine were distributed among the men, along with hundreds of extra longbows and thousands of arrows and bowstrings from the royal store.[87]

When Philip heard the confederates' formation described, he suddenly changed his mind about giving battle. His vanguard was pulled back, and he ordered that the French encampment be fortified with ditches and felled trees.[88] The reasons for this decision are explained differently in different sources. None of the French accounts seem very credible.[89] The English accounts mostly do not go much beyond accusing Philip of cowardice.[90] The most reasonable version is that of Jean le Bel:

> There was great strife and debate in the king's council among the lords and barons of France, for some said that it would be a great failure and a great dishonor if the king did not fight them, when he saw so near at hand, in his country, the enemies who had so burned and devastated his realm in his sight and knowledge. The others said on the contrary that it would be great folly if he gave battle, for he did not know what each person thought, nor if he harbored treason; and besides, on the other hand, the game was not on even terms, for if Fortune turned against him so that he were defeated, he would lose his life and all the realm; but if it turned out that it was the others who

---

86 Among the troops paid by the Wardrobe alone (essentially, the English contingent of the army) there were 57 new knights on 23 October, on top of ten new knights and one new banneret from the 22nd. The new bannerets whose names can be determined were: John Montgomery, Robert Ferrers, Robert Ufford the younger, Maurice Berkeley, Philip Weston, and Thomas Hatfield, the future Bishop of Durham. *WBWN*, 325–55.
87 "1339 Campaign Diary," 91; cf. 90. *WBWN*, 413, shows that 620 bows, 680 sheaves of arrows and 183 dozen bowstrings were handed out.
88 *RFR*, II:2:1092. Cf. Minot, "Songs on King Edward's Wars," in Wright, *Political Poems and Songs*, 68: "It semid he was ferd for strokes/ When he did fell his grete okes/ Obout his pavilyoune," supported by *Le Baker*, 66.
89 *Nangis*, 164, and the equivalent passages in *Grandes chroniques* and *Lescot*, have the king dissuaded from giving battle for four reasons: first, it was Friday, so the battle should be avoided out of reverence for God (apparently a reference to the old Truce of God); second, that the army had just ridden five leagues; third, that his men and his horses had not had food or drink all day; and fourth, that there was a dangerous passage between his army and the English. He was therefore advised to wait until the morrow, and accepted the advice, "which delay and advice turned to the very great dishonor of the king and all the realm. For when the King of England learned the power of the King of France, he departed around midnight and returned into the Empire; and thus was the King of France Philip defrauded, which made him very angry. He returned into France without having accomplished anything." *Grandes chroniques*, 9:173. While something like this (or the related story in *Chronographia*, 2:83–4, which gives the main emphasis to the obstacles to approaching the English) may explain why Philip did not press on to attack on Friday the 21st, it does little to explain why he did not give battle on Saturday the 22nd, when Edward was waiting in the fields belonging to Clairfontaine abbey.
90 Minot, "Songs on King Edward's Wars," in Wright, *Political Poems and Songs*, 68–9; *RFR*, II:2:1094; *Bridlington*, 148.

were defeated, he [Philip] would not have conquered the [realm] of England, nor the lands or the possessions of the other lords of England.[91]

Edward had more to gain from a battle, and Philip had less to lose from avoiding one. The French king was well aware of how much effort his cousin had put into mounting this invasion, and how deeply he had gone into debt to pay for it. He also knew that the Anglo-German army was having serious supply problems, thanks to the efforts of French troops.[92] Without a battlefield victory to redeem his travail, Edward's war effort might collapse. The same was not true of France, as some of Philip's advisers argued:

> Although the English had devastated and burned a large part of the realm, still they had gained little by it, for the king still had enough of it remaining to him; and if the King of England wanted to conquer the realm of France, he would need to make a large number of such *chevauchées*.[93]

At the end of the day, the leaders of the Anglo-German army decided that they had waited long enough.[94] They did not have the supplies to spend another day without moving.[95] Instead, they marched the short distance to Avesnes, in Hainault, coming within a league and a half of Philip's position in the process – and reportedly causing a panicked retreat among the French by doing so.[96] Once Edward's army returned into Hainault, the campaign was over. Although they had not fought the decisive battle they had hoped for, still the allies were reasonably content, as Jean le Bel explains:

> They had entered into the realm of France, remained there for some time while burning and laying waste the countryside, within sight of the king [Philip] with all his power, of which no one had ever seen the like. Yet they had waited for him in the field all day, just two short leagues away from him, in a flat place, without a river or the impediment of fortifications, and still he neither came to them nor showed himself nor made any appearance that he was about to move.[97]

---

[91] *Le Bel*, 1:163; cf. *Cont. Manuel, 1328–39*, 1265–6. Cf. also *Dynter*, 813, which specifies that the King of Bohemia and the Bishop of Liège pressed Philip to give battle nonetheless, but he answered "that he had now held and possessed the realm of France, peaceably, for more than twenty years; so it was not his intention to stake it on the outcome of a battle, which would perhaps last only one day, and the result of which was always very doubtful." Compare Vegetius, III.8, III.28.

[92] Giovanni Villani explains that Philip hoped to defeat Edward by blocking the passage on "a river" [presumably the Oise] over which Edward's supplies reached him. Villani, *Cronica*, 374; cf. Hocsem, *Chronique*, 290: "the King of England retreated . . . due to lack of victuals, which the men of the King of France did not allow to arrive."

[93] *Le Bel*, 1:165. The *Fr. Chron. London*, 73, similarly, has Philip say to his entourage that he would leave Edward in peace and allow him to expend all that he had, and more, so that all his realm of England would not be enough. Cf. also *Cont. Manuel, 1328–39*, 1266.

[94] *RFR*, II:2:1094.

[95] *Scalacronia*, 169; *Le Bel*, 1:164; Villani, *Cronica*, 373.

[96] *RFR*, II:2:1094; cf. *Bridlington*, 148.

[97] *Le Bel*, 1:164.

Le Bel left it to his readers to judge which side had done better in the campaign. In general, though, contemporary opinion was clear: the French should have given battle. One English author went so far as to claim that Philip, by his inaction, had forfeited the right to be called King of France.[98] As far away as Italy, people spoke of the great shame the campaign had brought on the Valois monarch.[99] Even in Philip's own realm, it was commonly said that the king had been excessively cautious, leading a great number of noblemen to have hats made of fox fur to symbolize their "detestation and mockery" of King Philip's "foxy" [cowardly] conduct of the affair.[100] Having failed to protect or avenge his subjects, he could only return to Paris "safe and sound, but with little honor."[101]

---

[98] *Fr. Chron. London*, 72, which also claims that the same title was then granted to Edward by "all the chivalry of Christendom." This was obviously affected by the author's hindsight after Edward adopted that title in January of 1340, but it is nonetheless very interesting that a contemporary should so associate the two events.

[99] *Storie Pistoresi (MCCC–MCCCXLVIII): Rerum Italicarum Scriptores*, ed. A. L. Muratori, ser. XI, vol. 5, 161 ("grande vergogna"). Cf. G. Villani, *Cronica*, 374 ("puose in viltá del re di Francia e de' Franceschi"). Cf. also *Bridlington*, 148.

[100] *Cont. Manuel, 1328–39*, 1266: "en detestacion et moquerie de la besoigne."

[101] Giovanni Villani, *Cronica*, 373.

CHAPTER EIGHT

"WITH SOROW ON ILKA SYDE": FLANDERS AND THE TWO KINGS OF FRANCE, 1340[1]

In war, numbers alone confer no advantage. Sun Tzu, IX.45[2]

"THE YEAR OF GRACE 1340," wrote the author of the *Grandes chroniques de France*, "was one of misery and confusion, for between the two kings nothing worthy of praise was done."[3] There is much truth to this observation, though Edward's naval victory at Sluys was one of the greatest triumphs of the war. Aside from that, neither king accomplished much militarily. The campaigning season ended with a truce which brought no great advantage to either side. This mediocre outcome was the result of a campaign in which both sides deployed massive armies, among the very largest of the war's 116-year course, paid for by yet another year of crushing taxation on both sides of the Channel.[4]

The most momentous event of the year, though, came much earlier, when on 26 January Edward III declared himself to be King of France as well as of England, and symbolically quartered his heraldic leopards with the lilies of France. Although Pope Benedict professed "great astonishment and amazement" at Edward's act,[5] this can hardly have been genuine, for there had been signs of its coming for at least three years.[6] At the death of Charles IV of France in 1328, Edward III, his nephew and therefore his closest male relative by a full degree, had been briefly considered as an heir to the throne. But, at the time, Edward was a minor under the control of his strong-willed mother Isabella and

---

[1] The quotation [with sorrow on every side] is from Minot, "Songs on King Edward's Wars," 72. Minot meant it to apply to the inhabitants of Tournai in 1340, but it is appropriate for the year as a whole.

[2] Griffith (ed.), 122.

[3] *Grandes chroniques*, 9:175. Cf. *Nangis*, 124.

[4] In England, the high level of taxation for yet another year brought the commons to the edge of rebellion (*Fr. Chron. London*, 82–3), and after the end of the campaign led to the greatest constitutional crisis of Edward's reign. In France, even the author of the semi-official royal *Grandes chroniques* was moved to complain at the oppression of the poor. *Grandes chroniques*, 9:175.

[5] *RFR*, II:2:1117.

[6] Edward had already used the title in a letter to the communes and Count of Flanders around December of 1338, one which the count had doubtless seen before he fled to Philip VI's court. Thus, Philip and the Pope must have been aware of it. See below.

her lover Roger Mortimer. The queen and Mortimer, whose conduct had scandalized the French court when they were there in 1326, were widely – and almost certainly correctly – believed to have been responsible for the horrible murder of Edward II just a year before King Charles' death. The fact that Edward was essentially a foreigner, despite his status as Duke of Aquitaine and a Peer of France, also impeded his claim. So the other peers agreed on Charles' next-closest male relative, Philip of Valois. Though ineffectual protests were sent from England, Philip was universally accepted as king. Until 1337, Edward never made any further public notice of his claim. When he did homage to Philip for his French possessions in 1329, and then in 1331 recognized this homage as liege, he explicitly recognized Philip's title.

Even before the outbreak of the Hundred Years War, however, Edward realized that his claim to the throne could prove as useful in France as Balliol's claim had been in Scotland.[7] Edward, in his role as Duke of Aquitaine and Count of Ponthieu, was not the only great noble of France who resented Philip's royalist, centralizing policies.[8] There was the potential that the Plantagenet could play on the internal divisions in France to bring some of the other peers to his side, drawing them away from the Valois king. The justice of his claim might not move them, but it could give French men and women who felt impelled towards him for reasons of self-interest an invaluable "excuse" for opposition to Philip. Once Edward made his claim to the throne, they could support him without unambiguously betraying their loyalty to the kingdom and crown of France, just as so many Scots had been able to switch their loyalty back and forth between Edward Balliol and David Bruce without being dishonored as traitors to their nation. Of course, few Scots other than disinherited exiles had acknowledged Balliol as the rightful king until he had won the battle of Dupplin Moor, and he had not gained really wide acceptance until after Halidon Hill. But, as we have seen, Edward III at the beginning of the war was planning for just such a battlefield victory in France.

In France, it was universally believed that the French exile Robert of Artois had planted the idea of prosecuting this claim in Edward's mind. This is probably not true, though the count may have helped develop thoughts which the Plantagenet had long entertained. Robert must indeed have had a full and subtle understanding of Edward's claim to the throne, since it was he who had taken the lead in arguing against the English king's pretensions in 1328.[9]

Wherever the idea came from, it was more fully discussed at the Great Council of 20–24 January 1337. The lords and prelates gathered in the Tower of

---

[7]   It should be noted that, at this time, Balliol's rule of Scotland was far from being a dead letter. David II was still a refugee in France; Balliol held the capital, Perth; and Edward III continued to dominate the Border counties ceded to him in 1334.

[8]   In a letter of July 1335, Benedict XII, perspicacious as always, had warned Philip of the danger this factor might present in an Anglo-French war. Printed in *BLF,* no. 90. See also J. Le Patourel, "Edward III and the Kingdom of France," *History* 43 (1958).

[9]   *Historia Roffensis,* fo. 79; *Chronographia,* 2:1; *Grandes chroniques,* 9:72n.

London, where (much to their "astonishment and wonder") the assembly was briefed on Edward's right to the crown of France, along with the less startling news of the French refusal to return the Aquitainian lands seized by Charles of Valois, the offers of peace made to Philip, and the efforts thus far made to secure allies in the Low Countries. On that first topic, the lords were reminded that Edward was in his twenty-fifth year, by the end of which he must either seek to reclaim the inheritance which should have come to him on the death of Charles IV, or lose it.[10] (This was a reference to the civil law principle that a minor, under the age of twenty-five, could not legally alienate his patrimony.)[11] Was not the son of a sister a nearer heir than the son of an uncle, they were asked, and should not the inheritance of a realm descend rather than ascend? The lords feared to reach any definite decision on undertaking a task which seemed so difficult, perhaps even impossible. After splitting into magnates and prelates to discuss the matter further, they finally decided that the king should once more send a solemn embassy to seek peace with Philip; but if peace were refused, then Edward should strengthen his naval forces and secure allies to help "against the King of France, who unjustly occupied the realm of France."[12] This amounted, in effect, to the council's permission for Edward to pursue his right to the French throne.[13] However, the king chose not to bring his claim into the public arena at that time. Up until early October, his correspondence always continued to refer

[10] *Historia Roffensis*, fo. 79: "Quibus, die Jovis proximo post predictas octavas [sancti Hillarii] in turri Londonie congregatis, fuit expositum de jure quod rex Anglie habet ad coronam Francie, et de detentione Vasconiae, ac de modis et viis oblatis regi Francie, et an expediret quod Rex Anglie in partibus transmarinis ad resistendum regi Francie amicos faceret magnos confederando. Item querebatur a magnis quod quia Rex erat in vicesimo quinto anno etatis sue, infra quod tempus regem oporteret petere vel perdere hereditatem suam." Cf. *EMDP*, 436: "dominus noster rex, ad discretionis annos jam perveniens, convocari fecit parlamentum," and *RFH*, 2:4:194: "Sanè, cum ad majorem Aetatem essemus provecti, metuentes grave nobis posse praejudiciam generari, si dissimulassemus ulterius de immiscendo nos Haereditate nostrae praedictae, omnia & singula, si quae per imbecillitatem & simplicitatem minoris Aetatis possimus dici fecisse, nobis praejudicialia in hac parte, statim, quatenus de Facto processerant, cum de Jure non tenuerant, Revocavimus effectualiter et expresse." The importance of this point has not been recognized.
[11] T. Cunningham, *A New and Complete Law Dictionary* (London, 1770), s.v. Gavel-kind: "By the custom of Gavel-kind an infant at the age of fifteen is reckoned of full age to sell his lands . . . but in this the customs of England differ from the Civil law, for the Civil law does not allow his dispositions till the age of twenty-five . . . If an infant [i.e. person not of age] bargain and sell his land by deed . . . yet may he plead non-age."
[12] *Historia Roffensis*, fo. 79v ["contra Regem Francie, injuste occupante Regni."]. It is interesting to note that the *Historia Roffensis* then goes on to note the honorable reception by King Edward of Robert of Artois the following week.
[13] Ibid.; *Scalacronica*, 167. The chroniclers' statements are supported by the fact that Archbishop Stratford, when defending himself against Edward III's accusations following the failure of the siege of Tournai, stated that the 1337 parliament had advised the king to go to war to recover France, and had also approved the alliance strategy. See Roy M. Haines, "An English Archbishop and the Cerberus of War," *The Church and War*, ed. W. J. Sheils (London: Ecclesiastical History Society/Basil Blackwell, 1983), 163.

to Philip as "King of France," even in war propaganda.[14] Edward did not give up the idea of reviving his claim to the throne, however. On 6 October 1337, not long after he had officially ratified his alliance with Emperor Ludwig, Edward had letters drawn up which his ambassadors could have used to appoint the Duke of Brabant, the Count of Hainault, the Marquis of Juliers or the Earl of Northampton as royal lieutenant in France. In the salutation of these letters, Edward was styled "Edward, by grace of God King of England and France, Lord of Ireland, and Duke of Aquitaine." Alternate versions reversed the order of "England" and "France." In these letters, and supplementary ones calling on the prelates, nobles and commoners of France to give their obedience to his lieutenant, it was specifically stated that the realm of France had devolved on Edward by legitimate succession.[15]

These letters were never used, and they may never even have been seen by anyone but the king's closest advisers. But, after 7 October, Edward carefully kept the way open for their deployment. He began to refer to the Valois king as "Philip, calling himself King of France,"[16] "Philip of Valois, who pretends himself to be King of France,"[17] or, most politely, simply as "our cousin of France."[18] In July of 1339, Edward removed any doubts as to what this was intended to suggest. In a long open letter to the Pope and the cardinals, he plainly stated that the realm of France "is known by all to belong to us by legitimate right."[19] Yet Edward did not go so far as to claim that he himself was the real King of France, though this was a natural consequence of his argument.[20] This was a way for Edward to use his claim as an implicit threat, a warning that he might play the succession card if the French refused to make peace on terms acceptable to him.

Between 1337 and 1340, however, his potential claim remained more valuable than an actual one would have been. As Balliol's case had shown, and Edward III's own exploratory diplomacy apparently confirmed, a claim to the throne was likely to gain him few if any French supporters until *after* he had demonstrated by victory in battle that he had a good chance of making his pretensions into reality. Edward's main allies were Imperials, rather than Frenchmen, so they did not need the "excuse" the claim could have provided to justify their support for him.[21] Furthermore, as Edward was well aware,

---

14 E.g. see *RFR*, II:2:994.

15 *RFR*, II:2:1001.

16 In a letter to the Pope on 17 October 1337, in *RFR*, II:2:1004, for example.

17 *RFR*, II:2:1034. The phrase is less awkward in Latin: "Philippum de Valesio, se Regem Franciae praetendentum."

18 E.g. *RFR*, II:2:1014. For other variations, see *RFR*, II:2:1043, 1086; Froissart, *Oeuvres*, 2:550. The significance of these appellations was not lost on French public opinion: see *Cont. Manuel, 1328–39*, 1262–3.

19 *RFR*, II:2:1086.

20 In other words, he was saying that he *should have been* King of France, not that he *was* or even still should be.

21 Though, as we have seen, they did require that Edward lead them as Vicar of the Emperor rather than as King of England.

declaring himself King of France would look rather absurd and impotent, considering that Philip was and had long since been universally recognized as king, and Edward appeared to have no way of making his own claim stick.[22] Also, it would shift his war to a more aggressive footing, making it one to *gain* his rights rather than defend them, which could be uncomfortable politically and religiously.[23]

Perhaps most importantly, by declaring Philip's kingship to be illegitimate, Edward would be dramatically raising the stakes in the war. If the war were over Scotland and Gascony, there was room for compromise. Philip could not lightly abandon his Bruce allies, and he had no desire to surrender the lands he and his father had conquered in Aquitaine, but still these were points on which he might make concessions if Edward's war went well. Edward I, after all, had gained similar terms from Philip the Fair even though the former's French campaigns had enjoyed little success. But if the issue of the war were who should rightly occupy the throne of France, then there could be no peace without an over-whelming military victory or defeat. Furthermore, once Edward had formally staked his claim to the crown, he could not easily or gracefully accept any form of compromise peace which did not at least offer suitable compensation for his rights to the throne (such as the division of the kingdom between him and the Valois). This problem was still plaguing the kings of England a century later, when the military advisor Sir John Fastolf pointed out that, if Henry VI agreed even to treat with the Valois on even terms, "it myghte be said, noised, and demed in all Christian londis where it shuld be spoken of . . . that alle [his and his predecessors'] werres and conquest hathe be but usurpacion and tirannie."[24]

Despite all this, Edward had seriously considered making the claim in 1337. He quite possibly would have done so in 1339 if he had won a battle at la Flamengrie.[25] Even his failure there likely contributed to the Plantagenet's decision to lay claim to the crown, for by doing so he would give Philip a major reason to give battle the next time their armies met. Without doubt, however, the main reason he took this major step was the chance to secure an alliance with the people of Flanders.

As noted in the last chapter, the English had instituted an embargo of wool

---

[22] *Le Bel*, 1:167–8; cf. *RFR*, II:2:1117; *Historia Roffensis*, fo. 88.

[23] Edward had consistently taken pains to cast himself as a man "having a peaceable heart" [cor habentes pacificum] and his war against France as a defensive one, claims which lost a good deal of credibility once he was trying to take Philip's crown. See *RFR*, II:2:1086, 994–5, 1004.

[24] Stevenson, *Letters and Papers*, 2:576. It should be noted, however, that Edward repeatedly showed that he *was* willing to give up his royal title in exchange for sovereignty over Aquitaine. See: J. J. N. Palmer, "The War Aims of the Protagonists and the Negotiations for Peace," *The Hundred Years War*, ed. Kenneth Fowler (London: Macmillan, 1971), and Rogers, "The Anglo-French Peace Negotiations."

[25] The letter to the Pope and cardinals cited above (note 19), which was issued as he prepared for the invasion of the Cambrésis, was probably intended to prepare the way for this eventuality. Cf. also the *Fr. Chron. London*, 72.

shipments mainly to put pressure on the Count of Flanders, whom Edward hoped could be brought into the Anglo-German alliance, or at least pushed into neutrality despite his personal Francophile leanings.[26] His county was among the most industrialized and densely populated regions of the world, and his people lived primarily by the cloth trade. Most of England's wool crop usually found its way to the great weaving cities of Ghent, Ypres, Bruges, and their satellites, where it was made into fine cloth for export. The weaving industry provided a livelihood for the masses, and a source of great riches for the urban elites. When wool from England stopped, so did the weavers' looms. Great numbers of Flemish workers were reduced to leaving the county to beg from strangers.[27]

The political history of Flanders in the first three decades of the fourteenth century was a tumultuous one.[28] Flanders had previously been almost independent from France, much like Aquitaine or Brittany. But in the aftermath of the Flemish alliance with Edward I in 1297, the French had occupied and practically annexed the county. Beginning in 1302, the common people of Flanders had risen against the occupying French, beginning a civil war that lasted intermittently until 1328, when the battle of Cassel finally crushed the Flemish independence party. But the tensions between Flemings and Frenchmen, and between rich and poor within the county, had by no means evaporated by 1337. In late December of that year, they erupted into an open rebellion against French control of the county, one spearheaded by a demagogue from Ghent named Jacques van Artevelde.

At first, the rebels were primarily concerned to get the English wool they needed to keep their people from starvation.[29] This they accomplished quickly, for by early February 1338, they negotiated an arrangement whereby Flanders would stay neutral in the war between the two kings, and England would allow the wool shipments to resume.[30] King Philip, however, reacted very badly to this news. In March of 1338, he executed Sohier de Courtrai, a popular and respected Flemish nobleman whom he suspected of having helped to bring about the Anglo-Flemish arrangement. This action, which was directly contrary to the chartered liberties of the Flemish towns (since Sohier had not been tried in a municipal court, as was his right), angered even those Flemings who were inclined to France. This was just the beginning. Philip then ordered that the walls of Ghent be cast down, and had Benedict XII put the city under interdict for its rebellion.[31]

---

26 Note the words of the count's *bailli* as reported in the *Chronographia*, 2:49.

27 *Chronographia*, 2:42, 44, 49.

28 For the most recent treatment, see William H. TeBrake, *A Plague of Insurrection* (Philadelphia: University of Pennsylvania Press, 1993).

29 *Chronographia*, 2:42–4, 49–51. Cf. *Nangis*, 162.

30 Lucas, *Low Countries*, 269–71; Sumption, *Trial by Battle*, 231.

31 See Sumption, *Trial by Battle*, 230–2; Lucas, *Low Countries*, 272–4. Sohier, one of the "leaders and governors of Flanders" at the time, was indeed engaged in negotiations with Edward III, even though he was receiving a pension from Philip VI: *DEB*, no. 357; *KdL*, 155;

Whether Philip acted more out of anger than policy, or whether he expected these sanctions to lead to the collapse of Artevelde's regime, the results for France were little short of disastrous. The leadership of Ghent, for its own protection, became actively anti-French. In late April, Artevelde's supporters defeated the men of the Count of Flanders (who remained personally loyal to Philip) in a pair of bloody if minor combats. Bruges and Ypres were brought under Artevelde's control, the former willingly, the latter after a brief siege.[32] Around this time, the neutrality agreement evolved into a "firm treaty of friendship" between England and the three great cities.[33]

By June, Philip had realized his mistake. Although Flanders was only a single county, its importance and its resources belied its rather small size. Ghent, Ypres and Bruges were all three among the ten largest (and richest) cities in the realm of France. The county's military strength was symbolized by the battle of Courtrai (1302), when an army of Flemish militiamen had crushed a major French army, killing about a thousand noblemen, "the glory of France made into dung and worms."[34] Under exceptional circumstances, the Flemings could put as many as twenty-four thousand soldiers into the field.[35] If all this were not enough, the county's good ports and proximity to England and to the Imperial Low Countries allies gave it a special strategic value. Edward III, according to Jean le Bel, believed that the Flemings could be of more assistance in the prosecution of his war "than the rest of the world put together."[36] Philip could ill afford to lose their assistance in the war, which was why he was so angry at the treaty of neutrality, but he could even less afford to have them go from neutrals to active enemies. So in early June, not long before Edward was due to arrive on the Continent, Artevelde managed to arrange it so that both kings officially recognized the neutrality of the commons of Flanders. Flemish merchants were to have full access everywhere. The people of the county were not to take part in the struggle between England and France, or aid either side in any way.[37] Neither side was to be allowed to damage the other within Flanders, or to cross through the county in order to attack the other.[38]

So things stood on the eve of Edward's planned 1338 campaign. When

Journaux du Trésor, 879, 904. Philip's power to have Benedict impose the interdict stemmed from the terms of the 1305 treaty of Athis-sur-Orgue, which had brought a temporary end to the Franco-Flemish wars. Cf. *Pakington*, fo. 190v.

32 *Chronographia*, 2:50–3; Lucas, *Low Countries*, 275–6.

33 On 8 May, Edward wrote to the aldermen of Ghent, Ypres and Bruges to express his joy and powerful contentment at hearing of the treaty. *RFR*, II:2:1035.

34 *Annales Gandenses*, 30.

35 Verbruggen, *Art of Warfare*, 167–9; cf. *RFR*, II:2:1130.

36 *Le Bel*, 1:168: "[les] Flamens, qui plus luy pouoient aidier à sa besongne que tout le remanant du monde." Cf. also *Grandes chroniques*, 9:162: Edward "saw well that he could not well get what he desired [venir à sa volenté] unless he had Flanders on his side."

37 This provision and the other neutrality terms referred to the commons and the bourgeois of the towns; the count, with his vassals and noble kinsmen who willingly joined him, could serve Philip outside of Flanders if they wished.

38 The Anglo-Flemish treaty is printed in *RFR*, II:2:1042–3. It was sealed on 10 June; the

Edward arrived on the Continent the next month, a representative of the leaders of the Flemish towns was waiting to meet with him. Through this man and through other contacts, Edward pressed the Flemings to join more fully into his alliance.[39] They declined to do so at that point, but they maintained close contact with the English over the following months. Once Edward's plans for a campaign in 1338 collapsed, and he gained the title of Vicar of the Emperor, he tried to use it to convince the Flemings to abandon their neutrality and join his side in time for the 1339 invasion. At first, in mid-November of 1338, he did so by summoning Count Louis, as a feudatory of the Empire, to aid him in reconquering lands lost by the Empire, on pain of forfeiture of all the fiefs he held of the emperor.[40] It is no surprise that this did not work, for Louis held vastly more land of Philip than of the emperor, and was in any case personally loyal to the Valois.

When Louis made no response to Edward's proposal, the English king tried some more powerful means of persuasion. Using Count Reginald of Guelders as his intermediary, the king sent the Flemings a truly remarkable letter, one in which he used the title of "King of France and of England" for the first time outside his own chancery.[41] The letter informed the Flemings that, since the Count of Flanders was the emperor's vassal, the latter would be ready to help them recover the castleries of Lille, Douai and Béthune, which had been taken from them by the kings of France. Once again, the count was required to attend the emperor or his vicar in order to renew his homage for his Imperial fiefs. In addition, more strikingly, he was required

in the name of the King of England, as King of France and England, to acknowledge what is right and reasonable, and attend the king to receive [*relever*] the fiefs which he holds of the crown of France, because he [Louis] is

---

king confirmed it on the 26th (ibid., 1045). For the agreement with France, given by Philip on 13 June, see *KdL*, 62–3.

[39] Lucas, *Low Countries*, 284 et passim.

[40] This was presumably just after 10 November, when Reginald of Guelders was invested with full powers to treat with Louis and the towns of Flanders, and Edward "instructed him to treat on behalf of the emperor for support in the war to recover his rights on the border." *DEB*, no. 537. Lucas, *Low Countries*, 316. Cf. *DEB*, no. 533; Froissart, *Oeuvres*, 2:549.

[41] Printed in Froissart, *Oeuvres*, 2:548–51; title at 549. Unfortunately, the document is not dated. It is certainly later than November of 1338, since it refers to the lack of response to the letters mentioned in the previous note. Allowing a reasonable period for a response, this suggests that the letter was sent in December of 1338 at the earliest. Since Reginald is referred to as Count rather than Duke of Guelders, it must have been written before 19 March 1339, when he received the latter title.

Lucas, *Low Countries*, 323, takes this document as having been issued the same time as a letter of the emperor announcing Edward's appointment as vicar to the men of Ypres, written 13 March 1339 (in Froissart, *Oeuvres*, 2:551–2); but since the Count of Guelders' letter (unlike the emperor's) addresses Count Louis as well as the commune, and asks the commune to try to overcome any hesitation on the count's part, it probably came earlier, before the count fled to St. Omer in late January of 1339. Indeed, it may even have been these proposals of Edward's that convinced the count to flee Flanders.

one of the Peers of France, and the King of England is the legitimate King of France.[42]

The towns of Ghent, Bruges and Ypres and the rest of the commons were requested to consider Edward's claims and advise the count to do the right thing and help the English king to recover his realm of France, which had been unjustly taken from him. Even if the count refused, the commons of Flanders were asked to rally to Edward as their sovereign, and aid him in recovering his rights.[43]

In exchange, the Count of Guelders was authorized to make momentous concessions on behalf of his liege-lord. Edward would restore the currency to the stability it had enjoyed under St. Louis, ending Philip VI's practice of devaluations which caused serious inflation and struck hardest at the most commercialized areas of France, such as Flanders. He would restore any lost customs or usages for the "profit and utility" of the craftsmen of Flanders; preserve the county from brigandage; and help the Flemings reconquer the three castleries, which he would perpetually reunite to the county of Flanders. He would establish a wool staple in Flanders and permanently revoke "all the sentences, fines, obligations and other servitudes which had been illegitimately imposed on them by the crown of France" – mainly a reference to the burdensome terms of the Treaty of Athis-sur-Orgue. He would agree not to make any treaties except by the consent of the count and people of Flanders. Finally, he would "accord to the land of Flanders all the liberties which it shall be in his power to give."[44]

Artevelde and his supporters might well have gone along with this proposal, but Count Louis would not so betray his liege-lord. So long as he was in Flanders, and so in Artevelde's power, however, he had little choice. It was probably to avoid entering into such an alliance with England that he fled his county in January of 1339. For the new regime in Flanders, this open break with their lord was very embarrassing. They informed Edward that they would prefer to remain in their current state of benevolent neutrality, for the time being at least. The obvious financial embarrassment of the English king probably contributed to this decision.

Over the ensuing summer and early fall, as the events of the Cambrai-Thiérache campaign described above ran their course, Artevelde was making every attempt to convince Count Louis to return, for his absence deprived the demagogue's government of the mantle of constitutional legitimacy. In September, when Philip wanted to try to make sure that Flanders would at least

---

[42] In Froissart, *Oeuvres*, 2:549–50: "Nous requérons aussi le comte de Flandre, au nom du roi d'Angleterre comme roi de France et d'Angleterre, de reconnaître ce qui est de droit et de raison, et de se rendre près du roi pour relever les fiefs qu'il tient de la couronne de France, car il est l'un des pairs de France, et le roi d'Angleterre est roi légitime de France."
[43] Ibid. A brief argument against the claim that the throne could not be transmitted through a woman was provided to help them convince the count.
[44] Ibid., 551.

stay neutral in the coming campaign, the French king persuaded his loyal vassal to return to the county. Artevelde took advantage of the count's return, Edward's offers, and Philip's dangerous situation to send an embassy to the French court, which arrived shortly after the standoff at la Flamengrie. The ambassadors asked for the return of Lille and Douai to Flemish jurisdiction, and threatened to take them by force if the Valois king would not grant them willingly.[45] Philip did not like rebels, and he did not like to be threatened. He refused. As soon as the embassy got back to Flanders with the news, Artevelde therefore reopened discussions with the English.[46]

Edward III, at this point, was already in the process of making plans for the 1340 campaigning season. After the stalemate at la Flamengrie, Edward's partisans had argued that he was the victor of the campaign, since he had ravaged the territory of Philip of Valois, and the French king had not dared to do anything about it.[47] Edward himself was under no illusions, however: he knew exactly how much effort, embarrassment and expense it had taken him to mount the 1339 *chevauchée*. He also knew that his whole aim for the campaign had been to bring Philip to battle, and that he had not succeeded in doing so. Despite all this, however, Edward had not abandoned the basic strategy which had guided the operation.

The flaw in the 1339 campaign seemed more in its execution than in its conception. He had, after all, *almost* pushed Philip into attacking the Anglo-German army. It seemed that with just a little more incentive, the English king might still get the decisive combat he desired. In 1339, Edward had not expected his adversary to want to avoid battle, and so he had not prepared properly for that eventuality. But Edward already had experience in bringing a reluctant foe to battle, in 1333, and it had been a good experience. The Scots had not wanted to fight in that year, but they had still done so when it came down to the choice of meeting the English in the field or losing Berwick. Lack of supplies and the onset of winter had prevented him from putting Philip in the same position with respect to Cambrai in 1339, but now that he knew what sort of an opponent he was up against, there was no reason he could not mount a more convincing siege in 1340.

Cambrai had been chosen in 1339 largely because it was technically an Imperial fief, and Edward's allies had hoped they might draw Philip into battle

---

[45] Sumption, *Trial by Battle*, 299; Hocsem, *Chronique*, 290; *Chron. Normande*, 42; *Chronographia*, 2:85–6.
[46] It has generally been suggested that Artevelde and his supporters turned to Edward because they feared an attack by Philip unless they had a strong ally to help protect them. (E.g., see Sumption, *Trial by Battle*, 299; Perroy, *The Hundred Years War*, 104–5.) It seems to me, however, that this was not a major factor. Philip had made more than a few concessions to keep them neutral, and if they had been willing to abandon their demands for territory outside Flanders, it is very unlikely that Philip would have pushed them into Edward's arms by attacking them. If he had intended to attack, he would probably not have allowed his faithful follower Count Louis to return to Flanders with the embassy.
[47] *Le Bel*, 1:164.

without having to cross into France. Under the changed circumstances of 1340, two obvious targets for a new siege presented themselves: Douai, the center of one of the three castleries which Flanders was seeking to recover, and Tournai.[48] Douai must have been particularly tempting to the eyes of William of Hainault, for it lay just a short way into France at the far end of the small county of Ostrevant, which had long been the subject of disputes between Hainault and France.[49] Holding it would greatly strengthen Count William's position in the county. The major problem with choosing Douai, however, was that it was upstream on the Scarpe river (a tributary of the Scheldt), from the other possibility, Tournai. Up to Tournai, the Scheldt flowed entirely through neutral Flanders and friendly Hainault. Thus, it could be used to bring food to a besieging army and prevent the supply problems which had forced the allies to abandon their siege of Cambrai the year before. If the allies moved directly on Douai without taking care of Tournai first, the French garrison there could make river transport difficult or impossible. Thus, Tournai was an ideal target for the 1340 campaign.[50] The possibility of Flemish help made it even more so. The Tournaisis was a shallow salient pinched between Hainault, to the south and the east, and Flanders, to the north. Thus, it could easily be accessed by troops and supplies from both those counties. A better situation for a siege could hardly be imagined.

Of course, though Tournai was a very substantial town,[51] its capture would not be of any great advantage to Edward III. This was nearly irrelevant, though, since *the purpose of the siege was not really to capture the city*: it was to put the city in certain and immediate peril of capture, so as to force Philip to come to its rescue. Edward's attitude towards the city itself was clearly indicated in the letter of credence he supplied to the ambassadors he was sending to treat with the Flemings on 4 January 1340.[52] In this document, Edward, as King of France, offered to hand the Tournaisis (along with the three castleries and the county of Artois) over to the county of Flanders. In return, the Flemings were to assist Edward in recovering his realm of France.

---

[48] Lille, the other major French city in the area, also coveted by the Flemings, was impossible to access from Hainault without marching through Flanders (which would violate the neutrality treaty, still in force when Edward was first making plans for the 1340 campaign) or the Tournaisis (which would endanger the lines of communication and supply).

[49] See Lucas, *Low Countries*, 195, and William's defiance in *KdL*, 137, for these disputes. Note that although Edward, in late 1339, could not count on William to join him in an invasion of France, he still could expect Hainault at least to continue to support his efforts within the borders of the Empire, which (combined with the neutrality treaty with Flanders, which kept the water-route down the Scheldt open) would give him and his other allies the access to Tournai and Douai they needed.

[50] Cf. *Le Bel*, 1:182, which suggests that the decision to besiege Tournai was based in large part on its value as a base for further campaigns against Lille and Douai, and into France up to Compiègne.

[51] According to a contemporary poem, the walls of Tournai were 9,000 feet in length, and protected by forty-seven towers. Froissart, *Oeuvres*, 25:365.

[52] *RFR*, II:2:1106.

Negotiations on this basis proceeded quickly. Although the formal treaty between Edward and the Flemings was not sealed until 29 March, when Edward could have it ratified by the parliament then sitting, it had been agreed in substance before 26 January.[53] On that date, in an elaborate ceremony in the Ghent marketplace, Edward III was solemnly crowned King of France.[54]

*

After about a month spent in Flanders, during which he visited Bruges and Ypres and also had notice of his assumption of the title and arms of King of France sent throughout northern France, Edward managed to secure permission from his creditors in Antwerp to return to England.[55] They were not happy to see him leave with his debts so far in arrears, but they realized that he could not pay them unless he could visit his realm to arrange for the collection of the money he needed. Edward arrived in the Orwell estuary on 21 February, and immediately plunged back into the activities which had occupied so much of his attention for the past four years: raising troops, ships, and especially money.[56]

The king summoned a parliament to meet at Westminster on 29 March; an assembly of 154 of the leading merchants of the realm was also to gather there two days earlier.[57] Edward had been trying to secure the parliamentary aid he needed to pay his allies' subsidies and wages since the previous October. At a parliament which met then, the Commons had taken the very unusual step of refusing to make a grant until they had returned to their communities to get popular approval for a new subsidy. When they met again on 19 January 1340, the Lords pressed them to make good their promise to grant the king the aid he so desperately required. Once again, their response was unusual – and very significant in the history of the development of parliament. They agreed to grant the king yet another massive aid, thirty thousand sacks of wool, but only if he would agree to the conditions set out in a letter of indenture they had prepared.[58]

---

53 Edward speaks in a letter dated 28 January of "certain conventions" agreed between him and the Flemings (*RFR*, II:2:1107) but they had doubtless been worked out earlier, before the coronation, since the basics of the agreement (including the territorial and commercial clauses, and a subsidy of £120,000, slightly lower than the £140,000 promised in the actual treaty) were announced during the ceremony. See the newsletter in *DEB*, no. 596, and the treaty, in *KdL*, 110–29. The treaty is dated "the Wednesday after mid-Lent," which Kervyn de Lettenhove wrongly gives as 23 March (actually a Thursday). "La mi-quaresme" here doubtless means "mid-Lent Sunday," (the fourth Sunday in Lent) the Wednesday after which was the 29th, the day of the opening of parliament (*RP*, 112). Cf. Mas Latrie, *Trésor*, 650 The treaty specifies the approval of parliament.

54 The ceremony is described in a newsletter in *DEB*, no. 596; see also *Le Bel*, 1:167 n.1. For a contemporary ditty circulated to explain the grounds for Edward's new arms, see *Pipewell*, fo. 14v.

55 Lucas, *Low Countries*, 366; *RFR*, II:2:1108, 1111. Special letters were addressed to Tournai, the three castleries, and the major towns of Artois. Ibid., II:2:1111.

56 *RFR*, II:2:1115 (date), 1114–16 (money); Sumption, *Trial by Battle*, 322 (ships and men).

57 *RFR*, II:2:1115; ibid., 1114; *RP*, 108; *Handbook of British Chronology*, 559.

58 *RP*, 107.

They had already made such frequent and substantial grants that they "were so impoverished they could hardly survive"; they could not understand how the king could possibly have spent it all. His own constant complaints at the paucity of revenues reaching him, which must have been widely known, tended to feed the Commons' suspicions that the king's financial problems arose from embezzlement and theft by his tax collectors. Therefore, they demanded an investigation of the use of the grants already made, with all current ministers to be suspended from their offices until they had rendered their accounts. Anyone found guilty of financial abuses was to be punished in exemplary fashion, without any pardons being given to anyone. All future expenditures were to be monitored, and indeed controlled, by a committee of peers answerable only to parliament. All of this, and several other petitions as well, would have to be accepted by the king, or there would be no grant of aid.[59] This was a matter of such constitutional significance that Edward's proctors could not assent without his personal approval, so they agreed to forward the petitions to the king.[60]

After this additional delay, and considering the £140,000 in new subsidies he had promised to the Flemings, Edward was more in need of money than ever before – and that is saying a great deal.[61] At the beginning of the 29 March session, the king's prolocutor explained the reason for the summons in the most Manichaean terms:

> Namely, how our lord the king needed to be assisted with a great aid, or he would be dishonored forever, and his lands on both sides of the sea in great peril; for he would lose his allies, and he would have to return personally to Brussels, and remain imprisoned there until the sums for which he was obligated should be fully paid. But if he were granted an aid, all these difficulties would cease, and the emprise which he had undertaken [*faite*] would be brought, with the help of God, to a good conclusion, and thus there would be peace and calm everywhere.[62]

The attitude of the Commons had not changed greatly since the last meeting, but they were willing to make some concessions. Provided that the king would

---

59 Ibid. The text of the petition is not to be found there, however. It can be found in A. W. Goodman, ed. and tr., *Chartulary of Winchester Cathedral* (Winchester: Wykeham Press, 1927), no. 297. Cf. *RP*, 113.

60 *RP*, 107–8. When the Lords reminded them of the urgency of the king's need for money, the Commons agreed to supply 2,500 of the 30,000 sacks immediately, whether or not the king granted their petitions.

61 Flemish subsidy: *KdL*, 120.

62 *RP*, 112: "C'est assavoir, coment nostre Seignur le Roi convendra estre aide d'un graunt Eide, ou il serra deshonurez a touz jours, et ses terres auxi bien par decea come par dela, en graunt peril; qar il perdera ses Aliez, et od tut cela il lui covendra en propre persone retorner a Brussell, et demorer y come prisoun, tan q' la soumme d'avoir en quele il se est obligez a eux soit pleynement paie. Et en cas q'il soit aidez, totes tiels meschiefs cesseront, et l'emprise quele il ad faite serra mene, od l'eid de Dieu, a bone fyne et par tant pees et quiete par tut." The last phrase is difficult to translate. On the king's obligation to return to Brussels if his immediate debts were not paid, see Lucas, *Low Countries*, 376.

accede to a list of petitions they had prepared, they were ready to make a two-year grant of the "ninth" sheaf, fleece, and lamb of the counties, and a ninth of all the goods of the burgesses of the realm.[63] In addition, the much-despised *maltote* of 40s. per sack of wool exported was authorized to continue until Whitsun of 1342, but after that the customs duties were to return to their traditional level of just 13s. 4d. Among other things agreed by the king in return for this grant was that the clause of the *Confirmatio Cartarum* forbidding taxation without parliamentary consent should be held to include the tallages which the king had heretofore been able to levy at will on his boroughs and demesne lands.[64] The king also agreed to permit an audit of the accounts of those who had received the money and wool contributed for the last parliamentary aid, conducted by individuals chosen by the parliament: a serious infringement on royal privilege.[65] These were the sort of constitutionally significant concessions which many other monarchs would have hesitated to make, but Edward did not. He was focussed on his goal. He just wanted to get as much cash as quickly as possible so that he could lead his grand army into France and pull Philip into an open battle where the French king could be thoroughly defeated.

Over the next three months, while Edward and his advisors worked to put together the English fleet and army necessary for that purpose, events on the Continent developed rapidly. The first news to reach England was good news: William of Hainault, who had abandoned the allied coalition when Edward led the army across the French border in 1339, formally defied Philip VI on 2 April, and returned more firmly than ever to the English camp. Philip's men, nominally acting on behalf of the Bishop of Cambrai, had for several months been making raids on William's territories in the Empire, especially the lands belonging to his uncle Jean d'Hainault who had so loyally supported Edward III.[66] Though William had actively sought to come to terms with the Valois king, the latter foolishly refused to have anything to do with him.[67] Philip remarked that since he had already been defied by fifteen princes, a sixteenth made little difference.[68] Indeed, the French were making rather obvious preparations for a full-scale attack on Hainault.[69] Under these circumstances, William had little choice but to turn to his English and Imperial allies for assistance.

They proved fully willing to come to his rescue. Edward had left the earls of Salisbury and Suffolk in Flanders (partly as his representatives, and partly as

---

63 *RP*, 112–13. This "ninth" was actually a tax of ten per cent; after the local parish had received the tenth sheaf, etc., in tithe, the king would get the ninth one, leaving eight for the producers. This innovative tax was expected to provide as much as £200,000, but proved extremely disappointing at first. See Fryde, *William*, 146–7.

64 Ramsay, *Revenues*, 178.

65 *Parliamentary History*, 254–5.

66 See *Récits*, 171; Williams's letter of defiance, in *KdL*, 136–40; Lucas, *Low Countries*, 383–4.

67 *KdL*, 136–40.

68 *Chronographia*, 2:107.

69 Lucas, *Low Countries*, 373, 388.

hostages for his debts), and they and Artevelde were particularly eager to begin military operations against France. The allies soon agreed that the assault on Tournai should begin earlier than previously planned, even though this meant opening the campaign before Edward III could arrive. Perhaps the English earls remembered how useful Balliol's early opening of the siege of Berwick had been. In any case, the allies now arranged to make a three-pronged advance on the French city, with Artevelde and the main Flemish army approaching from the north; the Hainaulters coming directly from their own county; and Suffolk and Salisbury conducting a small army of men from Ypres through the middle of Walloon Flanders, a fairly direct route which would give them the opportunity in passing to destroy a troublesome garrison of Genoese crossbowmen which the French maintained at Armentières.

Of these three contingents, two met with complete failure even before reaching Tournai, and the third accomplished nothing. The first to meet disaster was the force led by the English earls. Their advance towards Tournai took them just slightly to the north of Lille, so they decided to examine its defenses in case they were called on to besiege the town after the anticipated fall of Tournai.[70] Many years later, Froissart wrote of the English that they "never worried about it if they were not in great numbers."[71] He meant his remark as praise, and indeed the boldness of the English was, overall, to their great advantage in the war. But in this case it had nearly disastrous results: when Salisbury and Suffolk left their slow infantry army behind them for a quick cavalry reconnaissance of the city, they fell in with a portion of the garrison and were both taken prisoner, Salisbury being seriously wounded.[72] At a blow, Edward had lost two of his most loyal, experienced and competent commanders, by far the most important men yet taken by either side in the Anglo-French war. By comparison, the consequent retreat of the army of Flemings the earls had been leading was small beer.[73]

William of Hainault's army had only slightly better luck. Tournai was less than ten miles from his capital at Valenciennes, and his forces garrisoned the bridge-town of Antoing, just above Tournai on the Scheldt. Doubtless he originally intended to cross the river there. But when the time came for his army to advance, he decided to make a quick raid into Thiérache instead, to retaliate for the devastation already inflicted on Hainault by the French. It seemed that this

---

[70] *Nangis*, 167, implies that Lille was the main object of the earls' expedition, though this does not match well with the other sources.
[71] Froissart, *Oeuvres*, 7:333: "ne n'ont pas ressongné pour ce se il n'estoient point moult grant fusion."
[72] This is described in a number of chronicles, including: *Chronographia*, 2:98–103; *Le Bel*, 1:168–9; *Scalacronica*, 170, and *Murimuth*, 104–5, condemn the earls for their lack of prudence in making such a foolhardy reconnaissance. *Cont. Manuel, 1339–46* has a fairly detailed and very interesting account of these events, part of which can also be found (from a different manuscript) in the notes to the *Chronographia*, and which has also been printed in translation in Rogers, *Wars of Edward III*, 81–2.
[73] *Chronographia*, 2:98–104; Sumption, *Trial by Battle*, 311–12.

would be an easy and quick diversion, for there were hardly any French defenders in the area: Jean d'Hainault had already tricked them into concentrating elsewhere. As expected, the raiders met little resistance except at the substantial town of Aubenton, which they nevertheless took by assault and pillaged thoroughly, killing many of the inhabitants.[74] Meanwhile, however, the garrisons of Tournai and Lille took advantage of the count's absence to assault and capture his castle at Antoing. This deprived him of his only secure river crossing above Tournai, a very serious blow.[75]

By the time the Imperials returned to Valenciennes, they were already late for their rendezvous with the Flemings at Tournai. Rather than marching north of the target city to cross the Scheldt in Flanders, they decided to cross at Valenciennes and try to capture the French-held crossing over the Scarpe at Mortagne. That way, they would be "showing the flag" in the county of Ostrevant, which William claimed, as well as securing an approach to Tournai. This was a sound enough approach – though what the Imperials would have done after reaching Tournai is hard to imagine, since the Flemings by this point had already returned to Flanders – but its execution was very poor. French soldiers not only beat off the attack on Mortagne, they also succeeded in defending a barricaded ford a short way upstream against William's vastly larger force. The Count of Hainault returned to Valenciennes in complete failure to prepare for imminent approach of the French army.[76]

The third army, the one led by Jacques van Artevelde, managed to reach its destination without difficulties, encamping within view of Tournai around 10 April. Jacques soon received some news of his absent partners. The Imperials were still days away in Thiérache; the men of Ypres had gone home after their leaders were captured. The Flemish demagogue doubtless felt some satisfaction at having achieved his military objective when his noble colleagues had not, but he realized that it would be dangerous to remain in such an exposed position without them, for his army was not large enough to be secure even from a regionally organized French relief effort. Around the 13th, he and his men

---

[74] *Cont. Manuel, 1339–46*, fos 165v–66: "En l'an mil iij^c lx, tantost apres pasques [16 April], le conte de Henault, qui avoit rendu son hommage au roy, et ledit messire Jehan de Henault, desirant de soy vengier par engin, manda par menaces a Gales de la Baume (maistre des arbalesriers, qui estoit es frontieres de par le roy) que il se iroit veoir. Adonc ledit maistre cuidoit que les diz contes et messire Jehan deissent verite [et] manda plusieurs gens darmes qui estoient la de par le roy en plusieurs lieux es froniteres, et especialement au vidame de Laon qui estoit a Aubenton en Terasche, que il lui envoiast de sa gent. Si les lui envoia. Et lors ledit conte et messire Jehan, sachans que pou de gens avoit audit lieu d'Aubenton, vindrent la et ardirent la ville et tuerent hommes et femmes et prindrent ledit vidasme et occirent les duex fils dudit vidasme. Et ce fu fait secont jour apres que ledit conte ot rendu son hommage au roy sicomme dessus est dit."; also *Grandes chroniques*, 9:174, *Récits*, 171–4, and *Chronographia*, 2:104–5; Sumption, *Trial by Battle*, 310–11; Lucas, *Low Countries*, 385.

[75] Sumption, *Trial by Battle*, 313. He could cross the Scheldt at Valenciennes, but he would still find the Scarpe blocking his advance to Tournai.

[76] *Chronographia*, 2:107–8; Sumption, *Trial by Battle*, 313–14.

packed up their tents and returned to Ghent to await the arrival of their newly acknowledged king.[77]

In the middle of the next month, the French offensive which the allies had intended to draw away from Hainault began. It turned out to be almost – but not quite – as embarrassing for the French as the operations in April had been for Edward's men. It began well enough when an advance force led by Jean of Normandy (Philip VI's heir) and the Count of Eu, the Constable of France, marched from St. Quentin to Valenciennes in just four days, meeting no significant resistance on the way. Despite the Count of Eu's slightly absurd attempt to use a 50-year-old agreement between the King of France and the bourgeois of the town to convince them to surrender, however, the inhabitants of the town defended themselves vigorously.[78] The earls of Warwick and Northampton, valiant soldiers both, were present to help lead the defense. Their influence can perhaps be seen in the daring sally made by the garrison and the townsmen early on 23 May, the day after the French arrived. This was carried off so successfully that the French were entirely put to flight, losing their tents and a number of casualties. Normandy and Eu retreated back to the Cambrésis, where they began a rather less ambitious process of reducing the castles which the Hainaulters had held since the beginning of the 1339 campaign. Escaudoeuvres fell in the first week of June. The French then moved against the strong castle of Thun-l'Éveque, where they were joined by Philip VI himself. The castle held out for over two weeks, long enough for the Flemish and Imperial armies which had been gathering in anticipation of Edward's arrival to march to its rescue. From the 20th through the 23rd, the French and allied armies sat on opposite sides of the Scheldt, the water preventing the latter from rescuing the stronghold. On the 23rd, the garrison set fire to the remainder of the fortifications and slipped away to join their army. This, though neither side knew it yet, was to be the end of the border campaigns until high summer.[79]

While this second Cambrésian campaign was underway, Edward was making the final preparations for transporting his army to Flanders. The main fleet was due to assemble on 24 June, but Edward initially intended to cross about a fortnight earlier with the few dozen ships that were available by then.[80] When he was on the very point of departure, having already embarked most of the men-at-arms' horses, he received word that the King of France had deployed a huge armada at the mouth of the Zwin to block his passage and, if possible, capture his person.[81] Edward was glad to hear it. He disembarked his horses, intending to gather as many ships as possible, load them with soldiers, and attack the enemy immediately.

---

[77] Sumption, *Trial by Battle*, 312–13.

[78] See the Count of Eu's letter in *KdL*, 149–52.

[79] Sumption, *Trial by Battle*, 316–18; Lucas, *Low Countries*, 389–94.

[80] Around forty according to *Avesbury*, 310; around 60 according to *Historia Roffensis*, fo. 84v. Cf. also *Murimuth*, 105.

[81] *RP*, 118; *Avesbury*, 311; Jan de Klerk, *Edouard III*, 14; *Historia Roffensis*, fo. 84v.

For the last several years, the war in the Channel had gone back and forth, but generally the French had the better of it. Between late 1339 and early 1340, however, Philip lost most of the large galley fleet he had had at his disposal. First, a number of Genoese galleys in his service deserted for lack of pay; then an English surprise raid burned most of the remaining French galleys in harbor.[82] The alliance with Flanders had also boosted Edward's potential naval power very considerably.[83] The English, as we have seen, were always ready for a full-dress battle, and it now seemed that the circumstances were as favorable for a sea-fight as they would ever be. Furthermore, in a naval battle, unlike a land one, Edward could take the tactical offensive without disadvantage. This, combined with the fact that the French were evidently willing to fight, meant that he could for once be certain that he would not experience a frustrating standoff like the one at la Flamengrie.

If he did not move directly against the French fleet, it would almost certainly ruin his plans to attack Tournai. He could probably have managed to avoid the enemy fleet and land his troops at Dunkirk or Ostende, but, as he had explained at the March parliament, without great aid from England his war effort on the Continent could not proceed. If the money collected for the subsidies then granted to him could not reach him, he would not be able to pay his allies their subsidies or wages, and the whole effort would inevitably collapse. Thus, the Channel had to be kept open.

There was another issue at stake as well, one which he emphasized in his letter to parliament after the battle of Sluys. The English had known for some time that the French were planning a major invasion of England, possibly through Scotland. It was all too easy to imagine the two hundred ships and the twenty thousand men on them descending on Britain after the king had emptied the land of its best fighting men by leading them into France.[84]

Of course, grim as these possibilities were, they paled in comparison to what could be expected if the sea-battle Edward wanted did not go well. As Froissart observed, naval fights tended to be the cruelest, for there is nowhere to flee but into the sea.[85] On board the fleet would be Edward himself, along with the earls of Derby, Northampton, Warwick, Gloucester, Arundel, and Huntingdon, and the flower of the archers and men-at-arms of England.[86] Their loss would have left England prostrate. This outcome seemed all too probable, for the French ships were both more numerous and larger than any the English could conceivably gather on short notice.[87] The dangers were so great that Archbishop

---

82 Sumption, *Trial by Battle*, 265–6, 320.

83 The Anglo-Flemish treaty envisioned the Flemings (possibly with the aid of the Brabançons) providing twice as many ships as the English for a Channel defense fleet. *KdL*, 119.

84 *RP*, 118; cf. *Melsa*, 3:44.

85 Froissart, *Oeuvres*, 3:201.

86 For Derby through Gloucester, see E101/389/8, m. 11 (my thanks to Dr. Andrew Ayton for providing me with a summary transcript); for Arundel and Huntingdon, see Ayton, "Edward III and the English Aristocracy," 178.

87 By the time of the battle, even after surprisingly effective emergency efforts to reinforce

Stratford, the chancellor, vigorously opposed an attack on the French fleet, unless there was first enough delay to assemble a much more powerful fleet.[88] The archbishop felt so strongly on the matter that he resigned as chancellor and privy councilor and returned the Great Seal in protest when the king insisted on proceeding.[89] Edward then called on his most experienced admiral, Robert Morley, and John Crabbe, the Flemish ex-pirate, for their opinion. Their answer was almost verbatim the same as the chancellor's.

Edward exploded. He accused the two of having plotted with the archbishop to concoct a "premeditated sermon" to prevent him from making his crossing. "I will cross despite you," he declared angrily, "and you who are afraid, when there is nothing to fear, you stay at home!"[90] The two sailors then proved themselves to be of the high caliber that characterized so many of Edward's leading commanders. They insisted on their heads that, if the king made the passage immediately, he and all those with him would inevitably be cast into peril. But, if he were going, they would lead the way.[91]

Edward was mollified enough to compromise – influenced, perhaps, by the fact that the wind was in any case unfavorable for the crossing, and remained so until 23 June.[92] He wrote to each port in the north and south, and to London, for more ships. For a week, he and a few companions rode personally to all the ports within reach to collect ships, men-at-arms, and archers. This proved successful beyond anyone's hopes, for within ten days he had a sufficiency of ships, and so many archers and men-at-arms that he could select the best and send the rest home.[93]

"We hope," wrote Edward in an open letter to the towns of France the day before his departure, "that the King Above, who humbles the unjust for their misdeeds, and loves and exalts the just, will give us a sign of His favor."[94] The clergy of England were requested to pray for victory. Edward, however, was not relying entirely on divine intervention. He had put together a fleet, probably of 120 or 147 ships, which in addition to their crews were crammed with soldiers.[95]

Edward's fleet, the English managed to deploy only 147 ships (at most) compared to 200 or more on the French side. *Le Bel*, 1:179, remarks that considering the Frenchmen's larger and more numerous ships, "if God had not aided the English, they would not have had the power, or even a hope, of resisting the French."

[88] *Avesbury*, 311.
[89] Ibid; *RFR*, II:2:1129.
[90] *Avesbury*, 311: "Vobis invitis, transfretabo, et vos qui timetis, ubi timor non est, maneatis domi."
[91] Ibid.
[92] Wind: *Fr. Chron. London*, 76.
[93] *Avesbury*, 311–12; *Hemingburgh*, 355; *Pakington*, fo. 190v; *Historia Roffensis*, fo. 84v. Recognizing the gravity of the situation, the Bishop of Rochester even sent eight soldiers at his own cost; presumably others did as well. Ibid.
[94] *RFR*, II:2:1127 [Et speramus quod ipse Rex Excelsus, qui injustos propter suas injustitias humiliat, et justos diligit et exaltet, faciet nobiscum signum in bonum].
[95] The number of English ships is given in *Lanercost*, 333 (147) and Villani, *Cronica*, 377 (120). Other estimates are higher (e.g. 300 in *Fr. Chron. London*, 77; 260 in *Murimuth*, 105,

The pay record for the campaign shows some thirteen hundred men-at-arms and about a thousand archers aboard, but since some retinues are missing, and since in this emergency situation numerous soldiers were sent at local expense instead of the royal wage, Villani's assertion that Edward had two thousand men-at-arms and an ever larger number of archers may be correct.[96]

They left the Orwell estuary at dawn on 22 June, and reached the coast of Flanders the next morning.[97] The Bishop of Lincoln was put ashore with instructions to ride for Sluys and convince the Flemings to sail out from their ports to assist the English during the approaching battle. Sir Reginald Cobham and two other knights were to observe the French fleet from the land.[98] The English soon came within view of the enemy armada.[99] The French fleet had adopted a rather static defensive position under the direction of the two admirals of France, Hugh Quiéret and Nicholas Béhuchet, administrators with little naval experience who (as one French chronicler said of the latter) "knew better how to draw up an account than to conduct a naval war."[100] Their ships were arrayed in three lines, each ship linked to the next by a chain so that the English could not

and *Le Baker*, 68; 200 in Jan de Klerk, *Edouard III*, 15, and the *Historia Roffensis*, fo. 84v), but the sources unanimously agree that the French were much more numerous than the English, and since the numbers of the French ships are better known, it is clear that the smaller estimates for the English fleet should be preferred. (This conclusion is also supported by the relatively small number of English fighting troops aboard.)

French pay accounts indicate that the French fleet amounted to 171 ships and 29 galleys, barges, and bargots (counting Barbanero's three galleys, which were withdrawn before the battle). (l'Opital's accounts, discussed in Roncière, *Hist. de la marine française*, 438–43, have now been printed in *Clos des galées*, 2:20–64.) Edward III, in a letter written after the battle, states that the French had 190 ships, galleys and great barges, of which all but 24 were captured. [In *KdL*, 167: "Et si vous fesoms savoir que le nombre des niefs, galeyes et grant barges de nos enemys amounta à IX^{xx} et dis, lesqueles estoient touts pris, sauve XXIIII." For some reason, this has been generally misread as meaning 190 captured and 24 escaped. E.g. Lucas, *Low Countries*, 398 n.140; Sumption, *Trial by Battle*, 612 n.14.] The chronicles mostly report the French fleet as closer to 250 vessels. Villani, *Cronica*, 377; *Hemingburgh*, 356; *Knighton*, 2:18.

Edward III's figure of 166 ships captured (190–24) is roughly confirmed by Hocsem's figure of about 140 and William of Dene's tally of 160. Hocsem, *Chronique*, 295; *Historia Roffensis*, fo. 85. The latter source notes, incidentally, that the "large and beautiful" ships *Cog Seyndenys* and *Cog Sancti Georgii de Normannia* were among the prizes.

96 Villani, *Cronica*, 377. Pay rolls: See note 24, Chapter 9, below. Unpaid troops: note 93, above. An estimate of "the number of various men, lords, and archers who are about to cross over with the king," prepared in 1340 (though probably related to the Tournai army rather than the Sluys force) planned for wages for 2,590 men-at-arms (including the king, ten earls, 49 bannerets and 489 knights), 1,102 "gentz armez," and 7,952 archers, including 2,000 Welshmen, along with 12,000 sailors. PRO C47/2/33. The Sluys fleet may have been comparable in number of sailors, though it was substantially smaller in number of soldiers. The *Historia Roffensis*, fo. 85, estimates a total of 16,000 men aboard.

97 *RFR*, II:2:1129; Edward's letter in *KdL*, 166; *Pipewell*, fo. 14v, specifies the hour of tierce.

98 *Lanercost*, 333; *Hemingburgh*, 356; *Knighton*, 2:18.

99 *KdL*, 166; *Historia Roffensis*, fo. 84v.

100 *Chronographia*, 2:122.

pass through them.[101] They were heavily built up with wooden fortifications, so that some of the English considered them "so strongly equipped that it was too horrible to look at them."[102] Very few of the English ships had been so prepared for war. There was such a great number of the French vessels (over two hundred vessels, compared to probably 120 or 147 for the English), and some of their leading ships were so much larger than anything in the English fleet, that to some it seemed that Edward didn't have a hope of winning, unless by divine intervention.[103]

The men of Bruges thought so as well. Having been informed of Edward's arrival and intentions by Burghersh, they quickly sent ambassadors to the king where his fleet lay anchored off the Flemish coast, begging him for God's sake and his love of them that he not attack the French armada, considering the relative size of the fleets and the presence of the deadly Genoese galleys on the French side. They asked him to wait two days and rest his men, for they were manning and equipping a hundred ships to come to his aid, and he could have a certain victory.[104] This was sound enough advice, but now that he had sighted his enemy, Edward was in no mood to wait. Perhaps he thought that arranging a "certain victory" would not allow enough room for the sign of God's grace he had said he was hoping for.[105]

At the first sight of the English ships, on the 23rd, the most experienced sailor among the French leadership, a Genoese galley-captain and pirate known as Pietro Barbanero or Barbevaire,[106] advised the admirals to remove their chains and sail out onto the high seas. If they stayed where they were, he pointed out, the initiative would fall to the English, who could attack when the sun, wind and tide were in their favor. Béhuchet responded that it would be shameful to depart from their position once they had taken it: they would stand fast and

---

101 *Melsa*, 3:45; *Fr. Chron. London*, 76; cf. *Hemingburgh*, 356.

102 *Fr. Chron. London*, 76. Cf. *Hemingburgh*, 356.

103 *Le Bel*, 1:179 (divine intervention); cf. Delpit, *Collection générale*, 67–8. *Hemingburgh*, 356; *Knighton*, 2:18; *Murimuth*, 106; and *Le Baker*, 68, for the size and strength of the French ships. The disparity is confirmed by French accounts which show that the smallest French ships in the fleet were of 80 tons burden (Roncière, *Hist. marine française*, 439), while English fleets normally made use of ships half that size. Numbers: note 95, above.

104 Villani, *Cronica*, 377. This important passage is generally overlooked in modern accounts of the battle, so I will reproduce it here: "Quelli di Bruggia, come sentirono la venuta del re d'Inghilterra, gli mandarono loro ambasciadori alle Schiuse, pregandolo per Dio e per loro amore che non si metesse a battaglia contro l'armata del re di Francia, perocch'erano altrettante quanto la sua e più erano le galee genovesi, e ch'egli attendesse due giorni e riposasse sua gente, perocché di presente armerebbono cento cocche di buona gente in suo aiuto e poteva avere sicura vittoria."

105 *RFR*, II:2:1127.

106 Barbevaire in some sources, including French accounts (*Clos des galées*, 2:58) but Barbanero in Villani, *Cronica*, 377, and Pierre Barbenoire in *Cont. Manuel, 1328–39*, 1262, which adds that he was "un grant pirade de mer . . . qui moult de roberies et d'opressions avoit fait par maintes fois aux subgez du royaume [de France]."

await the outcome.[107] Perhaps he was worried that Edward might sail past his fleet into Sluys, and claim that the French had again been too cowardly to await battle.

The two admirals were not on the best terms. "The one could not stand the other," observes the *Grandes chroniques* simply.[108] Once Béhuchet, an administrator rather than a soldier and a man of common birth,[109] put the matter in terms of honor, the noble Quiéret could hardly argue for the more prudent course over the more *preux* one. Barbanero reacted angrily. He declared that if they would not take his advice, he would take the galleys under his command out of the fight. He then did precisely that, depriving the French fleet of the best ships it had for close-in fighting.[110]

The next morning the English sailed towards the French fleet.[111] Since they were approaching from the west, the early sun was shining full in their eyes. The wind was also not particularly in their favor.[112] So as to be able to attack under more advantageous conditions, they tacked farther out to sea to a position where they could use the wind and tide to carry them against the enemy. Not until they had the best possible conditions – late in the afternoon, in the event – did they advance against the enemy fleet.[113] The French, mistaking the English maneuvering for a retreat, had cast off their chains and ventured out a certain distance

---

[107] *Grandes chroniques*, 9:183. The chronicler makes this dispute seem to be immediately before the battle, but this is unlikely on two grounds. First of all, none of the many English chronicles which deal with the battle, often in some detail, mention the ensuing withdrawal of his galleys, something they would hardly have failed to bring up had it occurred within view of their fleet. Secondly, Barbanero's reason for withdrawing was the admirals' refusal to sail out to meet the English; yet this is precisely what they did the following day (see below). A further point is that, although the *Grandes chroniques* do not indicate any time gap between Barbanero's discussion with the admirals and the English attack, yet they also do not mention any time passing between the time the fleets first sighted each other (on the 23rd) and the battle. So the time compression could as well come after the dispute as before.

[108] *Grandes chroniques*, 9:184: "Et avint ceste desconfiture par l'orgueil des II admiraux, car l'un ne pooit souffrir de l'autre, et tout par envie."

[109] *Chronographia*, 2:123 n.1.

[110] *Grandes chroniques*, 9:183. But cf. *Chronographia*, 2:123 and 123 n.1.

[111] Froissart and the *Grandes chroniques* agree that the battle began at "primes," while the English chronicles uniformly have it begin in the afternoon (except *Pipewell*, fo. 14 v, which has the English attack at noon). Jan de Klerk, who specifically states that his account (written in 1347) is based on the testimony of eyewitnesses, says the English attacked "around evening" (omtrent der vespertide); *Van den Derden Eduwaert*, l. 1225 (*Edouard III*, 15). The former sources are probably beginning with the time the two fleets began to maneuver, and the latter starting with the point the ships actually came into contact.

[112] Froissart, *Oeuvres*, 3:195. The various chronicles give different accounts which are difficult to bring into accord with each other, or with modern calculations of the timing of the tides on that day. I have largely followed the argument set out by E. M. Thompson in his notes to *Le Baker*, 243–4.

[113] Froissart, *Oeuvres*, 3:195; *Fr. Chron. London*, 76; *Avesbury*, 312; cf. *Hemingburgh*, 356; *Murimuth*, 106; *Fr. Chron. London*, 77; Hocsem, *Chronique*, 295; *Historia Roffensis*, fo. 84v; and the letter of Edward III in Delpit, *Collection générale*, 67, for the time [bien apres houre de nonne, a la tyde].

in pursuit, only to find Edward's fleet turning about and heading towards them.[114]

As the two fleets approached each other, missiles from both sides filled the air, rapidly inflicting serious casualties on both sides.[115] Here the English archers had a tremendous advantage, for their longbows had better range, more accuracy, and a much higher rate of fire than the crossbows used by their enemies.[116] So heavy was the English fire, remarked one chronicler, that the French were unable to look outwards or keep their heads up. To many contemporary observers, the archers deserved the greatest portion of the credit for the victory: "the French and Normans, fired upon fiercely with arrows, were defeated by the English" one wrote simply.[117] Having the sun and wind at their backs was also helpful to the English at this stage.

Meanwhile the ships of Robert Morley's squadron made the first contact with the enemy (as he had promised), followed by those of the counts of Huntingdon and Northampton and Walter Mauny. Each ship grappled with a French vessel, and ferocious hand-to-hand fighting began.[118] Here, too, the English enjoyed a decisive superiority. Edward's ships were loaded with experienced soldiers, many of whom had served in his Scottish campaigns. Not a few had already been blooded at Halidon Hill or Dupplin Moor.[119] The French fleet, by contrast, was manned almost entirely by sailors – "poor fishermen and mariners . . . not so skilled at arms as the English" says the *Grandes chroniques* – who had never before faced the test of battle.[120] Although the French had some twenty thousand men engaged in the fighting (about 25% more than the English had), no more than 150 of these were men-at-arms.[121] On the other hand, however, the great height of many of the French ships, and their wooden fortifications, made them difficult to capture.[122] Still, ship by ship, the English conquered. King Edward himself was in the thick of the fight, risking his life with a boldness which

---

114 *Fr. Chron. London*, 76; *Avesbury*, 312; *Le Bel*, 1:178; cf. *Melsa*, 3:45; *Murimuth*, 106.
115 *Le Baker*, 68.
116 The relative merits of longbow and crossbow in this period were best demonstrated at the battle of Crécy (see below, Chapter 11) and at the naval battle of Winchelsea (see *Le Baker*, 110).
117 *Fr. Chron. London*, 77: "qe les Fraunceis n'avoyent poer de regarder ne lour testes sustener." The chronicler also gives part of the credit to the English crossbowmen and "enginours." See also Walsingham, *Historia Anglicana*, 1:227, and *Historia Roffensis*, fo. 85; cf. *Le Baker*, 110. Quotation: *Melsa*, 3:44.
118 *Hemingburgh*, 356; *Fr. Chron. London*, 77; Jan de Klerk, *Edouard III*, 15.
119 Of the four squadron leaders just mentioned, for instance, at least the latter three had fought at Halidon Hill, and Mauny had also been at Dupplin.
120 *Grandes chroniques*, 9:182. Béhuchet was accused by the same source of having recruited these men instead of noble men-at-arms because their wages were lower. There may have been some truth to this, for the French crown was under almost as much financial pressure as the English, and Béhuchet might well have supposed that the mariners' superior experience with ships would counterbalance their inferior skill at arms.
121 Roncière, *Hist. marine française*, 443. English: *Historia Roffensis*, fo. 85.
122 *Le Bel*, 1:179; *Murimuth*, 106; *Le Baker*, 68.

contemporaries described as astonishing in such a great lord. The decks of the Valois ships were literally ankle-deep in blood. Many French sailors jumped into the sea rather than suffer the cruel wounds inflicted by the enemy's swords and arrows.[123] Most drowned – so many that it was commonly said that if fish could speak, they would learn French.[124]

After an extraordinarily long, hard fight the entire first line of the French navy fell into English hands. The banners bearing the arms of Philip of Valois were cut down and replaced with Edward's quartered leopards and lilies.[125] This caused a panic in the French second line. Many sailors jumped into the water, or took to their small lifeboats, at the approach of the victorious English. Most of the overloaded boats capsized, sending their occupants to the bottom of the sea.[126] The Flemings who crowded the beaches to watch the progress of the battle disposed of any Frenchmen who managed to swim to shore.[127]

Securing this group of ships was much quicker and easier than defeating the first line, especially because large numbers of Flemish vessels were by now attacking the French in the rear,[128] but even so it was full night before it was accomplished. The exhausted English let things rest there until dawn.[129] During the night, some twenty-four small ships and galleys managed to escape; but the remainder of the French ships were captured the next day without notable difficulty.[130]

The smallest contemporary estimate for the total number of French casualties was "more than 10,000"; for once, this is probably too low.[131] There were over twenty thousand men on the French ships.[132] Only about one in eight of Valois ships escaped capture, and the proportion of individuals who survived was probably no higher.[133] English losses were far lower: a number of sources say

---

123 Jan de Klerk, *Van den Derden Eduwaert*, ll. 1253–6 ("Die coninc was . . . Bijden iersten daer men street/ Ende vacht mitter hant so seere,/ Dat wonder was van selken heere."), 1270 (blood) (Cf. *Edouard III*, 16). Walsingham, *Historia Anglicana*, 1:227; *Avesbury*, 312. The *Chron. Com. Flandr.*, 213, says that Edward fought so strenuously that he was "not unworthy of comparison with one of the Macabees."

124 A somewhat loose paraphrase of *Melsa*, 3:45.

125 *Hemingburgh*, 356.

126 Ibid., 356–7; *Le Baker*, 69.

127 *Melsa*, 3:45; *Nangis*, 169; *Chronographia*, 2:122.

128 *Chronographia*, 2:123 and 123 n.2.; *Cont. Manuel, 1339–46*, fo. 196v; cf. *Chron. Normande*, 45, and Edward's letter in *KdL*, 167.

129 *Murimuth*, 107; *Le Baker*, 69; *Fr. Chron. London*, 77.

130 *Fr. Chron. London*, 77; *KdL*, 167; cf. *Le Baker*, 69; *Knighton*, 2:18; *Hemingburgh*, 357; Jan de Klerk, *Van den Derden Eduwaert*, ll. 1300–1333 (escape). Jan de Klerk, however, describes fierce fighting on the second day, "described to me by eye-witnesses." *Edouard III*, 16. Size: *Chronographia*, 2:123; *Grandes chroniques*, 9:184.

131 Villani, *Cronica*, 378.

132 Roncière, *Hist. marine française*, 443; Lucas, *Low Countries*, 398–9; cf. *Chronographia*, 2:120 n.2.

133 Figuring that, as Edward III said, 24 out of 190 (the lowest estimate of the number of French ships) escaped. The ships that escaped were said to be small ones, and this is probably true since the French had their largest vessels in the front line. Writing after the battle,

only four to six hundred of Edward's men perished, though Adam Murimuth does give the figure of four thousand.[134] Corpses washed ashore all along the coast of Flanders.[135] Edward, like most of his subjects, took this victory to be the sign from God he had anticipated.[136] "From then on," wrote one contemporary with pardonable exaggeration, "Edward was lord of the sea."[137]

Edward III estimated that 5,000 men out of a total of 35,000 had escaped. *KdL*, 167. Most contemporary estimates give the number of Frenchmen who perished as 25,000 or more: *Knighton*, 2:18 (25,000); *Le Baker*, 69 (25,000); *Historia Roffensis*, fo. 85 (25,000); *Melsa*, 3:45 (55,000); Walsingham, *Historia Anglicana*, 1:227 (30,000); Jan de Klerk, *Edouard III*, 17 (30,000); *Lanercost*, 333 (30,000 killed or captured); *Chronographia*, 2:122 (30,000); *Avesbury*, 312 (30,000); etc.

[134] *Murimuth*, 109; *Le Baker*, 69. This fits well with Edward's own statement that his losses were "moderate in comparison" with the French casualties (*RFR*, II:2:1129: "cum laesione gentis nostrae modica respective"). Other English chroniclers (*Lanercost*, 333; *Anonimalle*, 16; *Melsa*, 3:45) give the figure of just 400 losses, and Jan de Klerk, who was in a good position to know, gives the comparable number of 600 (*Van den Derden Eduwaert*, l. 1278, *Edouard III*, 17); but these numbers may be too low, given Edward's remark and the agreement in all the sources that the fight for the first line was long and fierce. However, the widely reported fact that only four knights (whose names are given in several chronicles) were killed would seem to fit better with total casualties of 400 than 4,000. There is little evidence of casualties in the pay rolls. They could be read to imply that the Earl of Derby lost no men-at-arms but 17 of his 63 archers during the battle, while the Earl of Northampton lost 21 out of 154 men-at-arms but none of his 152 archers – but this is probably a sign of the peculiarities of the account rather than reliable evidence of casualties, since Walter Mauny for example seems to have *gained* a substantial number of men-at-arms on the day of the battle. Still, the simple lack of evidence of any heavy losses does tend to support the lower casualty figures. (Summary transcript of E101/389/8, provided by Dr. Andrew Ayton.) The estimate of the *Chron. Normande*, 45, of 10,000 English killed, is certainly inflated.

[135] Edward's letter in Froissart, *Oeuvres*, 167. Jan de Klerk says the very ocean was tinged with red. *Edouard III*, 17.

[136] Edward's three letters (*KdL*, 167: "Dieu Nostre-Seigneur ad assés de grâce monstré, de quoi nous et touts nos amys sumes tutdis tenus de lui rendre grâce et mercis." *RP*, 118; *RFR*, II:2:1129) and virtually all the English chroniclers, like Jean le Bel and Jan de Klerk, attribute the victory to the grace of God.

[137] Jan de Klerk, *Edouard III*, 19; *Van den Derden Eduwaert*, l. 1312 ("heere vander zee"). Cf. *RP*, 311.

CHAPTER NINE

"TO BRING OUR RIGHTFUL CHALLENGE TO A QUICK CONCLUSION":[1]
THE SIEGE OF TOURNAI, 1340

When the army engages in protracted campaigns, the resources of the state will not suffice.   Sun Tzu, II.4[2]

EDWARD, WHO HAD personally been involved in the thick of the fighting at Sluys, had taken a fairly serious wound in the thigh, so for a couple of weeks after the battle he remained on board his flagship, the *Cog-Thomas*, while the leg healed.[3] The leaders of the anti-French coalition, including Queen Philippa, visited him there to finalize their plans for the coming expedition. Edward was informed that the Valois host was on the borders of Flanders, ready to invade that county or the lands of his other allies in order to cause them as much harm as possible and to drive them out of the alliance.[4] Jacques van Artevelde pledged a huge number of Flemish soldiers in addition to the men provided by Edward and the Netherlandish princes.[5] Even in the extraordinarily rich and densely populated area where the campaigning was to take place, and even with the ease of water transport to Tournai, such a vast number of men could not comfortably be maintained in a single place indefinitely. As in 1335,[6] Edward decided to split his forces in two, partly for logistic reasons and partly because more could be accomplished by two armies than by one. He, the Netherlandish princes, and the majority of the Flemings would advance on Tournai and lay siege to it. Another large force of Flemings, bolstered by a small contingent of the stalwart English archers, would advance to St. Omer, a Flemish-speaking city on the

---

[1]   See note 30, below.
[2]   Griffith (ed.), 73.
[3]   *Chronographia*, 2:124 (wound); pp. 196–7, above (fighting); *KdL*, 167 (date). Edward had also received wounds in the head and hand according to *Cont. Manuel, 1339–46*, fo. 196v.
[4]   *RP*, 118; *Chronographia*, 2:124–5; cf. *Le Bel*, 1:180–2.
[5]   *RP*, 118. For the actual numbers, cf. Villani, *Cronica*, 378; Lucas, *Low Countries*, 408; Verbruggen, *Art of Warfare*, 167.
[6]   See Chapter 5, above.

border of Artois.[7] The latter force would be led by Robert of Artois, who claimed to have supporters inside the town who were ready to deliver it to him.[8]

Edward's biggest problem, as usual, was money. Back in England, yet another parliament was hastily summoned. On 12 July the assembled Lords and Commons listened attentively to a letter from their sovereign, recapitulating his victory at Sluys and briefly outlining his strategy for the coming months. As the king pointed out, it would take a great deal of money to provide for the massive army he had at his disposal, even aside from paying off his earlier debts. Once again, in a tiresome echo of the pleas he had been making ever since initiating the Low Countries strategy, Edward warned of the dire consequences which would follow unless he were immediately succored with a very large sum of money. If his allies and the soldiers he had retained were not paid the money owed them, they would leave his service; they might even go over to the enemy. The king, his lands, his children, and the men with him were therefore "on the point of perdition."[9] If he got the cash he needed, though, he hoped to find Philip at a disadvantage and defeat him.[10] As Pope Benedict observed, Edward wanted now to do on land what he had just done on the sea.[11]

Considering the very generous grant parliament had just made, they could not realistically be asked for more money. What they could do, and did, was help the king convert the two-year ninth they had already voted into an immediate lump payment. This was to be done via yet another impressment of thirty thousand sacks of wool: twenty thousand for the first year, and ten thousand in the second year. The money from the ninth was to be used to repay those who provided the wool before being applied to any other purpose. This was a generous arrangement, considering how very heavily burdened the people of England already were and had been due to the king's wars.[12] It probably could not have been made were it not for the popular enthusiasm generated by the battle of Sluys.

As soon as Edward received word of parliament's assent to these provisions, he instantly put his campaign plans into operation. A force of about fifteen thousand men, which had gathered at Cassel under the command of Robert of Artois, reached the vicinity of St. Omer on 24 July, burning the town of Arques

---

[7]   The author of the *Chronographia*, 2:125, describes these cities as "two keys of [Philip's] realm." Archers: Sumption, *Trial by Battle*, 340, says there were perhaps 1,000 of them, but does not indicate his source. The actual number may have been more like 150; cf. note 13, below.

[8]   *RP,* 118; *Chronographia,* 2:125. Artois' claims: *Chronographia,* 2:127; *Grandes chroniques,* 9:189.

[9]   *RP,* 118.

[10]   Ibid.

[11]   Déprez, *Préliminaires,* 338.

[12]   *RP,* 117–19, 122; The *English Brut,* 294, gives a vivid description of the popular response to the biennial Ninth recently granted: "wherfor, yf y shal knowliche the verrey threuth, the ynnere loue of the peple was turned into hate, & the commune prayrs into cursinge, for cause that the commune peple were strongliche ygreued." Cf. *Fr. Chron. London,* 83.

and all the land for miles around as it approached.[13] If Artois really did have partisans within St. Omer, however, they never had a chance to be useful.

Probably on the 25th, Artois received word that the main French army was on its way to relieve the besieged town. His force was nowhere near strong enough to stand up to the French king's army, even if well entrenched, especially since many of his Flemish troops were suffering from low morale.[14] His best hope to capture the town was therefore to take it by assault, ideally after having drawn the garrison out and defeated them where they did not have the benefit of walls. So, to put heart into his dispirited men, he told them that he had been informed that the town would be delivered to him as soon as he approached. On the morning of the 26th, thinking that they would drink the wines of St. Omer in the evening, Artois' men arrayed themselves in battle order outside the town, with the men of Bruges and England to the fore. Improvised ditches and fieldworks protected portions of their lines.[15]

The town held a large French garrison commanded by the Duke of Burgundy (who was also Count of Artois) and the Count of Armagnac, a skilled soldier with a great deal of experience in the Gascon theater who arrived on the same day as the Flemings.[16] With about twelve hundred men-at-arms in total, in addition to a large number of infantry soldiers, St. Omer held quite a good-sized garrison.[17] When the local men-at-arms in the town saw the Flemings arrayed in the fields, they issued out to skirmish with them. The Duke of Burgundy and the

---

[13] *Grandes chroniques*, 9:189–90. Numbers: The force included the contingents of Bruges, the Frank of Bruges, Ypres, and various smaller elements. (Ibid.) Bruges provided 6,547 men, and normally the Frank and Ypres together would be expected to provide half as many again as Bruges. Verbruggen, *Art of Warfare* (2nd edn), 167. Thus we can accept the French report written immediately after the battle which estimated the number of Flemings at 15,000 (*Le Bel*, 1:188 n.1). Date: Lucas, *Low Countries*, 406. Artois' force included two banners of English men-at-arms and a good number of longbowmen. *Chronographia*, 2:125 n.3, 129; *Grandes chroniques*, 9:191; *Murimuth*, 108. One of the bannerets may have been Walter Mauny (*Fr. Chron. London*, 78), though he is not mentioned in the best accounts of the fighting at St. Omer. Mauny was serving as a banneret, with a very large retinue of 8 knights, 58 esquires, and 136 archers during this campaign; this unusually large number of archers (more than were paid in the retinues of Lancaster, Warwick, and Gloucester combined), along with the high regard in which Edward held him, would have made him a natural choice to accompany Artois. (See E101/389/8, mm. 11, 14; a summary transcript of this document was kindly provided to me by Dr. Andrew Ayton of the University of Hull.) The other was Thomas Ughtred, a household knight who had fought in nearly all of Edward's Scottish campaigns. Ughtred had 25 archers in his contingent. Ibid., m. 14; *Murimuth*, 108; *Melsa*, 3:46.

[14] *Chronographia*, 2:127–8; *Grandes chroniques*, 9:189–90 (morale); *Chronographia*, 2:129, *Grandes chroniques*, 9:191 (news). The reports Artois had received of the French king's approach were correct. *Le Bel*, 1:188 n.1; *Chronographia*, 2:128.

[15] Fieldworks: *Chronographia*, 2:129. Date: *Le Bel*, 1:188 n.1, and *Grandes chroniques*, 9:191.

[16] Ibid., 190; Villani, *Cronica*, 378.

[17] Villani, *Cronica*, 378 (milledugento cavalieri). The *Tournai Bulletin*, 364, sets the garrison at 11,000. This may be inflated, as many of the figures in the bulletin are, but the *Chron. Pays-Bas*, 152, also gives figures of 2,000 men-at-arms and 10,000 infantry.

Count of Armagnac, who had been ordered not to leave the city until Philip arrived, remained inside.

The skirmishing lasted from midday to evening, until the Duke of Burgundy could no longer stand the sight of an enemy army in his county unchallenged. He called for the Count of Armagnac and his counselors. "My lords, how do you advise me?" he asked. "I do not see any way I can avoid being either dishonored or disobedient to the king today." The Count of Armagnac answered that, with the help of God and his good friends, he would be restored to the king's favor well enough – the implication being that his honor could not so easily recover from failing to attack an enemy on his lands, which casts an interesting if unintended light on how these men must have viewed King Philip's actions at Buironfosse. "Well then," replied the duke, "let us go arm ourselves, for God and St. George."[18]

The fight that followed was rather confused, even by medieval standards. The duke, with a relatively small force, charged directly against Artois' battle, which contained the English and the men of Bruges. After a good deal of back-and-forth, he was pushed back into the city, having suffered fairly heavy casualties.[19] Meanwhile, the Count of Armagnac with eight hundred men issued from another gate, circled around to the scene of the action, and slammed into the division of the men of Ypres. The Flemings broke and fled from his charge. Before the fall of night brought an end to the chase, the count had pursued them all the way to Arques, where they had encamped the previous night.[20]

As Armagnac's men returned towards St. Omer, they passed Artois' troops, who were marching in good order for Arques after the affray below the city walls. At first neither side recognized the other, which led to a few scuffles when the truth was realized; but all were too exhausted from the day's fighting to renew the combat in the night. When Artois reached Arques, he found the camp empty, for the men deputed to guard it had all fled. The watchfires were still burning, and the tents and other goods had all been abandoned.[21] Artois quickly marched off to rejoin Edward with the men that were left to him.[22] The French in St. Omer thoroughly plundered the camp the next day, capturing a great quantity of supplies and a large number of carts.[23]

---

[18] *Grandes chroniques*, 9:192–3; *Chronographia*, 2:130–1. On the timing, cf. *Murimuth*, 108.

[19] *Chronographia*, 2:131–2; *Grandes chroniques*, 9:193–6; *Fr. Chron. London*, 78–9 (which gives the French casualties at St. Omer as 5,210 including 95 knights, not, as one historian has recently written, 210,000); *Scalacronica*, 171.

[20] *Chronographia*, 2:131–2; *Grandes chroniques*, 9:194; Villani, *Cronica*, 378; *Scalacronica*, 171.

[21] *Chronographia*, 2:133–4; *Grandes chroniques*, 9:195–6; *Scalacronica*, 171.

[22] *Scalacronica*, 171; *Le Bel*, 1:187.

[23] Some 600 carts were captured. *Le Bel*, 1:189n. The figures given in the sources for the number of casualties on each side vary widely, but the Flemings probably lost around 3,000 men (*Grandes chroniques*, 9:196, *Chron. Normande*, 46; *Chron. Pays-Bas*, 152; 4,000 according to *Chronographia*, 2:134.) Jonathan Sumption's figure of 8,000 Flemings killed (*Trial by*

Meanwhile, Edward himself had advanced to the outskirts of the city of Tournai. His army at this point included over thirteen hundred English men-at-arms and somewhat under three thousand archers,[24] along with 5,455 infantrymen from Ghent, and perhaps another thousand Flemish men-at-arms.[25] After an unsuccessful attempt to capture the strong castle at Estaimbourg, he arrived at Chin, three miles down the Scheldt from Tournai, by 23 July.[26] He was there for nine days, during which he was joined by the Duke of Guelders, the Count of Hainault, and the Margrave of Juliers, who apparently brought with them even more than their quotas of men-at-arms per the agreements of 1338.[27]

Battle, 343) is certainly too high. It derives from a letter written almost immediately after the battle (*Le Bel*, 1:188 n.1) which reports *hearsay* that seven or eight thousand Flemings were killed: "l'en disoit que." Rumors generally exaggerate the extent of enemy losses. (Cf. *Chronographia*, 2:124n, which claims that at Sluys all but five of the English noblemen perished.) Furthermore, this would be an excessively high proportion of casualties to attackers, especially since the Flemings won part of the combat. The figure of 3,000 given by the *Grandes chroniques* and *Chron. Normande* is certainly to be preferred, especially since as pro-French chronicles they had no incentive to understate the scale of the victory.

French casualties were probably in the area of 750 men killed, but these were nearly all men-at-arms; as many as 95 dubbed knights may have perished. *Melsa*, 3:46; *Fr. Chron. London*, 77; *Murimuth*, 108. The *Tournai Bulletin*, 364, sets the French casualties at 600 killed, "lords of France, counts, barons, knights, and a great number of others." According to Murimuth, the English archers were responsible for most of the deaths among the French.

24 *Tournai Bulletin*, 361–2, and *Melsa*, 3:46, say 1,000 men-at-arms and 4,000 archers, but the surviving pay account for the expedition (which may be incomplete, but which also may include some troops under royal pay but not present with the army, e.g. those detached for service under Robert of Artois) indicates that Edward had about 1,000 archers at Sluys, rising to a peak of about 2,700 mainly thanks to the arrival of the arrayed contingents in early July, dropping to around 2,000 in early August, and back down to approximately 1,300 after 19 August (the drops mainly coming from the departure of the arrayed archers). According to the roll, his men-at-arms amounted to a few more than 1,300 at Sluys; the total fell only slightly over the course of the campaign. See PRO E101/389/8, mm. 11–16; I am grateful to Dr. Andrew Ayton of Hull University for providing me with a summary transcript of the record, on which the above calculations are based. See Ayton, "Edward III and the English Aristocracy," 179–81, for a discussion of the roll, which points out that there were probably a few hundred men who were present with the army but paid on different accounts.

Note that this is much smaller than the army planned in PRO C47/2/33, which called for a force of 2,590 men-at-arms and 8,967 infantry, including 7,952 archers – another indication of the severity of the king's financial difficulties.

25 Infantry (including "knapen" and "garsoenen"): Verbruggen, *Art of Warfare*, 167, and idem, *Het Gemeenteleger van Brugge van 1338 tot 1340* (Brussels: Com. Royale d'Histoire, 1962), 16. The *Tournai Bulletin*, 361, indicates that the Flemings contributed about a thousand men-at-arms on horseback (along with the less credible figure of 160,000 foot).

26 Estaimbourg: *Tournai Bulletin*. Chin, date: Lucas, *Low Countries*, 406. According to the campaign letter, Edward entered France on the 22nd.

27 The *Fr. Chron. London*, 78, has the Duke of Brabant arrive with 1,400 men-at-arms ["vij^{xx}. x. hommes à chival bien armez"; I take this to be an idiosyncratic way of writing "seven-score tens" of men rather than 150 men – seven-score *and* ten – which would be a more normal way of reading the figure, but makes no sense in context; note also that the same chronicler uses an "et" on p. 79 in "iiij^{xx} et xv."], and the Count of Hainault brought a comparable number. Brabant's treaty quota was 1,200, and Hainault's 1,000. For rough confirma-

A substantial portion of the Flemings who had retreated from St. Omer also arrived at this point. Thus, with the contingents of the allies – including the Duke of Brabant, who did not arrive until 11 August – Edward may have had about seven to eight thousand men-at-arms and somewhere very roughly in the area of fifteen to eighteen thousand infantry.[28]

Philip VI, meanwhile, had encamped with his army at Arras, some thirty-five miles away. He had assembled a very large host, which (including garrison forces in the area) comprised twenty-one thousand men-at-arms and 2,700 paid infantrymen.[29] This was roughly equal to the allies' host even in simple numbers, and since a man-at-arms was considered to be worth several infantrymen (or ten, according to contemporary texts on chivalry!), the French army was indisputably superior by the standards of the day, even without counting the large number of unpaid local infantry Philip also probably had available.[30] Yet, aside from a plan to move against the division of Edward's army before St. Omer (which was abandoned in the wake of events there),[31] the Valois king showed no inclination to oppose the invaders directly.

Of course, after the events at la Flamengrie, Edward had not really expected anything else. Still, he had his hopes. On the 26 July, while his army was still far below its maximum strength, he sent a provocative letter to his adversary:

Philip of Valois, for a long time we have importuned you, by embassies and all other reasonable ways that we know, to render to us our rightful heritage of

tion of the number of Brabant's men, see Verbruggen, *Art of Warfare*, 265. Hainault's surplus may perhaps be the contingent of Jean d'Hainault, whom the *Tournai Bulletin*, 364, credits with bringing "grant nombre des gentz." The letter also, however, gives the Count of Hainault's contingent as only 500 men-at-arms, plus around 8,000 foot (an improbably high figure). According to the *Chronographia*, 2:139, the Duke of Guelders brought 4,000 men. The *Tournai Bulletin* has Guelders and Juliers each arrive with 1,000 men-at-arms, but gives the Duke of Brabant's force as a greatly inflated 5,000 men-at-arms and 150,000 foot. This may be a confused statement of the totals the allies in combination were believed to have provided: 5,000 men-at-arms would be about right, and 150,000 is the number of foot which parliament was told the Flemings would provide.

The same source has the Count of Hainault arrive *after* the first skirmishes around the city's gate, which indicates that Edward had effectively opened the siege while he was still based at Chin.

[28] Villani, *Cronica*, 379, sets the total of men-at-arms in the army as 8,000. [Possibly, from the numbers in the notes above, 1,300 English, 1,400 Brabançons, 3,400 from Hainault, Guelders and Juliers, 1,000 Flemings, and an uncertain number of English troops in retinues like Robert of Artois' and the Bishop of Lincoln's, which do not show up in the pay roll, and various others.] Cf. *Chronographia*, 2:161 n.2. For the date of Brabant's arrival, see *Tournai Chronicles* in Froissart, *Oeuvres*, 25:350, but note that the *Tournai Bulletin*, 363–4, has the duke arrive only on 15 August. Infantry: 2,000 archers (based on the pay roll discussed in n.24, above); approximately 5,500 Ghent troops; the surviving troops from Bruges and the remnants of the other forces from the battle at St. Omer (say, a total of 6,500 men? Cf. Verbruggen, *Art of Warfare*, 167), and a few thousand more brought by the allied princes.

[29] Contamine, *Guerre, état et société*, 69, graphique III.

[30] *Chronographia*, 2:161 n.2. Ibid., 135, says it was the largest army ever seen in France.

[31] *Le Bel*, 1:188 n.1.

France, which you have detained from us for a long time, and very unjustly occupied. And because we can see well that you intend to persevere in your injurious detention, without making a reasonable answer to our demand, we have entered into the land of Flanders, as sovereign lord of it, and passed through the country. And we signify to you that, with the aid of Our Lord Jesus Christ and our right, and with the forces of the said land [of Flanders] and with our own people and allies, considering the right that we have to the heritage which you wrongfully keep away from us, we are drawing towards you in order to bring our rightful challenge to a quick conclusion, if you will approach. And because such a great force of men as we have assembled (as we think you have as well) cannot long hold together, without causing harm and destruction to the people and to the land, something which every good Christian should eschew, and especially princes and others who hold themselves for governors of men; therefore we greatly desire that the matter be concluded soon, and that, to avoid the death of Christians, as the quarrel is between you and us, that the debate of our challenge be conducted by our two bodies.[32]

Since Edward was a good deal younger than Philip, and much more skilled at arms, this offer might have seemed rather unchivalrous if made alone. So he offered two more options. The kings could each fight at the head of a hundred of their vassals; or the battle could be between the entire armies, in the fields before Tournai, within ten days. Edward's intention, as he said, was that once God had shown his will between them, peace could be restored among Christians.[33]

The main purpose of this challenge, of course, was to encourage Philip to come and give battle with his full army. Considering the superiority of the King of France's army, he would have been foolish to accept either of the other alternatives. But Edward was also making a sincere, if probably not very hopeful,

---

32 PRO, SC1/37/135: "Philip de Valoys, par lonc temps avoms pursui par devers vous, par messages & toutes autres voyes, que nous savisioms resonables, au fyn que vous nous vousissez avoir rendu nostre droit heritage de Fraunce, le quel vous nous avez lonc temps detenu, & a graunt tort ocupee. Et, pur ce que nous veoms bien, que vous estes en entente de perseverer en vostre injuriouse detenue, sanz nous fayre rayson de nostre demaunde, sumes nous entrez en la terre de Flandres, come seigneur sovereyn de ycele, & passe parmy le pays, & vous signefioms que, pris ovesque nous le eyde de nostre seigneur Jesu Crist, & nostre droit, ovesque le poer du dit pays, & ovesque noz gentz et alliez, regardauns le droit que nous avoms al heritage que vous nous detenez a vostre tort, Nous nous treoms vers vous, pur mettre bref fyn sur nostre droiture chalaunge, si vous voillez approcher.

Et pur ce, que si graunt poer des gentz assemblez, que viegnent de nostre part, & que bien quidoms que vous avierrez de vostre part, ne se purrount mie longement tenir ensemble, sans faire gref destruction au poeple & au pays, la quele chose chascuns bons Cristiens doit eschuer, & especialment prince, & autre qui se tignent governeurs des gentz, si desiroms mout, que brefs points se prist, & pur eschuer mortalite des Cristiens, ensi come la querele est apparaunte a nous & a vous, que la descuscion de nostre chalaunge se fesist entre noz deux corps." [Printed in *RFR*, II:2:1131.] It is interesting to note that in the record of the payment to the scribe who prepared the challenge, the letter is described as "missas domino Philippo de Valoys de veniendo coram Tournoi cum exercito pro iure sue declarando, quod clamat in regnum Francie." *DEB*, no. 458.

33 PRO, SC1/37/135.

offer of a way to avoid the effusion of Christian blood, and to let God show which claimant to the French throne had the better right.[34] Late medieval "just war" theory was based on the idea that war was essentially a judicial duel writ large, an appeal to the one "court" whose authority extended even to the quarrels of sovereign princes.[35] Edward expressed this principle himself in a letter to the Pope a few years later:

> As our Lord, who is the Sovereign Judge of our adversary and of us, at the disposal of Whom all things are placed, has ordained for us the crown of France as our right and heritage, which right our adversary has for a long time wrongfully held back from us . . . [we have therefore] brought our dispute into the hand of God.[36]

Of course, once the battle had been won, there was a political and propaganda advantage in representing it as divine judgment. But, as was the case with the battle at Sluys, Edward proclaimed his willingness to see the outcome of the combat as a sign from God even beforehand, and even when a more secular observer might not have given him particularly good odds of success. Throughout his military career, as has been shown above and will be further demonstrated below, Edward was always ready to stand the test of battle. There can be no doubt that part of the reason for his eternal confidence was his sincere belief in the principal of his famous motto, which still adorns the English royal arms: "Dieu et mon droit."[37]

If Edward's attitude had not changed since the autumn of 1339, neither had Philip's. A contemporary Brabançon chronicle records his initial response:

> After some moments of reflection, he answered that for many years he had possessed the crown in peace, that it was his legitimate heritage, that he had put it on his head by the unanimous consent of the Peers of France, and that no one but himself would have a single fleuron of it. Therefore, he did not think that he ought to accept a single combat; but as soon as he thought fit, he would give battle, and perhaps sooner than his adversary would like.[38]

In his official response, however, he dodged the issue of battle by professing ignorance of the identity of the "Philip de Valoys" to whom Edward's letters had been addressed; they were evidently not meant for him, he said, and so he would give no response. He added that he intended to cast Edward out of France "when it seems good to us" (he did not say how), and that any Christian blood shed

---

[34] There is no credible reason to doubt the sincerity of Edward's belief that such a contest would be an appeal to divine judgement. Cf. Ormrod, "Personal Religion of Edward III."

[35] For a brief summary, see Clifford J. Rogers, "By Fire and Sword: *Bellum Hostile* and 'Civilians' in the Hundred Years War," *Civilians in the Path of War*, eds M. Grimsley and C. Rogers (forthcoming).

[36] *Avesbury*, 379–80.

[37] [God and my right.] One of the best proofs of this is his eagerness to come to grips with the French fleet at Sluys, without even waiting for his own to gather fully (as described in the last chapter).

[38] Jan de Klerk, *Edouard III*, 21; cf. *Dynter*, 817.

would be the responsibility of the English king, who was the willful aggressor in the war.[39] From his subsequent actions, it is obvious that he preferred to rid himself of the invaders by means other than battle.[40] Indeed, his first thought on how to deal with Edward's siege of Tournai was an invasion of Flanders to draw the besiegers away from their prey. According to the *Chronographia regum Francorum*, the French abandoned this plan at the request of Count Louis, who did not want to see his county devastated.[41] It is easy to imagine that the constable, who had been in the English camp as an ambassador at the siege of Berwick, also contributed to this decision by reminding Philip how little the same strategy had availed the Scots.

As soon as he received Philip's response, Edward marched his men forward and began the formal siege of Tournai on 1 August 1340.[42] A group of local chronicles provide us with virtually a day-by-day account of events.[43] They describe the elaborate and effective defense preparations made by the garrison of the town (about four thousand men-at-arms plus a large number of infantry, commanded by the Constable of France, Raoul, Count of Eu) and its fifteen thousand inhabitants.[44] For nearly a month, however, there was no call on them to implement their careful plans to resist an assault. Though the besiegers cut off any supplies of food or other goods coming in, skirmished vigorously with any Tournaisians who sallied out from the walls, and bombarded the town with engines and small cannon (without, however, inflicting much damage), they made no more active attempt to capture the town until the end of August.[45]

39 *RFR*, II:2:1131. Philip is said to have added that the contest was unfair, since Edward was not risking anything that belonged to him; but if the English king would add the realm of England to the stakes, so that the victor should have both realms, Philip would be ready to accept the combat. Déprez, *Préliminaires*, 331; *EMDP*, 421n.
40 Jan de Klerk, *Van den Derden Eduwaert*, 133 (*Edouard III*, 23); *Chron. Com. Flandr*, 213.
41 *Chronographia*, 2:146–147. According to this source, Edward swore never to retreat until he had captured Tournai and its inhabitants, dead or alive. Similarly, the *Tournai Bulletin*, 364, says that after the Duke of Brabant's arrival, the king and his allies agreed firmly that they would lay siege to the town "until they had conquered it or they had fought with the King of France, if he would come to rescue it." Such declarations were very common in medieval warfare, intended to convince the defenders that their eventual fall was inevitable, and so to encourage them to negotiate a speedy surrender.
42 *Tournai Chronicles*, 346; *Le Muisit*, 128.
43 Especially *Le Muisit*, and the *Tournai Chronicles*.
44 Garrison: *Tournai Chronicles*, 347; Villani, *Cronica*, 379; *Tournai Bulletin*, 362; but cf. *Le Muisit*, 127. Inhabitants: Villani, *Cronica*, 379. This figure probably refers to the normal population of the town, rather than its population after the "useless mouths" were expelled. There was a great number of very distinguished French noblemen inside the town, including the constable, the Count of Foix, the two Marshals of France (Robert Bertran and Mathieu de Trie), the Count of Narbonne, Godemar du Fay, and others. *Le Bel*, 1:184–5, 184 n.4; 185 n.4; *Tournai Chronicles*, 347.
45 Preparations: *Tournai Chronicles*, 351, 357, 364 et passim; *Le Muisit*, 125, 129–30. Skirmishes: *Tournai Bulletin*, 362–3. That source notes that during one skirmish, Reginald Cobham and his men pressed the sally party so hard that the defenders had to close the port-

The reason for this was simple: Edward did not actually want to capture the town at this point. He wanted to draw Philip into a battle to rescue the town, and once it had been taken, that would be impossible. Of course, assaults would hasten the defenders' decision to negotiate a surrender, but they would also cost men, and Edward needed to save all his soldiers for the upcoming battle that was the real point of the whole operation.[46] So, for several weeks, the allied army sat before Tournai, skirmishing with French soldiers from the garrison and from the Valois king's host.[47]

Partly to gather supplies and booty, partly to revenge French raids over the winter, and partly to give the King of France incentive to give battle, the allies immediately began to launch major raids into the surrounding territory. The very first day of the siege, a detachment plundered and torched the town of Orchies. In further raids, St. Amand, Seclin, Cysoing, and Marchiennes suffered the same fate, along with a reported three hundred villages and hamlets. According to the local chronicler Gilles le Muisit, many of the men were killed, and the women and children taken prisoner.[48] One participant's account of the attack on St. Amand provides a good example of what these actions were like:

> And similarly, on Thursday the third day of August, the Count of Hainault, the Earl of Derby, and we other lords and companions made a *chevauchée* to the town of St-Amand, which was strong, and well enclosed by walls and by a water-filled moat all around, and stuffed with men-at-arms, a good 200 of them, and 600 light troops [*bideius*], aside from the people of the town. And so we scaled the walls of the town [*ensiglames la ville*] on several sides so that with the aid of God we captured it. And the people [*gentz*] who were inside were all killed except for a few who escaped. And twenty good destriers and coursers and many other goods were gained. And we had the town burned, the walls knocked down, and the moat filled, and we burned the countryside all around, and returned safely home. And none of our men were killed or wounded, except one knight and one esquire of the Count of Hainault.[49]

cullis on them, lest the English enter the city with them.
    Cannon were used by both sides, and the Count of Hainault even had a "mestre cannonier." *Tournai Chronicles*, 354. Ineffectiveness of bombardment: ibid., 354. Sallies and skirmishes: ibid., passim. First major assault, on 26 August: ibid., 355. Cf. also *Fr. Chron. London*, 79; *Chronographia*, 2:139; *Le Bel*, 1:192.
[46] Cf. the different analysis of Edward's intentions in Burne, *The Crecy War*, 59.
[47] The sources do not appear to bear out the claim of Lucas, *Low Countries*, 413, that the siege was "prosecuted with vigor" in the first two weeks of August.
[48] *Tournai Bulletin*, 363; *Le Muisit*, 129–30; *Récits*, 184, *Chronographia*, 2:140–3; *Tournai Chronicles*, 349, 352; *Fr. Chron. London*, 79; Lucas, *Low Countries*, 412; Déprez, *Prélimi-naires*, 332. They also burned the monastery at St.-Amand, and took many of the monks for ransom. Many mills were destroyed.
[49] *Tournai Bulletin*, 363. The mass killing of the inhabitants is confirmed by Jan de Klerk's *Van den Derden Eduwaert*, ll. 1556–8: "Sent Amants ende Orsijs ave/ Met brande ende mitten swaerde,/ Daermen man no wijf en spaerde."

This was just a small part of a deliberate policy whereby "the countryside all around the siege was seized, burned, and put to destruction," as the *French Chronicle of London* accurately summarizes.[50]

On 10 August, the consuls of Tournai sent two messengers to Philip to ask for succor.[51] The king had already begun his slow advance from Arras. He reached Béthune by 4 August, Lens by the 13th, and Douai – just seventeen miles from Tournai – on the 20th.[52] It might seem strange at first glance that it took Philip over a month to draw twenty-five miles nearer to his enemy, who was burning towns and villages of his realm every day – especially since the French army had already come within a few per cent of its maximum strength at the beginning of the period. The simplest explanation, given alike by the *French Chronicle of London* and one of Philip's own men-at-arms, was that the Valois king "did not dare give battle" to the allies.[53] Perhaps it would be more fair to say that he did not want to do so unless it became absolutely necessary; if he could break up the siege without fighting, as he had ended the invasion of the Thiérache, and avoid the risk of battle, that was certainly his preference, and indeed the wisest course.[54]

Nearly the entire month of August thus passed in a waiting game, with Philip hoping that Edward's army would collapse and Edward striving to hold it together until Philip would have to give battle or see the city fall. Time was working against both of them. As Edward had noted in his letter to parliament after Sluys, he still owed a great deal of money to his allies, and they were likely to desert him if not paid. When he first marched for Tournai, he expected the wool prest which parliament had authorized to solve this problem. Unfortunately for him, on 26 July the French had captured a convoy of thirty ships full of wool – a very substantial amount – which was probably the first installment of the twenty thousand sacks due to him.[55] With the knowledge of the parliament's grant, the English king's allies were willing to wait at least for a while longer. On the 28th, the king wrote again to England to remind his officials of the great amount of money he owed to his allies and the Flemings, and of the heavy expenses he had to bear. If he did not receive money quickly, he complained, he would lose the aid of his allies, his men, and his friends.[56] Edward's ministers in England replied on the 13th, explaining the problems and delays they faced, and expressing the hope that they would be able to send

---

50 *Fr. Chron. London*, 79. Deliberate policy: *Tournai Bulletin*, 364: "Et durant la dite sege ils [le Roi et toutz ses amys et alieqs] ount ordeynetz de faire chivacheecz tout enviroun le pays de gaster et destruire."
51 *Tournai Chronicles*, 349.
52 Lucas, *Low Countries*, 413.
53 *Fr. Chron. London*, 81; RTC, no. 6707. The man-at-arms, Guillaume Brouart, added that Edward III was "the most valiant man of Christendom." Guillaume was imprisoned for sedition despite his long service in Philip's armies.
54 *Le Muisit*, 133.
55 *Le Bel*, 1:189n.
56 Déprez, *Préliminaires*, 326n.

substantial payments soon.[57] This proved far too optimistic. They were meeting
the greatest difficulty in raising the subsidy voted by parliament, or collecting
the forced loan of wool. According to the *French Chronicle of London*, they
wrote to the king that they no longer dared make collections for fear of civil war:
"the people would rise up against them before they would give any more," they
said. So the king received virtually nothing.[58]

Edward's failure to make his promised payments to his allies only aggravated
internal tensions which were already becoming severe in his army.[59] Jacques van
Artevelde and Duke John of Brabant despised each other. Rumors of complicity
between the Brabançons and the French were rife in the Flemish and English
camps, and reached even to Italy.[60] Though the Duke of Brabant was not taking
bribes from the French, as was widely believed, still Laurence Minot's estima-
tion that "in hert he was unhale/ he come thare moste for mede [pay]" was
essentially correct.[61] He had been promised the largest subsidies of any of the
allies, and had not been fully paid. Edward's recent treaty with the Flemings had
specified that all wool exports from England should come through Bruges,
which meant the end of the profitable wool staple that had been established in
the duke's town of Antwerp.[62] Duke John's troops were even less willing to continue the siege than he was: by the end, they were threatening to depart with or
without leave, "in honor or in shame."[63] Even the Flemish soldiers were anxious
to go home.[64]

For all Edward's problems, though, his position was not much worse than
Philip's. The French king, as in 1339, had already incurred much disdain for his
evident lack of will to do battle with the allied army.[65] His camp stank
unbearably from the blood of the animals which were constantly being slaughtered to feed his army, and as September progressed his dispirited soldiers began
to complain of the growing cold.[66] More critically, he had received word from
the garrison of Tournai that they were out of money and food, and did not know

[57] *RP,* 122
[58] Collections: *Fr. Chron. London*, 82–3, quotation at 83: "ils n'oserent plus reddour faire
pur doute de guerre, et qe le poeple einz vodroyent lever encountre eux avant q'ils vodroient
plus doner." Cf. *English Brut*, 294; "Against the King's Taxes," *Anglo-Norman Political
Songs*, ed. I. Aspin (Oxford: Anglo-Norman Text Society, 1954), 111–14. In the aftermath of
the campaign, the king wrote "we were not aided or comforted with any goods out of our
realm at a time that, truly, if we had been aided with a small sum on time, we would have had
more honor than any prince has ever had, and so we would have brought our business to its
conclusion." Déprez, *Préliminaires*, 356; cf. *Le Baker*, 71.
[59] Lucas, *Low Countries*, 414–18, treats this subject with great thoroughness.
[60] Villani, *Cronica*, 380; Minot, "Songs on King Edward's Wars," 74; *Knighton*, 2:19;
Chron. Pays-Bas, 3:154.
[61] Minot, "Songs on King Edward's Wars," 74.
[62] Wool staple: *KdL*, 120.
[63] *Le Bel*, 1:207, cf. 208; Froissart, *Oeuvres*, 3:271.
[64] *Tournai Chronicles*, 361.
[65] RTC, no. 6707.
[66] *Le Bel*, 1:208.

how much longer they could hold out.[67] Food was growing scarce in the city, and food prices had soared to astronomical levels.[68]

Lack of food was one problem, at least, that Edward did not share. Meat was cheap and plentiful thanks to the cows, pigs and sheep which the foragers were constantly driving back to the army's camps.[69] In sharp contrast to the siege of Cambrai the previous year, the allies were this time supplied with a "great abundance" of all sorts of goods, which came in carts and river barges from as far away as Brabant.[70]

Food, however, was not enough to keep his army together very long. Something had to be done to speed up the siege. If the allies could pressure the defenders into making a surrender contract like the one agreed to by the Scots in Berwick in 1333, Edward's problems might be solved. A fixed date for the conclusion of the campaign would make it far easier to keep his army together until that point, just as Philip's assignment of a day for battle in 1339 had enabled Edward to keep the Low Countries princes from going home before then. It would also be more likely than anything else to push Philip into finally meeting the English in the field.

Beginning on 26 August, the English and the Flemings (the two parties most committed to the success of the campaign) began an all-out effort to convince the besieged to open negotiations for surrender. Major assaults tested the defenders' resolve on the 26th and 27th, and on 2 September.[71] These attacks were interspersed with slightly more subtle attempts to influence the townsmen.[72] "Every day men were sent to the gates to yell at the gates that they should surrender and that they would be betrayed by the lords who were then in Tournai [i.e. the garrison], and often said 'Eat your fill tonight, for you will not eat at all tomorrow.' "[73] One Fleming came to the Ste.-Fontaine gate on 27 August and yelled "Surrender, knaves, before you die of hunger, and we take your women."[74]

All of this failed to dent the defenders' loyalty to Philip or their determination

---

[67] *Le Bel*, 1:205, 192, 192n; *Tournai Chronicles*, 351; *Fr. Chron. London*, 80; *Chronographia*, 2:147; Villani, *Cronica*, 380.

[68] *Tournai Chronicles*, 364; *Fr. Chron. London*, 80, 79; *Chronographia*, 2:150, 150 n.1; *Le Muisit*, 131–2.

[69] *Fr. Chron. London*, 80.

[70] *Le Bel*, 1:191.

[71] *Tournai Chronicles*, 355–7. It was probably around this period that a charlatan posing as a sorcerer convinced Edward to pay a great deal of money for materials which were supposedly to be used to construct a flying wooden dragon capable of destroying the city with bolts of Greek Fire. The magician's best trick was making himself and the money disappear. *Chron. Pays-Bas*, 153–4.

[72] This was standard practice in medieval siege warfare.

[73] *Tournai Chronicles*, 357: "venoient les ennemis cescun jour cryer aulx portes que il se rendeissent et qu'il estoient trahis des seigneurs qui alors estoient en Tournay, et disoient souvent: 'Mengiés anuyt vo sof, car vous ne mengerés point demain.'"

[74] Ibid., 357: "Rendés-vous, larrons, par tant vous morrés de fain, et nous prendrons vos fames."

to hold out as long as possible.[75] But their prayers for relief finally seemed to have moved Philip of Valois – or perhaps he was already aware of the sentiment that, if the besiegers were forced to surrender, he might lose his realm and his honor as a result.[76] On 7 September, twelve days after the allies began their stepped-up attacks on the town, he advanced to Bouvines (where an earlier King Philip of France had put an end to an Anglo-German alliance in 1214), just six or seven miles from the English army. Everyone, except perhaps Philip himself, thought there would be a battle in the next few days. The garrison in Tournai thought so: they asked the townsmen for permission to sally out of the city when the combat began. The consuls granted the soldiers' request, provided that they agreed to return after the battle and pay their debts. The townsmen thought so too: they decided to send a thousand soldiers from the town to aid the king, dressed in uniform and armed at the expense of the rich bourgeois. These men were chosen and arrayed; captains were appointed; some of the men heard mass to prepare their souls.[77] The allies thought so: the Duke of Brabant and the Count of Hainault, who had been encamped on the far side of the river Scheldt, now crossed over to join the English on the side facing the French army,[78] and Edward used what funds he could find to make a last pay distribution to his troops.[79] Even John of Bohemia, one of Philip's closest advisors, apparently thought so, for he drew up a new will and testament on 9 September.[80] But the Valois king made no move, apparently lacking the will to attack soldiers reputed to be "the best in Christendom."[81] Rumors of battle spread through the allied host again on the 14th, and the troops drew up into full battle array in the fields of Orque.[82] But once again Philip failed to show. Meanwhile, bishops through-out France and England conducted religious processions, on the instructions of the Pope, to pray for peace between the two realms. Perhaps their prayers were having an effect.[83]

The disappointed allies tried to increase the pressure on Tournai, and so on the French king. The same night, the 14th, the English shot a large number of arrows into the town with messages attached. These promised the people of Tournai friendship and unity if they would surrender; "or if not, they [the besiegers] would capture the town by force and destroy them and their women and children."[84] To make this threat more credible – both to the people of

[75] Ibid., 356–8, 364; *Le Muisit*, 131.
[76] Jan de Klerk, *Van den Derden Eduwaert*, ll. 1745–9 (*Edouard III*, 24), has the Countess of Hainault express worry at this prospect: "Ende in die stad es honger groot . . . Die stad op moeten geven,/ Ic duchte ghij wart verdreven/ Uwes lands ende uwer eeren mede."
[77] *Tournai Chronicles*, 359.
[78] *Tournai Chronicles*, 358.
[79] This is implied by the timing given in *Le Baker*, 71.
[80] Déprez, *Préliminaires*, 334 n.8.
[81] Jan de Klerk, *Van den Derden Eduwaert*, l. 1750 (*Edouard III*, 24–5).
[82] *Tournai Chronicles*, 360.
[83] Déprez, *Préliminaires*, 335.
[84] *Tournai Chronicles*, 361.

Tournai and to the Flemish soldiers themselves, who by this point were growing anxious to return home – Artevelde had his carpenters construct a gigantic mobile siege tower in front of his tent.[85]

Into this tense situation stepped Jeanne, the dowager Countess of Hainault, who left the convent to which she had retired in order to try to make peace.[86] For her, this war was a family conflict: her brothers Philip of Valois and Charles of Alençon one side, and her son William and sons-in-law (Edward III, William of Juliers, and the emperor) on the other. She went to her brother and tearfully pleaded with him to send some of his nobles to treat with Edward for a truce. Philip made a face-saving show of resistance, repeatedly refusing to allow negotiations and even threatening the countess' son William with beheading.[87] The French king's obstinacy was probably not genuine: Jan de Klerk claims that Philip really considered himself to be in a difficult situation which he would be glad to get out of without fighting, if he could do so honorably, and the fact that he had made no move to attack before the countess' intervention makes this credible. It was politically impossible, however, to so abase himself as to ask for an enemy's grace. His public bellicosity, apparently yielding only reluctantly to the pitiful prayers of his own sister, let him proceed without too much loss of honor. The elaborate arguments in favor of peace presented by the papal nuncio Guillaume Ami, who had arrived in Philip's camp not long before, may also have helped to convince the French king to try negotiations. So he gave the countess permission to seek a truce, and promised not to attack for three days while she made her attempt.[88]

Outside Tournai, Jeanne turned all her powers of persuasion on her son-in-law, Edward.[89] He, too, had already been visited by a papal nuncio equipped with persuasive arguments for peace prepared by the brilliant Benedict XII.[90] Considering the imminent danger of his army's collapse from lack of pay, Edward could not refuse the countess' overtures out of hand. Personally, he did not want to agree to a truce, for he believed that the defenders of Tournai had only three or four days' more food, and he thought the army could be held together for that long.[91] Then, the Plantagenet believed, Philip would come and give battle rather than see the city fall; the affair would be settled once and for all; and he, Edward, would gain more honor than any prince had ever had.[92] But

---

85 Ibid.

86 *Chronographia*, 2:158; *Le Bel*, 1:202. Le Bel calls her "the good lady, the queen of good ladies."

87 Ibid., 203–4; *Chronographia*, 2:158.

88 Déprez, *Préliminaires*, 338–40; Jan de Klerk, *Edouard III*, 24–5.

89 *Chronographia*, 2:158–9; *Le Bel*, 1:203–4. According to le Bel, 204, John of Bohemia and Louis d'Aigimont were sent with her to Edward.

90 Déprez, *Préliminaires*, 340–2.

91 Villani, *Cronica*, 380: "Il re d'Inghilterra non volea intendere a trattato, conoscendo che la terra [Tournai] non si potea difendere né tenere per difetto di vittuaglia." *Le Bel*, 1:208, 207; *Le Baker*, 71.

92 See his letter in Déprez, *Préliminaires*, 356 (quoted in note 58, above).

he called in the leaders of his army to get their views. Jacques van Artevelde and Robert of Artois came out strongly opposed to negotiations.[93] William and Jean d'Hainault also inclined towards maintaining the siege, since the defenders of Tournai were on the verge of starvation.[94] Juliers and Guelders, it appears, were wavering.[95] But the Duke of Brabant had the last word. He warned his allies that it was only with the greatest difficulty that he had kept his troops at the siege as long as he had. They would leave in a day or two if a truce were not arranged, and he would go with them.[96] Edward, between Brabant's faintheartedness and his own lack of money, felt constrained to give in.[97] He unhappily agreed to send his most trusted counselors to meet with French representatives in the chapel of Esplechin between the two hosts.[98]

The negotiations went very quickly. They began on 23 September, and by the evening of the next day the two sides had agreed on terms, though it had grown too dark to write them down. So it was on 25 September that the Truce of Esplechin was drawn up, sealed, and officially proclaimed.[99] Although elaborate in detail, its terms were simple in essence. The truce was intended to freeze the war in place. No one on either side was to harm the other. The truce was to apply in Scotland, the Low Countries, the Channel, Gascony, the rest of France, and practically everywhere else the negotiators could think to mention. Each side would continue in possession of the lands it held at the time of the agreement. Merchants and other travelers would be allowed to go and trade freely from one obedience to another. Prisoners were to be freed on condition that they return to their captors at the end of the truce if they had not been ransomed in the interim. If a siege were in progress anywhere, it was to be lifted immediately, but the defenders were not to increase their garrisons or stores during the truce.[100] This clause, of course, applied to Tournai as well. When the seven commissioners from each side entered the city to examine the state of the stores, so that it could be assured that they would be the same at the expiration of the

---

[93]   *Chronographia*, 2:159.
[94]   *Le Bel*, 1:208. Adam Murimuth, however, claims that all the confederates except the Flemings were in favor of the truce, since it was useful to them (their towns and castles being restored), although it was useless to the King of England. *Murimuth*, 116.
[95]   The Pope, at least, suggested as much in the arguments he made to Edward for peace. Déprez, *Préliminaires*, 341n.
[96]   *Chronographia*, 2:159; *Le Bel*, 1:207–8; cf. Villani, *Cronica*, 380. Villani claims that Brabant had been influenced or bribed by Philip VI.
[97]   *EMDP*, 437; letters of Edward III and John Stratford in *Avesbury*, 326 and 332; *Murimuth*, 116; *Le Bel*, 1:208; Villani, *Cronica*, 380; Jan de Klerk, *Van den Derden Eduwaert*, ll. 1849–59 (*Edouard III*, 27); *Scalacronica* (ed. Maxwell), 112; *Grandes chroniques*, 9:208.
[98]   According to the *Chronographia*, 2:160, he assigned Henry Burghersh, William Clinton, Geoffrey le Scrope, Jean d'Hainault, William's deputy the Lord of Antoing, and the Lord of Cuyk to the negotiations. But cf. Lucas, *Low Countries*, 421.
[99]   *Le Bel*, 1:206, 206 n.1; *Tournai Chronicles*, 364–5; *RFR*, II:2:1135–7.
[100]   *RFR*, II:2:1135–7. The prisoners freed on parole included the earls of Salisbury and Suffolk, an important concession to Edward III.

truce, it was found that the defenders had only eight days' worth of food remaining.[101]

The biggest gainers from the truce were the Flemings. They got the free-trade provisions they needed to keep their export-based economy running. The agreement protected them, and the other allies, from French aggression once Edward had gone back to England. Moreover (by a document technically separate from the truce) Philip agreed to have Pope Benedict lift the interdict under which the county suffered, and further promised to invalidate permanently the terms of the treaty of Athis-sur-Orgue which had enabled him bring down the interdict in the first place.[102]

These terms were quite balanced in implication as well as form. Edward had gained Flanders (though it remained to be seen if he could keep it), but lost substantial territory in Aquitaine and Scotland. He had also escaped the imminent and shameful break-up of his army which his bankrupt finances threatened. Philip, for his part, had saved Tournai. More importantly, he had avoided battle once again. The French king had for a second time let his adversary expend gargantuan sums of money, but prevented him from gaining anything thereby. He probably hoped that Edward would be unable to muster the support (or the credit) for a third try.[103]

He was nearly right. Edward was thoroughly bankrupt.[104] He viewed the truce as a catastrophic missed opportunity, not a draw.[105] "The King of England could not [by means of the truce] salvage his reputation," observed a Rochester chronicler, "when by the instigation of the Flemings he had assumed the arms of the King of France, and styled himself King of France in letters sent everywhere, and [yet] had not obtained the kingdom."[106] The measure of Edward's disappointment was the icy rage he directed towards his administration in England, whose failure to supply him with the money he needed he could not begin to understand. The result, when the king returned to England as a virtual fugitive from his creditors, was a constitutional crisis of the first rank. Edward imprisoned most of his senior ministers, and would have done the same with the

---

101 Villani, *Cronica*, 380–1: "E se infra 'l termine non fosse fatto l'accordo, si dovea riporre la città di Torani nello stato ch'ella era, che non vi si trovò da vivere per otto giorni." See also *Le Bel*, 1:207; Déprez, *Préliminaires*, 356. Siege commissions: *RFR*, II:2:1136, clause VII.

102 *KdL*, 176–7. Yet, interestingly, Murimuth states that they were the only confederates who were opposed to the truce. *Murimuth*, 116.

103 Cf. *Le Bel*, 1:208.

104 On his situation after the Tournai campaign, see Déprez, *Préliminaires*, ch. 10; Lucas, *Low Countries*, ch. 12; Sumption, *Trial by Battle*, 359–69.

105 See his letter, quoted in Déprez, *Préliminaires*, 356.

106 *Historia Roffensis*, fo. 88. The chronicler adds that one might respond that Edward had been compelled to take the title by his need for Flemish help; yet no one in order to obtain help would name himself Sultan of Babylon or King of Heaven.

Archbishop of Canterbury if the latter had not taken sanctuary in his cathedral. That story, however, is beyond the scope of this work.[107]

The strategy that had guided Edward's conduct of the war from 1337 to the fall of 1340 was now in rubble. He had probably spent £500,000 in its prosecution,[108] more money than many medieval kings saw in their lifetimes. His unpaid debts to the Bardi and Peruzzi eventually led to the collapse of both houses, arguably setting back Europe's financial development for a generation. With their subsidies unpaid, his Imperial allies deserted him one by one.

Despite all this, Edward was not ready to give up the pursuit of his *droit*. In 1342, when a civil war in Brittany gave him the opportunity to add another peerage to his obedience in France, he brought another army to the Continent. But his operations there, like the ones conducted by his lieutenants in Gascony after the expiration of the truce, were little more than opportunistic sniping.[109] Not until 1346 would he again launch a full-scale effort to win the war. Not until then would his army again face off with that of Philip of Valois, at Crécy. By that time, though, Edward had developed a new strategy, one that was cheaper and could be conducted with his own national resources. The alliances and sieges which had been the focus of the 1339 and 1340 campaigns would be replaced with archers and *chevauchées*. But the ultimate goal would be the same: to bring Philip of Valois into decisive battle, where the will of God could be shown.

[107] Natalie M. Fryde, "Edward III's Removal of his Ministers and Judges, 1340–1341," *Bulletin of the Inst. of Historical Research* 48 (1975), is an excellent account.
[108] Sumption, *Trial by Battle*, 363.
[109] The Breton expedition of 1342–43 and Henry of Lancaster's campaigns in southern France in 1345–46 will not be covered in this book, primarily for reasons of space and focus. For Lancaster, see Sumption, *Trial by Battle*, and Fowler, *King's Lieutenant*. For Brittany, see Sumption and also the various works of Michael C. Jones, listed in the bibliography.

CHAPTER TEN

THE INVASION OF 1346:
STRATEGIC OPTIONS AND HISTORIOGRAPHY

> *Battles are short, but the victor's prize is enormous. Sieges*
> *waste time, and the town is rarely taken. Battles overcome*
> *nations and fortified towns, and an enemy beaten in battle*
> *vanishes like smoke.* Lisoius, seneschal of Geoffrey of Anjou[1]

ON 11 JULY 1346, after many delays, a fleet of some six hundred large vessels and a number of smaller ones sailed out from Portsmouth and from St. Helen's on the Isle of Wight.[2] On board, as an educated guess, were roughly 2,700 men-at-arms, 2,300 Welsh spearmen, 7,000 foot archers (English and Welsh) and 3,250 mounted archers, hobelars, and other troops – the largest British force ever to cross the Channel during the middle ages.[3] Edward III himself commanded the expedition; among the other leaders were his eldest son the Black Prince, the earls of Northampton, Warwick, Oxford, Arundel, Suffolk and Huntingdon, Lord Despenser "as an earl," the Bishop of Durham, Godfrey d'Harcourt, and lords Mortimer, Darcy, Mauny, Audley, Ferrers, Talbot, Burghersh, Morely and Ughtred, as well as Reginald Cobham, John Stirling, and Maurice Berkeley.

The fleet's destination was widely believed to be Gascony,[4] but the king had gone to great lengths to prevent definite intelligence of his plans from reaching the French. "No one could know for certain where he intended to sail, or in what place overseas he meant to land," wrote the royal clerk Adam Murimuth.[5] Even

---

[1] As quoted in the *Chroniques des comtes d'Anjou et des seigneurs d'Amboise*, given in Verbruggen, *Art of War* (2nd edn), 280.

[2] *Murimuth*, 199–200 (Burghersh's letter). For the delays, see *RFR*, III:1:67–86, esp. III:1:71. Number of ships: *Storie Pistoresi*, 222; cf. Villani, *Cronica*, 288; *Murimuth*, 198 (750 ships).

[3] See Appendix.

[4] Bartholomew Burghersh's letter to Archbishop Stratford, written after the landing in Normandy (in *Murimuth*, 200) claims that Edward intended to sail for Gascony, changing his mind only at the last minute due to the winds. This issue will be dealt with more fully below.

[5] *Murimuth*, 199. Cf. *Pakington*, fo. 195v: "en le Isle de Wyght . . . tient un counseil de ses prives et son purpos fuist si prive qe nul ne le savoit forsqe poy des gentz qi furent le plus privez de lui tanqe ils furent sur le mere; et puis singlerunt et avoient vent a voluntee tanqe ils viendrent a hogges." Secrecy measures included a prohibition on all traffic out of the

the captains of the ships did not know. They were given sealed orders, to be opened if the fleet were scattered by a storm, but otherwise they were instructed simply to follow the admirals.[6]

What the men of the expedition did know was that, once they arrived, they would have to be ready to withstand the test of battle. Edward made a "fair speech" to them, explaining once again the just cause he had for war with France: Philip had wrongly occupied Gascony, and also Ponthieu, which had been given to Edward by his mother. Furthermore, the Valois held even Normandy unjustly, for it had been taken unjustly in the time of King Richard around 1200 (not quite accurate, but close enough).[7] Edward's rather far-fetched remarks on Normandy here are, incidentally, a strong hint that he had already picked that duchy as his landing point. He continued his speech by propounding again his claim to the French crown through his mother. He asked his troops to bear themselves as doughty men, because he intended to leave the ships behind once he reached France.[8] They would have to be valiant and to conquer the land with sword in hand or all perish, for there would be no place to flee. Finally, he asked that any who felt fear or doubt at the thought of crossing stay behind in England with his goodwill. According to Villani, the English soldiers all responded with a loud shout that "they would willingly follow him, their dear lord, to the death!"[9]

Soon enough it became apparent that the fleet was not headed for Gascony. Instead, it made the quick crossing to the Cotentin peninsula of Normandy, arriving off the small port of St.-Vaast-la-Hougue the following morning. The French had anticipated the possibility of a landing in Normandy, though they did not consider it the most likely possibility, and the defense of the duchy's coasts had been entrusted to Marshal Robert Bertrand. Unfortunately for the marshal, the five hundred Genoese crossbowmen who had been stationed in the area for the preceding ten weeks had deserted, for lack of pay, just three days before the arrival of the invasion fleet. On the other hand, there was a bit of luck for the French: Bertrand had summoned all the men of the region to a muster of arms, which was to take place on the same day the English landed. With the men who

kingdom for a week after his final sailing date. *RFR*, III:1:85; letter of Edward III in *Le Bel*, 2:388.
6   Order to follow admirals: *Le Baker*, 79, and cf. *Le Bel*, 2:67–7. Sealed orders: Villani, *Cronica*, 389.
7   See Villani, *Cronica*, 388–9, for the speech.
8   As of course he did, after reaching the Seine area. Presuming Villani's account of this speech is accurate, this is another piece of evidence contradicting J. E. Morris' claim that "In 1346 it is an undoubted fact, though not sufficiently realized in history, that Edward III and his army were left stranded in Normandy simply because the fleet disappeared in complete defiance of orders . . . so that the army had to proceed as best it could, and Crécy was as it were an accident." *Welsh Wars*, 108. Edward was of course aware that leaving the ships behind had contributed to Beaumont and Balliol's victory in 1332; see above, Chapter 3.
9   Villani, *Cronica*, 389. Cf. his departure speech in 1359, the similarity of which may lend some support to Villani's reportage: Froissart, *Oeuvres*, 6:217.

gathered for this assembly and the remnant of his garrison soldiers, the marshal had some three hundred men-at-arms and seven hundred other local troops at his disposal. This was a small fraction of the strength of King Edward's army, but even a thousand men could do a great deal of damage if they struck by surprise and before the bulk of the English forces had landed. Intending to do just that, the French marshal led his men into the Bois de Rabey just west of the harbor and, as soon as an opportunity presented itself, arrayed them to attack.[10]

The highest-ranking Englishman yet ashore was the Earl of Warwick, the Marshal of England, whose duty it was to lead the vanguard.[11] Only a few horses had been unloaded, and Warwick probably had fewer men-at-arms to hand than Bertrand. Quite a number of English archers, however, had already disembarked. As soon as the earl saw the French force deploying for its attack, he mounted a horse of low quality (his own charger being still afloat), grabbed a lance and a shield, and charged right towards his enemies. Marshal Bertrand's forces were easily strong enough to defeat Warwick's improvised assault, but the French troops, doubtless overawed by the size of the English fleet which packed the expansive harbor in front of them, panicked and fled. There was a brief skirmish between the thirty men-at-arms who stuck by the marshal and the comparable force under Warwick, but Bertrand, his position hopeless, soon joined his more timid followers in flight.[12]

That, for the moment, was the only resistance mounted to the English invasion. After taking a leisurely five days to disembark, rest, and make final organizational arrangements, the king and his army rode into Normandy, where they found "the country fat and plentifully supplied with all goods, the granaries full of wheat, the houses full of all valuables, rich bourgeois, carts, horses and wagons, sheep, pigs, calves, bulls [and] cattle."[13]

The campaign which followed has been much studied, but much misunderstood. Both military and medieval historians have often found the strategy behind this great *chevauchée* "impossible to fathom."[14] A number, indeed, have concluded that there *was* no underlying plan: that the expedition was conceived "against every principle of the military art,"[15] and that the victory at its climax

---

10 *Acta Bellicosa*, 159 (crossbowmen, muster); *Récits*, 215–16 (Bertrand; 1,000 men total); and *Chron. St. Omer*, fo. 259: "Mais le bon Bertran, sire de Brisquebec, avoit assemble environ CCC hommes d'armes, et celle part se traist pour eulx deffendre l'arriver." Cf. also *Chron. Anon. Cant.*, 187.

11 He had received the office by royal grant in 1344 after the death of the Earl of Salisbury. *RFH*, 2:4:160.

12 *Récits*, 215; *Acta Bellicosa*, 159; *Chron. St. Omer*, fo. 259 ("Mais quant [Bertran] en eux cuida ferir, si vit ses gens qui ja s'enfuioient et ne demora que lui XXXe. Et pource se retraist, dolent et couroce."); Cottonian itinerary, in notes to *Le Baker*, 253; letter of Burghersh in *Murimuth*, 200; *Chron. Pays-Bas*, 168.

13 *Le Bel*, 2:76. This first week also saw attempts to win over the Normans to the Plantagenet obedience: see Chapter 11, below.

14 J. F. C. Fuller, *The Decisive Battles of the Western World and their Influence upon History*, ed. J. Terraine (London: Granada, 1970), 311.

15 Wrottesley, *Crecy and Calais from the Public Records*, p. iii.

was "an accident."[16] But it was a series of *chevauchées* like the 1346 campaign that eventually won for Edward the Peace of Brétigny – the most humiliating treaty inflicted on France until the twentieth century, which provided that the English king would take a full third of the realm of France, to be held in full sovereignty, completely independent of the French crown. This was not an absentminded slip on the part of the French monarchy: it was a rational, if painful, response to a desperate strategic and political situation created by the military efforts of Edward III. The evidence clearly shows that the Plantagenet's direction of the war between 1346 and 1360 was guided by a cogent overall strategy, one initiated by the Crécy campaign.

Although its roots stretched back at least to Edward's first campaign in 1327, the immediate impetus for the new strategy launched in 1346 came from the failed peace negotiations at Avignon in 1344, and the Earl of Derby's successful operations in the southern theater in 1345. Avignon showed Edward the limited potential of the war of opportunity he had sponsored in Brittany after the signing of the Truce of Esplechin in 1340.[17] Such limited actions threatened no vital interest of the French crown, and so they could not compel Philip to surrender something as important as his sovereignty over Aquitaine, much less his throne, nor even to risk a decisive defeat by offering battle on Edward's terms. No matter how successfully carried on, this style of warfare would not suffice to gain the English their political ends. Avignon made it clear to King Edward that he would have to mount a military effort commensurate with his ambitions, one which Philip could not afford to ignore.

The Earl of Derby's campaigns of 1345 demonstrated how vulnerable to invasion was much of France.[18] Derby's Anglo-Gascon forces had ridden wherever they wished virtually unopposed, capturing castles and towns and a king's ransom in booty and prisoners.[19] Derby's exploits also led to the French siege of Aiguillon in 1345–46. A garrison of Derby's followers held this strategically key stronghold, which he had recently captured, against a vast French army under Philip's eldest son Jean, Duke of Normandy. This left Edward with a political imperative – and, by the terms of Derby's indenture, arguably a

[16] Morris, *Welsh Wars*, 108. Cf. Lot, *L'art militaire et les armées au moyen âge*, 341; Liddell Hart, *Strategy*, 78.
[17] For the conference of Avignon, see E. Déprez, "La Conférence d'Avignon (1344)" *Essays in Medieval History Presented to Thomas Frederick Tout*, eds A. G. Little and F. M. Powicke (Manchester: Manchester U.P., 1925), and John Palmer, "The War Aims of the Protagonists and the Negotiations for Peace," *The Hundred Years War*, ed. Kenneth Fowler (London: Macmillan, 1971). For the operations conducted by Edward's lieutenants, see Burne, *Crécy War*, chs 3–4; Sumption, *Trial by Battle*, chs 11–12.
[18] For details, see Kenneth Fowler, *The King's Lieutenant: Henry of Grosmont, First Duke of Lancaster, 1310–1361* (London: Elek, 1969), chs 3–4; Sumption, *Trial by Battle*, ch. 13; Burne, *The Crecy War*, ch. 5, and also *Chron. St. Omer*, fos 254v–57v.
[19] Derby's profits from Bergerac (presumably including the battle of Auberoche) are said to have been no less than 52,000 marks. Knighton, *Chronicle* (ed. Martin), 188.

contractual obligation – to intervene and break the siege, in one way or another.[20]

In addition to these external military pressures, Edward had to satisfy his own *communitas regni*. Over the decade since the beginning of the war, the taxpayers of England had borne a tax burden that may have been higher than any other in all of European history up until then.[21] Yet, despite this vast expenditure, Edward seemed but little closer to his stated goal of recovering his rightful heritage of France.

The taxpayers of England were growing weary of paying what were supposed to be extraordinary war taxes on such a regular basis. At the parliament of June 1344 – the last before the 1346 campaign – Edward III asked the representatives of the community of the realm to advise him concerning the war. The response was unambiguous:

> They requested of our said lord the king, by unanimous assent, and each individual person of the Lords for himself, that he would make an end to this war, either by battle, or by a suitable peace, if he could get one; and that once our lord the king should be ready and equipped to cross over [to France] in order to take whatever God might grant to him for the successful completion of this business, that he not abandon his expedition until he had brought things to a conclusion in one way or another, not for letters, nor commands, nor requests of the Pope or anyone else. The king gave his full assent to this request.[22]

20 Derby's indenture specified that "the king has granted that if it should come about that the said earl should be besieged or pressed by so great a force that he cannot help himself without being rescued by the king's power, then the king will be bound to rescue him in one way or another, provided that he can be rescued by reasonable means [*convenablement*]." Fowler, *The King's Lieutenant*, 232. Of course, Derby was not besieged, in the strict sense, as he was not personally inside Aiguillon, but this was something of a technicality, especially since the Earl of Pembroke (who may well have had an equivalent clause in his indenture) was reportedly inside the besieged town (though cf. *Pakington*, fo. 195v). *Le Bel*, 2:67, and Froissart, *Oeuvres*, 4:376, give the relief of Derby first place in Edward's motivation for invading France.

21 England was probably the most-governed, and so most-taxed, realm in Christendom; and it takes little more than a glance at the tables in Ramsay's *Revenues of the Kings of England* to realize that the period from 1335–45 had never been equaled in terms of the tax burden borne by England. In addition to the taxation per se, the people had to bear the heavy weights of forced wool loans and royal purveyance; William of Dene's unpublished chronicle, for example, notes that after the 1344 grant "Rex et omnis milicia regni anglie die in dies . . . vectigalia per totum regnum per potenciam ab impotentibus et pauperibus et resistere' non valentibus congregare fecerunt nichil solvendo." ("The king and all the knights of the realm from day to day caused victuals to be collected by force from the poor, powerless, and unable to resist, paying nothing.") *Historia Roffensis*, fo. 90v. How this would compare to the tax burden sustained by, say, the Romans during the Punic Wars, is beyond my capacity to estimate; but it was almost certainly a record for the post-classical period.

The booty and ransoms which would later flood England, and so at least partially offset the cost of the war, had only just begun to appear in a major way in 1345, with Derby's capture of Auberoche.

22 *RP*, 148: "si prierent Touz d'un assent, & chescune singuler Persone des Grantz a par lui, a nostre dit Seign' le Roi, q'il vousist faire fyn de ceste Guerre, ou par Bataille, ou par Pees

In return, the parliament made a grant of a two-year subsidy – a substantial contribution considering the already heavy taxation of the preceding years. They imposed a special condition on the second year of the grant, however: it could only be collected if the king crossed in person to France in order to bring an end to the war.[23]

Under these circumstances, the preparations for a major invasion in late 1345 and early 1346 evoked no surprise.[24] The need to relieve Aiguillon, the recent demonstrations of English tactical superiority, Edward's personal military history, the mandate of parliament, and the failure of the peace talks at Avignon combined to ensure that the primary goal of the 1346 campaign would once again be to bring Philip VI to battle.[25] The campaigns of 1339 and 1340, however, had shown that this was no easy task – especially since Edward's actual intent, more precisely defined, was not just to secure a battle with the Valois army, but to do so on favorable terms. Practically speaking, this did not imply assuring numerical superiority for the English army (an almost impossible task), but rather utilizing the advantages of a strong position and the tactical defensive.[26]

The most obvious way for Edward to relieve Derby's men and secure a battle with the French army would be to sail for Bordeaux and from there march directly against Aiguillon. This approach would have a number of advantages. First, Bordeaux would provide the English army with a good port and a secure base of operations. Second, the very substantial army still in the field under Derby, which probably numbered somewhere around six thousand soldiers, would provide a welcome supplement to the host mustering in England.[27] Third,

---

convenable, s'il la purra avoir: Et que a quele heure que nostre Seign' le Roi serra prest & apparaillez de passer pur prendre ce que Dieux lui durra sur l'esploit de ceste Busoigne, que pur Lettres, n'autrez mandementz, ne priere du Pape, ne d'autry, il ne lest son veiage tan que il eit fait fyn en une manere ou en autre. A quele Priere le Roi ottroia pleynement." Note the similarity between parliament's petition and Edward's letter to Philip of Valois, written in the middle of the 1346 campaign: "we will remain in the realm [of France], without leaving, to carry out our war as best we can, to our advantage and the loss of our enemies. Therefore if you wish, as your letters purport, to do battle with us and to protect those whom you claim as your subjects, let it now be known that at whatever hour you approach you will find us ready to meet you in the field, with God's help, which thing we desire above all else for the common good of Christendom, since you will not deign to tender or accept any reasonable terms for peace." *CPR (1345–48)*, 517; PRO C66/219/m. 21d. Even after the battle of Crécy, at the beginning of the siege of Calais, Edward still had "no thought of leaving the realm of France until we have made an end to our war, with the help of God." Letter to Thomas Lucy, in Chandos Herald, *Black Prince*, 355.

[23] *RP*, 148: "si le Roi passe meismes & faite fyn des ditz Busoignes."

[24] For these preparations, see the records reproduced in Wrottesley, *Crecy and Calais*, passim.

[25] Readers familiar with the historiography of the 1346 *chevauchée* will realize that this assertion directly contradicts most of what has been written on the campaign. I will support my position below.

[26] Cf. my "Offensive/Defensive in Medieval Strategy."

[27] Sumption, *Trial by Battle*, 466, estimates Derby's army a bit earlier at 1,500 men in

the inherent strategic importance of Aiguillon, which dominated the confluence of the Lot and the Garonne, combined with the prestige and effort already invested in recapturing it, would make it nearly certain that the French would fight to maintain their siege.[28]

At the time, it was widely believed that Edward would take this course. Jean le Bel's chronicle and a letter written shortly after the landing in Normandy by Bartholomew Burghersh, a member of Edward's council, indicate that the king chose to make for the Cotentin only after the fleet's initial departure from Portsmouth. According to this version of events, persistently contrary winds (seen as a sign from God) and Harcourt's "counsel and exhortation" finally convinced the king of the value of the Normandy option while the fleet was anchored off the Isle of Wight, waiting for a chance to sail for Bordeaux.[29] An alternate possibility is that Edward planned a descent on Normandy from early on, spreading rumors of an invasion of Gascony just to deceive the French. The simple fact that the English went to such great efforts to conceal their plans – on the eve of his departure, Edward ordered that no ships be allowed to leave England for eight days after his departure, except the small Flanders expeditionary force under Hugh Hastings (who was ordered to search his own men for letters or messages before their departure) – lends some support to this view, since there would have been little point in taking such precautions in order merely to prevent the French from receiving *confirmation* of what they already expected.[30] This possibility is also given some support by the choice of Portsmouth (the typical point of departure for Normandy or the Seine) as the army's

Bergerac, plus 2,100 men-at-arms and 4–6,000 foot soldiers and mounted archers in the field, for a total of over 8,000. Reducing this figure by the 900 men of the garrison of Aiguillon (*Le Bel*, 2:57; cf. Villani, *Cronica*, 387) and some reasonable figure for minimal garrisons elsewhere leaves about 6,000 available for battlefield service.

28 Froissart says that in planning the 1346 campaign, Edward had many options, "et toutesfois cellui où il s'enclinoit le plus, estoit de aller lever le siége devant Aguillon *et de combattre les Franchois.*" ("and always the one to which he most inclined was to go to raise the siege of Aiguillon, *and to combat the French.*") *Oeuvres*, 4:376. Emphasis added.

29 Jean le Bel initially says simply that Edward intended "to enter into the realm of France and do there the worst that had ever been done," and that the troops summoned were instructed to "board the ships and to go with him to wherever he would go." However, le Bel does have Harcourt, while the fleet is anchored off Guernsey (an error for the Isle of Wight) advise the king to descend on Normandy (*Le Bel*, 2:67–8, 70). Burghersh's letter (in *Murimuth*, 200), says that Edward embarked still intending to go to Gascony, but changed his mind when the unremittingly contrary winds convinced him that God did not want him to take that course. Froissart's fourth redaction of his chronicle also gives this version of events: *Oeuvres*, 4:384–5. Just before the departure from the Isle of Wight, Edward wrote that his intention was to sail to wherever God and the wind should lead him in order to avoid any longer remaining where he was. Presumably he knew which way the wind was blowing and that this decision in practice meant sailing for Normandy.

30 For the security precautions, see Edward's letter, printed in an appendix to *Le Bel*, 2:338; *RFR*, III:1:85; *Murimuth*, 199; Villani, *Cronica*, 389.

gathering place rather than Plymouth or Southampton (the usual embarkation points for Gascony), though this is by no means strong evidence.[31]

In any case, Edward's own testimony is that he spent ten days on the Isle of Wight waiting, not for favorable winds, but for all his ships to gather. By 7 July, the fleet was assembled between Yarmouth and the Needles, and, according to the king's letter, he and his council decided to sail wherever the wind might take them in order to avoid any further delays.[32] Still, they must have had a destination in mind, for otherwise they could not have issued the sealed orders to the ships' captains. The mention of Normandy in Edward's departure speech, as given by Villani, suggests that by this point the plan to make for Gascony (if that ever was the plan) had been abandoned. On the 8th, the fleet put to sea heading west, but the wind reversed its direction so that the ships could not make any progress, and returned to Portsmouth. On 9 and 10 July, further attempts were made to reach the open sea. Finally, on the 11th, the fleet was able to gather between Portsmouth and St. Helen's, and proceed with favorable winds to Normandy.[33]

Although it is impossible to determine conclusively just when Edward decided against the Gascony approach, the logic behind the choice, even aside from the issue of the winds, is fairly clear. The idea of marching directly on Aiguillon would have been uncomfortably reminiscent of Edward's first great military success, the 1333 Halidon Hill campaign. "Uncomfortably" so because the English, advancing to break the siege of Aiguillon, would be cast into the role of the Scots of 1333, who had been forced to launch a disastrous attack on a strong English position in an ultimately unsuccessful attempt to rescue Berwick.

Philip had already, more than once, demonstrated his reluctance to fight an open battle with the English. As the standoff at la Flamengrie-Buironfosse showed, even if he were willing to do battle, he might not be prepared to take the tactical offensive. Edward would find it all too easy to visualize the invasion turning into a fiasco: the English could march the seventy miles up the Garonne

---

[31] Hewitt, "Organisation of War," 85, comments on the usual points of origin for expeditions to various destinations. E.g. in 1355, Edward III's fleet, bound for Normandy, sailed from Portsmouth to the Isle of Wight, and was stuck for a long time due to contrary winds, while the prince's fleet, bound for Gascony, gathered at Plymouth. See below, p. 295. It should be noted, however, that Portsmouth was chosen as the port for Gascon expeditions planned in 1294, 1325, and 1337. *RFR*, I:2:801; *RFH*, 2:2:129, 2:3:171.

[32] In *Le Bel*, 2:338.

[33] Edward issued warrants for Great Seal writs from Portchester and from the Isle of Wight on the 8th, and was at Freshwater on the southwest extreme of the Isle the next day. PRO, C81[Warrants for the Great Seal]/313 nos. 17793–6. On the 10th he was "at sea near the Isle of Wight," and on the 11th, at St. Helen's. *RFH*, 2:4:202. Burghersh (in *Murimuth*, 200) describes setting out for Gascony and being unable to make progress; the *Acts of War*, 27, notes the sudden reversal of the wind, the return to Portsmouth, and subsequent efforts "each day to reach the open sea." Note that Pakington's statement that the English "avoient vent a voluntee tanqe ils viendrent a hogges," (fo. 195v), and the *Acts of War*'s description of the winds and tides which took the fleet to Normandy as "favorable," also imply that Normandy had been adopted as the fleet's destination.

from Bordeaux to Aiguillon only to find Philip's army blocking their path to the fortress, his Genoese crossbowmen and communal infantry protected by strong fieldworks, and his renowned men-at-arms prepared to charge over a site chosen for its suitability for cavalry action. Under such circumstances, Edward would face almost certain defeat if he chose to abandon his Halidon tactics and lead his smaller army in an attack on his adversary. If, on the other hand, he drew his army into a defensive array, then Philip could simply wait him out. The English king would have to stand by helplessly as the 900-man garrison of Aiguillon – including the Earl of Pembroke, Walter Mauny and Alexander de Caumont, one of his most important Gascon supporters – was starved into surrender.[34] This result would not be considered a draw, but a clear victory for the French. The dishonor which had attended Philip at Buironfosse would here be transferred to Edward, for it would be the English monarch, not the French king, who would be seen as failing to protect his vassals as a good lord should. Such a perception would undermine, perhaps irreparably, the English king's strategy of presenting himself to the people of France as a more desirable monarch than Philip. And to make matters worse, the English army would eventually have to retreat, in the face of a numerically superior enemy, past the French garrisons of Le Mas d'Agenais and Marmande. With these unappealing prospects before him, it is little wonder that Edward decided against a direct approach on Aiguillon.

A second obvious possibility for the 1346 campaign would be an incursion from Flanders towards Paris. Like the Gascony option, this would provide the expeditionary force with a secure base of operations and a substantial number of reinforcements – Flemish communal infantry in this case. An advance on Paris would be hard for Philip to ignore, if not impossible; and if the Valois monarch did manage to avoid a battle in this case the shame would fall on him, not on Edward. A king who would allow his enemy to ride up to his capital, devastating and plundering all the way, and then let him simply ride away again, would be the very picture of impotence. Furthermore, since the main French army was at Aiguillon (about twice as far from Paris as Flanders is), Philip might even be forced to give battle with only a fraction of his potential might. In any case, he would almost certainly be forced to raise the siege of Aiguillon quickly and transfer the troops involved to the north, where they could help resist the invaders.[35]

The major problem with this option was that it seemed too much "business as

---

34 *Le Bel*, 2:57; Villani, *Cronica*, 387, makes it 1,200 men. The French nearly succeeded in starving out the garrison, who were constrained to eat their horses and cats before the siege ended. *Pakington*, fo. 195v.

35 This argument, according to Froissart, was made by Godfrey d'Harcourt (though in a different context: he was advocating a descent on Normandy). "Sire," Froissart has him say to Edward, "how could you lend them [the besieged] greater aid than to enter into the realm of France and immediately make war strongly? You will make a *chevauchée* with all your army to the gates of Paris, without finding anyone to impede you, or block your path; and by the expedition that you make through the realm of France the siege before Aiguillon will be raised of itself, for all the men-at-arms, wherever they may be, will be sent for to come to

usual." Edward had already tried invasions from the Low Countries twice, in 1339 and in 1340 (or three times, counting his failure in 1338), and his memories of those times were not happy ones. Then, too, he had been Vicar of the Empire, with nearly every major noble in the area as his ally. In the interim, all of these erstwhile supporters except the Flemings had abandoned him, and many were now active allies of the French, including even Edward's old friend, Jean d'Hainault.[36] If the Flanders approach had not worked then, why should it succeed in 1346?

Indeed, Edward did not need to look as far back as 1340 for a reason to make him hesitant to choose Flanders as a base of operations. Much more recently, in the summer of 1345, Ghent had gone through a political crisis which had required the king to bring an army to Flanders. Despite Edward's support, the long-time ruler of Ghent, Jacques van Artevelde, had been murdered by a mob. In addition, a rebellion in favor of the pro-French Count of Flanders had broken out, requiring a joint Anglo-Flemish operation (including a minor battle) to suppress it and restore the three cities' control.[37] The Anglo-Flemish alliance remained intact, but Edward and his council can hardly have relished the prospect of relying on such unstable allies.[38] With all of this taken into consideration, the English decided against the Flanders route for the main thrust of the 1346 invasion. The new campaign needed to differ radically from what had gone before, because Edward needed radically different results from it.

The third possibility, the one advocated by Godfrey d'Harcourt, a Norman exile who played much the same role as Robert of Artois had in earlier years, was a direct invasion of Normandy. A landing there would put the English just as close to Paris as would the previous option. By descending on the Cotentin, Edward could potentially *gain*, as well as use, a secure staging area: Harcourt, as the hereditary lord of St.-Sauveur-le-Vicomte, carried much weight in Norman politics, and he claimed that he could bring a number of noble supporters over to the English side.[39] If Edward could secure a permanent foothold in even a part of the Cotentin (especially if that part included the extremely strong castle of St.-Sauveur-le-Vicomte), he would have gained a significant prize, for the proximity of the area to England made it an excellent portal into France.

The biggest advantage of a descent on Normandy, however, would be its unpredictability. As military theorists from Sun Tzu onwards have often observed, the greatest strength of the strategic offensive is that the defender

meet you and combat you." Froissart, *Oeuvres*, 4:385. The earls of Warwick and Arundel are said to have agreed with this argument.

[36] *Chronographia*, 2:228; Lucas, *Low Countries*, passim; *Journaux du trésor*, 67 (Hainault).

[37] *Chron. St. Omer*, fos 258–58v.

[38] For details, see Lucas, *Low Countries*, 516–27.

[39] He was apparently even able to deliver a few, including Guillaume de Vaconges (*RTC*, no. 6544), Nicholas de Groucy, and Roland de Verdun (*Chron. Normande*, 75, n.1; *Grandes chroniques*, 9:271; Cazelles, *Société politique*, 152). See also *RTC*, nos. 5906, 6225. Villani, *Cronica*, 390, mentions that Edward was followed by many Norman gentlemen, and others, who were not enamored of French rule.

must everywhere anticipate attack, while the attacker may fall with all his strength on a fraction of his opponent's army.[40] Philip had to keep his forces – what forces he had outside of the army besieging Aiguillon – in a fairly centralized location, from which he could advance against an invader acting in any area. Thus Edward, so long as he avoided the most obvious approaches (from Flanders or Bordeaux), could expect to have a significant block of time to act unopposed by any organized defense.[41]

Nowhere could this time be put to better use than in Normandy. Most of the areas of the kingdom accessible by sea – Brittany, Saintonge, Gascony and the areas around Flanders – had already been fire-hardened by the earlier campaigns of the Hundred Years War. Normandy, on the other hand, was in Harcourt's words "the fattest, most bountiful land in the world, where we will [be able to] do our will; for the inhabitants are simple people, who don't know what war is."[42] Jean le Bel exaggerated somewhat when he wrote that the Normans "had never experienced war, nor seen men-at-arms," but it is true that their region was ill-prepared to deal with an invader.[43]

Thus, in the advance through Normandy, the English would have rich opportunities for plunder and destruction, uninhibited by the proximity of a strong enemy army.[44] Burning and looting the countryside and the poorly defended towns of the area would serve Edward's purposes in a number of ways: it would provide profit for his troops, bolstering their enthusiasm for the war;[45] it would undermine Philip's political and fiscal support by ruining his subjects and emptying their purses; and it would put strong pressure on the French king to stop the destruction of his people, or at least to avenge them, by giving battle.[46]

In the event, Edward chose to combine the Normandy and Flanders approaches. Five days after Edward's army sailed for the Cotentin, a second, much smaller force was sent to Ghent under Hugh Hastings, a baron and cousin of the King of England, who had recent experience leading an English contingent fighting in Flanders.[47] As the royal host rode east through Normandy, Hast-

---

40 *Art of War* VI.7–8, 13–15 (ed. Griffiths, pp. 98–9). Note that the validity of this proposition is *inversely* related to the speed of communications and movement. The more space the defender must cover with a set number of troops, the worse his situation is, and since military "space" is best measured by the *time* it takes to move information and troops across it, France of 1346 was much "bigger" than France of 2000, and thus harder to defend.

41 As Froissart has Harcourt say, "we will not find anyone there who will oppose us." *Oeuvres*, 4:384.

42 Froissart, *Oeuvres*, 4:386; cf. 381.

43 *Le Bel*, 2:77. Froissart, *Oeuvres*, 4:402, adds that the people fled before the English "like sheep before wolves."

44 In the event, as Harcourt had promised, the English king "passed through all of Normandy and plundered and burned large towns and others . . . no one resisting them." *Muisit*, 155.

45 Note that the army's backing for the war was doubly important during the middle ages, since the host included a large proportion of the most politically powerful men in the realm.

46 As Villani, *Cronica*, 394, says, Philip eventually pursued Edward after the English crossed the Seine "to combat him in the field, so that he would not destroy the countryside."

47 Villani, *Cronica*, 393. Recent experience: *Chron. St. Omer*, fos 258–58v.

ings' men were to accompany a Flemish army marching south to join up with Edward in the vicinity of the Somme.[48] The main army lost only a few hundred men and twenty small ships by this detachment,[49] but the total number of troops in the field against the French was increased by several thousand – the size of the Flemings' communal army.[50]

Given Philip's known indecisiveness as a military commander, any action which would add to his uncertainty could be expected to redound to Edward's favor. If Philip would find it troublesome to deal with two enemy armies in the field, in Gascony and in Normandy, how much more difficult would it be for him to deal with three! The "fog of war" (all the denser in that age of poor communications) would make it difficult for him to know how to respond to these diverse threats. With the Flemings in the field, he would have to maintain full-strength garrisons in the important towns and castles in that theater, even if he decided not to oppose them more actively.

The main thrust of the English attack, of course, would still come with the royal army in Normandy. That army would, for the reasons outlined above, thoroughly devastate the countryside of Normandy as it advanced towards Philip, at Paris or wherever he might be. The outcome, Edward hoped, would be a battle through which he could "make an end" to the war, as parliament had asked.

Still, Edward had to be prepared for the possibility that Philip would decline battle, no matter how severe the provocation. The Valois monarch had, after all, found it possible to avoid combat at Buironfosse and Tournai. But Philip had suffered "exceedingly great blame," even "detestation and mockery," for his seeming cowardice, and his prestige had declined greatly.[51] The French king's political standing had fallen even lower when, after the truce of Malestroit, he had continued to devalue the currency, leading to inflation and shortages of all sorts of goods, and – worse yet – had reinstituted the infamous salt tax, the "gabelle," which "created much indignation and ill-will against the king among

---

[48] Several sources, including the Tournai chronicler Gilles le Muisit (*Muisit*, 158; also Villani, *Cronica*, 393), state that Edward and the Flemings did intend to meet each other during the campaign, and this seems borne out by events; the suggestion of the Somme as the place chosen for the rendezvous, however, is merely my conjecture based on their actions and the timing of the two departures.

[49] Villani, *Cronica*, 393; Sumption, *Trial by Battle*, 498; Lucas, *Low Countries*, 554.

[50] The actual number of the Flemings in the field during the summer of 1346 is not given by any reliable source. The only even moderately realistic chronicler's estimate is Villani's figure of 20,000 (*Cronica*, 393), but even this is almost certainly too high. To get an idea of the real size of the Flemish army, we can observe that Ghent alone sent a contingent of some 4,000 men to the siege of Calais a few months later (Lucas, *Low Countries*, 553–40), and over 5,000 to Tournai in 1340 (above, Chapter 7). The Flemish field army in July/August included the levies from Bruges, Ypres, and the smaller towns as well as the Ghenters. Together they could well have equaled the 13,452 men whom, according to a Welsh chronicle cited by DeVries, "Siege of Calais," 156, the Flemings offered to supply for the siege of Calais.

[51] Froissart, *Oeuvres*, 3:44n: "trop grant blasme." In other manuscripts, "grant honte et grant deffaulte." Ibid., 3:44. *Cont. Manuel, 1328–39*, 1266: "And it was commonly said that he [Philip] had followed the counsel of 'foxiness,' because of which a large group of valiant knights and noble men had hats made out of fox fur, in detestation and mockery of the affair."

great and small alike," as even the semi-official *Grandes chroniques* admitted.[52] Edward had already gained an uncomfortable number of supporters in Flanders, Brittany, Normandy, Burgundy,[53] Périgord, the Agenais, and Poitou; now even in Compiègne people were beginning to whisper that "the King of England should better have obtained the realm of France than the king who held it," and that it was better to be ruled well by an Englishman than badly by a Frenchman.[54] A man-at-arms serving in the French army had to be prosecuted for proclaiming that Philip "had not dared to fight with the King of England . . . the most valiant man in Christendom."[55] Were Edward to enter into Valois territory for a fourth time, pillaging and ruining Philip's supporters at will, and once again escape with his loot, that opinion would be sure to spread; more and more people would come to agree with a Valenciennes chronicler that "no other King of France had ever made war so shamefully, so weakly, nor with such cowardice."[56] Philip's subjects might re-evaluate Edward's proclamation of

---

[52] *Grandes chroniques*, 9:235; see also 9:248 and *Récits*, 154–5. Philip's willingness to execute prominent men on suspicion of treason also continued to undermine his popularity, especially among the nobility. E.g. see *Récits*, 224–5: "never did a King of France . . . put to death so excessively many noble men, without cause, which was a shame; and if he was hated by their kin, it was no wonder."

[53] A substantial party of noblemen in Burgundy, led by the lords of Châlons and Neufchâtel and the Vicomte of St.-Just, had been drawn into supporting the Plantagenet party, and kept the Duke of Burgundy from contributing to the national defense effort. *Chron. St. Omer*, fo. 259; *Cont. Manuel, 1339–46*, fo. 165v; *RTC*, no. 6959; Denifle, *Désolation*, 52. Brittany and Normandy: *Grandes chroniques*, 9:248.

[54] Simon Poullet, a rich bourgeois of Compiègne (misidentified by le Muisit as a bourgeois of Paris), was executed for uttering those words at a dinner in 1346. *Le Muisit*, 171; *Grandes chroniques*, 9:269–70; *RTC*, nos. 6613, 6637; "Fragments inédits de la chronique de Jean de Noyal," 253.

Some idea of Philip's problems in this area can be gained by examining the roughly 150 entries in the *Registres du trésor des chartes* dealing with cases of lèse-majesté between 1337 and 1347, many of which, like the case of Bernard de Bailleul (no. 6279), involve the confiscation of goods from a "rebel partisan of the English."

[55] *RTC*, no. 6706. Guillaume Brouart, esquire, was denounced for sedition against the king, notably for saying that "nous [Philip] ne nous estions osé combattre au Roy d'Angleterre à Bouvines et que le dit Roy estoit le plus vaillant homme des crestiens." After being imprisoned for five weeks, he was freed on condition that he rejoin the army where he had served, notably at Amiens, Bouvines, Buironfosse and Calais. The pardon eventually granted to Brouart is not dated, but by its placement in the *Trésor des chartes* and the reference to Calais, it most likely dates to late in 1347. The remarks for which he was condemned, however, were presumably made after 1340 (the remark concerning Bouvines referring to Edward's siege of nearby Tournai) but before the battle of Crécy (which, if nothing else, absolved Philip of cowardice). At around the same time, one Jean de Lyons was imprisoned for six years for having proclaimed that, since Edward III was better able to cure scrofula with the "King's Touch" than Philip, the Plantagenet should be accepted as King of France. Cazelles, *Société politique*, 204.

[56] *Récits d'un bourgeois de Valenciennes*, 224–5, describing the point at which it seemed to some that Philip was unwilling to fight Edward while the latter was outside Paris: "Mais onques mès roy de France ne guerria sy honteusement, sy lachement, ne sy couwardement pour luy et pour tous ses pays." Cf. also *Le Bel*, 2:65–7.

Before entering the struggle with Edward III, Philip had fought one successful battle

1340 (in which he promised to restore good government, lower taxes and a strong currency, in addition to bringing peace to the realm), and his claim to the throne.

Philip was well aware, after all, that no crown could be held securely in the face of military defeat or incompetence. He had in his own entourage two once-sovereign princes (James of Majorca and Gautier de Brienne of Athens) who had lost their lands through military failure;[57] his "most beloved and most dear" ally in the war against Edward III, David of Scotland, had seen a rival crowned at Scone after the battle of Dupplin Moor; and his first cousin, Isabella, had successfully invaded England to dethrone her husband, Edward II.[58] Considering his propensity to see traitors everywhere, Philip could not have failed to appreciate the political consequences which would attend a decision to decline battle with the English king for a fourth time.[59] If his adversary rode up to the gates of Paris, Philip would find it most difficult to refuse the gambit yet again. Edward could reasonably expect the battle he sought, and could well hope to have it on tactical terms favorable to himself.

*

The rationale for the 1346 *chevauchée* outlined above flatly contradicts nearly all of the historiography on the subject. Almost every writer who has dealt with the campaign falls into one of two camps. One group, writing mainly before the Second World War, argued that "Edward's conduct of the campaign of Crécy shows no proof of any rational scheme"; that it was "discreditable to his generalship"; and that "Edward could order a battle and inspire his army with his own confidence, but he could not plan a campaign."[60]

The other school, led by H. J. Hewitt, agrees that the battle of Crécy resulted

against the Flemings, at Cassel in 1328, but he had also once previously (before his ascension) managed to avoid battle even after coming face-to-face with an enemy army. See Cazelles, *Société politique*, 42.

[57] The titular Duke of Athens, Gautier de Brienne, one of Philip's councilors (later Constable of France), was the son of the Gautier de Brienne who had been defeated by the Catalan company in the mud of the Cephissus in 1311, and lost his duchy as a consequence. The Brienne at Crécy had himself launched an unsuccessful military expedition to regain his Greek lands in 1331–32. He had also been driven out of Florence, where he had been tryant in 1342–43. James of Majorca had also been driven out of his realm by force.

[58] Philip refers to David as "amantissime ac dilectissime," as well as "praecarissime rex" and "carissime ac dilectissime consanguinee," all in one letter of 1346. In *Hemingburgh*, 421–3. David is in some ways a poor example of the vulnerability of a throne to military defeat, since his partisans were able to recover from two lost battles and restore him to power, driving out the pretender Edward Balliol, but the fact that David had been expelled from his own kingdom, even temporarily, must have given Philip food for thought.

[59] The first three being at Buironfosse (or la Flamengrie) in 1339, and at Bouvines (or Tournai) in 1340, and in Brittany in January 1343. Traitors everywhere: *Grandes chroniques*, 9:248.

[60] Fuller, *Decisive Battles*, 311; Oman, *History of the Art of War in the Middle Ages*, 2:126; William Hunt, "Edward III," *Dictionary of National Biography*, 51.

from Edward's strategic incompetence. These historians, however, do not see the 1346 *chevauchée* itself as being a "purposeless parade."[61] They believe that Edward's invasion was intended primarily to demonstrate his own power in contrast to Philip's impotence; to eliminate through pillage and burning the economic resources on which the Valois relied to fight their war; and then to escape "without having recourse to the near-ultimate sanction of a pitched battle."[62] Edward's failure thus lay in getting caught, not in having nothing to do.

The first group, which includes Sir Charles Oman, J. F. C. Fuller, B. H. Liddell Hart, George Wrottesley, and Edouard Perroy, among others[63] was strongly influenced by Napoleonic military theory, exemplified by the works of Antoine-Henri Jomini and Carl von Clausewitz. Despite the examples of the American Civil War and the First World War – which might have given them some insight into the importance of the tactical defensive in the English system of the Hundred Years War[64] – these historians failed to appreciate the differences between a straightforward Napoleonic *Niederwerfungsstrategie* (where the enemy army could simply be sought out and attacked) and a campaign aimed at provoking the enemy into taking the tactical offensive. This failure, combined with the mistaken assumption that good strategy requires confronting the enemy when he is numerically weaker, but avoiding him when he is stronger, made the Crécy campaign incomprehensible. Such a perspective is what led Oman to conclude that Edward was "a very competent tactician, but a very unskilful strategist."[65]

---

61 As Liddell Hart considered it to be. *Strategy*, 78.

62 Allmand, "The War and the Non-Combatant," 166; Hewitt, *Organization*, 117; Allmand, *The Hundred Years War*, 54–5. In the locations cited, these authors are discussing the fourteenth-century *chevauchées* in general; but they would all, I think, have included the Crécy campaign in that group. The first statement of this view of the *chevauchée* may have been the passing remark of Ferdinand Lot in his 1946 *L'art militaire et les armées au moyen âge*, 352–3, where he describes the Black Prince's expedition of 1355 as "one of the models of the warlike enterprises of the medieval style, where open battles and overly strong places were avoided, and the main activities were pillaging, devastating, burning houses and harvests across the country in order to ruin the adversary."

63 See note 60, above; Perroy, *Hundred Years War*, 119; R. Ernest Dupuy and Trevor N. Dupuy, *The Encyclopedia of Military History* (New York: Harper & Row, 1970), 357 ("Edward, who had scant stategical skill, [at Crécy] proved himself the master tactician of his time.") Cf. R. C. Smail, "Art of War," *Medieval England*, ed. A. L. Poole (Oxford: Clarendon Press, 1958), 153: "Edward seems to have had no greater strategic objective than to lead a raid through northern France"; Ferdinand Lot, *L'art militaire et les armées au moyen âge*, 341; Morris, *Welsh Wars*, 108.

64 In both these modern wars, as in the Hundred Years War, the power of rapid and lethal missile fire (whether from minié-ball rifles, machine guns, or yew longbows) to decimate attackers charging across open ground led to a marked superiority of the tactical defensive. Few modern strategists, however, have been as successful as Edward III in adapting their strategic approach to this tactical reality.

65 *A History of the Art of War in the Middle Ages*, 2:111. A striking example of Oman's overly battle-oriented approach to strategy can be found in ibid., 201: "the most surprising feature of the intermittent periods of war which lie between 1369 and 1396 is that no single

The second school – to which virtually every recent writer on the war belongs, including the outstanding historians C. T. Allmand, Kenneth Fowler, Maurice Keen, and Michael Prestwich – takes an almost opposite perspective on the role of battle in strategy.[66] According to this view, the medieval commander's opinion on giving battle would (in the words of John Gillingham) generally be "Don't. Well, you might occasionally, if you heavily outnumbered your enemy, if their morale was poor, their supplies short, if they were tired and poorly led, then in these circumstances you might, but otherwise, no."[67] Battle was too risky, and of too little benefit in an age when warfare revolved around sieges of fortified places.

With regard more specifically to the *chevauchées* of the fourteenth century, H. J. Hewitt wrote that the commander's aim "was not, as might have been supposed, to seek out the enemy and bring him to decisive combat . . . the king, the prince and Henry of Lancaster were not – or not usually – bent on that critical conflict of arms, nor did they refer to such an aim in their reports, nor did adulatory chroniclers attribute that aim to them."[68] The latter half of his statement, as we shall see, was flat-out wrong. More recent writers, while realizing this, have sustained Hewitt's general point by arguing that the contemporary statements to the effect that the English were looking for a fight in 1346 were jokes,[69] propaganda for distribution in England,[70] or attempts at deceit[71] which "cannot be taken seriously."[72]

On one issue both these historiographical camps are agreed: Edward, in 1346, had no intention of fighting Philip's larger army, if he could in any way avoid it.[73] He meant to do what damage he could before the French could gather an effective opposition force, then take advantage of his superior mobility to escape to Flanders. The battle of Crécy occurred only when Edward, having

---

pitched battle was fought in them . . . no new military discovery was made, save indeed Du Guesclin's ingenious if somewhat uninteresting proof that a successful war may be waged without accepting battles in the open."
[66] C. T. Allmand, "The War and the Non-Combatant," 166; Allmand, *The Hundred Years War*, 54–5; Kenneth Fowler, *The Age of Plantagenet and Valois*, 152; Tierney and Painter, *Western Europe in the Middle Ages*, 505; Michael Prestwich, *The Three Edwards*, 177–8, 180, 186; Maurice H. Keen, *England in the Later Middle Ages*, 135; Scott L. Waugh, *England in the Reign of Edward III* (Cambridge: Cambridge U.P., 1991), 17.
[67] John Gillingham, "Richard I and the Science of War in the Middle Ages," *War and Government in the Middle Ages*, eds J. Gillingham and J. C. Holt (Woodbridge: The Boydell Press, 1984), 82. Note that this important article has a wider scope than its title would suggest.
[68] *Organization of War*, 99–100.
[69] Barbara Emerson, *The Black Prince*, 34.
[70] Barber, *Life and Campaigns*, 13.
[71] Burne, *The Crecy War*, 154.
[72] Barber, *Edward, Prince of Wales and Aquitaine*, 59.
[73] Edouard Perroy, *The Hundred Years War*, 119. Cf. Philippe Contamine, *La Guerre de Cent Ans*, 29; Prestwich, *The Three Edwards*, 177–8 and 186; Jim Bradbury, *The Medieval Archer*, 105, 111; idem, *The Medieval Siege*, 157; Keen, *England in the Later Middle Ages*, 135; Liddell Hart, *Strategy*, 78.

failed to outmaneuver or outrun the French, turned to fight his hunter like a boar brought to bay. Thus, despite the English victory on the battlefield, the campaign reflected a failure of his generalship, and at its end the English "had achieved little of real strategic significance despite the scale of their victory."[74]

Two other writers, whose analyses of the Crécy *chevauchée* fit comfortably into neither of these schools, deserve to be briefly considered in this review of the historiography: Alfred H. Burne and Jonathan Sumption. Burne, a retired British artillery officer turned historian, authored the most militarily oriented history of the Hundred Years War.[75] Unlike most more recent writers, he believed that Edward did intend to fight in 1346. Unlike most earlier writers, he argued that Edward had a sophisticated plan to bring about a battle under the most advantageous possible circumstances.

According to Burne, the English plan in 1346 was essentially an operation on converging lines. After traversing Normandy, Edward would cross the Seine as quickly as possible. From there he would advance towards the Somme at Amiens, where he would meet his Flemish allies, who would have marched south from Ghent to meet him. Their powerful combined armies could then engage the single army of France on reasonably equal terms, and hopefully defeat it.

Jonathan Sumption's superb *Trial by Battle* – which contains the most recent, and without doubt the most painstakingly researched, account of the expedition – presents a different, less static, picture of Edward's motivations. Sumption argues that Edward initially intended for the invasion of 1346 to proceed without damage to the Normans, so that they could be won over to his side. It would be a "campaign of conquest," aimed at a permanent occupation of Normandy, comparable to the contemporary occupation of western Brittany. The king's control over his troops, however, was not strong enough for this approach to work, so he fell back by default on a strategy of devastation.[76] Although Sumption does not make it fully clear what he believes the English sought to achieve with this latter tack, he implies that Edward did his best to escape Philip's army without fighting.

With the exception of Burne, all these historians agree on that last point. Their descriptions of the campaign interpret all of Edward's actions with this assumed, and when this does not fit the English actions, merely comment that "at this point Edward's tactics seem obscure,"[77] or that they are "surprising."[78] Considering that (as we shall see) most of the contemporary sources claim that the English did everything they could to provoke the French into giving battle, it

---

[74] The quotation is from Sumption, *The Hundred Years War*, 532. For similar opinions, see Perroy, *The Hundred Years War*, 120; Lot, *L'art militaire et les armées au moyen âge*, 348.

[75] *The Crecy War* and *The Agincourt War*.

[76] *Trial by Battle*, 533.

[77] Richard Barber, *Edward, Prince of Wales and Aquitaine*, 58, re Edward III's decision to wait for Philip at Poissy.

[78] Ibid., 62, re his not attempting to escape Philip after the crossing of the Somme.

may seem puzzling that so many historians hold the opposite view. Before we turn to those sources, and a narrative of the campaign, therefore, we will have to complete our examination of the historiography of the subject by explaining briefly the reasons for this widespread belief.

The conviction that Edward was unwilling to risk a general engagement seems to come from two sources: the "inherent military probability" idea that no commander so outnumbered would wish to fight; and the fact that Edward was moving rapidly northwards, towards Flanders, immediately before Philip "overtook" him. Neither of these arguments stands up to careful consideration.

The "inherent military probability" idea, always risky, necessitates particular caution when applied to the mind of the medieval commander. Edward probably believed – and indeed had many good reasons to believe, since his earlier successes from Halidon Hill to Sluys had been phenomenal, and his claim to the French crown was a strong one – that God was on his side.[79] Both this belief and the complementary secular ethos of chivalry, which held that a good knight should "do the right thing, come what may,"[80] would have discouraged him from placing too much emphasis on the smaller size of his army. His personal character was well in accord with this motto, for "he dred neuer of none myshappes, ne harmes ne evyll fortune, that myght [be]falle a noble warryour."[81]

Furthermore, deficiency in numbers can be compensated for by superiority in tactics, equipment, discipline, leadership and morale. By the time of the invasion, as the preceding chapters have shown, many of the English soldiers and captains had become experienced veterans. More than a few had participated in the glorious victories of Halidon Hill, Morlaix, or Dupplin Moor. At Halidon Hill they had overcome odds of about 2:1; at Dupplin Moor, they won against odds of roughly 10:1. Clearly the victors of such engagements would not see a disadvantage in numbers as an insurmountable obstacle.[82] To paraphrase a

---

[79] See his letters to Clement VI (in *Avesbury*, 380–1), to Simon Boccanegra (quoted in Sumption, *Trial by Battle*, 380), to his council in England (PRO C81/314/17803) and to Thomas Lucy (in Chandos Herald, *Black Prince*, 355), etc. Consider also his conduct before the battle of Sluys (Chapter 8, above), and recall his motto, "Dieu et mon droit."

[80] The contemporary form of this saying, as given in Guillaume de Machaut's *Le confort d'ami*, a near-contemporary text on chivalry, was "fais ce que dois, adviegne que peut." François de Montebelluna also gives the same admonition. See Françoise Autrand, "La déconfiture. La bataille de Poitiers (1356) à travers quelques textes français des XIVe et XVe siècles," *Guerre et société en France, en Angleterre et en Bourgogne. XIVe–XVe Siècle*, ed. Philippe Contamine *et al.* (Lille: Centre d'histoire de la région du Nord et de l'Europe du nord-ouest, 1991), 95–6. For an expression of the same idea directly related to Edward III, see *Avesbury*, 456–7.

[81] *English Brut*, 333.

[82] Among the leaders of the English army at Crécy, for example, Richard Talbot and Thomas Ughtred had fought at Dupplin Moor (as had Fulk Fitzwarin, who may have served at Crécy: Wrottesley, *Crecy and Calais*, 89), while Edward III, Talbot, Bartholomew Burghersh, Ralph Basset, and the earls of Warwick, Oxford, Arundel, and Suffolk had fought at Halidon Hill (as Ughtred probably had also). The Earl of Northampton had been the commander at Morlaix,

contemporary poem on the battle of Halidon Hill, if the French outnumbered them by three to one it would be like "fifteen sheep against five wolves."[83]

Edward was in a much better position than are we to evaluate his own army in comparison with that of his enemy. The Valois host was relatively incohesive, lacking in missile capability, and had no tactical doctrine to match that of the English. Recent experience in Brittany and Gascony had given the king some idea of how important these factors were – though, as we have seen, these confirmations of English tactical strength were hardly necessary to convince him to pursue battle, which he had been doing in virtually every campaign since 1333.[84] Edward may not have expected to win as overwhelming and total a victory as we know with hindsight that he did; yet it seems equally unlikely that victory *per se* came as any great surprise to him. Philip's reluctance to force battle early on in the campaign indicates that he, too, was less than certain of a French victory. Indeed, Jean le Bel specifically states that the Valois monarch "had neither the boldness nor the courage to fight."[85] With God and his veteran army fighting for him, Edward was confident enough to risk battle, at least if he could fight it on his own terms.

The English movement towards Flanders in the second half of the campaign is generally interpreted as an attempt to slip away northwards and reach the coast before being overtaken, and thus to avoid battle.[86] In fact, however, this movement was intended to help keep the army fed and to secure the best possible situation before the sought-after confrontation. Edward had hoped to link up with his Flemish allies, who were supposed to be marching to meet him, or with the contingent he had ordered to sail for Le Crotoy, to counter the

where Reginald Cobham also fought. The following men, who served among the leaders of the Crécy *chevauchée*, had also been household knights or bannerets in the winter of 1333–34, and so had probably also fought at Halidon: the Earl of Northampton, William Fitzwarin, Thomas Bradestone, Maurice Berkeley, Rhys ap Griffith, John Lovel, Reginald Cobham. British Library, Additional MS 35,181 (Wardrobe account of Robert Tawton), m. 10 (and note John Lestraunge on m. 11).

83 *English Brut*, 288.

84 Thanks in large part to the signal victories of Crécy, Poitiers, and Agincourt, military and medieval historians have long been aware of the battlefield superiority of the English throughout most of the Hundred Years War. Reflecting the focus on these large-scale pitched battles, explanations for the English dominance have tended to emphasize the importance of the archers' clothyard shafts fired from prepared positions, on the indiscipline of French armies, and on the inherent superiority of disciplined infantry to cavalry. These explanations, however, are not fully adequate. After Crécy, French defeats can rarely be attributed to ill discipline; the inferiority of cavalry is even less relevant, since the French had no better luck when they made their attacks on foot. Furthermore, the English more than once proved that they could more than hold their own in cavalry actions. Although the longbow and the Halidon tactics were undoubtedly very important, credit must also be given to the sheer fighting élan of the English. As Napoleon said, in war, the moral is to the physical as three to one.

85 *Le Bel*, 2:86–7. See *Eulogium*, 208, for the concessions offered by Philip early in the campaign (Gascony and Ponthieu as Edward II had held them) in hopes of avoiding battle, and Edward's disdainful response.

86 This is the interpretation in Perroy, *Hundred Years War*, 119, for example.

endless stream of reinforcements to the Valois host. He also wanted to fight with his back to friendly territory in case of defeat.[87] Furthermore, Calais had been his destination from early in the campaign, so his path would have been sensible even if Philip had not had an army in the field at all.[88] But most important of all, Edward had to avoid the trap which Philip was trying to set for him, a trap precisely similar to the one the English had tried to set for the Scots in 1327.

Philip wanted to pin his enemy in place against an impassable barrier – the sea, the Seine or the Somme – just as Edward had earlier sought to trap the Scots against the Tyne.[89] Edward would then presumably do what he had done at la Flamengrie, and what he indeed did do at Crécy: draw up his army in a Halidon-style array. This formation relied on the strength of the tactical defensive for its effectiveness, however, and if the English were pinned between the French army and a natural barrier, then Philip would have no need to take the tactical offensive. Earlier, at la Flamengrie, after waiting for the French to attack, Edward had run out of food and been forced to move off back towards his base.[90] In 1346, too, he would have been unable to stand on the defensive for long without supplies. Then Edward would have had his battle – but on Philip's terms, not on his own.[91] Given that the French army was much larger and, indeed, better prepared for such an "open" battle, the outcome would not have been a Crécy or a Poitiers, except perhaps in reverse.

But Edward managed to avoid this trap by crossing the ford at Blanchetacque. When he had, thus, secured his line of retreat, he quickly found a good defensive position and halted to wait for Philip's army. This was not because his troops were too tired to escape the French;[92] it was, rather, precisely

---

[87] For Edward's desire to meet his allies, and the English army's need for food, see *Le Muisit*, 158–9; Villani, *Cronica*, 393. The capture of Le Crotoy after the crossing of the Somme led to the capture of "graunt plente du vitailles" on the eve of the battle of Crécy. *Avesbury*, 368. While still at Caen, Edward had written to his council that the Flemings should be informed that the English army would head for Le Crotoy at the mouth of the Somme. PRO C81/314/17803.

[88] This statement, which contradicts nearly all the modern histories of the campaign, will be supported below.

[89] Froissart, *Oeuvres*, 5:3, 7, makes it explicit that Philip blocked the Somme "affin que li roys englès, ne son host, ne peuissent passer, car il les volloit combattre à se vollenté ou affamer par delà le Somme"; "li rois de France . . . pensa bien que il encloroit le roy d'Engleterre entre Abbeville et le rivière de Somme, et le prenderoit ou combateroit à se volenté." (So that neither the King of England nor his army could cross [the river], because he [Philip] wanted to fight them at his pleasure, or starve them on that side of the Somme; the King of France . . . thought well that he would enclose the King of England in between Abbeville and the river Somme, and capture him or fight him at will.)

[90] Above, p. 172.

[91] Just as the English tried to do to the Scots along the Wear in 1327. Froissart, *Oeuvres*, 2:166–7. Edward would have found this possibility increasingly worrisome as the 1346 campaign went on and Philip's reluctance to attack became evident.

[92] An oft-expressed opinion; e.g. by Henry de Wailly, *Crécy, 1346: Anatomy of a Battle* (New York: Blandford Press, 1987), 53; Tierney and Painter, *Western Europe in the Middle Ages*, 502.

because from there he *could* get away. Thus, he could expect to be attacked rather than "besieged." The fact that he was trying to avoid Philip until he was able to cross the Somme, in short, does not mean that his stated goal of open battle was insincere.

This rather extended survey of the historiography of the campaign seemed necessary considering the unanimity of opinion that Edward was trying to avoid battle in 1346, a view which, if allowed to go unchallenged, would have undermined both the consideration of Edward's strategic alternatives at the beginning of this chapter and much of the analysis in the next chapter. Now that the ground has been cleared, we can turn to a close examination of the Crécy *chevauchée*, the paradigm for virtually all the major English campaigns for the remainder of the century.

CHAPTER ELEVEN

"TO MAKE AN END TO THE WAR BY BATTLE":[1]
THE CRÉCY CHEVAUCHÉE, 1346

> *Generally, he who occupies the field of battle first and awaits*
> *his enemy is at ease; he who comes later to the scene and*
> *rushes into the fight is weary. And therefore those skilled in*
> *war bring the enemy to the field of battle and are not brought*
> *there by him.*   Sun Tzu, VI.1–2[2]

THE CAMPAIGN OF 1346 which climaxed with the famous battle of Crécy
has, as the last chapter suggested, often been misinterpreted. As this chapter
will demonstrate more fully, Edward's goal for the campaign was to make an
end to the war by meeting his enemy in decisive battle, as he had tried to do in
1339 and 1340. This view of the English king's motivation in the campaign will
inform the entire narrative, greatly altering the familiar story of this remarkable
expedition.

After his landing at St.-Vaast-la-Hougue on 12 July, the English king spent
six days there to disembark the horses, to rest himself and his men, and to bake
bread.[3] To mark the start of what was intended to be the decisive campaign of
the war, the king knighted a number of the young nobles who had accompanied
him, including his own eldest son, the Black Prince.[4]

As part of the same ceremony, Godfrey d'Harcourt solemnly did homage to
Edward III for his Norman fiefs, acknowledging the Plantagenet as King of
France.[5] This was the first of several steps Edward took in an effort to bring the
Cotentin, if not the whole Duchy of Normandy, into his obedience. On the 13th
the king proclaimed that the persons and goods of clergy, women, old people

---

[1]   PRO C66/219/m. 21d (*CPR [1345–48]*, 516–17). See p. 260, below, for the text. Cf. also
the writ in Wrottesley, *Crecy and Calais*, 58.
[2]   Griffith (ed.), 96–7.
[3]   Although this seems rather a long time, a comparison with other expeditions suggests that
the delay was inevitable. In 1355, for example, the Earl of Lancaster landed at la Hougue with
a much smaller army, and took four days before marching to Carentan. Burne, *Crecy War*,
265.
[4]   He was not known by that name until after his death; but to avoid an unnecessary prolif-
eration of "Edwards" I shall often refer to him so.
[5]   *Acta Bellicosa*, 29.

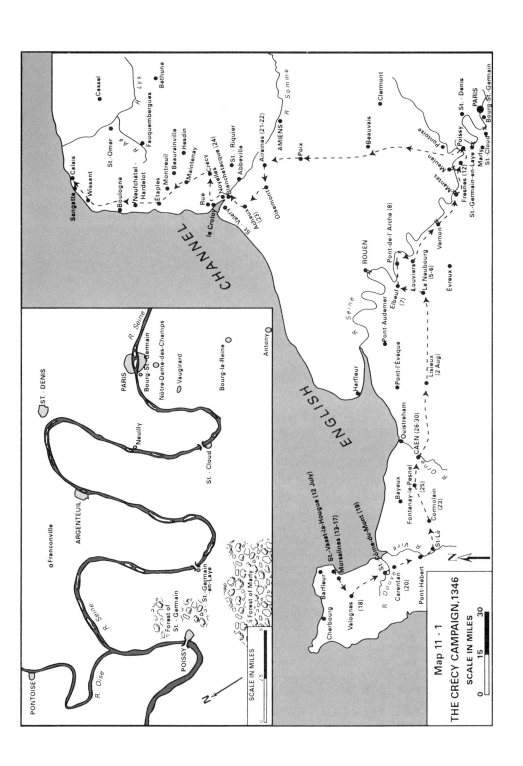

Map 11 - 1
THE CRÉCY CAMPAIGN, 1346

SCALE IN MILES

0   15   30

Inset map labels:

PONTOISE
R. Oise
o Franconville
R. Seine
ARGENTEUIL
R. Seine
Neuilly
St.-Cloud
POISSY
St.-Germain-en-Laye
Forest of St.-Germain
Forest of Marly
ST.- DENIS
PARIS
Bourg-St.-Germain
Nôtre-Dame-des-Champs
Vaugirard
Bourg-la-Reine
Antony
R. Seine

SCALE IN MILES
0   5   15

Main map labels:

CHANNEL

ENGLISH

R. Lys
Cassel
Béthune
Fauquembergues
R. A a
St.-Omer
Neuchâtel-Hardelot
Boulogne
Wissant
Calais
Sangatte
Étaples
Montreuil
Beaurainville
Hesdin
Maintenay
Rue
Crécy
Noyelles
Blanchetacque
St.-Riquier
Abbeville
Acheux (23)
St.-Valery
le Crotoy
Oisemont
Airaines (21-22)
R. Somme
AMIENS
Poix
Clermont
Beauvais
Pontoise
Meulan
Poissy
St.-Denis
PARIS
Fresnes (12)
St.-Germain-en-Laye
Marly
St.-Cloud
Bourg-St.-Germain
Nantes
Vernon
Pont-de-l'Arche (8)
Le Neubourg (5-6)
Louviers
Elbeuf (7)
Évreux
ROUEN
R. Seine
Pont-Audemer
Pont-l'Évêque
Lisieux (2 Aug)
Harfleur
Ouistreham
CAEN (26-30)
R. Orne
Bayeux
Fontenay-le-Pesnel (25)
Cormolain (23)
St.-Lô
R. Vire
Pont-Hébert
St.-Côme-du-Mont (19)
Carentan (20)
R. Douve
Valognes (18)
Morsalines (13-17)
St.-Vaast-la-Hougue (12 July)
Barfleur
Cherbourg

N

and children, and anyone else who would enter into his peace, should be
protected from harm or molestation, on pain of life and limb.[6] Local Plantagenet
supporters from the Harcourt and Clisson affinities were sent to incite the
people to rebel against the Valois king, bearing letters stating that Edward "had
come into this land not to lay it waste, but to take possession of it."[7] By the 17th,
many of the common people of the area had come into the English obedience
(which in practice seems to have meant paying ransom money to Edward's
troops, or at least providing victuals for sale).[8] The men-at-arms had fled or
retreated into the castles and strong towns, so that no one on the Cotentin
offered any active resistance to the invaders.[9]

   The proclamation, the letter-bearers, and Edward's later willingness to accept
the inhabitants of Valognes and Caen into his peace (on which see below) show
clearly that the Plantagenet planned to make the Cotentin, or if possible all of
Normandy, into another of the sally-ports he had gained around the periphery of
France, in Flanders, Brittany, and Guienne. There were good reasons to think
that all or part of the duchy might accept Edward's rule, or even welcome him.
Most importantly, Harcourt, as the hereditary lord of St.-Sauveur-le-Vicomte,
had been one of the powerful men of the Cotentin, and his ancestral seat was
well situated to provide a base of control for the entire peninsula.[10] Harcourt
doubtless played up his ability to win his former neighbors over to the Plantagenet allegiance, and his credibility would have been enhanced by Edward's
knowledge that there was still substantial resentment in Normandy over Philip's

---

6   *Acta Bellicosa*, 160: "nullus villas aut maniera incendere, ecclesias vel loca sacra depre-
dari, senibus, parvulis aut mulieribus quibuscumque regni sui Francie malum seu molestiam
inferre presumeret, seu quibuscumque personis aliis, nisi viribus instarent, malefacerent quo-
vismodo, sub pena vite et membrorum." *Historia Roffensis*, fo. 91: "ne quis sacrosancte
ecclesie religiosis presbiteris mulieribus parvulis neque alicui alteri se ad Regis pacem
reddere volenti de Regno Francie dampnum seu molestiam in personis vel rebus facerent vel
inferrent, sub pena et forisfactura membrorum et vite."
7   This statement is a generalization based on the case of the esquire Guillaume de Vacognes,
who was killed by the inhabitants of St.-Clément-sur-Gué (at the southeast corner of the
Cotentin) when he arrived at their town, inciting them to rebellion and bearing letters of the
King of England, saying that he "ne venoit pas en ycellui pais pour le gaster, mes pour en
prandre la saisine." Vacognes, in Calvados, was one of the Norman fiefs forfeited by Olivier
de Clisson when he went over to the Anglo-Montfort party in 1342. In 1343, though theoretically protected by the truce of Malestroit, Clisson was executed in Paris. It is little wonder
that his former vassals still bore ill-will against King Philip. *RTC*, nos. 6544, 5676.
   Note, incidentally, the phrase "en ycellui pais," which may be a reference to Normandy or
the Cotentin in particular, rather than France.
8   *Cont. Manuel, 1339–46*, fo. 163: "occirent ceulx qui ne se vouldrent rachater." But cf.
Villani, *Cronica*, 389: "rubando e ardendo e bruciando chi non volea ubbidire né dargli
mercato di vittuaglia."
9   Letters in *Murimuth*, 200–1.
10 It was an extraordinarily strong fortress, as the long siege of 1376–77 indicates, and sits at
the junction of roads to Valognes, Bricquebec, Portbail, la Haye, and Ste.-Mère-Eglise.

dishonorable execution of Olivier de Clisson (who had been a major Norman landholder) three years earlier. There was some reason to assume that members of the Harcourt and Clisson affinities who had lost their patrons to the Valois' purges might be willing to return to their old lords under Edward's sovereignty instead of Philip's. The first Valois king, after all, was widely viewed as tyrannical and cowardly, two traits not likely to endear him to the particularist and martial Norman nobility, especially when he was compared with the generous and valiant Plantagenet.[11] The spirit which had informed Edward's proclamation to the French people in 1340, in which he promised good and restrained government, a sound currency, moderate taxes, and protection to all who would acknowledge him as King of France (intentional contrasts with Philip's arbitrary rule, constant deflation of the coinage, high taxes, and failure to protect his subjects from Edward's armies) was still at work in 1346.[12]

Despite the king's proclamation, however, the general willingness of the common people of Normandy to enter his peace did not mean that they were in fact protected from "harm or molestation." On the 13th, while the more obedient of Edward's troops stayed with the ships, small groups of men-at-arms and archers spread out through the countryside for twenty miles around (i.e. throughout almost the entire peninsula), pillaging and skirmishing with any French soldiers they encountered, and "cheerfully and boldly set fire to the countryside around, until the sky itself glowed with a fiery colour."[13] The Welsh troops, in particular, acted "as if they were outside the king's jurisdiction," plundering and burning with abandon.[14] When those who had obeyed the royal proclamation saw the booty gained by their more audacious comrades, they felt cheated.[15] There was little or no chance of restoring the kind of discipline the king wanted thereafter, despite the best efforts of the constable and marshal of the host, and the offer of a 40 shilling reward for anyone reporting a malefactor.[16] The troops continued their daily marauding through the 17th.[17] As early as the 14th, a detachment of Edward's soldiers arrived at the substantial port of Barfleur, just north of la Hougue. The garrison had fled, and the town was plun-

---

11 See above, pp. 228–9.
12 *Avesbury*, 309–10.
13 Letters of Bartholomew Burghersh and of Thomas Bradwardine, Chancellor of St. Paul's, in *Murimuth*, 200–1; *Acts of War*, 28–9 (quotation).
14 [Wallensis tanquam exempti a jurisdictione Regis]: *Historia Roffensis*, fo. 91, which also accuses them of decapitating prisoners.
15 *Acta Bellicosa*, 160: "qui navibus noctuaverant . . . morigerosos et infelices se ipsos reputantes."
16 *Acts of War*, 28–9. The later burning of Carentan "pur riens qe le roy purroit faire" (Letter of Northburgh, in *Avesbury*, 358–9) and the burning of Valognes contrary to the king's command (see p. 243 below) show that discipline had not been established.
17 Letter of Thomas Bradwardine in *Murimuth*, 201. *Acts of War*, 28–9.

dered and burned, along with the vessels in the harbor.[18] The same force then advanced to Cherbourg, which it also destroyed.[19]

Considering the royal proclamation of the 13th, such widespread havoc seems rather surprising.[20] The contrast between the declaration and subsequent events led the most recent writer on the campaign, Jonathan Sumption, to reach the conclusion that Edward initially intended to make the 1346 invasion a "campaign of conquest" in which he would follow the pattern of the Brittany campaigns: capture a number of strongpoints to use as bases, and from them gradually intimidate the powerful nobles of the land into accepting his rule. In 1346, Sumption argues, the king abandoned that strategy when he discovered that he could not control his own troops. Their pillage and rapine in Normandy made it impossible for Edward to win the loyalty of the Normans, so the campaign "became a *chevauch[é]e*, a great mounted raid passing swiftly through the country before it disappeared."[21]

The first half of this analysis is essentially correct: it was indeed the indiscipline of the troops which foiled Edward's plans to secure a new base area in Normandy. However, Sumption places too much emphasis on this fact. Edward's strategy for 1346 never focussed on an attempt "to do . . . just as he had done before in Brittany."[22] His substantial efforts in Brittany, after all, had in the end done little to help him reach his war aims. Given the inherent slowness of a siege-based campaign of conquest, such an operation would also likely not have been of much benefit to the Earl of Derby's beleaguered men: so long as the invaders confined themselves to Normandy, there was no need for Philip to immediately lift the siege of Aiguillon.[23] Most importantly, even if he had succeeded in winning Normandy, that would not have served to fulfill the commission Edward had accepted from parliament: "to make an end to this war."[24] Thus, as the two campaign letters written on the 17th state, by that day – before the main body of the army had even left la Hougue – the king had already made clear his intention to make his way into France by way of the larger cities "to win his rights by force of arms."[25]

---

[18] Letter of Michael Northburgh, in *Avesbury*, 358–9. When Northburgh says that the English "thought to have found many people [gentz], but found none to speak of," he is evidently referring to soldiers, rather than the inhabitants, since other sources agree that a large number of the town's bourgeois were taken prisoner. *Le Bel*, 2:87; Froissart, *Oeuvres*, 4:388; *Acts of War*, 29.

[19] Froissart, *Oeuvres*, 4:388–9.

[20] Until I found the reference to the proclamation in the *Historia Roffensis* (note 6, above), it was known only through the *Acta Bellicosa*, and it seemed so odd that I was tempted to dismiss its existence.

[21] Sumption, *Trial by Battle*, 532–3 (cf. his Chapter 11).

[22] Sumption, *Trial by Battle*, 532–3.

[23] Cf. Froissart, *Oeuvres*, 4:385.

[24] See note 22, Chapter 10, above, and below, passim.

[25] Letters in *Murimuth*, 200–2 [pur conqerer soun dreit]. Note that while most French-English dictionaries translate "conquérir" as "to conquer or overcome," the primary defini-

Furthermore, if Edward's main objective had really been "to set up a permanent occupation in the territory through which he had passed," he would almost
certainly have garrisoned Barfleur (the second best port on the Cotentin, "very
strong" and easily supported from England) rather than allowing it to be burned
or, if it was burned against his orders, even afterwards.[26] The "large and rich"
port of Cherbourg would have been occupied, and its castle besieged; instead,
the town was burned and the castle left in enemy hands.[27] While he was interested in keeping towns like Valognes and Caen *if they could be held for him by
local Plantagenet partisans,*[28] Edward did not want to spare any men from his
field force for garrisons because he needed them for his *primary* purpose: to
seek out his adversary and do battle with him.

The first step on that quest was taken on the 18th, when Edward finally
decamped from Morsalines outside St.-Vaast and began his advance into
Normandy, "boiling with eagerness to meet his enemies."[29] The main body of
the army advanced to the "rich and worthy" town of Valognes, nine miles to the
southwest of La Hougue.[30] According to *The Acts of War of Edward III*, the
bourgeois of the town threw themselves at Edward's feet, asking only that he
spare their lives. He accepted their surrender and took them into his peace,
declaring that they should not be harmed, nor the town burned.[31] The next day,
however, the town was put to the torch and destroyed despite the royal order.[32]

The army had been divided into three divisions. The vanguard, nominally
under the command of the prince, included the constable (Northampton) and the
marshal (Warwick). The rear guard was led by Thomas Hatfield, the martial
Bishop of Durham, along with the earls of Suffolk, Arundel, and Huntingdon.
The main body, under the king's direct control, included about as many men as
the other two put together. The divisions marched separately, but converged on a

tion given by *Le Petit Robert dictionnaire de la langue française* (Paris, 1976), 331, is
"Acquérir par les armes"; hence the translation of the phrase above.

[26] The description of Barfleur is from Froissart, *Oeuvres* 4:388. In another redaction, he
points out that it had a "trop fors" castle which, however, was not garrisoned. (4:393). Northburgh's letter adds that Barfleur was "as good and large as Sandwich." (In *Avesbury*, 358–9.)
In the second redaction (4:391), Froissart says that Barfleur was pillaged but not burned, but
Northburgh's letter and the *Acts of War* (p. 29) far more reliable sources, state that it was
torched. *Le Baker*, 79, adds that la Hougue, too, was burned by the army.

[27] Froissart, *Oeuvres*, 4:393.

[28] His initial offer to the inhabitants of Caen to allow them to keep their lives *and goods* if
they entered his obedience is somewhat difficult to explain otherwise; if they had accepted,
what would he have gained? Cf. also the case of Carentan castle, noted below.

[29] Letter of Northburgh in *Avesbury*, 358. (The king and a portion of the army had moved
three miles inland, to Morsalines, on the 13th.) *Le Baker*, 82; *Acta Bellicosa*, 159. The quotation, "adversariorum obviam fervencium siciendo," is ibid., 160.

[30] *Acts of War*, 31; *Le Baker*, 255. All further indications of the army's movements, unless
otherwise noted, are from the itinerary established by F. Maunde Thompson, ibid., 252–7.
About this time, Montebourg and Nevilly were attacked unsuccessfully. *Lescot*, 71.

[31] *Acts of War*, 31; Sumption, *Trial by Battle*, 502.

[32] According to the contemporary campaign notes in *Le Baker*, 253; cf. *Acts of War*, 31.

prearranged spot each night. Thus spread out, they could forage, burn, and plunder all the more effectively.[33]

Two days after departing Valognes, slightly delayed by the need to repair the bridge over the Douve, the army arrived at Carentan. Although this good-sized town was fairly well fortified and garrisoned, the bourgeois, fearing a massacre, surrendered on being guaranteed their lives. The soldiers of the garrison at first retreated into the very strong castle, but then, seeing the English preparations for an assault, surrendered too.[34] When the Plantagenet departed the town, he left the castle occupied by two of Harcourt's Norman knights and a band of "*partisans anglais.*" They were later captured and beheaded.[35]

In view of the town's surrender – which, by eliminating the need to launch an assault, reduced the number of casualties suffered by the English – Edward did his best to prevent the town from being burned. This was a wise policy: since he aimed for a battle with Philip's larger army, he could not afford to squander any of his troops. Relatively gentle treatment of Carentan would have encouraged other towns to surrender, and save their homes from the torch, rather than hold out against him. To an extent this would have enabled him to have his cake and eat it too: he could have gained the most important advantages of a sack (loot to reward his troops, and Frenchmen angry with Philip for his failure to defend them) without the major cost of one (troops killed or wounded in the assault against desperate defenders), and with the additional bonus of appearing merciful. Unfortunately for Edward, his soldiers did not all understand the subtle strategic importance of precedent, and much of the town was burned "for all the king could do."[36]

With that example before them, the bourgeois of St.-Lô (a large and rich cloth manufacturing town) decided to resist the English.[37] They had done what they could to repair their broken walls and gather men-at-arms. Robert Bertrand and the Count of Eu (Marshal and Constable of France, respectively) arrived with all the French forces in the area to aid in their defense.[38] Together they stood ready to meet Edward's troops.

---

[33] *Le Bel*, 2:76; *Acts of War*, 29; cf. also *Chron. St. Omer*, fo. 262.

[34] *Le Bel*, 2:74, says the bourgeois surrendered "sauf leurs corps et leurs biens, et leurs femmes, et leurs enfans"; but Froissart, whose account of the incident is somewhat fuller (though much of it is taken nearly verbatim from le Bel), says only "lors corps, lors femmes et lors enfans." *Oeuvres*, 4:393. The castle is described as "fortissimum" [most strong] in the *Chronographia*, 2:53.

[35] *RTC*, no. 6225; *Grandes chroniques*, 9:271; *Lescot*, 71 and 71n. Some French chroniclers assert that the two Norman knights, Nicholas (or Guillaume) de Groucy and Roland de Verdun, were in command of the Valois garrison and sold the castle to the English. *Chron. Normande*, 75, 75 nn. 1–2; *Chronographia*, 2:223; Sumption, *Trial by Battle*, 504. It is, however, unlikely that they were in French service in 1346, however, since in August 1345 the estates of Verdun and of Guillaume de Groucy, confiscated for lèse-majesté, were granted to Marshal Bertrand's daughter. *RTC*, no. 5906; see also Cazelles, *Société politique*, 152.

[36] Letter of Northburgh, in *Avesbury*, 358–9: "pur riens qe le roy purroit faire."

[37] For the wealth and size of St.-Lô, see *Le Bel*, 2:77–8.

[38] Letter of Northburgh, in *Avesbury*, 358–9; *Acts of War*, 31. Eu, recently returned from

The English, having heard that the French were in force in the area and hoping that the constable might now be willing to fight, advanced towards the town in full battle array.[39] The sight of the disciplined English army seems to have thrown the French leaders into a panic. "When they saw that our men hastened against them," wrote an English eyewitness, "they fled by another gate at the rear of the town."[40] Some of the common people of the town nevertheless made an attempt at defense, but they were no match for the invaders. St.-Lô was conquered "with little effort," and a great number of the defenders were killed during the initial assault.[41]

Since the town had offered resistance, Edward made little effort to mitigate the violence of the sack. Many of the women in the town were raped. The English plundered everything worth taking. "No man alive," wrote Jean le Bel, "could imagine or believe the riches which were there acquired and robbed, even if he were told of it." A large number of the richer bourgeois were taken prisoner and shipped back to England to be held for ransom. Once the troops had finished with the town, they set it alight.[42] The message was clear: the towns of Normandy could not count on royal forces to defend them, but could expect the harshest treatment if they resisted the invaders.

The king had initially intended to continue southeast to Torigni the next day, but at the last minute he received some new information – probably that Robert Bertrand had assembled enough troops that he might be willing to offer battle – and decided to follow the retreating marshal to Cormolain. The advance troops who had been sent to Torigni set fire to the town, then hastened back to join the main body of the host. As the army advanced, pillagers spread out for five or six leagues to either side of the main line of advance, robbing, destroying, and burning "so that the enemy should know of their coming."[43] No attempt was made to defend Torigni or Cormolain, or any other of the towns on the way to Caen.

To that city, the largest in Normandy after Rouen, the Count of Eu and Robert Bertrand and their troops had retreated. Men-at-arms and armed commoners from all over the duchy, fleeing before the English advance, congregated there,

---

Aiguillon, had first gone to Harfleur to gather what men and ships he could. *Chron. St. Omer*, fos 259–59v.

[39] *Acts of War*, 30, specifically states that the English vanguard "drew themselves up in battle array against a possible enemy attack, *which, they hoped, was imminent.*" [Emphasis added].

[40] According to the strictly contemporary itinerary in Thompson's notes to *Le Baker*, 253 (the town was "estuffez de genz darmes; et quant ils vierent que noz genz lour presserent, ils fuyrent par un altre port aderere la ville.") The verb *presser* might be taken to mean that the men-at-arms fled only after the English had launched an assault (it can mean "assail" as well as "press" or "hasten") were it not that Northburgh's letter (*Avesbury*, 358–9) specifies that the men-at-arms left before the English arrived.

[41] Froissart, *Oeuvres*, 4:402 (effort); defenders killed: *Le Bel*, 2:78.

[42] *Le Bel*, 2:78.

[43] Quote from *Acts of War*, 31. Letter of Northburgh in *Avesbury*, 358–9; cf. *Le Bel*, 2:76–7, 80.

joining the contingents sent by King Philip to resist the English.[44] Their full number cannot be given with accuracy, but an educated guess would be that they included about fifteen hundred men-at-arms and Genoese mercenaries, as well as perhaps three times that many armored militiamen.[45]

The town, especially the old town, was strong. The inhabitants had repaired the eleventh-century walls of the old town and reinforced them with wooden palisades, while the new town was given some protection by the river Orne, which entirely encircled it, and by its fortified bridges. "Indeed," wrote an Englishman who served in the campaign, "it seemed impregnable."[46] Edward had already received information that he would not get past Caen without a fight.[47] Even so, he sent letters to the townsmen, offering to spare their lives and goods if the city were surrendered to him. Considering the strength of the force gathered there for the town's defense, and the fate of Carentan after its surrender, the bourgeois of Caen were hardly likely to accept. The commander of the town, the Bishop of Bayeux (who was Marshal Bertrand's brother), tore up the king's letter and sent the English messenger (an Augustinian professor of theology) into prison – a blatant violation of the medieval laws of war.[48]

The constable, at the insistence of the townsmen who formed such a large part of his army, decided to meet the English in the open field outside the city, in order to defend the unwalled suburbs. This was just what Edward and his men were hoping for.[49] But when the English army approached Caen early on the 26th, the morale of the bourgeois militia broke, and they fled back through the old town onto the Île-de-St.-Jean despite the efforts of the constable and marshals. The English entered into the undefended portion of the town, their advance guard drawing near the fortified bridge to the new town, which the French men-at-arms were preparing to defend. The English archers, without order or array, launched an unsupported attack on their enemies. They found

---

[44] *Le Bel*, 2:79, Froissart, *Oeuvres*, 4:405; *Acts of War*, 31. Letter of Burghersh in *Murimuth*, 202–3.

[45] The sources conflict wildly on this subject. The number above is based on 600 men-at-arms in the city (Northburgh, in *Avesbury*, 359) and another 200 in the castle (*Acts of War*, 33) along with the 500 crossbowmen who had recently left la Hougue, and 100 more in the castle garrison (ibid.), for a total of 1,400 professional soldiers, not far from the 1,600 men-at-arms reported by Edward III (PRO C81/314/17803). The total of 6,000 troops is based on the *Historia Roffensis*, fo. 91: "Tunc invenerunt ibidem [Caen] comitem Dieu constabularium Francie et camerarium de Tancrevile multosque alios circiter ad numerum vj milium bene armatorum missos per regem Francie ad defendendum villam." Jean le Bel says there were 8,000 bourgeois and craftsmen in the city. *Le Bel*, 2:78.

[46] *Acta Bellicosa*, 164: "Inexpugnabilis quidem apparuit." Cf. letters of Edward III, Michael Northburgh (op. cit.) and of Bartholomew Burghersh (*Murimuth*, 202–3), and the description of Meulan, "equipped, like Caen, with strong walls" in *Acts of War*, 35. The Count of Eu had considered it strong enough to hold out for forty days. *Acta Bellicosa*, 166; cf. Froissart, *Oeuvres*, 4:382.

[47] *Acts of War*, 31.

[48] Ibid.

[49] *Le Bel*, 2:80–1; Froissart, *Oeuvres*, 4:409; *Acta Bellicosa*, 164: "sperantes quodammodo in campis decentibus obviam habuisse."

themselves locked into hand-to-hand combat with some of the French men-at-arms. Edward, fearing that the archers would not be able to hold their own against the French, sent the Earl of Warwick to order them to retreat. Instead, the earl and his men were drawn into the mêlée themselves. Reinforcements piled in from both sides. Lightly armed Welshmen swam or waded across the Orne, bypassing the bridge, to attack the French from the rear.[50] The Genoese, who perhaps had wasted their bolts shooting at long range before the fighting heated up, ran short of ammunition.[51]

After a long and fierce struggle, the French at the bridge broke. Some, including the constable and Chamberlain de Tancarville (earlier that same day proclaimed a Marshal of France) fled to the upper stories of the bridge's fortifications. From there they surrendered after observing the English, especially the archers, running down and killing the fleeing French men-at-arms and soldiers "without mercy and without defense."[52] Some of the men defeated at the bridge managed to outrace their pursuers to the castle, where they found sanctuary. Others fled through the open gates of the town, but many of these (and the citizens of the town who joined their flight) were killed in the fields.[53]

Following the initial breakthrough into the old town, the English soldiers went on a rampage, pillaging, killing and raping.[54] A number of the common soldiers were killed or injured by desperate bourgeois who dropped heavy objects on them from the upper stories of their homes.[55] Some of the English knights made an effort to stop the troops from the killings and rapes which were so common in the aftermath of an assault.[56] The king, however, does not appear to have made any effort to restrain the sack at first. Indeed, in the evening, when he learned that several hundred of his soldiers had been killed or injured, he initially decided to have the town completely burned, and everyone in it put to the sword.[57] The townsmen had "cost him all too dear,"[58] and would have to be punished for it in order to discourage other towns from resistance.

According to Froissart, Edward was persuaded to show mercy by Godfrey of Harcourt. The logic of Harcourt's argument provides an interesting comment on Edward's strategy for the campaign:

> Dear sire, you should curb your wrath a little, and be satisfied with what you have already done to [the town]. You still have a very long way to go before you shall arrive before Calais, where you are aiming to go. In this town there

---

[50] *Acts of War*, 31–33; Burghersh in *Murimuth*, 202–3; Northburgh in *Avesbury*, 359; *Chron. Normande*, 76.

[51] *Cont. Manuel, 1339–46*, fo. 163: the defenders ultimately were defeated "pource que l'artillerie failly aux genevois qui la estoient en garnison."

[52] Froissart, *Oeuvres*, 4:406.

[53] See the sources cited in note 50 above.

[54] *Le Bel*, 2:83; *Chronographia*, 2:225.

[55] Froissart, *Oeuvres*, 4:412.

[56] *Le Bel*, 2:83.

[57] According to Froissart, at least. *Oeuvres*, 4:412.

[58] Ibid.

are still a great number of people who will defend themselves in their hostels and their houses, if they are attacked. It could cost you too many men, more than were lost during the assault on the town, which could cause your campaign to collapse; and if you retreat from the emprise which you have undertaken, it will turn greatly to your discredit. So spare your men, and know that within a month they will come in very handy to you; because it cannot be that your adversary King Philip will not have to ride against you with all his power and give battle, whatever the outcome may be. And you will yet encounter many combats, river-crossings, assaults and skirmishes, so that you will have need of [all] the men you have, and more. And without [more] killing, we will still be lords and masters of this town, and the men and women [of the town] will very willingly bring to us everything that they have.[59]

Whether or not Harcourt actually made such a speech, Froissart's version shows how the chronicler himself (a contemporary who served as one of Queen Philippa's clerks in England from 1362 to 1366) understood Edward's plans and motivations.[60] The reference to Calais, suggesting that the king intended to besiege that town from so early in the campaign, is usually dismissed as a sign of Froissart's unreliability.[61] Most historians agree that Edward decided to make for Calais only after his victory at Crécy.[62] It is possible that this is correct, and that Froissart erred in presuming that Edward's ultimate destination was part of his plan from the beginning. However, Calais was recognized by contemporaries (though not by all modern historians) as an invaluable prize for the English. To Froissart, Calais after its capture was what Edward valued most in the world, after his wife and children.[63] For the rest of the century, it proved the sharpest thorn in the side of the Valois monarchy.

---

[59] Froissart, *Oeuvres*, 4:412–13: "Chiers sires, voeilliés affrener un petit vostre corage, et vous souffisse ce que vous en avés fait. Vous avés encores à faire un moult grant voiage, ançois que vous soyés devant Calais, où vous tirés à venir, et si a encores dedens ceste ville grant fusion de peuple qui se deffenderont en leurs hostels et leurs maisons, s'on leur keurt seure, et vous poroit trop grandement couster de vos gens ançois que la ville fust essillie, par quoi vostres voiages se poroit desrompre, et se vous retournés sus l'emprise que vous avés à faire, il vous tourroit à grant blasme. Si espargniés vos gens et saciés qu'il vous venront très-bien à point dedens un mois; car il ne poet estre que vos adversaires li rois Phelippes ne doie chevaucier contre vous à tout son effort et combatre à quel fin que soit, et trouverés encores des destrois, des passages, des assaus et des rencontres pluiseurs, par quoi les gens que vous avés et plus encores, vous feront bien mestier; et sans occire, nous serons bien signeur et mestre de ceste ville, et nous metteront très-volentiers hommes et femmes tout le leur en abandon."

[60] Note that the passage in question, unlike much of Froissart's description of the campaign, was not based on the account of Jean le Bel.

[61] E.g. *The Dictionary of National Biography*, "Edward III," 56: "In spite of a remark attributed by Froissart to Harcourt, that Edward intended to march to Calais, his only idea as yet was to do as much mischief as he could in northern France, and then retire into Flanders before Philip could raise an army to intercept him."

[62] E.g. Sumption, *Trial by Battle*, 534; Burne, *Crecy War*, 207; Denifle, *La désolation des églises*, 2:48.

[63] *Oeuvres*, 5:230.

The reasons for the city's importance were not hard to discern: it was an excellent port (which before its capture provided shelter to French pirates, making it "most troublesome to England"[64]), so strongly defended that it would be almost impossible to take so long as it could be resupplied by sea.[65] And, of course, its close proximity to England made it an ideal entry point for English invasions of France: as Godfrey d'Harcourt later observed to the king, "once you hold the town of Calais, you will . . . wear the keys to the realm of France at your belt."[66] Edward III himself used it for that purpose in both of his two later expeditions to France, in 1355 and 1359–60, and several more major *chevauchées* were launched from the city later in the fourteenth century. Edward must have fully perceived how valuable the city could be to him – his adversaries certainly did, for their garrisoning decisions showed that they saw it as a potential target from early on.[67]

There is another reason why Edward could well have seen Calais as a sensible destination from the time he was at Caen. If the devastation of his *chevauchée* alone proved insufficient to provoke Philip into battle, a subsequent siege of Calais might do the trick. Once Edward had set up the siege of Calais, time would be on his side, and the ball would be in Philip's court. If Philip did nothing, Edward would gain a great prize. Nor would Edward have to worry about being "besieged" by Philip's army even as he himself besieged the city, for (with supplies from England easily available by sea) the English would have fewer supply difficulties than the French. The fiascoes at Tournai and Cambrai would not be repeated. And, once they had captured the city, the English could securely embark and return to their homes.

All of that is purely conjectural, of course, but there are two less speculative reasons to believe that Edward was in fact aiming for Calais from early on in the campaign, as Froissart says. One is that two other chroniclers agree that Edward was headed for Calais well before Crécy. Jean le Bel says (in a passage unrelated to the above quotation from Froissart) concerning Edward's movements near Beauvais that the king "did not want to stop to lay waste nor for any other reason, because he had no other intention but to besiege the strong city of Calais, since he could not be attacked [*estre combastu*] by King Philip, as he

---

64 *Lanercost*, 334: "infestissimam," which could also mean "most inimical," "most hostile" or "most dangerous." Cf. *RP*, 158: Calais, "the inhabitants of which have done so much damage to him [Edward] and to his people of England." The *English Brut*, 538, says much the same.

65 Cf. Villani, *Cronica*, 400. It took Edward a year to capture the city even after his victory at Crécy. The French and Burgundians failed in a major attempt to recapture it a century later, despite the advantage of the excellent Burgundian heavy bombards. Indeed, the English were able to hold on to Calais into the mid-sixteenth century.

66 Froissart, *Chroniques*, 4:242: "se vous avés, ensi que vous auerés, celle ville de Calais, vous auerés un grant avantage, et porterés les clefs dou roiaulme de France à vostre cainture."

67 Sumption, *Trial by Battle*, 535.

desired."[68] The *Brut* has the decision being made even before Edward left for France: at a parliament before his departure, according to that source, Edward "ordeynt hym to passe ouer see ageyne, to chastise the rebelles of Fraunce, and to lay seege to Caleis, which did gret harme about al the see-cost."[69] Both of these statements, along with Froissart's, could perhaps be dismissed as teleological errors, were it not for the support of the letter Edward wrote to his council on leaving Caen. In that letter, he asked them to send supplies to him at le Crotoy on the Somme, which shows conclusively that by then he had already decided at least to head in the direction of Calais.[70]

Harcourt's speech indicates some other things about Edward's strategy (as Froissart saw it, at least). It is yet another piece of evidence that Edward was expecting – and indeed bent upon – a passage of arms with King Philip. It also helps explain why Edward avoided attacks on strongly held fortifications in the course of the *chevauchée*: it was not only that they played little role in his strategy, it was also that he wanted to conserve his men for the battle he awaited.[71] Harcourt's request that the king be satisfied with what he had already done reflects the understanding that the town did need to suffer for having inflicted casualties on the English, so as to set a precedent favorable to Edward's army. The Norman lord was simply pointing out that the sack of the town had already done that much.

Seeing the sense of his councilor's argument, Edward proclaimed that no one should commit arson, homicide or rape. The bourgeois, grateful to escape with their lives, opened their homes and their coffers to the English, letting them plunder their goods as they wished.[72] This the soldiers did with enthusiasm: "the toun & the subbarbus vnto the bare wallys of al thing that myghte be bore & caryed out, was robbid and despoyled."[73] Among the most useful booty was a great number of horses.[74]

In addition to the plunder acquired in the town, the English captured many valuable prisoners. In the initial combat, 107 knights and six- or seven-score esquires were captured, along with the Count of Eu and the Sire de Tancarville. These, along with some four hundred rich bourgeois, were shipped back to

---

[68] *Le Bel*, 2:89: "n'y voulut point arrester pour exillier ne aultrement, car il ne tendoit à autre chose fors que à assiegier la forte ville de Calais, puisqu'il ne poeut estre combastu du roy Philippe, ainsy qu'il desiroit." Cf. the *Récits*, 229, which has Edward aiming for Calais just before the battle of Crécy.

[69] *English Brut*, 538.

[70] PRO C81/314/17803.

[71] Cf. *Grandes chroniques*, 9:274; *Acts of War*, 39.

[72] Froissart, *Oeuvres*, 4:413; *Acts of War*, 33.

[73] *English Brut*, 298 (paraphrasing Wynkeley in *Avesbury*, 362); *Acts of War*, 34 ("taking only jewels, clothing or precious ornaments because of the abundance"); *Le Bel*, 2:83; Froissart, *Oeuvres*, 4:407 ("until the varlets and servants were all rich, and took no account of silver money, but only of [gold] florins"), 4:413.

[74] *Récits*, 219.

England to await ransom.[75] Thousands more of all ranks perished, whether during the fight, in the chase afterwards, or during the sack.[76] On the English side, only one gentleman was slain, but several hundred other men were killed or wounded.[77]

The plunder and prisoners were sent to the fleet, which was some six miles up the Orne at the small port of Ouistreham. About two hundred ships had been following the king's progress along the coast, landing raiding parties to burn harbor towns and everything within five miles of the coast. In total, the sailors destroyed sixty-one built-up warships, twenty-three good-sized fishing boats, and a large number of smaller 20–30 ton vessels.[78]

During the five days the English army remained at Caen, the king held a council with all the great men of the host. They showed themselves ready and willing to accept Edward's rather Napoleonic plan and "hasten against our adversary, wherever he may be from day to day, as well as we can, trusting [*esperons*] firmly in God that he will grant us a good and honorable outcome to our emprise."[79]

Meanwhile, English raiding parties spread out from Caen, bringing the torch

75 Northburgh gives the number of captives as "to the number of 100 knights and six or seven score esquires" (*Avesbury*, 359); Burghersh says that 120 to 140 knights were taken, of whom 100 survived (*Murimuth*, 203); Edward III, in his earliest campaign letter (PRO C81/314/17803), gives the number of knights and bannerets taken as one hundred, with "and forty" inserted at a later time. The *Acts of War*, 33, says only 95 captives (presumably referring only to those of knightly rank). Jean le Bel gives no numbers, but Froissart says in his first redaction that the prisoners from Caen "par droit compte" amounted to 107 knights and more than 400 rich bourgeois. *Oeuvres*, 4:408. The figure of 107 knights captured is reliably confirmed by the contemporary campaign itinerary printed in *Le Baker*, 253 – an interesting comment on the accuracy of some details found in Froissart but not in other narrative accounts of the campaign. Cf. also *Récits*, 218, and *Chron. St. Omer*, fo. 259v; *Le Baker*, 80; Villani, *Cronica*, 390.

76 The *Acts of War*, 33, says 2,500 "apart from those killed in the pursuit across the fields"; Burghersh (*Murimuth*, 203) says that 5,000 men of all ranks were captured or killed. Villani, *Cronica*, 390, puts the total number killed at 5,000, while the *Récits*, 219, makes it 3,000. *Le Baker*, 80, says that a full 1,300 of the citizens who resisted the English were killed.

77 Froissart, *Oeuvres*, 4:412.

78 Northburgh in *Avesbury*, 359–60 ("five miles" is "ij. lieus od iiij." Ships are "lxj. [niefs] de guerre od chastel devaunt et derere, et xxiij. crayers, saunz autres maindres vasseaux plusors de xxj, come de xxx. tonels de vyn."); Burghersh in *Murimuth*, 203; Edward III, PRO C81/314/17803.

79 PRO C81/314/17803: "nous avons ia par lassent de touz noz grantz qi se monstrent de bone entiere et une volente pris purpos de nous hastier devers nostre adversaire queu part qil soit de jour en autre tant come nous purrons et esperons fermement en dieu qil nous durra bon issue et honorable de nostre emprise." Cf. letters of Edward III in *KdL*, 287, and of Burghersh in *Murimuth*, 203. The fact that, as Edward's letter mentions, *some* of the English ships had deserted does not justify the conclusion of J. E. Morris, *Welsh Wars*, 108, and Ferdinand Lot, *L'Art militaire et les armées au moyen âge*, 341, that Edward was "constrained to remain in France and seek an escape [*issue*] towards Flanders" against his will, the victory at Crécy being only an accident, the result of the lack of discipline of the English sailors. For the continuing acceptance of Morris' view, see Tierney and Painter, *Western Europe in the Middle Ages*, 501–2.

with them everywhere for miles around, "so that at least the men were not idle for lack of work."[80] The devastation they wrought, combined with news of the fate of Caen, terrified the citizens of Bayeux. Even though the English army had already passed them by, they immediately sent fifteen of the richest bourgeois to surrender the town to the Plantagenet monarch, and do homage to him.[81] The king's response is revealing: he refused to accept their allegiance until he could protect them from harm, showing that he had abandoned any idea of setting up a permanent occupation of Normandy.[82] His action also served to highlight, by contrast, *Philip's* failure to fulfill his royal duty to protect his subjects.

While still at Caen, Edward learned that his adversary had come in person to Rouen with a substantial army. On the 31st the English army set out again, making its way directly towards the French king.[83] As the *Historia Roffensis* says, "wherever he heard that his enemy Philip of Valois (the usurper of the realm of France) was, there [Edward] marched: what he desired most of all was to meet him in battle."[84] Again, as the king advanced, the soldiers spread out to lay waste to a band of territory about thirteen leagues broad.[85] By this point, this devastation was no longer against the king's will. Having left behind the area where he had hoped to secure a new base area (and abandoned that attempt as a lost cause), he was now concerned to harm and to provoke his enemy, and to allow his own men to enrich themselves.

By 5 August Edward had reached le Neubourg, sixty miles directly east from Caen and roughly twenty-five southwest from Rouen. On the 6th, a Sunday, he halted. Two cardinals, sent by the Pope to try once again to secure a peace, had joined the army four days earlier at Lisieux; now they finally had the chance to set forth their position. On behalf of the King of France, they offered to restore

---

[80] *Acts of War*, 34.

[81] Northburgh in *Avesbury*, 360; *Acts of War*, 34.

[82] Northburgh in *Avesbury*, 360: "meas il ne lez voleit receivre pur ascuns enchesouns et tantqe lez purroit salver de damage."

[83] Letter of Edward III in Chandos Herald, *Black Prince*, 352; Wynkeley in *Avesbury*, 362. The *Chronographia*, 2:225–6, states that Edward left a garrison of 1,500 men to besiege the castle of Caen, and that these men were later killed by Robert Bertran. It seems unlikely, however, that so major a loss could have gone unmentioned by the English chroniclers, as well as le Bel, Froissart, and all the English eyewitness accounts.

[84] *Historia Roffensis*, fo. 91v: "ubicumque hostem suum Philippum de Valeys regnum francie occupantem esse audierat querendo ambulabat, optans omni desiderio illum in proelio convenire."

[85] Jean le Bel's *Chronique* specifies that the breadth of devastation was one "journée" or more (2:85: "tant y eut wasté de bon pays et plus d'un journée de largesse"). In medieval French, a "journée" is usually a measure of area rather than of linear distance. But we can decipher le Bel's usage, since in the same place he also states that "entre la cité de Parys et le port de Hogues en Constentin . . . peut bien avoir V bonnes journées, ou VI, à aler le droit chemin." Since the actual road distance between St.-Vaast-la-Hougue and Paris is approximately 200 miles, we can calculate that for le Bel one "journée" equals 33–40 modern miles, or 12.3–14.9 medieval leagues. This is confirmed by his remarks on pp. 76–7 and 80 that detachments under the two marshals rode six or seven leagues on either side of the host, burning and wasting the land.

Gascony and Ponthieu to Edward in the manner his father had held them, i.e. as fiefs of the French crown. This was nothing more than had been offered at Avignon, however, and Edward rejected the proposal curtly.[86]

Just a few days earlier, Philip had been in the area with his army, apparently planning to challenge the invaders. It seems that he thought better of risking a battle with the formidable English host, however, for by the 6th he was back in Rouen. His change of plan may have resulted from receiving word that a second invasion of his kingdom – that of the Flemings, whose army set out for France on the second – had begun.[87] On the 7th Edward covered half the distance between them, halting at Elbeuf on the Seine. While he was there, he learned from a scouting detachment that Philip had broken the bridge at Rouen, abandoning the left bank of the river to the English.[88] A herald was sent to offer battle to the French army there, but Philip responded that he was not yet ready, and that he still awaited many of his men.[89] Many of those who *had* already joined his army were communal infantry who came "amazingly ill-armed and unwillingly," according to one chronicler.[90]

This answer was disappointing for Edward, who had hoped to come to grips with his enemy before Philip could gather his full strength.[91] Already the French army was large enough that it would be out of the question to try forcing a crossing against its opposition. Yet both Edward's immediate goal and his longer-range one – to fight the French king, and then to besiege Calais – required that he reach the opposite side of the Seine. He could not cross anywhere to his north: Rouen was the first bridge over the river. Up the Seine, in the direction of Paris, were seven more bridge towns: Pont-de-l'Arche, Vernon, Mantes, Meulan, Poissy, St.-Germain-en-Laye, and St.-Cloud. The pattern of the following week was set at the closest of these, Pont-de-l'Arche, where a quick English attack was held off by the garrison, which suffered heavy losses, until the main French army arrived, making further attacks pointless.[92] The English had to be content with burning the suburbs on their side of the Seine.[93] As the English army marched up the river, the French matched their daily marches on the opposite bank, so that the two armies could often see one

---

86 *Eulogium*, 208; *Pakington*, fo. 196 ("courtement").

87 Sumption, *Trial by Battle*, 512–13; "Itin. Phil. VI," 569 (Rouen).

88 Edward III, letter to Thomas Lucy in Chandos Herald, *Black Prince*, 352. Sir Thomas Holland and Sir Richard de la Marche are reported to have ridden all the way up to the broken bridge, shouting "St. George for Edward," killing two Frenchmen and wounding many others before they departed. *Récits*, 220.

89 Ibid. See also Froissart, *Oeuvres*, 4:425; *Historia Roffensis*, fo. 91v.

90 *Récits*, 219.

91 Ibid., 220, comments that Edward departed from the area of Rouen only "[when the King of England] saw that he could not have a battle with the King of France."

92 Sumption, *Trial by Battle*, 514; but cf. *Récits*, 221.

93 *Venette*, 41.

another across the water.[94] Eager to come to grips with his enemy, Edward was greatly annoyed by the Valois' unwillingness to cross over and fight.[95]

The castle at Vernon proved too strong to capture, though the town was burned. The bridge there, in any case, had been broken. The king was very disappointed when he saw that he could not cross the river.[96] The vanguard of the French army occupied Mantes before the English arrived there, so it could not be assaulted. At Meulan, the only one of the bridge towns which lay on the right bank of the river, the bridge was broken near the town side. The entrance to the bridge on the left bank, moreover, was defended by a strong fortification full of crossbowmen and men-at-arms. The English made a brief attack, routing a contingent of Amiens militiamen (who apparently made a sally against them), but ultimately retreated when several of their leaders were wounded by crossbow bolts.[97]

Convinced by the failure at Meulan that his prospects of seizing a bridge farther up the river were not good, Edward tried a somewhat different tack. Instead of the more than eleven miles per day they had been averaging since Elbeuf, the English covered only five miles, to Fresnes, on the 12th. Despite the shortness of the march, the English rose at dawn to give themselves time to put the area to the torch with special thoroughness.[98] At the same time they lifted the red banners which in the medieval laws of war symbolized immediate willingness to give battle to the death.[99] The author of the *Acts of War* explains that the Englishmen's intention was "so that their enemy could march up to encounter them, crossing from his side without fear."[100] By halting midway

---

[94] *Grandes chroniques*, 9:275; *Historia Roffensis*, fo. 91v; *Cont. Manuel, 1339–46*, fo. 163.
[95] Edward III, letter to Thomas Lucy in Chandos Herald, *The Black Prince*, 353.
[96] *Le Bel*, 2:85: "il fut moult dolent quant il vit qu'il ne pourroit passer la riviere." Cf. Froissart, *Oeuvres*, 4:420–1. According to the *Grandes chroniques*, 9:274, only a portion of the suburbs was burned.
[97] *Acts of War*, 35–6; cf. *Chron. St. Omer*, fo. 260: "la furent envoie un partie de ceulx d'Amiens a l'encontre de lui mais riens ne valu car tantost furent desconfis."
[98] *Acts of War*, 36; *Grandes chroniques*, 9:275. The town of les Mureaux near Meulan was reportedly razed to the ground.
[99] This is the most likely meaning of "vexilla flammea erigentes" (literally, "raising banners of flame") in *Acta Bellicosa*, 169; see the following note. For the significance of banners, and of red banners in particular, see Keen, *Laws of War in the Late Middle Ages*, 105, 107; cf. also *Acta Bellicosa*, 164; *Knighton*, 2:89.
[100] The translation here is uncertain due to the chronicler's attempt at literary style: "Aurora diei duodecimi, Anglici sunt armati ex omni parte vexillia flammea erigentes, ut eorumdem adversarius obviam posset erigere, intrepidi qua transirent." *Acta Bellicosa*, 169 [Cf. Barber, *Acts of War*, 36, which translates the sentence as "At dawn on the twelfth, the English armed themselves and raised fire-signals everywhere to encourage the enemy to attack and cross boldly at that point."] The verb "erigere," which the author chose to parallel the earlier phrase "vexillia flammea erigentes" (which itself is rather unclear, possibly referring to the raising of red banners, which in medieval warfare were often used as a sign of combat without quarter, or possibly being a metaphorical way of describing the flames sent into the sky by burning buildings, or possibly intended to combine the two images to suggest that the English raised literal flames which were reminiscent of the red standards of a fight to the finish),

between Mantes and Poissy, Edward was giving Philip an opportunity to make an unopposed crossing at either of those bridge towns. Since he could not cross over to Philip, he was trying to encourage Philip to cross to him.

The French king must have been tempted, for it pained him greatly to have to abandon his home territory to the enemy.[101] As the author of the *Grandes chroniques* pointed out, the area which Edward was about to enter contained "the principal residences and the special solace of the King of France."[102] It was, remarked the Italian chronicler Giovanni Villani, the finest and richest country in the world, having stood in repose and tranquillity without war for five hundred years.[103] But Philip knew that, so long as he could keep the English to the south of the river, time was on his side. As his advisers reminded him, the smoke of the fires set by the English could not waft away any part of his lands.[104] The Duke of Normandy had already been ordered to bring the massive Aiguillon army north to help resist the invaders. Philip could hold the Seine with a minimum of men and draw up the bulk of his army on the south side of Paris to protect his capital. Edward would then be faced with three unpalatable choices: to launch an attack on a prepared French position; to wait for Philip to attack, and so risk the arrival of the southern army; or to retreat ignominiously the way he had come, having apparently been faced down by the French. If, on the other hand, Philip crossed at Poissy or St.-Germain and took up a position to await an English attack, he ran the risk that Edward could simply maneuver around him and head for Paris, thus forcing the French to take the tactical initiative. So instead, with tears in his eyes, Philip ordered the towns of Poissy and St.-Germain-en-Laye (which were not strong enough to hold – for who expected a serious threat so close to Paris?[105]) evacuated, and the bridges there broken.[106]

The English occupied Poissy shortly thereafter. The vanguard encamped a little farther on at St.-Germain, within ten miles of Paris. In both places they found the bridges destroyed, but at Poissy the bridge's support piles were still in place in the water. Edward's practiced repair crew set to work immediately, so that by the afternoon there was a narrow beam over which individual soldiers could cross. Just then a substantial force of French soldiers, estimated in one of the campaign letters as one thousand horse and two thousand foot, arrived to guard the crossing. They came too late: in an example of the sort of routine excellence that gave them such a tremendous military reputation in this period,

---

though it literally means "to raise up," can be used, among other things, to mean "to march a body of soldiers up to a height" as I read it here.

101 Froissart, *Oeuvres*, 4:424.
102 *Grandes chroniques*, 9:275; cf. 279.
103 Villani, *Cronica*, 391.
104 Froissart, *Oeuvres*, 4:424.
105 As Venette says (*Venette*, 41): "the close approach of the English to Paris overwhelmed everyone in the city with stupefied amazement, for no one had thought ever to see such a thing." Cf. also *Grandes chroniques*, 9:277.
106 *Acts of War*, 36.

enough Englishmen made the crossing to meet the French soldiers' attack, and
the latter were driven off with very heavy losses.[107]

When Philip received reports of this action, he realized that he was in trouble.
Now that Edward could cross the Seine at will, the English could not be held
pinned while the French gathered their forces. As Jonathan Sumption has
observed, the geography of the area around Paris made the Valois king's
problem particularly acute.[108] Because of the bends in the river there, Poissy was
in practical terms much closer to Paris from the south than from the north. This
made it risky for him to move against Edward. If he approached from the south,
Edward could (if he wanted to avoid a battle) simply escape north and break the
bridge after him. This would give him a long head-start. If, on the other hand,
Philip approached from the north, Edward could make a dash for Paris and
assault the city long before the French king could reach his capital – a worrisome prospect, despite the precautions which had been taken for the city's
defense.[109] Philip had hoped to fight Edward on his own terms, rather than on
the English king's, but by this point he had gathered so many men (at least twice
as many as Edward had, and with a much higher proportion of men-at-arms)
that he would rather fight, even under somewhat unfavorable circumstances,
than let Edward escape unchallenged.

In a bid to prevent that last outcome, on 14 August Philip sent a letter to
Edward accusing the English king of being a false vassal and entering into
France full of arrogance and presumption to commit grave injustices against the
people of the realm. Expressing his confidence in God and his just cause, he
declared that he would await Edward in the field between the
Bourg-St.-Germain and the Vaugirard south of Paris, or alternately between
Franconville and Pontoise (north of Poissy), on the Thursday, Saturday, Sunday,
or Tuesday immediately following (the 17th, 19th, 20th, or 22nd); then the two

[107]The letter of Michael Northburgh (*Avesbury*, 367) and the *Acta Bellicosa* say that 500
Frenchmen were killed in this engagement. Wynkeley's letter (*Avesbury*, 363) says 1,000, and
the *Récits*, 223, says 1,200, "as well Frenchmen as Amiennois." *Le Baker*, 81, says 300 of the
enemy were killed. *Melsa*, whose account of the campaign is generally very accurate (though
it contains little not found in the campaign letters or the *Acta Bellicosa*), gives the figure of
800 enemy killed. *Knighton*, 2:36, says the French lost around 400 men-at-arms, and a "great
multitude" of commons. The lowest casualty figure is the one given by the *Chronographia*,
228: 200 men.

The estimate of 1,000 horse and 2,000 foot is from Wynkeley, in *Avesbury*, 363 (also given
by *Melsa*, 3:56). From the two letters cited, we learn that the Earl of Northampton and his
archers played the lead role in driving off the Frenchmen, who were mainly militiamen from
Amiens. The defenders of the crossing may have suffered from a serious morale disadvantage, in that they had already once before met and been handily defeated by the English,
outside of Meulan: *Chron. St. Omer*, fo. 260.

[108] *Trial by Battle*, 517.

[109] According to the *Récits*, 222, these included the construction of strong wooden barri-
cades in the streets, and an order for the bourgeois to carry heavy objects suitable for dropping on the enemy to the upper stories of their homes. The *Acts of War*, 36, adds that siege
engines were prepared in case the English decided to besiege the city. Cf. Froissart, *Oeuvres*,
4:424; Villani, *Cronica*, 392; *Cont. Manuel, 1339–46*, fo. 163v.

armies could do battle. "You who want to conquer this land," he wrote, "if you seek battle as you assert, should not refuse this offer." He closed by demanding that Edward certify in writing his intention to accept the terms offered, and refrain from burning and devastating in the interim.[110]

Edward was overjoyed at the news that his adversary was at last ready to fight. He told Philip's messenger that the French offer of battle was exactly what he wanted, and had always wished for. When the Valois army came, it would find the English prepared for the combat. The Plantagenet did not, however, intend to accept his enemy's demand that he cease laying waste the countryside in the interim. When the Frenchman asked where Philip would be able to find Edward, the king answered that he should look where he saw the light of flames from burning cities and towns.[111]

The same day that Philip had composed his letter, the English troops had burned St.-Germain, St.-Cloud, Retz, and a number of other towns and manors, some within two miles of Paris, so that everyone in the city could see the smoke blackening the air.[112] They "in particular burned the manor of Montjoye, the most pleasant of all the manors of the King of France, in order better to provoke Philip to fight."[113]

On the 15th, the English soldiers were forbidden to burn or pillage, nominally because it was the Feast of the Assumption of the Blessed Virgin.[114] The real reason was that, as the *Acts of War* comments, Edward was "awaiting the appearance of the enemy, which he heartily hoped to see."[115] He had good reason to hope that the Valois would indeed appear, considering the bellicose letter he had just received, and the final slap in the face he had given with the destruction of Montjoye. Of course, in the event of battle, Edward would want his men rested and concentrated, not spread out for twenty miles laying waste the countryside.[116]

The effect of this precaution, however, was to deceive King Philip. Edward had apparently intended for his verbal response to convey to his enemy just what the formal answer composed the next day said more clearly: he would gladly

---

110 The letter was given at St.-Denis. It is printed in a Latin translation of a lost French original in *Hemingburgh*, 423–5 (here at 424), and in the notes to Froissart, *Oeuvres*, 4:496–7, with slight differences; see also *Grandes chroniques*, 9:277; *Historia Roffensis*, fo. 91v. Note Philip's statement that Edward had asserted his desire for battle; this destroys any claim that Edward's expressions of his willingness to fight came only after the fact.

111 *Historia Roffensis*, fo. 91v.

112 *Venette*, 41; *Grandes chroniques*, 9:275.

113 *Melsa*, 3:56–7: "Anglici tamen non omiserunt quin villam de Sancto Clow, per unam leugam a Parisius distantem, necnon Sanctum Germanum de Lacu, et insuper manerium de Monte Gaudii, quod fuit magis delectabile omni manerio regis Franciae, combusserunt, ut Philippum magis ad pugnam provocarent."

114 *Acts of War*, 37.

115 Ibid.

116 This is in accord with Edward's own statement that he spent three days at Poissy "as much to await the enemy in case he wanted to give battle as to repair the bridge." Letter to Thomas Lucy in Chandos Herald, *The Black Prince*, 353.

accept battle should Philip come to attack him, but he would not let the French dictate the time or place of battle, nor would he accept the Valois' requirement that he stop devastating the countryside. These two reservations had been expressed in the remark that flames would mark his position for Philip to find him. Yet Philip's understanding was that Edward had accepted the challenge on the terms the Valois had set. The pause in the devastation on the 15th seemed to be a fulfillment of the demand that the English cease their destruction until the combat, and the flames of the previous day's burning of St.-Cloud (less than four miles southwest of Vaugirard) seemed to provide a signpost showing which of the two suggested battlefields he had chosen.[117] Thus, on the 15th, Philip left St.-Denis, crossed Paris with his army, and encamped near the Bourg-St.-Germain. He expected that on the 17th, in accord with the challenge which he thought Edward had accepted, there would be a battle on the plains there.[118]

In fact, however, the Plantagenet had no such intention. Advancing to Philip's chosen field of battle would have left the English in a very unfavorable position. Once the two armies were in contact, time would be on Philip's side. With his army sitting outside his capital, the Valois would have no supply problems at all; furthermore, if enough time went past, he would be able to trap his adversary between his own army and the Duke of Normandy's, which he had ordered north from Aiguillon. Under these circumstances, Edward would not be able to hold to a defensive formation and await Philip's attack. Even though his army was much smaller than the French one, Edward would have to take the tactical initiative, and across ground chosen and prepared by his enemy at that, or else withdraw in the face of an enemy ready to attack. Defeat would likely follow.

If, on the other hand, Philip came to Edward at Poissy, the English command over the river crossing would make it impossible for the French to "besiege" them there. The same logic that, from Philip's point of view, meant that from Poissy Edward could escape a battle, from Edward's point of view meant that he could *ensure* a battle, and ensure that it would be Philip who had to take the tactical initiative. The Plantagenet understood from his adversary's letter that the French intended to give battle, and he expected to see them outside of Poissy

---

[117] This makes comprehensible Gilles le Muisit's otherwise puzzling statement that Edward "ficte et cautelose fecit fieri incendia versus Carnotum, et, dimissa illa via, iter assumpsit ad contrarium." *Le Muisit*, 158.

[118] The reconstruction presented in this paragraph is based on the previously unknown verbal reply to Philip's challenge, as described in the *Historia Roffensis* (note 109, above); on the *Grandes chroniques*, 9:277; and also on *Chron. St. Omer*, fo. 260 ("roy d'Angleterre, qui a Saint Germain estoit et faint qu'il se vouloit traire vers Chartres"; "Roy Philippe de France qui estoit a Nostre Dame des Champs . . . et cuida que par illec ses ennemis deussent passer.") The rather pitiful feelings of betrayal, sorrow and anger openly displayed by Philip after he learned of Edward's departure confirm that he had expected the battle south of Paris. *Grandes chroniques*, 9:281; *Récits*, 224.

on one side of the Seine or the other. But, for the reasons described above, Philip did not appear.[119]

Considering what seemed to be a recurrence of Philip's famous reluctance to fight, the logical course was for the English to head north. Edward expected his Flemish allies to be operating in the area, and a juncture with them would provide a welcome addition to his strength before the battle with Philip. A fleet full of reinforcements and supplies from England might already be waiting for him at le Crotoy, in accordance with his orders from Caen. If he could make contact with his ships, or reach territory controlled by the Flemings,[120] his supply lines would be assured, so that he could not be "besieged" by his adversary. Then, once again, if Philip wanted a battle, Philip would be the one who would have to make the attack over unfavorable ground. If Edward could stay ahead of Philip's army all the way to Calais (which, says Jean le Bel, was now his destination, "since he could not be attacked [*combastu*] by King Philip, as he desired"[121]) the situation would be even better. If under those circumstances Philip still declined to attack, his reputation would sink to subterranean levels (a very significant political advantage to Edward, who still hoped to replace his adversary on the throne of France), and the English would eventually gain a great prize.

"So," wrote the king not long thereafter,

> when we saw that our enemies did not want to come and give battle, we therefore had all the countryside around burned and laid waste ... and we passed the bridge with our army, and in order better to draw our enemy into battle, we headed off towards Picardy.[122]

After the crossing on the morning of the 16th, the English sped directly north, averaging nearly fifteen miles per day through the 19th. As they went they continued to devastate a broad band of territory, as they had done in Normandy, as part of their effort to make the French king fighting mad (and to continue to accumulate booty).[123]

---

119 *Murimuth* [Nero MS], 246: "moram tridui apud Pussiacum factam, adventu regis Franciae exspectato pro bello optinendo, quem advenisse putaverunt, et non venit." Cf. Edward's letter to Thomas Lucy, in Chandos Herald, *The Black Prince*, 353 [below, note 120].

120 Le Muisit, a well-informed chronicler for these events, states positively that during his march north from Poissy Edward was aiming to meet with the Flemings. *Le Muisit*, 158.

121 *Le Bel*, 2:89: "il ne tendoit à aultre chose fors que à assiegier la forte ville de Calais, puisqu'il ne poeut estre combastu du roy Philippe, ainsy qu'il desiroit." Cf. *Récits*, 229.

122 Letter to Thomas Lucy, in Chandos Herald, *The Black Prince*, 353: "Et, quant nous veismes qe notre ennemiz ne vouloit venir pour doner bataille, sy fismes arder et gaster le paiz environ ... Et passams le pount avec notre hoste, et pour plus attraire notre ennemie a la bataille nous traiams devers Picardie." Cf. *Murimuth* [Nero MS], 246.

123 *Le Bel*, 2:89–91, 93–5; *Acts of War*, 38–9; Froissart, *Oeuvres*, 4:428, 432–3; *Chronographia*, 228. According to Villani, *Cronica*, 393, the English met some resistance at Pontoise, but eventually took the city by force and sacked it, putting to the sword all they found within except women and children. Even the long continuation of the *Manuel d'histoire de Philippe VI*, which is emphatic that Edward was fleeing and did not dare await battle, admits

At some point, probably on the evening of the 15th just before crossing the Seine, Edward composed and sent a formal response to his adversary's challenge, one far more elaborate and polished than the few words sent by messenger on the 14th, but essentially similar. The letter, which is often dismissed as "disingenuous" and intended "chiefly for consumption in [Edward's] own army"[124] by those who believe that the English were seeking to avoid battle, reads (in part) as follows:

we have come without pride or presumption into our realm of France, *making our way towards you to make an end to war by battle*. But although you could thus have had a battle, you broke down the bridges between you and us, so that we could not come near you nor cross the river Seine. When we came to Poissy and had the bridge there which you had broken repaired, and stayed there for three days, waiting for you and the army which you have assembled, you could have approached from one side [of the river] or the other, as you wished. Because we could not have a battle with you there, we decided to continue further into our realm to punish rebels against us and to comfort our friends and those faithful to us, whom you falsely claim as your subjects; and so we will remain in the realm without leaving to carry on the war as best we can, to our advantage and the loss of our enemies. Therefore if you wish, as your letters purport, to do battle with us and protect those whom you claim as your subjects, you can now show it: at whatever hour you approach you will find us ready to meet you in the field, with God's help, which thing we desire above all else for the common good of Christendom, since you will not deign to tender or accept any reasonable terms for peace. But we do not consider it advisable to [allow ourselves] to be cut off by you, or to let you choose the place and day of battle.[125]

---

that the English progressed "robant, ardant le pais, et occiant les bonnes gens, et gasta tout le Vimeu." *Cont. Manuel, 1339–46*, fo. 164.

[124] Sumption, *Trial by Battle*, 520.

[125] Emphasis added. PRO C66/219/m. 21d; *CPR (1345–48)*, 516–17. Dated 15 August (the day before Edward crossed the Seine) at Autes[?]. It is possible, however, that 'Autes' is Auteuil (identified in the two contemporary itineraries as "Auty" and "Autoille"), which does not appear on the king's itinerary until the 17th. *Le Baker*, 252–6. To add to the confusion, however, there is another Auteuil roughly fifteen miles southwest of Poissy (and, indeed, an Autoillet very close to that), where Edward could perhaps have found himself on the 15th. Indeed, this possibility is supported by the fact that Philip apparently believed that Edward, when he left Poissy, would move towards "Montfort" (Montfort-l'Aumary), which is on the direct road a short distance north of this latter Auteuil. *Grandes chroniques*, 277.

The more often used version of the letter given in the *Acts of War* (*Acta Bellicosa*, 171–2; also printed in Froissart, *Oeuvres*, 4:497 [with corrections on 5:551], and in English translation in Barber, *Life and Campaigns*, 38) is nearly identical to the enrolled form of the letter, but leaves out one key phrase in the first sentence of the text given above: it has "to make an end to the war" omitting the "by battle" immediately following. It also differs in being dated 17 August, variously at "Autel" (*Acta Bellicosa*, 172) or "Grantviller(?)" (by Kervyn de Lettenhove in Froissart, *Oeuvres*, 4:498). A Latin version (corresponding to the enrolled version with slight deviations, and dated 15 August) can be found in *Hemingburgh*, 425–6. The use of the past tense to refer to the time at Poissy perhaps suggests the later date of composition; but by the evening of the former date, Edward had already been at Poissy three

This letter is particularly valuable because it sets out all five of the goals of the 1346 *chevauchée* and (as we shall see) of later operations as well. First, and desired "*sovereinement,*" was the prospect of being attacked by a French army under favorable circumstances. Failing battle, the *chevauchée* at least served to comfort Edward's supporters (in this case, most notably his besieged vassals in Aiguillon), and to punish by fire and devastation those who failed to acknowledge his rule. In addition, the *chevauchée* was very profitable to the English, who acquired an "inconceivable" amount of plunder,[126] and even more than correspondingly costly to the French people (and to the French king, who could not tax the towns or areas he had failed to protect from devastation).[127]

The English army's departure for Picardy meant the failure of Philip's attempt to pin it against the Seine. But there was already a French army gathering on the Somme,[128] and the main bridge towns on that river were all strong, so Philip had the chance simply to shift his Seine strategy north to the Somme. Loudly and publicly complaining that he had been betrayed, the Valois marched his army back through Paris and set off in pursuit of his adversary.[129] His army paralleled the English on their march north, then, near the river, began to close in. Meanwhile, he had all the passages over the river reinforced or destroyed, "so that the English king and his host could not cross, because he wanted to do battle with them at his will, or starve them there by the Somme."[130]

Edward must have fully understood exactly what Philip was doing: the English monarch had, after all, tried to do exactly the same to the Scots in 1327.[131] Then he had failed. The Scots had chosen a position where they could defend themselves effectively if attacked, even against the larger English army,

---

days (including the 15th) without seeing the enemy, and had presumably already decided to push on the next morning, so the past tense could also be used in that case, even aside from the possibility that the tense reflected what Edward knew would be in the past by the time Philip received the document. In sum, the dating of the enrolled and Hemingburgh versions of the letters seems the most likely.

126 *Le Bel*, 2:90: "gaagnierent si grand tresor qu'on ne le pourroit croire ne penser."

127 This was true both practically (because devastated areas had no resources available with which to pay taxes) and also morally, for, according to medieval legal opinion, "kings had the duty to collect tribute from their subjects in order to repel external invaders and to suppress intestine wars, but . . . [should not] when they were incapable of defending their subjects." F. H. Russell, *The Just War in the Middle Ages* (Cambridge: Cambridge U.P., 1975), 265. For a variety of examples of tax remissions to devastated areas, see Rogers, "By Fire and Sword."

128 Sumption, *Trial by Battle*, 520.

129 *Grandes chroniques*, 9:278–80.

130 Froissart, *Oeuvres*, 5:2–3: "Enssi avoit li roys Phelippes fait pourveir les destrois et les passaiges sus le rivière de Somme, affin que li roys englès, ne son host, ne peuissent passer, car il les volloit combattre à se vollenté ou affamer par delà le Somme." Similarly, on 5:7: "li rois de France . . . pensa bien que il encloroit le roy d'Engleterre entre Abbeville et le rivière de Somme, et le prenderoit ou combateroit à se volenté." Cf. *Le Bel*, 2:98; *Récits d'un Bourgeois de Valenciennes*, 228; Chandos Herald, *Vie du Prince Noir*, ll. 231–5: "Car bien [Philip] quidoit avoir enclos / Les Englois, solonc mon purpos, / Droit entre le Sayne et la Somme / Et la endroit, ce est la somme, / Les quidoit il trop bien combatre."]

131 See above, p. 18.

and from where they could slip away if their enemy declined to make an assault. Edward no doubt remembered well how frustrating that had been, and now looked forward to placing Philip into the same position he himself had been in nearly twenty years earlier. But first he would have to cross the Somme to gain a clear line of retreat.

On 21 August, the invaders reached Airaines, within striking distance of the river, roughly midway between Abbeville and Amiens.[132] From there Edward sent out a strong reconnaissance party under the marshals with orders to find the most lightly defended crossing and seize it. They must also have been seeking information concerning the Flemings or the fleet. Of the latter they could have had no word, for it was still gathering in England. The Flemings, as the scouts probably learned, were bogged down at the siege of Béthune, some forty miles away from the river on the opposite side.

The scouting detachment made the loop from Airaines to Pont-Rémy, up the Somme to Fontaine-sur-Somme and Long, then back to the king by way of Longpré. The English attempted to capture the bridges at Pont-Rémy and Long, but found them too well defended. Fontaine and Longpré were pillaged and burned.[133] Godfrey d'Harcourt had heard that there was a ford across the river just below Abbeville (as, most likely, had Edward himself: Abbeville was the capital of his own County of Ponthieu, which he had visited as a youth[134]) but he did not know precisely where the crossing was.[135] The ford may well also have been familiar to Bartholomew Burghersh or some of the men in his retinue, for he had been seneschal of Ponthieu as recently as 1334.[136] So when the king got the bad news that none of the bridges between Abbeville and Amiens could be captured, he ordered that the army be ready at dawn to move out to the west. The following day, the 23rd, he sacked Oisemont and proceeded to Acheu, while raiding parties devastated the area all the way to St.-Valery on the Channel and scouts searched for the precise location of the crossing.

Meanwhile, King Philip arrived at Airaines, where his enemy had been just hours earlier. His counselors, believing that the English were trapped, advised him to wait there long enough for all his troops to arrive. They rather expected that Edward would find the ford at Blanchetacque, but since Godemar du Fay had been dispatched to guard the crossing with a strong "elite" detachment, they did not believe that the English king would be able to force a passage.[137]

[132] The inhabitants, terrified by the destruction of Poix, surrendered the town to the English, who therefore did not burn it on their departure. *Eulogium*, 209.

[133] *Le Bel*, 2:92–4; Froissart, *Oeuvres*, 5:4; according to the first redaction (5:2) they also made an attempt on Picquigny, though there is no other evidence for this.

[134] F.-C. Louandre, *L'histoire d'Abbeville et du comté de Ponthieu* (Abbeville & Paris: 1844), 213.

[135] Froissart, *Oeuvres*, 5:5; cf. 5:14. Harcourt's awareness of the ford is not surprising, since on the far side it exited near his niece's castle of Noyelles. *Récits*, 226.

[136] *RFR*, II:2:884.

[137] Froissart, *Oeuvres*, 5:8–9, 13–14. The best estimate of the size of the force guarding the crossing is from Michael Northburgh's campaign letter (*Avesbury*, 368): 500 men-at-arms and

With the help of a local informant, Edward did indeed find the ford.[138] As soon as the ebbing tide lowered the water there sufficiently, he ordered an attack on du Fay's troops. Despite heavy opposition, the English, led by a hundred men-at-arms and some archers under Northampton and Sir Reginald Cobham, managed to wade across and defeat the defenders, capturing many and killing more.[139] Godemar himself (severely wounded, according to Froissart) fled with the remnants of his troops.[140] This was a truly remarkable deed of arms on the English side, one of the many which gave them such a brilliant martial reputation during Edward's reign.

The forward elements of Philip's host arrived at the southern end of the ford just as the last of the English army made the crossing. The Plantagenet king prepared to resist a French attack while some of his troops under Hugh Despenser captured Noyelles-sur-Somme and le Crotoy, where they found a "great plenty of supplies" – but not the fleet. Others pursued the remnants of du Fay's command to the gates of Abbeville.[141] The food captured at le Crotoy was of critical importance, because the English were down to the very last of their bread supplies, living mainly on meat from captured cattle.[142]

The opposing armies faced off at Blanchetacque for the remainder of the 24th, and half the 25th as well. Edward, in accord with the spirit of his letter of challenge to Philip, offered to grant the French an unopposed crossing, promising a battle once they got across; but Philip declined to put his enemy's chivalric honor to so difficult a test.[143] Instead, he withdrew his army to Abbeville, planning to make use of the bridge there.[144]

After witnessing the departure of the French host, the English moved out,

---

3,000 armed commons. The latter included a large proportion of Genoese and other cross-bowmen. *Chron. St. Omer*, fo. 260v, however, suggests that du Fay's force may have been paralleling Edward's advance, rather than specifically guarding Blachetacque.

138 Whether this informant was a local named Gobin Agace who was bribed to reveal its location (Froissart) or a Yorkshireman who had been living for 16 years in the area (*Melsa*, 3:57), or an esquire in the retinue of Olifart de Ghistelle who was familiar with it from having crossed several times before (*Récits*, 226; cf. Froissart, *Oeuvres*, 5:31), is uncertain, but considering the fact that there must have been a trail leading to it from the road along the Somme, since the local cattle were accustomed to crossing there at low tide (*Chron. St. Omer*, fo. 260v), and considering the easily visible white stone which gave the ford its name (which means "white spot"), the English would likely have found it even without assistance.

139 Wynkeley in *Avesbury*, 363. For interesting little-known accounts of the crossing, see the *Récits*, 227–8, and *Chron. St. Omer*, fo. 260v. The standard accounts are in le Bel and Froissart.

140 Froissart, *Oeuvres*, 5:12–13; *Le Bel*, 2:96–8.

141 Northburgh's letter in *Avesbury*, 368; cf. Froissart, *Oeuvres*, 5:24; *Le Baker*, 81; *Chron. St. Omer*, fo. 260v.

142 *Le Muisit*, 158–9; Villani, *Cronica*, 394; *Historia Roffensis*, fo. 92. Cf. Froissart, *Oeuvres*, 5:26.

143 *Le Baker*, 82.

144 Edward III to Thomas Lucy, in Chandos Herald, *Black Prince*, 353–4.

"fearing nothing now that they had the river Somme behind them."[145] Those who hold to the theory that only the French wanted a battle in 1346 find it "surprising" that Edward did not take advantage of his head-start in crossing the river to escape to Flanders.[146] Instead he went rather slowly (especially considering that he had just acquired plentiful supplies), advancing only to the town of Crécy (nine miles from Blanchetacque as the crow flies) by mid-morning on the 26th.[147] The battlefield there was chosen by Harcourt, Warwick, and Reginald Cobham.[148] It was no coincidence that this group included men who had been among the leaders on the battlefields of Halidon Hill and Morlaix.[149] The king's intention, according to his own testimony, was to meet his adversary there.[150] To observers in his army, he seemed to have been made "merry and delightful" by the imminent prospect of battle.[151]

That same morning, Philip was just departing Abbeville, fourteen road-miles to the south. The French were so certain that Edward would try to flee before their much larger army that King John of Bohemia, one of Philip's most experienced military advisors, was mocked when he insisted that the English king would stand his ground.[152] But when the French marshals returned from a reconnaissance mission, they reported that "the English are encamped near Crécy-en-Ponthieu, and show by their array that they will await the King [of France] there."[153]

The strategic situation now was very different from what it had been at Poissy. In the event of a tactical standoff at Crécy, time would be on Edward's side, rather than Philip's. With the food captured at le Crotoy and their much smaller army, the English would have no more supply difficulties than the vast

---

[145] Froissart, *Oeuvres*, 5:24: "ne se esfréoient de riens, puisque il sentoient la rivière de Somme derrière euls."

[146] Barber, *Edward, Prince of Wales and Aquitaine*, 62.

[147] Crécy is nearly 16 ground miles from the ford, assuming they went around the forest of Crécy (as indicated by Froissart, *Oeuvres*, 5:23); but even that represents only a moderate pace. Furthermore, nearly half that distance would be on the road leading east from Rue to Crécy. If Edward had been seeking to outdistance the French, he could have covered the same distance directly north and been over the Authie at Nampont.

[148] According to Froissart, *Oeuvres*, 5:26.

[149] Warwick had been with Edward III at Halidon Hill and elsewhere; Cobham had probably also been there (he was a knight of the household by the following year; *WBRF*, fo. 223), and served at Morlaix, as well as at Cadzand, Sluys, and la Flamengrie; he was later to be constable of the Black Prince's army in 1355, and also fought at Poitiers. In his first redaction, Froissart adds Sir Richard Stafford to the group of those who selected the battlefield; it would be interesting to know if he had served with Lord Ralph at Dupplin.

[150] Letter to Thomas Lucy in Chandos Herald, *Black Prince*, 354: "et au darain quant nous voiams qil [Philip] ne vouloit illoques passer [le Somme] mez se tourna devers Abbevill, nous traams devers Crescy pour lui encontrer de lautre parte de la fforest." Cf. *Le Bel*, 105, and Froissart, *Oeuvres*, 5:25–6.

[151] *Murimuth* [Nero MS], 246: "rex Angliae . . . qui, cum intellexisset quod inimici tam prope fuissent, hilaris efficitur et jocundus, eo quod bellum festinanter optinere credidit."

[152] *Le Baker*, 82.

[153] Froissart, *Oeuvres*, 5:27; cf. 5:39.

and hungry Valois host. Dribs and drabs of reinforcements were constantly arriving for the French, but Edward could anticipate the appearance of two more substantial forces, from England and from Flanders.[154] The Duke of Normandy's army, much farther away, would not likely arrive until too late. Edward even had a good escape route if things developed in such a way that he needed one, for he controlled the Brunehart *chaussée* which could take him across the river Authie at Ponches.[155]

Thus, as Edward could anticipate, from Philip's point of view there was no reason to put off an attack. The Valois' attempts to checkmate his adversary had already failed twice, and if neither the Seine nor the Somme could stop the Plantagenet, then nothing between Crécy and Calais would even give him pause.[156] Besides, the French host was at least twice as large as the invaders' army, and perhaps as much as three times.[157] The English position was strong, but far from impossibly so – not like the one held by the Scots in 1327. Edward's military reputation was already impressive, but the French had their own "ancient military glory" to uphold.[158] If their king once again failed to attack the enemy who had ravaged his kingdom, he would be permanently tarred with the twin brushes

---

154 The account of Gilbert of Wendelyngburgh shows that at least two letters were sent by Hugh Hastings from Flanders to the king in Normandy, and that Hastings received other letters from the king, which he forwarded to the Marquis of Juliers. Furthermore, the king's letter to his council from Caen ordered that Hastings be informed of his plan to progress towards le Crotoy. So it would have been reasonable for Edward to assume that help was on its way from Flanders. PRO E372/191/49; C81/314/17803.

155 G. F. Beltz, "The Battle of Cressy," *Archaeologia* 28 (1844), 178. There are, in any case, many crossings over the Authie.

156 It is true that the *Chron. St. Omer* says of the bridge at Maintenay, to which Edward advanced after the battle, that "le passage estoit moult fort car peu de gent l'eussent bien deffendu contre lui," but he could have gone another way, and in any case had already done well enough at forcing difficult river crossings, as at Poissy and Blachetacque.

157 The chroniclers usually say four or more times. Froissart, in different redactions, says six or eight times (Froissart, *Oeuvres*, 5:25–6; cf. 5:37). The *Récits*, 224, says five times. The smallest ratio given by a contemporary chronicler is 3:1, though this may be intended to refer only to men-at-arms (Villani, *Cronica*, 401, cf. 396). Furthermore, Edward III in his letter to Thomas Lucy (Chandos Herald, *The Black Prince*, 354) says that at the battle Philip had 12,000 men-at-arms of whom 8,000 were noble knights and esquires; the rest were probably the 4,000 Italian crossbowmen who, according to the *Storie Pistoresi*, 222, were with the French king. (For a clear example of crossbowmen being counted as men-at-arms, see Delachenal, *Histoire de Charles V*, 1:163.) This matches well with the statement of Villani, *Cronica*, 392, that in a muster outside Paris King Philip found he had 8,000 "cavalieri" and more than 60,000 foot sergeants, of whom 6,000 were Genoese crossbowmen. Of course, the figure of 60,000 is not reliable, but it seems safe to say that Philip had about 8,000 men-at-arms, 4–6,000 professional mercenaries, mostly Genoese crossbowmen, and a large number of other common infantry, including large town militia contingents. *Chron. St. Omer*, fo. 261v, notes that the Genoese and other infantry were so numerous "que tous les champs en estoient couvers." Thus, Philip's men-at-arms and mercenaries alone matched the total numbers of the English host, and with the infantry he may conceivably have commanded three times as many troops as Edward did.

158 Petrarch, quoted in Boutruche, "The Devastation of Rural Areas," 26.

of cowardice and impotence. Relying on the support of his warlike vassals for his struggle against a charismatic soldier – reputed "the most valiant man in Christendom" even within the French army – who claimed to be the rightful holder of Philip's own crown, the Valois king could ill-afford such stains on his reputation.[159] So anxious for battle had he become, by this point, that immediately after hearing mass on 26 August he issued out of Abbeville in disorder and with only a few men, waiting neither for friends nor strangers. When those of his council observed this, they wondered greatly what he had in mind, but none dared to ask. Finally one of them did come up and say to the king, "Sire, what are you thinking, that you ride thus, so close to your enemies, without awaiting the princes who follow you?" King Philip answered that he was no longer at all certain how close they were, and added "My dear friends, if I am under way, everyone will follow me."[160] The proud barons of his army were, if anything, even more eager to come to grips with the invaders than was their king, and did indeed scramble out after him. Philip paused long enough to array them into four divisions, with the bulk of the infantry under the marshal and the Master of Crossbowmen in the vanguard, then set off for Crécy.

So that afternoon, on 26 August 1346, the battle around which the two kings had been dancing at last took place. Because of Edward's skillful strategic conduct of the campaign, however, it was fought on his terms and not on his adversary's. Fully sorting out the details of the battle which followed would require an additional chapter, if not a book. Since this book is a study of strategy and not tactics, a relatively short treatment will have to suffice.[161]

The English army was divided into three battles, which deployed in column. The first two each comprised a thin but solid core of dismounted men-at-arms flanked by two wings of archers, angled forward so that "they did not impede the men-at-arms, nor did they attack the enemies head-on, but shot arrows like thunderbolts into their flanks."[162] The substantially smaller rearguard manned

159 *Trésor des chartes*, no. 6706; see note 55, p. 229, above.
160 *Chron. St. Omer*, fos 261–61v.
161 The following summary of the battle is based on the accounts of Le Baker, Froissart, and Jean le Bel. Details from other sources are cited as such.
162 *Le Baker*, 83–4: "Sagittariis eciam sua loca designarunt, ut, non coram armatis, set a lateribus regis exercitus quasi ale astarent, et sic non impedirent armatos neque inimicis occurrerent in fronte, set in latera sagittas fulminarent."
  There are a number of other possible interpretations of the sources concerning the English formation; the one suggested here seems most probable to me. With the battles one behind the other, they would appear from the front as a single battle of men at arms flanked by two of archers. This would explain assertion of the *Récits* (p. 231) that "ne fist que deux batailles d'archiers à II costés en la manière d'un escut." [There were only two battles of archers on [the] two sides, in the manner of a shield.] The last portion of the phrase probably suggests a cross-section of the concave inner surface of a shield, a "(" shape, with the flanks thrown forward. The *Récits* place the Prince of Wales' battle (i.e. the vanguard) in between these two wings of archers, and the king, the Bishop of Durham, and the other lords behind him, sitting on their shields and awaiting the outcome, which again fits the idea that the other two battles were ranged behind the prince's (and is supported by the St. Omer chronicle's statement that

an improvised fortification made up of the army's wagons. In front of the entire line the English had dug many small holes, each about one cubic foot, to trip up the enemy horses.[163]

Some of Philip's advisers, seeing the English dispositions, recommended waiting until the next day, so that the French would have time to rest and organize before making an assault.[164] The king would have nothing of it, however. He ordered to the fore the large force of four to six thousand professional Italian crossbowmen who accompanied his army.[165] They began to fire at the English, but quickly discovered that they were completely outmatched by the English longbowmen, who could fire farther and much faster with deadly effect. The situation of the Italians was made doubly worse by the fact that their large shields, or *pavises*, which they normally used to give them cover in the field, were still in the rear with the baggage: Philip would not wait for them to be brought up.[166] Unable to stand against the archers' arrows, the Genoese broke and fled, having accomplished nothing. The French leaders, believing that the

---

Edward did not don his full armor. *Chron. St. Omer*, fos 261–2). This would also match well with the statement of the *Chron. Com. Flandr.*, 218, that the other two divisions of the English army were arrayed "ut, si immineret necessitas, primae succurrerent aciei," and with the description of the ideal formation in Pisan, *The Book of Fayttes of Armes and of Chyvalrye*, 80. Charles the Bold's *ordonnance* of 1476, similarly, called for four lines of infantry, each three ranks deep, with archers on the flanks (and cavalry on the far flanks). Hale, *War and Society in Renaissance Europe*, 59. This interpretation also fits with le Baker's statement that the archers were like wings on the side of *the army* of the king, not of "the battles" of the king. Also, many sources make it clear that the prince's division did almost all of the fighting (e.g. Knighton, *Chronicle* (ed. Martin), 62; *Murimuth*, 264), which would only make sense if the French could not attack the other divisions without going through his. It is hardly likely that an army far superior in numbers would concentrate its attacks almost entirely on one-third or one-half of the frontage of its enemy's line. Finally, *Chron. St. Omer*, fos 261v–62, has the prince's division form up in the fields near the windmill, then the king's division "after" [empres] it, with the baggage behind the second division [par derriere eulx] guarded by the rearguard.

I would argue that Froissart's famous statement that the archers were deployed "in the manner of a harrow" likens the archers to the tines of the harrow, spaced in checkerboard fashion in a formation longer than deep. One standard interpretation of this phrase, followed by Oman among others, that it means a shape, like the one sketched below, is rather far-fetched if one really looks at a medieval illumination of a harrow. Cf. the discussion in Bradbury, *Medieval Archer*, 95–108.

163 *Le Baker*, 83; cf. *Chron. St. Omer*, fo. 262, *Chron. Pays-Bas*, 172.

164 This group very likely included Philip's nephew, the Count of Blois, who had commanded the defeated French army at Morlaix.

165 *Storie Pistoresi*, 222; Villani, *Cronica*, 392.

166 For Philip's "undue haste," see *Venette*, 43; *Chron. des quat. prem. Valois*, 16; *Le Muisit*, 161–2; *Cont. Manuel, 1339–46*, fos 164–64v ("suivoit a coite d'esperon . . . tant angoisseux et aire"; "desirant de soy mesler a eulx se appareilla et fist crier moult hastivement et la ala avec son ost avec petit d'ordonnance de bataille") and see also *Chron. St. Omer* fo. 262: "Vers les ennemis s'en vint le Roy de France si grant a leure que oncques homs ne vist en fait de guerre si tost chevaucher" and "autres dirent que puis que aux champs estoient venus alencontre de lui que honte seroit si seurre si ne leur couroit; et a celui conseil s'assenti le Roy,

crossbowmen were either cowards or traitors to turn tail so quickly, ordered that they be attacked. The Italians who managed to survive both the English arrows and the sudden onslaught of the French cavalry picked themselves up off the ground and, many of them, switched their fire to take vengeance on the men-at-arms who had struck them from behind.[167]

The French were so numerous that the men at the rear of their deep formation could not see precisely what was happening at the front. But they could hear the cries of the Genoese, set upon from before and behind, and the screams of horses wounded by the English arrows. Thinking that these sounds were coming from the English, and overconfidently worrying that the battle might end before they had the chance to take part, the French chivalry in the rear pushed forward.

Meanwhile, though badly disarrayed by its passage through the Genoese, the front battle of the Valois army charged against the English men-at-arms. Clothyard arrows darkened the sky, falling "thicker than rain" on the French cavalry. Men were killed and wounded. Uncontrollable horses, maddened by the arrows in their flesh, wreaked havoc on the French array. It is difficult for charging cavalry to break a steady line of heavy infantry under the best of circumstances; by the time the charging men-at-arms met the English, their circumstances were far from the best. They were stopped dead in their tracks, still suffering from the lethal enfilading fire of the longbows.[168] The press from behind made it impossible for them to recover. As at Dupplin Moor, a large number of men were crushed or smothered to death, without a wound on them.[169]

The Frenchmen, whose valor exceeded their wisdom, mounted three general attacks against the English, each comprising several distinct charges. The Count of Blois, a veteran of Morlaix, tried dismounting and leading his men forward on foot, but, therefore unable to retreat, he was overwhelmed and killed.[170] One group of French men-at-arms dispersed a block of archers and broke into the English forward battle, which was nominally under the command of the Black Prince; the prince's standard fell and he himself was (according to some French accounts) briefly captured. The men-at-arms of the English second battle moved forward to reinforce their shaken comrades; the prince was rescued and the line

jassoit ce que ce feust contre le volente de ceulx qui de guerre savoit."
Other sources, notably Froissart's chronicles, suggest that Philip wanted to delay the battle until the next day, but that his men-at-arms refused to draw back, and so the engagement was forced upon him. This view is accepted by Tourneur-Aumont (*Bataille de Poitiers*, 212), among others. The undoubted fact that the battle was opened by the Genoese archers makes this unlikely, however – as professional soldiers they were not the type to act so intemperately, nor would they have proceeded into combat without their pavises (*Chron. Pays-Bas*, 172; *Le Muisit*, 162) unless ordered to do so.
[167] *Chron. St. Omer*, fo. 262: "lors se releverent les Genevois et se commencierent a vengier."
[168] Cf. Rogers, "Efficacy of the Longbow."
[169] *Le Baker*, 84.
[170] *Chron. St. Omer*, fo. 262v.

restored.[171] Welsh soldiers passed through the thin line of English men-at-arms to finish off the enemy wounded. Each failed assault left hundreds of men and horses dead on the ground to impede the next attack.[172]

Some knights from the Empire who were in King Edward's division, who did not understand the new manner of fighting demanded by the infantry-based English tactics, approached him to protest the slaughter: "Sire, we wonder greatly that you allow so much noble blood to be shed, for you could make great progress in your war and gain a very great deal in ransoms if you were to take these men prisoner." The king answered only that they should not marvel, for thus it had been ordered, and thus it had to be.[173] This was not mere bloodthirstiness. Given the numerical inferiority of the English, Edward could not afford for any of his men to be distracted by securing (or then guarding) prisoners while the actual battle raged, especially since one of the keys to the Plantagenet army's success was maintaining a solid formation while fighting an enemy in disarray. Collecting captives meant breaking ranks.

The fate of the aged and blind King of Bohemia, John of Luxembourg, is a metaphor for the entire French army. When he heard how his comrades were being cut down, he asked his vassal Alard de Baseilles (who, according to Froissart, had been the strongest advocate of delaying the attack until a better opportunity arose) to lead him into the midst of the press. Blindly striking at friend and foe alike, he was finally brought down with a mortal wound, and his loyal companions with him.[174]

By nightfall, the French left alive were stampeding towards the rear. King Philip did his best to rally them, crying out "My lords, to where are you fleeing? Don't you see your king in the field, with his face towards his enemies?" His reproaches were ineffectual, however: "not for anything he could think of to say would they turn back, but continued on their way like defeated men."[175] In this desperate situation, the Valois did not try to stay out of danger. He was reportedly unhorsed twice, and wounded three times.[176] His banner-bearer was killed at his side. Finally he was led off the field by Jean d'Hainault, miserably leaving the sacred Oriflamme of St. Denis and his other royal banners behind in the

---

[171] *Chronographia*, 2:232–3; *Chron. Normande*, 81. Cf. *Récits*, 232–3 and *Chron. Com. Flandr.*, 218. The *Chronographia* says that the prince's captor was the Count of Flanders (who in fact died in this fight).

[172] Villani, *Cronica*, 398.

[173] *Chron. St. Omer*, fo. 262v–63: " 'Sire, moult avons grant merveille que vous souffrez que tant de noble sang soit espanduz. Car par les prendre a Rancon vous pourriez eschever grant partie de vostre guerre et en eussiez tresgrant Raencon.' Et le Roy si respondi que point ne s'esmerveillasent car la chose estoit ainsi ordonnee et ainsi convenoit qu'elle feust."

[174] *Chron. St. Omer*, fo. 262v; Froissart, *Oeuvres*, 5:53–8. For the identification of the "Monk," see ibid., 475–6.

[175] *Chron. St. Omer*, fo. 263.

[176] In his neck and thigh, and with an arrow stuck in his jaw according to the *Eulogium*, 210–11; in neck, hand and stomach according to the *Storie Pistoresi*, 222. Writing immediately after the battle, Richard Wynkeley said only that Philip was reported to have been wounded in the face by an arrow. In *Murimuth*, 216.

mud.[177] He was lucky to have survived: another king, John of Bohemia, lay dying on the field. Among the others killed were Philip's younger brother the Count of Alençon; his nephew the Count of Blois; the Count of Flanders; at least seven more counts and viscounts, eight great barons including an archbishop and a bishop, eighty bannerets, and 1,542 knights and esquires who had been done to death in the small area before the prince's battle, aside from others killed in other parts of the field. A great number of common soldiers also perished, the Italians in particular having been virtually wiped out.[178] Even the men who escaped, according to Villani, "were all wounded with arrows."[179] In addition, the English took many noble knights and esquires prisoner after the fighting was decided. Edward's troops suffered far fewer losses than their defeated enemy, as was usually the case in medieval warfare: few of the French attacked the archers, while the English men-at-arms were protected by their armor and their tight formation. In total they may have lost three hundred men-at-arms and a few archers.[180]

The victors of Crécy remained on the field through the night, without breaking their formation even to eat or drink.[181] Before dawn the next morning the Duke of Lorraine, ignorant of the previous day's battle, arrived on the field with three thousand men-at-arms and four thousand infantry he was leading to join Philip's host. They were routed by the men of the earls of Warwick and Northampton, reportedly with two thousand or more killed, including the duke himself and a hundred of his knights.[182] On the following day, as the heralds wandered the blood-soaked field tallying the dead,[183] detachments were sent to

---

[177] Villani, *Cronica*, 399; Wynkeley in *Avesbury*, 363.

[178] Edward III to Thomas Lucy in Chandos Herald, *Black Prince*, 354. Froissart, *Oeuvres*, 5:74. Of these 1,542, six hundred were reported to be belted knights. *Storie Pistoresi*, 223. *Le Baker*, 85, says that in total the number of knights and men of higher degree [militarium et superioris dignitatis] killed exceeded 4,000, aside from a number of other men whom no one cared to count. Cf. also *Chron, Normande*, 82; *Chronographia*, 2:235. The *Storie Pistoresi*, 223, says that all 4,000 of the Genoese were killed. Cf. also Villani, *Cronica*, 399–400.

Many of the contemporary sources also include the exiled King James of Majorca among the dead, but this is apparently incorrect: Mas Latrie, *Trésor*, col. 1736; *Petit Thalamus*, 349.

[179] *Cronica*, 400: "e tutti i fuggiti erano fediti de saette"; cf. 398: "che non v'ebbe cavallo de Franceschi che non fosse fedito [delle bombarde e saette]."

[180] *Le Bel*, 2:108, says that the English lost 300 knights; but since he also says that the French lost 1,200 knights when they only lost some 1,500 men-at-arms, the figure of 300 for the English should probably be taken to refer to all men-at-arms, especially since dubbed knights were relatively rare in mid-fourteenth century England. There were likely not more than 750 knights in the entire army. Richard Wynkeley, writing immediately after the battle, claimed that the English lost only two knights and a squire, and a few Welshmen killed in pursuing the French. (In *Avesbury*, 363.) Though le Bel's figures seem inherently more credible, Wynkeley was in a much better position to know the truth, and it is not impossible that his claim is correct.

[181] Edward III to Thomas Lucy, in *Avesbury*, 354; Northburgh in ibid., 369.

[182] Villani, *Cronica*, 399; Northburgh in *Avesbury*, 369.

[183] *Chron. St. Omer*, fo. 263, gives an idea of how this was accomplished: King Edward, according to this source, granted to his soldiers that they might keep all the valuables they might find, provided that they brought him the surcoats ["torincles"] of the fallen.

pursue the fleeing remnants of the enemy, and break up any groups trying to rally. According to Edward III, a total of four thousand French men-at-arms, Genoese, and other soldiers were killed that day, 27 August.[184] Back on the battlefield, the English were pulling the wounded out of the piles of slain to bind their wounds, and preparing the dead of both sides for burial.[185] Among the bodies the searchers found John of Bohemia, still barely breathing. He was rushed to King Edward's pavilion, where he was tended to by the royal physicians, but it was too late to save his life.[186]

The most noble of the dead were committed to a nearby abbey. Edward and the nobles with him, draped in mourners' black, paid great honor to the body of the King of Bohemia, out of respect for his age, his chivalry, and his courtesy to Englishmen who had been captured in war.[187] Through the heavy mist which cloaked the field drifted the solemn sounds of masses sung to honor the dead and to thank God for the victory.[188]

Edward had finally got the passage of arms with his adversary he had sought for so many years, and it had turned out just as he had "firmly trusted."[189] He was not alone in attributing his victory to the hand of God. "Oh Holy of Holies, Our Lord, God of Hosts, how great is your power, in heaven and in earth and especially in battle!" wrote Giovanni Villani within a year or two of the battle. "Sometimes, indeed often, You give a few men the power to defeat giant armies, to show Your power and abase the arrogant and the proud, and to punish the sins of kings, nobles, and the people." In this battle, the chronicler added, God had well shown his power, for the French were three times as many as the English.[190] However much of the credit may go to the English longbowmen or to divine intervention, some must be reserved for Edward's successful strategy. His goal in the campaign was to get Philip to attack the English army in open battle, and that goal was met.

On the 28th, Edward and his soldiers packed up their booty and set out for Calais. As they marched, the marshals of the host again led out detachments of

---

184 Edward III to Lucy in Chandos Herald, *The Black Prince*, 354. According to Holinshed, *Chronicle*, 640, four times as many of the commons were killed on this Sunday than had perished during the main battle on Saturday.
185 Villani, *Cronica*, 400: "e consagrare il luogo e dare sepoltura a' morti cosí a' nimici come agli amici, e trarre i fediti tra' morti e fargli medicare." According to Villani, those of Philip's common soldiers who survived were allowed to take their pay and depart.
186 *Chron. St. Omer*, fo. 263.
187 Villani, *Cronica*, 400 (mourning); *Pakington*, fo. 196: "il fuist homme de graunt age et avoit este noble chivaler et curteys devers gentz Dengleterre quand ils furent pris de guerre." The last is probably in particular a reference to his intervention on behalf of Suffolk and Salisbury in 1340; cf. *Le Baker*, 68.
188 Masses: Villani, *Cronica*, 400; cf. *Pakington*, fo. 196. Mist: Holinshed, *Chronicle*, 640.
189 See p. 251, above.
190 Villani, *Cronica*, 400–401: "santo de' santi nostro signore Iddio dell'oste, quant'è la potenzia tua in ciele e in terra e spezialmente nelle battaglie! che talora bene sovente fa che meno gente e potenzia vincono gli grandi eserciti, per mostrare la sua potenzia e abbattere le superbie e gli orgogli, e punire le peccata de' re e de' signori e de' popoli." Cf. *Murimuth*, 248.

coureurs who devastated the countryside through which they passed, burning Saint-Riquier, Fauquembergues, Beaurainville, Saint-Josse, Wissant, Étaples, and Neufchâtel-Hardelot, and the suburbs and rural areas surrounding Boulogne and Montreuil.[191] On 3 September, they arrived before Calais, "which was held to be one of the strongest towns in the world."[192] The capture of that city, after the longest and most elaborate siege of the war, is the subject of the next chapter.

---

[191] *Le Bel*, 2:109–10; *Knighton*, 2:39; *Récits*, 232–3. He also passed through Maintenay, and probably burned it too. *Chron. St. Omer*, fo. 264.

[192] Quotation: *Le Bel*, 2:110. Date: Le Baker, and Thompson's itineraries say the 4th (*Le Baker*, 86, 253, 255; cf. *Le Bel*, 2:110 n.6), but Edward's letter to Thomas Lucy (Chandos Herald, *Black Prince*, 355) is dated "devant Calais, le iij Jour de Sept," the date also given by the reliable *Avesbury*, 372).

CHAPTER TWELVE

"IN PURSUIT OF HIS QUARREL":
THE SIEGE OF CALAIS AND THE YEAR
OF MIRACLES IN RETROSPECT

*Those skilled at making the enemy move do so by creating a
situation to which he must conform; they entice him with
something he is certain to take, and with lures of ostensible
profit they await him in strength.* Sun Tzu, V.20[1]

THE SIEGE OF CALAIS, which lasted from 3 September 1346 to 4 August
1347, was probably the largest single military operation undertaken by England
until the modern period. According to pay records, some thirty-two thousand
British troops served at the siege for all or part of its eleven-month course, even
aside from the crews of the nine hundred ships, barges, balingers and victuallers
that supplied the army.[2] There were 13 earls, 44 barons and bannerets, 1,046
knights, 4,022 esquires, 5,104 mounted archers and vintenars [commanders of
20 infantrymen], 500 hobelars, 15,480 English foot archers, 4,474 Welsh troops,
and 314 masons, carpenters, smiths, engineers, tent-makers, miners, armorers,
gunners, and artillery men, among others.[3] They lived in an elaborate fortified
camp which Edward dubbed Villeneuve-le-Hardi: "Bold New Town." By the
end of the siege, it included solidly built houses lining well-ordered streets,
butcher shops, bakeries, a market square, and all sorts of shops, where goods
supplied from England and Flanders by sea could easily be purchased, "as if he
intended to stay for ten or twelve years."[4] The Plantagenet kept his army there
though the cold of winter and the heat of summer, despite disease and boredom,

---

1 Griffith (ed.), 93.
2 Grose, *Military Antiquities*, 278. Calculations based on the total amount of wages paid and
the wage rates indicate that, on *average*, somewhere in the area of one-third of these troops
were in the siege lines at any one time. Doubtless, however, there was wide variance; the *Historia Roffensis*, fo. 92v, says Edward had few men with him over the winter, which means he
must have had relatively many in the spring and summer.
3 Ibid.; cf. Wrottesley, *Crecy and Calais*, 204, for somewhat different figures. The number
for the esquires includes some constables, centenars, and ductors. According to the version of
the total roster in Wrottesley (which, like the one in Grose, is an abstract derived from the lost
Wardrobe Book for the campaign), the naval component included 738 ships and 9,355 mariners.
4 Froissart, *Oeuvres*, 5:85–6: "ensi que dont que il deuist là demorer X ans ou XII."

despite constant harassment by a French army at Boulogne, regardless even of a
Scottish invasion of England and a French invasion of Flanders. Part of the
reason for his determination, as Villani observed, was his desire to gain a strong
port and a place of refuge in France.[5] But still more important (as the reader will
by now not be surprised to hear) was the English king's hope that the siege
would draw Philip into another battle, where the war could finally be brought to
an end.

As with the Crécy *chevauchée* which preceded it, the siege of Calais has
often been misinterpreted. The analysis of the great French historian Edouard
Perroy, whose understanding of military affairs did not equal his political
insight, is almost absurd:

> Victor [at Crécy] against all expectations, Edward had not sufficient strength
> to exploit his success. He persisted in his intention to re-embark. First he must
> reach a port. He chose Calais, . . . which he thought he could carry without
> delay. But siege warfare was at this time so badly equipped that, in the case of
> a town with stout walls, only treachery or starvation could get the better of
> resolute defenders. The siege went on and on . . . Calais surrendered on
> August 4th, 1347.[6]

The idea that Edward, desiring to take ship again for England, would
abandon the port of le Crotoy (which he had already taken, and where he had
long since ordered the fleet to arrive), then underestimate the time needed to
capture a city by ten or twenty times, but stay there anyway for a year, just to
capture a port, is easily dismissed. Yet even A. H. Burne, a military historian,
basically accepts Perroy's rationale.[7] Other scholars have dismissed the siege of
Calais as an almost trivial afterword to the campaign or a serious strategic
mistake on Edward's part.[8] But, for the reasons indicated in the last chapter, the
capture of Calais was a great advancement to the English war effort, not a sign
of Edward's lack of "sufficient strength to exploit his success."

The siege, however, had an ulterior motive beyond the aim of capturing the
Gibraltar of the North. Edward had promised parliament that he would not leave
France until he had made an end to the war, and he could easily see that Crécy,
though it had been a severe blow to the French monarchy, had not won the war.

---

[5]   Villani, *Cronica*, 402.

[6]   *The Hundred Years War*, 119–20.

[7]   *The Crecy War*, 204: "Calais . . . presented a very tempting target. The English army was
sadly in need of warlike stores of all kinds: boots and horse-shoes were worn out and thin;
transport vehicles were in need of repair; above all, the stock of precious bows and arrows
needed replenishment. But a wide stretch of water separated the army from a renewal of all
those things, and a powerful French fleet roamed these waters; St. Vaast and Caen were now
far distant." Cf. also the recent work of Plaisse, *Grande chevauchée*, 79.

[8]   E.g. R. C. Smail, "Art of War," *Medieval England*, ed. A. L. Poole (Oxford: Clarendon
Press, 1958), 155: "So great a success [as Crécy] gained for Edward only Calais." Similarly,
Lot, *L'art militaire et les armées au moyen âge*, 348: "As brilliant as the victory of Crécy was,
it merely assured for the English the security of their retreat." DeVries, "Siege of Calais,"
136, cites a number of similar opinions.

A *second* battlefield defeat, however, might well cause the Valois government to collapse entirely – especially if Philip were this time among the slain or captured. True, while Edward waited at Calais Philip might well be able to gather an even larger army than the one he had led at Crécy,[9] but Edward was never one to let an enemy's numerical superiority concern him. Furthermore, Edward's position at Crécy had not even approached the strength of the defensive lines he prepared outside of Calais.[10] And if the English were stronger, the French were weaker (except perhaps in sheer numbers) for they had lost both their best military leaders and their confidence. So, if Philip could be induced to give battle again, Edward could await the result with some confidence.

The Plantagenet's letters from Calais show clearly that such a course of events was exactly what he had in mind. The very day he arrived before the town he wrote back to England, ordering that reinforcements and supplies be sent to him. Did he need those men for the siege? No; he needed them because he had heard that Philip "has ordered his forces to assemble anew, so that he can give battle to us once again."[11]

> And so [he continued] we trust firmly in God that He will continue to grant us His grace in the same way He has done up to now. And so we have now moved to the sea so that we can be resupplied from England, with men-at-arms as well as military equipment and other necessaries, because the journey we have made has been long and continual. But we have no thought of leaving the realm of France until we have made an end to our war, with the help of God.[12]

The next day, Michael Northburgh wrote that he had heard that the king intended to besiege Calais.[13] But the steps Edward took for this operation prove, as his own letter suggests, that the siege of Calais was designed primarily to draw Philip into a second battle to finish the war, and only secondarily to capture the town. The army the king gathered for the siege was very large, as noted above – on average, over the course of the siege, a third larger than the force commanded by the Black Prince at the battle of Poitiers, and doubtless much larger still at times.[14] Such a substantial army was hardly necessary to guard against sallies from the defenders, or even to encircle the land side of the

---

9 Cf. Villani, *Cronica*, 403: "The King of France after his defeat returned to Paris and summoned all his realm and his friends in order to gather more men than the first time [i.e. Crécy], to take vengeance on the King of England and raise the siege of Calais." I cannot agree with the assessment of DeVries, "Siege of Calais," 133, that "There was little prospect of a French relieving army arriving after the loss at Crécy." As the letters of Edward III cited below clearly show, a relieving army is precisely what Edward expected to face. Furthermore, Philip did in point of fact assemble a large relieving army, though it did not approach Calais until the very end of the siege.

10 *Cont. Manuel, 1339–46*, fo. 165v: "il fist telle forteresse de fossez et de paalis que nul ny pouoit entrer en son ost sans grant peril"; also *Chron. St. Omer*, fos 267, 271v.

11 Letter to Thomas Lucy, in Chandos Herald, *Black Prince*, 355.

12 Ibid.

13 Northburgh, in *Avesbury*, 369.

14 For Poitiers numbers, see below, p. 352; for Calais, see p. 274, above.

town to prevent it from being supplied or reinforced.[15] Edward's army could only have been intended to match a French relief army. This is confirmed by the writs the king sent to England, demanding reinforcements, "the King's enemy, Philip de Valois, having collected a great force at [Compiègne] to attack him."[16] Edward did not, however, send for help from his Flemish allies. "The King of England said that he had plenty of fighters and archers, enough to resist his adversary Philip . . . without the help of the Flemings," explains the *Chronicon comitum Flandrensium*, "and that he desired nothing else, except to be able to meet the French in battle anew."[17]

In the face of these preparations, and after the disaster at Crécy, Philip had no stomach for another fight. Calais was powerfully fortified –"one of the strongest towns in the world"[18] – and well garrisoned and supplied. It would be extremely costly to take by assault, if that were possible at all, and the marshy ground made mining or the use of heavy siege engines impossible. Gold was pouring out of Edward's pockets every day to pay for the siege. Thus, the French king could hope that the town would be able simply to outlast its besiegers, as Cambrai and Tournai had done – that Edward would give up or go broke and depart for England without the need to risk a battle. So Edward's hope for a rapid challenge from the French went unrealized.

But Philip underestimated his adversary's tenacity. Edward declared that "neither for winter, nor for summer would he depart until he had the town at his mercy, unless King Philip would come to combat him, and defeat him."[19] If Philip did not come and break the siege, Edward proposed to ride out in search of his adversary as soon as Calais fell. As he informed his parliament, he still intended to fulfill his earlier promise to pursue the war in France without returning to England until he had brought the conflict to a close.[20]

While he waited to see whether or not Philip would come to break the siege, Edward proceeded with such siege operations as could be carried out without

---

[15] Judging by the map in Sumption, *Trial by Battle*, 536, a mere 3,500 yards of trenches would have sufficed to enclose the town, even allowing a distance of 300 yards between the walls and the first trenches (for protection against the town's artillery). The town held only some 6–7,000 inhabitants of all ages and both sexes.

[16] Wrottesley, *Crecy and Calais*, 102–3.

[17] *Chron. Com. Flandr.*, 220: "Dicebat enim rex Angliae se habere pugnatorum et sagittariorum copiam sufficientem ad resistendum adversario suo Philippo, qui regnum Franciae sibi debitum injuriose et nequiter occupabat, et hoc absque adjutorio Flamingorum, et quod nihil aliud affectare, nisi quod denuo posset cum Gallicis ad proelium convenire." This was in response to rumors, in the fall of 1346, that Philip was preparing an army to rescue Calais.

[18] *Le Bel*, 2:110.

[19] *Le Bel*, 2:111: "Adonques assiega le noble roy la bonne et forte ville de Calais, et dit que pour yver, ne pour éste ne s'en partiroit tant qu'il l'eust à sa voulenté, se le roy Philippe ne se venoit la combattre à luy et le desconfit." Note also *Lescot*, 75.

[20] *RP*, 158. "Et que apres ceste Conqueste [de Caleys] il soi voleit trere devers son Adversaire en la pursuyte de sa querele, saunz retourner en Engleterre avant q'il eust fait fyn de sa guerre par dela, od l'eide de Dieu."

costing him the men he needed for the battle he hoped to have soon. He prepared a defended camp and slowly tightened his noose around the town until nothing could get in or out.[21] Both to supply his army and to harm his enemies, he plundered, burned and devastated the area for many miles around.

Philip tried everything he could think of to get Edward to abandon the siege. He sent an army into Flanders – the same plan he had considered but not implemented when the allies besieged Tournai in 1340 – and had it besiege Cassel. When the communes of Flanders sent an army led by Edward's loyal ally the Duke of Guelders, the French broke their siege and retreated to St. Omer rather than face battle.[22]

The French king also tried writing to his ally David King of Scots, begging him to invade England so that Edward would have to leave France.[23] Edward had plenty of advance warning of this threat, for even before the battle of Crécy the regent at Windsor was already expecting an invasion from Scotland.[24] Edward well realized the danger this posed, since "all the flower of the good chivalry of England" was with him at Calais or in Gascony with the Earl of Derby. But, determined to maintain the siege of Calais until Philip would have to give battle or see the city fall, the English king refused to deplete his army in France to protect the north of England.[25] In the event, this proved a wise decision. The Archbishop of York and the northern barons dealt with the invasion well enough: while Edward remained at Calais, they defeated the Scots at Neville's Cross, and captured King David himself in the process. Four other Scottish earls were captured, and the slain included two earls more and the constable, marshal, chamberlain and chancellor of Scotland.[26]

There is no need to describe the details of the skirmishes, *chevauchées*, small-scale naval combats, and other minor events which enlivened the siege of Calais.[27] The essential point is that Edward succeeded in cutting off all supplies coming into the town, until the inhabitants and garrison began to starve. Meanwhile, neither side did anything of great significance, though an English raiding force did manage to burn Thérouanne and capture Arnoul d'Audrehem.[28] It took a long time, but by late June of 1347 the defenders of the town were reduced to

---

21 See Sumption, *Trial by Battle*, ch. 15, for more detail.
22 Villani, *Cronica*, 403; but cf. *Chron. St. Omer*, fos 268v–272v.
23 Froissart, *Oeuvres*, 5:122; *Pluscardensis*, 292; Villani, *Cronica*, 40; *Knighton*, 2:41; *Pakington*, fo. 196v. Two of these letters may be found in *Hemingburgh*, 421–3. It should be noted that these are both dated before the beginning of the siege – before even the battle of Crécy. But doubtless Philip continued to encourage his ally to invade England after the opening of the siege.
24 *RFR*, III:1:89; *RS*, 674.
25 Froissart, *Oeuvres*, 5:122–3.
26 For the impression made by Edward's determination in the face of this invasion, see DeVries, "Siege of Calais," 137. On the Neville's Cross campaign, see Clifford J. Rogers, "The Scottish Invasion of 1346," *Northern History* 34 (1998).
27 There are many interesting details of these actions in *Chron. St. Omer*.
28 *Chron. St. Omer*, fo. 264v.

desperate straits. With a pathos only slightly tainted by melodrama, the garrison commander wrote to his king:

> Right dear and dread lord, know that, although the men are all well and of good courage, yet the town is in dire need of wheat, wine, and meat. There is nothing left which has not been eaten, not dogs nor cats nor horses; so that we cannot find anything to live on in the town unless we eat human flesh. Earlier you wrote that I should hold the town so long as there should be food. We are now to the point that we have nothing more on which to live. So we have agreed among ourselves that, unless we have succor soon, we shall sally forth from the town into the open field, to fight for life or death. For we would rather die honorably in the field than eat one another. Therefore, right dear and dread lord, apply whatever remedy shall appear appropriate to you; for, unless counsel and remedy are soon applied, you will never more have letters from me, and the town and we who are inside it will be lost. Our Lord grant you a good life and long and give you the will, if we die for you, to requite it to our heirs.[29]

The besiegers captured the message, and if Edward had been focussed primarily on taking the town, he could have simply kept it. Instead, he had it delivered to Philip under his privy seal, along with a personal message asking the French king to hasten to the Calesians' aid.[30] This provides clear evidence, were it in doubt, that Edward preferred another battle with Philip to a successful resolution of the siege.

The Valois was now faced with an unhappy choice analogous to the one the Scots had been forced to make in 1333: he could either launch a potentially fatal attack on a prepared English position, or else abandon his loyal servitors and subjects, losing the extremely valuable town of Calais, and giving the English a permanent foothold in northern France. Edward thought that Philip would make the former choice. He already knew that the French king had been preparing to gather a large army since May,[31] and may well have received reports describing King Philip's reaction to the news from Calais: he "was very distressed at heart, and said that he would never rest easy until he had rescued them."[32]

That army set out for Calais from Hesdin between 15 and 17 July 1347.[33] Edward's Flemish allies shadowed Philip's march, meanwhile rushing reinforcements (they had promised to provide the fantastic number of thirty thousand

---

[29] *Avesbury*, 386. On the hunger inside the town, cf. the *Grandes chroniques*, 9:311, and *Chron. St. Omer*, fo. 273v, which say much the same thing.

[30] *Knighton*, 2:48.

[31] In response, the king sent writs to the absent barons of England, asking them to join him without waiting for shipping for their horses. Wrottesley, *Crécy and Calais*, 121. On the large size of the French army, see DeVries, "Siege of Calais," 146, and *Chron. St. Omer*, fo. 275v ("fu son ost si tresgrant a raconter que merveilles seroit").

[32] *Chron. St. Omer*, fo. 274; cf. also fo. 275.

[33] On the 17th, Philip moved from Hesdin to Le Coupelle (*Itinerary*, 577), though *Chron. St. Omer*, 275v, which gives the main stages on the march correctly, has the army move out on the 15th.

men) into the English camp.[34] Ten days later the French host came within sight of the near-starved defenders, and of the besieging army. Both parties were over-joyed. The garrison expected imminent salvation, and Edward thought that he would at last have his battle, as he wrote to England:

> Our adversary of France has encamped with all his forces near Mountoire, which is only three French leagues from our host, and we can see their tents and lodgings from our said host, so that we hope that with the aid of our lord Jesus Christ we will soon have a good battle [*journée*] according to our just quarrel, to the honor of us and of all our realm, so we ask you to pray devoutly for us.[35]

Neither the besieged nor the besiegers would get their wish. When Philip arrived with his great army, intending to combat his enemy and break the siege, he sent his marshals to examine the English defenses. Edward was so strongly entrenched that, when they returned, they told their king briefly that there was no way even to approach the English "unless he wanted to suffer worse losses than at Crécy."[36] According to the *St. Omer Chronicle*, the French king was also taken aback by the strength of the Flemish army which had marched to support Edward.[37] Furthermore, the morale of his own troops seemed dangerously low.[38] So the most he could do was offer to parley.

Negotiations were held, but they came to nothing. At first, the French nego-tiators tried to make favorable surrender terms for the town a precondition of further peace talks. The English were not interested; they knew they would soon

---

34 This appears to be the meaning of Edward's undated letter, transcribed in *Lescot*, appendix VIII, which reads in part: "Et sachez que les gentz de Flandres containent tutdiz lor bon port devers nous et vuillent estre prest pour nous aider de trente mille persones et sur ce ils ont ja comencez de costeer nosditz enemys sur leur venue devers nous." The *Chron. St. Omer*, fos 275v–76, does claim that they did indeed bring 40,000, but cf. Verbruggen, *Art of Warfare*, 167.

35 Printed in *KdL*, 302: "nostre adversaire de France ove tut son poair s'ad herbergé de costé Mountoire qui n'est que trois lieuwes frauncèses de nostre host, et si poons bien veoir leurs tentes et leur logger hors de nostre dit host, sique nous espérons, ove l'aide de Nostre-Seigneur Jésu-Crist, sur eux hastivement avoir astive bele journée, selonc nostre droite querèle, à l'honnour de nous et de tut nostre roialme, pur quoi vous prions que dévoutement facés prier pur nous."

36 *Le Bel*, 2:157: "luy dirent à brefves parolles qu'il n'y avoit passage par où l'ost du roy poeut aprochier l'ost des Angloys, s'il ne vouloit mettre ses gens à perte mielx qu'ilz ne furent à la bataille de Cressy." It is significant that one of these marshals, Édouard de Beaujeu, had fought at Crécy, and would later (at Ardres in 1351) be one of the few fourteenth-century French commanders to defeat an English force in the field.

Note that this testimony undermines the contention of some pro-French writers (such as le Muisit and the *Chron. Normande*) that Edward used the three-day negotiating period to dig field fortifications for his army. It would in any case have been very odd if Edward, having failed to prepare a defensive position during the year he sat before Calais, would then sud-denly decide to do so after the French army's arrival.

37 *Chron. St. Omer*, fos 275v–76.

38 The men he summoned, according to *Cont. Manuel, 1339–46*, fo. 165v, came only "moult tardivement et preceusement."

enough have the town under any terms they wished. Philip's negotiators, after much prodding, eventually offered the restoration of Guienne and Ponthieu as fiefs in return for a general peace. Edward's negotiators dismissed this offer out of hand: it was "much too small."

Philip's next suggestion was rather more to the English liking: the French king offered to arrange a fight on a fair field. Edward could now see that the French would not be enticed into attacking his field fortifications, but he also had reason to be confident of the outcome of a fight even away from them. So, as he says in his letter describing the negotiations, he accepted.

The French king had most likely made his offer as a face-saving device, calculating that Edward would not be so rash as to abandon his strongly entrenched position when the town was already virtually his. But, as we have seen, the Plantagenet wanted a battle even more than he wanted Calais. The French negotiators, surprised by Edward's assent, backpedaled, trying to bring the surrender terms for the town back into the deal.[39]

Le Bel offers a contrasting account of the results of Philip's challenge to battle away from Edward's field fortifications. According to his chronicle, when the French offer was brought to Edward, the king responded

> I have been here for nearly a year, as he [Philip] saw and knew; he could have come sooner if he wanted to. But he has left me to remain here so long that I have had to spend largely of my own; and I think that as a result I shall soon be lord of the good town of Calais. So I am not advised to do everything as he wishes, for his convenience, or at his pleasure, nor to abandon that which I have conquered (or intend to conquer); and if he cannot approach [my army] by one way, he can approach it by another.[40]

When Philip received this word, he was greatly dismayed, "and no wonder, when he had gathered so many noble lords, from such distant lands, and yet saw that he would have to retreat without doing anything."[41]

This speech of Edward's, with its echoes of his letter of 15/17 August 1346 (see above, pp. 260–1), and indeed of the Scots' answer to his own similar proposal at Weardale in 1327, carries the ring of truth. But, though le Bel is well informed, he could hardly have known the situation better than Edward himself. It could be claimed that Edward, in his letter, was simply inventing his offer to accept Philip's challenge, for propaganda purposes. Considering the detail of Edward's letter, however, this would require wholesale fabrication on his part,

---

[39] The negotiations are reported in some detail in the letter of Edward III to the Archbishop of Canterbury, written immediately after Philip's departure, in *Avesbury*, 392–3; Cf. *Knighton*, 2:50–1.

[40] *Le Bel*, 2:158: "je suys ci, il a prez d'ung an, à sa veue et sceue; plus tost y fust venu, s'il eut voulu; mais il m'a lessé cy demourer si longuement que ge i ay despendu largement du mien, et cuide avoir tant fait que briefment seray seigneur de la bonne ville de Calais. Si ne suys pas conseillié de tout faire à sa devise, ne à son aise, ne à son plaisir, ne d'eslongier ce que j'ay conquis ou pensé à conquere; et s'il ne poeut passer par une voye, s'il voit par l'aultre."

[41] Ibid.

not merely putting a favorable slant on his reporting. Such an action does not at all fit with my understanding of the king's character; under the circumstances, and considering their histories and characters, I am much more prepared to believe that Philip would back away from a battle than that Edward would.[42]

The two accounts, however, can be reconciled. According to le Bel, the formal negotiations between the two sides began only *after* Edward made the speech described above. Edward may have refused Philip's initial offer hoping that the latter could be goaded to attacking the strong English position before Calais.[43] By the time the French brought up the proposal again during the formal negotiations, Edward had become convinced that Philip would let Calais fall rather than attack the English entrenchments. So, at that point, he accepted the offer (as he says in his letter) and issued safe-conducts for four French representatives to come to his army, to join with four of his own men to form a battlefield-selection committee. This reversal of his position would also explain the consternation of the French negotiators at his acceptance, who, "when they heard this response, began to change the terms of their offers, and to speak of the town all over again, as well as leaving aside (*entrelessant*) the battle, so that they would not stick with anything definite."[44]

The French wanted to bring up the town's surrender terms again, to which the English would not agree, so the discussions went no further. The next day, Philip, having been signaled by the garrison that the town was about to surrender, decamped before dawn and departed in haste, burning his tents behind him.[45] According to Gilles le Muisit's chronicle, immediately after the French king burned his camp and withdrew, word spread in his army that the King of England and his men were coming after them. Philip at that stage did

---

[42] Jonathan Sumption, however, doubts the veracity of Edward's letter, saying "no sensible person in Edward's strong position could have accepted" the French proposal. *Trial by Battle*, 580. The results of nearly every English fight with the French during Edward's reign suggest, however, that it would have been perfectly "sensible" for Edward to want to do battle with Philip here as well, even if he had to abandon his entrenchments to do so. Furthermore, Edward's agreement to give battle is reported in a number of other chronicles, including *Reading*, 104, and *Knighton*, 2:50–1, and (somewhat differently) *Melsa*, 3:66. Perhaps most telling in support of this version of events is the *English Brut* (544), which *criticizes* Edward for his response: Philip "sent to Kyng Edward, and askit hym whedir he durst feight with hyme the iij[de] day, about euensonge tyme, and leve the seege. And Kyng Edward onon, without eny counsaile or avisement acceptet gladly the day; and yette much of his pepill wer seke and ded on the fflux." The negative cast of this report makes it unlikely that the statement of Edward's willingness to fight was merely a loyal affirmation of the king's propaganda.

It should also be noted that in 1355 Edward was again willing to come out from Calais to do battle with the French – see below, pp. 301–303.

[43] Cf. *Chron. St. Omer*, fos 271v–72.

[44] Edward III in *Avesbury*, 393.

[45] *Avesbury*, 395–6; *Le Baker*, 90–1; *Le Muisit*, 182, *Chron. St. Omer*, 276–276v. See also the *English Brut*, 544: "When the Kyng of Fraunce wist verely that he [Edward] wold feight, with-out eny avisement or long tarying he sette his loggynges on fyre, and went cowarly his way," and Walsingham, *Historia Anglicana*, 1:271.

not stop short and prepare for battle; instead, he hastily retreated to Tournai.[46] This offers further evidence that Philip's earlier offer to give battle provided that Edward left his entrenchments was not sincere.

Seeing their king depart without having done anything to aid them, the despairing garrison sought terms from Edward. At first the king did not want to offer any terms: the citizens of Calais, by resisting so long, had cost him dearly of men and money. He thought they – the garrison in particular – should suffer equivalently. His advisors, especially Queen Philippa and Walter Mauny, eventually convinced him to cool his anger a little. If the garrison were executed for having done its duty by holding out so long, Mauny argued, then in the future Edward's own garrisons would fear to hold out against the French as long as they could, lest they too be executed. Heeding the advice of his counselors, the king eventually agreed to give the bourgeois and the garrison their lives, though the gentlemen in the garrison were held for ransom.[47] On 4 August he received the keys to the city.[48]

As Edward took possession of his prize, soldiers from his army harried Philip's retreating host. To make his hold on Calais more secure, Edward had those of the inhabitants who would not swear loyalty to him evicted, offering their homes and businesses to English émigrés. As he tried to decide what to do next, his first thought was to stay in France and launch a *chevauchée* "in order to win our war as quickly as we can."[49] Receiving word that Philip had issued summons for another army and intended to advance once again on the English (who were now much fewer in number, most of the army having returned to England after the conclusion of the siege), Edward took counsel with all the important men remaining in his court. With their advice, wrote Edward, "we have decided to do battle with our said adversary if he comes against us . . . and to make a *chevauchée* forward into the realm of France in order to recover our rights, and to take [whatever] grace and fortune which God shall give to us, if he [Philip] does not come."[50] He ordered that every soldier who could be found sail for Calais as quickly as possible.

---

[46] *Le Muisit*, 182.

[47] *Le Bel*, 2:160–7; *Chron. St. Omer*, fos 276v–77, adds an independent and more contemporary account of this famous scene, printed in Rogers, *Wars*, 143–4.

[48] Molinier, *Étude du vie . . . d'Audrehem*, 15n.

[49] Edward III in *Avesbury*, 393: "nous pensoms de chivaucher sur lexploit de nostre guerre si en haste com nous purrons, od leaide de Dieu." (Note that "exploiter" in medieval French means "to carry out," "to perform successfully," "to accomplish," etc. In this context, I have translated "sur lexploit ne nostre guerre" as "to win our war"; an alternate possibility would be "to carry on our war.") Cf. his plans at the very beginning of the siege (to take Calais and then pursue Philip to make an end to the war), in *RP*, 158, and the letter quoted in note 50, below,

[50] Letter of 6 September 1347, printed in *Le Bel*, 2:350: "Por ce que nous avons certeines novelles qe nostre adversaire de France, par cause qe doné lui est entendre qe grant partie de noz gentz sont departi de nous et retournez as parties d'Engleterre, fait assembler tout le poair qu'il poet avoir pur venir sur nous là ou nous sumes . . ., et nous pensantz ove l'eide de Dieu d'arester son compassement et malice en celle partie, par avis, conseil et deliberacion de tous

While he waited for the arrival of the French, and of his own reinforcements, Edward sent his captains out on a series of short raids – burning the town of Fauquembergues south of Calais, among other places – but one of the raiding parties, under the Earl of Warwick, was attacked and driven off with losses near St.-Omer. This fiasco, the loss of a supply fleet on its way to Calais, and the exhaustion of his men and his finances eventually convinced him that another great *chevauchée* was not immediately practical.[51] Furthermore, since Philip's new army failed to materialize, the Plantagenet's hope for another battle was dashed yet again. So, in mid-September, he agreed to a truce with Philip, to last until the following July. The terms, unsurprisingly, were very favorable to the English.[52] Then King Edward went home to London, where he was met by the rapturous citizens of his capital, and honored by his subjects all over the kingdom.

In the end, the English king had broken his promise not to leave France until he had brought the war to an end. King Philip still sat on his throne in Paris, still unwilling to surrender sovereignty over Aquitaine. But those who emphasize this side of the story, or suggest that the English "had achieved little of real strategic value in spite of the scale of their victory" at Crécy, are seriously underestimating Edward's accomplishment in 1346–47.[53] Jonathan Sumption has recently written that "Crécy was a political catastrophe for the French crown, but its military consequences were small because Edward III did not have the manpower to set up a permanent occupation in the territory through which he had passed."[54] This entirely misses the fact that one of the primary goals of Edward's military strategy was precisely to cause "a political catastrophe for the French crown," and that the strictly military consequences of the victory were themselves profound and lasting. Calais, which probably could not have been taken without the fight at Crécy, gave Edward the perfect base for future military operations against the Valois. Aiguillon had been relieved, and the main French army drawn away from the southern theater, freeing the Earl of Derby to *chevauchée* to Poitiers and back, capturing that city as well as Bourg, Blaye, Châteauneuf, St.-Jean-d'Angély, Lusignan, and half a dozen other important places.[55] A striking number of the Plantagenet's most dangerous enemies, from

les grantz esteantz de lez, nous avons pris certein acord de combatre ové nostre dit adversaire en cas qu'il viegne par devers nous en la manere susdite, et en cas q'il ne viegne point de chivaulcher avant en roialme de France pur nostre droit recoverir, et de prendre la grace et l'aventure qe Dieu nous dorra."

51 *Le Muisit*, 186–8; *Chron. St. Omer*, fo. 277v.
52 *RFH*, 3:1:20–2. The terms were favorable to the English mainly in that they solidified the gains recently made in the south by Henry of Lancaster, and in that they benefited the Flemings, Edward's allies.
53 Sumption, *Trial by Battle*, 532. See also DeVries, "Siege of Calais," 136, which cites some similar views.
54 Sumption, *Trial by Battle*, 532.
55 *Chron. St. Omer*, fos 266–66v has some interesting details on the Gascon war of this period, especially regarding the capture of Lusignan. See also the *Cont. Manuel, 1339–46*, fos 165–65v, and *Avesbury*, 372–4.

the King of Scots to John of Bohemia and Charles of Alençon, were dead or captured, unable to oppose him further. Froissart struck to the heart of the matter when he commented that because of the casualties suffered in the battle, "the realm of France was afterward much weakened in honor, strength and counsel."[56]

On the political level (which, properly speaking, cannot truly be separated from the military/strategic in war), the Valois monarchy was gravely weakened, already beginning to tumble down the rocky slope that would lead to the Treaty of Brétigny fourteen years later. Royal revenues collapsed as each town and region scrambled to prepare its own defenses.[57] Edward, by contrast, was at his personal aphelion. His soldiers had taken so much booty from the realm of France that there was hardly a lady in England without adornment of plundered French cloth or jewelry.[58] Some of his followers had overnight become fabulously wealthy, like Sir Thomas Holland who gained 80,000 florins for the ransom of the Count of Eu.[59] Partly in consequence, enthusiasm for the war ran high among the armigerous classes, and even among the common people – a marked contrast to their attitude in 1344. The Flemings were confirmed in their loyalty to Edward, despite the lavish economic and political concessions offered to them by a desperate King Philip. "To the English," wrote Thomas Walsingham, "it seemed almost as if a new sun had arisen, because of the abundance of peace, the plenty of material goods, and the glory of [their] victories."[60] Edward's prestige was so high that parliament would deny him nothing. Even an (arguable) majority of the Electors of the Holy Roman Empire offered him the Imperial crown not long thereafter, describing him as "the most worthy, most vigorous, most powerful knight in Christendom" – an offer he declined because he was too busy with his own affairs.[61] Truly it was, from the English point of view, a year of miracles.

At the parliament which met in March 1348, Edward gave ominous warnings

---

[56] Froissart, *Oeuvres*, 5:64–5: "la perte pour les François fu moult grande et moult horrible . . . par lesquels li royaumes de France fu moult depuis afoiblis d'onneur, de poissance et de conseil."

[57] See Sumption, *Trial by Battle*, 540, 560–1.

[58] Walsingham, *Historia Anglicana*, 1:272.

[59] Wrottesley, *Crecy and Calais*, 269.

[60] *Historia Anglicana* 1:272: "videbatur Anglicis quasi novus sol oriri, propter pacis abundantiam, rerum copiam, et victoriarum gloriam."

[61] *RFH*, 3:1:34; *Knighton*, 2:55; *Scalacronica*, 301; *Le Baker*, 97; discussion in Offler, "England and Germany," 628–30. Offler's claim that "Edward had in fact been disingenuous in pretending in May [1348] that he might still be ready to go on with the Wittelsbach scheme" is debatable, since it is not clear that Edward in fact did that. His letter of 10 May (*RFH*, 3:1:34) says he is sending representatives to answer the electors' proposal, but does not say what that answer was; it could very well have been a clear "no." Indeed, this seems most likely, since (as Offler says) after the message of 10 May was delivered, "Nothing more is heard of Edward's candidature."

that the French were not keeping the truce, and that they were in fact preparing an invasion of England.[62] He was probably preparing the way for another invasion of France in 1349, and another attempt to "make an end to the war by battle." Any ideas he may have had in this direction were thoroughly derailed by the Black Death, which struck England later in 1348. This gave the French something of a respite to recover from the war, though doubtless they would have preferred to have suffered from another of Edward's *chevauchées*. As it was, Edward III did not bring another army to France until 1355; but even then, despite the eight-year recovery period which the French had gained, it took only another five years before France was completely in shambles, and Edward had a treaty securing for him a third of France to rule as part of his own sovereign domain. The three years of campaigning it took to solidify his victory – 1355, 1356, and 1359–60 – will be dealt with in the next four chapters.

---

[62] *RP,* 200.

CHAPTER THIRTEEN

"GIVING THE FRENCHMEN SHARPER PROVOCATION TO FIGHT": THE TWIN *CHEVAUCHÉES* OF 1355

> *Boldness subservient to the direction of intelligence is the mark of a hero: this sort of boldness does not consist in making gambles contrary to the nature of things, in clumsy offenses against the laws of probability, but rather in forceful action in support of decisions made in accordance with higher calculations carried out lightning-fast and only half-consciously by Genius, which is the intuitive perception by the judgement of what is right.*   Clausewitz, *Vom Kriege*, III.vi.[1]

FOR EIGHT YEARS AFTER the fall of Calais, there was neither full war nor full peace in France. Despite intermittent renewals and revisions of the Truce of Calais,[2] there were skirmishes, raids, sieges, and ambushes; there were, however, no full-scale campaigns like those of 1339, 1340, or 1346. The general pause in the fighting was due in part to the impact of the Black Death, which struck in 1348. Perhaps even more important, though, was the hope that the war could be resolved, and a "proper peace" for England won, without further campaigning: that Philip's twin failures at Crécy and Calais had already done the trick.

The records of the peace negotiations in these years are scarce, and one authority has even questioned whether any significant activity took place.[3] Yet it is clear from reliable narrative sources that, with the encouragement of the Holy See, peace negotiators from the Valois and Plantagenet courts met at least occasionally over the eight years before the start of the negotiations in 1353 which led to the Treaty of Guînes.[4] While Philip of Valois lived, there was little hope of a compromise, though in 1348 there was some movement towards arranging a new battle to settle the outcome of the conflict. Unsurprisingly, it was the

---

[1] *Vom Kriege*, 267.

[2] *RFH*, 3:1:36, 44, 54, 60, 69–70, 72, 73, 82, 85.

[3] Palmer, "War Aims," 59: "During the next few years [i.e. 1347–53] an almost total obscurity descends upon the negotiations, an obscurity which may well conceal a lack of significant activity."

[4] *Le Baker*, 98, 100; Leland's summary of *Scalacronica* (ed. Maxwell), 116–17; *Knighton*, 2:58, 60; see also *RFR*, 3:1:39, 40–1, 44, 52, 53, 55, 56, 69.

French king who refused this proposal.[5] The basic problem remained the same as it had been since 1340: Edward would not give up his claim to the French throne for anything less than a restored Aquitaine held by him as an alod (i.e. in full sovereignty, not as a fief of the Valois monarchy); Philip was not prepared even to consider this possibility. But Philip died in 1350, to be succeeded by his son, Jean II (later known as "the Good," though it is doubtful that he deserved this appellation).

During the beginning of the new king's reign, the war did not go much better for the French than it had under Philip. At the end of Philip's reign, in late 1349 into early 1350, there had been a breakdown in the series of truces which had kept fighting to a minimum since shortly after the fall of Calais.[6] Henry of Lancaster took the opportunity to *chevauchée* up the Garonne all the way to the gates of Toulouse, laying waste a thirty-mile broad strip of French lands and capturing forty-two towns and castles on his way, and burning the city's suburbs when its defenders refused a challenge to do battle.[7] Around the same time, Edward III and the Prince of Wales foiled an attempt to capture Calais by treachery, in the process taking prisoner the leading knight of France, Geoffrey de Charny, and killing or capturing over two hundred other nobles.[8] Within a week of Philip's death in August of 1350, Edward followed up his personal victory at Calais with a naval battle off Winchelsea, where he inflicted a bloody defeat on a French-allied Castilian fleet.[9] Only in Poitou, where a personal quarrel drove Edward's erstwhile ally Raoul de Caours into the French camp and resulted in the death of Sir Thomas Dagworth, did events clearly favor the Valois.[10]

The next year an Anglo-Gascon force inflicted another serious defeat on a small French army at Saintes, capturing Marshal Nesle and Arnoul d'Audrehem, and killing or capturing another six hundred noble men-at-arms.[11] This did not prevent the Valois from recapturing St.-Jean-d'Angély and Lusignan, but, in return, towards the end of the year, the English established themselves in Rouergue, occupying St.-Antonin and Cas.[12] Also in 1351, Henry of Lancaster

5   *Le Baker*, 98; *Knighton*, 2:60.
6   There had also been an interval without a truce between 8 July and, apparently, 5 September 1348 (*RFH*, 3:1:20, 38, cf. 36), then another between 25 October and 13 November 1348 (ibid., 3:1:44). A truce was then extended until 16 May 1350 (ibid., 3:1:48). That truce, however, had collapsed by October 1349, apparently broken by the French, who besieged Tonnay-Charente. Fowler, *King's Lieutenant*, 85–6.
7   Ibid., 84–8; *Knighton*, 2:66; *Le Baker*, 108; *Jurades d'Agen*, 187, cf. 262.
8   *Avesbury*, 408–10; *Le Baker*, 103–7; *Historia Roffensis*, fo. 100.
9   Winchelsea [Espagnols-sur-Mer]: *Le Baker*, 109–11, *Knighton*, 2:67; Froissart, *Chroniques*, 4:88–98; *Historia Roffensis*, fos 100v–101.
10 Michael Jones, "Les capitaines Anglo-Bretons et les marches entre la Bretagne et le Poitou de 1342 à 1373," 365–6; Fowler, *King's Lieutenant*, 88–92.
11 Saintes: *Chron. Normande*, 97–8; *Avesbury*, 413; *Le Baker*, 115; Froissart, *Chroniques*, 4:107–8, 336; Burne, *Crecy War*, 232–3.
12 Lusignan and St.-Jean-d'Angély: Favreau, *Ville de Poitiers*, 156. St.-Antonin, Cas: DeVic and Vaissette, *Hist. Gén. Languedoc*, 9:641.

led a short but devastating *chevauchée* in Artois and Picardy, burning the suburbs of Boulogne, capturing many forts, and laying waste to le Portel, Etaples, Alette, Faucquembergues, Thérouanne, and on up to St.-Omer.[13] The small battle at Ardres, where an English raiding party of five hundred under John Beauchamp was defeated by a French force more than twice its size, did not suffice to compensate for these reverses, especially since Marshal Beaujeu was killed in the process of winning his victory.[14]

The year 1352 was even worse for Jean II: the key fortress of Guînes was captured by a surprise English escalade during truce-time (probably with the complicity of the garrison commander), and Walter Bentley led a small English force in defeating a much superior French army at Mauron in Brittany, where some forty-five members of Jean's new Order of the Star (a rival to the Garter) were killed or captured, along with almost eight hundred other men-at-arms.[15] In the south, the English held large areas of the Agenais, Périgord and Quercy, and the Valois situation seemed likely to get worse before it got better.[16] The small-scale warfare of this period was not benefiting the French, and there was every reason to expect that their situation would decline precipitously if Edward returned to active campaigning. The remarkable English record of success on battlefields large and small did not bode well for French prospects in the event of another set-piece combat, but what other choice was there for the Valois monarch if Edward did launch another Crécy-style *chevauchée*?

---

[13] Lancaster in Picardy: *Le Baker*, 115; *Knighton*, 2:68. In this *chevauchée*, Lancaster's forces also burned some 120 French ships in the ports along the coast, and brought a great deal of booty and raided cattle, along with many prisoners, back to Calais. Not long thereafter, around Lent, Walter Mauny and Robert Herle successfully led another substantial raid from Calais.

[14] According to *Le Baker*, 116, 1,500 French men-at-arms defeated 300 English men-at-arms and as many archers. *Knighton*, 2:86 gives the total number of French soldiers as 2,000 and lowers the number of English archers to 200. Froissart, in his detailed account in his third redaction, gives the English 300 men-at-arms and 200 archers, and in his first redaction gives the number of French troops as 420 men-at-arms and 700 well-armed "brigants." *Oeuvres*, 5:295–302. Leland's summary of the *Scalacronica* (ed. Maxwell), p. 117, says the French were "iiii tymes doble as many as the Englishce men." According to varying manuscripts of the *Chron. Normande*, 101–2, either 700 or 140 Englishmen were captured in this defeat.

[15] Avesbury, and Bentley in *Avesbury*, 415–17; the *Chron. Normande*, 105, which is in general less reliable than Avesbury, claims however that the English slightly outnumbered the French, 1,500 to 1,400.

[16] Breuils, "Jean Ier, Comte d'Armagnac," 47; DeVic and Vaissette, *Hist. Gén. Languedoc*, 9:637. In November/December 1352, the jurats of Agen wrote to the king and the Count of Armagnac that the town was in danger of being lost, because the state of the region was so bad that the common citizens were ready to flee to other areas if the war continued. See *Jurades d'Agen*, 260, 254–5; 262; 325–7; 246 and 279, 245, 219, 288, 308, 336. In January of 1353, they wrote to the newly elected Pope Innocent VI to describe "la paubretat en que [el pais] es per la guerra, ni cum se pert del tot, e que a luy plassa far patz entre lo Rey nostre senhor e l rey d'Anglaterra"; in August of the same year, they declared that all the other towns between the Lot and the Garonne had made *patises* with the English, and that they were ready to do so as well, since the king could not defend them, and the English daily harmed, captured and robbed them, so that they did not dare work their heritages. Ibid., 301–2, 328–9.

The political situation was no better for Jean than the military one. In the
wake of the battle of Winchelsea, the Castilians – perhaps the most important
allies of the French – agreed to a twenty-year truce with England.[17] This was
partly, but only partly, balanced by Jean's success in regaining the allegiance of
Louis de Male, Count of Flanders, who for a while had gone over to the English
side.[18] Meanwhile, two developments illustrated the strength of pro-English
feeling which Edward III's chivalry and prowess had encouraged among the
martial French nobility. First, Raoul, Count of Eu and Guînes and Constable of
France, returned from England where he had been a prisoner since 1346. He was
vocal in his praise of Edward III, who had treated him well during his captivity.
The constable may even have come to a secret agreement to support Edward,
since shortly after his return to his homeland he was arrested by King Jean and
shown a mysterious secret letter which induced him to confess to some sort of
treason (the details were not revealed), after which he was summarily beheaded
without trial, "because of which everyone was sad and angry, and the king
severely criticized and less beloved."[19] A similar situation arose when Thomas
de la Marche, Jean II's bastard brother, traveled to Westminster in order to fight
a judicial duel before Edward III. When Thomas, victorious, returned to his
half-brother's court, he too was full of praises for Edward's famous nobility and
justice. Although he also professed his loyalty to Jean, the French king was so
angry that he reportedly condemned Thomas to death for the crime of *lèse-
majésté*, though the sentence was not carried out.[20] But if a Constable of France
and a son of Philip of Valois were willing to praise Edward III's chivalry openly
at the court of Jean II, it left little room for the new king to employ the type of
cautious, Fabian strategy which had led to accusations of cowardice and
renardie ["foxiness"] against his father in 1339, 1340, and before Crécy. This
was all the more true because the people and the nobles of France, as Froissart
notes, blamed the king greatly, behind his back, for his tyrannical behavior.[21]
Another hard blow to Jean's position came somewhat later, on 1 March 1353,
when Charles of Blois (an English prisoner since the battle of Roche-Derrien in
1347) agreed to a settlement of Breton affairs which, had it been implemented,
would at minimum have made the duchy neutral in the Plantagenet–Valois
struggle, freeing up substantial English resources for use elsewhere, and which
at maximum could have made a reunited Brittany an active participant on

17 *RFH*, 3:1:70–1 (1 August 1351); *Avesbury*, 412–13; *Le Baker*, 116. Interestingly, Edward
in the treaty is titled King of England and France. The Anglo-Navarrese treaty in *RFH*, 3:1:70
(given as 1 August 1351) appears to be misdated.
18 Fowler, *King's Lieutenant*, 96–102, discusses this well.
19 *Le Baker*, 113–14, and see note, ibid. p. 283, against the rumors of an affair with Queen
Bonne as the cause of the execution; Knighton, *Chronicle* (ed. Martin), 122–4; Froissart,
Oeuvres, 5:303–6; *Le Bel*, 2:198–200 (quotation).
20 *RFR*, 3:1:199, 205; *Le Baker*, 112–14, 283; Froissart, *Chroniques*, 4:123–5.
21 Ibid., 125. Froissart also links the unjust treatment of the Count of Guînes with the sale of
the castle of the same name to the English in 1352, an example of the practical military consequences which could come from unpopularity.

Edward's side.[22] And, of course, all of this came in addition to the political and economic turbulence which swept through French society in the aftermath of the Black Death.

This appreciation of Jean's insecure military and political situation makes comprehensible what otherwise would be "the most mysterious episode in the entire war," as J. J. N. Palmer considered it to be: the negotiation of the draft Treaty of Guînes in 1353–54.[23] Not long after the French reverses at Mauron, Guînes and Agen (where in September 1352 Boucicaut was again captured in a skirmish, along with seven other Knights of the Star),[24] Pope Clement VI died, and Innocent VI was elected to replace him. Though Innocent leaned even more towards the French side than his predecessor had, he was eager to end the war between Valois and Plantagenet. His kinsman King Jean was equally anxious for peace, and encouraged the Pope to work for an Anglo-French accommodation. Since there seemed to be little chance that this could be achieved by a French military victory, Innocent and Jean were ready to pursue negotiations on the basis of a compromise which Edward III had suggested in 1340 and 1346: the English king would give up his claim to the crown of France, and would receive in exchange sovereign possession of the lands his predecessors had held in France.[25] The main benefit to be gained by the Valois king was simply peace.[26] The loss of some portion of his kingdom would guarantee that he would not lose all of it.

The negotiations began in the spring of 1353, and continued for a year.[27] Towards the end of that period, in early 1354, Jean's domestic weakness was made even more manifest when his vassal Charles the Bad, King of Navarre, Count of Evreux, and one of the richest nobles of France, flagrantly murdered Jean's favorite Charles de La Cerda (also known as Charles of Spain), the Constable of France; defied the Valois king; and sought help from the English.

---

[22] Bock, "Documents," Appendix I, esp. pp. 84–5. Note that the agreement was not ratified. Bock, p. 66, argues that Edward intended "to enter into an alliance with Charles de Blois and to make use of his assistance against the French King in the same way as he had used the help of his German allies some ten years earlier." This seems to me to be overstated. Clauses 2 and 3 of the treaty seem clearly to envision a neutral Brittany, with the duchy becoming an active participant in the fight only if Blois requested Edward's aid – presumably if Jean refused to accept Breton neutrality and attacked the duchy. The fact that Edward is referred to in the preamble as "Roi dengleterre," not "de France et dengleterre," indicates that the portion of clause 2 where Blois' aid against Edward's enemies is subject to the condition "sauuant sa ligeance et son honour devers autres" refers to Jean II. Cf. Robert of Avesbury's understanding: *Avesbury*, 418–19.

[23] Palmer, "War Aims," 58.

[24] *Le Baker*, 121; Devon, *Issues of the Exchequer*, 159; cf. *Jurades d'Agen*, 291, which suggests the Constable of France and the Count of Armagnac may have been involved in this fight as well.

[25] *Le Baker*, 123 (which specifies the Duchy of Aquitaine and the counties of Artois and Guînes); Bock, "Documents," 70 and 70 n.8.

[26] Note the parallel with the Treaty of Northampton in 1328.

[27] It seems that in September 1353 the citizens of Agen were aware of the possibility of a peace or long truce being made soon. *Jurades d'Agen*, 330.

In March, Jean managed to patch up this dangerous breach by the Treaty of Mantes, in which he pardoned the King of Navarre for the constable's death and gave him extensive lands in Normandy – most of the Cotentin – in place of lands Charles should have inherited but which the Valois kings had thus far kept in their own hands.[28] Then, on 6 April 1354, at Guînes, the diplomats of Jean II and Edward III sealed a draft treaty for perpetual peace. The terms (which were ratified, on the French side, by the Archbishop of Rouen, the bishops of Beauvais and Laon, the king's chamberlain, and two other nobles) were a triumph for Edward III.[29] He was to receive, as alodial possessions without obligation for homage, the Duchy of Aquitaine, the counties of Poitou, Touraine, Anjou, Maine, Ponthieu and Limousin, and the Calais Pale. These territories comprised roughly three times as much land as Edward had held in France at the beginning of his reign. Furthermore, a firm treaty of friendship was to be made between France and England, and any other alliances which would impede it were to be cancelled and annulled by the Pope – a provision which was apparently directed at the reciprocal elimination of the Franco-Scottish and Anglo-Flemish alliances.[30] Edward had gone to war with Philip VI in 1337 over Scotland, over French interference in his government of Guienne, and over French refusal to return the portions of Aquitaine conquered by Charles of Valois in the War of St. Sardos and promised to him in the treaty of 1329: all three of these issues were, by the draft treaty, to be resolved entirely in Edward's favor, and extensive areas which had not been in English hands since the days of King John were thrown in for good measure. In short, if this treaty had been ratified, Edward III would have finally succeeded in winning his war with France and would have been well positioned to return to the subjugation of Scotland.

The fundamental reason for these concessions was of course the crushing French defeat at Crécy, and indeed the Treaty of Guînes is perhaps the strongest retort to those who depict the 1346 *chevauchée* as strategically barren.[31] While the agreement was not in fact ratified in 1354–55 (representatives of both sides, the English ambassadors equipped with documents empowering them to renounce Edward's claim to the throne once the treaty was ratified, came to Avignon in the middle of winter, but at the last minute the French proctors renounced the agreed-upon terms[32] – doubtless inspired by the Count of Armag-

---

28 For these events, see Delachenal, *Histoire de Charles V*, 1:71–87.

29 For a contrary view, that "It was the English, not the French, who had been brought to a surrender" with the Treaty of Guînes, see Fowler, *King's Lieutenant*, 128–43, quotation at 130.

30 The draft Treaty of Guînes is transcribed in Bock, "Documents," Appendix II. On the cancellation of alliances, cf. article 31 of the Treaty of Brétigny (*RFH*, 3:2:5).

31 This surrender may have been, as Perroy remarked, "flagrant," but it was not also "gratuitous": Edward III's harsh and skillful campaigns had made peace necessary, even at a high price. *Hundred Years War*, 129.

32 Letters of Edward III in *RFH*, 3:1:109, 122 (especially telling); Bock, "Documents," 76–7, 94–7; *Avesbury*, 421; *RP*, 264; *EMDP*, 297, 298; Knighton, *Chronicle* (ed. Martin), 126–7. The commonly-held view that the English were responsible for the failure to ratify the peace is incorrect; see the discussion in Rogers, "Anglo-French Negotiations."

nac's impressive turning of the tide in Gascony[33]), the Treaty of Brétigny which closed the first phase of the war in 1360 followed the same general outlines. The Crécy *chevauchée* had brought Jean II to the edge of an agreement to surrender a sovereign, expanded Aquitaine and to abandon the Scots, but it took the additional pressure of the 1355 and 1356 campaigns to push him over. After all, he may have reasoned, if he chanced another battle and won, the situation would be redeemed, and if (as perhaps seemed more likely) he lost, he could hardly be much worse off than if he sealed the Treaty of Guînes.

From the English standpoint, Jean's renunciation of the tentative agreement was a disappointment, but one for which there was an obvious remedy. The success of the English war effort had clearly almost persuaded Jean of the need for peace at any price; what was therefore called for was active campaigning in France to remind the Valois king just how high the cost of continued warfare would be. Since it had not been possible to make peace at Avignon, Edward is said to have remarked, he would make war in France more vigorously than ever before.[34]

The simplest way to take the offensive on the Continent would be to launch a *chevauchée* from Calais, but in the aftermath of the collapse of the Guînes agreement, an even more promising alternative presented itself. The scheming Charles of Navarre, not content with the gains he had made with the Treaty of Mantes, secretly approached the Duke of Lancaster in Avignon and offered to assist the English in bringing down the Valois monarchy. Since Charles, like Edward himself, had a claim to the French throne through his mother,[35] he proposed to divide France with the Plantagenet.

---

[33] The advantage on the Agenais front in 1353 had not gone clearly to either side – the English took Lusignan-Petit near Agen, Beauville, and several surrounding places, and the larger town of Ste-Livrade-sur-Lot, and repeatedly raided the environs of Agen; the French besieged St.-Antonin in Rouergue and Féneyrols in the Agenais, captured and destroyed Monbalen, and retook Clairac. In 1354, however, things went all in the French favor, with the submission of the lords of Beauville, Roquecor, and Seysses, and with the recapture of Monsempron and Port-ste-Marie in January and Tournon, Madaillan, Prayssas, and – most important by far – Aiguillon in June. Breuils, "Jean Ier," 45–52; DeVic and Vaissette, *Hist. Gén. Languedoc*, 9:645–6. It is highly significant that one of the French ambassadors at Avignon was in fact Count Jean. *Knighton*, 2:78.

[34] Froissart, *Chroniques*, 4:134.

[35] It is often remarked, indeed, that Charles' claim was better even than Edward's: both were direct descendants of Philip IV, and Charles' descent was through Philip's eldest son (Louis X, whose sole progeny was Joan, Queen of Navarre, mother of Charles), while Edward's was through Philip's youngest daughter, Isabella. E.g. cf. Perroy, *Hundred Years War*, 128. This is poor logic, however: Edward's claim was based on the simple fact that at the time of the death of Charles IV in 1328, he was the deceased king's closest male relative (the equivalent of which, incidentally, was also John of Montfort's grounds for claiming Brittany, though Edward has sometimes been accused of hypocrisy for supporting Montfort); since Charles of Navarre had not been born at that time (much less at the time of the death of his grandfather, Louis), he was ineligible for the succession. The English case is given, quite elaborately, in *EMDP*, 434–52, esp. 438, 451–2. It is worth noting that as impartial an observer as

Since Charles controlled the Cotentin and several key towns in Normandy (including Evreux, Pont-Audumer, and Breteuil)[36] this gave Edward the opportunity to begin a new campaign there with the base which he had attempted to establish in 1346 already prepared for him. Charles could also supply a welcome, though not a great, accession to the forces Edward would have available to fight the second Crécy which might develop from a new *chevauchée* in the duchy.[37] Thus, the English king began to prepare for a substantial expedition under his own command to go to Charles' assistance in Normandy.[38]

Within a few weeks of these developments, a delegation of powerful Gascon noblemen arrived in London to argue that when the truce expired in midsummer of 1355, Edward should take the offensive in the south of France, rather than (or

St. Brigitte of Sweden concluded that Edward's claim to the throne was superior to Philip's: Cazelles, *Société politique*, 72–3.

36 According to Contamine, *Guerre de Cent Ans*, 36, his holdings in Normandy after the February 1354 Treaty of Mantes amounted to "half of Normandy."

37 In 1356, Philip of Navarre brought 100 local men-at-arms to serve on Lancaster's Norman *chevauchée*, in addition to the garrisons the Navarrese were maintaining in various places in Normandy.

More important than the men-at-arms, it was anticipated that the Navarrese would arrange horses for Edward's men, so that they could economize on shipping and load their vessels only with men and supplies. *Avesbury*, 425; *Anonimalle*, 33.

There was also, of course, the potential that Charles' kingdom of Navarre in the Pyrenees, and his powerful ally the Count of Foix (Froissart, *Chroniques*, 4:131), could help in the Guienne theater.

38 There is a widespread belief that the English plan for 1355 called for *three* expeditions: the Black Prince's from Guienne, Henry of Lancaster's to Normandy, and Edward III's from Calais. E.g. see Burne, *Crécy War*, 246; Prestwich, *Three Edwards*, 179. This is however incorrect. Only two armies were originally planned; the Calais expedition was essentially a redirection of the Normandy force undertaken when (as will be explained below) the English learned that Charles of Navarre had betrayed them. King Edward had definitely planned to command the Normandy expedition himself – just before the fleet sailed out of the Thames in July, he made preparations for the government of his realm during his absence, and Walter Mauny's speech to parliament in November makes it clear that it was the king's own fleet which sought unsuccessfully to sail to Normandy in July and August. [*RFR*, 3:1:305]; *RP*, 264. However, it may be that this was kept secret in order to confuse the French. It was the Duke of Lancaster's streamer, rather than the king's, which flew from the mast of the flagship of the fleet in the Thames, and even a source as well informed as Robert of Avesbury thought that the fleet was Lancaster's (even though he noted that the king was "in mari cum dicto duce"). *Avesbury*, 425–6. Cf. *Knighton*, 2:80; *Le Baker*, 125.

Some historians have also followed Froissart's assertion that Edward III planned to lead an army to Normandy himself, send the prince to Gascony, and send a third force of 500 men-at-arms and 1,000 archers under Henry of Lancaster to Brittany. This seems internally credible, and is lent some support by the fact that the king appointed Lancaster his Lieutenant in Brittany in mid-September. Froissart, *Chroniques*, 4:135–6; *RFH*, 3:1:112–13. This, however, is so late that it seems probable that, upon learning of Navarre's defection, Edward considered sending the forces he had gathered to Brittany under Henry, but then decided instead to take them (and Lancaster himself) to Calais. Note that while Froissart lists the lords gathered for the armies of the prince and the king, he does not give any names for Lancaster's force.

as well as) the north. In Guienne, since the departure of the Earl of Lancaster in 1351, the war had not gone badly for the Plantagenet cause, but neither had it gone especially well. The battle of Saintes had been won that year, but the town of St.-Jean d'Angely had been lost. Count Jean I of Armagnac, King Jean's lieutenant in Languedoc, had launched several devastating raids into regions held by men loyal to Edward III, counterbalancing the Anglo-Gascons' frequent raids in the Agenais. In the summer of 1354, however (after the initial agreement on the Treaty of Guînes) the French turned the tide of the struggle in the region with an unbroken string of successes, recapturing a number of Plantagenet strongholds: Prayssas, Tournon, the Albret stronghold of Madaillan, and also (most seriously) the key fortress of Aiguillon at the Lot-Garonne confluence.[39] This was a disappointing epilogue to the impressive Anglo-Gascon successes gained under the leadership of Henry of Lancaster in 1345–47 and 1349.

The Gascons wanted more than fiscal and military support from England: they also wanted a captain of the king's own blood, preferably the Prince of Wales himself. The prince was twenty-four years old[40] and already a mirror of chivalry and a heroic figure for his much-publicized feats at the battle of Crécy, on tournament fields, in the fight at Calais in 1350, and at the battle of Winchelsea. He was generous, proud, forceful and fierce, characteristics well suited to the leader of an Anglo-Gascon *chevauchée*. What is more, he was as eager to go to Guienne as the Gascons were to receive him.[41]

In early April of 1355, the king held a Great Council at Westminster. Two cardinals who had come to press for an extension of the truce were firmly informed that previous truces had been abused by the French, to the great harm of Edward's subjects and adherents on the Continent, and that the king did not intend to grant another. No: since Jean had refused peace, he would have war.[42] The same council agreed that the prince should go to Gascony with the earls of Warwick, Suffolk, Salisbury and Oxford, a thousand men-at-arms, two thousand English archers, and a large number of Welshmen.[43] The king's own expeditionary force, envisioned as the main campaigning army, was to be two or three times larger, partly because the prince would be able to gather far more local

---

[39] Breuils, "Jean Ier," 48–52; *Jurades d'Agen*, 328–9, 352–7. The *Chron. Pays-Bas*, 178, also notes the fall of the castles of Lusignan (which had earlier been recaptured by the English in June 1353: *Jurades d'Agen*, 353) and "Lendin" and many others.

[40] The same age Edward III had been in 1337, by which time he had already won the battle of Halidon Hill and brought Scotland to the verge of subjection.

[41] Chandos Herald, *Vie du Prince Noir*, 63.

[42] *Avesbury*, 425 (council, cardinals, truce); *RFH*, 3:1:122 (refuses truce); [*CCR 1354–60*, 210] (war).

[43] *Avesbury*, 424; cf. Chandos Herald, *Vie du Prince Noir*, 63–4. The number actually sent was probably somewhat smaller, perhaps 1,000 men-at-arms, 1,000 horse archers, 300–400 foot archers, and about 170 Welshmen. Hewitt, *Black Prince's Expedition*, 20–1.

reinforcements.[44] If all went well, both armies would be under way in time to reach France not long after the expiration of the truce on 24 June.[45]

Considering the brief gap between these decisions and the scheduled departure times, delays for gathering ships, provisions and troops were remarkably short. For twenty-three years the royal administration had been organizing military activity on a nearly annual basis; the success in readying two separate armies for a quick departure from England shows that the experience had borne some fruit in the area of improved efficiency and competence. Fortunately (as it turned out) for Edward III, that competence did not extend to controlling the weather, and contrary winds kept the two fleets bottled up in port for weeks on end.[46] Only with difficulty was the king able to take his ships from Greenwich (which they reached around 10 July) to Sandwich and Portsmouth, where they remained immobile until 15 August. A major effort then took the fleet up to Winchelsea and the Isle of Wight. From there they made several more attempts to reach France despite strong storms and rough waters, but each time they were driven back to England.[47] The prince's fleet, meanwhile, sat frustrated and bored in Plymouth harbor, waiting for better weather.[48] Favorable winds finally rose, and the ships bound for Bordeaux took the open sea on 9 September.[49]

Meanwhile, while King Edward's fleet remained stuck in Portsmouth waiting for its own favorable winds, the situation in France changed dramatically. Some of Lancaster's spies, who had been sent to check out the situation in Normandy, returned with startling news. The King of Navarre had made peace with Jean II, and was planning to lead the English army into a trap. Cherbourg, where the Plantagenet fleet was expected to land, had been packed with thousands of men-at-arms ready to ambush the expeditionary force.[50] Even once this plot was discovered, the large numbers of French troops sent to garrison the ports of Normandy made a landing there impractical. On 12 September the

---

44 The prince's force in 1355 was roughly half Gascon; the king's comprised about 2,000 English men-at-arms, 1,000 more from Flanders, Brabant, and Germany who assembled at Calais, 2,000 horse archers, and about 4–5,000 foot archers and heavy infantry (hominum armatorum). *Avesbury*, 428; *Knighton*, 2:84; *Le Bel*, 2:212.

45 *Avesbury*, 421; *Récits*, 274.

46 *Register of Edward, the Black Prince*, 3:493.

47 *Avesbury*, 425–6.

48 Hewitt, *Black Prince's Expedition*, 38–40, demonstrates that much of the delay in the prince's departure was the result of delays in finding and readying sufficient naval transport, but none of his evidence shows that the fleet was not ready to depart by early August, a month or more before it actually sailed. Thus we can accept the chroniclers' statements that contrary winds delayed the prince.

49 *Black Prince's Expedition*, 40.

50 Spies, trap: *Avesbury*, 426. Date: the *Anonimalle*, 32, has Edward delayed by contrary winds for eight weeks, which would be until around 4 September. The Treaty of Valognes between Charles of Navarre and Jean II was sealed on the 10th. On the 12th, King Edward announced that he would sail for Calais on the 29th. Since Charles and Jean had been negotiating for some time before the ratification of their treaty, Edward could well have gotten word of their rapprochement even before the 10th. It would be interesting to know if Charles' betrayal was discovered before or after the prince's departure on 9 September.

expedition was called off. But, as Jean le Bel remarks, Edward did not leave
matters so, as he wanted to get some use out of the army he had readied for
action.[51] The king dismissed his men, who were worn out from their long time at
sea, so that they could get some rest, but he ordered that they hold themselves in
readiness to rejoin him for an expedition to Calais, which was to leave on Michaelmas (29 September). Since that would give time for the fleet which had
carried the prince to Gascony to return to England, the expedition would be
freed from the extremely tight constraints on shipping which had previously
held. Edward therefore sent for the horses and other equipment which according
to the original plan would have been left behind.[52] "And I want it known
throughout France," he proclaimed, "that soon I will arrive there, and do battle
with King Jean, and lay waste the land as far forward as I can."[53]

The subsequent campaign has been a source of puzzlement for many historians,[54] perhaps because many of them have accepted Jean II's perspective on
it rather than Edward III's.[55] When considered in the context of Edward III's
strategic history, however, the 1355 Picardy *chevauchée* comes into clearer
focus. It was meant simply as a gauntlet thrown down before Jean II, a challenge
to battle, as the 1339 campaign had been a challenge to Jean's father. Jean was
more concerned with the forms of chivalry and knightly virtue than his father
had been, as the creation of the Order of the Star attests. It would be going too
far to call him bold, but neither was he burdened (or blessed?) by the caution
bordering on timidity that Philip VI had displayed. Furthermore, by rejecting the
Treaty of Guînes, the Valois had implicitly announced that he was ready for a
fight. As we have seen, Edward III was never one to shy away from a full-out
combat, and, having assembled an army capable of doing battle, he wanted to
make sure that his adversary would have a chance to attack it. Sir Walter Mauny,
acting as the king's prolocutor, said as much to parliament shortly after the end
of the campaign:

> because he could not have the peace, and the said alliance [with Charles of
> Navarre] could not be maintained, and also because his adversary was making
> himself strong with men-at-arms and others on the marches of Calais, our
> same lord [King Edward], thinking to have a battle there quickly, arranged
> with his said navy and people to cross the sea towards Calais. After which
> passage . . . he began to lead them out of Calais on November second, and
> made his way into the realm towards the places where, by spies and otherwise,

---

[51] *Le Bel*, 2:211; *Récits*, 276–7. 12 September: *Avesbury*, 427.
[52] *Avesbury*, 427. The passage to Bordeaux took about eight days (Hewitt, *Black Prince's Expedition*, 40, 42). Horses, equipment: note 37, above, and Froissart, *Chroniques*, 4:138.
[53] *Le Bel*, 2:211; cf. *RP*, 264.
[54] Burne, for example, called it the "most baffling campaign of the whole war," though in fact he seems to have understood it fairly well. *The Crecy War*, 248.
[55] As usual, many of the historians who have considered the campaign have refused to accept Edward's statements that he was seeking a battle in this campaign. E.g. Delachenal, *Histoire de Charles V*, 1:129; Tourneur-Aumont, *Bataille de Poitiers*, 386.

he understood that his said adversary then was, as he wanted to have a battle with him.[56]

The army sailed for Calais in late October, arriving around the 26th. For four days the troops disembarked their horses and rested from the journey.[57] A thousand men-at-arms from Flanders, Brabant, and Germany, who had heard the news of Edward's intentions, were waiting there to join his army: a sure sign both of Edward's extraordinary martial renown, and of the profits which his campaigns were expected to bring to participants. These men brought his total strength up to some ten thousand soldiers: three thousand men-at-arms, two thousand mounted archers, and the rest foot archers and other infantry.[58] Shortly after his troops had recovered from their transit and the volunteers had been integrated into the army's structure, Edward heard the news that King Jean had come to Amiens with a very large army. The English king thereupon announced that "he would go to those parts and show him [Jean] the flames and smoke of his country."[59] So, on November second, he took his army the short distance from Calais to Guînes. Once he had come near Ardres, the next day, he began to burn and lay waste the land, as always on such operations.[60] [Map 13-1] After the invaders were safely past, the large French garrison of the town, under the command of Marshal Audrehem, issued out from its base to harass the English rear and prevent supplies from reaching them from Calais.[61] Another detachment of French troops withdrew in front of the English advance, carrying out a classic scorched-earth policy to further exacerbate the invaders' supply problems.[62]

Though Edward's army was much smaller than the main French force, he was anxious for battle.[63] At first it seemed that King Jean shared this attitude.[64] As his enemies marched to Alquines, and from there southeast, he sent Sir Jean le

---

56 The last phrase, "s'il voleit aver eu la bataille ovesque lui," is translated loosely. *RP,* 264. Note also *Avesbury,* 427.

57 *Le Bel,* 2:212.

58 Numbers: *Avesbury,* 428; cf. *Knighton,* 2:84, *Le Bel,* 2:212. Avesbury notes that the infantry included 500 uniformly clad archers sent by London at the city's own expense.

59 *Le Bel,* 2:212; cf. *RP,* 264.

60 Ibid.; *Le Bel,* 2:213; *Anonimalle,* 33; *Avesbury,* 428.

61 1,000 men following three leagues behind the English, according to the *Récits,* 277, 279. Cf. Froissart, *Oeuvres,* 5:329.

62 *Avesbury,* 428–9: "Johannes . . . cum suo exercitu retrocessit et, praecedens regem Anglie, in quantum potuit, devastavit victualia, ne Anglici uterentur eisdem." Cf. *Le Baker,* 126, and *Knighton,* 2:84.

63 *Le Bel,* 2:213: ("si vouloit combatre au roy de France et à toute sa poissance enmy son pays"); *RP,* 264. On the size of the French force, cf. *Récits,* 278–9.

64 And, indeed, it even seems so in retrospect, despite the outcome of the campaign. After the fact, Jean wrote concerning Edward's departure: "Unde tacti dolore cordis intrinsecus tanto sit dolor noster acerbior quanto majori fraude fuimus hostium nostrorum non solum ibi set alibi circonventi, dum idem Rex Anglie, qui fingebat se eodem tempore animo bellandi venire . . . bellum ex parte nostra sibi et suis instanter oblatum respuens, eo vitato . . . in Angliam celeriter retrocessit." Quoted in Delachenal, *Histoire de Charles V,* 1:129n; cf. 128–9.

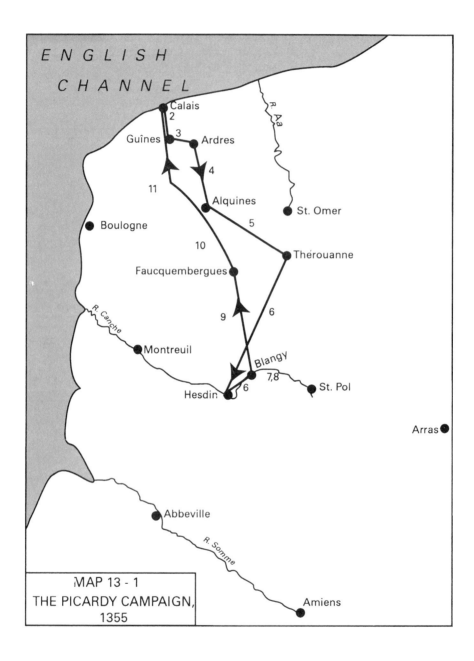

E N G L I S H
C H A N N E L

Calais
2
Guînes   3   Ardres
4
11
Alquines
Boulogne   5   St. Omer
10
Thérouanne
Faucquembergues
9   6
R. Canche
Montreuil
Blangy
7,8
6   St. Pol
Hesdin   6
Arras
R. Aa
Abbeville
R. Somme
Amiens

MAP 13 - 1
THE PICARDY CAMPAIGN,
1355

Maingre, called Boucicaut, who had been captured not long earlier in Gascony and released on parole, to visit Edward's army. The *Scalacronica* says that the knight had been ordered to deliver a formal challenge to battle, and to negotiate for a time and place; Avesbury says merely that he came to examine the strength and order of the invaders' force.[65] Probably he was doing both.[66]

Boucicaut encountered the invaders' army not far from Thérouanne, on 5 November. He was brought before King Edward, who greeted him gracefully and asked for news of Jean. Boucicaut replied that he thought the king was at Amiens (just where he had been when Edward left Calais.)[67] "Holy Mary!" exclaimed King Edward in surprise and annoyance. "Why is he waiting for me there, when he has so great a force and sees his land burned and devastated by so few men?"[68]

Edward did not want to leave the French king with any excuse for avoiding a battle. He called over three of his knights and ordered them to lead the Frenchman through all of the English forces, so that he could accurately tell the French king the size of the army opposing him. Boucicaut was impressed by the quality of the English troops – "martial men, ready for battle and wonderfully spirited"[69] – but surprised by their small number.[70] The next day, as the army lay waste to the land around Hesdin and Blangy,[71] without hearing any news of the Valois, Edward called Boucicaut back before him. "Sir Boucicaut, do you know what you shall do?" he asked.

> I know well that I could have more than 6,000 écus for your ransom, if I wished. You go say to your lord that I have burned his country up to here, because I thought he would come to extinguish the flames. And tell him I will wait here for three days, so he will find me if he wants to come; and if he does

---

65 Leland's notes of the missing portion of the *Scalacronica* (ed. Maxwell, pp. 118–19): "apon this King John of Fraunce, sumwhat to redubbe the rebuke of King Edwardes acts in his realme, sent his marescal to King Edwarde, that he should apoint a day by gages." This is supported by *Nangis*, 229. See also *Avesbury*, 428.

66 Froissart's claim that Boucicaut was simply returning himself to captivity because he had not raised his ransom seems somewhat unlikely, though perhaps that is because of modern bias. *Oeuvres*, 5:324–5.

67 I.e. over 50 miles road distance away. The date, like all the dates I give in this section, is based on the presumption that the stages noted by the Bourgeois de Valenciennes correspond to daily marches (with a three-day halt, as reported by le Bel, at Hesdin-Blangy); since this works out perfectly with the known starting and ending dates of the expedition, this calculation seems justified. *Récits*, 277–9.

68 *Le Bel*, 2:213. Cf. *Avesbury*, 428. The surprise and annoyance are my inference. The former may have been due to the English belief that King Jean was personally leading the force which was conducting a scorched-earth withdrawal before Edward's army. Ibid.

69 *Avesbury*, 428: "viris utique strenuis et ad proelium promptis et mirabiliter animosis."

70 *Le Bel*, 2:213; however, *Avesbury*, 428, has Boucicaut surprised at the power of the English force, considering the other army in Gascony.

71 *Récits*, 279. Avesbury describes the position as "ultra villam de Hoden versus Amyens." *Avesbury*, 429. Note that this represents a fairly long march generally *towards*, not away from, King Jean's reported position.

not come, I'll return the way I came . . . If you will pledge to bear this message just as I have said it to you, I will quit you of your ransom.[72]

The three-day interval was carefully calculated to allow just enough time for Jean to move his army to Edward's position, providing he acted promptly and with vigor on receiving the knight's message.[73] It was also the longest amount of time Edward could practically allow to his rival, for already the English troops were running seriously low on supplies. They had already run out of wine that day.[74]

For the three promised days (6, 7, and 8 November), Edward remained in the vicinity of Blangy, only a few miles from the future battlefield of Agincourt. The French army, however, did not show; it seemed that the famous Valois aversion to battle had once more come to fore.[75] This perception may not have been very accurate: it appears that Jean, rather than being averse to battle, was simply not ready for it, since his army was not yet fully assembled.[76]

Disappointed, but probably not very surprised, Edward decided to return to Calais. The season was late, and the French forces in the area had been very successful in their efforts to prevent the English from supplying themselves adequately. For the whole of the waiting period, the Plantagenet troops had been reduced to the unhealthy practice of drinking water, for they were unable to secure any wine, and food was also scarce.[77] Edward, as Mauny said to parliament, had at first expected his invasion to sting his adversary into giving battle quickly; now that this expectation had been dashed, there was insufficient reason to prolong the campaign.

Still, the English king knew that he had not left Jean much time to respond to his challenge, and so there continued to be hope that the Valois might still be persuaded to give battle. Thus, the invaders fell back at a moderate pace; some troops swung west to take advantage of the relatively unspoiled lands around Boulogne, while others apparently took a more direct northerly route.[78] During the retreat, Edward did not cease "laying waste to all the country, so that he

---

[72] *Le Bel*, 2:214. Cf. the similar account in Froissart, *Oeuvres*, 5:325, 327–8. Froissart exaggerates the duration of Edward's stay at Blangy.

[73] Allowing one day for Boucicaut to travel the 40 miles to Amiens, and two days for the army to make the return trip. Such a pace would leave the French soldiers very tired by the time they reached the field, and might require Jean to leave his slowest troops behind – offering significant advantages to Edward. Cf. *Récits*, 279.

[74] *RP*, 264; *Knighton*, 2:84.

[75] *Avesbury*, 429: "videns vecordiam sui adversarii eventum belli expectare nolentis"; *Le Bel*, 2:214; *RP*, 264. Many historians (e.g. Favier, *Guerre de cent ans*, 191) have accepted Jean II's claim that this offer to await the French was a mere deception, but there is no real support for this belief.

[76] Froissart, *Oeuvres*, 5:328.

[77] Ibid.; *RP*, 264; *Knighton*, 2:84.

[78] *Avesbury*, 429 and *Le Bel*, 2:214 (Faucquembergues-Boulogne); *Récits* (Faucquembergues-Alquines), and Froissart, *Oeuvres*, 5:329, for the more direct route.

would be giving the Frenchmen sharper provocation to fight."[79] By Wednesday 11 November, the invaders were back in Calais.

The English must have received some indication that this provocation was having an effect, for when Edward reached his base his council advised him to camp in the fields outside the strong city walls and await the coming of the French army.[80] The accounts of this campaign from the French side are very poor, but from letters written by King Jean after the fact it appears that he was almost as eager for battle as was his adversary, and that his failure to meet the invaders around Blangy had been due more to inability to act with the requisite speed than desire to avoid a fight.[81] Thus, when apprised that the Plantagenet had not sought refuge behind the walls of Calais, King Jean sent Marshal Audrehem to deliver a challenge to battle. His council, reasonably enough, felt confident that Edward would accept.[82]

Marshal Audrehem carried the French king's message to Calais without delay, arriving on Thursday the 12th.[83] In the presence of the Duke of Lancaster, the Earl of Northampton, and Sir Walter Mauny, he informed King Edward that Jean was willing to do battle on the following Tuesday, the 17th (an interval which would have given him plenty of time to gather in all the French forces in the region, and the reinforcements still trailing in from the summons to Amiens), provided that Edward would fight on a fair field away from Calais. The English lords responded with a counter-proposal: in order to avoid the shedding of Christian blood, as much as possible, Edward would fight Jean one-on-one in a sort of judicial duel to determine which of them had the better right to the realm of France. Or, if Jean preferred, the two kings could be joined by their eldest sons, or by an additional two, three, or four noble knights, chosen from among their closest relatives.[84] In any case, the loser would surrender his right to the French throne to the victor. This offer may seem quaint, almost absurd, to a modern reader, but it should not be seen as a mere bit of chivalric frippery, a propaganda ploy, or even a cynical attempt to match men acknowledged as among the best knights in the world (as Edward III, the Black Prince, and Henry of Lancaster all were) against a family not quite their match in the arena of arms.[85] Edward III, so far as we can tell, was a sincere Christian, if not

---

79 *Reading*, 122: "totam patriam supponens vastitati ut gentem Franciae acrius provocaret ad pugnam." *Le Bel*, 2:214; *Avesbury*, 429.

80 *Récits*, 279; cf. *Le Bel*, 2:215 (on the provocation).

81 See the letters excerpted in Delachenal, *Histoire de Charles V,* 1:128–9, and also *Récits*, 279 and Froissart, *Oeuvres*, 5:326, 329.

82 *Récits*, 279.

83 *Avesbury*, 429.

84 *Avesbury*, 429–30; *Le Bel*, 2:215 and Froissart, *Oeuvres*, 5:326, 330 (fair field). Froissart, *Oeuvres*, 5:330, has the French side lead off with an offer to fight on a mutually agreed-upon field with either the full armies, or 100 against 100, or 1000 against 1000. This is certainly possible.

85 Of course, if Jean had opted for the combat involving the eldest sons, it would have had to have been delayed until the Black Prince could be recalled from Aquitaine. In this context it is

a very sophisticated one, and high chivalry was almost a second religion for him. The resonance of his offer with the latter belief-system is obvious, as is its relation to the ancient judicial custom of trial by battle. But Edward's proposal was also, in his terms, a deeply Christian act. If Jean accepted – and even more so if he agreed to a duel of family against family – it held out a reasonable possibility, though not a guarantee, of resolving the issue of the war without the slaughter, rape, devastation, destruction of churches, and other evils which inevitably came with the prosecution of war (especially when that war was conducted primarily by means of *chevauchées*). Even more important, Edward was falling back on the old conception of "trial by battle" as an appeal to the court of God, an opportunity to let Him issue a judgement between them. There can be little doubt as to how the Plantagenet thought Heaven would rule: he had, after all, chosen *Dieu et mon droit* as his motto.[86]

Whether less certain of divine favor, less confident in their king's knightly prowess, or simply aware that the proposed stakes were unbalanced (since Jean was asked to risk what he already held, whereas Edward only put up what was so far a largely unrealized claim), the French negotiators turned down the English proposal, and reiterated their initial suggestion. The Englishmen expressed willingness to do battle, but declined to grant the French so much time to prepare. They offered to fight on the next day, Friday, or the day after.[87]

Once again the French rejected this proposal, insisting that they would not be ready to fight until Tuesday. It began to seem to the English that the Valois representatives were not sincere in their expressed desire for a battle, but rather were simply trying to get Edward to bankrupt himself by the useless expenses of keeping an army under arms while they prevaricated and delayed.[88] Perhaps they remembered King Philip's expressed intention to use just such a strategy against the Count of Hainault fifteen years earlier.[89] There was also a risk that French stalling and the onset of winter would make the Channel uncrossable and leave Edward and his men stuck in Calais.[90] To guard against this possibility, the English negotiators put forward a proposal which took the French completely by surprise. They would agree to the date which King Jean preferred, but with a special condition added to guarantee that the French really did mean to fight: the

worth noting, however, that King Edward had brought two of his teenaged sons (probably Lionel of Antwerp and John of Gaunt) along on the expedition. *Le Bel*, 2:215.

[86] Furthermore, his three earlier appeals to the divine court (Halidon, Sluys, and Crécy) had all gone in his favor.

[87] Ibid.; cf. *Le Bel*, 2:216, who has the English declare that they do not wish to fight at the convenience of the French, who had already been given an opportunity to do battle, especially since the English troops had been tired by their exertions. According to Froissart, *Oeuvres*, 5:326, the Valois army was at this point encamped on the heights of Sangatte, so Edward's suggestion for a battle within the next two days was not impossible.

[88] *Avesbury*, 430, and cf. *EMDP*, 298, for the Englishmen's general perception of French dishonesty in negotiation.

[89] Froissart, *Oeuvres*, 3:192–3.

[90] *Le Bel*, 2:214.

negotiators on each side would offer themselves as hostages. A group of experienced knights from both sides would jointly choose a fitting battlefield, and if, on the agreed upon day, King Jean did not appear there ready for battle, then the French hostages would surrender themselves to the English as prisoners of war. The English hostages would be bound by the same terms to surrender themselves if King Edward failed to show.[91]

The details of these negotiations are reported only by an English source – the well-informed Robert of Avesbury – and he does not give the exact words of the proposal. It seems very likely, however, that the English negotiators framed their offer in such a way that the burden of action was explicitly or implicitly put on the French, that in other words the English would only have to offer battle, whereas the French would have to take the tactical offensive and deliver it. The tactical offensive was generally considered a tremendous disadvantage by late-medieval soldiers,[92] a view which Edward III's successful defenses at Halidon Hill and Crécy had strongly reinforced. King Jean, it seems, was eager to face King Edward on the battlefield, and would doubtless have been overjoyed if the English had been willing to abandon their proven tactical system and assume the burden of the offensive; but he was not willing to be put in a position where he would be virtually compelled to charge a steady English army positioned to receive his attack. The French negotiators, after a brief consultation among themselves, rejected this proposal too. The Englishmen made one last try, offering to set 25 June as the day of battle (which would certainly have given plenty of time for Jean to prepare, but would also have allowed Edward the chance to return to England and gather a whole new army); this offer found no more favor than the others.[93]

That was the end of the discussions. It had become clear that the French were not willing to give Edward the kind of battle he wanted, one in which he would be able to receive a French attack and make full use of his English archers' skills. The king had, furthermore, learned by this time of the recent *coup de main* by which the Scots had captured Berwick.[94] Once he realized that he was not going to get a fight on his own terms in France, he grew anxious to get back to England and deal with the situation in the north. So he gave his final answer to the French representatives: "During the ten days when I *chevauchéed* in France and lodged before Blangy, I sent to inform him [King Jean], as you know, that I wished only for battle. Now other news has reached me; so I will not fight at the convenience of my enemies, but according to the desires of my friends."[95] The English unilaterally announced that they would stand ready for battle on the

---

91 *Avesbury*, 430.
92 See my "Offensive/Defensive in Medieval Strategy."
93 *Avesbury*, 430.
94 Froissart discusses this rather circumstantially, saying the news arrived on the same day the French brought their challenge (*Oeuvres*, 5:330), and it would be surprising if such important news took more than a week to reach the king at Calais. Note also Knighton, *Chronicle* (ed. Martin), 136.
95 Froissart, *Oeuvres*, 5:331. Cf. *Le Bel*, 2:215–16, and *Récits*, 280.

day which the French had chosen but, since nothing more was said about a joint commission to choose a battlefield, this meant that they would hold a strong defensive position, most likely the very one chosen by Edward III when he expected the arrival of Philip VI's army outside Calais in 1347.[96] So, says Avesbury, "the King of England waited there until the said Tuesday; no Frenchmen came."[97]

Edward immediately discharged the foreign soldiers in his army, giving them their wages and various bonuses, and hastened back to England to deal with the Scottish situation.[98] The whole expedition to Picardy had lasted barely over two weeks, but in that time, according to the *Scalacronica*, the English had burned out several hundred parishes.[99] They had also bearded King Jean in his own realm, making him appear to be as reluctant to face the test of battle as his father had been. These accomplishments sufficed to ensure that King Edward returned to his realm "much praised."[100]

*

Substantial though the damage done to the realm of France by Edward III's Picardy campaign was, it could not begin to compare with the havoc wrought by the Black Prince's army during the Languedoc *chevauchée* which was going on at the same time. Over the course of eight weeks, Prince Edward's little Anglo-Gascon army traversed the breadth of France, from Gascony to the Mediterranean and back, pillaging and burning a broad band of Valois lands on either side of its advance, striking, says Robert of Avesbury, "a severe blow against the inhabitants of all the lands from Bordeaux up to Narbonne, up until then not in the obedience of the King of England (excepting, just as is appropriate, the people of the lands of the Count of Foix, who freely received him, and those of Juliac, who surrendered themselves to the prince)."[101]

This "severe blow," as Avesbury's careful caveat suggests, was delivered with a certain precision, so as to maximize its utility as a tool of Plantagenet policy. Edward III's own vision of the strategic purposes of the *chevauchée*, as expressed in the letter of 1346 discussed in Chapter 11, provides an ideal lens through which to examine the Black Prince's *grande chevauchée* of 1355. As we have seen, the English king, in response to Philip's challenge to do battle at an appointed place and time, declared that he was continuing his *chevauchée* in order "to punish rebels against us and to comfort our friends and those faithful

[96] *Avesbury*, 430.
[97] *Avesbury*, 430; cf. *RP*, 264, and *Récits*, 280 (Jean "ne se osoit partir de Saint-Omer").
[98] *Avesbury*, 430; Nicolas, *Controversy between Scrope and Grosvenor in the Court of Chivalry* (London: Samuel Bentley, 1832), 2:198; *Récits*, 280. Most likely Edward could not have returned any earlier in any case, since it took time to gather shipping for the crossing.
[99] 700 according to *Scalacronica*, 303 (Leland's summary of the missing portion). This seems exaggerated, however, and may be a mistranscription of the missing original.
[100] *Avesbury*, 431.
[101] *Avesbury*, 432.

to us, whom you falsely claim as your subjects . . . [and] to carry on the war as best we can, to our advantage and the loss of our enemies." These – and of course also the desire for a decisive battle on favorable terms which always characterized the English approach to strategy in this period – were the same considerations which guided the Prince of Wales in the conduct of his first independent campaign.

"To comfort our faithful friends" was the first goal to emerge as the prince and his Anglo-Gascon council planned their expedition out of Bordeaux; "to punish rebels" proved to be the obverse of the same coin. As noted above, one of the main reasons the Gascon lords had applied to their king-duke for aid and a leader was because of the incursions into English-held Guienne conducted by the Count of Armagnac, Jean II's lieutenant in Languedoc. With the reinforcements which the prince had brought from England, the Gascons felt themselves strong enough to retaliate for the damage they had suffered, and they were most anxious to do so.

Thus, the County of Armagnac became the first target for the destructive energies of the Anglo-Gascon forces.[102] Departing Bordeaux on 5 October, the six thousand or so men of the prince's army[103] followed the Garonne southeast up to Langon, where they turned directly south to reach Bazas, a substantial town (and episcopal seat) at the edge of the Landes. [Map 13-2] The French probably expected that the prince's men would from there turn southeast, skirting the edge of the wastelands, to advance through Casteljaloux to Aiguillon at the confluence of the Lot and the Garonne, and from there into the Agenais.[104] The regions south of the Garonne had seen little action thus far in the war: of Henry of Lancaster's major operations, for example, only the raid of late 1349 had been directed south of that river. Since the earl's departure, the French had recaptured the strategic strongpoints of Aiguillon and Tonneins, and it would not have been surprising if the prince had directed his efforts towards recovering those key positions, rather as Jean of Normandy (now King Jean) had done in 1346 at Aiguillon.

But, as noted above, the prince's initial strategy was not focussed on *places*,

---

[102] Armagnac was still the commander of the main French army in the region, and it may well be that a secondary reason for beginning the campaign by devastating his lands was that such a course would help to provoke the count into giving battle. Certainly this route was *not* chosen, as Breuils thinks, because the prince feared an encounter with Armagnac. "Jear Ier," 56.

[103] About 1,000 English and 500 Gascon men-at-arms, 2,000 English archers, and 2,000 Gascon light infantry (*bidaus*), plus the "varlets" whom the Gascons brought, according to Froissart, *Oeuvres*, 5:344; over 6,000 total according to *Vie du Prince Noir* (ll. 643–4).

[104] This was such a natural presumption that Froissart even after the fact assumed that this was what the English had done – he has the English cross the Garonne at Porte-Ste.-Marie just south of Aiguillon. The Count of Armagnac almost certainly was operating under the assumption that the English campaign would take this direction, for he had stationed himself at Agen (not far up the Garonne from Aiguillon), around the time the prince left Bordeaux. Breuils, "Jean Ier," 54.

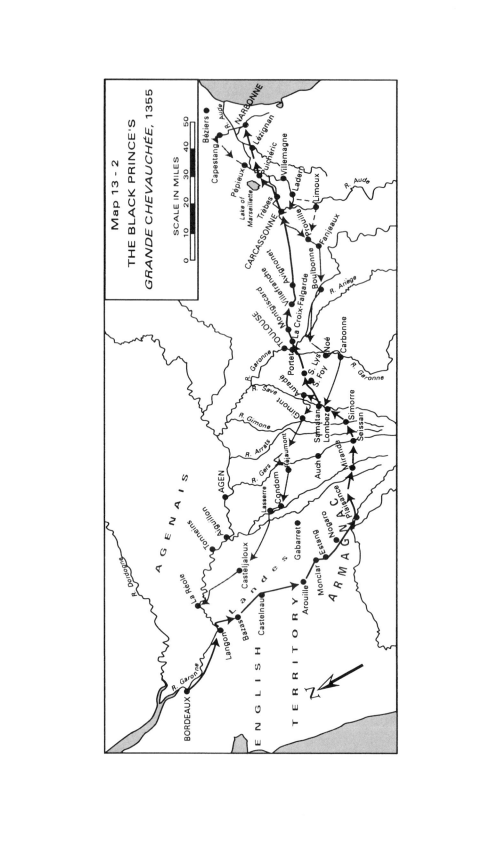

Map 13 - 2
THE BLACK PRINCE'S
GRANDE CHEVAUCHÉE, 1355

SCALE IN MILES

0 10 20 30 40 50

but rather on *people*: friends to comfort, and rebels and enemies to punish. His blows would be aimed to strike those who had most harmed the English position in Gascony, and also to land where they would have the biggest impact.[105] Thus, after a day's rest, Edward led his troops directly south from Bazas, to Castelnau in the middle of the desolate Landes. From there, a single hard march brought the army up to the southern edge of the moorlands, poised to break into the rich and fertile county of Armagnac. There the Anglo-Gascon leaders divided their forces into the usual three battles and unfurled their banners in sign that they were about to enter hostile territory and to begin making war.[106] The vanguard was placed under the Earl of Warwick and Sir Reginald Cobham (the constable and the marshal of the host); the prince commanded the center; the earls of Salisbury and Suffolk had charge of the rearguard.[107]

The first stronghold on the road leading out of the Landes was the castle of Arouille. Guillaume Raymond, its captain, had already been engaged in secret negotiations with the English. At the prince's arrival, he promptly surrendered the castle and three nearby towns under his control, including Juliac, and became a "loyal Englishman." The army lodged for the night in these four places, which since they had willingly returned to the prince's obedience were spared from destruction.[108] Those who wished to do so made forays from the encampments of the main army to collect provisions, forage, and plunder from the more recalcitrant inhabitants of the area, partly for their own profit, partly in order to do "in general all they could in order to bring the countryside to [King Edward's] peace,"[109] by punishing the people for what the Plantagenets considered their rebellion.[110] The Anglo-Gascon army spent the next twelve days, from 12 to 23 October, destroying the lands of the Count of Armagnac with careful

---

105 Froissart (*Oeuvres*, 5:339) notes that they struck a land "where the English had never been before."

106 On the significance of banners, see Keen, *Laws of War*, 106–7. The march from Castelnau to Arouille, covering nearly 25 miles in a single day, caused the loss of numbers of horses. *Le Baker*, 128. It was probably pressed so hard for two reasons: first, so that the army would not have to camp for the night in the relatively inhospitable Landes, and, second, to insure that their strike against Armagnac would have the benefit of an initial surprise.

107 *Le Baker*, 129 (cf. 296–7), gives this information and more. The first division also included Lord Beauchamp of Hache, Sir Roger Clifford, Sir Thomas Hampton, seneschal of the Landes, and seven unnamed Gascons as bannerets. The prince's division also included the Earl of Oxford, Lord Burghersh, Lord Lisle, Lord Willoughby, Lord de la Warr, Sir Maurice Berkeley, Lord Bourchier, Lord Roos, the Captal de Buch, the Mayor of Bordeaux, the Sire de Caumont, and the Sire de Montferrand as bannerets. The Sire de Pommiers accompanied the two earls in the rearguard. It is interesting to note that the expedition thus included nearly a third of the Knights of Garter. Cf. also Froissart, *Oeuvres*, 5:343.

108 *Le Baker*, 129; Black Prince, in *Avesbury*, 434 [Juliac]. Hewitt makes no mention of this. It seems likely that the other two were Mauvezin-d'Armagnac and Créon d'Armagnac, which – along with Arouille and Bellevue – had been occupied by the French shortly before the start of Edward III's reign. Chaplais, *War of St.-Sardos*, 258.

109 *Le Baker*, 129.

110 This whole area had been part of the English duchy of Guienne up until 1307.

thoroughness.[111] "At this," as the prince later wrote to the Bishop of Winchester, "the liegemen of our honored lord, whom he [Armagnac] had previously harmed, were much comforted and reassured."[112]

By the time the Plantagenet troops had completed their west–east traverse of Armagnac on the 23rd, they had occupied (aside from Arouille and Juliac) Monclar, and burned Gabarret, Estang, Panjas, Galiax, Mirande, and the rich town of Plaisance, among many other places.[113] The possessions of the Church – notably the town of Bassoues, which belonged to the Archbishop of Auch, and the great Cistercian monastery of Berdoues – were spared from destruction by the prince's concern; a few of the stronger places of the region, such as Nogaro, were saved by their own strength.[114]

From Armagnac, the Anglo-Gascon forces entered the County of Astarac, finding it mostly abandoned in advance of their approach. The prince, like his father, was a firm believer in seeking a decisive battle (provided he would be able to fight it on his own terms),[115] so after burning the "wealthy and well-stocked" towns of Seissan, Simorre, Villefranche, and Tournan, along with Samatan, a larger center, he turned sharply northeast in the direction of Toulouse, where the count was reported to be assembling an army.[116] Having reached Ste.-Foy and St.-Lys on the 26th, Edward sent out detachments to burn the suburbs of Toulouse (only fifteen miles away), to see if King Jean's lieutenant would venture out from behind its walls, and to scout for a crossing over the Garonne in case he would not. Although his leading elements fought well in a skirmish with the French just outside of Toulouse, they were not able to burn the built-up areas outside the town walls, for the simple reason that the burghers of the city, at Armagnac's order, had already done so themselves, so that the Plantagenet army would not be able to profit from them or use them as bases for an assault on the city. According to Froissart, no fewer than three thousand houses went up in flames in this incident.[117]

Toulouse was one of the greatest cities of France, described by contempo-

---

[111] Black Prince, in *Avesbury*, 434. Careful thoroughness: From the 12th to the 22nd, the Anglo-Gascon troops advanced only about 25 miles. Between the 23rd, when they passed out of Armagnac, and the 26th, they covered 30 miles. See also the list of places destroyed in Breuils, "Jean Ier," 55 n.3.

[112] In *Avesbury*, 434.

[113] Ibid., and list in Breuils, "Jean Ier," 55 n.3. The document he quotes now seems to be lost.

[114] *Le Baker*, 130.

[115] The course of the campaign, described below, shows he was anxious to come to grips with Armagnac's army. In general, cf. *Chron. CCCO*, fo. 179, and *Chron. Anon. Cant.*, 195–6.

[116] Itinerary: *Le Baker*, 129–31; Wingfield, in *Avesbury*, 440. It is worth noting that Seissan, the first town entered in Astarac, was burned "against the Prince's strict orders." Le Baker does not explain why the town was to be spared. Samatan: Black Prince, in *Avesbury*, 434. Armagnac in Toulouse: Ibid. Froissart, *Oeuvres* 5:344, claims that the Anglo-Gascon army had Toulouse as its destination right from the start.

[117] Itinerary: *Le Baker*, 131. Skirmish, suburbs: Froissart, *Oeuvres*, 5:339, 344–5.

raries (with some exaggeration) as "not much smaller than Paris,"[118] and packed with troops – mainly the untried men of the city militia, but also a substantial force of men-at-arms and professional soldiers under Armagnac's command. The constable, Jacques de Bourbon, and Marshal Clermont were with the royal lieutenant.[119] Such numerous defenders, if fighting behind walls to compensate for their lack of skill, would be formidable indeed. In the open country, however, Prince Edward knew that his army's greater skill and experience would make it more than a match for the raw levies of the Toulousain. Thus, on the 27th, the prince drew up his three divisions in full battle array and marched them under their battle-standards into the fields outside the city.[120] At the same time small groups of outriders set fire to all the surrounding countryside, to encourage the people of Toulouse to issue out and defend their lands.[121] The men of the city were ready to accept his gambit and do battle, but King Jean's lieutenant forbade them, observing that they were not as accustomed to arms as the Gascons and the English: it would be enough, he said, for them to defend the walls of their city.[122] The recent desertion of several companies of Italian mercenaries in his employ may have been decisive in convincing him that it would be unwise to give battle.[123]

Another reason for Count Jean's unwillingness to risk the uncertainties of a general engagement was that he appeared to have effectively blocked the Anglo-Gascon army's advance without the need to fight.[124] He had broken all the bridges over the Garonne except those of Toulouse itself, and the river would be virtually impossible to ford if the crossing were opposed. Downstream from Toulouse, all the major crossings as far as Tonneins (past Aiguillon) were in French hands. Thus, presuming that the count proved able to avoid the sort of error that had allowed Edward III to get across the Seine at Poissy in 1346, the invasion would be contained, and the prince left with little choice but to turn back towards Bordeaux.

---

118 Froissart, *Oeuvres*, 5:344.

119 Breuils, "Jean Ier," 57.

120 Froissart, *Oeuvres*, 5:345.

Hewitt, *Black Prince's Expedition*, 57, sets this episode after the crossing of the Ariège and describes it as follows: "An attack on Toulouse from the south may have been considered and rejected. Some slight demonstration (probably a reconnaissance in force) within view of the city walls was apparently made, and there was pillage and burning in the locality." But Froissart is clearly describing a formal offer of battle, with the three English divisions arrayed in full battle order, not a mere reconnaissance in force, and it only makes sense that this challenge would have been offered before rather than after taking the risks of crossing the rivers.

121 This is implied in *Le Bel*, 2:220: the English "firent leurs batailles assez prez de la cité de Thoulouse et ardirent tout le pays d'entour, que oncques nul n'issy de Thoulouse pour le deffendre."

122 Froissart, *Oeuvres*, 5:345. *Le Bel*, 2:220, says that Armagnac, Bourbon, Clermont, and the other lords sent by King Jean to the area had four times more men-at-arms than the prince at this stage. Cf. n. 174, below.

123 Breuils, "Jean Ier," 57.

124 *Le Baker*, 131: "gentes illius terre . . . se putantes per aquas istas securos."

Unfortunately for the French, however, the English were by then past masters at the art of river-crossing, and Count Jean was even less on his guard than King Philip had been. The summer had been an unusually dry one, and the river waters were at their lowest level in twenty years. This gave the prince an opportunity which his own decisiveness allowed his enemies no time to counter. On 28 October, the day after the demonstration before the walls of Toulouse, he pushed his men over previously unknown fords over both the Garonne (just above Portet)[125] and also the Ariège, at Lacroix-Falgarde. None of the local people had anticipated the possibility of a crossing because the Garonne was "swift, rocky, and absolutely terrifying," and the Ariège was even worse. No one had ever taken horses across there before.[126] The whole operation took place within an hour's hard ride from Toulouse, but the army was across before the French were able to mount any opposition.[127] The difficult crossing cost the Anglo-Gascon army a few lives, but it put the prince into a new region, one where the inhabitants had believed themselves secure from the ravages of war. The people here hardly knew what to do when faced with the unaccustomed threat of an advancing army. Their fortifications were mainly of earthwork, and often in poor repair where they existed at all. From here, as the prince later wrote, "not a day passed when we did not capture towns, castles and fortresses."[128] Hewitt is right to point out the boldness of this stroke, but his claim that the prince's decision to bypass Toulouse and leave a hostile force in his rear was "contrary to military prudence" and "audacious to the point of the foolhardy" exaggerates the danger Armagnac posed. The prince was sufficiently confident in his army's military superiority to trust it to fight Armagnac's force either then or later, and the danger posed by an enemy in his "rear" was a very different thing than it would be in later eras, when an army had to be supplied from its base of operation. Living off the land, the prince had no real "lines of communication" to be "cut." There might be some risk that the French would be able to use the Garonne to trap the invaders and prevent them from returning home, but if he was able to cross it moving eastwards, why would he not be able to do the same when returning west? Even if the French were by then better prepared, the prince's experiences of 1346 had shown him how effectively

---

[125] Froissart, *Oeuvres*, 5:339 gives the crossing point as "Port-Sainte-Marie dallés Toulouse." He is probably conflating Portet and Porte-Sainte-Marie, the strong bridge-town just above Aiguillon. *Parvus Thalamus*, 351, is clearer: "passeron los Engleses Girona sobre portel."

[126] *Le Baker*, 131: "rigidam, petrosam, et mirabiliter terribilem."

[127] Portet is about five miles upstream from Toulouse, Lacroix-Falgarde about seven miles. The prince and le Baker thus understated the distance when they, respectively, described the fords as "one league above Toulouse" and Lacroix-Falgarde as one mile from Toulouse. But the crossing cannot have been closer to Toulouse than Portet, unless the course of the river has greatly changed since then, since from there the Garonne and the Ariège flow together. The army may have crossed the Ariège some small distance downstream from Lacroix-Falgarde, which is where they lodged for the night (*Le Baker*, 131).

[128] Inhabitants: *Le Baker*, 131. Fortifications: Letter of the seneschal of Carcasonne in *Hist. Gén. Languedoc* 9:655; Froissart, *Oeuvres*, 5:345; Black Prince, in *Avesbury*, 434.

his English archers could clear away the defenders of a ford or a repaired bridge, as they had done at Poissy and Blanchetacque.[129]

At first the locals' lack of experience with war led them to overestimate their own ability to resist the invaders. At the town of Montgiscard, the first[130] place Prince Edward came to after Lacroix-Falgarde, the inhabitants were prepared to defend their earthen walls. But the English recognized the weakness of the fortifications, and decided to launch an assault. They knocked breaches in the walls and attacked from all sides. The defenders put up a good fight, wounding many of their enemies with arrows and stones, but were soon overwhelmed. The men-at-arms of the Anglo-Gascon army, unenthusiastic at the risks posed by close-quarter fighting and by the possibility of fire, largely stood aside and let the light troops sack the town. This they did with all the brutality to be expected of a medieval army taking a defended town by storm: many noncombatants were killed, everything of value was seized, and what was left was put to the torch.[131]

The next day, after passing through Baziège and Villefranche (which were pillaged) the army reached Avignonet, a substantial cloth-producing town belonging to King Jean. The fifteen hundred houses of the unwalled town provided lodging for the army, though the prince, in accordance with his usual custom, stayed in a tent in the field. Most of the inhabitants had fled, but many of the richer bourgeois had taken refuge in the hill-fort outside the town; like the inhabitants of Montgiscard, they were placing an undue reliance on earthwork walls. Once again the English archers cleared the ramparts while other soldiers breached the fortifications. This time, in addition to collecting a substantial booty of material goods, the English took many of the rich townsmen prisoner in order to hold them for ransom.[132] The same pattern was repeated at Castelnaudry, which was almost entirely destroyed on the 31st.[133] In addition to these towns, the invaders pillaged "all the castles around there."[134] By the following day, the havoc wrought in these sacks had made its impression. An unnamed town attacked by a detachment while the main army rested opened negotiations before it was stormed, and successfully offered a ransom of 10,000

---

[129] Hewitt, *Black Prince's Expedition*, 55–6.

[130] Or possibly the second, since Castanet (closer to Lacroix-Falgarde) was also burned, though no details of events there are known. *Parvus Thalamus*, 351. Looking at the road network there, however, it seems likely that it was the Anglo-Gascon vanguard which hit Castanet while the prince's own division moved to Montgiscard.

[131] Froissart, *Oeuvres*, 5:345–6; *Parvus Thalamus*, 351; Dossat, *Le Languedoc . . . Trésor des Chartes*, no. 1766.

[132] *Le Baker*, 132; Froissart, *Oeuvres*, 5:346–7; *Parvus Thalamus*, 351. The town was burned on the departure of the English: Dossat, *Le Languedoc . . . Trésor des Chartes*, no. 1170.

[133] *Le Baker*, 132; *Le Bel*, 2:221; Froissart, *Oeuvres*, 5:346; *Parvus Thalamus*, 351; Dossat, *Le Languedoc . . . Trésor des Chartes*, no. 1764.

[134] *Parvus Thalamus*, 351. Along with these was the town of Mas-Stes-Puelles. Dossat, *Le Languedoc . . . Trésor des Chartes*, no. 1755.

florins for the safety of the inhabitants and their goods.[135] Alzonne, however, was put to the torch on 2 November.[136]

On the 3rd, the army reached Carcassonne, one of the great cities of southern France, described by le Baker as "larger than London inside the walls."[137] There were seven thousand hearths just in the new city or "Bourg," in addition to those of the fortified old town, the "Cité." The Bourg had no fortifications worthy of mention, aside from the walls of its houses and a system of chains strung across the avenues of the city in order to block cavalry. Nevertheless its inhabitants were determined to attempt a defense: there were, after all, several times as many men of military age among the citizens of the town (aside from the many who had taken refuge there from the surrounding areas) as there were troops in the Anglo-Gascon army.[138] Perhaps they were inspired by the long resistance of Calais in 1346–7, for many of the inhabitants of that city who had been expelled after its conquest by Edward III had found their way south to Carcassonne.[139]

Numbers, however (as the Count of Armagnac had warned the citizens of Toulouse) are of little value when not accompanied by skill and discipline. The prince's vanguard quickly routed the municipal militia which manned the chains, sending them flying to the refuge of the strongly fortified old town. The Bourg was found to be full of supplies and valuable booty, and in addition many rich bourgeois were captured and put to ransom. As usual when a town was taken by storm, many of the townswomen were raped.[140]

The Anglo-Gascon army rested in the Bourg on the 4th, the 5th, and part of the 6th, the troops scavenging for more treasures while their leaders looked for a way to assault the Cité, a most tempting prize.[141] In this they were unsuccessful, for the fortifications were too strong for a simple assault to succeed, and it would have been a violation of the prince's general strategy to delay for a regular siege. While they were looking, however, they received an embassy from the citizens inside the old town, who offered him the truly immense sum of 250,000 gold écus if he would refrain from burning the Bourg.[142]

---

[135] *Le Baker*, 132. *Knighton*, 2:84, suggests this practice of ransoming towns was quite common on the prince's itinerary: "patriam sub tributo et subjectione ex omni parte subjecit." Cf. also Mullot and Poux, "Itinéraire du Prince Noir," 305, 310 n.7.

[136] Mullot and Poux, "Itinéraire du Prince Noir," 299.

[137] *Le Baker*, 132: "ampliorem Londoniis infra muros"; Wingfield described the city as larger, stronger, and finer than York. In *Avesbury*, 440.

[138] *Le Baker*, 132; Froissart, *Oeuvres*, 347–8; Black Prince in *Avesbury*, 435 (refugees).

[139] Denifle, *Désolation des églises*, 48n.

[140] Froissart, *Oeuvres*, 5:348–9 (rout, supplies); *Le Bel*, 2:221 (riches, rapes). The rout was accomplished easily enough that neither le Baker nor the prince mentions the fight described by Froissart, but le Baker does note that on this day the Anglo-Gascon army was drawn up in full battle array, and that men took the order of knighthood, which indicates that a fight was expected.

[141] *Le Bel*, 2:222; *Le Baker*, 133.

[142] *Le Baker*, 133; cf. also the petition of the clergy, in Jeanjean, *Incursion du Prince Noir*, 30–1. By comparison, 250,000 écus was at this time enough to pay 2,000 skilled craftsmen (e.g. artillerists) for a year; a "large cannon" could be purchased for just 3 écus. Napoleon III

"Offered the gold," reports Geoffrey le Baker's chronicle, "the prince responded that he had come to seek justice, not gold; to take cities, not sell them. Then, since the citizens remained in fear of the French usurper and did not wish to obey their natural lord (or else did not dare to do so because they feared the revenge of the aforesaid French usurper), the prince ordered the next day that the town be put to the torch, religious buildings being spared."[143] This incident is crucial to understanding the strategy behind this campaign, for it demonstrates clearly that the havoc wrought by the Anglo-Gascon army was intended to do more than enrich the invaders at the expense of the people of Languedoc – that this *chevauchée*, in other words, was *not* merely brigandage on a massive scale[144] guided "by no consideration of strategy."[145] There was a strong element here of political theater, albeit theater of a particularly brutal and bloody kind. By burning the Bourg of Carcassonne, and openly linking its fate to the citizens' failure to obey their "natural lord" (i.e. Edward III as King of France), the prince was making an announcement to all Frenchmen that, even if they lived far from the normal conflict zones, King Jean could not protect them; only by satisfying the claims of the Plantagenets could they be secure. Those who obeyed the Valois monarchy were considered in rebellion against Edward III, and could expect the usual fate of rebels: fear of retribution from King Jean was no excuse for failure to obey King Edward, for they ought to have more fear of the Plantagenet than of the Valois.[146]

---

and I. Favé, *Études sur le passé et l'avenir de l'Artillerie* (Paris: J. Dumaine, 1846–1871), 3:88. In 1364, the war taxes owed by the good-sized town of Pontoise amounted to just 3,000 écus. M. Bruchet, "La Guerre de Cent Ans dans le Vexin: Documents communiqués a la société par M. Max Bruchet, Archiviste de la Haute-Savoie," *Bull. et. Mém. de la Soc. histor. et archéol. de l'arr. de Pontoise et du Vexin* 15 (1893), doc. IV.

   This sum is so large that some historians have found it impossible to accept, and have guessed that the amount offered was actually only 25,000 écus. However, given the large population of the city, even 250,000 écus might not amount to more than 10 écus (under £2 sterling) per person, which does not seem excessive.

[143] *Le Baker*, 133: "Offerentibus aurum princeps respondit quod huc non venit pro auro set iusticia prosequenda, nec ut venderet set caperet civitates. Unde, civibus in timore coronati Francorum persistentibus, nec suo domino naturali volentibus obedire, seu revera non audentibus pro vindicta predicti coronati, princeps die crastina iussit burgum ita incendi quod domibus religiosis parceretur."

[144] Tourneur-Aumont, *Bataille de Poitiers*, 78: "L'enterprise du prince de Galles n'était qu'une razzia de pirate affamé"; cf. pp. 77, 82, 85, 88, 175; Delachenal, *Histoire de Charles V*, 1:189; Favier, *Guerre de Cent Ans*, 190.

[145] Delachenal, *Hist. Charles V*, 1:126: "L'expédition ne fut, d'ailleurs, déterminée par aucune considération d'ordre stratégique; elle n'eut d'autre but que la ruine du pays où passa l'invasion anglaise." Cf. Favier, *Guerre de Cent Ans*, 189; *Hist. Gén. Languedoc* 9:651–2n.

[146] This is largely consistent with Hewitt's interpretation, *Black Prince's Expedition*, 59–60. However, I think he misses the mark when he writes that "though in the inconsistencies of human affairs it was expedient to connive at various practices in the troops, he [the prince] had not, so far, been a party to a sordid transaction of the kind proposed [viz. the ransoming of the town]. In the light of Edward III's claim, the people of Carcassonne had to be regarded as his father's subjects and, since they offered resistance, as rebels and therefore as his father's enemies. As Edward's lieutenant, he could not bargain with them." First, I know of no

From Carcassonne two more major cities were still within striking distance: Limoux and Narbonne. The former was closer by, about fifteen miles south along the Aude; the latter was significantly larger, but would require pressing on still farther from English-held territory, almost to the Mediterranean Sea. Behind and to the north of them there were two armies gathering strength, one at Toulouse under Count Jean and the other at Ambian under Jacques de Bourbon, the constable. Typically, the prince chose the bolder option, deciding to aim for Narbonne.

As they rode through the Toulousain and the Carcassonnais, Prince Edward's agents had been collecting records from city halls and tax-collectors' houses so that they could keep track of the damage they were doing to their enemy's fisc. They could calculate that the royal taxes paid by the towns they had destroyed thus far reached to many tens of thousands of écus annually, and they knew that Narbonne was if anything larger and richer even than Carcassonne.[147] The French had thus far shown no inclination to try to put an end to the devastation – according to le Bel their forces merely trailed along a day behind the prince's army, and had not killed even one of the Anglo-Gascons, despite the opportunities offered by the dispersion which naturally came with the invaders' efforts to burn a five-league-wide band of the countryside[148] – and if they were to make the attempt, so much the better would that please the prince, who was as battle-oriented as his father. Limoux could be struck on the return, unless a still more tempting target presented itself. So forward went the army, marching through Trèbes to Rustiques on the 6th, then burning Puichéric, crossing the Aude at Castelnau, and continuing through Lézignan to Canet on the 7th.[149] Lézignan, owned by a friend of the prince, was surrendered to the Anglo-Gascon army, and spared from harm.[150]

reason to think that the prince would have considered such a transaction "sordid" or that he could not bargain with rebels or enemies; consider the fact that Edward III himself would later make a similar pact with the dukes of Bar and Burgundy to spare their lands during the 1359–60 campaign. The issue was not that there was anything inherently wrong with accepting a *patis* payment; rather, it was that the destruction of the Bourg would be *more effective* as a means of progressing towards the English war aims.

[147] Records, calculation: Wingfield, in *Avesbury*, 442. Narbonne: *Le Baker*, 133.
[148] *Le Bel*, 2:221, 220 (five leagues).
[149] *Le Baker*, 133; *Parvus Thalamus*, 351 [Puegayric]. For Trèbes and Canet, see also Froissart, *Oeuvres*, 5:340–1, 349–50; for Lézignan, *Le Bel*, 2:221 (*contra* Mullot et Poux, "Itinéraire," 302–3). Le Baker notes that the army passed the castle of "Botenake" [Bouilhonnac] on the left; this fits with the route through Trèbes. Froissart notes that Trèbes and the nearby town of "Ourmes" were spared after paying a ransom (12,000 écus in the latter case) to the invaders; the Bourgeois of Valenciennes adds the story – probably fanciful, but perhaps with some element of truth to it – that when the former town was entered, Bérard d'Albret found a woman in labor, who delivered a son in his presence, then begged him to have the baby baptized, and to stand as his godfather in the ritual. The Gascon baron granted her request, and, for his new godson's sake, ordered the protection of the town. *Récits*, 282. Hewitt and Mullot and Poux state that Trèbes was burnt, though without citing evidence. *Black Prince's Expedition*, 60; "Itinéraire du Prince Noir," 302.
[150] *Le Baker*, 133.

The next day the prince reached Narbonne, which was treated much as Carcassonne had been.[151] The army remained in the expansive suburbs of the city, which contained some three thousand homes, for two more days, plundering it thoroughly while vigorously probing the defenses of the old town to see if that too could be taken.[152] Meanwhile the prince's outriders visited the towns and villages for some fifteen miles around (or as far as twenty-five miles, according to Jean le Bel), plundering many and ransoming a few.[153]

Having inflicted another heavy blow on France, the prince and his council once more had to decide whether to carry on or to turn back. The rich cities of Béziers and Montpellier were in striking distance to the northeast, but it was growing late in the campaigning season, and with the rich haul taken from Narbonne the army's wagons and saddlebags were already overstuffed with plunder.[154]

Still, the *chevauchée* had been such an outstanding success thus far that it must have been very tempting to continue it. The inhabitants of Montpellier were sufficiently convinced that the Anglo-Gascon army was about to pay them a visit that they destroyed their own suburbs to strengthen their defenses, as the citizens of Toulouse had done. Refugees from the entire region streamed towards the papal city of Avignon; the Pope himself reportedly did not feel entirely secure.[155] Indeed, he sent two bishops to try to arrange a truce between the prince and the lieutenant of King Jean. The envoys halted thirty miles away from the Anglo-Gascon army and sent one of the Pope's sergeants-at-arms to seek a safe-conduct for them.

As one of his arguments to persuade the English of the wisdom of negotiating, the papal sergeant-at-arms doubtless warned them that a large French army (reportedly comprising eleven thousand men-at-arms and a huge number of communal infantry) was coming up on their flank and rear; the same infor-

---

151 *Le Baker*, 133; Le Baker states that the Aude was crossed at "Chastel de terre" [probably Castelnau-sur-Aude] on the 8th, but this is evidently an error: the crossing must have been made on the 7th since Rustiques and Canet are on opposite sides of the river. It was presumably the Orbieu which the army crossed on the 8th.

152 *Parvus Thalamus*, 351 [prezeron lo borc e cremeron, e combateron la ciutat en tant que agron mot giens paor de lur vida].

153 They are known to have held Capestang (11 miles north of Narbonne) for a ransom of 40,000 écus (though this was apparently not collected), and to have appeared before the gates of Béziers, over 14 miles northeast of their base; Jean le Bel says they even went another ten miles beyond Béziers, to St. Thibéry. Capestang: Froissart, *Oeuvres*, 5:340–2, 351, and Mullot and Poux, "Itinéraire du Prince Noir," 305–6. Béziers: Denifle, *Désolation des églises*, 2:901; *Parvus Thalamus*, 351; Mullot and Poux, "Itinéraire du Prince Noir," 305 n.9; and Chandos Herald, *Vie du Prince Noir*, l. 648 (which wrongly says it was taken by the prince). All three: *Le Bel*, 2:221.

154 Plunder: Froissart, *Oeuvres*, 5:352; *Récits*, 283. Mid-November was quite late in the season, considering that they had three weeks' travel time to reach Bordeaux again; cf. pp. 164–5, 165 n. 44.

155 *Avesbury*, 433.

mation was gained from interrogated prisoners.[156] These reports proved decisive in shaping the course of the remainder of the campaign, for the prince saw in them an opportunity for the one thing which the *chevauchée* had thus far failed to accomplish. He had already "much comforted" his vassals, inflicted severe punishment on those who failed to acknowledge his father's right to the French throne, enriched his friends beyond measure, and more than correspondingly impoverished the Valois treasury: the four goals which, as noted above, had been set out by Edward III for continuing his Crécy *chevauchée* in 1346. But of course the greatest impact of the 1346 expedition had not come from the desolation inflicted on the French countryside, great though that had been: rather, it had come from the battle of Crécy itself, where the prince had literally won his spurs. Now, it seemed, there was another opportunity to inflict a telling battlefield defeat on the French. "We took counsel as to where it would be best for us to go; and, because we had reports from prisoners and from others that our enemies had gathered and were coming after us in order to fight with us," wrote the prince, "we turned back towards them; and we expected to have a battle within the next three days."[157]

Meanwhile, so that he would have a better chance of surprising his enemies, the prince kept the papal messenger in custody without even reading the letters he had brought. After taking the time to fire the Bourg of Narbonne thoroughly on the morning of 10 November, the Anglo-Gascon army marched due north to the castle of Aubian. For the next two days Prince Edward pressed his men to make what speed they could, loaded down as they were with plunder. They camped in the open on the 11th, after a long, waterless westward march over difficult trails during which they had been forced to give their horses wine to drink, that being the only liquid available.[158] They hoped to strike the French

---

[156] Numbers: *Anonimalle*, 35. This is offered some support by le Bel, who says that the French had three times as many men in the field as the English. *Le Bel*, 2:222. Prisoners: Black Prince, in *Avesbury*, 435. Cf. also Mullot and Poux, "Itinéraire du Prince Noir," 305.

[157] Black Prince, in *Avesbury*, 435: "Et illesqes preismes nostre counsail vers ou nous purrons mieltz trere; et, par cause qe nous avons novels de prisoners et aultres qe noz enemys estoient assemblez et venoient apres nous pur nous combatre, nous retournasmes devers eux, et quidasmes daver eu la bataille deinz les trois jours ensuantz." Hewitt, in discussing the campaign from this point forward, seems to waver back and forth between, on the one hand, being convinced that from Capestang the English were "determined to avoid contact with Armagnac's army" and to carry their booty back to Bordeaux "without endangering the column," and, on the other hand, acknowledging that the prince expected battle within three days of turning back and that he might have wished to overtake the retreating French as they withdrew to Carcassonne. *Black Prince's Expedition*, 63. On balance, though, Hewitt finally concludes that there was "a determination on the prince's part to avoid a large-scale action." Ibid., 65; cf. the similar views of Tourneur-Aumont, *Bataille de Poitiers*, 87, 85; Delachenal, *Hist. de Charles V*, 1:127; Jeanjean, *Incursion du Prince Noir*, 42. This interpretation can hardly be sustained in the light of the clear statements of the prince, Wingfield, and the *Anonimalle* that the prince was pursuing the French, and the other details of the campaign as related below.

[158] *Le Baker*, 134. On the same day they burned the town of Ouveillan. Mullot and Poux, "Itinéraire du Prince Noir," 305; G. Mouynès, *Inventaire des archives communales de la ville de Narbonne* (Narbonne: Caillard, 1877), 1:437.

army the next day, but when they reached the towns of Pépieux and Azille, where (as captured French scouts revealed) the Count of Armagnac and the constable had been planning to spend the night, they discovered that the Valois forces had received reports of their approach before dawn, and hastily retreated to the west.[159] It is evident that the French leaders in Languedoc had already adopted a strict strategy of avoiding battle with the English (one comparable to that later followed by Charles V and du Guesclin) – a fact puzzling to many historians who fail to appreciate that the skill and experience of the Anglo-Gascon army made it more than a match for the larger French army it faced, and who mistakenly see the English as trying to avoid rather than come to grips with Armagnac's force.[160]

The prince's next steps, as Hewitt notes, are "most difficult to trace." However, the route described by all the more recent accounts (Mullot and Poux's, Jeanjean's, Hewitt's, and Barber's), which has the Anglo-Gascon army swing north of the (now dry) lake of Marseillette and head west on the 13th, passing north of Carcassonne to lodge around Pennautier on the 14th, is almost certainly incorrect.[161] Le Baker says that on the 13th the army made another "long and waterless" march to reach "Lamyane," a poor place with few houses and little water. Then on the 14th, he continues, they turned towards Guienne, leaving the lake, the city of Carcassonne, and the whole of the previous journey to their *right*,[162] and lodged at the end of the day with the rearguard at "Alieir," the prince on a riverbank across a bridge near "Puchsiaucier" (where the center stayed), and the vanguard at the good town of "Pezence." On the 15th, entering the open country, they made a long march to reach the abbey of Prouille, meanwhile destroying Limoux, Fanjeaux, "Vulard," and Lasserre.

Since the account in le Baker, clearly based on a campaign diary written during the *chevauchée*, provides by far the most detailed and accurate narrative we have of this expedition, we should not accept any proposed route which directly contradicts its statements. But if the Anglo-Gascon army had followed the route given by Mullot and Poux and their followers, it would have passed the

---

159 This sequence of events was rather complex to reconstruct. The prince says that, on leaving Narbonne, he expected battle within the next three days – i.e. either by the 12th or by the 13th, depending on whether he was counting the 10th, the day of his departure, as the first of the three. Wingfield says "the third day, when we should have come upon them, they had news of us before dawn, and retreated"; this would then, again, be either on the 12th or the 13th. (In *Avesbury*, 435, 441.) I conclude that it must have been on the 12th, because that was when Geoffrey le Baker reports that they reached Pépieux and Azille, where they learned that the French leaders had planned to spend the night. *Le Baker*, 134; note also *Parvus Thalamus*, 351. This would suggest that the difficult march of the 11th avoided the main routes to enhance the probability of a surprise attack on the following day.

160 E.g. see Jeanjean, *Incursion du Prince Noir*, 17, 42; comments of August Molinier in *Hist. Gén. Languedoc*, 9:651–2.

161 Mullot et Poux, "Itinéraire," 306–10; Jeanjean, *Incursion du Prince Noir*, 42–4; Barber, *Edward, Prince of Wales*, 118 (map); Hewitt, *Black Prince's Expedition*, 51 (map), 63.

162 *Le Baker*, 134: "Sabbato revertentes versus Vasconiam, reliquerunt a dextris piscinam de Esebon et carkasonam et totum iter pristinum."

318

landmarks mentioned on its *left*, not its right. In order to pass them on its right, it would have to be travelling south, not north, of them, and therefore of the Aude.[163] Le Baker's statement that it was only *after* the march of the 13th that the army turned towards Guienne, i.e. turned west, then makes complete sense: the prince must have marched south on the 13th, and then turned west for the next day's march. (By the other route, the turn towards Gascony would have been made during the 13th, not on the 14th.) This also explains why the march of the 13th was waterless, and the place chosen to encamp small and dry: moving south from Pépieux, Azille and Laredorte,[164] the prince must have crossed over the Montagne d'Alaric into the mountainous region northeast of the Plateau de Lacamp, reaching the hamlet of Villemagne ("Lamyane") at the end of the day,[165] then turning west (towards Guienne) and leaving Marseillette and Carcassonne to the north (the right) on the following day, probably following the route through Serviès to Villar-en-val to Ladern-s-Lauquet. From there, it seems, the first two divisions took the northwest fork, leading them across the Aude and beyond, to the banks of what is now the Canal du Midi, beside the bridge between Pech-Redon and Sauzens (i.e. "Puchsiaucier"). There the prince encamped; the vanguard pressed on a very short distance to Pezens, which it captured and occupied. Meanwhile the rearguard took the southwest fork from Ladern to lodge at St.-Hilaire ("Alieir"), from where it was poised to strike Villar-St-Anselm ("Vulard") and Limoux the next day (thus lessening our surprise at the well-attested attack on that city, which is a long way off from the line between Pezens and Prouille, where the prince lodged the next day).[166] This

---

[163] Mullot and Poux offer the hypothesis that this is explained by the Anglo-Gascons' perception that the lake of Marseillette appeared to be like a river, so that its "right bank" was its northern shore. This is not credible for several reasons, however. First, le Baker clearly says that the army left its previous route as well as Carcassonne and the lake to its right, and neither a route nor a city can reasonably be said to have a right bank. Second, even if they had thought it was a river, they would have seen its southern, not its northern, shore as the "right bank," by analogy with the Aude and the other rivers of the region, which flow east to the Mediterranean. Third, le Baker explicitly notes that the lake was unusual in that it had no water flowing in or out, so the English clearly did not "doubtless view it as running water."

[164] Mullot and Poux do offer evidence for the destruction of several villages *northwest* of Pépieux (Livinière and Ventajou) and of Peyriac-Minervois, west of Azille, but these were probably hit by outriders on the 12th, before the army turned south. Mullot and Poux, "Itinéraire du Prince Noir," 307, 310.

[165] Mullot and Poux's identification of "Lamyane" as the deserted tenement of la Mejane/Lamigran is phonetically attractive, but unsustainable for two reasons. First, as already noted, it cannot be reconciled with le Baker's statement that the army was leaving its old route (etc.) to its right rather than its left. Second, Lamigran is only six or seven miles from Pépieux and Azille: hardly the "longum iter" described by *Le Baker*, 134. Mullot and Poux, "Itinéraire du Prince Noir," 307.

[166] The identifications of place-names I suggest here may seem unlikely to anyone who has not attempted to follow le Baker's itinerary on a map, but they are overall better than the alternatives suggested by those who presume the prince took the more northerly route. Barber, for example, identifies "Alieir" (my St.-Hilaire) as Villepeyroux, "Puchsiaucier" (my Pech-Redon/Sauzens) as Pennautier and "Vulard" (my Villar) as Montréal. *Life and Campaigns of the Black Prince*, 66.

route south of the Aude would also explain why Froissart describes the English army as moving from Narbonne to Limoux rather than to Carcassonne: he was describing the path of the Plantagenet rearguard.[167] Lastly, the route I describe solves a final problem with the more northerly route: le Baker describes the army as entering a "fair region, long and broad" on the 15th, which implies that on the preceding days they had been in rougher terrain. This fits with a route through the highlands south of the Aude, but not with one through the plains to the north of Carcassonne.

On 15 November, then, the vanguard and center marched west to Fanjeaux (which they captured) and the abbey of Prouille, seizing and destroying Montréal and Lasserre on the way. Meanwhile the rear division demolished Villar and the rich city of Limoux (leaving, says Froissart, not one of its four thousand houses standing) before turning northwest to Routier.[168] With the three divisions once more relatively close together, the prince spent the next three days marching west towards the Garonne, still wreaking havoc across a broad swathe of land as he went, sparing only certain territories belonging to the Count of Foix (the enemy of the Count of Armagnac). Once they reached the Garonne, the men of his vanguard graphically demonstrated their facility with river crossings: first they waded across single-file near Noé, much to the amazement of the locals who made a weak effort to oppose them, then, a short distance upstream at Marquefave, they switched sides again so that they could strike the town of Carbonne unexpectedly from the unwalled eastern side (which involved a third transit of the river).[169]

The prince later described this whole phase of the campaign, from the 12th to the 18th, as a pursuit of the French army which had escaped him at Azille.[170] During the night of the 19th (which the army spent at Carbonne, resting from the previous days' efforts) Edward received reports that the main force of the French (including Armagnac, the constable, Marshal Clermont, and the Prince of

---

167 Froissart, *Oeuvres*, 5:342.
168 *Le Baker*, 135; Froissart, *Oeuvres*, 5:352–3 for Montréal, Routier, Limoux; Mahul, *Cartulaire . . . Carcassonne*, 4:286, 3:311, 3:257 for Fanjeaux and Montréal; Dossat, *Le Langue-doc . . . Trésor des Chartes*, no. 1765 for Fanjeaux. The match between towns and divisions is my inference. On Limoux, see also Denifle, *Désolation*, 2:94 (size), Jeanjean, *Incursion du Prince Noir*, 45 (letter showing Limoux was "destructa et per majorem partem concremata"); Mullot and Poux, "Itinéraire du Prince Noir," 311 n.2 (documentary evidence that the city was "in magna parte combuste et trucidate"). The last authors also state that Villasavary was burned.
169 *Le Baker*, 136; Black Prince in *Avesbury*, 435. On the long-standing feud between the houses of Foix and Armagnac, cf. Vale, *Origins*, passim.
170 Black Prince, in *Avesbury*, 435: "Et sur nostre retourn devers eaux, ils se retournerent devers Tholouse. Si lez pursuismes a grandes journees tantqe pres Tholouse; od nous preismes nostre chemyn a passer Geronde a une ville appelle Carboun, iij. lieues de Tholouse." Similarly Wingfield in ibid., 442. I see no justification for Richard Barber's view that this was a propagandistic distortion, "a prudent retreat . . . made to look like a pursuit of the French forces in the region, whereas the prince was probably doing his best to get a weary army safely back home." *Life and Campaigns*, 49.

Orange) had come out of Toulouse and encamped a short distance from the Anglo-Gascon rearguard, which had been involved in skirmishes with them.[171] The natural conclusion was that the French, who with their five large divisions substantially outnumbered the invaders, had finally mustered the confidence to give battle; the prince, of course, was more than willing to accept such an offer.[172] On the 20th, he assembled his three divisions, marched a mile closer to the reported location of the enemy, and then halted in an advantageous position to form up his troops and ready them for battle.[173]

The French troops learned of the proximity of their enemies when, as so often happened in medieval warfare, one of the soldiers in the battle formation halooed at a hare and the others took up the call. French scouts, coming to investigate, spied the battle-ready Anglo-Gascon army and in a panic rushed back to their camp. It turned out that the Valois army's leaders, despite the greatly superior numbers of their force,[174] were by no means ready to risk an open fight with their enemies: instead they hastily packed up and retreated to the north "without giving or taking a blow of lance or sword," as the Anonimalle chronicler contemptuously remarked.[175] Nipping at their heels came a small force of the best knights in the English contingent – Bartholomew Burghersh, John Chandos, James Audley, Baldwin Boutetourt, Thomas Felton, and a few dozen others – which the prince had sent to find out what had happened to the enemy forces. This reconnaissance party struck the tailguard of the retreating enemy and captured over thirty men-at-arms, massacred some carters, and destroyed the supplies they were carrying.[176]

As soon as the prisoners confirmed the Valois army's retreat, the Prince of Wales set his vanguard, under the Earl of Warwick, in pursuit.[177] Despite the delay in getting started, the soldiers of Anglo-Gascon army covered roughly eighteen miles that day, a sign of their eagerness to come to grips with the

---

[171] Black Prince in *Avesbury*, 435–6.

[172] *Anonimalle*, 35: "Et quant le dit prynce les vist, egrement se myst encountre eaux pur les avoir done bataille." As noted earlier, Hewitt (*Black Prince's Expedition*, 65) and Jeanjean (*Incursion du Prince Noir*, 42), in accord with Tourneur-Aumont, *Bataille de Poitiers*, 85, claim on the contrary that the prince was doing his best to avoid a battle.

[173] *Le Baker*, 136: "in campo apto ordinarunt ad prelandum."

[174] *Chron. Jean II et Charles V*, 55, says the French force was larger by half; *Le Bel*, 2:222, makes it three times larger than the prince's army; the latter estimate is supported by King Jean himself, who later wrote that "nobis fuerat de eisdem partibus pro certo rescriptum, per litteras et nuncios speciales, quod numerus gencium nostrarum in armis numerum hostium nostrorum ibidem multipliciter excedebat." Delachenal, *Hist. de Charles V*, 1:130n.

[175] *Anonimalle*, 35.

[176] *Le Baker*, 136–7; Black Prince, in *Avesbury*, 436.

[177] *Anonimalle*, 35: "le counte de Warrewyk les dit Fraunceis od toute lavaunt garde de dit prynce enchaceaunt tanqe al cite de Gemounde." This pursuit was clearly determind by the path of the fleeing French army; Hewitt is wrong to imply that the path followed from Carbonne was chosen in order to get the army back to Bordeaux as quickly as possible, "to avoid a large-scale action," and to "resist the temptation to chase attackers back towards Toulouse." *Black Prince's Expedition*, 65.

French. At the end of the day, however, the pursuit was blocked by the deep and difficult river Save, on the far banks of which, between Sauveterre and Lombez, the Valois forces had encamped. The frustrated prince could see his enemies' campfires burning but, since they had broken the bridges over the river and night was falling, he could not reach them.[178]

The next day, a rainy Saturday, Edward set out northwards to find a way across the river. After a difficult journey over a poor, muddy, road he found a crossing-place near the castle of Auradé, where his army encamped for the night. The following day they hastened along the opposite bank of the Save back towards Lombez, but, with the day growing late, the prince discovered that his enemy had withdrawn northwest, over the mountains, to shelter around the strong fortress of Gimont.[179]

It was too late to give battle that day, but the leaders of the Plantagenet army took the wise precaution of sending a detachment to capture the castle of Aurimont, which would supply them both with a forward base to observe the French and also a secure crossing over the river Gimone, should one prove necessary the following day. The castle was captured, its substantial garrison being driven with loss to the refuge of Gimont's walls.[180]

The prince, by his own report, fully expected that on the next day the French would finally do battle, so the Anglo-Gascon army was drawn up in the fields before dawn to await the enemy, the carters and other noncombatants having been left behind at Aurimont.[181] As he might by now have expected, however, events proved the French less eager for a fight than he was. During the night (as he learned from his scouts while the Anglo-Gascon army stood arrayed in the

---

178 From Carbonne, according to le Baker, the prince reached "Muwos" – probably either Monès (about 16 miles) or Mauvesin (about 14). *Le Baker*, 137. The prince himself says he encamped opposite Sauveterre and Lombez, which would indicate a total journey of at least 18 miles from Carbonne. In *Avesbury*, 436.

179 This southward movement explains why the detachment sent to Aurimont is described by le Baker as being dispatched "to the right"; it also fits with the description of the French army's position as on the other side of the mountains below Gimont. *Le Baker*, 137. Hewitt (*Black Prince's Expedition*, 66 and map, 51) wrongly has the prince advance directly west from Auradé to Aurimont.

There is no need to look (as Breuils, "Jean Ier," 58, does) for unknown "grave and ineluctable" reasons, such as the supposed defection of some of his troops, for the count's retreat to Gimont. He took shelter in Gimont for the same reason he had been fleeing from the prince for days: he did not think he would win a battle.

180 *Le Baker*, 137; cf. Black Prince, in *Avesbury*, 436. Hewitt's description of the French imposing a check on the English at Gimont and offering "sufficient resistance to hold the English force at bay till midnight" (*Black Prince's Expedition*, 67) is misleading: the prince states fairly clearly that the French withdrew into Gimont at the approach of the leading English troops.

181 Black Prince, in *Avesbury*, 436; *Le Baker*, 137. It may seem surprising that the prince expected the French to give battle, considering that they had been fleeing before him for several days. The answer may be that he had already heard that the Count of Armagnac was promising to do battle with him; he did later learn that the count's failure to keep such promises had led to a fight between the count and the constable. *Le Baker*, 138.

fields) the bulk of the French army had decamped and retreated, probably to Auch, leaving only their leaders to occupy the nearly impregnable stronghold of Gimont.[182]

On discovering this the prince held a council (as always at the turning points of the campaign) to discuss what to do next. "Since we understood that they [the French] did not want a battle," he later reported, "it was agreed that we should return to our own borders."[183] It was another five days before the army's banners were furled, a period which included some hard marches and a successful assault on the town of Réjaumont, but this was all rather anti-climactic after the French flight from Gimont.[184] By 2 December, having dismissed most of his troops, the prince was at La Réole. There he held a council to make plans for the winter and to take stock of the campaign just completed.

Froissart's judgement was that Prince Edward's *chevauchée* had been "very honorable and very bold;" few contemporaries, among the chivalric classes at least, would have disagreed with this assessment. Geoffrey le Baker remarked how the campaign amounted to a defeat for the French, "since they repeatedly fled in terror from the vicinity of their adversaries, the English, who had sought them out by long and hard marches."[185] Jean le Bel was even more scathing towards the French: "the lords of France always followed [the English], but never attacked them, even though they were three times more numerous, for which they were much blamed. I don't know how they could stand themselves for not having at least struck at the tail [of the army], unless they were enchanted or ensorcelled."[186]

Certainly the Gascon lords who had loyally persevered in their support of the

---

[182] Black Prince, in *Avesbury*, 436; *Le Baker*, 137.

[183] Black Prince, in *Avesbury*, 436. Hewitt quotes this statement without any acknowledgment that it contradicts his general view that the prince, in returning towards Bordeaux, was striving to *avoid* fighting. *Black Prince's Expedition*, 67.

[184] The route of the Anglo-Gascon army in this period, according to *Le Baker*, 137–8, was: in the open on the 24th; past Fleurance to St. Lary ["Silarde"] to Réjaumont on the 25th; halt on the 26th; to Lasserre ["le Serde"] the next day; then across to English-held Mézin. The march of the 24th was particularly hard because of lack of water; horses were given wine to drink, and many were injured because they could not keep a steady footing.

The invaders had hopes that the enemy would try to defend one of the rivers which was crossed during this period, and so bring on a fight, but this did not occur. Hewitt's failure to understand the prince's battle-seeking strategy has led him to misinterpret le Baker's text on this point. Apparently referring to the chronicler's statement that the English "preterierunt aquam, ubi sperabant inimicis obviasse" (*Le Baker*, 137), Hewitt writes: "In one place, he clearly states that it was hoped that a river the army had crossed would serve as a barrier against the enemy." *Black Prince's Expedition*, 66, cf. 67.

[185] *Le Baker*, 137: "respeccione armorum fuerant disconfecti, presertim cum sui adversarii, scilicet Anglici, ipsos per itinera longa et mala diu quesitos et pluries e vecinio repertos solo terrore profugos fugaverint."

[186] *Le Bel*, 2:222. The precise translation of the second sentence is debatable, though the import is clear: "Je ne sçay comment ilz se pouoient tenir qu'ilz ne feroient en la queue au mains, s'ilz n'estoient enfantosmez ou escorcellez." Cf. note 174, above, on the size of the French army.

Plantagenet cause were greatly encouraged by this striking demonstration of English military superiority. The vast haul of treasure brought back by those who had joined the prince on his expedition also did more than a little to raise the spirits of Edward's Gascon subjects. "They seized," le Baker tells us, "no small wealth from the land of the enemy, enriching their own country."[187] Froissart agrees that the Black Prince and his men secured a "very great profit" from the expedition, acquiring "so many goods, fine supplies, and so much good wine, that they didn't know what to do with it all."[188] According to Jean le Bel, they found an "unbelievable" amount of wealth, so that even the common troops paid no attention to silver coins, goblets, tankards or furs, being interested only in gold florins, brooches and jewels. The men-at-arms had gained so much profit, he wrote some six years later, that "those who survive are still better off for it; and, after their deaths, their heirs will be too."[189]

Of course, everything thus gained by the Anglo-Gascon army was also a loss to the French. But the harm inflicted on the subjects of King Jean was far, far greater than the amount gained by his enemies, for throughout their *chevauchée* the English and the Gascons had been careful to inflict as much damage as possible even when doing so brought no profit to them. They had consistently burnt the towns and villages of the countryside rather than merely plundering them (though some were spared after paying ransoms); they had made mills (a major concentration of productive capital in the period) special targets for destruction,[190] and when they had found greater stores of wine than they could either drink or bring with them, they had taken the time to destroy what remained.[191] In the words of Edward III's challenge of 1346, "to the loss of our enemies" was at least as important a goal as "to our profit."

The key document for this aspect of the *chevauchée* is the summary report written by Sir John Wingfield to the Bishop of Winchester, who, significantly, was then Treasurer of England. It is worth quoting at length:

> I am certain that since the beginning of this war against the King of France, there has never been such destruction in any region as on this *chevauchée*. For the countryside and good towns which were destroyed in this *chevauchée* found more money each year for the King of France in support of his wars than did half his kingdom (excluding the annual devaluation of the money and the profits and customs which he takes from Poitou), as I could show you from good records found in various towns in the tax-collectors' houses. For Carcassonne and Limoux, which is as large as Carcassonne, and two other towns nearby Carcassonne, find each year for the King of France the wages of a thousand men-at-arms and, in addition, 100,000 old écus, in support of the war. And I know, by the records we found, that the towns which we destroyed

---

[187] *Le Baker*, 138–9.
[188] Froissart, *Oeuvres*, 5:353, 351; cf. 347.
[189] *Le Bel*, 2:221–2.
[190] *Le Baker*, 131, 132, 135.
[191] *Le Baker*, 134.

around Toulouse and Carcassonne, along with Narbonne and the Narbonnais, found each year an additional 400,000 old écus in aid of his wars, as the citizens of the large towns and other people from the area, who should have good knowledge [of the matter], have told us.[192]

Note that the prince and his advisers were so concerned with this aspect of the *chevauchée* that they went to the effort of confirming the tax records they collected with a second source, the testimony of influential citizens. And Wingfield's figures are not as incredible as they might seem. In 1329 the King of France had a document prepared to estimate how much a war in Gascony would cost him, and where he could find the necessary money. The men who prepared that study expected to get more money from Carcassonne alone than from Champagne, Anjou, Maine, Touraine, Valois, Chartres, Senlis, Vermandois, Amiens, Bourges, Sens, and Tours combined. Toulouse was expected to provide even more than Carcassonne,[193] and then there was Limoux, also of comparable size, and Narbonne, which Wingfield described as "only a little smaller than London."[194] In all, some five hundred "towns, places and castles" were sacked during the course of the expedition.[195] In the long run it would become clear that the indirect effects of this *grande chevauchée* had been as damaging to the French crown as the immediate devastation, but for the moment, the Plantagenets could certainly rest assured that they had indeed "struck a severe blow" against their enemies.[196]

Though the prince had not been able to bring the French to battle, he had accomplished all four of his other goals in a way that must have far exceeded anyone's expectations.[197] As the summary report of the campaign noted, King Edward's vassals were "much comforted and reassured"; his enemies, on the other hand were "in a severe state of shock" (*mult estonez*).[198] It remained to be seen if France would be able to sustain many more such hammer blows, but the Prince of Wales and his father immediately started planning how and where to inflict the next ones.

---

[192] *Avesbury*, 442. The *Anonimalle*'s claim (p. 35) that the English destroyed eleven "bones cites" and 3,700 "villages" on this *chevauchée* is doubtless an exaggeration, but it is certainly evocative.

[193] M. Jusselin, "Comment la France se préparait à la guerre de Cent ans," *Bibliothèque de l'école des chartes*, LXXIII (1912), doc. II (Touraine and Sens in doc. III). Froissart (*Oeuvres*, 5:344) says that Toulouse was not much smaller than Paris.

[194] In *Avesbury*, 441. To this list of major cities could be added Montpellier, the suburbs of which were destroyed by the French themselves in a panic at the prince's approach. *Le Bel*, 2:222.

[195] According to a list which was once to be found among the Gascon Rolls, according to A. Breuils, "Jean Ier," 55n.

[196] *Avesbury*, 432.

[197] And yet Auguste Molinier, failing to appreciate that the prince was (rightly) willing to fight even much larger French forces, claimed that "the enterprise of the Prince of Wales was absurd in itself; and just the fact that he attempted it proves that this bold knight had none of the qualities of a general." DeVic and Vaissette, *Hist. Gén. Languedoc*, 9:651.

[198] Wingfield, in *Avesbury*, 442.

CHAPTER FOURTEEN

"TO MAKE *CHEVAUCHÉES* AND HARM HIS ENEMIES": THREE CAMPAIGNS OF EARLY 1356

> *In the practical art of war, the best thing of all is to take the enemy's country whole and intact.*   Sun Tzu, III.1[1]

WHEN THE PRINCE OF WALES' cavalcade returned to English Guienne, its packhorses stumbling under the weight of plundered gold and silver,[2] there was no doubt in anyone's mind that his campaign had been a great success.[3] He had not been able to bring Armagnac to battle, but the count and his royal master had suffered for their restraint, while Edward III's subjects had been both avenged and enriched. The king's improvised *chevauchée* in the north, though not so dramatic as the prince's expedition, was also considered a moderate success, increasing his own stature and honor at the cost of his adversary.[4]

The full value of these two campaigns, however, did not become clear until 1356, when events in the north and the south brought the Plantagenets' strategy to the brink of complete success. The most immediate after-effects of the twin *chevauchées* came in Aquitaine, where the prince took advantage of his enemies' demoralization[5] to fight a dispersed and remarkably successful winter campaign of conquest in Saintonge and along the Isle, Dordogne, Lot and

---

[1] Lionel Giles trans., in T. R. Phillips (ed.), *The Roots of Strategy* (Harrisburg: Stackpole, 1985), 26.

[2] Froissart, *Chroniques*, 4:173.

[3] Modern historians have not all been equally clear on this point, however, Auguste Molinier, for example, commented that "Les résultats politiques et militaires de cette expédition étaient bien faibles, le prince de Galles n'avait conquis ni un pouce de territoire français ni une forteresse; mais l'effet moral de cette longue course, de ce pillage fut incalculable; mal commandés, les hommes d'armes des Valois se défièrent de leurs chefs et perdirent cette confiance en eux-mêmes qui a toujours fait la plus grande force des armées françaises; ravagée, toute une partie du Languedoc paya moins facilement les subsides qu'il fallut lui demander les années suivantes." Of course, the demoralization and impoverishment of the French to which Molinier refers were among the prince's primary goals for the campaign, and should certainly be seen as both "political and military results." DeVic and Vaissette, *Hist. Gén. Languedoc*, 9:652n.; cf. Jeanjean, *Incursion du Prince Noir*, 48, 57.

[4] *Avesbury*, 431.

[5] See Breuils, "Jean Ier," 60; DeVic and Vaissette, *Hist. Gén. Languedoc*, 9:663. As the latter shows, the panic in the French countryside was so great that the authorities had to take steps to stem an exodus of refugees fleeing into Catalonia.

Garonne rivers. By the spring of 1356, his efforts had established an English presence as far east as Périgueux and Castelsagrat – meaning that, north of the Garonne, they were past the frontier of the duchy as it had been before the War of St. Sardos in Edward II's reign.[6] The details of these operations are difficult to disentangle, as we must rely on a single report quilled by Sir John Wingfield on 22 January for most of the details, and many of the place-names are impossible to identify with full certainty. The following reconstruction of events therefore of necessity involves some guesswork, but the overall picture is certainly correct.

The prince's first step, after a short rest, was to divide his Englishmen and those Gascons staying with him for the winter operations into four or five divisions of about 1,000–1,500 men each. These divisions spread out in various towns along the frontiers of English control, from where they could "make *chevauchées* and harm his enemies."[7] The work of inflicting general harm on the enemy in the style of the *grande chevauchée* just completed, however, was only half their duty. The French, as Wingfield noted just before the beginning of the winter operations, were in a state of virtual paralysis, giving Prince Edward an excellent opportunity to capture many places and to extend the limits of the Plantagenet obedience.[8] The first of these forces, led by Captal de Buch and Bartholomew Burghersh, consisted of six hundred men-at-arms, a similar number of Gascon foot-sergeants, and 240 archers. These troops cleared eastern Saintonge of two remaining French strongholds (Plassac and Montendre), then proceeded north to garrison the Charente. [See Map 14–1.] By the end of January 1356, they had established themselves in Cognac, Taillebourg, Tonnay and Rochefort. The second group, under the Earl of Warwick, was based at La Réole. It too did impressive work in January, capturing the walled bridge-towns of Clairac on the Lot and Tonneins on the Garonne, just downstream from that river's confluence with the Lot, as well as Bourg St.-Pierre near there. These feats, along with the capture of Lévignac and the twin castles of Bouglon, cut off the main French base remaining in the area, Marmande, from the north-west, north, south-east, south, and south-west.[9]

---

[6]   The 1307 border ran just short of Castelsagrat, and some forty miles west of Périgueux. See Vale, *Origins of the Hundred Years War*, map I.
[7]   Wingfield to the Bishop of Winchester, in *Avesbury*, 442 (quotation). Numbers: Wingfield to Stafford in ibid., pp. 446–7.
[8]   Wingfield to Winchester in *Avesbury*, 442. Edward's success in doing just that demonstrates that Jeanjean's remark on the 1355 campaign that the prince "had burned more than 500 places, but he had not conquered an inch of land" is rather short-sighted (aside from being simply wrong, since during the *chevauchée* the prince did garrison several places in the Juliac area). *Incursion du Prince Noir*, 48.
[9]   Most of these details are based on Wingfield's letter to Stafford, reporting the action between 23 December and 22 January, in *Avesbury*, 445–7. Wingfield has Buch's force (which also included the Sire de Montferrand and the Sire de Curton) raiding from the named Charente towns at the end of that period; it is my inference that the same group was responsible for the capture of Plassac [Plasak] and Montendre [Mountoundre]. It was probably (based

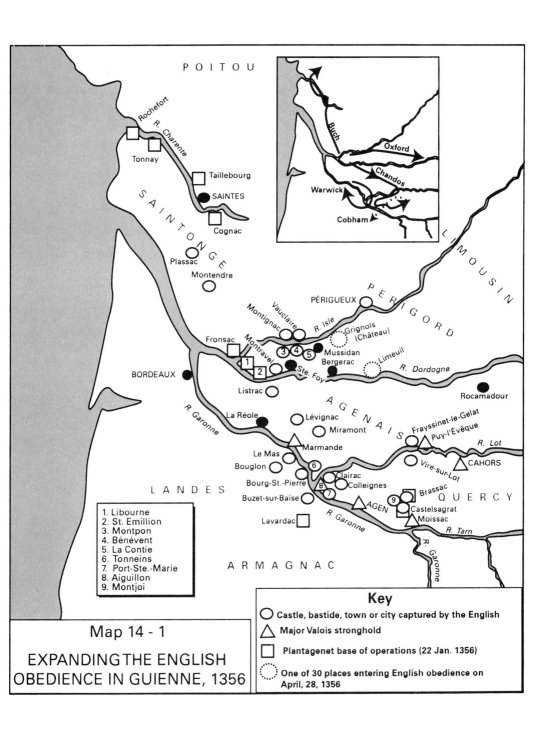

POITOU

Rochefort

R. Charente

Tonnay

Taillebourg

SAINTES

S A I N T O N G E

Cognac

Plassac

Montendre

Buch

Oxford

Chandos

Warwick

Cobham

L I M O U S I N

PÉRIGUEUX

P É R I G O R D

Montignac

Vauclaire

R. Isle

Grignols
(Château)

Fronsac

Montravel

Mussidan

Bergerac

Limeuil

R. Dordogne

1

3 4 5

2

BORDEAUX

Ste. Foy

Listrac

A G E N A I S

Rocamadour

R. Garonne

La Réole

Lévignac

Miramont

Frayssinet-le-Gelat

Puy-l'Évêque

R. Lot

Le Mas

Marmande

Vire-sur-Lot

CAHORS

Bouglon

6

L A N D E S

Bourg-St.-Pierre

Clairac

Colleignes

Brassac

Q U E R C Y

Buzet-sur-Baïse

8

7

9

Castelsagrat

AGEN

Moissac

Lavardac

R. Garonne

R. Tarn

1. Libourne
2. St. Emillion
3. Montpon
4. Bénévent
5. La Contie
6. Tonneins
7. Port-Ste.-Marie
8. Aiguillon
9. Montjoi

A R M A G N A C

R. Garonne

Key

◯ Castle, bastide, town or city captured by the English

△ Major Valois stronghold

☐ Plantagenet base of operations (22 Jan. 1356)

◌ One of 30 places entering English obedience on
April, 28, 1356

Map 14 - 1

**EXPANDING THE ENGLISH
OBEDIENCE IN GUIENNE, 1356**

Two other groups made deep raids into Quercy and the Agenais. The first, a thousand men under the earls of Suffolk, Oxford and Salisbury, Elie de Pommiers, and Raimond de Montaut, Sire de Mussidan, started by clearing the Isle river between the prince's base at Libourne and Mussidan, capturing Montpon, Montignac, Vauclaire, Bénévent, and La Contie.[10] From there, around 9 January, they began a *chevauchée* up the Dordogne towards Rocamadour. No further details of their expedition are known, but they sufficiently impressed the lord of Limeuil (an important castle over sixty miles upstream from Libourne) that he joined the English side in April.[11] The second division, a comparable force led by the prince's main advisors, John Chandos and James Audley, took a wandering course. From St.-Emillion they captured the castle of Montravel, crossed the Dordogne there, took Listrac-de-Durèze, then swept eastwards into Quercy. Just short of Puy-l'Évêque, they captured Frayssinet and Vire-sur-Lot.[12] There they crossed the river, turned back west, and seized the walled town of Port-Ste.-Marie on the Garonne, possibly taking Colleignes on their way. From Port-Ste.-Marie, they advanced against Agen.[13] It was too strong to capture, and its defenders stayed safe behind their defenses, so Chandos and his company

on its placement in the list) also this group, or else the Earl of Oxford's group, which captured the castle of "Pusdechales," which I have been unable to identify.

The same letter states that Warwick had captured Tonneins [Tonynges] and Clairac [Cleyrak]; listed with them as a "ville enclose," is "Burgh seynt Piere," which was apparently a walled suburb of Tonneins, probably on the opposite side of the Garonne. See Chaplais, *War of St. Sardos*, 264. If my identification of "ij. chastels appellez Boloygnes, qe sount bien pres lun de lautre" with Bouglon south of Marmande is correct, it was doubtless this same group which captured them. The earl's base at La Réole [Riole] is given by Chandos Herald, *Vie du Prince Noir*, l. 669.

10 Wingfield in *Avesbury*, 446 [Mounpoun, Mountanak, Valeclare, Benavaunt, Contdestablison]. All of these are easily recognized except "Contdestablison," which is probably a conflation of Contie and *d'establison* ("garrisoned"). I infer that it was the Sire de Mussidan's group, stated by Wingfield to be on *chevauchée* towards Rocamadour (see next note), which secured the area around Mussidan.

11 Chandos Herald, *Vie du Prince Noir*, ll. 671, 673, has Salisbury and Suffolk based at Ste.-Foy and St.-Emillion near Libourne. The other details are based on Wingfield in *Avesbury*, 447. The identification of "Nostre Dame de Rochemade" as Rocamadour is supported by Froissart, *Oeuvres*, 25:234. Hewitt unhelpfully calls it "Notre Dame de Rochemade," and conflates the raid of Suffolk etc. with that of Burghersh and Buch's division into Anjou and Poitou, but this is not supported by the sources, and furthermore does not make much sense. *Black Prince's Expedition*, 88. For Limeuil, see *Avesbury*, 449. The connection between his submission and Oxford's raid is my inference.

12 Chandos Herald (*Vie du Prince Noir*, ll. 686–8) has Chandos and Audley undertake their *chevauchée* "Dusqe a Caours et vers Agent." Cahors is the capital of Quercy, so the Herald is likely referring to an advance towards Frayssinet [Frechenet] and Vire-sur-Lot [Viressch], just into Quercy, which Wingfield (in *Avesbury*, 446) lists among the captured castles. Lamothe-Montravel ["Moun Ryvel"] and Listrac ["Lystrak"] are on the path from Libourne to there. Chandos' and Audley's company, not including the elements under Baldwin Boutetort at Brassac or those under Cobham at Lavardac, comprised over 300 men-at-arms, 300 sergeants, and 150 archers, and had adequate supplies to last until June. Ibid.

13 Chandos Herald, *Vie du Prince Noir*, l. 688, has Chandos and Audley capture Port-Ste.-Marie, which Wingfield also lists among the captured towns (*Avesbury*, 446), after riding

destroyed the bridges and mills outside the walls, captured and garrisoned an unnamed castle nearby, then moved east to take two walled towns and a bastide north of Moissac – Castelsagrat, Brassac, and Montjoi. These three strongholds enabled them to control the Séounne valley, and keep Boucicaut and his men, who had arrived to defend the area, bottled up in Moissac.[14] While most of this division remained in Castelsagrat and Brassac, a detachment of English and Gascon troops under Reginald Cobham returned to Port-Ste.-Marie, crossed the Garonne, seized Buzet-sur-Baïse, and established a southern flank for the prince's armies at Lavardac.[15]

Thus, the prince had done a great deal to reassert English control over areas of Aquitaine lost by his grandfather to the French. This was done partly by the most direct method: capturing and garrisoning important strongholds, especially those located on the main rivers which were the arteries of southwest France. Marmande, Aiguillon, and Agen, which remained centers of Valois power along the Garonne, were contained by rings of Plantagenet garrisons. Chandos' men, stationed at the outer edge of what had been Edward I's Duchy of Guienne, held the French garrisons at Moissac on the Tarn and Puy-l'Évêque on the Lot in check. The Plantagenet presence on the Isle, with the capture of the five castles around Montpon, was solidly in place well east of where the duchy's border had been in 1307.[16]

Despite this impressive exploitation of the opportunities presented in the aftermath of the Narbonne *chevauchée*, the prince did not rest on his laurels. When Wingfield wrote his letter to Stafford on 22 January, Burghersh and Buch were on a *chevauchée* into Anjou and Poitou with the lords of Montferrand and Curton; Suffolk, Oxford, Salisbury, Elie de Pommiers, and the Sire de Mussidan had not returned from their drive towards Rocamadour; Chandos' and Cobham's companies were out on raids in their zones; and Warwick had ridden towards Marmande "in order to destroy their supplies, and everything else of theirs that he could destroy."[17] In the course of this raid, the earl probably seized Miramont and its strong castle northeast of Marmande, thus completing the isolation of that French stronghold.[18] Meanwhile, the prince reassembled elements of his

---

"vers Agent." The "Collier" listed by Wingfield is probably Colleignes north of Port-Ste.-Marie. It could have been captured by Warwick's division rather than Chandos'.

14 Wingfield in *Avesbury*, 446 [Chastel Satrat, Brassak, Mounjoye].

15 Ibid. Wingfield has Cobham "retourne arere vers Lavedak" (BL, MS Harley 200, fo. 133v; the printed version has "Lanedak") after the capture of Castelsagrat; Buzet-sur-Baïse [Wingfield's "Buset"], near the confluence of the Baïse and the Garonne, is about five miles off the road between Port-Ste.-Marie and Lavardac. Lavardac was a property of the English crown: *RFR*, III:1:129.

16 For the 1307 border, see the map in Vale, "The War in Aquitaine," 70.

17 Wingfield in *Avesbury*, 446–7. While at Castelsagrat, Chandos strengthened the works there, and gathered cattle by the hundred. Hewitt, *Black Prince's Expedition*, 89–90.

18 *Avesbury*, 450, notes that "the Earl of Warwick subjugated . . . a certain walled town in *Kersyn* called *Mirabeu*, with a very strong castle." Since Mirambeau is quite far from La

dispersed army and sent them up the Isle to Périgueux, the capital of Périgord. The Count of Périgord, with papal backing, attempted to secure the safety of the city by paying an *appatis* to the prince but, as with the *Bourg* of Carcassonne in the previous campaign, Edward was more interested in demonstrating Plantagenet power than in adding to the already substantial pile of treasure he had won on the 1355 *chevauchée*. His father the King of England, he wrote in answer to the count's proposal, had all the wealth he needed, and had supplied him with abundant gold and silver, so that he did not lack for money. He would not let the town buy its safety for gold or silver, but rather would punish and discipline the inhabitants of the Duchy of Aquitaine by force of arms until they abandoned their rebellion against his father, King Edward, and returned to his allegiance and obedience. Days after this response was delivered, the city fell to Captal de Buch.[19]

The lords of Aquitaine got the message. On 28 April, a group of powerful nobles – Jean Galard, Sire de Limeuil; Gaillard Durfort, Sire de Grignols; Bernard Durfort; and the Sire de Caumont – switched to the Plantagenet allegiance. With them they brought thirty castles, walled towns, and forts, including the key town of Le Mas, doubling at one stroke the gains the prince's men had already made.[20]

For many of these lords, whose holdings largely fell within the boundaries of the pre-St. Sardos Duchy of Guienne, this change was relatively easy.[21] Those areas which had not been under Plantagenet rule in living memory reacted differently to the English campaigns, but in ways which in total cost the Valois king even more than did the defection of thirty towns and castles. The most dramatic result of the prince's raid came in Toulouse, where, says Froissart, the Count of Armagnac was "much hated" for his failure to engage the English during the Narbonne *chevauchée*. Armagnac's position was not helped by the sympathetic letters which Jean II sent to the towns which had been destroyed,

Réole (or Quercy), in Saintonge not far from Montendre, and furthermore Mirambeau was still in French hands after Poitiers (*Le Baker*, 155), Avesbury probably has made a mistake for Miramont, a substantial town and key road junction northeast of Marmande. It is possible, however, that Warwick, after a raid towards Marmande, returned to one of the bases north of Agen, then launched another *chevauchée* in the opposite direction, during which he might have captured Mirabel in Quercy. Hewitt simply calls it Mirabeau in Quercy, without further identification. *Black Prince's Expedition*, 89.
[19] *Avesbury*, 457: "castigare, disciplinare, militari omnes habitatores ducatus Aquitanniae, dicto domino regi patri suo rebelles, et ad pristinam ipsius legeanciam, pro suis viribus, revocare, ac sibi obedientes in sua justitia manutenere." After Périgueux was captured, its defenses were repaired and it was garrisoned with a force of 100 men-at-arms. Hewitt, *Black Prince's Expedition*, 89. The castle remained under French control. *Vie du Prince Noir*, ll. 691–701.
[20] *Avesbury*, 449–50.
[21] Cf. *Gascon Calendar of 1322*, 140–1, 144; *War of St. Sardos*, 39, 259, 261, 263, 212; *RTC*, nos. 3178, 3709, 4591, 5529, 7078.

which excused the king for his failure to defend them by, in essence, shifting the blame onto Armagnac.[22]

More hostility was directed at the royal lieutenant throughout the Midi because of his role in imposing the painful costs of improving the region's defenses against the likelihood of a new Anglo-Gascon *chevauchée*. Armagnac's responsibilities included the destruction of any fortifications which were not strong enough to be defended effectively, lest they be seized, strengthened, and used as bases by the English.[23] The nobles of Languedoc whose insufficiently strong châteaux were torn down in accordance with this policy, like the inhabitants of bastides whose walls were demolished and who in some cases were forced to abandon their homes, obviously resented this policy: for them, the medicine was worse than the disease.

Even where Valois officials were not ordering demolitions and expulsions, they were directing defensive preparations which imposed heavy burdens on the people of Languedoc. A massive program of fortification construction began in dozens of towns and cities. In Narbonne, royal deputies decreed that the services of all skilled construction workers in the town would for up to five years be reserved for the city's new walls, and that as many men and women of the town as necessary would assist them in their work. At Millau, each household in the city had to supply a laborer to work on the walls one day in every eight. Similar efforts were made everywhere.[24] The costs, of course, ultimately came out of the taxpayers' purses, whether through local taxes or indirectly through the heavy taxes granted by the Estates of Languedoc in March.[25]

All these burdens, of course, could have been avoided if Armagnac, who had commanded a much larger force than the prince's, had defeated Edward in battle. The fact that the Anglo-Gascon army had escaped without battle was especially galling to the bourgeois of Toulouse, for they had tried to convince the count to allow them to issue out against the invaders when the *chevauchée* first drew near their city. Armagnac had then (as we saw in the last chapter) not only forbidden them to do so, but had also required them to destroy their own suburbs.[26] In 1357, when Armagnac tried to enforce an unpopular tax, these tensions would break out into a genuine tax revolt and a virtual civil war between Jean II's personal representative in Languedoc and the largest city of the region.[27] Already in early 1356 they left the Valois political position in the

22 See Jean II's letter of 18 December to the consuls of Montpellier in Delachenal, *Histoire de Charles V,* 1:130n: "dolemus insuper et amare tristamur quod quia nobis fuerat de eisdem partibus pro certo rescriptum, per litteras et nuncios speciales, quod numerus gencium nostrarum in armis numerum hostium nostrorum ibidem multipliciter excedebat, nec poterant evadere sine bello."

23 Noël, "Town Defence," 19, 29.

24 Ibid., 27–9; 58–9, 102, 241; Jeanjean, *Incursion du Prince Noir*, 49–57.

25 They granted a double subsidy of 6d on the pound (sales tax) and fixed *taille* of a gold *mouton* per hearth. Delachenal, *Histoire de Charles V,* 1:132.

26 Froissart, *Chroniques*, 4:161–2.

27 Breuils, "Jean I," 62–3; cf. Froissart, *Chroniques*, 4:382.

south much weakened, and added to the mass of the pressures pushing the French government into a more aggressive, and more dangerous, military stance.

This discord was bad enough for the French cause, but the situation in the north of the realm was even worse. Arras and much of Normandy rose in open rebellion against Jean, and elsewhere as well "the King of France was severely hated in his own realm."[28] The fundamental reasons were the same as those which had prompted unrest in the south: high taxes and failure to resist the Plantagenet invaders (both, it should be noted, results of the 1355 *chevauchées*).[29] Edward III was well informed of the troubles in France: the account of the Arras uprising in the chronicle composed by the court registrar of the Archbishop of Canterbury is noticeably superior to that contained in the semi-official *Grandes chroniques de France*.[30] As the former explains, the lesser citizens of Arras were reacting to the imposition of new taxes which Jean II had levied to pay the cost of the war with England. The bourgeois complained that they could not afford such a subsidy, since they had suffered greatly from the depredations of the English (most recently the preceding November, when there had been panic in the town at the threat of an English siege[31]), and King Jean had done nothing to defend them. Instead, he had only imposed nearly unbearable burdens on them, and spent their subsidies fruitlessly. They had reached the point that they refused to pay any more: they would rather take responsibility for the defense of the city themselves, and let the king and the rest of realm do the same.[32] Leading burgesses who refused to go along with the rebellion were killed by the lesser folk of the town.

In Normandy, especially upper Normandy, the response to the new taxes was much the same. "God's Blood, God's Blood, this king is a bad man," declared the Count of Harcourt (nephew of Godfrey d'Harcourt) at the meeting of the Norman Estates at Valdreuil, "and not a good king, and truly I will guard myself against him."[33] More importantly, he told the bourgeois of Rouen that if they

---

[28] *Récits*, 283: "le roy de France fut durement enhays en son royalme."
[29] As Philippe de Mézières observed later in the century, it is precisely these factors which could be expected to inspire rebellion in late medieval France: "Because of the taxes and the widespread devastation resulting from feeble defence, your people begin to complain and to say that they have been more harassed than free men should be. From such oppression are born treason and rebellion." *Le Songe du Vieil Pelerin*, ed. and tr. G. Coopland (Cambridge: Cambridge U.P., 1969), 2:76, French on 2:386.
[30] *Avesbury*, 457–8; *Chron. Jean II et Charles V*, 62.
[31] Froissart, *Chroniques*, 4:141.
[32] *Avesbury*, 457. The uprising began on 5 March 1356, just after news reached the city of the 1 March concession by the reassembled Estates of a new head tax, which was to be in addition to the substantial grant already made in December. The main towns of Picardy, significantly, had not been present at this second meeting of the Estates, so it is little wonder that they objected strongly to the royal government's attempt to impose taxes which they had not granted. *Chron. Jean II et Charles V*, 1:62, 60; cf. Froissart, *Chroniques*, 4:175.
[33] Delachenal, *Histoire de Charles V*, 1:139 n.6, citing the testimony of Friquet de Fricamps. Cf. *Chron. Jean II et Charles V*, 64.

accepted the new gabelle they would be no better than serfs, that he would not allow it to be levied in his lands, and that any royal official who tried to collect it there would suffer for the attempt. The King of Navarre, Charles the Bad, who was also Count of Evreux and one of the largest landholders in Normandy, said the same, and a number of other local lords joined them in a sworn confederation to block the taxes. Thus, throughout March and into April, they were virtually rebels against the commandments and ordinances of the king, and their revolt was beginning to spread to other areas.[34]

The risk this posed to the Valois monarchy was obvious. It was less than a year since Charles of Navarre had murdered the constable, Charles de la Cerda, and conspired with the English; it was less than a decade since Godfrey d'Harcourt had first done homage to Edward III as King of France. Charles enjoyed great influence with his brother-in-law, the dauphin, Charles Duke of Normandy, and had earlier, reportedly, been involved with him in plots against King Jean. What might not happen if the Harcourts and Navarrese were allowed to continue in open defiance of royal authority?

Jean did not wait to find out. The scene is famous: on 5 April, preceded by Marshal d'Audrehem bearing a naked sword and followed by a hundred armored men-at-arms, the king burst into the feast-hall in Rouen where Charles of Navarre, Charles of Normandy and the Count of Harcourt were dining with a large number of friends. "Nobody move," called out the marshal, "no matter what you see, unless you want to die by this sword!"[35] Jean, his countenance dark, strode past the frightened guests, up to the high table. Dismayed, the men seated there rose up to pay their respects to the king, but he ignored them. His arm lanced out, he grabbed the King of Navarre by the cowl, and roughly pulled him in. "Up, traitor!" he said, "you are not worthy to sit at the table of my son. By the soul of my father, I do not intend to drink or eat until you are dead."[36]

There were scuffles, protests, proclamations of innocence and pleas for mercy. Despite the best efforts of the Duke of Normandy, the King of Navarre was cast into prison, along with the lords of Préaux, Cleres, and Tournebu, and Louis and William d'Harcourt. Jean, Count of Harcourt, Jean Malet the Sire de Graville, and two others were not so lucky. They were bound to a pair of carts, pulled out to the Field of Pardon behind the castle of Rouen, and decapitated. Their naked bodies were then hung from the gibbet there, and their heads set atop it.[37]

This brutal action struck many of Jean's subjects as tyranny of the worst kind. He claimed that his victims had been traitors, but he gave no specifics: even to his son the dauphin, he said only "They are evil traitors, and they will soon

34 Froissart, *Chroniques*, 4:175: "tant que pluiseur aultre pays y prisent piet." Cf. *Chron. Jean II et Charles V,* 64.
35 Froissart, *Chroniques*, 4:177; *Chron. Jean II et Charles V,* 1:62.
36 Froissart, *Chroniques*, 4:178.
37 *Chron. Jean II et Charles V,* 1:63–5.

reveal their deed. You don't know everything I know."[38] But promised revelation
never came. Charles of Navarre continued to protest his innocence, and Edward
III – never one to pass up an opportunity for a propaganda coup – issued letters
to the Pope, the emperor, and many others, in which he depicted the Valois king
as unchivalrous, tyrannical, and dishonest:

> In order to justify his massacre, it is said, Jean claims to have letters of the said
> king [of Navarre] and nobles, in which they conspired to betray him, and hand
> over the Duchy of Normandy to us, and even promised to do the work . . . We
> say the truth in the words of a king, and faithfully testify in the court of God,
> that the said king and nobles were not conspiring with us on anything, nor
> were they supported or favored by us; rather, we call them our strong
> enemies.[39]

Many Frenchmen were more prepared to believe Edward than their own
monarch. "King Jean was much criticised for the killing of the said lords," notes
the *Chronique des quatres premieres Valois*, "and because of this much ill-will
was directed at him by the nobles and by his people, and especially those of
Normandy."[40] Support for the King of Navarre, which inherently carried an
implication of dissatisfaction with the Valois régime, was very widespread.[41]
The strongest reactions, of course, came from Godfrey d'Harcourt and Charles'
brother Philip of Navarre. After unsuccessfully seeking release of their imprisoned relatives, they renounced their homages to Jean II,[42] seized control over
much of Normandy, then turned to Edward III for help. The Plantagenet, of
course, was more than happy to give it.

*

When the first Navarrese envoys reached England in mid-May, they brought
word from Philip of Navarre, Charles' brother, that he had raised the entire
Cotentin against Jean II, and that Navarrese garrisons also held Pont-Audemer,
Breteuil, and the comital capital of Evreux at the other end of Normandy. It was
clear that French forces would soon move against these three outposts of rebellion. Philip desperately needed English assistance, and, as it happened, King

---

38 Froissart, *Chroniques*, 4:179.
39 *RFH*, 3:1:123 [14 May 1356]. Note that Delachenal characterizes this letter as saying
"Jamais aucune entent n'a existé entre le roi d'Angleterre et la noblesse normande," which
would be clearly false. But this is taking "nusquam" ["no-where," or "in nothing," or "on no
occasion"] to be the equivalent of "nunquam" ["never"] – which it can be. However, it seems
more likely that Edward meant "in nothing": "in nothing did they conspire with us," i.e.
"there was no plot, they did not conspire with us on anything"; not "never did they conspire
with us, there was never any plot."
40 *Chron. des quat. prem. Valois*, 37: "Moult fut blamé le roy Jehan de l'occision des diz
seigneurs et moult en fut en la malivolence des nobles et de son peuple et par especial de
ceulx de Normendie."
41 Delachenal, *Histoire de Charles V*, 1:157–9.
42 Philip's admirable letter renouncing his fealty to Jean II is printed in Froissart, *Oeuvres*,
5:551–2.

Edward was in a fairly good position to grant it, having recently returned from a relatively major campaign in Scotland.

As noted in the last chapter, the Plantagenet had been recalled from Calais the previous fall by word of a Scottish *coup de main* against Berwick. On returning to England, he promptly turned his attention to the affairs of the north. The first step was the recapture of the city of Berwick, which posed little difficulty for the English. While Edward III stayed at Newcastle directing the assembly of an army which had been ordered to muster there by 1 January, he sent ahead a detachment of 120 miners from the forest of Dean and elsewhere who began to tunnel under the city walls.[43] They had nearly completed their work when the royal host arrived on 13 January. The tiny garrison of 130 men who had been left to guard the city had no hope of resisting, and there was certainly no prospect of a relief army coming to their rescue, so they promptly surrendered. Generous as usual in such cases, Edward allowed them to depart with their goods as well as their lives, even though in practice this meant they were permitted to profit from the plunder they had taken from the English citizens of Berwick.[44]

Once the city was secured, the army advanced to Roxburgh, where it arrived by the middle of January. Meanwhile, Edward III had persuaded Edward Balliol to surrender to him his rights to the throne of Scotland, in exchange for an annual pension of £2,000. In a ceremony on the 20th, Balliol provided his liege-lord a charter to that effect, and personally handed over the crown of Scotland, along with a handful of earth and stones from his kingdom.[45] When the Plantagenet and his army marched north a few days later, the royal banner of Scotland was among those displayed by the English king.[46]

At first all this seems rather puzzling. Edward III was still in the middle of his great war with France, and had no more resources to spare for the conquest of Scotland than he had since 1337. By accepting (indeed, engineering) Balliol's cession, was he not binding himself to a more vigorous prosecution of what was likely to be a costly and difficult effort in the north with little prospect of any success commensurate with the effort which would be required – especially since he already had a legal claim to most of Scotland up to the Firth of Forth, less than half of which he actually had any control over?

To understand what the English king was up to, his actions of January 1356 must be seen in the context of his ongoing negotiations with David II, still his captive since the battle of Neville's Cross a decade earlier. The Bruce king, eager to regain his freedom and his throne and (like so many other of Edward's

---

43 Newcastle: *RFR*, III:1:315. Miners: *Avesbury*, 450.

44 *Avesbury*, 450–1; *Fordun*, 373; *Pluscardensis*, 297 (plunder). This generosity served to minimize the time, money, and lives the king had to spend on the conduct of sieges.

45 *RFH*, 3:1:114–18 (documents); *Fordun*, 373 (ceremony).

46 The army departed Roxburgh on either the 27th (*Avesbury*, 454) or, more probably, the 24th (*Knighton*, 2:85). Banner: *Avesbury*, 454.

"enemies" who came to know him well)[47] apparently attracted to the chivalric and charismatic English monarch, had relatively quickly proved willing to grant a peace settlement on terms acceptable to the Plantagenet. At first Edward III had tried to procure a settlement similar to the 1336 Treaty of Newcastle. The Disinherited were to be restored; David was to do homage for Scotland and provide military service. Edward also tried to persuade his childless brother-in-law to settle the inheritance of the kingdom onto either Edward himself, or one of his children (David's nephews by marriage), instead of Robert Stewart (who had abandoned the King of Scots at Neville's Cross).[48] Robert Bruce's son was not prepared to go quite that far, but he made an attractive counter-offer, probably in the fall of 1350. Precisely what this entailed is very difficult to disentangle, and over the next two years of negotiations the terms under consideration varied somewhat, but throughout this period three key elements seem to have remained constant: the Disinherited were to be restored; there would be a peace or a long truce so that Edward III could focus on his war with France; and David (provided he died without a legitimate heir, as now seemed probable) would settle the succession of the Scottish throne on Edward's third son, John of Gaunt.[49] Such an arrangement would have been more than satisfactory for Edward III.[50] Unfortunately for the two kings, however, the community of the realm of Scotland was not as eager to regain its head as David was to recover his freedom. This was of course especially true of Robert Stewart, the regent during David's captivity, who stood to be both deprived of his power and disinherited of the kingdom by the proposed treaty. He managed to block the implementation of each proposed version of the accord, with the help of the other Scottish lords who were happy with the current situation, in which the lack of a strong royal government allowed each of them to rule in his own territory.[51] A new Anglo-

---

[47] E.g. Raoul, Count of Guînes and Eu and Constable of France; Olivier de Clisson; and Thomas de la Marche, Bastard of France (all either executed for treason or threatened with execution by Valois kings after a stay in Edward's court); William Douglas of Liddesdale, Thomas of Mar and Thomas Stewart (Earl of Angus); and Jean II and David II themselves after their capture at Poitiers and Neville's Cross. For the Scots, see Campbell, "England, Scotland, and the Hundred Years War," in Rogers (ed.), *Wars of Edward III*, 215, 222. One could reasonably add Guy of Flanders (on whom cf. *DEB*, 181), Philip of Navarre, and Marshal Boucicaut (*Le Bel*, 2:214) to this list.

[48] See the text of David's petition in A. A. M. Duncan, "*Honi soit qui mal y pense*: David II and Edward III, 1346–52," *Scottish Historical Review* 67 (1988), 138–9; note particularly sentence [2a]. Duncan's interpretation of David's attitude to the proposal (ibid., 116–120) is preferable to Balfour-Melville's (*Edward III and David II*, 15–16).

[49] Duncan, "David II and Edward III," does some brilliant detective work in pulling the evidence together. There were also to be concessions on the English side, varying at different stages in the negotiations; the most important (aside from peace and David's release) appear to be a willingness at least to put aside the question of English suzerainty over Scotland during a thousand-year truce (in the August 1351 terms, though not necessarily before or after) and that the Disinherited would pay a moderate cash compensation to the current holders of their restored lands.

[50] Ibid., 121–2 (clause 2).

[51] Scottish lords: Leland's abstract in *Scalacronica* (ed. Maxwell), 117. David II, on his

Scottish treaty, this one a simple ransom agreement, was drawn up not long after the conclusion of the Anglo-French Treaty of Guînes in 1354. Its terms were so generous, however, that it seems likely Edward III and David II had a secret agreement that the King of Scots would continue, once freed, to work for an arrangement along the lines of the settlement described above. Stewart's supporters may have suspected as much, which could explain why the treaty was never implemented by the Scots.[52]

Still, by securing the Bruce king's personal acceptance of satisfactory peace terms, Edward III had gone a long way towards settling Scottish affairs to his liking. A second, lesser, problem was posed by Edward Balliol, for the Plantagenet had promised his vassal not to compromise his claim to the northern kingdom without his consent. Yet Balliol certainly realized that by 1356 there was very little prospect of his ever regaining control over Scotland, even with Edward III's wholehearted support. Thus, as we have seen, the Plantagenet was able to buy him off at a cost which, though by no means trivial, would be small enough if it cleared the way for a favorable and honorable end to the war.[53]

release, would doubtless have been able (with Edward III's support) rapidly to restore a measure of strong royal government, and in the long run it would be expected that John of Gaunt, with his father's example and support, would have been able to increase the crown's power in Scotland greatly. Rejections: Duncan, "David II and Edward III," 123–5 (1351), 132 (1352).

52 Treaty: *RFH*, 3:1:99 (ransom of 90,000 marks). Generosity: compare to the agreement of 1350–51 (Duncan, "David II and Edward III," 123–4), which required a ransom 2/3 as large, *and* the restoration of the Disinherited, *and* a Plantagenet succession, and perhaps more, *and* was made before the Treaty of Guînes, which had it been implemented would have put the Scots in a desperate position. Secret arrangement: in the negotiations leading up to the treaty, Edward III seems still to have aimed at a definitive peace settlement which would have acknowledged David as King of Scots, since just two weeks before the completion of the ransom treaty (as also in 1351) he promised Edward Balliol that the latter's rights in Scotland would not be compromised by the negotiations *unless* a treaty were completed. He would not have had any need to negotiate with Edward Balliol concerning the latter's rights in Scotland if only a ransom treaty (which would not affect Balliol's claims) were in the offing, nor would he have been likely to make such a concession to David without getting his way on the succession issue. *RFH*, 3:1:97–8. Also, Edward III and David II had already in earlier negotiations envisioned the possibility of using a secret clause to get around opposition to the arrangement they both favored. Duncan, "David II and Edward III," 122 (clause 4). It seems that David was not unwilling to see John of Gaunt rather than Robert Stewart (who had abandoned him at Neville's Cross, and then blocked every attempt to get him out of prison) succeed him, and the secret clause, if indeed it existed, most likely envisioned that once free he would work towards a "new" treaty which would cancel his ransom and return to Scottish control the lands occupied by Edward III in exchange for a Plantagenet succession and the restoration of the Disinherited. The 1357 Treaty of Edinburgh – another simple ransom treaty, this one implemented – may also have had a similar secret clause (or understanding), since in 1363–64 David agreed to and put before the Scottish parliament just such an agreement. *RFH* 3:2:82–3.

53 Especially considering that Balliol was then somewhere around 70 years old, and so it cannot have been expected that the £2,000 pension would be paid out for many years. (In the event Edward died in 1364.)

Thus, in late January of 1356 only one thing stood between Edward III and victory in the now 24-year-old Second War of Scottish Independence (via a revival of the terms of 1350–52): the obstinacy of the Scottish people and nobility. The king's past experiences in Scotland suggested that this obstacle could be overcome by the overwhelming application of brute force, as it had been (albeit briefly) by the great invasions of 1333 and 1335. It seems, in other words, that his strategy in 1356 was to use the opportunity presented by the aggression against Berwick to take a great army into Scotland, so that he could apply pressure directly to the Scottish commons and magnates, who otherwise had little motive to support the peace arrangements agreed by the two kings.

Of course, this analysis does not explain why Edward III had Balliol transfer the kingship directly to him, or why he marched into Scotland under the lion banner, suggesting that he intended to make himself (as Avesbury calls him) the new King of Scots,[54] instead of finalizing an agreement with David II personally and then sending his army north under the Bruce king to put down any of his "rebellious" subjects who refused to accept the treaty. The reasons are not difficult to guess, however. As the experiences of two successive Balliols had demonstrated, the Scots were not eager to be ruled by a king who openly owed his throne to English military support. David's greatest asset, the thing that most contributed to his potential ability to solidify a permanent peace with England on Edward's terms, was his legitimacy, and putting him at the head of an invading army of foreigners would only have destroyed that legitimacy.

It seems, thus (though there is no direct evidence to support this conclusion) that the Plantagenet was using his purchased claim to the Scottish throne as a bargaining chip, a way to say to the Scots that they had better compromise by accepting a Plantagenet succession in Scotland – one which, by the terms of the 1351 agreement, would at least keep Scotland an independent realm – lest they provoke him into a war of conquest to assert his direct lordship. Just as he was willing to surrender his claim to the French throne in return for an end to Valois claims to sovereignty over his French possessions (and a free hand in Scotland), so too he was probably aiming to surrender his direct claim to the Scottish throne in return for the acceptance of his son's eventual rule over Scotland (and a truce or peace which would allow him to concentrate on his French war).

At first it seemed that the invasion of 1356 might lead to a quick negotiated mass surrender of the Scottish nobility, just as the invasion of 1335 had done. Shortly after the large English host – comprising three thousand men-at-arms and many thousands of hobelars and archers[55] – left Roxburgh, Lord William Douglas (the slayer and successor of the other William Douglas, the knight of Liddesdale who had been captured at Neville's Cross and then done homage to Edward III) approached the king and asked for a truce of eight or ten days. Aves-

---

[54] *Avesbury*, 455.
[55] *Avesbury*, 454. The chronicler's figures for the infantry are clearly much exaggerated, but it would not be surprising if Edward had roughly 10,000 hobelars, horse archers, and foot archers.

bury claims that he said this was "so that he might address the magnates of Scotland, and draw them into [Edward's] obedience and liegeance." Knighton adds that other Scottish nobles also seemed willing to enter Edward's fealty.[56] In fact, however, there was little prospect of a direct submission to Edward III as King of Scots; the negotiating commission granted by the steward a few days earlier was actually to treat for the release of King David.[57] It seems likely that the chroniclers were slightly confused and that the Scots were actually offering to reconsider the proposal for a Plantagenet succession which had been put before the Scottish parliament two years earlier.

It is impossible to know whether the Scots were seriously considering negotiating a compromise peace along those lines or (as Avesbury indicates) whether this was merely a cynical move to buy time for the evacuation of their people and goods into caverns, the deep forests, and the lands north of the Forth. In either case, they certainly pursued the latter precautions during the truce period, at the end of which Douglas sent word that they did not wish to enter the Plantagenet's peace. Edward's response, typically, was that if they did not wish for peace, they would have sharp war. Dividing his army into three battles, which with little fear of Scottish resistance spread out over the unusually large area of sixteen to twenty leagues' breadth, the English king marched north towards Haddington. Nothing was spared from the torch, not even the fine church and monastery there.[58]

Near Edinburgh, the English army rendezvoused with a substantial fleet which had been sent ahead of them there. Campaigning in Scotland, especially in winter, posed severe logistic difficulties, which could only be met by sea transport. This was all the more true because of the success with which the Scots had emptied out the country during the truce period, so that on the march north the miserable English found nothing but water to drink, and also suffered a dearth of bread.[59]

According to Fordun, Edward's intention was now "to destroy and ruin Scotland both near and far, and indeed to devastate it utterly." He apparently planned to march from Lothian towards Perth, but contrary winds kept his fleet from advancing north past the Firth of Forth, leaving him stuck in Lothian for over a week in early February.[60] His troops ravaged the area so severely that this episode has ever after been known in Scotland as the "Burnt Candlemas." While his ships were waiting for better weather, they instead got a severe storm which

---

56 *Avesbury*, 455: "pacifice loquens, in dolo petiit inducias decem dierum, ut interim posset alloqui magnates regni Scocie et ipsos allicere ad obedientiam et ligianciam ipsius novi regis Scociae." *Knighton*, 2:85: "multi de magnatibus Scotorum venerunt et habuerunt colloquium cum rege Edwardo quasi vellent venire ad fidem regis; et super hoc assignatus est dies de responso. Et rex cum populo suo quievit in pace per Viij. dies."

57 *RFH*, 3:1:114 (17 January). It also covered negotiations towards a final concord between the realms.

58 *Avesbury*, 455; *Knighton*, 2:85; *Fordun*, 374.

59 *Knighton*, 2:85; *Avesbury*, 455–6.

60 *Fordun*, 374.

sank a few of them and completely dispersed the rest. Had it not been for this gale, writes a Scottish chronicler, nothing would have prevented him from laying waste to all of Scotland, but as it was he was constrained by lack of supplies to retire towards England without having broken the resistance of his enemies.[61] He had, however, succeeded in teaching his enemies the unwisdom of attacking his lands even if he were absent, for what he could not immediately defend, he could at least avenge.

After the army reached Melrose, where it began to break up, Edward received word from Henry of Lancaster – who had made a foray deeper into Scotland – that he had learned that the Scots were preparing for a fight. The king, of course, responded by riding with a small retinue directly to the duke, to see what might develop. By doing so, ironically, he avoided an ambush which had been set for him by William Douglas. Another party of Englishmen, returning south, triggered this trap, and suffered significant losses as a result.[62] Edward, meanwhile, returned to England without further incident. On 18 April – not long before the arrival of the Navarrese envoys in England – a partial truce was concluded with Scotland.[63] Before the next year was done, the Scottish parliament ratified a ransom treaty for David II, on essentially the same terms they had declined to implement in 1354.[64]

*

On 2 May, King Edward formally refused a papal suggestion that he resume peace negotiations with France, noting that previous discussions had never led to a concrete result.[65] Between the king's return to England and then, the Plantagenet court had considered the possibilities for the campaigns of the upcoming season. The prince's *grande chevauchée* would of course have to be followed up with another major expedition. The very success of the 1355 effort ensured that this would not require additional support from England, for the Gascons themselves could be expected to provide all the men he might need.[66] Thus, when news of the Norman situation reached England about two weeks later, the Plantagenet was already planning some sort of campaign in the north of France, but still retained plenty of flexibility in the details of its deployment.

In late May and early June (when the initial two envoys were joined by Martin of Henriquez),[67] the Navarrese worked to forge an alliance between their lord and King Edward. They asked for immediate succor by a thousand soldiers and a supply of money, so that they could hold out long enough to be of service

---

[61] *Fordun*, 374; *Avesbury*, 455–6.

[62] *Knighton*, 2:85; *Avesbury*, 456; *Fordun*, 374.

[63] *RFH*, 3:1:122. It was technically a truce between William Douglas and the Earl of Northampton, but that for practical purposes ensured there would be no major warfare on the Scottish border.

[64] The treaty of Edinburgh. See Duncan, "David II and Edward III," 134, and n. 52, above.

[65] *RFH*, 3:1:122.

[66] Arrangements were made in March, however, to ship some horses and supplies to the prince. *RFH*, 3:1:120, 121.

[67] Ibid., 3:1:122, 123.

to King Edward later. They also wanted guarantees that any suitably major French prisoner captured would be exchanged to free King Charles, and that they and their supporters would be indemnified with English lands if they were driven out of France. The English were willing to accept the first two of these requests, and to promise that no peace would be made with France which did not ensure full restitution of confiscated lands to those of the Navarrese who were willing to do homage to King Edward. The royal council also advised that Edward grant to Philip lordship over substantial lands in eastern Normandy, except for the territories and rights belonging to the Duke of Normandy, which would be reserved to the Plantagenet.[68] Edward was also prepared to grant the Navarrese request that Champagne and Brie be returned to them, if he succeeded to the French throne and could dispose of those counties.[69]

That contingency, however, remained a long way off. Meanwhile, Valois troops had moved into position around Pont-Audemer and Breteuil, strong fortresses which protected the approaches into Normandy from Rouen and Paris, respectively. If the English wanted to keep the support of the house of Evreux, they would have to act quickly, both to reassure rebels who might otherwise decide to seek King Jean's grace, and to keep the most valuable Navarrese possessions available for future use against the French. Within a few days of Sir Martin's arrival, therefore, Edward III dispatched to Normandy the force he had been assembling for an expedition to Brittany, with Henry of Lancaster, his best general, at its head. Perhaps no other man, even among the talented group of military leaders which surrounded the Plantagenet king, could have done as much with such as small army as Duke Henry was to do.

On 18 June, eight hundred English archers and five hundred men-at-arms disembarked at St.-Vaast-la-Hougue, where some of them had last been ten years earlier under very different circumstances. They were met there by Philip of Navarre, Godfrey d'Harcourt, and a round hundred Norman men-at-arms, accompanied by a like number of local archers. Sir Robert Knolles had also brought up a force of three hundred men-at-arms and five hundred archers from the garrisons of Brittany. Lancaster thus initially had some 2,300 men with which to face French forces which may have totalled ten times that many soldiers.[70]

---

[68] Edward would also have the right to keep any other Norman territories he wished, provided that he compensated the Navarrese with other equivalent lands.

[69] The key documents for these negotiations are the instructions given by Philip to his envoys and a memorandum of Edward's council concerning his proposals. (Printed in *KdL*, 378–81, where it is identified as belonging to April 1356. Considering that Philip's messengers were not even granted safe-conducts until May, however, it is fairly certain these proposals and counterproposals date to May.)

[70] Bulletin in *Avesbury*, 463. The bulletin gives the total number of archers as 1,400 after mentioning only 800 from England and 500 from Brittany; the logical conclusion is that the Norman men-at-arms brought 100 archers with them. However, the *Chron. Jean II et Charles V*, 67, claims the Anglo-Navarrese army amounted to around 4,000 troops, and Jean le Bel claims Lancaster had nearly 2,600 men-at-arms and a great number of infantry – a figure which precisely matches the one from the *Chron. Jean II et Charles V*, if the "great number of infantry" refers to the 1,400 archers. This suggests that the 900 men-at-arms with which Lan-

His earlier campaigns in Guienne had been marked by remarkable speed and boldness, combined with a noteworthy ability to capture enemy towns through assault and negotiation. His boldness, however, was one which favored surprise attacks and slashing hit-and-run raids. That is not to say that he was unwilling to face the test of open battle on reasonably even terms, but he did not have the absolute faith in divine favor and English archery which made Edward III happy to invite an attack by enemies twice or thrice as numerous. Lancaster's mission was to relieve Pont-Audemer and Breteuil (Evreux having already fallen to the French on 9 June),[71] and he would do whatever was necessary to accomplish his business. He would even take reasonable risks to go beyond his initial mission parameters, to strengthen the Anglo-Navarrese position or harm the French. To do these things he was prepared to fight, even outnumbered, if necessary, but for him a major battle was rather an impediment to his task than an overriding goal in itself.[72] As Jean le Bel put it, "the Duke of Lancaster, who was wise and expert in arms, realized well that the French army was so strong that by attacking it he might lose more than he would win."[73]

The expeditionary force required a few days to recuperate from its sea-crossing (a rest especially necessary for the trans-shipped warhorses of the men-at-arms), but by 23 June it was at Carentan, on the edge of the Cotentin, ready to set forth into enemy territory. Lancaster's first destination was Pont-Audemer, a fair-sized town near the mouth of the Risle. The English soldiers reached it in four evenly-spaced marches, via Torigni (where they rested for a day), Evercy, Argences, and Lisieux. The French made no effort to resist their advance, not even at the heavily fortified bridge at Corbon, which was described in the campaign bulletin as "the strongest passage in the realm."[74] Each day as

---

caster began the campaign may have received substantial reinforcements from the strongly-manned Navarrese garrisons of Normandy *en route* (so to speak). Cf. also Froissart, *Oeuvres*, 5:367.

Ibid., 5:366, gives almost the correct figures for Lancaster's contingent (he says 400 men-at-arms and 800 archers, increased in the third redaction to 500 and 1,000), and notes that the earls of March and Pembroke accompanied the expedition; we know from the bulletin that John Montfort, the young Duke of Brittany, also served on the *chevauchée*.

The size of the French army which eventually faced Lancaster at l'Aigle is given in the bulletin as 8,000 men-at-arms (the same number as at Crécy) and 40,000 infantry, a figure reduced by Froissart to 10,000 men-at-arms and 20,000–30,000 infantry. *Oeuvres*, 5:369–70. These are presumably exaggerated, but there is good reason to expect that the French army in Normandy was significantly larger than the force of approximately 16,000 which Jean led at Poitiers, considering that the French king had dismissed much of his communal infantry prior to that battle. See below.

[71] *Chron. Jean II et Charles V*, 68; *Le Bel*, 2:226n.

[72] For Lancaster's previous experience as an independent commander in Gascony, see Fowler, *King's Lieutenant*, chs 4, 6; Sumption, *Trial by Battle*, ch. 13, and Burne, *Crecy War*, ch. 5. On his attitude to battle in 1356, see the campaign bulletin quoted below, p. 346, and *Le Bel*, 2:227. In general, see Fowler, op. cit., 220.

[73] *Le Bel*, 2:227: "qu'ilz pourroient plus perdre à ferir sur eulx que gaagnier."

[74] *Avesbury*, 463: "un tres graunt forteresse et le plus forte passage que soit de realme."

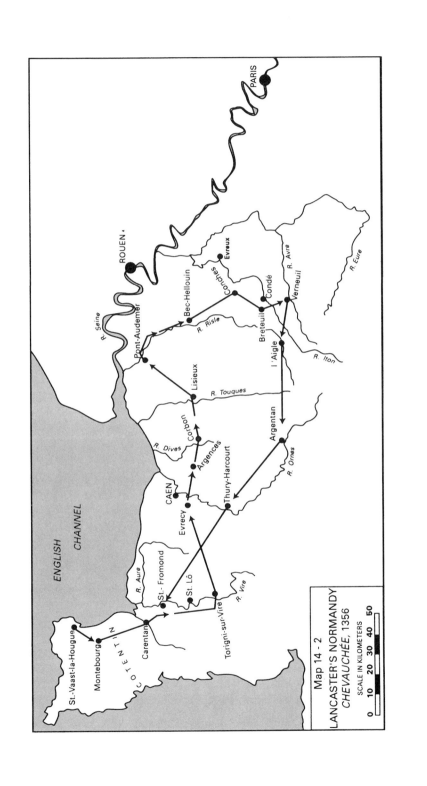

ENGLISH

CHANNEL

St-Vaast-la-Hougue
Montebourg
C O T E N T I N
Carentan
St.- Fromond
St. Lô
R. Aure
Torigni-sur-Vire
R. Vire

R. Seine
ROUEN
PARIS

Pont-Audemer
Bec-Hellouin
R. Risle
Conches
Évreux
Condé
Breteuil
Verneuil
R. Avre
R. Eure
l'Aigle
R. Iton

Lisieux
R. Touques
Corbon
R. Dives
Argences
Thury-Harcourt
Argentan
R. Ornes
CAEN
Evrecy

Map 14 - 2
LANCASTER'S NORMANDY
CHEVAUCHÉE, 1356
SCALE IN KILOMETERS
0 10 20 30 40 50

they went, the Englishmen captured whatever fortresses were too weak to resist them, collected prisoners, plunder and supplies in great plenty, burned the countryside, and in particular brought with them all the horses they could find.[75]

The Valois troops in position around Pont-Audemer, under the command of the Master of Crossbowmen of France, had been besieging the Navarrese stronghold for eight or nine weeks.[76] They had, however, apparently been ordered not to engage the English without the support of the main French army, so as soon as they received word of the crossing at Corbon (west of Lisieux) they broke camp and retreated in unseemly haste, leaving behind their siege engines and much of their other equipment, including even crossbows and pavises.[77] Duke Henry would not be given the opportunity to stage another devastating dawn attack like the one he had led against the French at Auberoche ten years earlier.

His little army had arrived just in time to effect the relief of the town, for the besiegers had dug mines to within four feet of its outer walls.[78] There was now great pressure for the duke to act with speed, for the French, having learned his position and gotten some idea of his weakness, could be expected to act – whether by advancing against him, or merely by pressing the siege of Breteuil. Even so, he stayed at Pont-Audemer for an additional two days in order to secure the castle from a renewed siege, a process which involved stocking it with a year's worth of supplies and filling in the mines the French had made. Henry also reinforced the garrison with fifty men-at-arms and the same number of archers, from his own retinue, and installed a new castellan, Sir Johann de Luk of Brabant.[79]

On 2 July, still with no evidence of any sense of urgency, Lancaster led his men to the famed abbey of Bec, some thirteen miles up the Risle. The next day the army picked up speed, covering over twenty-eight miles to reach the French-held town of Conches in time to assault and capture it. The English also seized the outer bailey of the castle, and burned it down. A short march on the 4th carried the army to its second main objective, the King of Navarre's strong castle of Breteuil. As at Pont-Audemer, the besiegers departed before the duke's arrival, though this time in better order. The castle's defenses had not been compromised, so all that was necessary was for it to be resupplied; this was accomplished quickly.

Only a few miles away from Breteuil lay Verneuil, the strategically positioned capital city of lower Normandy,[80] and there was as yet no sign of the

---

[75] Ibid., 465; *Chron. Jean II et Charles V,* 68. Cf. Froissart, *Oeuvres,* 5:367.

[76] *Chron. Jean II et Charles V,* 67.

[77] Bulletin in *Avesbury,* 463; *Chron. Jean II et Charles V,* 67–8.

[78] Bulletin in *Avesbury,* 463.

[79] Ibid.

[80] The campaign bulletin refers to it as "appelle le chief de Normandy," and Knighton (whose account of the action is largely derived from the bulletin) departs from his source to say it is called "one of the keys of Normandy" [una clavis Normanniae], and adds that it is partly in Normandy, partly in the Ile-de-France. *Avesbury,* 464; *Knighton,* 2:86.

French army.[81] Lancaster gladly took the opportunity to strike a blow against the French and enrich himself and his army at the same time. The same day that Breteuil had been relieved, the English pressed on to take the town of Verneuil by assault. They took many prisoners and seized a great deal of booty, but as always in such cases the richest men of the area had secured themselves and their goods in the strongest element of the defenses, in this instance the famous Grey Keep constructed by Henry I. Since King Jean had still made no sign of his appearance, Duke Henry decided to try to crack the hard shell to reach the pearl within. The assault began that very evening, and continued all through the next day. The attackers lost a number of men to crossbow bolts and cast stones, but pressed the assault until Wednesday morning, when the defenders agreed to surrender, provided they were allowed their lives and freedom.[82] The English got the rich store of goods inside, and Henry ordered that the captured keep be demolished before their departure. This took the rest of the day on Wednesday. That evening, Duke Henry received a report that the French army had finally reached Condé-sur-Iton, next to Breteuil.[83] That put the French in easy striking distance of the English army, and Lancaster had enough experience in surprise attacks not to risk being taken unawares. He immediately had his men issue out of the town and take up battle positions in the fields.[84] The Valois army, however, did not make an appearance.

It is somewhat surprising that the English did not take advantage of that night, the 6/7 June, to begin their retreat towards the Cotentin before the French could establish contact. Perhaps Henry did not yet realize just how large the French army was, or perhaps he wanted to rest his hard-worked men, and was counting on Valois timidity to hold his enemies back for another day. If that was his calculation, it proved correct. The English spent all day on the 7th in the

---

81 It was probably still in Rouen. See below, note 83.

82 The bulletin says the keep surrendered at primes, while Knighton makes it at tierce. Knighton also notes that the English made use of a strong ram (*hordicium*) which was wonderfully effective in bringing down the walls of the castle. *Avesbury*, 464; *Knighton*, 2:86.

83 *Knighton*, 2:86. This source does not mention Condé by name, but it gives the distance (five leagues), which matches with the French position at Condé reported in *Chron. Jean II et Charles V,* 68. The sources do not enable us to reconstruct Jean's itinerary with certainty, but based on information given by the chronicles, it appears to have been as follows. The king issued summons as soon as he learned of the English landing, with the soldiers ordered to assemble at Poissy, near Paris, and at Beauvais, from where they could advance either to Paris or to Rouen. Jean took up a position at Mantes near the end of June, and was there when, probably late on the 30th, he received a report that Lancaster had passed the bridge of Corbon and appeared to be heading for Rouen. He rode the fifty-odd miles from Mantes to Rouen on 31 June and 1 July, with his army following behind as best it could. He remained halted at Rouen on the 2nd through 4th of July, waiting for his full army to gather. By the evening of the 2nd he would have learned that Lancaster had departed southwards from Pont-Audemer, but he was not ready to set out in pursuit until the morning of the 5th. When he did so, he pressed his troops and made good time, reaching Condé by mid-afternoon of the 6th. Froissart, *Oeuvres*, 5:369 (to 7/4); *Chron. Jean II et Charles V,* 68, and *Knighton*, 2:86 (to 7/6). Cf. Burne, *Crecy War*, 272–3, for a different reconstruction.

84 *Knighton*, 2:87.

fields outside Verneuil, resting but arrayed and prepared for a French attack. Jean, however, spent the day where he began it, at Condé, resting his forces after their two-day forced march from Rouen.[85]

The French chroniclers assert that the Valois was eager to come to grips with his enemy, and indeed it would be surprising if that were not the case. His army was vastly superior to Lancaster's in numbers, and he was reportedly much moved by the plight of his subjects whose lands had been ravaged by the Anglo-Navarrese force.[86] He had never had a better opportunity to inflict a serious defeat on the English. Bearing all this in mind, it is at first glance hard to understand his inactivity on the 7th. Why did he not attack?

The most likely answer to that question is suggested by the message he sent to the English commander on the 8th, after Lancaster's army had retreated to l'Aigle, and the French had pursued him up to Tobeuf, just two or three miles behind him.[87] "Two heralds came to milord the duke on behalf of the king," reports the campaign bulletin, "and they told him that the king knew well, because milord had ridden into his realm for such a long time, and tarried so close to him at Verneuil, that he had come in order to have a battle – which he would have, willingly, if he wanted it."[88] Jean, in other words, had not felt impelled to rush to give battle on the 7th before his men were rested and ready because he did not see the Anglo-Navarrese army as a prey which might escape his grasp if he did not act quickly enough, but rather as a challenger who would happily fight if given an opportunity. It seems that, for all his protestations about English "deceit," the Valois monarch realized that Edward III really had, during the Picardy *chevauchée* the previous season, made a sincere offer of battle, which had been withdrawn only because the French had not acted to meet its terms, and because the English had been low on supplies.[89] Failing to appreciate fully the differences in this situation – that he faced Henry of Lancaster and an army of 2,500 (or at most 4,000), rather than Edward III and an army of 10,000 – King Jean now presumed that the English would await his attack, so long as it was clear that an attack was indeed coming.[90]

Duke Henry's answer to the heralds might have enlightened him, had he understood it properly. "Milord answered them that he had come into these parts in order to take care of certain business, which he had well completed, thanks be to God, and was now returning from doing that to the place where he had other business; and, if King Jean of France wanted to bother him on his way, he would be ready to meet him."[91] According to Knighton, the duke added that he did not

---

[85] As noted above (note 83), the French army probably departed Rouen on the morning of the 5th, and covered the 50-odd miles to Condé by mid-afternoon on the 6th. For such a large army, this was a fast pace. Cf. Froissart, *Oeuvres*, 5:370.

[86] Froissart, *Oeuvres*, 5:370.

[87] Bulletin in *Avesbury*, 464 (English); *Chron. Jean II et Charles V,* 68–9 (French).

[88] In *Avesbury*, 464.

[89] Above, pp. 300–1, 297 n. 64.

[90] Froissart, *Oeuvres*, 5:370.

[91] In *Avesbury*, 464.

intend to do anything covertly: the French would be able to find him easily enough if they simply looked for the flames which would be rising behind him.[92] On the face of it, this was a statement that Lancaster did *not* intend to await battle, though he would defend himself if the French overtook him and attacked him. However, the reply contained clear echoes of the answers given by Edward III to similar challenges in 1346 and 1355, and in both those instances Edward had been willing to hold still long enough for his enemies to attack him if they wished to (as the Scots had waited for Edward in 1327).[93] This, combined with the bellicose "appearance, countenance and visages" of the English, and the fact that they had been drawn up in battle array on the previous day, convinced the king that his enemies would await him, or at least that they would not try to escape him.[94] Thus, on the evening of the 8th, he did not press on through the potentially dangerous l'Aigle forest, but instead encamped on the far side of it and set strong watches, thinking that there was a good chance that Henry would try to make up for his inferior numbers with an ambush or a night attack.[95]

Scouts sent out the next morning reported that a detachment of two hundred Navarrese soldiers had taken up a position blocking the road. They were not pressed, for the French army was busy making preparations and forming up in battle array. Around noon, as the pennons and banners of the royal host led the men forward, the Navarrese took to horse and spurred hastily to the west. Just then some locals arrived with the news which the blocking force had kept the French scouts from ascertaining: the English army had departed from l'Aigle in the middle of the night, and was now many miles distant.[96]

The Valois host was far too large to hope to make up for the lost time and overtake Henry's raiders, who were making remarkable speed in their retreat towards the Cotentin.[97] There was nothing to do but return to Breteuil, begin the siege anew, and wait for word of the *chevauchée* which the Prince of Wales was expected to lead from Bordeaux.[98] The wait was not a long one.

---

92 *Knighton*, 2:87.

93 See above, pp. 20, 260, 299–304; also in 1339 (pp. 168–70).

94 Froissart, *Oeuvres*, 5:370: the English "monstroient, par samblant, contenance et visage, qu'il se vorroient combatre"; "Li rois de France et li François cuidièrent bien ce jour combatre."

95 Ibid. (expectations, watch); *Chron. Jean II et Charles V*, 69 (forest).

96 Froissart, *Oeuvres*, 5:371; cf. *Récits*, 288; *Chron. Normande*, 110. Froissart notes that elements of the army broke off to reinforce various Navarrese castles in the area, which certainly seems probable.

97 *Chron. Normande*, 110. Lancaster took his force from L'Aigle to Argentan (28 miles) the first day; from there 30 miles to Thury-Harcourt ["Turreye"; this cannot be Torigni (as it is read by the editor of Avesbury, and by Burne) which would require a march of some 61 miles in a single day] on 10 June; and the next day a final very long march to St.-Fromond (40 miles). Bulletin in *Avesbury*, 465.

98 *Knighton*, 2:87; but cf. Froissart, *Oeuvres*, 5:368, which says he pursued for three days without drawing closer to them.

CHAPTER FIFTEEN

"EAGER FOR BATTLE BECAUSE OF THE PEACE WHICH USUALLY COMES WITH IT": THE POITIERS CAMPAIGN, 1356

> *The general principles applicable to an invading force are that*
> *when you have penetrated deeply into hostile territory your*
> *army is united, and the defender cannot overcome you.*
>
> Sun Tzu, XI.30[1]

THE MOST IMPORTANT CAMPAIGN of the Hundred Years War, the Black Prince's *chevauchée* of 1356, is also the most studied,[2] and the most controversial. The battle which came at the climax of this expedition far surpassed even Crécy in importance, for at Poitiers King Jean II of France was not only defeated, but also taken prisoner. The dauphin, Charles, and the king's brother, the Duke of Orléans, fled the field. Thousands of other noblemen were killed, and thousands more captured. Of the three highest military officers of the realm, two were killed – the constable and Marshal de Clermont – and the other, Marshal d'Audrehem, was captured. With its military strength crushed and its political leadership decimated, the kingdom of France was virtually prostrate. Though a treaty of peace was not signed for another four years, the results of the prince's *chevauchée* made an English victory in the first phase of the Hundred Years War almost inevitable. The unintended "side-effects" of the king's captivity were, in the long run, even more significant, for the need to pay his tremendous ransom led directly to the transformation of France from (in the terms of the historians of state-formation) a "domain state" to a "tax state," one in which the crown possessed extensive fiscal powers independent of the Estates.[3]

Like the Crécy campaign of 1346, the Poitiers *chevauchée* has often been interpreted as "nothing but the razzia of a ravenous pirate,"[4] a simple booty-collecting expedition rather than the execution of a strategic plan aimed at

---

[1] Griffith (ed.), 134.
[2] Tourneur-Aumont, Hewitt, Lampe, and Moisant treat it in great detail, as do the authors who have given more general accounts of the war – Burne, Delachenal, etc.
[3] J. B. Henneman, *Royal Taxation in Fourteenth Century France: The captivity and ransom of John II* (Philadelphia: American Philosophical Society, 1976).
[4] Tourneur-Aumont, *Bataille de Poitiers*, 78.

obtaining a decisive political result.[5] When his attempts to escape a pursuing French army and avoid battle failed, the argument runs, the prince was forced to fight, and once again the tactical prowess of the English soldiers rescued their leaders from a disaster nearly brought on by incompetent generalship.[6] Prince Edward's words to the contrary, stating that during the campaign he had been seeking rather than avoiding battle, have been dismissed as the "official version," designed to sway public opinion in England after the fact, and rather different from reality.[7]

By now, the reader will not be surprised to learn that I do not agree with this traditional understanding of the *chevauchée* of 1356. However, the sources for this campaign are even more mutually contradictory for this expedition than is normally the case, and the argument that Poitiers was a "battle which difficult circumstances constrained the prince to fight"[8] against his will is more credible than the corresponding case for 1346. On balance, though, it appears that the various accounts can be reconciled, and that the resulting narrative fits very well the pattern set by the Crécy campaign and the prince's own *grande chevauchée* the year before: the prince intended to do general harm to the wealth and political support of the Valois monarchy while enriching himself and his men through plunder, but he was also, as Geoffrey le Baker says, "eager for battle, because of the peace which usually comes with it."[9] If the English won the battle (as Prince Edward expected they would, provided that they were able to fight it using the defensive tactics which had so often proved successful for his father), then the peace would be a peace of victory.

Like the previous year's expedition to Narbonne, the summer campaign of 1356 was intended to be conducted in loose coordination with operations in the north of France. Henry of Lancaster was to ride out from Brittany, and King Edward from Calais. All three forces would aim for the river Loire, near the Ile-de-France,[10] where they might perhaps join forces. More specific plans would have been pointless, for invasion forces could be delayed by the vagaries of wind

5   Delachenal, *Histoire de Charles V,* 1:189, 190, 190–1 n.6; Oman, *History of the Art of War in the Middle Ages,* 2:160; cf. also Hewitt, *Black Prince's Expedition,* 101.
6   Hewitt, *Black Prince's Expedition,* 105; Philippe Contamine *et al., Histoire militaire de la France. 1: des origines à 1715* (Paris: Presses Universitaires de France, 1992), 130; idem, *Guerre de Cent Ans,* 39; Labarge, *Gascony,* 140; Bradbury, *Medieval Archer,* 111 ("The Black Prince had certainly been trying to evade the French army in his march"); Perroy, *Hundred Years War,* 130–1; Oman, *History of the Art of War in the Middle Ages,* 2:160–3; Liddell Hart, *Strategy,* 78; Morris, *Welsh Wars of Edward I,* 129–30; cf. also Allmand, *Hundred Years War,* 17; Fowler, *Age of Plantagenet and Valois,* 59–60.
7   Delachenal, *Histoire de Charles V,* 1:209–20; Tourneur-Aumont, *Bataille de Poitiers,* 253; Moisant, *Prince Noir,* 52.
8   Köhler, cited with approval by Delachenal, *Histoire de Charles V,* 1:190–1 n.3; see also the historians cited in note 6, above.
9   *Le Baker,* 141–2.
10 Bartholomew Burghersh's letter to John Beauchamp [hereafter cited as *BB*], in *KdL,* 386; the prince's letter to the Bishop of Worcester [hereafter *PW*] in H. T. Riley, *Memorials of London Life in the XIIIth, XIVth, XVth Centuries* (London, 1868), 207. Cf. also *Scalacronica,*

and weather, and the slowness of communication made precise coordination impossible. The commander in each theater had to be prepared to fight his own war if necessary.

Both politically and militarily, the Plantagenet position in Aquitaine had improved tremendously since the prince's arrival on the scene. The small campaigns of the winter and spring, as described in the last chapter, had done much to consolidate the military superiority gained by the moral effect of the great Languedoc *chevauchée*. Before undertaking another major expedition, however, the prince needed to carry out a similar solidification of the political gains he had made. At his first arrival in Bordeaux, he had received the homages of the local nobility and of others who had come to his court, but many Gascon lords had not been there – including of course the ones who had then been in the Valois obedience, such as the lords of Caumont, Grignols, and Limeuil. The prince therefore summoned a great assembly of the Plantagenet subjects in Aquitaine, including both nobles and representatives of the towns: a parliament in all but name. The proceedings were opened by a speech in which the prince reminded the delegates that he had been made his father's lieutenant in Gascony. The letters patent which set out his authority in the duchy were read aloud. The prince then announced that he planned to do more than take possession of Gascony: he intended, on his father's behalf, to demand the crown of France as his right and heritage.

In what was doubtless a stage-managed performance, he then asked the counsel of the assembly as to how he could best accomplish these objectives. "Many" of the assembled Gascons advised him that his best course of action would be to meet the King of France on the field of battle. Hearing this, the prince observed that he would not be able to do that unless the people of the duchy provided him with substantial aid, both in military service and in goods. If, however, they would grant him a subsidy of a fifteenth part of their goods, as the people of England were accustomed to doing, then he would willingly undertake to do so. Considering the successes he had already won, it is no great surprise that this unprecedented tax was immediately and without contradiction granted to him. Edward then closed the parliament by setting a date for the new expedition to begin, announcing that he would not consider as a friend anyone who failed to appear on the assigned day, ready and equipped to go with him, and to stand with him when it came to a fight.[11]

173; *Chron. des quat. prem. Valois*, 46. The French were aware of the prince's intention to cross the Loire, as is shown by the letter printed in Delachenal, *Histoire de Charles V*, 199 n.4.
[11] The details of this very important assembly are, unfortunately, known only by a brief account in a little-known manuscript chronicle, *Chron. CCCO*. (Though there are even briefer references to it in *Reading*, 123; *English Brut*, 307.) The credibility of its narrative, however, is somewhat increased by the relationship which it apparently bears to the chronicle composed by William Pakington, clerk and treasurer of the Black Prince's household in Gascony, during his patron's lifetime. Cf. Clifford J. Rogers and Mark Buck, "Three New Accounts of the Neville's Cross Campaign," 70–1.
The Corpus Christi chronicle's account is as follows (fos 178v–79): "puis il [the prince]

Bergerac was picked for the gathering place. It was a good choice, since from there the prince could strike north, northeast, east, or southeast to hit regions where the pain of the war had not been much felt, at least not since Lancaster's campaigns of 1346–47. The French would have to prepare everywhere, and so would be weak everywhere, improving the prince's chance for a victory if his enemies proved willing to fight. Even where he did not, in the event, lead his troops, the mere potential for an invasion would have effects beneficial to the Plantagenet war effort. Towns and local communities would press King Jean for protection or for peace, and would divert their tax revenues into preparing their own defenses.[12]

Of these options, the route northward held many advantages. First, it offered the greatest opportunities to enrich the prince's men and impoverish the Valois fisc, for the wealthy cities of Limoges, Bourges, Tours, and Poitiers all lay within reach – a string of jewels worthy of comparison to Toulouse, Carcassonne, Narbonne, and Limoux. Second, it would take the Anglo-Gascon army directly towards the only French force in the region which might be willing to give battle (just as the advance to Toulouse had done in 1355). This summer the defense of Languedoc had been entrusted to King Jean's 18-year-old son, Jean,

fist assembler les plus graunts seignurs de la terre et la comuniulte pour ly faire feaute et homage, lour monstrant come il fust seisi de la terre de Gascoine come heir a soun pier par ses lettres patents, les queux furent apertement leux devant celle assemble. Et il lour monstra outre qe il vorreit auxi demander le Roiaume de Fraunce, depart soun pier, pour soun droit et sa heritage. Et sur celles points il demanda lour counsaille; et plusours de eux ly dona counsaille d'encountrere le Roy de Fraunce en force des armes. Et le prince, enseignant lour, dist qil ne poiast ceo parfourmer saunz lour eide sibien as armes comme es biens, adjoustaunt qe sils vorreient eider par le quinzime de lour biens solunc la coustume d'Engleterre qe adonqes il voleit voluntiers enprendre celle affaire: qe meintenant sanz contredite ly fust graunte. Et le prince assigna une jour a tous qe ove ly vorrent aler et esteer de lour appariller, et ceux qe ne furent prests a celle jour de venir ove ly, il ne les tiendreit mie ses leals amys."

The tax was apparently never collected, probably because the prince gained so much wealth from the Poitiers *chevauchée* (particularly from the ransoms of Frenchmen captured at the battle) that there was no justification for the taxation. Cf. Barber, *Edward, Prince of Wales and Aquitaine*, 117.

Barber, ibid., takes this passage as a description of the assembly held on the prince's initial arrival in Guienne, but the Corpus Christi chronicle makes it quite clear that it concerns a second assembly held after the Languedoc *chevauchée*: "Apres ce qi[ls] furent venux a Burdeux ils assemblerent les gents de celles parties pour une counsaille faire endreit de celle matier pur qi le prince commencea a chivacher es armes en la terre solonc le poiar ly graunte parount plusours villes soi parlour eindegre rendirent a prince et altres ly contresteerent et plusours soi mistreount en sa grace ly fesaunt asseurance par serement qils fecount devers luy come devers lour verreie seignour. *Et puis* il fist assembler les plus graunts" [emphasis added]. *Chron. CCCO*, fo. 178v.

12 See Noël, "Town Defence," passim; Breuils, "Jean Ier," 60; *Le Baker*, 139. Cf. also the case of Arras in 1355, above, Chapter 14.

Count of Poitiers,[13] who was believed to be based at Bourges.[14] Third, and perhaps most important, the advance towards the Loire held out the possibility of a junction with the armies which Henry of Lancaster and King Edward were expected to be leading out from Brittany and Calais towards the Ile-de-France.[15]

The Prince of Wales himself left Bordeaux for La Réole on 6 July, and from there moved to Bergerac on the 22nd,[16] but his army was not fully mustered until August. Once the host was ready to begin its *chevauchée*, Edward sent word of his impending departure to his father in England, confirming that he would aim for the Ile-de-France.[17] As one might expect after the previous campaign, the turnout among his Gascon subjects was substantially better than it had been in 1355. Indeed, so many soldiers appeared, proclaiming their readiness to follow him into any peril, that his counselors became worried that such a large expedition might leave the duchy defenseless against the counterstrikes which the Count of Armagnac was expected to make. They therefore advised the prince to leave a portion of the gathered host behind, and this he did.[18] So, when the Anglo-Gascon army set out on its first march into French territory on 4 August,[19] it again included only about six thousand troops: three thousand men-at-arms, two thousand English archers, and a thousand other infantry.[20] It was a very small force to lead on a campaign expressly aimed at an "encounter

[13] Delachenal, *Histoire de Charles V,* 133.

[14] The prince is explicit on this point: "nous prismes nostre chemyn par le pais de peregort et de Lymosyn et tout droit vers Burges en Were ou nous entendismes davoir troues le fitz le Roi le counte de Peytiers." Letter of the prince to the mayor and commune of London, in H. T. Riley, *Memorials of London Life in the XIIIth, XIVth, XVth Centuries* (London, 1868), 204. Hereafter, this letter will be cited using the abbreviation *PL*. I have given all the quotations from *PL* and *PW* in expanded form (rather than indicating abbreviation marks with apostrophes, as Riley does, so that he for example gives the word "nostre" as "n're").

Note that the prince's letter is clear on the point that he was aiming for the Count of Poitiers, not for Bourges per se; Hewitt seems to have missed this point. *Black Prince's Expedition,* 100–1.

[15] *PW,* 207. The prince specifically says this was the most important reason for this course ["souvraignement"]. Burghersh (*BB,* 386) and the prince both indicate that their destination was the Ile-de-France, but the former's language is clearer.

[16] *Scalacronica,* 172; *Reading,* 123; *Anonimalle,* 35.

[17] *PL,* 204.

[18] *Le Baker,* 140, 143; *Chron. CCCO,* fos 179–79v: "les Gascoines vindrent tout prests ly offerants ensuire et devant aler en tous perilles. Et sur ceo le prince councella ovec ses barons et seignurs et, par lour avys, il lour enmercia de lour bone et fraunc volunte; et les uns il prist et mist en soun hoste, et les autres remanda a lour parties."

[19] *Eulogium,* 215.

[20] *BB,* 387 (Burghersh was in a position to know). Le Baker raises the number of men-at-arms by 1,000 (*Le Baker,* 143), but other chroniclers make the prince's army even smaller (e.g. 1,900 men-at-arms and about the same number of archers according to *Reading,* 126; 3,000 men-at-arms, 1,000 archers and 1,000 sergeants according to *Chron. Anon. Cant.,* 196). Cf. also M. Villani, *Cronica,* 526, and the discussion in Delachenal, *Histoire de Charles V,* 1:193–7.

in arms" with the King of France;[21] but then, as Froissart later observed, "the English, and all the various men-at-arms on their side, never let it worry them if they were few in numbers."[22] Certainly the earls of Warwick, Suffolk, and Oxford (all veterans of Halidon Hill as well as Crécy) would not have been unduly daunted by the prospect of fighting a larger enemy army.

For three and a half weeks the invaders made their way towards Bourges without meeting any significant resistance, traveling at a moderate pace so as to leave plenty of time for a thorough devastation of the French countryside.[23] A campaign diary incorporated into the *Eulogium Historiarum* of the monk of Malmesbury provides us with a detailed itinerary which, despite the difficulty of identifying some of the places mentioned, makes it possible to trace the prince's path with a fair degree of precision [see Map 15-1].[24]

As drawn here, however, the map of the prince's itinerary seems to contradict the descriptions of the English route given not only by certain other chroniclers, but also in the report of Bartholomew Burghersh, one of Prince Edward's right-hand men, whose testimony cannot lightly be discarded. Writing shortly after the campaign, he described the prince as having "*chevauchéed* through Agenais, the Limousin, Auvergne, and Berry, and beneath the Loire, from Nevers, which is the entrance to Berry, through there [Berry] up to Tours."[25] Matteo Villani,

---

21 *Chron. CCCO*, fo. 179 ("d'encountrere le Roy de Fraunce en force des armes").

22 Froissart, *Oeuvres*, 7:333.

23 Hewitt, *Black Prince's Expedition*, 104, notes the slowness of the army's progress (just sixty miles forward in the week leading up to the arrival at Vierzon) and concludes that "such conduct cannot be related to a serious effort to meet the English king or the Duke of Lancaster or the Count of Poitiers." Why not? We do not know when he expected Edward III to reach the Ile-de-France, and in the event (as we shall see) his arrival was quite well timed to meet Lancaster, considering that the two forces had to move in near-total ignorance of each others' progress. As to the Count of Poitiers, the prince was hoping that as Jean's lieutenant he would be in command of a large army and so willing to fight; if this were the case, then what need would there be to hurry to meet him?

24 Based mainly on the *Eulogium*, 215–18, I have reconstructed the following itinerary for the start of the campaign. 6 August, Périgord. 7, Périgueux (Delachenal: Château l'Évêque). 8, château Ramefort, cn. de Valieul (Delachenal). 9, Brantôme. 10, Quinsac ["Quisser." Babinet suggests Bussière Badil, but Quinsac is better both from sound and from position.] 11, St.-Martin-le-Pin ["Merdan." Babinet identifies this as Marthon; Delachenal considered it (like "Quisser") still unknown; Hewitt thinks it is Nontron.] 12, Rochechouart. 13, Abbey of la Péruse [Hewitt says the Benedictine priory of Peruche near Confolens, but from his map this may be just a variant spelling of la Péruse.] 14, Lesterps. 15, halt. 16, Bellac. 17, capture of two unnamed castles, and a town where the wife of Jacques de Bourbon resided (identified by Delachenal, 198, as le Dorat). 18, halt. 19, Lussac-les-Eglises. 20, St.-Benoit-du-Sault. 21, Argenton-sur-Creuse. 22, halt. 23, prince at Châteauroux, vanguard at Villedieu-sur-Indre ["Burgo Dei." Delachenal, *Histoire de Charles V*, 1:198, and Babinet think it is Déols; Lampe, *Schlacht bei Maupertuis*, 19, argues for Bourges.], rearguard at St.-Amand Montrand [Barber thinks St.-Maur]. My reasons for departing from the variant identifications noted above are in each case based on locations and names only; the reader can judge for himself based on a good map.

25 *BB*, 386. The presence of the prince's army in Auvergne is also noted in Froissart, *Oeuvres*, 5:383–5 (and in several chronicles which merely summarize Burghersh's letter).

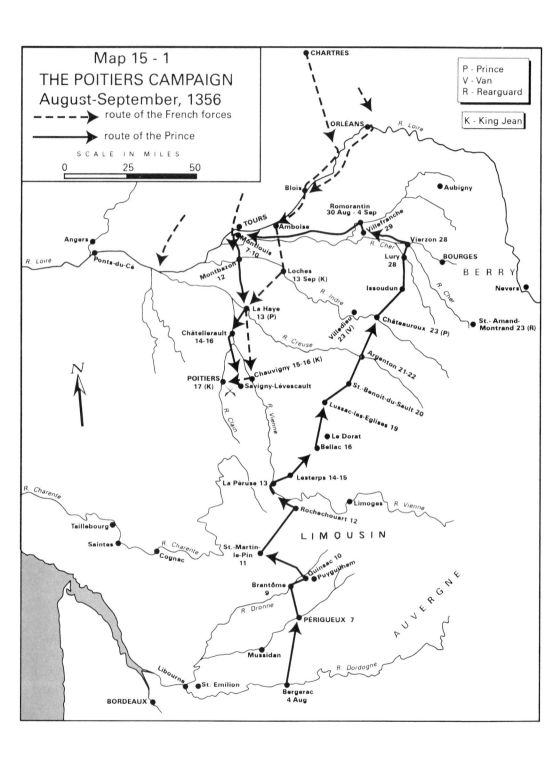

Map 15 - 1
THE POITIERS CAMPAIGN
August-September, 1356
- - - → route of the French forces
——→ route of the Prince

SCALE IN MILES
0   25   50

P - Prince
V - Van
R - Rearguard

K - King Jean

CHARTRES
ORLÉANS
R. Loire
Aubigny
Blois
Romorantin 30 Aug - 4 Sep
Villefranche 29
Vierzon 28
TOURS
Amboise
Angers
R. Cher
BOURGES
R. Loire
Ponts-du-Cé
Montlouis 7-10
Montbazon 12
Loches 13 Sep (K)
Lury 28
BERRY
R. Indre
Issoudun
Nevers
La Haye 13 (P)
Villedieu 23 (V)
Châteauroux 23 (P)
St.- Amand-Montrand 23 (R)
Châtellerault 14-16
R. Creuse
R. Cher
N
Chauvigny 15-16 (K)
POITIERS 17 (K)
Savigny-Lévescault
Argenton 21-22
St.-Benoit-du-Sault 20
R. Clain
R. Vienne
Lussac-les-Eglises 19
Le Dorat
Bellac 16
La Péruse 13
Lesterps 14-15
R. Charente
Limoges
R. Vienne
Rochechouart 12
LIMOUSIN
Taillebourg
Saintes
R. Charente
Cognac
St.-Martin-le-Pin 11
Quinsac 10
Puyguilhem
AUVERGNE
Brantôme 9
R. Dronne
PÉRIGUEUX 7
Mussidan
R. Dordogne
Libourne
St. Emilion
Bergerac 4 Aug
BORDEAUX

similarly, says that the prince "coasted the Loire up to Orléans," and other chroniclers note appearances at Limoges, Bourges, Aubigny, and Amboise, which like Nevers, Auvergne and the Loire are well to the right-hand side of the line of march depicted.[26]

The resolution to this apparent contradiction is suggested by the *Eulogium* itself, which notes that on 23 August, when the prince was at Châteauroux, his vanguard was at "Burgo Dei" [Villedieu on the Indre], while his rearguard occupied "Seynt Yman" [St.-Amand Montrand].[27] This gives a concrete example of a general point made several times above: that an army on *chevauchée* typically advanced in widely separated divisions, to facilitate foraging and to lay waste to the widest possible area. Fourteenth-century chroniclers often speak of a band of destruction eight to fifteen leagues (19–36 modern miles, even assuming a short Parisian league) wide;[28] here we see the encampments of the three divisions of an army spread out over a remarkable breadth of *forty-nine* linear miles.

Thus, the line depicted on map 15-1 must be seen as merely tracing the epicenter of a broad swathe of desolation, with one division advancing to its left, and another ranging typically some forty miles to its right, via the Auvergne, St.-Amand Montrand, Nevers, along the Loire through Berry, and across to Aubigny.[29] Places in between the main bodies were likely to face attacks or outright destruction, as Limoges and Bourges did, along with the "many towns of 500 and of 1000 hearths and larger and smaller" described by Villani as having been pillaged and burned by the Anglo-Gascon army during this *chevauchée*.[30]

Up through 28 August, when the prince passed the border of Aquitaine's greatest historical extent[31] and captured Vierzon, the Anglo-Gascon army met very little resistance. Many towns were left abandoned at the approach of the

Delachenal, viewing Burghersh's statement as irreconcilable with the itinerary of the *Eulogium*, wrongly describes the letter as useful only from the point at which the prince entered Berry. *Histoire de Charles V,* 197n.

26 M. Villani, *Cronica,* 526. Limoges: *Le Bel,* 2:229. Bourges: Froissart, *Oeuvres,* 5:384 ("le chité" of Berry is Bourges), 386 (suburbs burnt and skirmish); *Le Bel,* 2:229; documentary evidence in Froissart, *Chroniques,* 5:111. Aubigny ("villam de Daubene"), *Eulogium,* 218. Amboise: *Le Bel,* 2:231. Froissart also indicates an English advance from Bergerac into Rouergue, around Rocamadour, then into the Auvergne, back and forth over the Allier – i.e., roughly, a west–east traverse along the Dordogne, then north along the Allier to Nevers; a route which fits well with Burghersh's words. *Oeuvres,* 5:378–80.

27 *Eulogium,* 218.

28 See Rogers, "*Bellum Hostile* and 'Civilians,' " for some two dozen examples.

29 After Romorantin, it appears, the three divisions began to march much more closely together, so that they would remain in supporting distance of one another in case they encountered the French army, as they expected to do.

30 Limoges and Bourges: note 26, above. Quotation: M. Villani, *Cronica,* 526.

31 Lury, on the Cher, which used to be the border between the duchy and the realm of France, according to the *Eulogium,* 218, cf. 219. It is worth noting that the member of the prince's army who kept the diary on which this account is based (note the use of the first person, "nos," on p. 221) was both aware of and interested in this fact.

invaders, or surrendered at their demand. A few castles and fortified churches were taken by assault after attempts to defend themselves.[32] But there was no sign of any organized French opposition – a key factor in allowing the English and Gascons to spread out as much as they did, thereby allowing them to do as much damage as they did. Even at Bourges, where the English had hoped to meet an army under the Count of Poitiers, no large force dared come out from behind the city walls to challenge the invaders.[33] The prince had therefore decided to aim for the Loire, in the hope of crossing over and forming a junction with his father or with Henry of Lancaster.[34]

While the prince had been ravaging France for nearly three weeks, King Jean had been maintaining the siege of Breteuil and preparing to meet the Anglo-Gascon *chevauchée*, which he had anticipated. When, in the middle of August, he got word of Prince Edward's advance, he granted favorable terms to the garrison in order to conclude the siege quickly, dismissed the communal foot troops who would not be able to maintain the pace expected for the coming campaign (and whose value on the battlefield was doubtful),[35] then brought the rest of his army to Chartres, which had been assigned as the gathering-point for a full royal host. He arrived there on the 28th;[36] on that same day, a reconnaissance party which he had sent south of the Loire made contact with the outriders of the prince's rearguard, under Sir John Chandos and Sir James Audley,[37] near Aubigny (which the English had just sacked and burned).[38] The Frenchmen were routed, many being killed and several captured. From these prisoners the prince learned two important pieces of information: first, that a larger Valois force under Boucicaut and the Lord of Craon was also scouting for his location, and, second, that Jean himself was drawing near Orléans, intending to give battle to the English in the vicinity of Tours.[39] Since that was just what the prince wanted, he decided to turn west and head directly for Tours, with scouts following the course of the Loire to search for intact bridges which would enable

[32] Ibid. Aside from two walled towns captured near Périgueux (*Eulogium,* 218), it does not appear that any of the captured places were garrisoned.
[33] *PL*, 204 (count); Froissart, *Oeuvres*, 5:386 (Bourges). Count Jean was in fact miles away at Decize at this time. Delachenal, *Histoire de Charles V,* 1:199n.
[34] *PL*, 204; *PW,* 207; *BB*, 386; *Le Bel*, 2:230. According to Froissart, *Oeuvres*, 5:385, 386, the prince at this stage received word that King Jean was at Chartres with a large army, and that he had blocked the passages of the Loire.
[35] Froissart, *Oeuvres*, 5:381–2; *Chron. des quat. prem. Valois*, 46; Delachenal, *Hist. Charles V,* 1:186 n.2.
[36] *Le Bel*, 2:230n; *Chron. des quat. prem. Valois*, 46.
[37] Cf. *Le Baker,* 140, on these two.
[38] *Eulogium*, 218–19.
[39] *PL*, 204: "disoient les ditz prisoners qe le dit Roi avoit pris certein purpos de combatre ovesqe nous a quele heure nous estoioms sur le chymyn envers Tours et encostoavit devers Orliens"; cf. *Le Baker,* 140 [Siquidem ingresso Pictaviam nuncirunt exploratores quod coronatus adunavit exercitum copiosum, presens apud Aurelianum], 141 [Postea redierunt exploratores, nunciantes quod coronatus Francorum descendit Turoniam castrorum acies ordinaturus]; *Vie du Prince Noir,* ll. 739–43; and (for a different understanding) Froissart, *Oeuvres*, 5:385–6.

him to cross over to meet his adversary (or his compatriots, if they were in the area) even sooner.[40]

The next day, the 29th, the prince's army followed the river Cher up to the town of Villefranche. On the way, some of his men encountered another party of French scouts, this time belonging to the detachment under Craon and Boucicaut. The eight men-at-arms who fell into the hands of the Sire de Caumont confirmed to the prince that the French planned to meet him in battle. "At this," the *Eulogium Historiarum* tells us, "he rejoiced greatly."[41] Later in the day there was another skirmish, this time the result of an ambush laid by Craon, Boucicaut, and their men for an English foraging party under Lord Willoughby. The ambush was initially successful, and the French took a number of English prisoners and recovered the booty the foragers had been carrying back to the main body of the Anglo-Gascon army, but before they could secure their gains the French were set upon by a large number of English reinforcements from the marshals' division and compelled to flee.[42] Many of the Frenchmen were killed or captured in a vigorous pursuit, but the two barons and the best-mounted of their men managed a narrow escape into the castle of Romorantin, roughly forty miles south of Orléans, and fifty east of Tours.[43]

The rest of the Anglo-Gascon forces concentrated around the fortress the next day, Tuesday 30 August, and fixed their tents outside the town, so that their enemies were trapped within. On Wednesday Edward ordered an assault and succeeded in capturing the outer walls, but Boucicaut and his companions retreated to the extremely strong tower-keep called the "Dongoun," and beat off their enemies' vigorous attempts to take it.[44] At this the prince called a council to consider whether to make further attempts to seize the keep and its occupants, or to proceed with the *chevauchée*. The decision was to stay where they were and besiege the French lords in the Dongoun.[45]

This decision produces a major problem for the many historians who believe that the Anglo-Gascon army aimed to avoid battle during this *chevauchée*.[46]

---

40 *Le Bel*, 2:229–30; *Anonimalle*, 36. Cf. also *Chron. des quat. prem. Valois*, 45–6.

41 *Eulogium*, 219: "Eodem die nova venerunt principi quod rex Franciae voluit congredi cum eo, unde multum laetatus est." Simlarly, *Vie du Prince Noir*, ll. 739–44: "De Chartres se sont departy/ Et chivacherent, sanz nul sy,/ Tout ensi par devers Tours./ Mout par fu noble lour atours./ Lui Prince en oy novelles/ Queux lui semblerent bons et beles." Cf. Hewitt's understatement, in *Black Prince's Expedition*, 105.

42 Froissart, *Oeuvres*, 5:387–91; *Eulogium*, 219.

43 Froissart, *Oeuvres*, 5:387–8; *Eulogium*, 219; *PL*, 204–5.

44 *Eulogium*, 219. The editor's emendation of "Jovis" to "[? Martis]" is, incidentally, unnecessary. The prince arrived at Romorantin on Tuesday (*Le Baker*, 141), and the *Eulogium* notes that he fixed his tents outside the town for three days – i.e., until *Thursday* ("et hoc fuit die Jovis"). See also Froissart, *Oeuvres*, 5:387–8, 391–2; *Le Baker*, 141.

45 *Le Baker*, 141.

46 Barber, *Edward*, 135, says "The prince decided to invest the castle, a decision which seems remarkable when his most urgent need was to cross the Loire. But the prince did not yet know either that the Loire was impassable, or that John's army was on the move." Yet he *did* know that Jean was nearby, had blocked the Loire, and intended to fight him, as shown above (nn. 34, 39).

Boucicaut and Craon were valuable prizes, but hardly worth fighting an unwanted battle over; and with the French royal army believed to be only a day and a half away at Orléans,[47] a fight would be difficult to avoid if King Jean were bent upon one. The difficulty for these historians is increased by the fact that the prince not only chose to stay at Romorantin and continue the attacks, but in the event stayed in the town for a total of six days – Tuesday the 30th through Sunday the 4th – even though the French lords surrendered on the fifth day (Saturday 3 September).[48] Why would someone seeking to avoid a battle stay motionless for six days, with his enemy less than two days away?[49]

The answer, of course, is that he would not, and that the prince was not seeking to avoid a battle. In fact, Geoffrey le Baker makes it quite clear that the long stay at Romorantin was motivated by exactly the opposite consideration. The prince, notes the chronicler, "desired above all else to engage [King Jean's] force," but judged that it would be better to await Jean's attack than to seek him out. Edward reckoned that a close siege of the French lords in the keep ought to provoke the French to come and break it – after all, the royal army was already nearby, and Jean was reported to be eager to fight. Thus the prince and his council decided not to leave Romorantin until the trapped knights were captured, unless they could be very certain of a battle otherwise.[50] This was an old Plantagenet stratagem, a version of the same one that Edward III had used at Berwick in 1333, Tournai in 1340, and Calais in 1347. It was designed to ensure that the burden of action would fall on the French, who would need to attack in order to break the siege, thus leaving the tremendous advantages of the tactical defensive to the English.[51]

---

[47] *Le Baker*, 141, and above, note 39. The English, indeed, thought that Jean at Orléans was only ten leagues away, even closer than the city actually was.

[48] *Eulogium*, 220.

[49] Historians who hold to the battle-avoiding view of the *chevauchée* tend to explain away this episode as a foolish error on the prince's part, a diversion which cost him time, gained no real military advantage, and gave Jean the opportunity to catch him (e.g. Hewitt, *Black Prince's Expedition*, 105, 101; Delachenal, *Histoire de Charles V*, 1:201), the result of chivalry overcoming good sense (Lampe, *Schlacht bei Maupertuis*, 22).

[50] *Le Baker*, 141: "consulcius diiudicans immotus expectare coronai feritatem preliaturam quam querere forsan non exspectaturam potenciam, cum qua summe concupivit conserere manus bellatrices, estimans preterea quod obsidio congesta provocare deberet Gallicos ad eius demolicionem, finaliter sentenciavit se non recessurum de loco subacto quosque conclusi forent capti seu dediti, nisi forte bellico certamine cogeretur." The *Anonimalle*, 35–6, confuses the details, inventing an eight-day respite given by the prince to the French, but it does get the purpose of the siege correct: "pur veer si soun dit adversere de Fraunce les [viz. Boucicaut and Craon] vouldreit ascune rescus faire." Galbraith is overly hard on the chronicler when he claims that "The account of the siege of Romorantin is apparently a wilful perversion of the truth." Ibid., 164.

Although there was no respite, it is certainly possible that Edward did allow the garrison to send a messenger to inform the French king of their plight – as the Scots had been allowed to do in 1333, and as the message of the garrison of Calais had been forwarded to Philip in 1347. In any case, Lampe is wrong to say that "the sources are silent" concerning the reasons for the siege. *Schlacht bei Maupertuis*, 22.

[51] Cf. my "The Offensive/Defensive in Medieval Strategy," 158–61, 164. Barber, *Edward,*

King Jean, however, was not yet ready to engage the prince. His army was still gathering at Chartres and Orléans, so he did nothing while the English attacked the keep of Romorantin with "fire, mine and engine" on 1, 2 and 3 September. On that last day, seeing that their lord was not going to come to rescue them, and unable to respond effectively to the fires set by the English siege engines, the defenders finally surrendered unconditionally to the mercy of the prince.[52] He not only spared their lives; he even released them on parole.[53] Most likely, he had Boucicaut carry some sort of provocative challenge to King Jean, just as the knight had done in Picardy the previous November.[54]

Either on that same day or on the following one, Sunday the 4th, the prince received reports from his scouts that King Jean was moving down the Loire to Tours, with his divisions arrayed for battle.[55] Edward therefore spent Sunday resting his men and ordering them to tend to their arms and armor, so that they would be ready for a fight.[56] The next day, as le Baker reports, "the prince, eager for battle because of the peace which usually accompanies it, directed the day's march towards the usurper."[57] During the 5th and 6th, the main body of the army followed the course of the Cher directly towards Tours, while scouts searched the banks of the Loire for a ford or other crossing so that they might cross over to engage the French – unsuccessfully, since Jean had ordered all the bridges broken and defended, and the water of the Loire was high due to heavy rainfall.[58] Each night the Anglo-Gascon outriders could see the campfires of their opposite numbers on the far side of the river.[59]

On the 7th, the Plantagenet army reached the town of Montlouis on the Loire,

---

258, explicitly discounts le Baker's statement that the prince was eager for battle and using the siege to provoke a fight, but he does not note the similar statement by the *Anonimalle*, nor give any reason for discounting le Baker, who is along with the *Eulogium* the best source for the campaign.

52 *Eulogium*, 220; *BB*, 386 (quotation); *Le Baker*, 141; Froissart, *Oeuvres*, 5:389, 395. Le Baker has the surrender on the 6th day of the siege, presumably counting Monday the 29th (before the prince and the bulk of the army arrived).

53 *Anonimalle*, 36; *Le Bel*, 2:231.

54 Such a challenge is not recorded in the sources, but it was nearly a "standard operating procedure," as seen above in the chapters on 1333, 1339, 1340 (outside Tournai), 1346, 1347, and 1355 (in Picardy).

55 *Le Baker*, 141.

56 *Eulogium*, 220.

57 *Le Baker*, 141–2. The scouts reported Jean's advance towards Tours, "unde princeps, avidus belli propter pacem que solet bellum comitari, adversus coronatum castra direxit." Cf. Barber, *Edward*, 135–6, who again ignores le Baker and says "news now seems to have reached the prince that *the comte de Poitiers* was at Tours . . . and he therefore headed westwards." [Emphasis added.]

58 *Eulogium*, 220; *Le Bel*, 2:231 (route); *Le Baker*, 142 (scouts, bridges); *Anonimalle*, 36 ("il ne purroit trover pount ne passage sur la ryver de Leire de corere sur soun adversere de Fraunce"); *Scalacronica*, 173, *Reading*, 123; *BB*, 386.

59 *Le Baker*, 142 ("quorum" probably refers to the French forces rather than Lancaster's). Cf. Hewitt, *Black Prince's Expedition*, 107.

just a few miles up from Tours.[60] King Jean was believed to be close by, and it was known that his sons, the counts of Poitiers and Anjou, were inside the city with Marshal Clermont and a large force.[61] The prince also received news, probably on the 8th, that Henry of Lancaster was following the Loire eastward, as quickly as he could, to form a junction with him.[62] The prince therefore decided to maintain his position outside of Tours, hoping that the French would come out and give battle.[63] He waited there on 8, 9, and 10 September, making a few attempts to burn the suburbs of Tours (which failed because of a spurt of rainy weather), but his enemies stayed put, protected by the city walls and by the Loire.[64]

The key to understanding his stay outside Tours and his movements in the next few days is the same as the key to Edward III's actions around Poissy a decade earlier. Fourteenth-century English armies relied on their superior skill and discipline, combined with the power of the longbow and the advantages of the tactical defensive, to counterbalance the overwhelming numerical superiority almost invariably possessed by the French. The usual Valois riposte to this strategy was to attempt to pin the English in place against the sea or an uncrossable river, so that they could be starved until they were forced to take the tactical offensive or to surrender. The trick to conducting a successful *chevauchée* was not to avoid battle, but to avoid a trap of that sort.[65] This would have been easy enough, given the slow speed of communications and the even slower movements of a French royal host, were it not for the fact that the Plantagenets' battle-seeking strategy regularly forced the English armies into close

---

60 The *Eulogium*'s "Aumonk" [from "au Mont-Louis"?]. See Charles de Grandmaison, "Séjour du Prince Noir à Montlouis," *Bulletin de la Société des Antiquaires de l'Ouest* ser. 2, v. 8 (1898), 150–5.

61 Jean: *Le Baker*, 142; cf. *PW*, 207. Anjou, Clermont: *PL*, 205. Poitiers: *BB*, 386.

62 *PL*, 205: "Et a nostre departir d'illeoqs nous prismes le chemyn pour passer ascuns daungers des eawes et en entente davoir encountree ovesqe nostre tres cher cosyn le ducs de Lancastre de qi nous aviens certeins novelles qil se voillent afforcier de trere devers nous." Cf. *Anonimalle*, 36: "En quele temps [while the prince was at "Baugemounde" outside Tours – either "Aumonk" or Montbazon?] viegnt le duk de Loncastre od tout soun poer devaunt les cites de Angers et de Tours pur passer leawe de Leire" and M. Villani, *Cronica*, 532. Delachenal writes that if the prince later wrote that at this time he had not abandoned all idea of meeting up with the Duke of Lancaster, it was intended to influence, after the fact, public opinion in England. This makes little sense to me: why would public opinion look on him more favorably because he was waiting for the Duke of Lancaster? Indeed, in the aftermath of his victory at Poitiers, why would he need to lie to his subjects in order to boost his popularity, which was already as high as human prestige can be? And if, as Delachenal believes, the prince was waiting neither for Lancaster nor for King Jean, then why *did* he stay outside of Tours for four days? *Histoire de Charles V*, 1:203, 1:205–6.

63 *Le Baker*, 142: "fixit tentoria juxta Turoniam, ubi, expectans quator diebus, serans coronatum una leuca distantem preliaturum." Cf. *BB*, 386.

64 *Eulogium*, 220–1; *Le Baker*, 142. Le Baker and Burghersh (*BB*, 386) have the prince remain before Tours for four days; presumably this includes the 7th, the day of his arrival in the vicinity.

65 Cf. Froissart, *Oeuvres*, 5:413, and my "Offensive/Defensive in Medieval Strategy."

proximity with their enemies, in order to offer them the chance for a decisive
encounter, provided it was fought on English terms.

So long as the prince believed that his enemies were advancing from Orléans
or Chartres to Tours along the northern coast of the Loire, his position on the
southern bank of the river was just where he wanted to be. From there, he could
offer battle to the French with little risk that they would be able to cut off his line
of retreat and so compel him to fight at a disadvantage. Furthermore, the Loire
would serve as a shield for his foraging parties, so that it would be difficult for
the French to use their much-favored logistic strategy against him. Thus it was
not until he learned that King Jean had turned aside from the route to Tours,
crossed the Loire at Blois, and moved to get between the English and their base
that Prince Edward left his position, hoping to get back in front of the French.[66]

*

Let us pause for a moment to consider the generally accepted understanding of
this portion of the campaign, which varies substantially from the interpretation
given above. In *The Black Prince's Expedition of 1355–1356*, H. J. Hewitt
assesses this period after the departure from Romorantin as follows:

> Neither the prince nor Lancaster had sufficient strength for a battle with the
> army of the French king . . . Prudence dictated that the prince . . . should with-
> draw. . . . The best way from Romorantin to Bordeaux lay in going west along
> the Cher and, at some suitable point, turning south. . . . The march to Tours is
> then a first step towards Bordeaux . . . while the decision to start the journey
> southwards by way of the Loire valley was wise, the halt at Tours served no
> purpose. . . . The safety which might be held to lie in a few days' start and in
> the superior speed of a smaller army, had been thrown away.[67]

Hewitt's version of these events is a natural consequence of beginning from
the assumption that the prince was seeking to avoid battle. Yet there is a major
problem with this perspective on the prince's movement, even aside from the
fact that it ignores or directly contradicts the statements of *all* the best sources
for the campaign as to the prince's motivations.[68] It takes only a glance at a map
to realize that "the best way from Romorantin to Bordeaux" did *not* lie "in
going west along the Cher" to Tours[69] – especially not if the intent was to avoid

---

66 *Le Baker*, 142: "intellexit quarto die quod coronatus, ad Blaviam x. leucis a tergo principis
preterioratus, per pontem duobus opidis munitissimis intersituatum Ligerim transivit atque
versus Pictaveium properavit.

  Ea coronati declinacione principi comperta, pinceps revertebatur festinanter, intendens iter
coronati preocupasse." Also *Scalacronica*, 173. On the French movements, see Froissart,
Oeuvres, 5:396–8.

67 *Black Prince's Expedition*, 105–7.

68 Cf. *PL*, 205; *Le Baker*, 141–2, 144; *Eulogium*, 219; *Chron. CCCO*, 179.

69 The road distance from Romorantin to Chauvigny, along the route he actually took, is
about 116 miles; if he had taken the hypotenuse instead of the two sides of the triangle (i.e.
gone via Valençy and Chatillon), the distance would have been only 79 miles – a saving of
about two days' march time.

a battle with the King of France, who, as we have seen, was believed to be *moving towards Tours*.[70] And, of course, if the prince had indeed been motivated merely by "a desire to get his plunder and his small army back in safety to Bordeaux," then the halt for four days at Montlouis would make little sense.[71]

As already noted, however, eagerness to fight a battle did not mean willingness to be cut off and constrained to fight on his enemy's terms. Thus, when he learned that the French had crossed the Loire upstream from his position, Prince Edward hastened to get across the Cher and the dangerous Indre, taking up a position at Montbazon so that he would again have an advantageous position from which to offer battle if King Jean advanced directly towards him.[72] The next day, however, he learned that he had not succeeded in getting in front of the French army, which had reached the Indre at Loches, east and slightly south of his position.[73] The Cardinal of Périgord arrived in his camp with a large entourage of clerics and magnates, "preaching of piety and mercy," and trying to arrange a truce between the adversaries. These emissaries also announced that King Jean intended to come to do battle with him in two days, on Wednesday 14 September. The cardinal attempted to arrange a truce, but Prince Edward, with a battle in the offing, made it clear that he was not interested in a truce.[74]

If, however, the prince were to wait at Montbazon for his adversary's advance on Wednesday, it would come from the south, and the Plantagenet would then have lost the advantages his position on the river brought him.[75] On Tuesday, therefore, he made a long march southwards to the next major river, the Creuse.[76] If the French king did indeed mean to come fight him – rather than to entrap him – he could do so at La Haye on the Creuse as well as at Montbazon on the Indre.

That night Prince Edward received bad news: a report that, as he had feared, it was indeed King Jean's intention to get ahead of the English and cut off their retreat, rather than to advance directly against them. The Valois was afraid that

---

[70] See p. 361, above.

[71] Oman, *A History of the Art of War in the Middle Ages*, 2:161; cf. Labarge, *Gascony*, 140. On the prince's concern to get his plunder back to Bordeaux, cf. *Eulogium*, 222: "Princeps vero ultra modum equitabat reliquendo viam quae ducit de Cha[v]igne ad Poyters sed ultra campos ad inimicos suos festinando *nec habendo respectum ad cariagium suum*." [Emphasis added.] Note also the prince's lack of interest in making a truce while at Montbazon (below).

[72] *Le Baker*, 142: "Ea coronati declinacione principi comperta, princeps revertabatur festinanter, intendens iter coronati preoccupasse." Indre, Montbazon: *Eulogium*, 221.

[73] *Le Baker*, 142 ("intendens iter coronati preocupasse, quod not fecit.") Loches: Froissart, *Oeuvres*, 5:396.

[74] *Eulogium*, 221; *PL*, 205 (note that "estoiens non plus plenement certifiez" is probably a misreading for "estoienz nous plus . . .").

[75] He could not simply switch to the opposite side of the Indre and await Jean there, threatening a retreat northwards if Jean refused to attack, because the dauphin continued to hold Tours with 1,000 men-at-arms and a large number of infantrymen – who could both keep the English from crossing the Loire, and also severely hinder the English foraging efforts if the prince tried to outwait his enemy. *Eulogium*, 221.

[76] Ibid. The march was about 34 miles.

his adversary would flee before his army and escape battle, just as Henry of Lancaster had done at l'Aigle the previous year.[77] Edward did not want to let his enemy get in front of him, but he also did not want to move off too quickly, lest Jean decide the chase was hopeless and give up the pursuit, as he had done in Normandy.[78] He therefore made a rather short march to the southwest, to Châtellerault on the Vienne.[79]

Once again we see the delicate balance between avoiding a trap and not avoiding battle. If the prince's intent had indeed been to avoid a fight, he would have spent the next two days moving south up the Vienne or the Clain, which would have put him only one day's march from English-held Cognac.[80] King Jean could not possibly have intercepted him.[81] But the Plantagenet did not want to escape from the French; he wanted to fight them. This was, it should be remembered, the proud young man who had led the first division of the English at Crécy, when a French army vastly superior in numbers had gone down to ignominious defeat; many of his councilors had also helped overcome terrible odds at Halidon Hill.

Wednesday, when the Anglo-Gascon army first reached Châtellerault, was the day when the Valois monarch had proposed to give battle to the English at Montbazon. Now, with no more rivers against which he might be trapped between his army and the English-held Charente, King Edward's son wanted to find out if his adversary was still willing to cross swords. He therefore stayed put on the Vienne for two full days, waiting to see what the King of France would do.[82] Moisant's description of this halt as "prudent inaction . . . which can only be explained by the desire to *avoid* battle" is simply absurd.[83]

---

[77] *Eulogium*, 221: "nova venerunt principi quod rex Franciae vellet praecedere nos, nam multum dubitavit si forte princeps fugeret viso exercitu Francorum." Froissart, *Oeuvres*, 5:397–8.

[78] Nor, indeed, did he wish to suffer the reproach of having fled precipitously in the face of the enemy.
   M. Villani specifies that the prince had received a report on Lancaster's June *chevauchée* before departing Guienne. M. Villani, *Cronica*, 526.

[79] *Eulogium*, 221. This was an advance of only 15 miles. He had thus covered about 59 miles over four days – hardly the "precipitous march" described by Moisant, *Prince Noir*, 52.

[80] Assuming 30-mile marches, which would have been hard but not impossible, even with his baggage – he had just made the 34-mile march from Montbazon to La Haye in a single day.

[81] It was a remarkable feat for Jean to cross the Chauvigny bridge on the morning of the 16th [and indeed he may not have crossed until the 17th; that is the implication of the *Eulogium*, 221, which however cannot be trusted as implicitly for French movements as for English ones]; if the prince, on the other hand, had not halted more than overnight at Châtellerault, he could easily have reached Poitiers by midday on the 15th, and thus retained over a day's "lead" on the French.

[82] *PL*, 205: "desmourasmes quatre [sic] iors ettendauntz de savoir plus la certein de lui [Jean]." The "quatre jours" presumably include Wednesday, when the prince arrived, and also Saturday, when he left before dawn.

[83] Emphasis added. *Prince Noir*, 52. If you are fleeing from someone who is well behind you and moves more slowly than you, the best way to escape him is not to stop and try to figure out where he is. However, cf. Tourneur-Aumont, *Bataille de Poitiers*, 192.

The idea of awaiting the French on the Vienne had to be abandoned when, late at night on Friday the 16th, the prince's scouts reported that King Jean had, by unusually fast marching, slipped south around the English position and gained another bridge over the river at Chauvigny.[84] Once again the English faced the prospect of being pinned against a river they had hoped would protect their line of retreat. On the other hand, however, the scouts' reports indicated (correctly) that the French had lost track of their enemy's position. Thus, the threat was balanced by a new opportunity for a surprise attack, in which there would be no need for the tactical strength of the defense. So, says the *Euolgium Historiarum*, "the prince had it proclaimed that all the baggage train should cross the bridge that night so that in the morning the army would not be impeded from . . . hastening against their enemies."[85] The prince explains his own plan as follows: "Jean came with his army to Chauvigny . . . to cross the same river towards Poitiers. On hearing this, we decided to hasten towards him on the road which he would have to take, in order to fight him."[86] This is doubtless sincere, though some historians of the campaign have considered it an idle boast.[87] The English clearly hoped to fall on the French army while it was in the middle of crossing the Vienne, but they arrived too late, despite leaving Châtellerault before dawn and riding cross-country with all possible speed, leaving the baggage-train to follow as best it could.[88]

The main body of the French had already gone past when the leading elements of the Anglo-Gascon army struck a surprised body of seven hundred men-at-arms[89] of the French rearguard, "their heads covered with ostrich-plumed chaplets . . . rather than bascinets."[90] This encounter probably took place somewhere in the vicinity of Savigny-Lévescault, rather than the generally accepted location of La Chabotrie.[91] In any case, three French counts were

---

[84] *Anonimalle*, 36; *Eulogium*, 221; *Scalacronica*, 173 (from prisoners). Froissart says that Jean reached Chauvigny late on the 15th, and crossed the river either on the 16th or (in some variants) the 17th.

[85] *Eulogium*, 221–2; similarly *Anonimalle*, 36–7; cf. also M. Villani, *Cronica*, 528.

[86] *PL*, 205: "prismes purpos de hastier devers lui sur le chemyn qil devereit passer pour estre combatuz ove lui." Cf. M. Villani, *Cronica*, 528; *Eulogium*, 222.

[87] E.g. Delachenal, *Histoire de Charles V*, 1:205–6: "Aux termes de la lettre qu'il écrivit au maire et aux aldermen de Londres – et le moine de Malmesbury l'a répété apres lui – le prince de Galles aurait cherché à recontrer l'ennemi. Ceci nous parait étrange, au premier abord, et a tout l'air d'une fanfaronnade." Delachenal does, however, qualify this statement in his next sentences, leaving the matter unresolved; but then on p. 209 he returns to his initial conclusion. Cf. also Tourneur-Aumont, *Bataille de Poitiers*, 192–3. On the other side, cf. Burne, *Crécy War*, 285.

[88] *Scalacronica*, 173; *PL*, 205, *Le Baker*, 142. Baggage: *Eulogium*, 221–2; *Anonimalle*, 36.

[89] *PL*, 205.

[90] *Anonimalle*, 37. Cf. M. Villani, *Cronica*, 528, who indicates that part of the reason for their surprise was a bit of Anglo-Gascon trickery. Froissart, *Oeuvres*, 5:399–400, similarly has the French strike an English scouting detachment, and pursue it right into the middle of the English army.

[91] This was a very difficult conclusion to reach, and must be considered highly tentative. The location of the fight is given as "Chabutorie" in one version of Burghersh's letter, and

captured in the fight, along with another 240 men-at-arms killed or captured.[92] The rest fled, some towards Poitiers, some towards Chauvigny; Edward, aware of the risk of a French counterstrike, did not pursue with his main force, but some of his men did chase the fugitives as far as that latter town.[93] This pursuit effectively forced the prince to encamp his army near the site of the skirmish, so that the men involved in the chase would be able to find his army to rejoin it.[94] He therefore took up a position in the woods by a small stream (which did not provide enough water for his army), probably between Savigny-Lévescault and Tercé.[95] Then he waited to see if the French would respond that evening. Jean,

---

"Tanne" (probably a misreading for "Cavne") in another; in both cases this is said to be a castle where the King of France stayed the previous night. *BB*, 386; *Chartulary of Winchester Cathedral*, no. 370. *Reading*, 124, says the skirmish took place "propre La Chaveney"; the *English Brut*, 307, makes it "faste by Cha[v]eney," and *Avesbury*, 417, indicates it was "in via ducente de Chaveny versus Poitiers." The *Eulogium* places the combat at the exit of a large woods, reached by the prince after leaving "viam quae ducit de Cha[v]igne ad Poyters," and then notes that the prince made camp that night in the same woods. All of this is made more confusing by the fact that the various forms of "Chaveny/Cavne/La Chaveney/Chavigne" could very well be Savigny-Lévescault rather than Chauvigny, as suggested by *Chronique des règnes de Jean II et Charles V*, 72, which is clearly referring to Savigny when it describes "un chastel de l'evesque de Poitiers, appellé Chavigny."

Indeed, there are a number of reasons to conclude the skirmish did take place near Savigny ["La Chaveny"/Cavne] rather than the usually given location of La Chabotrie, an enclosed farmstead belonging to the hamlet of le Breuil l'Abesse just east of Poitiers: (1) Savigny, unlike La Chabotrie, is well off the road from Chauvigny to Poitiers, as the *Eulogium* suggests; (2) it seems much more likely that the King of France, knowing his enemies were in the vicinity, would spend the night in the bishop's castle of Savigny than that he would halt just short of Poitiers in a simple enclosed farm; (3) Burghersh's letter describes Chabutorie/[C]a[v]ne as a "chastelle," a term which fits Savigny but not La Chabotrie; (4) the prince's letter and Froissart (*PL*, 205; Froissart, *Oeuvres*, 5:400) indicate the encounter took place about three leagues from Chauvigny, which is about right for Savigny but too close for La Chabotrie; (5) the *Chron. Jean II et Charles V* says the prince was encamped near Savigny on Monday; on Sunday he had marched towards Poitiers from his camp which was near the site of the skirmish (notes 94–97, below); this is still possible if the skirmish took place in the vicinity of Savigny, but makes no sense if it happened near le Breuil l'Abesse. Finally (6) Savigny, being further east than La Chabotrie, makes more sense as the location of the encounter given that the prince's initial intent was to cut the French off at the river crossing. *Scalacronica*, 173; cf. *Anonimalle*, 37, and *PL*, 205.

For the traditional view, see Delachenal, *Histoire de Charles V*, 1:209.

92 *BB*, 386; *Scalacronica*, 173, says over 100 captured; larger figures in *Anonimalle*, 37; M. Villani, *Cronica*, 528–9.

93 *Eulogium*, 222; *PL*, 205; *Scalacronica*, 173.

94 *PL*, 205: "et puis les pursuievrent noz gentz tanqe a Chaveny [i.e. Chauvigny] bien a treis lieus loyns purquoi il nous convienoit logger cel jour a plus pres de celle place [where the skirmish took place] qe nous poiens pur recoiller noz gentz." See also Froissart, *Oeuvres*, 5:402.

95 *Eulogium*, 222; *Anonimalle*, 37; *PL*, 205; *Le Baker*, 142. The sources are clear that the encampment was near the site of the skirmish – the prince, in other words, did not "press on further that very day, to snatch at the possibility of getting well south of Poitiers before the French army could deliver its blow," as Hewitt claims. *Black Prince's Expedition*, 110. The location between Savigny and Tercé – i.e. in the middle of the Bois de Savigny – is about the

however, on receiving word of the English attack, simply arrayed his forces in a defensive posture on a hill outside the walls of Poitiers.[96]

Early on Sunday morning, having reassembled his men, the prince took a step which is very confusing to those who believe he was aiming to avoid a battle with the French: he began a march directly towards King Jean's position outside Poitiers.[97] After the skirmish of the 17th, Edward recognized he was in a dangerous position. Considering the proximity of the French, and the vigor they had recently displayed, and the fact that at Poitiers they were well positioned to block a march towards English-held St.-Jean d'Angély or Cognac, it would be very difficult for the Anglo-Gascon army to escape to Bordeaux without a fight.[98] Of course, the prince did not particularly *want* to get back to Bordeaux without a fight, but, paradoxically, it was of great importance for him to be *able* to do so. So long as he was in a position where he could safely escape to Bordeaux, he could afford to offer battle to the French; under those circumstances, if Jean wanted a battle, the French would have to take the tactical offensive, and if the French took the tactical offensive, then Edward was confident he could win. But if he did not have the ability to retreat safely, then the Valois would have the opportunity to try to hold him in place until he starved or was forced to take the tactical initiative, which considering the disparity in force between the two sides would doubtless have been disastrous. This was precisely the threat Edward realized he faced on 18 September 1356.[99]

The prisoners taken on the previous day, however, had doubtless confirmed what earlier reports had said: King Jean was eager to fight with the English, and had proclaimed as much to his men.[100] There was, then, reason to hope that if the Anglo-Gascon army presented itself in battle array in front of the French camp, Jean might attack immediately, rather than attempting the safer but less glorious tactic of letting hunger do his fighting for him.[101] The men in the prin-

---

right distance to Chauvigny, and also explains how the prince could on the next day move towards Poitiers (see note 97, below), and still find himself between Savigny and the Bois de Nouaillé (*Petite chronique Française*, cited in Delachenal, *Histoire de Charles V,* 1:211n).

[96] *Anonimalle*, 37; *Eulogium*, 222 (Francos nolle pugnare).

[97] Delachenal, *Histoire de Charles V,* 1:209–10, and Tourneur-Aumont, *Bataille de Poitiers*, 253, for example, simply refuse to believe this, but it is clear from all the sources, French as well as English. The two best sources, the prince and the *Eulogium*, are explicit on this point, as is the *Scalacronica*. *PL*, 205: "lendemeyn prismes nostre chemyn tout droit devers le Roi"; *Eulogium*, 222; *Scalacronica*, 173; see also *PW*, 207. Finally, the *Chronographia* and the continuator of Guillaume de Nangis both agree that the two armies were approaching *one another* when the cardinal intervened. (*Chronographia* 2:260: "Franci et Anglici sibi apropinquassent"; *Nangis*, 239: "Appropinquantibus autem utriusque partis aciebus.")

[98] M. Villani, *Cronica*, 526. Froissart, *Oeuvres*, 5:403.

[99] Froissart, *Oeuvres*, 5:413; M. Villani, *Cronica*, 529; *Le Bel*, 2:236.

[100] With a formal oath according to Froissart, *Oeuvres*, 5:383.

[101] This latter possibility was all the more worrisome because the English had kept their troops close together – and so unable to forage effectively – for the last few days, because of

ce's army who had been with Edward III in 1339 and 1340, like those who had stood with him waiting for a French attack outside Calais in 1347, must have realized the dangers of a plan which relied on Valois aggressiveness for its success, but there was no better alternative.

Thus it was that the Anglo-Gascon army was marching towards Poitiers before dawn on Sunday the 18th. When English scouts brought word that they had located the French army, arrayed for battle, in the fields one league southeast of Poitiers, the prince halted, dismounted his men-at-arms, and ordered his troops for battle.[102] The earls of Warwick and Oxford had command of the vanguard; the prince led the second division, and the earls of Suffolk and Salisbury had the third.[103] Shortly after Edward's men resumed their march towards the French position,[104] the Cardinal of Périgord, whom he had earlier rebuffed at Montbazon, rode up from the French army,[105] ready to make another last-minute attempt to arrange a truce. At first Prince Edward showed little inclination to listen to him. "Speak your proposal quickly," he reportedly said to the legate, "lest time be lost to preaching which would better be spent fighting."[106] The cardinal opened by warning him that the King of France, the most powerful prince on earth, was approaching with a great army, intending to destroy the Plantagenet and his army. This did not have the desired effect, for that was exactly what Edward hoped to hear. "I rejoice greatly, then," he answered, "that the King of Heaven, the King of Justice, will today show and declare to which claimant the inheritance of the realm of France rightfully belongs!"[107]

---

the imminent risk of battle. As a result, they were now seriously lacking in supplies. Knighton, 2:88: "supplies began to fail in the prince's army, to such an extent that he had to meet them in battle, or else foolishly turn his back on the enemies." Cf. *PL*, 205; Froissart, *Oeuvres*, 5:402, 415 (await the enemy's attack); 5:398, 419, 435 (supplies); 5:413, 414, 435 (hunger option).

[102] *Le Baker*, 142; *PL*, 205: "alasmes a plus pres de lui qe nos poiams prendre nostre places et nous mesmes a pie et en arraie de bataille et prest de combatre ove lui." Cf. *Anonimalle*, 37.

[103] *Le Baker*, 143. At this point the French would have been near Chantemerle, and the English in the area of Carthage.

[104] *Le Baker*, 143 (ad hostium venacionem resumendos).

[105] Where he had been given permission to try to arrange a peace by pointing out that the French might be able to gain a negotiated victory without risking the uncertainties of battle. M. Villani, *Cronica*, 530.

[106] *Eulogium*, 223: "Dic propositum tuum velociter, quia jam non vacat tempus praedicandi sed potius pugnandi."

[107] *Chron. CCCO*, fo. 179v: " 'Nous vous consaillons qe vous retournetz qar le plus pussant Roy terrene ove soun poair vous approche a graunt force des armes pur vous et les voz perdre et destruir et pour ce nous counselloms qe vous retournez et eiez pite et mercie de vous mesmes.' Et le prince lour respoundi: 'Jeo moy resjoie graundement qar le Roy celestre et le Roy de droiture monstra et declara huy cest jour a quelle partie le droit de leritage de Roiaume de Fraunce appartient. Jeo ne voile retourner mes ove ferme corage poursuire voile le droit commence par leide de Roy toutpuissant.' " Cf. *Vie du Prince Noir*, ll. 825–34, and ll. 848–52: "Si accorder ne voillent ceste foitz/ Je sui ci tut prest pur attendre/ La grace de Dieu, au voir entendre,/ car nostre querelle est si veraie/ Qe de combatre ne m'esmaie." Also *Chron. des quat. prem. Valois*, 51; Froissart, *Oeuvres*, 5:404.

The cardinal quickly changed his tack. Would it not be better, he asked, if France and England could be at peace, and the two nations could devote their efforts to a crusade against the unbelievers, rather than shedding Christian blood?[108] The legate added to the pragmatic strength of his argument by pointing out that the French, "hoping to gain a cheap victory over the English," had taken up positions such that the prince's men would not be able to spread out, and so would come in a few days to suffer greatly for lack of supplies, "for which reason the King of France appeared to have the victory in hand: that was the way of things, by the logic of war."[109] Considering the danger of the prince's situation, the cleric concluded, it would be showing inordinate pride and presumption if he refused to negotiate, and God would judge against him for it.[110] If, on the other hand, the prince would agree to truce talks, then he would, God willing, get an honorable peace.[111] Considering all these arguments, on the advice of his council, the prince agreed to begin discussions, "neither fearing battle nor rejecting peace."[112]

The cardinal immediately returned to the King of France and secured his agreement to go ahead with peace talks. The legate soon rejoined the prince and informed him of the king's willingness to proceed. Parties from each side then met in between the two hosts, and began to negotiate.[113] After discussions lasting most of the day, the English made an offer which reflected the peril of their situation. The precise details vary from chronicle to chronicle, but the scope of the concessions the prince was prepared to offer appears clearly enough. It seems that Edward offered to return all the prisoners he had taken and all the places and lands he had captured in the past three years, as well as paying a substantial but hardly crippling indemnity of 100,000 écus and even promising not to take up arms against Jean for seven years. The main provisions, however, were to be subject to the approval of King Edward, a condition which substan-

---

108 *Eulogium*, 223. Cf. *Scalacronica*, 173; *Le Baker*, 144; *Vie du Prince Noir*, ll. 812–16; Tourneur-Aumont, *Bataille de Poitiers*, 225–6.

109 M. Villani, *Cronica*, 529, thus analyzes the situation ("sperando avere degl'Inghilesi buon mercato; e misonsi a campo presso al campo del duca a meno di due leghe parigine, in parte che gl'Inghilesi non si poteano allargare; ed erano per venire in pochi dí in gran soffratta di vittuaglia . . . per la qual cosa al re di Francia pareva avere la vittoria in mano, e cosí era per ragione di guerra.") and later (p. 530) says the Cardinal of Périgord "con savie parole gli [the prince] mostrò il pericolo dov'era egli e tutta la sua oste." Cf. ibid., 534; Froissart, *Oeuvres*, 5:413; *Chron. des quat. prem. Valois*, 53.

110 M. Villani, *Cronica*, 530: "conchiudendo disse, che acciocché Dio non guidicasse la sua causa per disordinata presunzione e superbia in cotanto pericolo quanto egli era." Cf. *Vie du Prince Noir*, ll. 817–20.

111 *Scalacronica*, 173; *PL*, 205; *Le Baker*, 144; M. Villani, *Cronica*, 530.

112 *Le Baker*, 144 (nec bellum timuit nec pacem recusavit); *PL*, 205; *Vie du Prince Noir*, ll. 848–56; M. Villani, *Cronica*, 530.

113 *PL*, 205; *Scalacronica*, 174; *Anonimalle*, 37; *Vie du Prince Noir*, 72; cf. M. Villani, *Cronica*, 531.

tially reduced their force.[114] The prince, nonetheless, would not budge on this point.[115]

These terms have led many historians to conclude that the Prince of Wales was intent on avoiding battle.[116] As we have seen, however, it was not *battle* that Edward wanted to avoid. Rather, as Froissart notes, "the English and Gascons mainly worried that the French would hold them there, as if besieged, without fighting: it was this plan that worried them the most."[117] Jean le Bel is equally clear on the English motivation: "they offered these things more because they were worried that Jean would starve them" than because they were afraid of fighting his army.[118] The only significant source suggesting that the prince wanted to avoid a fight is Chandos Herald's poem, which says that "willingly, *it seems to me*, he would have avoided the battle if he could have;"[119] but this

---

114 *Chron. Normande*, 113; *Chron. Pays-Bas*, 186; *Le Bel*, 2:233; Froissart, *Oeuvres*, 5:414 [first redaction]. In his second redaction (ibid., 416) Froissart adds that his information on the negotiations came directly from eyewitnesses in the Cardinal of Périgord's entourage, and that Jean insisted that the prince and 100 of his knights surrender to prison. M. Villani, *Cronica*, 531, says his offer was that he would restore the lands and prisoners taken in the last three years, pay an indemnity of 200,000 nobles; and, in order to strengthen the peace, the prince asked for the hand of one of Jean's daughters, with Angoulême, as a fief of the French crown, for a dowry. This was all to be subject to ratification by King Edward, but the prince promised to secure that rapidly.
Le Baker, 144, by contrast, has the prince concede only a truce until Christmas.
115 *Scalacronica*, 174: "Ly prince luy disoit touz iours qen ceo qil auoit poair il se acorderoit uoluntiers, et ceo ne passeroit il my." *Vie du Prince Noir*, ll. 855–6, 841–4: "Eins en ferray tout mon pooir./ Mais saches qe, tut pur voir,/ je ne puisse pas ceste matiere/ Accompler sanz le roi mon piere." M. Villani, *Cronica*, 531. It is possible, however, that the prince went so far as to offer to remain King Jean's prisoner himself until the other terms were accomplished. *Chron. Normande*, 113; *Chron. Pays-Bas*, 186; cf. Froissart, *Oeuvres*, 5:416.
116 Delachenal, *Histoire de Charles V*, 1:210 n.3; cf. Hewitt, *Black Prince's Expedition*, 111, 117, where he speaks of "a fight in which [an English] victory appeared most improbable and even survival doubtful."
117 Froissart, *Oeuvres*, 5:413: "Li princes . . . et ses conssaux se veoient enclos ou fort dou royaumme, et se doubtèrent de premiers li Englès et li Gascon, que li Franchois ne les tenissent là ainsi que pour asségiés sans combattre: c'estoit li ordonnanche qu'il resongnoient le plus." Cf. 5:435, 419–20: "au voir dire, il [the English] ne ressongnoient point tant le bataille que il faisoient ce que on ne les tenist en tel estat, ensi que pour asségiés et affamés" and M. Villani, *Cronica*, 529–30, 534.
118 *Le Bel*, 2:236: the English before the battle "n'avoient gousté de pain III jours devant; pour tant offrirent ilz les choses dessus dites, car ilz doubtoient plus que le roy Jehan ne les affamast que sa bataille." Cf. *Le Baker*, 144 (nec bellum timuit).
119 *Vie du Prince Noir*, ll. 1066–1068: "Et volentiers, a ma semblaunce, vousist la bataille excuser, s'il le pooit devoider, mais bien veoit qe lui covient faire." On the Herald's uncertainty, note also l. 885. Supporting the Herald, however, *Wyntoun* 2:495, says "wyth- owtyn dowte the Inglis men/ Fayne away wald have bene then;/ Bot that thai mycht noucht than lychtly,/ Thai war abowte thame swa mony,/ Off welle bodyn Frawns men,/ Agayne ane ay as to set ten,/ Na nane proffyre wald thai here/ Off mesowre for pryd of thare powere." Yet the chronicler's "wyth-owtyn dowte" actually does inspire some doubt, since it implies a deduction rather than a report. In contrast, the (comparably late) *Chron. des quat. prem. Valois*, 54, says that even after the first several French attacks, the English "cuidoient avoir eu victoire."

hardly outweighs the more contemporary and less hesitant testimony of Jean le Bel, much less the words of the *Eulogium Historiarum*, of the Corpus Christi chronicle, of the chronicle of Geoffrey le Baker, and of the prince's own campaign bulletin, all of which indicate that the Plantagenet was more than willing to fight.[120] Furthermore, the Herald's opinion goes against what he himself reports of the words of the prince ("our quarrel is so righteous, that I am not worried by a fight") and the Earl of Warwick.[121]

In any case, the negotiated terms were carried by the Cardinal of Périgord to the King of France, who met with his council to consider them. According to Villani's detailed account of the proceedings, Jean, seeing a prospect of gaining suitable amends for the damage done to him without having to risk another Crécy, was favorably disposed towards the proposals.[122] Marshal Clermont agreed.[123] One of the king's closest counselors, the Bishop of Châlons, however, was less amenable, particularly because he saw the proviso requiring ratification by King Edward as an escape clause which could leave the French with no gains at all. He arose before the council and spoke out:

> Sire, if I recall correctly, the King of England and the [prince] who is nearby, his son, and the Earl of Lancaster, his cousin, have for a long time inflicted much shame upon you, and committed shocking outrages against your entire realm, over and over again, defeating your father in the field, with the loss of kings and of great barons, and have cut up your forces on the sea, and burned and depopulated your realm in various places: tell me, Sire, what revenge have you taken, that without shame to you and your whole realm, this peace can be made? You have in your hands your mortal enemy, with a great many English and Gascon barons and knights (who have done such great harm and so many evils, even aside from the ones I recounted to you, to you and to your realm)

---

[120] *PL*, 205: "hastier devers lui . . . pour estre combatuz ove lui . . . prismes nostre chemyn tout droit devers le Roi . . . et alasmes a plus pres de lui qe nos poiams prendre nostre places et nous mesmes a pie et en arraie de bataille et prest qe combattre ove lui [when the cardinal came] . . . s'ils voilont la bataille ou trere devers nous en lieu qe nestoit mye tres graundment a nostre desavauntage qe nous le preindreins et ensint estoit fait sur quoi le bataille se prist." *Le Baker*, 144: the prince agreed to treat, "neither fearing battle nor rejecting peace" [nec bellum timuit nec pacem recusavit]; earlier (pp. 141–2): "immotus exspectare coronati feritatem preliaturam quam querere forsan non expectaturam potenciam, cum qua summe concupivit conserere manus bellatrices . . . princeps, avidus belli propter pacem que solet bellum comitari, adversus coronatum castra direxit." It has been argued that the prince, for propaganda purposes, had a motive to give the impression that he wanted to fight when what he really wanted was to escape, but this makes little sense to me. After he had fought and won, it seems to me, he stood to gain even more glory by saying "the French were so vastly much stronger than we were that I was constrained to try to retreat, but God did not allow this to occur, and instead gave us a great victory" rather than saying that he had sought a battle.
[121] *Vie du Prince Noir*, ll. 743–4, 851–2 ("Car nostre querelle est si veraie / Qe de combatre ne m'esmaie"), 909–18. Cf. also Froissart, *Oeuvres*, 5:420, 436.
[122] M. Villani, *Cronica*, 531.
[123] *Le Baker*, 144. He had recently received very favorable treatment from Edward III, when prosecuting a case in the court of chivalry in London; this may have made his intervention suspect. Devon, *Issues of the Exchequer*, 159.

and now God has reduced them and enclosed them in such a way that they cannot retreat, nor can they move off to the right or to the left. They have few supplies, and do not await succor: On you it rests, my lord, to take your revenge nobly, and yet I see you negotiating to let them go – and, what is more, without their certain faith or the confirmation of their promises! . . . And therefore I counsel that you not delay the conquest any more, lest you see the vengeance for the offenses you have suffered, and the full victory that God has arranged for you, escape through the delays of your negotiating and your taking counsel.[124]

Marshal d'Audrehem, William Douglas, and Geoffrey de Charny (the royal banner-bearer, an author of texts on chivalry, and widely considered the best knight in France) all strongly agreed with the bishop. Douglas, who had brought a troop of two hundred Scottish men-at-arms to serve King Jean, argued that the French had superior numbers, were more rested and better supplied, and would be fighting on their own ground, for the defense of their homeland and under the eyes of their king: "in the ordinary course of things," he predicted, "the English cannot prevail."[125]

These speeches had a powerful effect on the king, who was filled with resolution to fight.[126] The Cardinal of Périgord was summoned back in, and Jean haughtily informed him of his decision: "We do not wish for [Prince Edward] to depart without a battle. Now we shall see if he can stand against us in our own land and resist our power."[127]

The cardinal unhappily brought word of the French decision back to the English camp. "Sire," he said, "I have worked hard in order to be able to bring peace, but I was not able to do so in any way, and therefore you will have to seek to be a valiant prince, and think on your defense with sword in hand, because you will have to give battle to the French: no other hope of accord or peace remains."[128] The prince received this word calmly, without any sign of distress.[129] "You can bear witness," he answered, "that I accepted the peace agreement in good faith, and that it was not our fault it failed: now that our adversary rejects it, I have faith that God will be on our side."[130] He then asked the cardinal to pray earnestly that God would grant the victory to the side with the more just cause, and to give him his blessing and absolve his sins.[131] Once the legate had departed, the prince summoned his bannerets and the captains of

---

124 M. Villani, *Cronica*, 532–3.
125 *Le Baker*, 144. For a different understanding of Douglas' stance, cf. *Chron. des quat. prem. Valois,* 53.
126 M. Villani, *Cronica*; *Le Baker*, 144.
127 *Chron. CCCO*, fo. 180: "le Roy de Fraunce nient assentant mes il dit orguillousement: 'Nous ne voloms [q]'il departira de nous saunz bataille. Ore nous verroms s'il poet esteer encontre nous en nostre terre et countresteer nostre poair.' " Cf. *Chron. Normande*, 113.
128 M. Villani, *Cronica*, 533. Cf. *Scalacronica*, 174.
129 M. Villani, *Cronica*, 533; cf. ibid., 527 and Froissart, *Oeuvres*, 5:436.
130 M. Villani, *Cronica*, 533.
131 *Chron. CCCO*, fos 179v–80.

his archers and sergeants for a speech preparing them for the likelihood of battle on the morrow.[132]

Even once the main issue of the negotiations had fallen through, secondary points continued to be discussed. The French king offered his adversary a truce over the night of the 18th/19th, provided that the English would agree not to try to slip away under cover of darkness, as Lancaster had done at l'Aigle. Edward had no intention of agreeing to such a proposition, for it was only by threatening such an escape that he could pressure his enemy into attacking him rather than starving him out. "To this the very noble lord the prince replied sharply that he had not come there . . . by his assent, but against his and all his supporters' wishes; and he [the prince] would stay and go at his own pleasure despite him and all his men . . . and if he [Jean] was afraid of him and his men, *he* [the prince] would willingly grant *him* a truce and respite."[133] Since both sides had declared that they were ready to fight rather than talk, the last issue of the negotiations was a discussion of how to agree upon a set battlefield, "so that the battle could not in any way fail."[134] This was thought necessary, by the French at least, because of the difficulty of the ground between the two armies' current positions.[135] But since the English were counting on that very factor to help them overcome the French numerical superiority, no agreement was reached. "You see here the field and the place," said Warwick in closing. "Let each do his best . . . and God will aid the side with the more just cause."[136] Before sunrise the next day, the cardinal returned to make one last try to arrange an indefinite truce for further discussion, but Edward refused, seeing that his men were beginning to suffer from lack of supplies, while the strength of the French army was increasing substantially by the hour.[137]

The breaking dawn of Monday 19 September thus found the two armies arrayed for battle in the fields between Savigny-l'Évescault and the woods of Nouaillé.[138] As was often the case in medieval battles, the day opened with a standoff. As the prince later reported, neither side wanted to give the other a great advantage by undertaking an attack across the broken terrain which separated them.[139] The French could afford to wait thus for as long as necessary, but

---

132 M. Villani, *Cronica*, 532–3. *Le Baker*, 145–6, gives versions of two separate speeches, one to his knights and another to his archers. Cf. also Froissart, *Oeuvres*, 5:436.

133 *Anonimalle*, 37–8; also *PL*, 205–6; *Scalacronica*, 174.

134 *PL*, 206. Cf. *Vie du Prince Noir*, 73.

135 *PL*, 205–6. On "ascuns forces," see Greimas, *Dictionnaire de l'ancien Français*, s.v. "force," def. 3 (and cf. def. 7). See also *Chron. des quat. prem. Valois*, 50–1.

136 *Vie du Prince Noir*, ll. 913–18: " 'Veiez ci la champaigne et la place / Chescun qui poet son meillour face./ . . . Dieux voille conforter le droit / Ou il semble qe meillour soit.' " Note the provocative tone here, and even moreso in ll. 909–12. Cf. *Scalacronica*, 174.

137 *PL*, 205; *Scalacronica*, 174; *Eulogium*, 223; *Le Baker*, 144; cf. *Chron. des quat. prem. Valois*, 53; Froissart, *Oeuvres*, 5:419–20, 435.

138 *Petit chronique Française*, quoted in Delachenal, *Histoire de Charles V*, 212 n.2. Cf. *Chron. Jean II et Charles V*, 72.

139 *PL*, 206: "et demourerent les batailles d'une part et d'autre tote noet chescun en lour place et tanqe le demein entour un prime[;] et pur ascuns forces [i.e. difficulties] qe estoient

the English could not. "So," as the prince himself later reported, "because of a lack of supplies, and for other reasons, it was agreed that we should take a path traversing their front, in such a way that if they wanted the battle, or would come towards us in a place which was not too greatly to our disadvantage, we would fight them."[140]

That, of course, was what the French were waiting for.[141] They knew the danger of assaulting a steady, immobile infantry formation, and understood that they would do much better if they could strike the English while the latter were on the march. The Anglo-Gascon leaders' task, then, was to manage the disengagement so skillfully that they would be ready to conduct an effective defense when the French attack came.[142] This they succeeded in doing.

The details of the ensuing conflict are difficult to disentangle, largely

parentre les ditz batailles nulz ne voloit a autre taunte davauntage demprendre a venir l'un sur l'autre"; *Fordun*, 376 (version B): "princeps Anglie . . . primo cum Gallicis, qui in aciebus suis stabant immobiles, congredi aperte non audebant." Cf. *Chron. Jean II et Charles V,* 71–2; *Chron. Pays-Bas,* 186 ("pour le bastaille atendre"). See also note 135, above. Froissart has the battle start at primes, so this standoff apparently lasted about an hour. *Oeuvres,* 5:434.

140 *PL,* 206: "Et pour defaute des vitailles si bien pour autres enchessons acorde estoit qe nous deveriens prendre nostre chemyn encosteant par devant eux en tieu manere qe s'ils voilont la bataille ou trere devers nous en lieu qe nestoit mye tres graundement a nostre desavauntage qe nous le preindreins." The last verb, as Delachenal notes, is rather obscure. It could be a form of *prendre* (Delachenal, *Histoire de Charles V,* 1:228 n.3), meaning "we would take [it]," i.e., "we would accept the battle." (Cf. the next line – "le bataille se prist" – and Edward III's usage in 1347: "nous acceptasmes lour offre et prendrissoms le bataille," in *Avesbury,* 393.) It could also (as Delachenal does not consider) be the Old French verb "preindre" – to crush, to assail, to press, to overcome [them]. (Greimas, *Dictionnaire de l'ancien Français,* s.v.) In either of those two cases, the meaning would effectively be "to fight" (as I gave it, above) though the latter reading would imply a more aggressive stance by the English. The reading Delachenal himself prefers (as do Hewitt, *Black Prince's Expedition,* 118, and Tourneur-Aumont, *Bataille de Poitiers,* 235), taking "preindreins" to be the equivalent of "préviendrions," (we would precede [them], be the first) clearly makes less sense, on both linguistic and content grounds.

On the prince's use of "encosteant," cf. *Scalacronica,* 174, and Froissart, *Oeuvres,* 5:390, 391, which suggest a meaning of "moving parallel to." The word is obscure but the meaning of the phrase is clearly a motion along the front of the French formation towards its flank – i.e. traversing its front. It may be that the prince intended to invoke the image of a ship moving along the coast of the land.

Note the prince's willingness to fight provided that the enemy would come to him ("trere devers nous"), which is clearer in light of the prince's preceding sentence stating that neither side wanted to accept the disadvantage of making the attack. Cf. also Fordun, *Chronica,* 376 (above, note 139) on this point.

Overall, though there are questions about the nuances of his language, the prince's general meaning is clear enough, not "intentionally obscure" as Hewitt (who lists several possible interpretations, but not including the one I give above) states. *Black Prince's Expedition,* 118.

Concerning the logic of the prince's decision, see also M. Villani, *Cronica,* 534.

141 Cf. *Chron. des quat. prem. Valois,* 51.

142 *Vie du Prince Noir,* ll. 1092–5; Cf. Tourneur-Aumont, *Bataille de Poitiers,* 285–6.

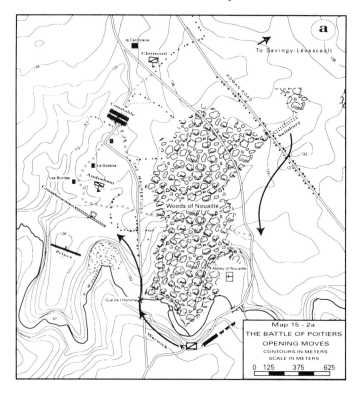

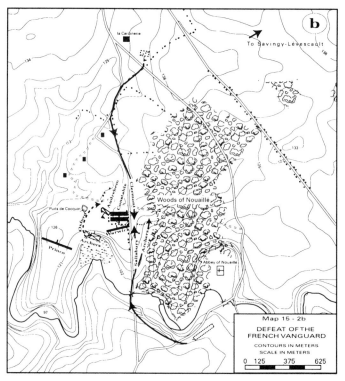

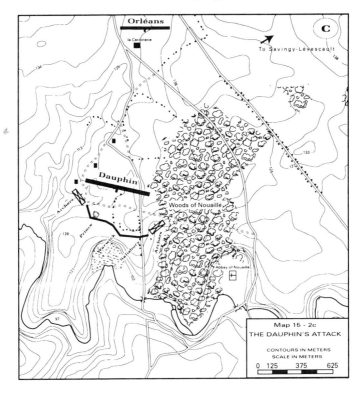

Map 15 - 2c
THE DAUPHIN'S ATTACK

CONTOURS IN METERS
SCALE IN METERS

0   125   375   625

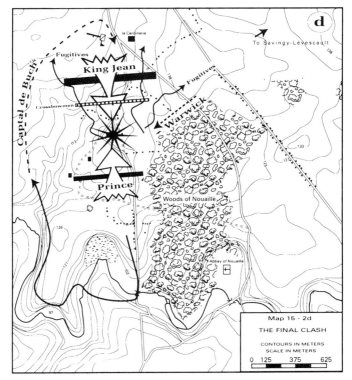

Map 15 - 2d
THE FINAL CLASH

CONTOURS IN METERS
SCALE IN METERS

0   125   375   625

because of uncertainties over the precise location of the fighting,[143] and this book is not the place to make a fully documented attempt to resolve the points under dispute – especially since my reconstruction of the battle is substantially different from that presented by earlier writers, and so would require bulky justification. On the other hand, since the aim of the prince's strategy was to achieve a tactical victory, we must understand his battlefield success in order to comprehend the foundation of his strategy. I will therefore present a narrative of the battle as best I could unravel it, without spending much space to explain (beyond citing my sources) why I resolved many controversial issues in the way I did. A more complete discussion of the points in dispute will have to await a separate treatment.[144]

The prince's division began the action by moving towards the French right flank, to a good fighting position on a vine-covered hill from which it could block a French advance down the "Maupertuis"– the "bad road"[145] which led south just to the west of the Nouaillé woods.[146] Next the Earl of Warwick, with the troops of the vanguard, conducted the English wagons south across the Miosson river by the narrow bridge at Nouaillé.[147] The rear division, under Salisbury and Suffolk, held its position. (See map 15–2a.)

King Jean had assigned a mixed force of mounted and dismounted men-at-arms, heavy infantry, and crossbowmen to keep watch on the English. His two marshals, d'Audrehem and Clermont, each commanded a small wing of mounted knights and esquires, selected from the best-armored in the royal host, while the veteran constable Gautier de Brienne (the exiled Duke of Athens) led the bulk of the first division.[148] Brienne's troops, in accordance with the advice given by Sir William Douglas, were prepared to fight on foot.[149] Farther back

---

[143] The best analysis of the battlefield is in ibid., 251–3; see also Tourneur-Aumont's aerial photograph and maps, at the end of his book, on which my maps are based.

[144] Meanwhile let me acknowledge that I do not claim to have resolved definitively every questionable point; the obscurities of the sources make it impossible to be certain of the correctness of any interpretation. I have taken into careful account the views of Delachenal, Hewitt, Babinet, Burne, Galbraith, and Tourneur-Aumont in reaching my own conclusions.

[145] See discussions in Tourneur-Aumont, *Bataille de Poitiers*, 239–44; Hewitt, *Black Prince's Expedition*, 113. See also *Chron. Normande*, 112; Froissart, *Oeuvres*, 5:402; *Chronographia* 2:260. The last source is particularly clear that Maupertuis is an area of fields, not a building or hamlet.

[146] *Le Baker*, 146; Cf. *Eulogium*, 224; *PL*, 206; *Scalacronica*, 174. It seems that the prince moved down the slope east of the Nouaillé woods, crossed the Miosson southwards at the bridge at Nouaille, then recrossed farther west at the Gué de l'Homme, and climbed up to Hill 126, where he took up his position. Cf. *Vie du Prince Noir*, ll. 1085–88, 1144.

[147] *Anonimalle*, 38; *Vie du Prince Noir*, ll. 1083–4.

[148] *Vie du Prince Noir*, 74; *Le Baker*, 143; *Lescot*, 102; *Chron. des quat. prem. Valois*, 51; cf. Froissart, *Oeuvres*, 5:406–7.

[149] *Le Baker*, 143 (Douglas); *Le Bel*, 2:232, says the decision to fight on foot was taken "out of dread for the archers, who always killed their horses, as at the battle of Crécy." On Douglas at Poitiers, see also *Pluscardensis*, 297–8; *Fordun*, 376. Hewitt's criticism of Jean's decision to have his army fight dismounted is unwarranted. The terrain was not suited to a cavalry charge, and Crécy had already shown that, in any case, horses were too vulnerable to English

were three more divisions of the French: the first under the dauphin, the second under Jean's brother the Duke of Orléans, and the last (probably only a small mounted reserve), under the king himself. In all – though the sources are very far from clear on this point – there were probably 10,000–12,0000 men-at-arms, in addition to some 2,000 crossbowmen and 2,000 other infantry, so that the prince's men were outnumbered by well over two to one.[150]

When the vanguard observed the motion of the Anglo-Gascon army, Marshal d'Audrehem pressed strongly for an immediate cavalry charge by the small element of the vanguard which had remained mounted, in order to fix the English long enough for the rest of the army to come up. Clermont, however, did not believe that there was much danger of the English escaping, and was highly unenthusiastic about the prospect of an unsupported attack against the English.[151] He therefore held back while his colleague charged towards Prince Edward's men-at-arms[152] with the infantry of the vanguard following close behind.

When they saw the two elements of the French vanguard advancing towards the prince, Warwick's men-at-arms, who were also still mounted, recrossed the Miosson at the Gué de l'Homme and swept up the slope to strike the leading French infantry (mainly crossbowmen and their *paviseurs* [shield-bearers]) in the flank. The attack was highly successful, and the French were immediately

archery for a mounted attack to have much chance of succeeding. Furthermore, the prospect of fighting on foot was not as unnatural to the French as he implies. *Black Prince's Expedition*, 117, 126.

150 *Vie du Prince Noir*, ll. 736–8 and pp. 68–76, passim. *BB*, 387, gives the French army as 8,000 men-at-arms and 3,000 infantry; the former figure is repeated by *Le Baker*, 143, and the *Scalacronica*, 175. The *Anonimalle*, 38, suggests, however, that this total may be *exclusive* of the men-at-arms (1,600 according to Froissart, *Oeuvres*, 5:426) who fled with the dauphin and the Duke of Orléans, and of those who had been struck down in the first three attacks on the English line: "Den apres viegnt le roi de Fraunce od son graunt bataille et od touz qe a lui voldrent relyer; le noumbre par estymacioun des gentz darmes viii m^i bacynetz et des pavasers et aublasters et de pedaille graunt noumbre, fuant le Dolphyn et ses deux freres." If so, Burghersh is not inconsistent with the Herald.

I tend to prefer Chandos Herald's figure of 10,400 men-at-arms (or more, if it is assumed that the king's division was more than a 400-man élite reserve force) to Burghersh's for two reasons: first, it is more detailed (with figures for each division of the French); second, the Herald implies (e.g. ll. 737, 993) that his numbers are based on a French muster list ("estille," "nombre"; cf. the accuracy of ll. 1521–2).

Other good sources also tend to support the Herald's numbers rather than Burghersh's smaller ones. Note *Chron. Normande*, 114; M. Villani, *Cronica*, 529; *Le Bel*, 2:230; Froissart *Oeuvres*, 5:421; *Pluscardensis*, 299–300, and *Fordun*, 376. See also Hewitt, *Black Prince's Expedition*, 114; Delachenal, *Histoire de Charles V*, 1:215–19.

151 *Vie du Prince Noir*, 79; *Scalacronica*, 174. Cf. also M. Villani, *Cronica*, 537. Edward III's recent lavish gifts to Clermont may help explain d'Audrehem's suspicion of the former. Devon, *Issues of the Exchequer*, 159 (and cf. *Le Baker*, 147).

152 Contrary to Hewitt's natural assumption (*Black Prince's Expedition*, 115), the prince apparently did not have any archers in his division (*Le Baker*, 148 – Earl of Oxford). This is not entirely surprising, since he commanded the "center" division, and the normal English practice was to have the archers form in wings on the flanks.

driven back.[153] (See map 15–2a.) The men-at-arms of the vanguard then
dismounted and arrayed themselves while the rest of Warwick's troops hurried
forward to take up their positions below and to the right of the hill on which the
prince's men-at-arms stood. The earl's archers formed on Edward's immediate
right, in a morass formed by a bend of the Miosson river, where the ground
made them secure from a cavalry attack; the rest of the vanguard held the line of
a thick hedge which ran from west to east up a slope.[154] To the right of his
position, where the "bad road" which gave its name ("Maupertuis") to the area
ran, there was a single broad gap in this hedge. Marshal Clermont decided to try
to rescue the situation by driving through it and hitting the English vanguard in
the flank and rear. His attempt, however, was foiled by the Earl of Salisbury,
who anticipated the French move and brought up his men-at-arms to block the
gap.[155] These troops, ably assisted by the archers of the rearguard (who formed
up behind the hedge and, at the extreme right, along the edge of Nouaillé
woods) drove the French cavalry back with heavy losses.[156] (See map 15–2b.)

The portion of the French line opposite the Earl of Warwick was at first able
to maintain the fight without too heavy losses, despite the defensive advantage
the hedge provided to the English, because the earl's archers were unable to
achieve their usual results with their longbows – though they did keep the
French crossbowmen from being of much use to their side. The men-at-arms of
Audrehem's battalion, on their heavily barded horses, had been provided with
large leather shields which, linked into an overlapping wall, proved quite effective in deflecting the English arrows. They took up a position between the
archers and the main body of the constable's men, so that they acted as a living
shield for their comrades.[157] Observing this, however, the Earl of Oxford rallied
a portion of the longbowmen, and brought them over past a small zigzag in the
hedge to where they could fire into the right flank of the French cavalry.[158] The
arrows, striking the French destriers in their unprotected hindquarters, instantly
dispersed the line of men-at-arms who had been shielding the flank of the
constable's line as it fought with Warwick's men. Some of the horses crashed
through the French formation behind them, trampling numbers of men-at-arms.

[153] *Anonimalle*, 38; cf. *Eulogium*, 224; *Le Baker*, 147 [circa "equites nostri"]; cf. Froissart,
Oeuvres, 5:426 (bataille des Allemans).
[154] *Le Baker*, 147 [declivum marisco], 148 [primaque classe]. Note that the "marisco" would
have been more extensive than usual in 1356 because of the high rainfall recently experienced
(ibid., 142).
[155] *Le Baker*, 147–8; *Anonimalle*, 38; *Vie du Prince Noir*, 80. Cf. Froissart, *Oeuvres*, 5:405;
Chron. Normande, 114–15.
[156] *Le Baker*, 147–8; cf. *Vie du Prince Noir*, ll. 1189–92. Note that with the archers on the
left in the swamp and those on the right along the woods, the English effectively had the two
wings of archers described in the *Chron. Normande*, 114 (and Froissart, *Oeuvres*, 5:405; M.
Villani, *Cronica*, 536).
[157] *Le Baker*, 148. Cf. *Eulogium*, 225.
[158] *Le Baker*, 148. The zigzag in the hedge is not specifically mentioned, but it is the obvious
place for them to have moved to. Cf. M. Villani, *Cronica*, 537–8.

Now the archers were able to strike the French infantry with full effect, just as Salisbury's archers were doing on the opposite side of the field.[159] Brienne's men could not make any headway against the English men-at-arms behind their hedge, so they were effectively held in place as "sitting ducks" to the fire of the archers. Firing yard-long arrows at short range from bows with draw-strengths of over 100 pounds, the English yeomen were able to drive their shafts right through the armor of the Frenchmen, provided that the angle of impact was correct.[160] The effect of this was so great that several chroniclers report simply that "the first French division was defeated by the arrows of the English."[161] Soon this first stage of the battle was over, the Valois forces having been utterly crushed.[162] Of the leaders of the vanguard, the constable and Marshal Clermont were dead. Marshal d'Audrehem, wounded, was taken captive. The English did not pursue the fugitives, and took few prisoners, for they knew there was much fighting yet to come.[163]

The second division of the French army, four thousand men-at-arms under the dauphin and King Jean's uncle the Duke of Bourbon, came forward without delay to resume the struggle.[164] (See map 15–2C.) As it advanced, however, the wounded and frightened survivors of the constable's division fell back through and around it, demoralizing and breaking up the new wave of assaulting troops.[165] Meanwhile, there was enough time for the men-at-arms of the prince's division to come down to join Warwick's troops behind the hedge. The English casualties during the first stage of the fighting had been light, and though Warwick's and Salisbury's men were tired, the pause between the stages of the French attack allowed them time to catch their breath; the men of Prince Edward's division had not yet been heavily engaged.[166] The advance under fire of the French men-at-arms, on the other hand, inevitably left them tired and disordered by the time they reached the English lines.[167] Furthermore, the six thousand men of the Anglo-Gascon army outnumbered the dauphin's division by 3:2 (though the Valois had more men-at-arms). Considering these factors, and the boost to their morale gained by their easy defeat of the constable, and the efficacy of the English longbowmen, it is no surprise that the Plantagenet troops emerged from this fight, too, with a complete victory. The Dauphin

---

159 *Le Baker*, 148; M. Villani, *Cronica*, 537.
160 *Le Baker*, 147: "coegerunt saggitas armis militaribus prevalere." See also my "Efficacy of the Longbow."
161 *Chronographia*, 2:262; *Chron. Pays-Bas*, 187; *Chron. Normande*, 116n; *Knighton*, 2:89; Froissart, *Oeuvres*, 5:425, 439; cf. M. Villani, *Cronica*, 537–8.
162 Duration: *Le Baker*, 149; Froissart, *Oeuvres*, 5:439; *Knighton*, 2:89.
163 *Le Baker*, 148; Froissart, *Oeuvres*, 5:439; *Chron. Normande*, 115, but cf. *Knighton*, 2:89.
164 *Vie du Prince Noir*, 74–5; *Le Baker*, 149.
165 *Le Baker*, 149; Froissart, *Oeuvres*, 5:440.
166 *Le Baker*, 149.
167 See my "Offensive/Defensive in Medieval Strategy." The advance over a substantial distance, while wearing armor, would be moderately tiring in and of itself, but in the adrenaline-charged, heart-pounding circumstances of battle, with every muscle tensed against the anticipated impact of the densely falling English arrows, it could be quite exhausting.

Charles' men, however, fought harder and held out longer than the constable's division (which had included a substantial proportion of foreign troops and mercenary infantrymen).[168] It did not collapse until Charles' own banner-bearer was taken prisoner; even then the remnants of the division made an orderly retreat.[169] Behind them, however, they left a great number of their men killed or captured (though the English did not break their formation to pursue), including the slain Duke of Bourbon.[170]

It is impossible to be sure just what happened with the next division, that of the Duke of Orléans, because the sources are so mutually contradictory, but it seems most likely that the duke himself fled the field rather than enter the killing-ground in front of the men-at-arms of the Anglo-Gascon army.[171] With him he took about half the men of his command – 1,600 fresh men-at-arms under 57 banners – and some of the survivors of the first two actions, including all four of Jean's sons who were on the field.[172] One of these, however, Philip, the youngest (and the future Duke of Burgundy) slipped away and rejoined his father.[173] Jean later wrote that he had ordered his sons to leave the field, and this may well be true, though the king probably did not intend for them to be accompanied by so many troops.[174] The remainder of the division seems to have made a half-hearted attack, which was beaten off with little difficulty, then fallen back to join the king.[175]

The French soldiers of the first three divisions who were still fit for combat, and had not fled, coalesced around the royal reserve battalion, which included a specially selected striking force of four hundred knights on well-barded horses, under twenty-three banners, who had up until now remained mounted.[176] Even these men, however, along with the king himself, now sent their destriers to the

---

[168] *Le Baker*, 149; *Chron. des quat. prem. Valois*, 53; but cf. *Scalacronica*, 174 (fight); M. Villani, *Cronica*, 534–5; Froissart, *Oeuvres*, 5:407, 426; Delachenal, *Histoire de Charles V*, 1:232 (foreigners).

[169] *Lescot*, appendix XIV (banner-bearer); *Le Baker*, 149 (orderly retreat).

[170] *Le Baker*, 149. One exception, notes Baker, was Sir Maurice Berkeley, who plunged into the dauphin's retreating division, then was overpowered and taken prisoner.

[171] A number of sources indicate that Orléans' battle did make an attack (below, note 175), but this probably occurred after the duke himself had departed, since Froissart, *Oeuvres*, 5:426, and M. Villani, *Cronica*, 538 specify that he left with a large number of fresh men-at-arms.

[172] *Eulogium*, 225, and BL MS Sloane 560, fo. 58 (banners); Froissart, *Oeuvres*, 5:426 (1,600; the narrative is a bit confused but the number matches well with the number of banners, and the inclusion of the king's sons fits); *Vie du Prince Noir*, l. 1003 (total).

[173] Cf. M. Villani, *Cronica*, 539.

[174] Letter in Ménard, *Histoire de Nîmes*, 2:182. Cf. *Chron. Normande*, 116; *Chron. Jean II et Charles V*, 74; *Chron. des quat. prem. Valois*, 54, 56–7.

[175] *Scalacronica*, 174; *Anonimalle*, 38; but cf. *Chron. Normande*, 115, 116n; *Chron. des quat. prem. Valois*, 52–3.

[176] *Anonimalle*, 38; *Chron. Pays-Bas*, 187; Size of reserve force: *Vie du Prince Noir*, 76–7, but cf. *Knighton*, 2:89 (2,000 men-at-arms). Note that the size of the prince's reserve was also 400 men: *Le Baker*, 150.

rear.[177] The result was a very large force, including a substantial number of crossbowmen – presumably the ones from the constable's division who had been driven off by the English archers and by Warwick's cavalry charge at the start of the battle.[178] Its numbers were deceptive, however, for most of the Frenchmen had already been beaten once, and even those who had not yet been engaged had observed a once-despised enemy, whose fate had seemed sealed, cut down three successive French attacks. The new division's morale was, inevitably, brittle.[179]

The English, however, were not in much better shape. All of the prince's men, except for a small mounted reserve which had been kept out of the fighting, were exhausted after three consecutive contests. Hardly a one of the men-at-arms remained unwounded, and the archers were critically low on arrows.[180] But, since a typical medieval army divided only into three battles, many of them had assumed that the third French attack was the last, and that they had already won the battle. Thus, large numbers of troops (particularly from Warwick's division)[181] had broken their formations to pursue the remnants of Orléans' force and take prisoners.[182] Their feeling of triumph, however, made their shock all the deeper when the king's division crested the ridge behind which it had been sheltered, revealing to them that the French were not yet defeated.[183] Many of the Anglo-Gascon soldiers then cursed the fact that the prince had, at the beginning of the campaign, detached so many troops to guard Guienne in his absence.[184] One, standing near the prince, cried out in despair that they were undone. "You lie, you fool," answered King Edward's son, "and speak the worst slander if you say that I could be defeated and yet still alive!"[185]

Although their morale was shaken, the Anglo-Gascon soldiers did not break. Their victories over the last three French attacks provided them with some hope, and the realization that there was no safety to be gained by fleeing through enemy territory stiffened their resolve. As King Jean's huge division ponderously marched towards them, many of the bowmen took advantage of the pause in the action to dart out from their cover, into the open field, where they could pull already-fired arrows from the ground, from corpses, and from "half-dead wretches" too badly wounded to fall back with their comrades.[186] From all over

177 M. Villani, *Cronica*, 538; *Scalacronica*, 174; Froissart, *Oeuvres*, 5:427; cf. *Le Baker*, 150.
178 *Anonimalle*, 38; *Le Baker*, 150.
179 *Le Baker*, 143; *Pluscardensis*, 300; cf. *Nangis*, 240; Froissart, *Oeuvres*, 5:425.
180 *Le Baker*, 150; *Knighton*, 2:89.
181 *Knighton*, 2:89–90; cf. *Scalacronica*, 174–5.
182 *Knighton*, 2:89; *Vie du Prince Noir*, 82; *Anonimalle*, 38; *Chron. des quat. prem. Valois*, 54.
183 *Vie du Prince Noir*, ll. 1249–50; *Le Baker*, 150; *Scalacronica*, 174.
184 *Le Baker*, 143 (at the beginning of the battle, but doubtless here too).
185 *Le Baker*, 150: "Mentiris," iniquit, "pessime vecors, si me vivum posse vinci blasfermeris." This is rather difficult to interpret; on the use of "blasfemeris," cf. ibid. 147. I am not sure if the thought le Baker intends to convey is "As long as I am alive we can still win," or "if I don't win I will at least die in the attempt."
186 Ibid.

the field, troops rallied towards the prince's banner and prepared to meet this new foe.[187] Some others, however, fell back until they were absorbed by the vanguard.[188]

Jean's dismounted men-at-arms were preceded by crossbowmen, who engaged the archers in some long-range missile dueling without much effect. The Englishmen began to fire at the main body of the French as soon as it came into range, but the French kept their heads down, and advanced behind a line of men who had formed their shields into an interlocking wall, so the arrows' effect was limited, especially because the archers did not have enough arrows to maintain the dense hail of fire which had earlier proven so effective.[189]

Fully appreciating the danger of his situation, Prince Edward took two important steps. First, he allowed Captal de Buch, one of the Gascon barons, to take a force of sixty men-at-arms and a hundred archers and work his way around towards the French rear, from where he could make a surprise attack at the critical moment of the battle. (See map 15–2D.) This, however, caused a new wave of dismay among the rest of his army, for the soldiers saw the captal's banner moving to the rear and thought he was abandoning a doomed ship.[190] To keep his men's strained bravery from snapping, the prince gave an order as surprising as it was inspired: "Banners, *advance!*"[191]

Military writers throughout the ages have noted that nothing has such a great impact on the mind of an army as the unexpected. An English attack was certainly that. Doubtless it shook the French morale; it also, however, played to the Valois army's strength. King Jean still had many more men-at-arms than the prince (perhaps more than double the number), and many of these were fresh. Since this time the Anglo-Gascon army, like the French one, was moving forward, it would not have the advantage of stronger order which came from immobility in the face of an attacking enemy. Inspired though they might be by Prince Edward's example and by the realization that flight would likely mean death – they could all see that the French king had raised a red banner, signi-

[187] *Anonimalle*, 38; *Chron. Normande*, 115; cf. also *Knighton*, 2:89–90.

[188] *Scalacronica*, 174. This may however be a confused reference to the "withdrawal" of the captal's men (see below).

[189] *Le Baker*, 151; *Knighton*, 2:89. That is not to say that the longbowmen's arrows made no contribution to this phase of the battle: cf. the *Chron. Normande*, 115; *Chron. Jean II et Charles V*, 72.

[190] *Le Baker*, 151. Cf. Froissart, *Oeuvres*, 5:422–3.

[191] *Vie du Prince Noir*, 82, 83; *Le Baker*, 151; *Anonimalle*, 38; M. Villani, *Cronica*, 538–9; cf. *Nangis*, 240; *Fordun*, 376; cf. *Chron. des quat. prem. Valois*, 58; Froissart, *Oeuvres*, 5:440–1. Froissart has Chandos advise the prince to strike directly for King Jean, the enemy "center of gravity" ["celle part gist tous li fors de le besongne"].

Modern historians have generally followed Froissart in describing this attack as a cavalry charge, but no other source describes the prince's men as mounting up, and such a course of action seems improbable. Froissart, *Oeuvres*, 5:425–7, 440–1; Hewitt, *Black Prince's Expedition*, 121, 124; Barber, *Edward*, 144; Burne, *Crecy War*, 305–6; Delachenal, *Histoire de Charles V*, 1:239.

fying that no prisoners were to be taken[192] – it seems unlikely that the Plantagenet forces could have prevailed in a long, head-on contest of force against force.

The fight, after the two armies struck each other, was fierce. The English archers, who quickly found themselves without any arrows, cast away their bows and instead either threw rocks or, picking up lances, swords and shields, took their chances in hand-to-hand combat with the better-armed French.[193] The prince's forward movement was quickly checked by King Jean's men, who began to push the English back.[194] The French were beginning to break into the English formation when, just in the nick of time, the Earl of Warwick, having been warned of the prince's fight by some of the men who had fled from King Jean's fresh division, brought his men back to the field. These troops formed up on the French flank with a loud cheer which greatly encouraged the Englishmen and dismayed the French. They renewed the fight with vigor.[195] Not long thereafter, the captal appeared in the French rear, at the crest of the hill the French had descended, cheering loudly, with the banner of St. George flying.[196] His archers, firing into the less-protected backsides of the Valois troops, were extremely effective.[197]

It can be presumed with near certainty that when Jean formed up his division for this final attack he put his freshest men in front. The men whom the captal struck, then, were the ones who had already been defeated under the constable, the dauphin, or as part of Orléans' force. This new test was more than they could face. The king's division began to dissolve from the rear.[198] Since the captal and the prince were too busy fighting to pursue, the first to depart the field were able to reach their horses and escape without much risk.[199] The spirit of defeat, of retreat, of panic spread, while the Plantagenet soldiers, with renewed confidence, pressed their adversaries with redoubled energy. King Jean cried out for his men to stay, but few heeded him.[200] Soon it was all over. When the banner of the fleurs-de-lis fell, those who were still able to do so fled, pursued now by the Plantagenets, all the way to the gates of Poitiers.[201] The king was a prisoner, as

---

192 *Knighton*, 2:89; cf. Keen, *Laws of War*, 104. Chandos Herald also has the French king repeatedly insist that the English should all be put to death regardless of rank; e.g. ll. 972–9.

193 *Le Baker*, 151; *Knighton*, 2:89; *Chronicon Anglie monacho Sancti Albani*, 36–7.

194 *Scalacronica*, 174; cf. Froissart, *Oeuvres*, 5:428, 446.

195 *Knighton*, 2:90; *Scalacronica*, 174

196 *Le Baker*, 152. Cf. Froissart, *Oeuvres*, 5:425. Note that these two events – Warwick's return and the captal's surprise attack – may actually have been just one, considering that the captal and many of the Gascons were part of Warwick's division. Ibid., 5:421. However, the sources noted above do suggest that there were two separate events.

197 *Le Baker*, 152. Cf. Froissart, *Oeuvres*, 5:425.

198 Cf. *Le Bel*, 2:234–5.

199 M. Villani, *Cronica*, 539.

200 *Vie du Prince Noir*, ll. 1344–7. On those who fought to the last around the king, see *Chron. des quat. prem. Valois*, 55.

201 *Le Baker*, 153; *Anonimalle*, 38; *Vie du Prince Noir*, 85–6; Froissart, *Oeuvres*, 5:452; *Le*

was his young son Philip who, too small to fight himself, had stood by his father, calling out "watch out there, Father! To the right!" or "To the left!" wherever he saw an attacker.[202]

Other prisoners included the armored Archbishop of Sens, seventeen counts or viscounts, twenty-two bannerets (including Marshal d'Audrehem and the seneschals of Saintonge, Tours, and Poitou), and over 1,900 other men-at-arms. Those killed included the Duke of Bourbon, the constable, Marshal Clermont, the Bishop of Châlons, Sir Geoffrey de Charny (Jean's own banner-bearer) and nearly 2,500 other noble men-at-arms, aside from an uncounted number of lesser men.[203] These losses, as the *Chronique des quatre premiers Valois* notes, were "a great harm, a great pity, and damage irreparable" for France.[204] The war was not yet over, but it was already won.[205]

Bel, 2:235–6; *Chron. des quat. prem. Valois*, 56–7. The battle was over by "basse nonne" according to Froissart, *Oeuvres*, 5:434.

[202] M. Villani, *Cronica*, 539. Cf. *Pluscardensis*, 299–300, *Chron. Pays-Bas*, 187.

[203] *PW*, 390–2. The other English sources vary, but most are in this area. See *Eulogium*, 225 (and BL MS Sloane 560, fos 58–58v); *Scalacronica*, 175; *BB*, 387.

French chronicles typically report lower numbers, e.g. the 800 killed and 1,700 captured given by the *Chron. Jean II et Charles V*, 72–3. I prefer the English sources, both because they come first hand, and because the English, who held the field, were in the better position to get an accurate count.

Barber displays unwarranted cynicism when he says that the prince's claim of 2,446 men-at-arms killed "means nothing more than 'a great number'." There is no reason to suppose that the English failed to assess their victory by having the slain counted, as they did for example at Crécy (see above), especially since Knighton specifically says they did so. *Chronicon*, 2:92. Cf. Hewitt, *Black Prince's Expedition*, 137.

[204] *Chron. des quat. prem. Valois*, 56. Cf. *Le Bel*, 2:248; Froissart, *Oeuvres*, 6:272.

[205] As Delachenal says, "the treaty of Brétigny is the direct consequence of the capture of Jean II." *Histoire de Charles V*, 1:244. For a more contemporary opinion, see the petition of Philip of Navarre printed in *KdL*, 400, which holds that it is "entirely clear" that the capture of Jean II and others at Poitiers equates to Edward's "final victory over his adversary who calls himself King of France." It is also worth noting that the First Treaty of London, settled in May of 1358, provided for the transfer of various lands "as entirely as he [Jean II] held them on the day of the battle of Poitiers." In Delachenal, *Histoire de Charles V*, 2:403.

CHAPTER SIXTEEN

"COURTING COMBAT TO MAINTAIN THE RIGHT OF THEIR LORD, BUT NOT FINDING ANY TAKERS": THE REIMS CAMPAIGN AND PEACE, 1359–1360

> *If we wish to compel the enemy to fulfill our will, we must impose on him a situation more disadvantageous than the sacrifice we demand of him.* Clausewitz, *Vom Kriege*, I.i.4[1]

SIR CHARLES OMAN once wrote that "the political results of Poictiers [sic] were, owing to the king's captivity, very considerable, but the immediate strategical results were *nil*."[2] Such a division between political and strategic results is highly artificial: the battle was a strategic success to precisely the extent that it brought Edward III closer to achieving his war aims, which it did both dramatically and immediately. At Avignon in 1354, the French had demonstrated determination to fight on rather than concede sovereignty over the territories demanded by Edward III; in the aftermath of Poitiers, they showed themselves eager to treat for a final peace between France and England, even if it meant returning to the concessions contemplated in the draft Treaty of Guînes. By the middle of December 1356, arrangements to reopen peace negotiations had already been made. The deadlock which had always previously prevented finalization of a peace agreement had been broken by the capture of King Jean and the virtual disarmament of France at Poitiers.[3] There were still difficult details to resolve (mainly the size of the king's ransom and the extent of the territorial transfers) but the basic principle on which a peace could be built, as initially negotiated in 1354 – that Edward would surrender his rights to the crown of France in exchange for a sovereign, independent Aquitaine and a free hand in Scotland – was quickly re-established, and on that basis the outline of a peace treaty was agreed upon as early as March of 1357.[4] Even before then, the two

---

1 *Vom Kriege*, 92.
2 *History of the Art of War in the Middle Ages*, 2:175.
3 Deadlock broken: before the end of 1356, Jean was urging his subjects to accept "whatever good and honorable peace can be made" [Guesnon, "Documents inédits," 244.] Disarmament: *Le Bel*, 2:248: "il avoit poy de gens ou royaume avecq quielz on se poeut appuyer, car tous estoient ou mors ou pris"; cf. also *Anonimalle*, 43. Note Clausewitz, *Vom Kriege*, I.i.4, p. 92 (worst situation).
4 Edward III's instructions to Prince Edward concerning the negotiations are published in

sides arranged a truce until Easter of 1359 in order to allow the negotiations to proceed unhindered.[5]

And yet, as most readers of this book will be aware, the treaty of final peace was not ratified by both sides for another three years, years which must be accounted the most miserable ever endured by France. Before the conclusion of the Treaty of Brétigny, innumerable French towns and villages were sacked and burned; thousands of individuals were raped, tortured, mutilated, or killed, from Picardy to the Agenais and from Brittany to the Auvergne; the French agricultural and mercantile economy was cast into ruin; the kingdom was riven by multi-faceted civil war and by the most famous peasant uprising of the middle ages, the *Jacquerie* – and all this *before* Edward III launched his massive invasion of 1359–60, which only worsened the situation of a realm already near collapse.[6] Granted that the French were beaten in 1356, and that they knew they were beaten, why did it take so much time and so much human suffering before Edward III gained the "honorable peace" he had so long pursued?

There are two basic answers: first, that the very divisions which made the Valois kingdom so weak that it had to accept peace on Plantagenet terms also made King Jean too weak to compel his subjects to accept and effect the peace terms he twice negotiated; second, that Edward III insisted on a favorable resolution of certain conflicts between his court and the papacy before he would finalize the peace. When Edward discovered that negotiation with his captive alone, no matter how successful, could not get him what he wanted (since, on the one hand, a peace treaty not supported by the dauphin and the Estates of France could not be implemented, and, on the other, the Pope showed little willingness to give ground on the collateral issues), he once more turned to the use of his military might to force his adversaries to meet his demands. For a time, these demands grew so as to be commensurate with the additional effort he was being forced to make and with the new opportunities which France's near-collapse seemed to offer, but in the end the two sides returned, essentially, to the terms of the agreements of 1353–54 and 1357–58. The Plantagenet did not, thus, get as much as he might have wanted, but he did get more than anyone in 1337 could reasonably have expected him to secure. He had begun the war against the House of Valois in order to end French interference in Scotland and Gascony, and to recover the lands occupied by Charles of Valois in 1324; the Treaty of Brétigny gave him all this, with Poitou, the Angoumois, Bigorre, Guare, Rouergue, Quercy, Guînes, the Calais Pale, and the promise of 3,000,000 écus of French gold thrown in for good measure.

Before the start of Edward's last great invasion of France in 1359, at least

---

Bock, "Documents," 98–9; see also *Chron. Jean II et Charles V,* 107; *RFH,* 3:1:140; *Knighton,* 2:99, and Rogers, "Anglo-French Negotiations."

5   *RFH,* 3:1:133–6.

6   As Charles of Navarre declared to Charles of Normandy in August 1359: "il veoit bien, si comme il disoit, que le royaume estoit sur le point de estre destruit." *Chron. Jean II et Charles V,* 242–3.

four different peace agreements were reached.[7] The precise terms of the settlement which was presented to the dauphin and his council in January of 1358 and to the English parliament the following month are now unknown, but they probably differed little from those of the Treaty of Guînes, except for the addition of a large cash ransom for King Jean.[8] Such terms would be surprisingly generous – the French doubtless expected Edward to try to extract greater concessions than the ones negotiated in 1354, now that he had ravaged much of southern France, won a second great battle, gained control of western Normandy and significant portions of the Agenais, Périgord, and Poitou, and captured the French king – which would explain why the dauphin and his council pronounced themselves very pleased with the proposals.[9]

Edward's parliament, which met from 5 to 26 February 1358, was also well inclined to the conclusion of peace, but insisted that England take advantage of Jean's captivity to pressure the Pope, who was perceived as being virtually a French ally – "The Pope has become French, and Jesus has become English: now we'll see who does more," read a graffito popular after the battle of Poitiers[10] – into making concessions in two areas analogous to English war aims towards France. First, they sought a renunciation of the papal claim to suzerainty

---

7 These were the agreement of 18 March 1357; the terms presented to the dauphin in January 1358 (which despite the interval were probably almost the same; cf. *M. Villani (Porta)*, 2:121); the "First Treaty of London" of May 1358, and the "Second Treaty of London," of March 1359. See below.

8 The fact that several months of negotiations took place between this agreement and the drafting of the First Treaty of London suggests that the terms were significantly different, but there is no reason to presume that the terms of that document were particularly more favorable to either side than the initial arrangement. It seems unlikely that the latter was any harsher than the First Treaty of London, given the positive reception it was given in Paris (*Chron. Jean II et Charles V*, 144). On the other hand, it also seems unlikely that it was much easier, for the agreement of May 1358 was already quite generous to the French: certainly its territorial provisions were little more exacting than the Treaty of Guînes, which the French had almost accepted even before the capture of the king. My guess is that the terms of the Treaty of Guînes were accepted as a starting point for the negotiations, and that over time there was a certain give-and-take, with the demand for Maine, Anjou and Touraine abandoned in exchange for a generous definition of Aquitaine (as in the May 1358 agreement).

9 Ibid. (reception). Edward exercised direct control over most of the Cotentin, having purchased the inheritance of Godfrey d'Harcourt's lands there including the viscounty of St.-Saveur-le-Vicomte [*RFR* III:1:346], and much of the rest of Normandy was under the control of Philip of Navarre, who had done homage to Edward as King of France and Duke of Normandy (*RFH*, 3:1:128) and been appointed Edward's lieutenant in the duchy (*RFH*, 3:1:161). For the Agenais and Périgord, see Chapter 15, above, and also *RFR* III:1:391, 397, 399, 403, 405. The Plantagenet presence in Poitou is indicated by the appointment of Olivier de Clisson as one of Edward's lieutenants "in Ducatu de Peytou" in July 1359. PRO C67/37 m. 10.

10 *Knighton*, 2:94: "quia papa semper favebat Francis, et eos fovebat in quantum potuit contra Anglos, et propter miraculum quod deus tribuerat victoriam tam paucis viris contra tantam multitudinem Francoram, scriptum erat in pluribus locis in Vienna et in multis aliis locis, Ore est le Pape devenu Franceys e Jesu devenu Engleys. Ore serra veou qe fra plus, ly Pape ou Jesus."

over and tribute from England which dated back to the days of Innocent III and John Lackland. Second, they insisted on an end to the court of Rome's interference in the administration of royal justice against "criminal churchmen" in England, particularly regarding papal protection of Thomas de Lisle, the Bishop of Ely.[11]

Immediately on the close of the parliament, an embassy was dispatched to Avignon to pursue these concessions, but the two cardinals who had mediated the Anglo-French negotiations despaired of a favorable result,[12] apparently aware that Innocent VI had no intention of backing down in his conflicts with Edward, despite his strong desire to see peace made and Jean II released.[13] Meanwhile, Anglo-French negotiations on the points left unresolved in the initial agreement continued to make good progress. By early May, the two royal councils had resolved nearly all the differences, to the point where the two kings, after some personal negotiations, embraced, kissed, exchanged rings, dined together amicably, and announced to all that an end to the war was at hand.[14] The terms of this new concord, the "First Treaty of London," survive in draft form.[15] The territorial elements of the treaty were closely comparable to those agreed at Guînes, except that Maine, Anjou, and Touraine were to be retained by the Valois monarchy, while Edward was to receive the Angoumois and Quercy (which in 1354 he had been prepared to consider releasing)[16] as part of the Duchy of Aquitaine, along with Saintonge, Poitou, the Limousin,

---

[11] *Scalacronica*, 177: "quelis comunes desagreerent en playn parlement a Loundres ou tail du dit tretice, si ensy ne fust qe autre addicioun ne fust aiouste. Ceo fust qe le pape releissast pur ly et sez successours tout le contracte qe le roy Johan auoit fait par endenture et par attournement au patronage le apostoil en le temps Innocent; et qe le seint pier cessast de chos qen le hour sentremist peniblement. Quoy com lez genz de lay Engles disoint estoit grantement countre la coroun, qar meisme le hour lez justices le roy estoint personelement escomengez pur processe de vn iugement qils auoint fait en le bank le roy encountre Thomas de Lile, euesque de Ely"; Letter of Jean II, 18 May, in Delachenal, *Histoire de Charles V,* 2:64n: "leur a semblé que à la reparation des ditz griefs le Pape et les cardinaux enclineroient plus legerement pour faveur de nostre delivrance"; Second Treaty of London in *Kdl*, 429 (below, note 23). Cf. *Reading*, 129–30; Aberth, *Criminal Churchmen*, passim (the Ely affair), 171 (the treaty). The dispute over the fate of Ely had resulted in the excommunication of some of Edward's councilors, and even the exhumation of some of them who had died in the interim. Aberth's statement that parliament "rejected the treaty because it distrusted a mediator who had just excommunicated the King's justices" underestimates the parliament's appreciation for the significance of Edward's jurisdictional conflict with the Pope: it was the substance of the dispute with the court of Rome, not distrust of a mediator, which posed a problem for the ratification treaty.

[12] *Scalacronica*, 177.

[13] Desire: *RFH*, 3:1:140, 3:1:160; *Knighton*, 2:103.

[14] This was on 8 May. Letter of Jean II in Delachenal, *Histoire de Charles V,* 2:66n; *M. Villani (Porta)*, 2:200; *Chron. Anon. Cant.*, 208. See also *Le Bel*, 2:254.

[15] Published in Delachenal, *Histoire de Charles V,* 2:402–11.

[16] Secret instructions to Lancaster in Bock, "Documents," 95, article 4. Lancaster was authorized to give up the Angoumois and Quercy ["Caourzin"] *provided* that these territories were not found to be part of the Duchy of Aquitaine as it had been held by any previous King of England.

Périgord, Bigorre, Gaure, the Agenais, the Calais Pale, and the counties of Guînes and Ponthieu. These lands would be held by Edward in full sovereignty; in exchange, he would give up his claim to the crown of France and stop making war on the Valois.[17] There were two other exchanges comprised in the treaty: King Jean would pay 4,000,000 écus (equal to £666,667, a phenomenal sum, the equivalent of the "normal" [non-Parliamentary] revenues of the English crown for some twenty years[18]) for his ransom, and would abandon his alliance with Scotland in return for Edward's equivalent action towards Flanders.[19] It should also be noted that, contrary to earlier historians' interpretations, the treaty did provide for the eventual restoration of Valois sovereignty in Brittany.[20]

The Plantagenet was offering unexpectedly mild terms to his defeated adversary, and he wanted to make sure that his generosity was not mistaken for weakness. In a separate document, he made it clear that if the French did not punctually and perfectly fulfill their obligations under every single point of the agreement, the whole deal would be off, the entire treaty null and void, and both sides as free as they had been before its conclusion.[21] Furthermore, there were

---

[17] There is no clause explicitly stating that Edward would renounce his claim to the French crown comparable to the one in paragraph 11 of the Treaty of Brétigny, but it is clearly implicit in the phrase "le dit adversaire pour lui et pour toutes *ses heirs rois de Ffrance*," and in the fact that the document, entitled "La trattié et la parlaunce de la *paix*" (pp. 405, 402, emphasis added), envisioned "paix finales et perpetuels alliances et amistiez entre les roys et les roialmes de Ffrance et d'Engleterre" (p. 407). (It is not quite right, however, to state that the title King of France is "freely bestowed" on Jean II in the text of the treaty; in fact he is always called "l'adversaire de Ffrance" or some version thereof. Cf. Palmer, "Negotiations for Peace," 61.) Le Patourel, "Treaty of Brétigny," makes an unconvincing argument to the contrary, which has however been widely accepted; for a full discussion, see Rogers, "Anglo-French Negotiations."

[18] Harriss, *King, Parliament and Public Finance*, 523–6; Kaeuper, *War, Justice and Public Order*, 62; Fowler, "Truces," 204–5. The figure of twenty years is very rough; the revenues varied substantially from year to year, and furthermore different totals for "normal" revenues are reached depending on exactly which sources are comprised within that term. Looked at another way, £666,667 was probably greater than the sum total of all the coinage in circulation in England at that time. Waugh, *England in the Reign of Edward III*, 80.

[19] The clause relating to Scotland (on p. 407 of Delachenal's transcription) has often been omitted in summaries of the contents of this treaty, but considering its importance as the fulfillment of one of Edward's main war aims, it deserves emphasis. That Edward III and Jean II would have agreed with that statement is indicated by the fact that the French insisted on receiving Edward's renunciation of his rights to the French crown before they would end the Scottish alliance (or formally transfer sovereignty over the ceded lands in France); everything else they were willing to do in advance. PRO E30/164.

[20] See the mistaken view of John Le Patourel, "Edward III and the Kingdom of France," 178; "Treaty of Brétigny," 24, 31; cf. Fowler, *King's Lieutenant*, 210. Discussed in Rogers, "Anglo-French Negotiations." See the text of the treaty in Delachenal, *Histoire de Charles V*, 2:410–1.

[21] Document transcribed in Delachenal, *Histoire de Charles V*, 2:67n. This was doubtless also a reflection of Edward's distrust of the French, arising from his perception that they had often failed to live up to the terms of their agreements and treaties, including the treaty of 1329 and the draft treaty of 1354, among others. Cf. his letter to the Pope in 1355: *RFH*, 3:1:122.

some points left to be negotiated in the future, such as the precise schedule for the ransom payments, the details of the resolution of the Breton succession dispute and the full list of hostages to be handed over as security; the final completion of the peace remained contingent on French fulfillment of all these anticipated agreements, and on the favorable resolution of the conflicts between Edward and the Pope as well.[22] This last factor should not be underestimated, for Edward openly declared that he was inflexibly resolved that no peace would be finalized until his business with the court of Rome was "brought to a perfect and successful conclusion."[23]

Had this treaty been implemented, France might have been spared many of the miseries of the following two years. The war would have been over, and this study would now have reached its natural end. Unfortunately for France, however, the dauphin was unable to raise the first payment of the ransom (600,000 écus, or £100,000) by the stipulated date of 1 November,[24] and Pope Innocent declined to resolve the affair of the Bishop of Ely in the Plantagenet's favor. Had Edward wished to do so, he might simply have allowed the French more time to collect the necessary money (as he did when King David of Scotland fell behind in his ransom payments, and indeed as he later did for Jean II himself[25]) and continued to put diplomatic pressure on the court of Rome. The events of the past summer in France, however, had convinced him that he had an opportunity to press for greater concessions from the French.[26] He had always argued that he was of right entitled to the crown of France, or at least to the restoration of the full Angevin Empire (including Normandy, Maine, Anjou, and Touraine as well as Greater Aquitaine); his willingness to accept less had represented a concession on his part for the sake of peace, nothing more. If he could become King of France in fact as well as in name, then he could restore peace as well as recovering his full rights of inheritance without compromise. In the fall of 1358 when the French failed to meet the first installment of the ransom, much more so than in the previous spring, this seemed like a realistic possibility. The French default and the Pope's intractability gave Edward the chance to pursue this possibility without dishonoring his sworn word.

---

[22] Terms remaining to be negotiated: First Treaty of London, in Delachenal, *Histoire de Charles V,* 2:410–11. Pope: implied by Jean II's letter, quoted ibid., 66 n.1. Note also *RFH*, 3:1:171–2.

[23] As shown by the following clause of the Second Treaty of London (March 1359): "Item, pour les explois d'aucunes besoingnes touchans le roy et le royaume d'Engleterre en la court de Romme, messagiers seront envoiés à la dicte court d'une part et d'autre, qui feront toute bonne et loiale diligence au miex qu'il pourront à l'exploit de mesmes les besoingnes; *et toutes fois a esté dit et ouvertement de par le roy d'Engleterre protesté et oultrement déclairée son entention que le pais ne se pourra jamais faire entre les roys, se non que mesmes ces besoingnes soient parfaitement exploitées.*" Printed in *KdL*, 428, emphasis added.

[24] Delachenal, *Histoire de Charles V,* 2:72; cf. *Le Bel,* 2:272; Froissart, *Oeuvres,* 6:104 ("car les rentes et les revenues dou dit duc . . . estoient toutes perdues"); *Chron. des quat. prem. Valois,* 62, on the poor state of the royal revenues.

[25] *RFR,* III:1:533; *RFH* 3:2:56.

[26] Cf. *M. Villani (Porta),* 2:363–4.

It takes only a glance at the situation in France to understand both why the dauphin was unable to raise the needed 600,000 écus and why Edward III believed the time might be right for him to seize Reims and Paris. In the words of contemporaries, the noble realm of France was then "overwhelmed, and trampled under foot,"[27] "on the verge of destruction,"[28] "in peril of being lost"[29] and "tormented and war-ravaged" from one end to the other.[30] Brittany, Picardy, Normandy and the Gascon frontiers had been laid waste by year after year of garrison warfare. The Black Prince's *chevauchées* of 1355 and 1356 had devastated southern Languedoc and much of the region under the curve of the Loire. The Ile-de-France, having suffered through the Jacquerie and the even more destructive suppression of the uprising in May–June 1358, as well as the depredations of Anglo-Navarrese *routiers* and the almost equally damaging French garrisons,[31] was in terrible shape. The chronicler Jean de Venette's depiction of the state of his native Beauvaisis in 1359 gives some idea of the realm's troubles:

The English destroyed, burned, and plundered many little towns and villages in this part of the diocese of Beauvais, capturing or even killing the inhabitants. The loss by fire of the village where I was born, Venette near Compiègne, is to be lamented, together with that of many others near by. The vines in this region, which supply that most pleasant and desirable liquor which maketh glad the heart of man, were not pruned or kept from rotting by the labors of men's hands. The fields were not sown or ploughed. There were no cattle or fowl in the fields. No cock crowed in the depths of the night to tell the hours. No hen called to her chicks. It was of no use for the kite to lie in wait for the chickens in March of this year nor for the children to hunt for eggs in secret hiding places. No lambs or calves bleated after their mothers in this region. The wolf might seek its prey elsewhere and here fill his capacious gullet with green grass instead of rams. At this time rabbits and hares played freely about in the deserted fields with no fear of hunting dogs, for no one dared to go coursing through the pleasant woods and fields. Larks soared safely through the air and lifted their unending songs with no thought of whistling attacks of eyas or falcons. No wayfarers went along the roads, carrying their best cheese and dairy produce to market. Throughout the parishes and villages, alas! went forth no mendicants to hear confessions and to preach in Lent but rather robbers and thieves to carry off openly whatever they could find. Houses and churches no longer presented a smiling appearance with

---

27 *Le Bel*, 2:268 ("Ainsy le noble royaume de France, le plus noble des nobles, qui soloit estre le reffuge de seureté et de paix, estoit adoncques, sans justice, foulé et confondu").

28 *Chron. Jean II et Charles V*, 242–3.

29 *Chron. des quat. prem. Valois*, 99–100.

30 Froissart, *Oeuvres*, 6:115 ("Ensi estoit ensonnyés et guerryés de tous lés li royaumes de France en toutes ses parties"). Cf. also the document of 1359 reproduced in A. Germain, "Projet de descente en Engleterre . . ." *Publications de la société archéologique de Montpellier*, 26 (1858), 425–7, especially clauses 2–4, 9–15.

31 French garrisons: Denifle, *Désolation des églises*, 2:244, cf. 252; note also *Chron. Normande*, 127–8; *Venette*, 105, 113.

newly repaired roofs but rather the lamentable spectacle of scattered, smoking ruins to which they had been reduced by devouring flames. The eye of man was no longer rejoiced by the accustomed sight of green pastures and fields charmingly colored by the growing grain, but rather saddened by the looks of the nettles and thistles springing up on every side. The pleasant sound of bells was heard indeed, not as a summons to divine worship, but as a warning of hostile incursions, in order that men might seek out hiding places while the enemy were yet on the way. What more can I say? Every misery increased on every hand, especially among the rural population, the peasants, for their lords bore hard upon them, extorting from them all their substance and poor means of livelihood. . . .Yet, their lords did not, in return, repel their enemies or attempt to attack them, except occasionally.[32]

This picture, extreme as it may appear, is broadly supported by the testimony of other contemporary chroniclers, letters, and documentary evidence. The *Grandes chroniques* state that the dauphin's men, in suppressing the Jacquerie, "laid waste the entire area between the Seine and the Marne."[33] "It is very doubtful," wrote the provost of merchants of Paris to sum up the same situation, "whether this country, which used to be very fertile for wheat and wine, won't be entirely wasted and dead this year, or that there will be anyone to take care of the vines and pick the grapes, or anywhere to put the wine, since the casks in the villages are all burned, as are the villages themselves."[34] A pardon granted some years later which notes the burning of seventeen villages near Paris by the "valets" of the dauphin's army at this time simply adds another point of confirmation.[35] Froissart comments repeatedly that broad areas of France had been left uncultivated because the war made it too dangerous for the laborers to go into the fields, and this is confirmed by a letter of the regent himself.[36]

Meanwhile the Anglo-Navarrese garrisons and "Free Companies" which held Poissy, St. Cloud, Juilly, Meaux, la Ferté-sous-Jouarre, Mauconseil, Clermont, Corbeil, Chevreuse, Chaumont, Melun, Creil, and literally hundreds of other towns and fortresses,[37] robbed merchants, sacked and plundered towns and villages, raped women, and held for ransom individuals and cities alike, torturing the former and burning the latter if they could not or would not pay.[38]

---

32 *Venette*, 93–4 (*Nangis*, 293–4, leaves out about half of this).
33 *Chron. Jean II et Charles V,* 188; cf. ibid., 187 and *Le Bel*, 2:259.
34 See the letters printed in Froissart, *Oeuvres*, 6:468, 469. Cf. also *Le Bel*, 2:264.
35 *Chron. Jean II et Charles V,* 187n.
36 Froissart, *Oeuvres*, 6:224: "il faisoit si chier temps parmi le royaulme de France et si grant famine y couroit, pour le cause de ce que on n'avoit III ans en devant riens ahané [alt: labouré] sus le plat pays"; ibid., 6:235: "li pays, II ans ou III en devant, avoit estet toutdis si guerryés que nuls n'avoit labouret les terres"; also 6:90, 118, 271–2. Letter of the dauphin cited in Denifle, *Désolation des églises*, 2:244; cf. 252. See *Chron. Normande*, 145–6, for a general assessment of the state of France.
37 Luce, *Histoire de Bertrand du Guesclin*, 1:459–509; *Chron. des quat. prem. Valois*, 82, 84, 87–8, 101, 104; *Le Bel*, 2:245–85; *Chron. Jean II et Charles V,* 142–234; Froissart, *Oeuvres*, 6:35–191; *Venette*, 72–86.
38 For broad treatments see Rogers, "*Bellum Hostile* and 'Civilians',", and Michael Jones,

Among the many places sacked by the *routiers* between May and November of 1358 were Nemours, Meaux, Vitry, Arpajon, Châteauneuf-sur-Loire, Châtillon-sur-Loing, and the suburbs of Amiens; Evreux, a Navarrese city, was burned by royal troops.[39] The garrison of Beauvoir in the Bourbonnais dug a large pit which they kept filled with a great fire and called "Hell"; when the local people they captured were unable to pay the sums demanded of them, the soldiers cried "to Hell with them!" and threw them into the burning hole.[40] Despite the terrible depredations inflicted by these men and others like them, they met almost no resistance by local or royal forces. Bands as small as a few hundred men, and even smaller, coursed the countryside even of the Ile-de-France without meeting any opposition.[41]

The vision of a kingdom in smoldering ruins which inspired the prose of Jean de Venette was essentially a bottom-up viewpoint, the common man's perspective; looking at the overall political situation from the top down, however, did not make the situation appear more favorable for the Valois monarchy. As early as October of 1356 the Estates-General and especially the citizens of Paris had risen up in virtual rebellion against the dauphin's government, one which quickly became intertwined with the Navarrese war against the Valois. There were scenes reminiscent of the French Revolution: the dauphin's counselors murdered in his bed-chamber by a bourgeois mob; the terrified prince himself forced to wear one of the parti-colored blue-and-red hats which symbolized loyalty to the cause of the Estates-General and the Parisian bourgeoisie above his bloodstained robe; calls for a parliamentary committee to assume the government of the realm.[42] By June of 1358, the leaders of the Parisian uprising went so far as to try to have Charles the Bad proclaimed "universal captain throughout the realm" in opposition to the "bad government" of the regent.[43] During this period, according to the *Grandes chroniques*, most of the people of Languedoïl supported either the Parisians or the Jacques:[44] except for the

---

"War and Fourteenth-Century France," *Arms, Armies and Fortifications in the Hundred Years War*, eds Curry and Hughes (Woodbridge: The Boydell Press, 1994).

[39] *Chron. Jean II et Charles V,* 175–6, 215–17. Places destroyed or damaged by the *Jacques* in this period include Ermenonville, Thiers, and Beaumont-sur-Oise. Ibid., 178.

[40] Jean Cabaret, *La Chronique du Bon Duc Loys de Bourbon*, ed. A. M. Chazaud (Paris: SHF, 1876), 19.

[41] *Le Bel*, 2:270, 275, 250; Froissart, *Oeuvres*, 6:35, 94, 99; *Venette*, 66.

[42] *Le Bel*, 2:254, *Chron. Jean II et Charles V,* 149–50; *Scalacronica*, 178, 180; *Chron. des quat. prem. Valois*, 60, 62, 69; *Chronographia*, 2:264–5; *Chron. Normande*, 118, 123–4. Interestingly, the last two chronicles (which are closely related) suggest that the murder of the marshals of Normandy and Champagne by Etienne Marcel's men, and the humbling of the dauphin, was prompted by the latter's too-favorable response to the proposed treaty with England. *Chronographia*, 2:264; *Chron. Normande*, 123.

[43] *Chron. Jean II et Charles V,* 185–6. See also Delachenal for all this.

[44] *Chron. Jean II et Charles V,* 181: "avoit lors pou de villes, citez ou autres en la Langue d'oyl, qui ne fussent meues contre les gentilz hommes, tant en faveur de ceulz de Paris qui trop les haioient, comme pour le mouvement du peuple." Cf. also *Le Bel*, 2:253, 270.

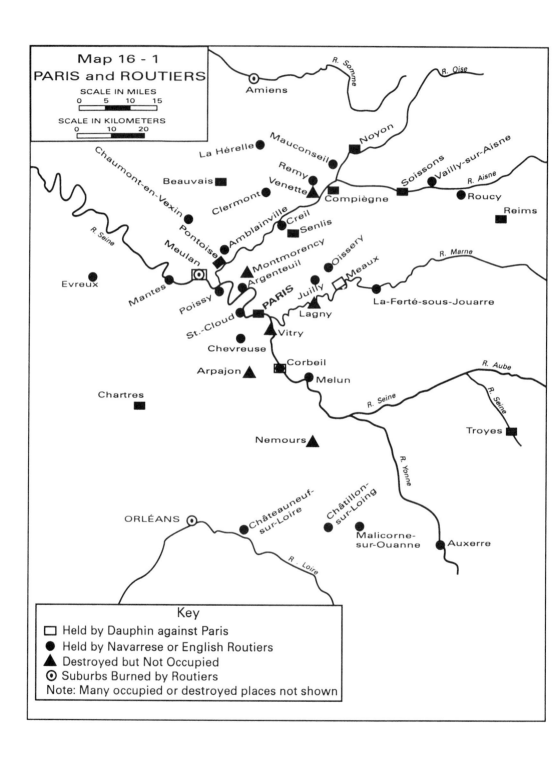

Map 16 - 1
PARIS and ROUTIERS

SCALE IN MILES
0   5   10   15

SCALE IN KILOMETERS
0   10   20

Key
☐ Held by Dauphin against Paris
● Held by Navarrese or English Routiers
▲ Destroyed but Not Occupied
◉ Suburbs Burned by Routiers
Note: Many occupied or destroyed places not shown

nobility (which itself was not much loved), the Valois monarchy seemed to have alienated much of its natural support.

By early August, after making war on the bourgeois for over a month, the dauphin had regained control over Paris (the first time he had genuinely controlled the city since October of 1356), the Jacquerie having already been suppressed in June by the massacre of a reported twenty thousand peasants, the innocent along with the guilty,[45] but the civil war between Duke Charles and Charles of Navarre continued in full flame.[46] Another small war broke out between the townsmen and the garrison of Rouen, leading to much devastation in the area.[47] In September, Arpajon and the suburbs of Amiens were burnt; the next month Anglo-Navarrese routiers including Robert Knolles (fighting under Navarrese auspices, because of the truce between England and France) captured Châteauneuf-sur-Loire, Châtillon-sur-Loing, and Malicorne-sur-Ouanne in the Orléannais, Oissery in Multien, and Amblainville just three leagues outside of Paris. The capital city, like Beauvais and Rouen, was practically besieged by the many garrisons surrounding it.[48] [Map 16–1]

With the realm in such turmoil, it is easy to understand why the regent – compelled to spend what resources he could gather on the maintenance of an army if he were to have any hope of restoring effective Valois control over Languedoïl – found it difficult (and probably impossible) to raise the 600,000 écus for the first installment of King Jean's ransom, especially considering that up until August the Parisians were refusing to contribute "a single penny."[49] Yet, although the dauphin did make some progress towards raising the necessary money between then and October, there is no documentary evidence that he offered a partial payment to Edward III or that he sought to arrange a new schedule for the ransom, nor were the hostages stipulated in the treaty handed over to the English.[50] Considering the fate of the agreements of 1329, 1334, and 1353–54, Edward had good reason to be suspicious when it came to French non-fulfillment of agreed peace terms. Although historians have usually viewed the English king as aggressively "seiz[ing] the opportunity afforded by their increased internal difficulties to tear up the treaty and press for an even more

---

45 *Chron. Jean II et Charles V,* 187; *Le Bel,* 2:260, 259: "Si alerent ces gens d'armes de ville en ville . . . si y ardirent et roberrent tout aussi bien sur les ungs comme sur les aultres, car ilz n'avoient point loisir de faire enqueste"; cf. *Chron. des quat. prem. Valois,* 76; Froissart, *Oeuvres,* 6:58 (200 villages burned by Charles the Bad in suppressing the Jacques).
46 *Chron. des quat. prem. Valois,* 87: "Moult fut grieve au pais de France et cruelle la guerre d'entre le roy de Navarre et monseigneur le duc de Normendie. Car moult de gens en furent mis à mort, mainte pucelle corrumpue, mainte preude femme violée, mainte bonne personne destruicte et gastée, mainte eglise, mainte ville et mainte maison arse et bruie, et maint enfant en devindrent orphelins et povres mendians."
47 Ibid., 78.
48 *Chron. Jean II et Charles V,* 215–20; cf. *Chron. des quat. prem. Valois,* 96, 84; *Knighton,* 2:100.
49 *Chron. Jean II et Charles V,* 195; cf. also *Le Bel,* 2:254.
50 See Rogers, "Anglo-French Negotiations."

generous settlement,"[51] it should be remembered that it was in fact the *French* who, whether through inability or unwillingness to implement its terms, allowed the First Treaty of London to fall into abeyance.[52] Indeed, the fact that Edward waited two full months past the due date of 1 November before he began to make any military preparations suggests that he may not have been as eager to see the treaty's demise as has usually been assumed.[53]

As already noted, the French default, combined with the Pope's intransigence, made the First Treaty of London null and void, and reopened all the issues which had been settled by that agreement, including Edward's claim to the French throne. It may be that Edward promptly seized the chance to press for better terms; it may be that he merely accepted the fact that there was no peace treaty in effect, either de facto or de jure, and that he therefore had to prepare to resume prosecuting the war. Either way, he had to settle on a strategy for the forthcoming campaign. Considering the state of the realm, would it be any wonder if Edward III thought that the people of France might welcome a strong soldier-king who could restore order? With English and Navarrese garrisons encircling Paris and raiding the capital city's environs with impunity,[54] why should he not presume that its capture was within his means?[55] Under the circumstances it would have been surprising had he decided upon any other course than a bid to make real the title which he had first formally assumed in 1340, and to which he believed himself legitimately entitled.

Unlike the other major French campaigns of the war to date, this one was to be financed by Edward's own resources rather than a parliamentary grant. The force gathered for the expedition was nevertheless to be the second largest sent to the Continent during the war, after the one which fought at Crécy.[56] It was also to be the best-equipped army Edward had ever assembled; indeed, England arguably never sent out a superior expeditionary force until the Egyptian expedition of 1882.[57] The scale of the resources thus committed by the English royal

---

[51] Palmer, "War Aims," 59; cf. ibid., 61; see also Perroy, *Hundred Years War*, 137; Contamine, *Guerre de Cent ans*, 44–5.

[52] Rogers, "Anglo-French Negotiations."

[53] The first order for bows and arrows to be sent to the Tower was issued 2 January; commissions of array were appointed only on 12 January. *RFR*, 3:1:414–16.

[54] *Chron. Jean II et Charles V*, 215.

[55] Cf. the opinion of the author of the *Chron. des quat. prem. Valois*, 99–100: if the King of Navarre and the dauphin had continued to make war on each other during Edward's invasion, the English king might more easily have captured the forts and bridges held by the Navarrese, and "le royaume de France seroit en peril d'estre perdu."

[56] Ayton, "English Armies," 31. Sometimes said to be the largest, but at about 10,000 men plus an unknown number of unpaid Germans and other foreigners from among those who had gathered at Calais, it was substantially smaller than the army of 1346. It is worth noting here, however, that the Reims army was only slightly larger than Edward III's army in 1355, which was in the field at the same time as the Prince of Wales' large force in Languedoc.

[57] Major General George Wrottesley, who was as well qualified as anyone to assess the matter, made that claim in 1898 about the Crécy army, but I think it has to be said that the army of 1359 was still better provided. *Crecy and Calais from the Public Records*, 9n. *Le Bel*,

fisc helps explain why this could not be simply another *chevauchée* on the model of 1346, 1355, and 1356. The Valois monarchy had already been undermined, weakened, and pressured enough. Now was the time for the *coup de grâce*: the capture of Reims, where French kings had for centuries been anointed and crowned, followed by the re-coronation of Edward III as King of France and the subsequent occupation of Paris.

As preparations for this massive effort continued through the winter of 1358–59, Jean of Valois grew increasingly desperate. Historians have generally accused him of being selfishly concerned only with his own release, yet this is clearly not fair. He had enough contact with his kingdom to realize just how desperate its situation was, and his belief that one of the main causes of his nation's ills was his own absence is not as "puerile" as it has sometimes been portrayed.[58] Whatever Jean's weaknesses, it is difficult to imagine that the Estates-General or the King of Navarre would have dared to have act towards him in the ways that they did towards his young son Charles. He certainly would not have been as passive in dealing with the *routier* garrisons as was the regent.[59] Even before the miseries of 1358, it had seemed in Paris that the realm was "devastated and in danger of being entirely destroyed and lost;" by early 1359 that danger was all the more immediate and grave.[60]

In order to fend off the further devastation of his kingdom and the very real risk that he might lose it entirely to Edward III, King Jean pressed his adversary to reopen the peace talks. For the reasons discussed above, however, the English king had little motive to make a new treaty which might well meet with another French default, but would certainly in the meanwhile allow the French to consolidate the recovery begun in August, continue improving the fortifications of Reims and Paris (both greatly strengthened during the summer of 1358),[61] and in general ready themselves to meet the forthcoming attack. The sack of Lagny-sur-Marne in January of 1359, and the capture of Auxerre by Robert Knolles in early March, can only have served to strengthen Edward's determination and deepen Jean's despair.[62]

It is conceivable that it was the fall of Auxerre, a hundred miles *southeast* of Paris, which convinced the Valois that further resistance was hopeless, although there would only barely have been time for word of the disaster to reach him before, on 18 March, he persuaded King Edward to extend the truce until 24

2:290, calls it "le plus grand appareil que on avoit jamais veu en celluy pays n'en aultre." Cf. ibid., 299, 294; *Chron. des quat. prem. Valois*, 97–8; *Knighton*, 2:105.

58 Cf. Perroy, *Hundred Years War*, 136; Delachenal, *Histoire de Charles V*, 2:82 ("une complète inconscience ou d'un monstrueux égoïsme").

59 In the case of Charles the Bad, this is suggested by his efforts to prevent Jean's ransom. See the dauphin's letter in Froissart, *Oeuvres*, 6:477. More generally, cf. Froissart, *Oeuvres*, 6:272.

60 *Chron. Jean II et Charles V*, 78.

61 Reims: Jones, "War and Fourteenth-Century France," 118–19; Paris: Froissart, *Oeuvres*, 6:53.

62 *Chron. Jean II et Charles V*, 225–8.

June. In order to prevent the upcoming expedition, Jean made important new concessions, offering to give Edward everything which he had ever asked for short of the crown itself: sovereignty over all the lands included in the First Treaty of London, plus Maine, Anjou, Touraine, Brittany and even Normandy – Henry II's full Angevin Empire reconstituted, the eastern half of France from top to bottom. In exchange, Jean would gain peace, and the renunciation of Edward's claim to the crown of France.[63]

The treaty also responded to the English fears of French dissembling with a clever clause which was added to the usual provision of hostages and swearing of oaths. King Jean was to declare by the upcoming Pentecost whether or not he would be able to fulfill the treaty's terms completely; if so, then he would see to it that all the French lords in England, whether prisoners or otherwise, would do homage and fealty to Edward III for the lands they held in his half of the kingdom by 1 August.[64] Since the prisoners of the battle of Poitiers (many of whom were still in England) included the counts of Tancarville and Ventadour, the Bishop of Le Mans, the Viscount of Rochechouart, Marshal d'Audrehem, the lords of Sully, Dinan, Derval, Amboise, Montagu, Crâon, Arx, Turpin, and Castillon, the captain of Poitiers, and the seneschals of Poitou, Saintonge, and Touraine, all of whom would presumably be required to perform the appropriate homages, this would be a major and nearly irrevocable step towards the imple- mentation of the treaty, and one which would not depend on the wholehearted support of the dauphin or the Estates. Another noteworthy clause was directed at Charles of Navarre, who had played an important role in bringing about the failure of the first treaty: if he tried to block the new agreement or refused to return to the obedience of King Jean, then King Edward would be bound to aid the Valois monarch, as his new ally, against the King of Navarre. The two working in concert would presumably have little difficulty in bringing even slip- pery Charles the Bad to heel.[65]

The terms of this Second Treaty of London did, however, incorporate two significant concessions to the French. The First Treaty, as noted above, had demanded a ransom of 4,000,000 écus (£666,667) for King Jean. Of that sum, £100,000 was to be paid before the king's release, then £66,667 within that same year, then the remainder in annual installments of £100,000.[66] The Second Treaty was significantly more generous. First, by its terms the 4,000,000 écus were to cover the ransoms of King Edward's other French prisoners as well as of

---

[63] This is quite specific in the treaty: "bon acort et paix perpétuelle se prendront entre les deux roys," (p. 413), "Et ceste chose facite et afinée, renoncera le roy d'Engleterre au nom, à la couronne et au royaume de France, si avant come il demourra au roy de France parmi ce traittié." (p. 425). Thus Le Patourel's passing statement that the Second Treaty was little more than a mere " 'ransom treaty' " ("Treaty of Brétigny," 32, cf. 29) must be based on his misun- derstanding of the ransom payment terms, on which see Rogers, "Anglo-French Negotia- tions."

[64] In *KdL*, 429.

[65] *KdL*, 427 (treaty clause); Froissart, *Oeuvres*, 6:477 (interference with First Treaty).

[66] In Delachenal, *Histoire de Charles V*, 2:407.

King Jean himself – a provision probably worth upwards of £50,000.[67] The first installment of the ransom was kept unchanged at £100,000, to be paid by 1 August; this was not excessively difficult, considering that the French had long since been working to collect money for the ransom, initially with the aim of reaching that amount nine months earlier, and also considering that any money which had been raised for the ransoms of the other prisoners could potentially be redirected to this combined payment. The schedule for the payment of the remainder of the ransom was left undetermined, though the two royal councils were required to settle it by the end of the just-extended truce (24 June 1359). This was presumably intended to make the payment terms easier for the French. Most significantly, if I read the somewhat obscure ransom clause of the document correctly, the Second Treaty of London provided that once the first 3,000,000 écus of the total had been paid in London, King Edward would cancel the remaining debt. Thus, in effect, the ransom was reduced to 3,000,000 écus, with an obligation for a further 1,000,000 serving as a bond for prompt payment.[68] The importance of this reduction should not be underestimated: 1,000,000 écus was the equivalent of £166,000 – twenty times the annual revenues produced by the estates of Henry of Grosmont, Duke of Lancaster, Earl of Derby, Lincoln and Leicester, and lord of extensive Welsh lands, the greatest magnate in England.[69] Considering that twenty times the annual revenue of a property was generally considered a fair purchase price, the reduction of the ransom by 1,000,000 écus may well have been intended as a *relatively* even exchange for the addition of the Duchy of Normandy, or the counties of Anjou, Maine and Touraine to the lands included in the First Treaty.[70] The Second Treaty was certainly viewed as less generous to the French than its predecessor, but, comparatively speaking, it was only moderately harsh.[71]

Still, the difference between the two treaties was great enough that the majority of the convocation of the Estates-General which met in late May – sparsely attended because of the great dangers involved in travel to Paris through the garrison-infested countryside – chose, after much debate and

---

67 See Rogers, "Anglo-French Negotiations." Since the treaty clause simply speaks of "des autres prisons françois," it is quite possible that it was intended to cover *all* the unransomed prisoners of the Poitiers campaign, even those whom the king had not acquired, with the presumption that he would be responsible for compensating their captors. In that case, those covered by the provision would also include the Archbishop of Sens (who eventually brought 48,000 écus ransom for the Earl of Warwick: *RFH* 3:2:57), Marshal Boucicaut, the counts of Nassau, Vaudemont, Roucy, etc.

68 These terms have often been misunderstood by modern historians. See Rogers, "Anglo-French Negotiations."

69 Fowler, *King's Lieutenant*, 172.

70 Perhaps even for all of them, when it is considered that the acquisition of the Dauphiné cost Philip VI and Jean II only about 400,000 écus in total (200,000 florins plus money paid in life-rents to Dauphin Humbert). Delachenal, *Histoire de Charles V*, 1:30, 34–5.

71 This runs counter to the generally accepted historical interpretation of the treaty; see Rogers, "Anglo-French Negotiations," for discussion.

dissension,[72] to reject the treaty as "neither acceptable nor practicable."[73] The terms were too hard, they said: they would rather continue to suffer their current troubles than to see the realm of France so greatly diminished.[74]

Edward's next step was to remind the French that their alternative to making peace was not merely to continue bearing their current ills, but rather to suffer a whole new collection of miseries which he intended to prepare and bring to them. He publicly declared that he would enter France with a powerful army "and remain there until he had ended the war by an honorable peace."[75] Preparations for the expedition had ceased almost entirely since the agreement of the treaty, but now they were resumed with vigor in response to the "troublesome and urgent news" from France.[76]

It was now early June, and the English government immediately changed the previously set target date for the mustering of the army from 16 June, which had become unrealistic, to 21 July, then 1 August.[77] Furthermore, somewhat surprisingly, the king actually made deep cuts in the number of troops which the commissions of array were ordered to provide, perhaps because it was already becoming clear that shipping would be scarce, or perhaps in order to keep the wage costs for the expedition manageable – an especially important factor considering that the strategy for the campaign envisioned the possibility of a long siege at Reims or Paris, for long sieges meant high wage bills.[78] In any case, all the usual difficulties manifested themselves: troops of inferior quality arrayed so that the selection process had to be repeated, inadequate shipping available, and so on.[79]

The armigerous classes, at least, supported the preparations for the campaign with enthusiasm. There was not a lord or esquire in England, says Froissart, who was not ashamed to remain behind "when they saw the king, their lord, whom

---

[72] According to *Le Bel*, 2:289: "quant ilz eurent bien longuement conseillié, *si ne furent ilz pas d'acord*, car ladite paix sembloit aux *aucuns* trop grieve." (Emphasis added.) It seems thus an overstatement to say that it was "summarily rejected." Le Patourel, "Treaty of Brétigny," 20.

[73] *Chron. Jean II et Charles V,* 234–6 ("Le quel traictié fu moult desplaisant à tout le peuple de France. Et après ce que ilz orent eu deliberacion, ilz respondirent au dit regent que le dit traictié n'estoit passable, ne faisable.")

[74] *Le Bel*, 2:289: "ledit paix sembloit aux aucuns trop grieve pour le royaume de France en pluseurs manieres, et eurent plus chier à endurer le meschief où ilz estoient et cil où le roy Jehan estoit, et attendre le plaisir de Dieu, que à consentir que le noble royaume fust ainsy amendry et departi par laditte paix."

[75] *Le Bel*, 2:289–90 (dist sy hault que chascun le pouoit bien ouïr que avant ce que l'aoust fust passé, il vendroit si poissaument ou royaume de France qu'il y demourroit tant qu'il avroit fin de guerre ou paix à son honneur); *Reading*, 133 (protestans se nolle reverti ad propria usquequo guerram terminaret); cf. Froissart, *Oeuvres*, 6:271.

[76] PRO C67/37 m. 16: "nova ardua et urgenta"; see *Reading*, 132, and *Le Bel*, 2:289 for Edward's anger.

[77] PRO C67/37 m. 16 (from Trinity [16 June] to 21 July), m. 14 (to 1 August).

[78] Reductions: ibid., mm. 14–16.

[79] Arrayed troops: ibid., 14.

they loved so much, was going."[80] Indeed, more knights and esquires signed on for the campaign than had participated in the Crécy *chevauchée* (before the Black Death). Not only was the gathering army large, it was exceptionally well equipped with items not formerly accustomed to be carried with armies. In addition to the usual accouterments of war, Edward had provided for the acquisition of a thousand carts (some sources say even more) to carry the army's supplies, as a means to counter the problems posed by the impoverished state of the French countryside. Having become all too familiar with French and Scottish scorched-earth techniques, the English monarch also brought large numbers of hand-mills for grinding grain, so that the French could not impede his progress greatly by burning their own mills. There were portable bread-ovens, and forges to repair arms and shoe horses in the field. The most ingenious addition to the army's usual equipment was a small fleet of three-man leather boats, which enabled the army to secure fresh fish (especially important during Lent), and which were also doubtless used to facilitate river crossings.[81]

While King Edward was readying his invasion force, a large number of foreign men-at-arms from Flanders, Hainault, Brabant, Meissen, Holland, Burgundy, Savoy and elsewhere, eager to serve under the most renowned soldier of Christendom, collected at Calais. Some, like Henry of Flanders (founding Knight of the Garter, and one of Edward's companions-in-arms since 1340) had been summoned to join the royal expedition, but many more, like the Margrave of Meissen, had come on their own initiative, hoping to gain their shares of the honor and wealth which had come to those serving in the earlier English *chevauchées* in France. Because of the delays in the Plantagenet's departure, many of these men had used up their cash, or even pawned their horses and armor, awaiting his arrival. They were growing restive, and it seemed that the situation might turn ugly.[82]

In this situation, the king naturally turned to his most experienced soldier-statesman, the 59-year-old Henry of Lancaster. The duke was sent ahead with a retinue of three hundred men-at-arms and two thousand archers, with instructions to make what use he could out of the crowd of foreign soldiers, so long as he got them out of Calais.[83] After arriving in the port a little after 29 September,[84] he warned the assembled troops that it would be some time before the rest of the royal army arrived. Duke Henry proposed, however, to make a *chevauchée* into France, to gain what plunder and do what harm to the French

---

80 Froissart, *Oeuvres*, 6:217. This appears to have been surprisingly close to true: in 1360, according to the county's sheriff, there was not a single hale knight left in Northumberland, because so many were absent on military service. Prestwich, *Armies*, 55.

81 *Le Bel*, 2:299, 312–13; Walsingham, *Historia Anglicana*, 1:287 and *Chron. CCCO*, fo. 181 (mille charettes).

82 *Le Bel*, 2:290–5.

83 *Le Bel*, 2:291; *Scalacronica*, 195; Froissart, *Oeuvres*, 6:212–13.

84 *Knighton*, 2:106; the date is implicitly confirmed as the force's departure date from England by the change in the wages received by numbers of men-at-arms in Farley's pay accounts (*WBWF*), e.g. Henry Burton on fo. 110v.

they could. This was a rather risky course, for his combined forces can hardly have exceeded six thousand men, and the French had long since been expecting an invasion from Calais.[85] A quarter-century of military successes, however, had raised England's martial reputation so high that, as the *Anonimalle* chronicler reports, "a hundred Frenchmen neither wished nor dared to meet twenty Englishmen in the field, nor to give them battle."[86]

Lancaster's little army therefore met no opposition from the French as it made a broad circuit via St. Omer, Béthune, Mont-Saint-Éloi, Arras, Bapaume, and Péronne, then down the Somme to Bray-sur-Somme (attacked unsuccessfully) and Cerisy.[87] At the last-named town, where the army found a good supply of bread and crossed the river, a messenger arrived bearing news of Edward's arrival at Calais. The duke's men returned promptly to meet him, glad to be headed back after a month during which they had often been short of bread and wine.[88] As they went, they paralleled the route of a smaller force under the Roger Mortimer, Earl of March, who had crossed over six days before the king and made a *chevauchée* down the coast as far as Étaples (which he burned) before returning to Calais.[89]

A few miles outside of the city Lancaster's troops encountered the royal army, which had crossed the Channel on 28 October,[90] as it began its march towards France. The foreign troops immediately petitioned the king for money to compensate for the expenses they had incurred while waiting for him, but after consulting with his advisors Edward declined to offer them anything more than a small sum for travel homewards: he had brought with him, he said, enough men to do the business he had in mind, and insufficient money to pay more. He did offer, however, to let them accompany his army without pay if they wished, in which case he would grant them a generous share of the plunder gained if the expedition went well. A number of them chose the latter option, either ashamed to go home without participating in the main event or anxious to try to recover some of their losses.[91]

*

The subsequent campaign can be divided into five portions: the advance to Reims, the siege of that city, the advance to Guillon and the ransoming of Burgundy, the threatening of Paris, and the reforging of the peace. Although each of these phases was in some way distinct, the only major turning point in

[85] *Le Bel*, 2:291, gives the total number of men-at-arms as around 2,000; in one redaction Froissart lowers this to 1,000 (*Oeuvres*, 6:205).
[86] *Anonimalle*, 43: "apayn c Fraunceis ne voidreount ne oseount vint Engleis en chaumpe encountrere ne a eux bataille doner."
[87] Froissart, *Oeuvres*, 6:205–6; *Le Bel*, 2:291–2; cf. *Anonimalle*, 44 (Cambrai, St. Quentin).
[88] Froissart, *Oeuvres*, 6:205–6; *Le Bel*, 2:291–2; *Scalacronica*, 187.
[89] *Scalacronica*, 187; le Bel's statement (deleted by Froissart) that Lancaster returned via the mouth of the Somme is probably a confusion with Mortimer's expedition.
[90] *RFR*, III:1:452.
[91] *Le Bel*, 2:294–5; Froissart, *Oeuvres*, 6:212.

terms of strategy was the end of the siege of Reims in January, and the conduct of the campaign by the English was fairly uniform throughout [Map 16–2]. The French defense was even more constant, for it consisted almost entirely of holding the major cities with strong garrisons, emptying out the countryside, and waiting for the English to go away – a strategy essentially no different from the one Philip VI had employed against Edward in 1339.

The first stage of the campaign, the advance towards Reims, was carried out in a manner typical of the other English *chevauchées* of the era. As usual, the army separated into three divisions advancing along parallel routes, in this case spreading out even farther than normal due to the impoverished state of the countryside (the result of years of warfare and bad harvests, worsened by French scorched-earth policies), which imposed the necessity to disperse more widely in order to find sufficient provisions to feed the soldiers and sufficient plunder to make the expedition profitable for them.[92] The band of desolation between the divisions stretched for some forty-five to fifty miles from flank to flank.[93] In one important way, however, this *chevauchée* departed from the pattern of the Crécy, Languedoc, and Poitiers campaigns: no major towns or cities were sacked or burned by the invaders in their advance towards Reims. As we have seen, the very devastation wrought by those earlier *chevauchées* had provided the impetus for a massive wave of refortification in France, and the inhabitants of the *bonnes villes* were now reaping the benefits of their huge investments.

During the first stage of the march, as the army advanced to the Somme, the three divisions stayed widely separated the whole way; as a result, they were able to devastate the countryside of virtually the entire portion of France north of that river.[94] Even the nominally Imperial Cambrésis was not spared, for Edward, attracted by the relative plenty of provisions to be found there, elected to treat it as Valois territory.[95] Aside from a single unsuccessful night-raid on the headquarters of the Earl of Stafford, the French did not put up any active resistance to the English.[96] The latter, however, did not press the matter by attacking St. Omer, Béthune, Abbeville, Arras, Bapaume, Péronne, or any of the other large walled towns of the region.[97] Any time expended on besieging one of these places could better be spent on Reims, and their defenses were too well prepared

---

[92] *Reading*, 133, is unusually explicit on this point: "diviso exercitu suo in tribus turmis *propter victualia*" (emphasis added); cf. *Scalacronica*, 189.

[93] Map; *Anonimalle*, 45 (each battle "tiegnt de autre lieu a xx ou xxx lieus chivachaunt et destruyaunt toutz la pays"); e.g. with the center of the king's division at Fesmy-le-Sart (Froissart, *Oeuvres*, 6:234) and the prince's at Nesle (*Scalacronica*, 187), a distance of approximately 36 miles as the crow flies, with their divisions' flanks doubtless farther out.

[94] I.e. in combination with Lancaster's and Mortimer's preliminary *chevauchées*.

[95] Froissart, *Oeuvres*, 6:233. Edward III's division traveled the route St. Omer, past Arras, Cambrésis, Thiérache, Laonnois. The Prince of Wales went via Montreuil, Hesdin, Nesle, Ham, Vermandois. Lancaster's route was in between these two. *Scalacronica*, 187–8.

[96] *Knighton*, 2:106–7; *Scalacronica*, 187.

[97] Though, according to *Chronographia*, 2:290, they did unsuccessfully attack Bray-sur-Somme and Crépy-en-Laonnois; but this may be an erroneous reference to the Duke of Lancaster's attacks on Bray and Cerisy before Edward's arrival (see above).

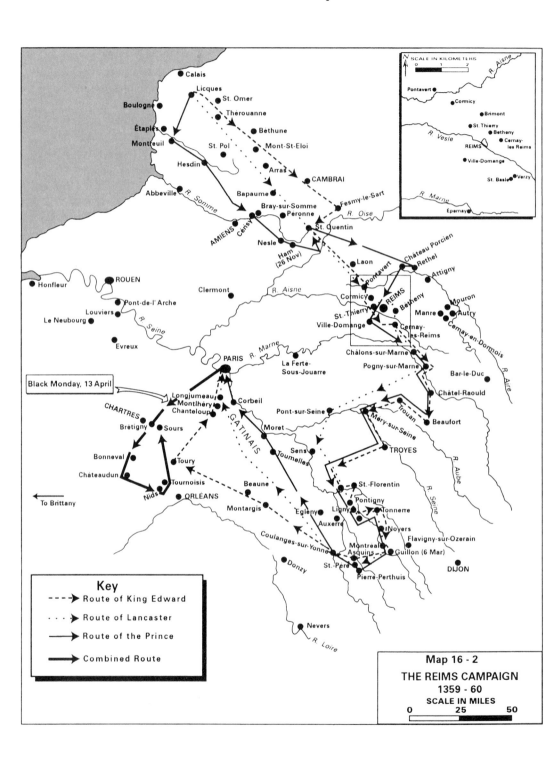

Black Monday, 13 April

To Brittany

Key
--→ Route of King Edward
···→ Route of Lancaster
—→ Route of the Prince
⟹ Combined Route

Map 16 - 2

THE REIMS CAMPAIGN
1359 - 60

SCALE IN MILES

0   25   50

to allow the uncontested occupations or the rapid escalades which had led to the sacking of so many walled towns during the Crécy and Languedoc *chevauchées*.

After some three weeks of slow marching, during which the three divisions had maintained only loose contact with one another, the whole army concentrated at St. Quentin on 28–29 November in order to coordinate the approach to Reims.[98] There was still no sign of the army which the dauphin was supposed to be gathering to resist the invaders,[99] so the logistic benefits of a dispersed deployment continued to determine the style of the English advance. The prince's division took the route southeast to Rethel (which he attacked unsuccessfully) and Château-Porcien, then southwest to the monastery of St.-Thierry, where he took up lodgings.[100] The king took the direct route, farther to the west, crossing the Aisne at Pontavert, then moving south and east to set up his headquarters at the monastery of St. Basle near the town of Verzy southeast of the city in early December.[101] Roger Mortimer, the marshal of the host, was based at Bétheney, just north of the besieged city.[102] There was no regular investment like the ones outside Calais in 1346 or Berwick in 1333: all three divisions were quartered in the scattered villages of the countryside, as directed by the marshals of the host, where they could find shelter from the extraordinarily rainy December weather.[103] Each lord, notes Henry Knighton, set up his own court and kept Christmas as merrily as if he were in England.[104] The siege of Reims, which was to last for the next forty days, was thus carried on in the fashion of a distant blockade, with pillagers and patrols serving to make the approaches to Reims so dangerous that only the bravest messengers risked breaking the cordon.[105] This approach was about as effective in cutting the city off from supplies as a more formal siege could have been.

Unfortunately for Edward, their isolation from the rest of the country had little effect on the defenders of Reims. They had long known of the English plans to besiege the city,[106] and had consequently provided themselves with ample supplies for a long period of self-sufficiency.[107] There was some anxiety in the city, especially when the townsmen received word that the relief army

---

[98] *Knighton*, 2:106.

[99] Letter of the dauphin, printed in Delachenal, *Histoire de Charles V*, 2:438: "est nostre entencion . . . de les combatre"; *Récits*, 301: "s'en ala mettre le siége devant Raims, cuidant et désirant que Charles le régent . . . le combatesiest."

[100] *Scalacronica*, 188 (Rethel, Château-Porcien); Froissart, *Oeuvres*, 6:231.

[101] Delachenal, *Histoire de Charles V*, 2:153–4 (date); Froissart, *Oeuvres*, 6:231 (St. Basle); according to *WBWF*, fo. 61, he spent Christmas, the Feast of St. John (27 December), and Epiphany (6 January) all at "Virzey." See also *RFR*, III:1:453; *Lescot*, 208

[102] Barber, *Edward, Prince of Wales*, 162.

[103] *Knighton*, 2:107 (dispersion); *Le Bel*, 2:299–300 (rain); Froissart, *Oeuvres*, 6:231 (marshals).

[104] *Knighton*, 2:107.

[105] Froissart, *Oeuvres*, 6:247; Delachenal, *Histoire de Charles V*, 2:157, 157 n.2.

[106] At least since they were specifically warned by the regent on 10 July (Delachenal, *Histoire de Charles V*, 2:145–6); note also Froissart, *Oeuvres*, 6:191, 247.

[107] *Chron. des quat. prem. Valois*, 100.

which the dauphin had promised had been recalled to Troyes,[108] but in reality their position was very strong. After a crash program of fortification, the city was strong enough that it could not be taken by assault.[109] There was no real possibility for the English to mount a long siege similar to those of Calais in 1346–47, Tournai in 1340, or Berwick in 1333, for the simple reason that there was no secure water route from England to Reims, and without that an encircling army could not long be maintained, especially in winter. Even keeping the army in place for forty days, which was as much as Edward could manage, required sending foraging detachments as far afield as Warcq and Donchery on the eastern border of the kingdom of France at the Meuse river, fifty miles northeast from Reims.[110]

Meanwhile the dauphin's troops continued their assiduous avoidance of combat with the English. There were fairly frequent small skirmishes between foraging parties and the garrisons of castles on the edges of the English zone of operations, and one group of Englishmen made a daring raid as far as the suburbs of Paris, but aside from these the only major military events involved English attacks on outlying walled towns or fortresses.[111] On 29 December the Duke of Lancaster, accompanied by John of Gaunt, Roger Mortimer, and John Chandos, assaulted and captured the well-fortified town of Cernay-en-Dormois.[112] This success was followed up over the next few days by the capture and destruction of Autry and Mouron on the Aisne, the inhabitants having fled at the duke's approach.[113] Eustache d'Auberchicourt and his *routiers* had earlier taken Attigny on the Aisne by a surprise escalade, and, having found the town well stocked with wine, now made a very welcome present of some of it to the king and the prince.[114] Bartholomew Burghersh meanwhile made use of some of the miners brought along by Edward III to capture the strong keep of the town of Cormicy, north of the city, where the lord of Clermont was captured on 6 January.[115]

These actions were mere sideshows, however. While they were going on, and the English magnates remaining around Reims were holding their Christmas courts in borrowed manor-houses, the main issue of the campaign was being

---

[108] Delachenal, *Histoire de Charles V,* 2:158, cf. 438.

[109] Fortification: Jones, "The War and Fourteenth-Century France," 118–19; impossible to storm: Froissart, *Oeuvres,* 6:253; letter of the regent, quoted Delachenal, *Histoire de Charles V,* 2:158n4; cf. Venette in *Nangis,* 297.

[110] Froissart, *Oeuvres,* 6:235–6, 232.

[111] Ibid., 6:235 (skirmishes); *Scalacronica,* 188 (Paris).

[112] *Knighton,* 2:107–8; *Scalacronica,* 188.

[113] *Knighton,* 2:108; I read "Meuran" as Mouron rather than Manre (*contra* Moranvillé, "Siège de Reims," 97; Delachenal, *Hist. Charles V,* 2:160; Barber, *Edward, Prince of Wales,* 162), on linguistic as well as geographic grounds, though Manre ("Menre") apparently also fell into English hands around this time: see *KdL,* 435.

[114] Froissart, *Oeuvres,* 6:190, 232; *Scalacronica,* 188.

[115] *Knighton,* 2:108–9; *Scalacronica,* 188 (date); *RFR,* III:1:417 (indenture for service of 43 miners and 4 smiths from the forest of Dean).

decided inside Reims. The fortifications of the city were too strong to be taken by storm without excessive casualties, if they could be taken at all.[116] In any case, the English king wanted to be received by the city, not to take it by assault: if Reims were to surrender to him, the bishop of the city (who had many times publicly boasted of being a distant cousin of Edward III, and who had been involved in the revolutionary activity of the Estates-General of 1356)[117] could doubtless be persuaded to formally acknowledge the Plantagenet's right to the crown and to perform the ritual anointing with St. Remy's sacred oil. For Edward to be successful in gaining the recognition of his title by the people of France, this was almost a *sine qua non*.[118]

In pursuit of this goal, the Plantagenet gave strict orders making the region immediately around the city off-limits for pillaging.[119] This policy aimed primarily to avoid incurring the ill-will of the citizens, in hopes of encouraging them to surrender to Edward, but also was meant to address the logistic difficulties of staying in one place for a long time: "King Edward commanded on pain of hanging," Jean le Bel tells us, "that no one should burn anything in any town, except for one or two houses, in order to ransom the others more effectively."[120] In addition, the king made it known to the episcopal city's inhabitants that if they submitted to him he would "make the[ir] city great, and exalt it above all the other cities of France," and promised to treat them all with magnanimity.[121] It was only after approximately two to three weeks of this kid-glove treatment passed by without result that Edward tightened the noose around the city to increase the pressure on the citizens, threatening them with the desolation of the countryside and the rigors of a long siege.[122] The stick, however, proved no more effective than the proverbial carrot.

By early January, three facts were becoming obvious. First, as Edward had perhaps expected all along, the dauphin was not about to risk a battle to break the siege.[123] Second, the people of Reims were not going to surrender their city

---

116 *Le Bel*, 2:302; cf. Jones, "War and Fourteenth-Century France," 118–19.

117 Delachenal, *Histoire de Charles V*, 2:155. In the interim he had become counselor of the dauphin, but still the townsmen of Reims considered that there was a significant risk of his betraying the city to the English. Ibid., 156.

118 Consider the well-known impact of the coronation of Charles VII by Joan of Arc.

119 *Knighton*, 2:107; *M. Villani (Porta)*, 2:383.

120 *Le Bel*, 2:301; cf. *M. Villani (Porta)*, 2:404.

121 *M. Villani (Porta)*, 2:383.

122 Ibid., and the dauphin's letter, quoted in Delachenal, *Histoire de Charles V*, 2:158 n.1.

123 On 26 December the dauphin wrote to the people of Reims that he had recalled the constable, who had been dispatched to aid them, but promised to send a new relief force as soon as possible. Quoted ibid., n.2. Moranvillé ("Siège de Reims," 98) accepts this at face value, but considering the unwillingness of the dauphin to face the test of battle during the rest of the campaign, it was probably an empty promise meant to encourage the defenders in their resistance. Concerning Edward's expectations, however, cf. *Récits*, 301: "the said King of England . . . went to lay siege to Reims, believing and desiring that Charles the regent, Duke of Normandy, would fight with him."

to him. Third, the army had exhausted all the supplies which could be squeezed from northern Champagne.[124] It was time to move on. But where?

A march west along the Marne to Paris was doubtless expected by many.[125] The capture of the capital would have been comparable to the occupation of Reims in terms of its impact on French public opinion, and there was some reason to believe that a faction of the Paris bourgeoisie might welcome Edward's arrival. The support which the people of the city had lent to what was virtually a revolutionary movement against the dauphin just eighteen months earlier demonstrated that their loyalty to the Valois dynasty was not absolute, and the period since then, with Anglo-Navarrese garrisons wreaking havoc in the Ile-de-France without much opposition from the dauphin, had given them little reason to strengthen their attachment to Jean II or the regent.[126] Even if no overt movement to give the city up to Edward III emerged, the regent's precarious political position might conceivably compel him to accept a challenge to battle outside Paris. These calculations were all very uncertain, but clearly there was no other target for the army which had a better prospect of leading to Edward's goal of an honorable peace, or even an equal chance of doing so.

Whatever the strategic merits of an advance on Paris, however, another factor militated strongly against that course. The area between Reims and Paris, both south and north of the Marne, had for some time been a center of *routier* activity. It had also suffered the devastation of both the Jacquerie and the counter-revolutionary excesses of the nobles. As a result, it had grown as desolate as any region through which the English army had thus far marched. Especially in the middle of January it would be difficult to support an army there.

A movement up the Marne into southern Champagne, on the other hand, would bring the invaders into one of the few areas of France thus far largely spared the ravages of *chevauchées*, rebellions, and continual garrison warfare. Where there had been peace, there would be food, wine and fodder to be expropriated. Once again the English might find themselves in the happy situation of entering a region where the people (like those of Normandy in 1346 or Languedoc in 1355) "did not know the meaning of the word war," and where fortifications had been allowed to fall into desuetude. This would once again provide the English king with the opportunity to enrich his friends and to distress his enemies in a region which thus far had provided a secure reserve of manpower and money for the Valois war effort.

Of all these factors, the determining ones were the two sides of one coin: by going south and east the army could find enough supplies to make it through the

---

124 Froissart, *Oeuvres*, 6:232, 235, 253.
125 Cf. *Le Bel*, 2:304.
126 Indeed, some Parisian bourgeois were reportedly involved in a plot to kill the dauphin, and allow Navarrese soldiers into the city, in December 1359. *Le Bel*, 2:303; *Chron. Jean II et Charles V*, 252–3. Matteo Villani notes that the dauphin, even after the suppression of Marcel's party, "was neither loved nor obeyed as lord, either by the people or by the barons." *Cronica* (ed. Porta), 2:272; cf. 274–5, and (elsewhere), 386.

winter without undue hardship; if it went west, it might go hungry.[127] The horses, in particular, were already suffering from lack of forage combined with the debilitating effects of the miserable, wet, winter weather. Edward decided to turn southeast, towards Châlons and Troyes. Behind him, however, he left Eustache d'Auberchicourt with a strong band of *routiers* based at Attigny, Autry, Manre, and several other fortresses.[128] These troops continued to plunder the entire region, striking as far west as Pierrepont in the Laonnois, as far north as Mézières, and as far east as Stenay.[129] Peace did not return to northern Champagne in the wake of Edward's departure.[130]

The areas which the English entered after leaving Reims around 11 January were neither as impoverished nor as well defended as the one they were leaving.[131] The army was able to find enough victuals in the vicinity of Châlons to sustain itself there for a week while the bridge over the Marne was reconstructed, and the king successfully treated with representatives of the Duchy of Bar for a *patis*.[132] Still, supplies were tight enough that, considering also the approach of Lent, a number of the Germans who had thus far accompanied the English army departed for their own country from near Troyes in early February. A few of them, notably the Margrave of Meissen, received substantial gifts from the king in aid of their expenses.[133] The strength of the royal army nevertheless did not decline appreciably, for Captal de Buch and James Audley arrived (coming from their strongholds of, respectively, Clermont in the Beauvaisis and la Ferté-sous-Jouarre in Brie) to join the prince's division.[134]

---

127 On the importance of this consideration, cf. Froissart, *Oeuvres*, 6:253 (Quant il eut là tant estet qu'il li commenchoit à anuyer, et que ses gens ne trouvoient riens que fourer et perdoient leurs chevaux, et estoyent en grant mésaise de tous vivres, s'il ne l'avoient aporté avoecq yaux, il se deslogièrent); cf. 274 (tousjours en quérant le plus cras pays pour mieux trouver à vivre).

128 Treaty in *KdL*, 435; *Le Bel*, 2:304; Luce, *Jeunesse de Bertran*, 463.

129 Froissart, *Oeuvres*, 6:260–1.

130 This is in accordance with his declared strategy of leaving garrisons throughout France to carry on his war until the whole country was conquered. Below, p. 413; cf. *Anonimalle*, 49.

131 Delachenal, *Histoire de Charles V*, 2:160–1 (date); *Le Bel*, 2:304, 306; *Chron. des quat. prem. Valois*, 101 (more plentiful region).

132 *Scalacronica*, 188–9, *Anonimalle*, 45. The latter source gives the duchy's ransom as 200,000 florins, though this probably represents a confusion with the ransom of Burgundy. The *Scalacronica*'s use of "faillerent" here probably means "completed" rather than the more usual "lacked"; cf. Greimas, *Dictionnaire*, s.v. "faillir," def. 3. Many such agreements were made during this campaign on a smaller scale: *M. Villani (Porta)*, 2:404, 406, 408.

133 *Scalacronica*, 189; *Le Bel*, 2:307–8; *WBWF*, fo. 71v (gift of £120 to the margrave, departing for his own lands, and three smaller similar gifts to other individuals on 3 February). Despite the generalization of le Bel and the *Scalacronica*, however, more of the foreigners apparently stayed with the English than left. Larger numbers of departure gifts were given later – six on 1 March, and nearly fifty at the very end of the campaign. Ibid., fos 72–72v.

During early February, the English army was spread out between Troyes and Méry. Froissart, *Oeuvres*, 6:253.

134 *Scalacronica*, 189.

While the Duke of Lancaster's division crossed the Seine at Pont-sur-Seine (formerly the base of Eustache d'Auberchicourt's *routiers* in the area)[135] and swept south past Sens, the other two elements crossed the bridge at Méry and turned south to St. Florentin.[136] After an unsuccessful attack on that town and a short pilgrimage by the army's leaders to the tomb of St. Edmund Rich (once Archbishop of Canterbury) at Pontigny, the prince's division was forced by lack of fodder to separate itself again from the rest of the army, taking up a new position west of Auxerre at Égleny while the rest of the army moved in the opposite direction, to Tonnere.[137]

The last-named town was captured by assault and proved to be well stocked with supplies: this coup provided the entire army with wine and other victuals to last for a week.[138] From there, after they had rested, the English continued due south to Montréal and Guillon, which the king occupied on Ash Wednesday, 18 February. One of his captains, John Harleston, had some weeks earlier seized the extraordinarily strong neighboring castle of Flavigny-sur-Ozerain, which because it was considered impregnable had been used to store a huge quantity of victuals. These proved sufficient to maintain the entire English army for a month. From there, Edward planned to continue southeast deeper into Burgundy, where he expected to find plenty of supplies to sustain the army for all of Lent.[139]

Throughout this period, the French had occasionally managed to capture some of the English "varlets" as they were engaged in foraging, and occasionally even archer or two. About this time, however, they managed to take prisoner a bigger prize – a highly regarded young member of the king's household, Geoffrey Chaucer. Evidently men with a good eye for quality, his captors demanded a stiff ransom from the young gentleman, towards which King Edward made a gift of £16.[140]

Shortly thereafter, a delegation arrived from the court of the young Duke of Burgundy, whose capital at Dijon was now in easy striking distance for the English. They reportedly found King Edward in good humor – this expedition was, after all, allowing him to combine two of his favorite occupations, war and hunting, as he had brought his falcons and greyhounds with him from

135 Froissart, *Oeuvres*, 6:116–17, cf. 163.

136 *Chron. Jean II et Charles V,* 254; cf. *Scalacronica*, 189; Froissart, *Oeuvres*, 6:253 (St. Florentin).

137 I.e. the prince moved southwest while the king moved southeast; Egleny and Tonnerre are about 25 miles apart. Prince: *Scalacronica*, 189. Pilgrimage: *Anonimalle*, 45; *WBWF*, fo. 61.

138 Froissart, *Oeuvres*, 6:254. The town was captured, but not the castle, which was defended by the Master of Crossbowmen of France.

139 Froissart, *Oeuvres*, 6:254; *Scalacronica*, 189.

140 Chaucer received £16 of the king's gift "in subsidium redemcionis sue" on 1 March. *WBWF*, fo. 72. Especially considering that the phrase "in subsidium" indicates that the total ransom was even higher, this was a large sum, what one might expect to see paid by an esquire or even a knight, though Chaucer is not given a rank in the entry. Varlets: ibid., fos 71–2.

England.[141] The offers brought by these supplicants can only have improved his mood, for they ultimately agreed to pay a ransom of 200,000 *moutons* (enough to cover almost three months' worth of the wage bill he had been accumulating for the expedition) in exchange for his promise not to overrun the duke's territories for the following three years. Of almost equal importance was an implied agreement that, if Edward should be crowned as King of France at Reims within that period, the young duke would lend the Plantagenet his support.[142]

By the time the negotiators for the two sides had concluded this Treaty of Guillon on 10 March, spring was approaching. The new season brought with it fine sunny weather and growing fodder for the horses, making an advance on Paris more practical. When it departed in that direction, the English army left in its wake a number of *routier* garrisons, occupying the castle of Ligny and several other places, just as Auberchicourt's men had been left to harry Champagne.[143]

The region south of the capital was one of the ever-fewer areas of France which had not yet seen one of Edward III's armies marching through, though it had been forced to bear the scourge of Robert Knolles' *routiers* for the past year or so.[144] To make sure that the local people fully experienced the pain they had thus far been spared, the army resumed its slow and widely dispersed march north, again devastating a swathe of land up to forty-five miles wide.[145] Only those who paid heavy indemnities to the invaders to purchase *patises* were spared.[146] Many of the churches in the region had been fortified and stocked with supplies by the local people; numbers of these were taken by the English, either seized by assault or surrendered when Edward's men positioned siege engines against them.[147] Some of the English outriders meanwhile undoubtedly reached as far as the right bank of the Loire, just opposite where the prince's

---

141 *WBWF* (wages of falconers and huntsmen); *Le Bel*, 2:301, 313; Froissart, *Oeuvres*, 6:257.
142 The treaty is printed in *RFR*, III:1:473. I say an implied agreement because in fact the clause only stated that, if Edward were crowned and Duke Philip did *not* support him, then the protection granted to his duchy would be revoked. An explicit agreement to accept Edward as King of France would have been impossibly damaging politically for the Burgundians if Edward did not prove successful. The well-informed Florentine chronicler Matteo Villani, however, certainly believed that the Burgundians were at that time secretly hostile towards the Valois cause, and that the treaty envisioned the Duke of Burgundy assisting at King Edward's coronation as King of France, under certain circumstances. Villani, *Cronica* (ed. Porta), 2:404, 406.

   On 1 March, the king gave a gift of £16 to Jean de Guillon, knight of Burgundy, whom he was sending into England, and two days later another messenger was sent to Avignon – presumably bearing word of the basic structure of the treaty. *WBWF*, fo. 72.
143 See the document in *KdL*, 439.
144 Froissart, *Oeuvres*, 6:54.
145 Map 16–2; *Récits*, 304. E.g. with the king's division at Toury while the prince was at Moret, about 42 miles apart.
146 *M. Villani* (ed. Porta), 2:406; *Le Bel*, 2:306; e.g. the county of Donzy-le-Pré. *Chron. Jean II et Charles V*, 255.
147 *Scalacronica*, 192; Venette, in *Nangis*, 302.

coureurs had carried the torch less than four years earlier on their way north from Bordeaux. Froissart's description of a realm devastated from one end to the other was in truth no exaggeration.

The Plantagenet's near approach to Paris was not viewed with equanimity by the regent and his council. On the last day of March, when the invaders reached Chanteloup and Longjumeau not far south of the capital, a group of Edward's councilors received an embassy from the dauphin's court seeking to reopen the peace negotiations. The English agreed to a meeting, which was held on Good Friday, 3 April, but this came to nothing because they insisted on terms that the French considered excessive – essentially the implementation of the Second Treaty of London.[148]

One reason for the English king's unwillingness to make any major concessions at this point is that he still had hopes of provoking the French into giving battle. Perhaps he remembered how his last stay in the city's suburbs, in 1346, had seemed to spur Philip VI into fighting at Crécy. Perhaps, as Henry Knighton reports, the dauphin had previously "promised" to do battle with the invaders.[149] In any case, after burning Montlhéry, Longjumeau, and other towns on Good Friday and Holy Saturday, then solemnly observing Easter at Chanteloup,[150] the king led his army to just outside the walls of Paris on 7 April, the troops fully arrayed in their combat formations under their unfurled banners, with trumpets and clarions blaring a challenge to the defenders.[151] The English army had already ravaged the countryside of the entire area, so that (according to Jean de Venette, who was inside the city at the time) not a man or woman was left in any of the towns in the region.[152] The capital was packed to bursting with refugees, including the inhabitants of the suburbs immediately outside the city's defenses, which had been destroyed by Parisians themselves lest the English make use of them in an assault on the city.[153]

Heralds were sent to invite the French to come out and fight. Edward even went so far as to propose a battle before the walls, with the promise that if he were defeated he would go away and never again claim the throne of France.[154]

Despite King Edward's bellicose display, however, the French army remained shut up behind its defenses.[155] The king, angered by the French inactivity, ordered the burning of the remaining suburbs of the town "in order to provoke them to fight." Though the flames and smoke of neighboring villages, for the

[148] *Chron. des quat. prem. Valois*, 115; *Chron. Jean II et Charles V*, 256–7; *Knighton*, 2:110–11; but cf. Froissart, *Oeuvres*, 6:280–1.

[149] *Knighton*, 2:111 (expectantes praelium de his qui in civitate Parisiensi erant sicuti eis ante promiserant.) Possibly a reference to the dauphin's letter, quoted above, note 99.

[150] *WBWF*, fo. 61; Venette, in *Nangis*, 301.

[151] *Chron. Jean II et Charles V*, 257–8; *Knighton*, 2:111; *Anonimalle*, 46; cf. *Le Bel*, 2:307.

[152] Venette, in *Nangis*, 302 (from the Seine to Étampes and beyond); cf. *Récits*, 304.

[153] Venette, in *Nangis*, 303.

[154] Froissart, *Oeuvres*, 6:265–6; *Reading*, 135–6; *English Brut*, 310; Walsingham, *Historia Anglicana*, 1:288.

[155] *Knighton*, 2:111; Froissart, *Oeuvres*, 6:256.

second time in the war, could be seen from the very walls of Paris, the French stayed in their fortifications.[156] Edward's army withdrew to the region of Montl-héry, where it stayed almost another week.[157] The regent's only response to his enemies' presence outside Paris was to send out another peace embassy on the 10th, which however had no more success than the previous one.[158]

It was probably about this time that Captal de Buch, who had been sent to Normandy to try to arrange for Charles the Bad's cooperation in capturing Paris, returned with the news that the King of Navarre was unwilling to accept Edward's proposals.[159] Since the capital was far too large and well garrisoned to be stormed by an army of only about ten thousand men, unless by the aid of a faction of the citizens, this rebuff meant that the English could see little prospect of capturing the city. The army the regent had collected inside its walls was large enough that, without Navarrese cooperation, it would be impossible to encircle the city with small detachments as had been done outside Reims, so a siege was essentially out of the question, especially for an army which had already been on campaign for nearly half a year. Besides, after almost two weeks nearly stationary south of the city, the army's horses were running out of forage.[160]

Edward therefore made another bid to draw the dauphin into battle, once again forming up the army and sending heralds to deliver a challenge to his adversary, but Charles kept his troops under tight rein and stayed behind Paris' gates.[161] Edward, frustrated, announced his intention to march west along the Loire to Brittany, rest in friendly territory for the summer, and then return to besiege Paris in September.[162] The baggage train had already set off in that direction, while the army waited to see if the French would do battle. The Duke of Lancaster, meanwhile, was to remain in the Orléannais and the Gâtinais, in charge of the many castles held by the English in the area.[163] These, and the

---

156 Venette, in *Nangis*, 303 (smoke and flames; referring to burning of 5–6 April); *Knighton*, 2:111 (Edwardus inde graviter motus jussic dare incendio magnam partem suburbiorum ut eos provocaret ad pugnam); *Scalacronica*, 193; *Chron. Jean II et Charles V*, 258.

157 *Scalacronica*, 193.

158 *Chron. Jean II et Charles V*, 258; *Knighton*, 2:111; *Reading*, 136; *Scalacronica*, 193.

159 Buch sent from the army in Beauce to Navarre in Normandy: *Scalacronica*, 192–3. Back by 12 May: Froissart, *Oeuvres*, 6:281.

160 *Scalacronica*, 193, but cf. *M. Villani (Porta)*, 2:407–8.

161 *Chron. Jean II et Charles V*, 259.

162 Froissart, *Oeuvres*, 6:273: "se volloit aller cel esté rafrescir en Bretaingne et en Nor-mendie, et laissier convenir les fortrèches qui pour lui se tenoient ou royaumme de France, et tantost après le Saint-Jehan-Baptiste [i.e. his *decollatio*, 29 August] que li bleds et les vignes meuriroient, revenir devant Paris"; 279: "Li intention dou roy Édowart d'Engleterre estoit tele que il enteroit en ce bon pays de Biausse et se trairoit tout bellement sus celle belle, douce et bonne rivière de Loire, et se venroit tout cel esté jusques apriès aoust rafreschir en Bretagne, et tantost sus les vendenges, qui estoient moult belles apparans, il retourroit en France et venroit de rechief mettre le siége devant Paris."

163 *Knighton*, 2:111 (Tunc movit se rex in alias partes et tradidit custodiam castellorum quae sunt in partibus de Orlions et Catenesia duce Lancastriae.) The Gâtinais is the region roughly between the Essone-Rimarde and Seine-Loing rivers.

other fortresses held by Edward's subjects in the Ile-de-France, Brie, Champagne, Picardy, Ponthieu, the Vexin, Normandy and elsewhere would meanwhile continue to "harry and make war on the realm of France, and so torment and beat down the cities and good towns of France that they would willingly accept him [as king]."[164]

The first step in implementing the new strategy was a long march into Beauce, to the southwest of Paris, on Monday 13 April. That day may have been the decisive moment of the campaign. The fine, warm spring weather which had accompanied the army since its departure from Guillon[165] turned suddenly fearsome. Dark stormclouds swept in, dumping massive hailstones on the English columns as they trod onwards through icy, penetrating mists, so bitter cold, that men fell by the way, frozen to death."[166] A large number of the baggage-horses carrying the army's supplies and accumulated plunder perished, as did some of the troops.[167] The storm was so heavy, according to Froissart, that "it seemed the heavens would crack, and the earth open and swallow everything up."[168]

Terrible as this day was, its physical effects were not great enough to weaken the English army significantly. The Englishmen continued on into Beauce over the following days, still burning the countryside for miles around.[169] The army in Paris stayed there, rather than risk pursuing a still redoubtable foe. If we can trust the testimony of Froissart on this matter, however, Black Monday (as the day of the storm was called) had "much humbled" King Edward, making him

---

[164] Froissart, *Oeuvres*, 6:279 ("lairoit ses gens par ces forterèces, qui guerre faisoient pour lui, en France, en Brie, en Campagne, en Pikardie, en Pontieu, en Vismeu, en Vexin et en Normendie, guerryer et heryer le royaulme de France et si taner et fouler les cités et les bonnes villes que de leur volenté il s'acorderoient à lui.")

[165] Venette, in *Nangis*, 300.

[166] *A Chronicle of London, 1089–1483* (London: Longman, 1827), 64.

[167] *Knighton*, 2:111–12, states that the Earl of March (who had in fact perished earlier, on 27 February, of a fever – *Scalacronica*, 189; J. Taylor, "A Wigmore Chronicle, 1355–77," *Proc. of the Leeds Phil. and Lit. Soc.; Lit. and Hist. Section* 11 (1964–6), 87), Guy of Warwick (eldest son of the Earl of Warwick), Lord Robert Morley and his son, and many other noble knights and esquires, among many others [gentes absque numero], were killed in the storm, along with no fewer than 6,000 horses. Many soldiers were forced to burn their tents and other gear for lack of carriage as a result. *Reading*, 139, also states that "plura millia hominum et equorum itinerando, quasi per vindictam, subito interierunt." These statements are pretty clearly great exaggerations; it should be borne in mind that many English magnates shipped more horses back to England at the end of the campaign than they had brought with them. The Prince of Wales, for example, came to France with 1,369 horses and returned with 2,114, and of the men-at-arms' appraised warhorses only 1,203 were lost over the entire course of the campaign for the whole army. E101/393/11, fo. 79; Ayton, *Knights and Warhorses*, 265–70. Cf. also *Chron. Normande*, 152; *Scalacronica*, 193–4; Froissart, *Oeuvres*, 6:273; Venette, in *Nangis*, 308; *English Brut*, 311 ("suche a storme & tempest [th]at non of our nacioun herd ne sawe neuere non such"); *Chron. CCCO*, fo. 181v: "il feust si graunt tempest de greille et neife [sic] sourdant es parties dela dount plusours del hoste le Roy chierount mortz a terre."

[168] Froissart, *Oeuvres*, 6:273: "il sambloit que li chiels deust s'en partir, et li tierre ouvrir et tout engloutir."

[169] Venette, in *Nangis*, 308, Cf. *Reading*, 137; *English Brut*, 311.

more willing to listen to the Duke of Lancaster and the Prince of Wales, who had for some time been urging him to resume peace negotiations with the French.[170] Froissart's version of Duke Henry's arguments has the ring of truth:

> My lord, this war which you are carrying on in the realm of France is . . . excessively costly for you; your people gain by it, you lose [money] and spend time. All things considered, if you continue to make war according to your plan, you will use up your whole life, and it will be difficult to reach your goal even then. If you take my advice, you should get out of it and take the offers presented to you while you can exit with honor; for, my lord, we could lose in a day more than we have conquered in twenty years.[171]

The Plantagenet's plan to recuperate in Brittany and then return to Paris was certainly feasible – what could or would the dauphin do to prevent it? – but even if he did come back with fresh forces in the autumn, there was no guarantee that they would do any better than this army, which had not been able to secure the capital or Reims for the English king, and which had "courted combat to maintain the right of their lord without finding any takers anywhere."[172] The situation was thus something of a stalemate.

Considering that Edward had always proclaimed his battlefield successes to be divine signals of the justice of his cause, it is easy to imagine that the combination of a political check (the retreat from Paris) and an unexpected and awe-inspiring storm might seem to him a sign from God that the time had come to make peace.[173] According to Froissart, Edward's response to the hailstorm was, "as he has since confessed," to "turn himself towards the church of Our Lady at Chartres, and religiously [vow] to the Virgin . . . that he would accept of terms of peace."[174] There is no reason to doubt the chronicle's testimony: had not the king always said he was willing to accept any just and reasonable offer in order to end the war?[175] And had he not already admitted, in 1358, that the provisions

---

170 Froissart, *Oeuvres*, 6:281: "qui moult le humilia et brisa son corage." Prince of Wales as a main peacemaker: Chandos Herald, *Vie du Prince Noir*, ll. 1540–3; *Chron. des quat. prem. Valois*, 116; cf. also *Knighton*, 2:99.

171 Froissart, *Oeuvres*, 6:281.

172 *Scalacronica*, 196: "queraunt batail dauoir derenez le droit lour siris, qe ne trouerount nul part countenaunce a ceo faire"; *Récits*, 301: "Et pour ce estoit-il [Edward] descendus sy avant qu'il désiroit avoir bataille; mais nuls ne vint encontre luy"; cf. *Chron. Normande*, 149.

173 Froissart, *Oeuvres*, 6:273: "elle [the storm] li mua et canga, car il fu inspirés adont de la grâce de Dieu." "Adont y eut en l'ost aucuns souffissans hommes qui dissoient que c'estoit une verghe de Dieu envoyée pour exemple, et que Dieux monstroit par signe qu'il volloit que on fesist pès." Cf. *Chronographia* 2:294, *Lescot*, 145 and note the possible reference in King Jean's letter, quoted in Delachenal, *Histoire de Charles V*, 2:199 n.3 (peace made "ainsi que par divin miracle"). The issue of Edward's religious motivation in this instance is discussed further in Rogers, "Anglo-French Negotiations."

174 Froissart, *Oeuvres*, 6:282.

175 Most recently just as he left Paris: "Le count de Tankiruille enueint hors de la cite en le houre, requist tretice du counsail le dit roy Dengleter, qe ly fust responpu qe lour dit seignour prendroit toutdiz resoun toutez houres." *Scalacronica*, 193. A particularly significant statement to this effect (given its audience) is the one he made in a private communica-

of the First Treaty of London were sufficient to allow him to make peace with honor? What clearer sign from Heaven could he ask for to tell him to do so?

Such considerations were enough to inspire King Edward, after a period for consideration and to ensure that the gesture would not appear to be a sign of weakness, to despatch a messenger to the dauphin's court with letters indicating that he was willing to renew the negotiations for a final peace. The regent and his councilors responded eagerly, and quickly dispatched an ambassadorial party to meet with Edward's men.[176] For two weeks the English stayed in Beauce near Orléans, their foraging parties skirmishing with the French, while the royal councils informally discussed terms under the mediation of the Abbot of Cluny and Sir Hugh of Geneva, an envoy from the Pope who had earlier been one of Edward III's captains.[177] Formal negotiations resumed on May first in the small village of Brétigny near there, and two days thereafter agreement had been reached on the terms of a final peace, though wrangling on minor points delayed the formal conclusion of the treaty until the 8th.[178] The price the French were required to pay for peace was very close to what it had been in May of 1358 by the First Treaty of London. The ransom for King Jean, now also to include Edward's other French prisoners, was reduced to 3,000,000 écus (the additional 1,000,000 écu bond of the Second Treaty of London was omitted), but the valuable[179] county of Rouergue, comparable in size to Touraine or Anjou, was added to the lands due to King Edward.[180] The French were to end their alliance with Scotland, and Edward was to abandon his special relationship with Flanders. The Plantagenet was to hold all the lands surrendered to him in full sovereignty, as a "neighbor" to the Valois kingdom; in exchange, he would renounce his rights to the French crown and to the remainder of the old Angevin Empire.[181]

For the purposes of this study, two questions need to be answered concerning

---

tion to the Prince of Wales in 1342 during his expedition to Brittany: *Avesbury*, 341; see also his letter to the emperor of November 1356, *RFR* 3:1:343.
[176] *Chron. Jean II et Charles V*, 259–61.
[177] Ibid.; *Scalacronica*, 194–5; cf. Froissart, *Oeuvres*, 6:280.
[178] *Chron. Jean II et Charles V*, 262 (1 May); Delachenal, *Histoire de Charles V*, 2:198 n.3 (3 May). For the text of the treaty, see *RFH*, 3:1:202–9.
[179] Some idea of the county's value is given by M. Jusselin, "Comment la France se préparait à la guerre de cent ans," *Bibliothèque de l'école des chartes* 73 (1912), doc. III, which shows that Valois planners around 1331 expected to raise more (12,000 l.t.) from Rouergue for the financing of a Gascon campaign than from Maine, Anjou, Touraine, and Orléans combined. In a slightly earlier plan (doc. II), Rouergue was expected to provide well more than Quercy and Périgord combined.
[180] How these two changes should be balanced against one another is open to debate, but in my opinion – considering that the transfer of Rouergue, unlike the payment of the fourth million of the ransom, could be carried out more-or-less immediately, and so had the major advantage of being more a "bird in hand" – the Treaty of Brétigny was neither much more nor much less beneficial to the English than the First Treaty of London. (Cf. Prestwich, *Three Edwards*, 182; Le Patourel, "Treaty of Brétigny," 32, for contrary views.)
[181] As things worked out, for reasons that are still in debate, these last exchanges of renunciations (concerning sovereignty and the crown, and Scotland and Flanders) were never carried out, a fact which contributed greatly to the renewal of the war in 1369, but they never-

the Treaty of Brétigny. First, to what extent should it be reckoned a success for the English king? Second, how far should that success be attributed to the campaign of 1359–60, and to Edward III's strategic conduct of the war in general?[182]

The recent historiography of the subject has tended to answer these questions in a fashion most unfavorable to Edward III's reputation as a military commander.[183] Philippe Contamine claims that the Plantagenet accepted the Treaty of Brétigny "only to avoid a military disaster, which he believed to be imminent." Kenneth Fowler argues that the campaign was an expensive "failure of strategy" which had "achieved nothing." John Le Patourel, the first major proponent of this interpretation, went so far as to call the campaign a "great victory" for the dauphin's battle-avoiding strategy and to describe the treaty itself as "the measure of [Edward III's] fear, his disillusion, and the growing strength of the French government."[184]

Although there is a grain of truth to these evaluations, they are overall highly misleading. The campaign of 1359–60 was not exactly a defeat for Edward III, and still less was it a victory for the dauphin.[185] Yes, lack of supplies had forced the English to leave Paris after merely burning all the villages and farms surrounding the capital city – but the fact remains that there was an unchallenged English army laying waste to the heart of France, not a French army besieging London or ravaging Middlesex. There is no evidence whatsoever that the English were faced with "imminent disaster";[186] on the contrary, it is hard to

theless clearly should be considered as among the provisions of the treaty. On the need for separate renunciations relating to the Scottish issue, see PRO E30/164; *RFH*, 3:2:20–1.

182 The following paragraphs are based on Rogers, "Anglo-French Negotiations."

183 This view of the 1359 campaign is, moreover, not limited to recent writers: in J. E. Morris' view, the expedition was "a hopeless failure" (*Welsh Wars of Edward I*, 129–30); Edouard Perroy called it a "lamentable escapade" and concluded that "the failure for the Plantagenet was obvious." *Hundred Years War*, 138.

184 Contamine, *Guerre de Cent ans*, 47; Fowler, *King's Lieutenant*, 209–11; Le Patourel, "Edward III," 189 (cf. 177–8, 189: the military situation of May 1360 was "desperate"; "the treaty of Brétigny-Calais registers Edward's defeat"); idem, "Treaty of Brétigny," 32, 33 ("It was the French, then, who were victorious at Brétigny"). Tourneur-Aumont, similarly, says the Treaty of Brétigny "was a retraction, an avowal of weakness." *Bataille de Poitiers*, 390.

185 Compare Jean le Bel's rubric: "Vouz pouez cy veoir quelles marches du royaume de France le roy d'Angleterre gasta et raenchonna et combien de temps il y demoura sans estre empeschyé." *Le Bel*, 2:305; cf. 311–13; consider also Froissart, *Oeuvres*, 6:271–2, 279–80.

186 Le Patourel, "Treaty of Brétigny," 32. He gives no citation in support of this claim. Philippe Contamine supports his identical view (*Guerre de Cent ans*, 47), with a reference to the *Chron. des quat. prem. Valois*, 117 (as well as to Le Patourel), but that chronicle actually says only that his army was "half-starved" and that Edward was about to be compelled to leave France because of his lack of supplies – a statement also supported by *Knighton*, 2:112, who says that after Black Monday "oportuit necessario redire versus Angliam, sed deus transtulit miseriam necessitatis in honorem regiae majestatis." Other sources dispute this, however (e.g. *Le Bel*, 2:312; Walsingham, *Historia Anglicana*, 1:289), and in fact the army did not starve during the more than three weeks between Black Monday and the sealing of the

see how the French posed much threat even to the small and isolated garrisons which Edward had left scattered behind him like caltrops (many of which the French were unable to recover by force even after the conclusion of the treaty, having instead to buy out the occupying *routiers* with large cash payments[187]), much less to his main force. Indeed, some in England believed that the garrisons could within a short time have completed the conquest of France for King Edward, if he had been willing to let them.[188]

It is difficult to see how the dauphin could have stopped Edward from, at a minimum, plundering the as-yet unspoiled regions of Anjou and Maine and then returning to the Ile-de-France in the next autumn or spring. The best that Charles' Fabian strategy could accomplish was a stalemate, and it would be a stalemate almost unbearably painful for France to maintain, if it could be maintained at all.[189] The economy was collapsing, people were afraid to work the lands, and famine seemed imminent. As Froissart explained, wise men in the French court "worried that [France] could not bear such burdens much longer" and "would be in excessively great peril" if the war continued for the summer.[190] The English king's demonstration of the sorry fate in store for the French if they continued to resist him explains why the Treaty of Brétigny was, to a great extent at least, actually implemented, unlike the First Treaty of London which it otherwise closely resembled. If, as Lancaster said, the English might "lose in a day more than we have conquered in twenty years," that could only happen if the

---

peace, despite the logistic difficulties of staying relatively stationary. In any case, even if Edward had been forced to move into relatively untouched Beauce, Maine and Anjou, or even all the way to his bases in Brittany, that would not quite qualify as a "désastre militaire."

[187] Chaplais, "Documents . . . Brétigny," 18–19, 42–5; cf. *Le Bel*, 2:304.

[188] *Anonimalle*, 49: Because of the peace, many captains gave up their strongholds in accordance with Edward's orders, "a graunt perde et damage al roy Dengleterre et a ses heirs pur toutz iours, quare bien pres toute la communalte de Frauns fuist en subieccion et raunsoun a eux et si purroient les ditz captayns od lour gentz deinz brieff [temps] avoir conquis la roialme de Frauns al oeps le roy Dengleterre et ses heirs sil les voldroit avoir soeffre." Cf. Froissart, *Oeuvres*, 6:95: the regent earlier worried that "par tels gens se poroit perdre li royaulme de France dont il estoit hoirs." See also ibid., 271–2, 279–80.

[189] Froissart, *Oeuvres*, 6:279 ("Adont estoient en Paris li dus de Normendie [etc.] qui imaginoient bien le voiage dou roy d'Engleterre, et comment il et ses gens fouloient et apovirssoient le royaulme de France, et que ce ne se pooit longement tenir, ne souffrir, car les rentes des signeurs et des églises se perdoient généraument partout."); note also Jean's own statement that one reason for accepting the Treaty of Brétigny was the probability that the future would be worse for the French than the present [below, p. 420]; cf. also *Chron. Normande*, 149, 149 n.8.

[190] Froissart, *Oeuvres*, 6:271–2: "li dis royaummes estoit durement blechiés et grevés de cief en qor, se doubtoient que il ne peuist longement porter si grant fès, car on ne pooit aller en nulle marce dou royaumme de France qu'il n'y euist Englès ou Navarrois qui constraindoient si les bonnes villes, que nulle marchandise n'y pooit aller, ne venir, et ossi le plat pays que les terres demoroient en ries et les vignes à labourer, par quoy grant famine et grant chiereté de temps y apparoient"; 280: "il veoient le royaulme de France en si povre estat et si grevé que en trop grant péril il estoit, se il attendoient encores un esté."

[191] Le Patourel, "Edward III and the Kingdom of France," 178: "If, a year later, Edward was

dauphin chose to risk a major battle, and that would equally carry the chance for Edward to gain in a day what twenty years had not yet enabled him to win: the success of his bid for the crown. The Plantagenet was accepting a great and certain triumph in exchange for an even greater but uncertain possibility, a fact which reflects well on the 47-year-old king's wisdom. The Treaty of Brétigny did not give the Plantagenet everything he had hoped for, but it *did* give everything he had sought at the beginning of his war with France, and much more besides. To call it a defeat is comparable to arguing that the Germans "lost" the war of 1870–71 because the peace terms negotiated by Bismarck were less exacting than those sought by Moltke – except of course that no one in Germany remotely contemplated imposing conditions comparable to what Jean II and the dauphin agreed to surrender to Edward III. Weigh Alsace-Lorraine against Gascony, Ponthieu, Calais, Guînes, Saintonge, the Angoumois, Poitou, the Limousin, Périgord, the Agenais, Gaure, Bigorre, Quercy and Rouergue and it becomes evident just what sort of "overwhelming defeat"[191] the English had suffered in 1359–60.

Granted, as I think it has to be, that the Treaty of Brétigny set the seal on the victory of Edward III in his twenty-four year war with Valois France,[192] we still must return to the question of the fundamental cause of that victory. Sir Charles Oman again missed the essential unity of war and diplomacy when, on this subject, he wrote that

> The Peace of Bretigny was extorted from the French, not by reason of strategical successes, but rather through the desire of the captive King John to get back to his realm, and by the profound desire for peace at almost any price which was felt by a majority of his subjects. And so King Edward won, not by the sword but by the pen, the immense districts for which he surrendered his unreal claim to the royal crown of France.[193]

The historian was essentially correct when he attributed the French acceptance of the treaty to Jean's desire to escape captivity and the eager desire for peace of the French people.[194] The Valois king said much the same in his letters explaining the terms of the peace to his subjects, though with much more elaboration of the reasons for the populace's desperation for an end to the war:

---

prepared to give up his claim and his title for considerably less territory [than provided by the Second Treaty of London], this was due to the overwhelming defeat he had suffered in the winter of 1359–60."

192 It is legitimate to term the Treaty of Brétigny as ending a war rather than merely a phase of the "Hundred Years War" (a name of nineteenth-century origin: see Fowler, *Age of Plantagenet and Valois*, 13–15), since the treaty was intended as a final peace settlement rather than a truce arrangement. Consider the view of Sir Thomas Gray, who served on the 1359–60 campaign: "and thus the war was extinguished, on the said day and year, the which war had at that time lasted twenty-four years" [et ensi la guerre estanche le iour et lan susditz, quel guere auoit en le hour duree vint et qatre aunz]. *Scalacronica*, 196. Matteo Villani says almost the same thing: *M. Villani (Porta)*, 2:433; cf. also Venette, in *Nangis*, 309.

193 *History of the Art of War*, 2:196–7.

194 Cf. Froissart, *Oeuvres*, 6:272.

The wars which have lasted for a long time between our very dear lord and father formerly king of France, during his life, and after his decease between us on the one side and the King of England our brother, who claimed to have a right to the said realm, on the other side, have brought great damages not only to us and to you, but to all the people of our realm and of neighboring realms and to all Christendom, as you yourselves well know: for because of the said wars many mortal battles have been fought, people slaughtered, churches pillaged, bodies destroyed and souls lost, maids and virgins deflowered, respectable wives and widows dishonored, towns, manors and buildings burnt, and robberies, oppressions, and ambushes on the roads and highways committed. Justice has failed because of them, the Christian faith has chilled and commerce has perished, and so many other evils and horrible deeds have followed from these wars that they cannot be spoken, numbered or written . . . therefore, considering and thinking on the evils abovesaid – and that it seemed in truth that even greater [evils] could have followed in time to come – and that the world suffered so many anguishes and sorrows because of the said wars, and having pity and compassion on our good and loyal populace which so firmly and so loyally has held itself in true constancy and obedience towards us, exposing bodies and goods to all perils and without avoiding expenses and outlays, which we ought never to forget; we have therefore recently undertaken discussions and negotiations of peace. . . . In order to put an end to the wars and the evils and sorrows spoken of above, because of which the people have suffered such abuse, as is said above, more than for the deliverance of our person, and for the honor and the glory of the King of Kings and the Virgin Mary and for the reverence of the holy Church, of our holy father the Pope and his said nuncios, we have consented and do consent to, ratify, will and approve [this treaty of peace].[195]

The parallel with the preamble to the Treaty of Northampton is striking. The French in 1360, like the English in 1328, were ready to make peace even at the cost of extraordinary political concessions because that was the only way they could bring an end to the "killings, slaughters, crimes, destructions of churches, and ills innumerable" inflicted by the devastating *chevauchées* of a highly mobile, tactically superior army which could neither be trapped nor directly attacked and defeated. An added factor for the French monarchy was of course the captivity of the king himself, as Oman noted and Jean II admitted (in the process of downplaying its importance). The problem with the historian's formulation that Brétigny was won "not by the sword but by the pen" is, of course, that it was English *soldiers*, not English *diplomats*, who had made Jean a prisoner, won the mortal battles, slaughtered the people, burned the towns, manors and buildings, plundered and oppressed the common people, ruined France's economy, and destroyed the Valois ability to maintain good order, thus instilling the "desire for peace at almost any price" of which Oman speaks.

    War, as defined by Carl von Clausewitz, is "an act of violence intended to

---

[195] Bardonnet, *Procès-verbal de l'delivrance à Jean Chandos, commissaire du roi d'Angleterre, des places françaises abandonnées par le traité de Brétigny* (Niort: 1867), 136.

compel the enemy to fulfill our will," and, though there are many ways to this end, "the defeat and destruction of the enemy army is the surest commencement" for any of them.[196] Because the tactical superiority of the defense was even greater in the fourteenth century than in Clausewitz's day (when the philosopher of war still recognized it as "the stronger form of warfare"), however, the overthrow of a battle-shy enemy was a particularly difficult proposition. At first, after stubborn French support of Scottish independence pulled Edward into the war against the Valois, he tried to defeat his French adversaries just as he had defeated the Scots: by using a siege to draw them into decisive battle on his own terms. Despite the remarkable efforts Edward made to stretch the limits of medieval governance and finance, however, in 1339 and 1340 alike this approach failed in the face of Philip's resolute employment of a Vegetian battle-avoiding strategy. It was not until 1346, when the English king switched to a new strategy based on *chevauchées*, in which devastation served both to undermine the Valois government and to provoke the French to fight, that he succeeded in bringing the French to the general engagement he had so long sought and making that "surest commencement" of which Clausewitz wrote. By 1360, thanks to the repeated hammer-blows delivered in 1355, 1356, and 1359–60, the French had plumbed the depths of what Clausewitz termed "the worst state that a combatant can experience," the state of being disarmed.[197] "If we wish to compel the enemy to fulfill our will, we must impose on him a situation more disadvantageous than the sacrifice we demand of him."[198] The Treaty of Brétigny was signed and ratified by the French because, great as those sacrifices were, the current situation was worse, "considering and thinking on the evils abovesaid, and that it seemed in truth that even greater could have followed in time to come."[199]

Over the six centuries since, France has been so completely defeated only once: in 1940. For the humiliation of 1360 to have been inflicted on the mightiest realm in Christendom by a nation with only a fraction of her population and wealth, and which at the start of Edward III's reign had been considered a military backwater, her soldiers inferior even to the ill-equipped Scots, represents a martial accomplishment the likes of which very few men have ever matched.

This triumph owed much to Edward's command circle – the Black Prince and Henry of Lancaster, Suffolk and Warwick, Oxford and Huntingdon, Northampton and Beaumont, Chandos and Audley, Walter Mauny and Captal de Buch, and so many other bold and competent leaders – and much to his soldiers,

---

196 *Vom Kriege*, I.i.2 (pp. 89–90); VIII.iv (p. 875): "Was aber auch das Hauptverhältnis des Gegners sein mag . . . so bleibt doch die Besiegung und Zerstörung seiner Streitkraft der sicherste Anfang und in allen Fällen ein sehr wesentliches Stück."

197 *Vom Kriege*, I.i.4 (p. 92).

198 Note 1, above.

199 Cf. *Vom Kriege*, I.i.4 (p. 92): "die Nachteile dieser Lage dürfen aber natürlich, wenigstens dem Anscheine nach, nicht vorübergehend sein, sonst würde der Gegner den besseren Zeitpunkt abwarten und nicht nachgeben."

his rock-solid men-at-arms and his lethal longbowmen. But, as this study has shown, much of the credit for the successful prosecution of the war is due directly to Edward III, who consistently pursued a strategy balancing siege, devastation and pursuit of battle which, if simple, was fundamentally sound. His enemies, with some justification, considered him "the wisest and shrewdest warrior in the world."[200] Not only did the king guide the war effort intelligently, he inspired those who helped him fight it with some of his own spirit of confident, chivalric boldness combined with pragmatic realism. More than any other's, the Treaty of Brétigny was *his* victory.

[200] *Chron. des quat. prem. Valois*, 114: "le plus sage guerroier du monde et le plus soubtil." The latter adjective can also mean clever or skillful. Cf. the opinion of Edward Balliol: "qui alios principes in strenuitate praecellit." Charter in *Avesbury*, 452.

APPENDIX

The Strength of the Army
at La Hougue, 1346

In the absence of detailed pay records, it is impossible to determine with any certainty the strength of the English army at the time Edward III landed in France in 1346, but there is enough information available to make an educated guess. My best estimate is that it comprised, in round figures, 2,700 men-at-arms, 2,300 Welsh spearmen, 7,000 foot archers (English and Welsh) and 3,250 mounted archers, hobelars, and other troops, for a total of about 15,250 men.

These figures are based primarily on the summary of Walter Wetewang's lost wardrobe book, as published in Wrottesley's *Crécy and Calais*. (There are also other versions of these abstracts published elsewhere; their value and the problems of using the Wetewang abstracts have been well discussed by Andrew Ayton.)[1] Although this record has often been presented as giving a "snapshot" of Edward's army at a particular time at the siege of Calais, in fact it includes everyone who served at any point over the sixteen-month expedition, and in some cases counts them twice if they served in two different retinues. This record, in other words, includes all the retinues who served only at Calais as well as those who served from the start of the campaign, and since it does not give the information on dates of service found in a full account, it is impossible to know just who served when.[2] To make a rough estimate, I have assumed that the retinues were at their maximum strength at the start of their service, and that that is the number listed in the Wetewang abstracts; this assumption could certainly be questioned, but I think it is probably fairly close to correct.[3]

To estimate the strength of the army at La Hougue, it is necessary to eliminate the retinues which were created or joined the army only after the end of the *chevauchée* through France. Of the magnates, I exclude the retinues of

---

1   Ayton, "English Army and the Normandy Campaign."
2   This fact will be easily understood by anyone who has worked with the other Wardrobe wage accounts. The list of retinues cannot represent a particular time, since it includes people who were never in the army at the same point. Ayton, "English Army and the Normandy Campaign," 267–8.
3   Over the full period of the expedition, the *average* strength of the army was only about one-third of the full total of 32,000 troops given, in cost terms; this can be calculated simply by calculating the daily wage bill for the roster given in the summary total of the Wetewang accounts as printed in Wrottesley or Grose, multiplying by the number of days in the expedition, and then dividing by the actual wage cost of £127,201 2s. 9½d. given in one version of the abstracts (Grose, *Military Antiquities*, 278). The army strength at La Hougue was, thus, certainly well above the average strength, and probably its maximum strength, since many troops returned to England early in the siege.

Lancaster and Pembroke (in Gascony at the time of the landing), Stafford (probably in Gascony)[4] and Kildare (who was in Ireland).[5] The lists of the leaders of the English army given in the *Acts of War* and the *Chronicle of St. Omer* enable us to determine that most of the simple bannerets' retinues listed in Wetewang's accounts were already present from the landing at La Hougue.[6] The exceptions are Walter Mauny (in Gascony), Hugh Hastings (in Flanders), John Montgomery and John Maltravers (probably in Flanders),[7] Thomas Lathom, and the last seven retinues listed in this section: John Howard, John de Louedale of Brabant, Fulk de la Freiyne of Ireland, William de Groucy (of Normandy), Ogier de Montaut, Sire de Mussidan, Peter of Spain, and Henry of Flanders. Of these, there is some evidence which hints that Howard and Lathom may have been present for the *chevauchée*,[8] but I have still excluded them because that evidence is not strong, they not listed in the *Acts of War* or *Chron. St. Omer* rosters, and I prefer to err on the side of smaller numbers. Groucy I retain in the total because stronger evidence indicates that his contingent was with the king from early in the *chevauchée*.[9] The others I exclude for the same reason as Howard and Lathom (also, Henry of Flanders was presumably with Hastings in Flanders, and de la Freiyne definitely came later with Kildare).[10]

For the knights serving as independent heads of retinue, it is apparent that a number of those listed, particularly towards the end of the list, only took on their role as heads of retinue late in the campaign, when their earlier captain died or returned to England (e.g. Adam de Asshehurst from the retinue of the deceased William de Kildesby, or William Marmion from the Bishop of Durham's

---

[4] Wrottesley, *Crecy and Calais*, 156 [Middelnye], and note that Stafford is not in the leaders' lists in *Acts of War* and *Chron St. Omer*, but to the contrary cf. Wrottesley, *Crecy and Calais*, 186 [Daundeville]; *Le Bel*, 2:105.

[5] Wrottesley, *Crecy and Calais*, 183.

[6] *Acts of War*, 29; related list in *Chron. St. Omer*, fos 261v–62. These lists also make it possible to identify nearly all the bannerets who were present but not heads of their own retinues; this fact minimizes the risk that the banneret heads-of-retinue assumed the latter status only after the *chevauchée* with the break-up of larger retinues of which they had been part.

[7] Montgomery: Wrottesley, *Crecy and Calais*, 173 (Bruyn), 171, and Sumption, *Trial by Battle*, 498; but he is said by the *Chron St. Omer* to have been present with the army at Crécy. Maltravers: the *younger* John Maltravers was on the *chevauchée* in the retinue of Richard Talbot, and was not a banneret (since Talbot's retinue included no other bannerets); therefore the head of retinue was probably the *elder*; he had been banished and was given permission to return to England during the siege of Calais; thus he was not in England at the start of the campaign and cannot have sailed with the fleet. Wrottesley, *Crecy and Calais*, 130, 98, 194 (younger); 267, 195 (elder).

[8] See Wrottesley, *Crecy and Calais*, 186 (Howard), which may however be referring to a period rather than to the location of service, as is pretty clearly the case for Thomas of Haukestone (below, note 12). Lathom in late June was described as "about to set out with the King," (Wrottesley, *Crecy and Calais*, 89, and cf. 94), but the same had been said of Hugh Hastings (ibid., 97) who went to Flanders. The placement of Lathom's name in ibid., pp. 206 and 197, may suggest he went to Flanders with Hastings, Montgomery and Maltravers.

[9] Ibid., 148.

[10] Ibid., 183.

retinue)[11] or when they brought reinforcements from England to Calais, as Thomas de Haukestone did in January 1347.[12] It is likely that all the Calais-only retinues were listed after the full-campaign retinues; the question is then where in the list the former begin and the latter stop. A good guess is that the break-point comes at John de Cobham, who seems to have joined the siege of Calais late,[13] and whose retinue sticks out for its large size after much smaller retinues. I have therefore counted in my estimate the simple knights' retinues only from Sir William de Warenne (whose presence at Crécy, incidentally, is testified to by the *Chron. St. Omer*'s list) to John Ward. This is admittedly only a guess, but the numbers involved in this section are in any case not large, so an incorrect guess here does not change the broad picture.

The next section of the Wetewang abstract deals with the officers of the household; I have included the full retinues for Wetewang, Thoresby, Weston and Kildesby, but not Islip, who was in England until after the start of the siege. These units in total amount to 166 men-at-arms, 169 mounted archers, and 11 foot archers.[14] In the retinues of the Controller of the Household and of William atte Woode, including the household esquires and the king's archers, I count 235 men-at-arms, 438 mounted archers (and sergeants-at-arms and paunceners), and 52 foot archers.[15]

The grand total for all these retinues amounts to 2,650 men-at-arms,

---

11 See ibid., 85, 200 (Asshehurst); 141, 201 (Marmion); similarly Philip le Despenser (ibid., 87, 201) and Thomas Colville (101, 200).

12 Thomas de Haukestone may have begun the campaign with the king, but if so returned early (perhaps with Huntingdon). Wrottesley, *Crecy and Calais*, 139, 176. He was in England at the time of Crécy, then served as marshal for a small army of reinforcements brought to Calais. *RFH*, 2:4:204; Wrottesley, *Crecy and Calais*, 112. His own retinue of 49 men apparently served at Calais only from January 1347 (Wrottesley, *Crecy and Calais*, 176); this group was probably part of the army for which he was marshal, which is probably the same as the 715 men who appear under his name in the *Brut* version of Wetewang's accounts (*English Brut*, 540).

It seems from the numbers (which match fairly closely though not precisely) that the combination of the Haukestone contingent and the Ward contingent in the *Brut* list are the same as the combined categories "de servitio" through "archers from counties" in the Wrottesley version. This total apparently comprises three main groups: the arrayed contingents that crossed to La Hougue with the king; Haukestone's small reinforcing army; and the large number of foot archers arrayed for the siege. It seems that the "archers from counties" section in the Wetewang version probably refers only to the last group, since the 4,502 foot archers in the "Other English Soldiers" group must be mostly archers from the counties too. But the "Other English Soldiers" group does seem to include Haukestone's force as well as those present from the start of the campaign, so to get the initial strength of arrayed troops I have added the categories from "de servitio" through "Other English Soldiers" (in Wrottesley) and then deducted the strength of Haukestone's force (based on the *English Brut*).

13 Wrottesley, *Crecy and Calais*, 135.

14 *RFH*, 2:4:202 (Islip); Wrottesley, *Crecy and Calais*, 201–2; *English Brut*, 540, for Weston; he and Kildesby and Thoresby and Wetewang are all listed among the bannerets in the *Acts of War*'s list, and from Wrottesley, *Crecy and Calais*, 151, it appears that Weston's unit was independent.

15 Wrottesley, *Crecy and Calais*, 201–3; cf. *English Brut*, 539–40.

including 651 knights of all degrees (excluding clerks). The same units also include 2,476 mounted archers, hobelars, etc., and 192 foot archers.[16]

My estimate for the number of Welsh spearmen derives from simpler calculations. About 7,000 Welshmen were summoned for the campaign,[17] so it is easily credible that the 4,580 Welsh troops reported in the Wetewang abstracts (not counting the Prince of Wales' retinue contingent) actually participated in the campaign from its inception.[18] I have figured half the Welshmen as archers, and half as spearmen, which is how they were summoned for this campaign.

The figure of 3,250 for mounted archers (etc.) is the total of 2,476 from the retinues, plus 194 "de servitio," 362 from the cities (all hobelars), and 531 from the "Other English Soldiers" category (including the 109 crossbowmen), less the 313 who probably came in Haukestone's force in January.[19] The equivalent calculations for the foot archers, with the addition of half the Welshmen, produce a total of 7,003.[20]

The grand total in my estimates of 5,295 English, non-retinue archers, hobelars, etc., matches well with the government's orders to raise 5,773 men, mostly foot archers, from the shires and cities for the start of the campaign, though it would indicate a somewhat surprisingly high level of success in meeting quotas.

Note that the totals thus calculated match passably well with Jean le Bel's estimate of 4,000 men-at-arms, 3,000 Welshmen, and 10,000 archers.[21]

---

[16] The chronicles, however, tend to support a higher figure, of 3,000–4,000, for the men-at-arms: Hocsem, *Chronique*, 345 (3,000); *Le Bel*, 2:105–6 (4,000), and the *Storie Pistoresi*, 222 (4,000).

[17] Ayton, "English Army and the Normandy Campaign," 261–2.

[18] Wrottesley, *Crecy and Calais*, 193, 199, 203–4; counting the 8 Welshmen in Sir William de Warenne's retinue, but not the 513 Welshmen listed in the Prince of Wales' retinue, who were probably later reinforcements; cf. Wrottesley, *Crecy and Calais*, 129.

[19] Wrottesley, *Crecy and Calais*, 203; for Haukestone, *English Brut*, 540, and note 12, above.

[20] For the reasons given in note 12, above, I have not included any of the 10,806 foot archers listed in the separate "from the counties" heading, presuming that these were reinforcements brought during the siege. I have also not counted any of the 862 troops listed under the headings of Netherlanders, "Overlanders," Hainaulters, or Lorrainers, whom I guess to belong only to the siege, though this is certainly open to question. The centenars and vintenars of the "Other English Soldiers" category were counted as foot archers.

[21] *Le Bel*, 2:105–6.

BIBLIOGRAPHY

This bibliography lists primarily works which are cited in the notes. Many works which, though not cited in the notes, contributed to the author's background understanding of the period and events covered in this book (for example the various studies of the cost or distant origins of the Hundred Years War, or works and sources dealing with the English intervention in Iberia under Edward III, studies of Edward I's or Henry V's wars, books on medieval military technology, etc.), have been excluded. However, a few particularly noteworthy or relevant publications have been included even if never specifically cited in the notes.

Many of the chronicles and documentary collections in the notes are cited using abbreviated notations (e.g. *RFH* or *Le Muisit*), for which see the list on pp. xiv–xviii. For a number of works, more than one edition is listed here and used in the notes. The fact that an older edition is referred to in some places, rather than a newer edition, should not be taken to imply that the older edition was considered superior. Rather, the use of multiple editions usually reflects the fact that the research for this book was undertaken over eight years in several different cities, with access to different libraries.

I. Unpublished Documentary Sources

Documents from the following record classes in the Public Record Office, London, are cited in this book:

C47	Chancery Miscellanea
C49	Chancery and Exchequer: Parliamentary and Council Proceedings
C61	Gascon Rolls
C66	Patent Rolls
C81	Warrants for the Great Seal
E101	Exchequer, Accounts Various
E372	Exchequer, Pipe Rolls
E359	Exchequer, Lord Treasurer's Remembrancer, Enrolled Lay Subsidies
PRO31	Roman Transcripts
SC1	Ancient Correspondence

Various documents from the collection of the British Library have also been used. The most important by far is the Wardrobe account book of Robert Ferriby, 1334–1337. BL MS Cotton Nero C VIII.

II. Unpublished Chronicles

London, British Library

Additional MS 18462. Fifteenth-century copy of the French *Brut* to Halidon Hill.

Cottonian MS Caligula A XIII and Harleian MS 624. *Chronica Monasterii de Pipwell*. Citations are to the earlier Caligula MS.

Cottonian MS Cleopatra D III. A later redaction of the French *Brut*, similar to the English version.

Cottonian MS Faustina B V. The *Historia Roffensis*, attributed to William of Dene. [An edition is currently under preparation by Dr. Mark Buck.]

Cottonian MS Tiberius A VI. Epitome of the Chronicle of William de Packington, Clerk and Treasurer of the Black Prince's Household in Gascony.

Royal MS 20 A XVIII. Long *Brut* continuation in French, 1307–1329.

Oxford, Bodleian Library
MS 240. *Historia Aurea.*

Oxford, Corpus Christi College Library
MS 78. A *Brut* continuation, unconnected to any published version for our period.

Paris, Bibliothèque Nationale
MS Fr. 693, fos 248–79v. An anonymous chronicle related to the garrison of St. Omer, covering the years 1342–1347. [I am currently working on an edition of this chronicle.]

MS Fr. 693, fos 155–66. A second continuation, for 1339–1346, of the *Manuel d'histoire de Philippe VI*.

III. Printed Documentary Sources

Benoit XII (1334–1342). Lettres closes, patentes et curiales se rapportant à la France, ed. Georges Daumet. Paris: Bibliothèque des écoles française d'Athènes et de Rome, 1920.

Bock, F. (ed.) *Das deutsch-englische Bundniss von 1335–1342: Quellen*. München: C. H. Beck'she Verlag, 1956.

Bock, F. "Some New Documents Illustrating the Early Years of the Hundred Years' War." *Bulletin of the John Rylands Library* 15 (1931).

Calendar of Documents Relating to Scotland, ed. Joseph Bain. Edinburgh: HMSO, 1887.

Calendars of the Close Rolls (London: HMSO, 1892–1945).

Calendars of the Patent Rolls (London: HMSO, 1891–1942).

Carolus-Barré, L. "Benoit XII et la mission charitable de Bertrand Carit dans les pays devastées du nord de la France. Cambrésis, Vermandois, Thiérache. 1340." *Mélanges d'archéologie et d'histoire* 62 (1950).

Cartulaire et Archives des communes de l'ancien diocèse . . . de Carcassonne, ed. M. Mahul. Paris: Didron, 1863.

Cazelles, R. "Lettres closes, lettres 'de par le roy' de Philippe de Valois." *Annuaire-bulletin de la Société de l'histoire de France* (1958).

Chaplais, P. *English Medieval Diplomatic Practice. Part I, Documents and Interpretation*. London: HMSO, 1982.

Chaplais, P. "Some Documents Regarding the Fulfilment and Interpretation of the Treaty of Brétigny (1361–1369)." *Camden Miscellany, Vol. XIX*. Camden Society, 3rd ser., 80 (1952).

Chaplais, P. *The War of Saint-Sardos, 1323–5*. Camden Society, 3rd ser., LXXXVII (1954).

Chartulary of Winchester Cathedral, ed. and tr. A. W. Goodman. Winchester: Warren & Son, Ltd., 1927.

The Controversy between Sir Richard Scrope and Sir Robert Grosvenor in the Court of Chivalry, ed. Sir N. H. Nicolas. London: Samuel Bentley, 1832.

Delpit, J. *Collection générale des documents français qui se trouvent en Angleterre*. Reprint of 1847 edition. Geneva: Slatkin, 1971.

Devon, F. *Issues of the Exchequer, Henry III to Henry VI, from the Pell Records*. London: J. Murray, 1837.

Dorat, Y. *et al*. (eds) *Le Languedoc et le Rouergue dans le Trésor des Chartes*. Paris: CTHS, 1983.

Ellis, H. (ed.) *Original Letters Illustrative of English History*, 3rd series. London: R. Bentley, 1846.

Exchequer Rolls of Scotland. Vol. 1: 1264–1359, eds J. Stuart and G. Burnett. Edinburgh: HMSO, 1878.

Foedera, conventiones, litterae etc., ed. Thomas Rymer. The Hague, 1739–45.

Foedera, conventiones, litterae etc., ed. Thomas Rymer, revised edn by A. Clarke, F. Holbrooke and J. Coley. London: Record Commission, 1816–69. [Note: For a concordance between the two editions, see Hardy, T. D. *Syllabus (in English) of . . . Rymer's Foedera*, vol. I. London: Longman's, Green & Co., 1869.]

François de Monte-Belluna. "Le *Tragicum argumentum de miserabili statu regni Francie* de François de Monte-Belluna (1357)," ed. A. Vernet. *Annuaire-bulletin de la Société de l'histoire de France* (1962–3).

Het Gemeenteleger van Brugge van 1338 tot 1340 en de Namen van de weerbare Mannen, ed. J. F. Verbruggen. Brussels: Commission Royale d'Histoire, 1962.

Germain, A. "Projet de descente en Engleterre . . ." *Publications de la Société archéologique de Montpellier* 26 (1858).

Grose, Francis. *Military Antiquities Respecting a History of the English Army*. London: T. Egerton, 1801.

Historical Papers and Letters from the Northern Registers, ed. J. Rain. London: Rolls Series, 1873.

Jassemin, M. "Les papiers de Mile de Noyers." *Bulletin philologique et historique du comité des travaux scientifiques*, an. 1918 (1920).

Les Journaux du trésor de Philippe VI de Valois, suivis de l'ordinarium thesauri de 1338–1339, ed. Jules Viard. Paris: Imprimerie Nationale, 1899.

Jurades de la ville d'Agen (1345–55), ed. Adolphe Magen. Auch: Cocharaux, 1894. [= *Archives Historiques de l'Agenais*, tome 1er.]

Jusselin, M. "Comment la France se préparait à la guerre de Cent ans." *Bibliothèque de l'école des chartes* 73 (1912).

Laurence Minot. "Songs on King Edward's Wars." In Thomas Wright (ed.) *Political Poems and Songs Relating to English History Composed during the Period from the Accession of Edward III to that of Richard III*. London: Rolls Series, 1859–61.

Laurent, Henri. *Actes et documents anciens intéressant la Belgique conservés aux archives de l'état à Vienne, 1196–1356.* Brussels: Lamertin, 1933.

Miret y Sens, J. "Lettres closes des premiers Valois." *Moyen Âge* 20 (1917–18).

Moranvillé, H. "Rapports à Philppe VI sur l'état de ses finances," *Bibliothèque de l'École des chartes* 48 (1877).

Northern Petitions Illustrative of Life in Berwick, Cumbria and Durham in the Fourteenth Century, ed. C. M. Fraser. Gateshead, Northumberland: Surtees Society, 1981.

Nijhoff, I. A. *Gedenkwaardigheden uit de Geschiedenis van Gelderland,* vol. I. Arnhem: P. Nijhoff, 1830.

Pierre Dubois. *Summaria brevis et compendiosa doctrina felicis expedicionis et abbreviacionis guerrarum ac litium regni Francorum,* ed. Hellmut Kämpf. Berlin: Teubner, 1936.

Quicherat, J. "Récit des tribulations d'un religieux du diocèse de Sens pendant l'invasion Anglaise de 1358." *Bibliothèque de l'école des chartes* 3e ser., 4 (1857).

Register of Edward, the Black Prince, ed. M. C. B. Dawes. London: HMSO, 1930–1933.

Registres du Trésor des Chartes, eds J. Viard and A. Vallée. Paris: Archives Nationales, 1979–84.

Riley, H. T. *Memorials of London and London Life in the XIIIth, XIVth, and XVth Centuries, 1276–1419.* London: Longman's, 1868.

Rotuli Parliamentorum, vol. II, ed. J. Strachey *et al.* London: Record Commission, 1783.

Rotuli Scotiae in Turri Londinensi et in Domo Capitulari Westmonasteriensi asservati, vol. I: Edward I – Edward III. Ed. David Macpherson. London: Record Commission, 1814.

Stevenson, J. (ed.) *Letters and Papers Illustrative of the Wars of the English in France during the Reign of Henry the Sixth, King of England.* London: Rolls Series, 1861–4.

Stones, E. L. G. *Anglo-Scottish Relations 1174–1328: Some Selected Documents.* London: Nelson, 1965.

Timbal, P.-C. (ed.) *La guerre de cent ans vue à travers les registres du Parlement (1337–1369).* Paris: Centre national de la recherche scientifique, 1961.

Treaty Rolls. Vol. II, 1337–1339, ed. John Ferguson. London: HMSO, 1972.

The Wardrobe Book of William de Norwell, 12 July 1338 to 27 May 1340, ed. Mary Lyon *et al.* Brussels: Commission Royale d'Histoire, 1983.

Wright, Thomas (ed.) *Political Poems and Songs Relating to English History Composed during the Period from the Accession of Edward III to that of Richard III.* London: Rolls Series, 1859–61.

Wrottesley, G. *Crecy and Calais from the Public Records.* London: Harrison and Sons, 1898.

IV. Printed Chronicles (and miscellaneous primary sources)

"1339 Campaign Diary." In Jean Froissart, *Oeuvres*, ed. Kervyn de Lettenhove. Bruxelles, 1870 etc. Reprint, Osnabrück: Biblio Verlag, 1967. Vol. 18, 84–96.

Acta Bellicosa. In J. Moisant, *Le Prince Noir en Aquitaine, 1355–6, 1362–70*. Paris: Picard, 1894.

Acts of War of Edward III. In Richard Barber (ed.) *The Life and Campaigns of the Black Prince*. Woodbridge: The Boydell Press, 1986. [Translation of *Acta Bellicosa*.]

Adam Murimuth. *Adae Murimuth. Continuatio Chronicarum*, ed. E. M. Thompson. London: Rolls Series, 1889.

Andrew of Wyntoun. *Orygynale Cronykil of Scotland*, ed. David Lang. Edinburgh: Edmonston and Douglas, 1872.

Annales Gandenses, ed. and tr. H. Johnstone. London: Nelson, 1951. Reprint, Oxford: Clarendon, 1985.

Annales Paulini. In W. Stubbs (ed.), *Chronicles of the Reign of Edward I and Edward II*, vol. I. London: Rolls Series, 1882.

The Anonimalle Chronicle 1307–1334, ed. Wendy R. Childs and John Taylor. York: Yorkshire Archaeological Society [Record Series vol. CXLVII], 1991.

Anonimalle Chronicle 1333–1381, ed. V. H. Galbraith. Manchester: Manchester U.P., 1927.

Barber, Richard (ed. and tr.) *The Life and Campaigns of the Black Prince*. Woodbridge: The Boydell Press, 1986.

The Book of Pluscarden [Historians of Scotland, v. X], ed. and tr. Felix J. H. Skene. Edinburgh: William Patterson, 1890.

The Brut or the Chronicle of England, ed. F. W. Brie. London: Early English Text Society, 1906–8.

Chandos Herald. *The Black Prince by Chandos Herald*, ed. H. A. Coxe. Roxburghe Club, 1842.

Chandos Herald. *La Vie du Prince Noir*, ed. Diana B. Tyson. Tübingen: Max Niemeyer Verlag, 1975.

Christine di Pisan. *The Book of Fayttes of Armes and of Chyvalrye*. London: Early English Text Society, 1932.

A Chronicle of London, 1089–1483. London: Longman, 1827.

Chonicon Angliae ab anno Domini 1328 usque ad annum 1388, auctore monacho quodam Sancti Albani, ed. E. M. Thompson. London: Rolls Series, 1874.

Chronicon comitum Flandrensium, in J. J. de Smet, ed. *Corpus Chronicorum Flandriae*, vol. I. Brussels: Commision Royale d'Histoire, 1837.

Chronicon de Lanercost, MCCI–MCCCXLVI, ed. J. Stevenson. Edinburgh: The Bannatyne Club, 1839.

Chronicon Domini Walteri de Hemingburgh, ed. H. C. Hamilton. London: English Historical Society, 1849. [Includes continuations of Guisborough's chronicle.]

Chronique des Pays-Bays, de France, d'Angleterre et de Tournai. In J. J. de Smet (ed.), *Corpus Chronicorum Flandriae*, vol. III. Brussels: Commission Royale d'Histoire, 1856.

Chronique des quatre premiers Valois (1327–1393), ed. Siméon Luce. Paris: Société de l'histoire de France, 1862.

Chronique Normande du XIVe siècle, eds A. and E. Molinier. Paris: Société de l'histoire de France, 1882.

Chronographia regum Francorum, ed. H. Moranvillé. Paris: Société de l'histoire de France, 1891–7.

Edmond Dynter. *Chronique des Ducs de Brabant*, ed. P. F. X. de Ram. Brussels, 1854–60.

Eulogium historiarum, ed. F. S. Haydon. London: Rolls Series, 1858–63.

French Chronicle of London, ed. G. J. Aungier. Camden Society, XXVIII (1844).

Galbraith, V. H. "Extracts from the Historia Aurea and a French Brut (1317–47)." *English Historical Review* XLIII (1948).

Geoffrey le Baker. *Chronicon*, ed. E. M. Thompson. Oxford: Clarendon, 1889.

Gesta Edwardi Tertii Auctore Canonico Bridlingtonensi. In W. Stubbs (ed.) *Chronicles of the Reigns of Edward I and Edward II*, vol. II. London: Rolls Series, 1883.

Gilles le Muisit. *Chronique et Annales*, ed. H. Lemaître. Paris: Société de l'histoire de France, 1906.

Giovanni Villani. *Cronica*. In Roberto Palmarocchi (ed.) *Cronisti del Trecento*. Milan: Rizzoli, 1935.

Grandes chroniques de France, ed. Jules Viard. Paris: Société de l'histoire de France, 1920–53.

Guillaume de Nangis *et al. Chronique Latine de Guillaume de Nangis de 1113 à 1300, avec les continuations de cette chronique de 1300 à 1368*, ed. H. Géraud. Paris: Société de l'histoire de France, 1843.

Hellot, A. "Chronique parisienne anonyme de 1316 à 1339, précédée d'additions à la chronique française dite de Guillaume de Nangis." *Mémoires de la Société de l'histoire de Paris et de l'Ile-de-France* XI (1884).

Henry Knighton. *Chronicon*, ed. J. R. Lumby. London: Rolls Series, 1895.

Henry Knighton. *Knighton's Chronicle, 1337–1396*, ed. and tr. G. H. Martin. Oxford: Oxford Medieval Texts, 1995.

Istore et croniqes de Flandres, ed. Kervyn de Lettenhove. Brussels: F. Hayez, 1879–80.

Jan de Klerk (a.k.a. Boendale). "Edouard III, roi d'Angleterre, en Flandre," tr. Octave Delpierre. In *Miscellanies of the Philobiblon Society* 10 (1867). [French translation of *Van den Derden Eduwaert*.]

Jan de Klerk (a.k.a. Boendale). *Van den Derden Eduwaert*, ed. J. G. Heymans. Nijmegen: ALFA, 1983.

Jean Cabaret. *La Chronique du Bon Duc Loys de Bourbon*, ed. A. M. Chazaud. Paris: Société de l'histoire de France, 1876.

Jean de Bueil. *Le Jouvencel*, ed. Léon Lecestre. Paris: Société de l'histoire de France, 1887.

Jean de Hocsem. *La Chronique de Jean de Hocsem*, ed. Godefroid Kurth. Brussels: Commission Royale d'Histoire, 1927.

Jean de Venette. *The Chronicle of Jean de Venette*, tr. J. Birdsall, ed. R. A. Newhall. New York: Columbia University Press, 1953.

Jean Froissart. *Chroniques*, ed. Siméon Luce *et al.* Paris: Société de l'histoire de France, 1869–1957. [NB: citations to Froissart, *Chroniques*, are to this edition; citations to Froissart, *Oeuvres*, are to the Kervyn de Lettenhove edition.]

Jean Froissart. *Oeuvres*, ed. Kervyn de Lettenhove. Bruxelles, 1870 etc. Reprint, Osnabrück: Biblio Verlag, 1967.

Jean le Bel. *Chronique de Jean le Bel*, eds Jules Viard and Eugène Déprez. Paris: Société de l'histoire de France, 1904.

John Barbour. *The Bruce*, ed. A. A. M. Duncan. Edinburgh: Cannongate Classics, 1997.

John of Fordun, *Chronica Gentis Scotorum* [Historians of Scotland, v. I], ed. William F. Skene. Edinburgh: Edmonston and Douglas, 1871.

John of Fordun. *John of Fordun's Chronicle of the Scottish Nation* [Historians of Scotland, v. IV], ed. W. F. Skene, tr. F. J. H. Skene. Edinburgh: Edmonston and Douglas, 1872.

John Fortescue. *De Laudibus Legum Anglie*, ed. and tr. S. B. Chrimes. Cambridge: CUP, 1942.

John of Reading. *Chronica Johannis de Reading et anonymi Cantuariensis, 1346–1367*, ed. J. Tait. Manchester: Manchester U.P., 1914.

Liber Pluscardensis [Historians of Scotland,vol. VII], ed. Felix J. H. Skene. Edinburgh: William Patterson, 1877.

Matteo Villani. *Cronica*. In Roberto Palmarocchi, ed. *Cronisti del Trecento*. Milan: Rizzoli, 1935.

Matteo Villani, *Cronica*, ed. G. Porta. Parma: Fondazione Pietro Bembo, 1995.

Récits d'un Bourgeois de Valenciennes, ed. Kervyn de Lettenhove. Louvain: Lefever, 1877.

Richard Lescot. *Chronique (1328–1344), suivie de la continuation de cette chronique (1344–1364)*, ed. J. Lemoine. Paris: Société de l'histoire de France, 1896.

Robert Avesbury. *De Gestis Mirabilibus Regis Edwardi Tertii*, ed. E. M Thompson. London: Rolls Series, 1889.

Rogers, Clifford J. "A Continuation of the *Manuel d'histoire de Philippe VI* for the Years 1328–39." *English Historical Review* 114 (1999).

Rogers, Clifford J. and Mark Buck. "Three New Accounts of the Neville's Cross Campaign." *Northern History* 34 (1998).

Rogers, Clifford J. "An Unknown News Bulletin from the Siege of Tournai in 1340." *War in History* 5 (1998).

Stewart, William. *The Buik of the Croniclis of Scotland; or a metrical version of the history of Hector Boece*. London: Rolls Series, 1858. [All citations are to volume 3.]

Storie Pistoresi (MCCC–MCCCXLVIII) (*Rerum Italiacarum Scriptores*, XI, vol. 5). ed. L. A. Muratori. Città di Castello, 1907.

Sun Tzu. *Sun Tzu. The Art of War*, ed. and tr. Samuel B. Griffith. Oxford: Oxford U.P., 1971.

Taylor, John. "A Wigmore Chronicle, 1355–77." *Proc. of the Leeds Phil. and Lit. Soc.; Lit. and Hist. Section* 11 (1964–6).

Thomas Burton. *Chronica Monasterii de Melsa*, ed. E. A. Bond. London: Rolls Series, 1866–8.

Thomas Gray. *Scalacronica*, ed. and trans. Sir Herbert Maxwell. Glasgow: James Maclehose & Sons, 1907.

Thomas Gray. *Scalacronica*, ed. Joseph Stevenson. Edinburgh: The Maitland Club, 1836. [Citations in text are to this edition unless otherwise noted.]

Thomas Walsingham. *Historia Anglicana*, ed. H. T. Riley. London: Rolls Series, 1863.

Tournai Chronicles. In Jean Froissart, *Oeuvres*, ed. Kervyn de Lettenhove. Bruxelles, 1870 etc. Reprint, Osnabrück: Biblio Verlag, 1967. Vol. 25, 344–65.

Vegetius (Flavius Vegetius Renatus). *The Earliest English Translation of Vegetius'*

De Re Militari, ed. Geoffrey Lester. Heidelberg: Carl Winter Universitätsverlag, 1988.

Walter Bower. *Scottichronicon*, ed. D. E. R. Watt *et al.* Aberdeen: University of Aberdeen Press, 1987–1996. [All citations are to vol. 7.]

V. Secondary Sources

Note: Among the many secondary sources cited here, a few deserve special note as providing excellent narratives of Edward III's campaigns and diplomacy, often in greater detail than given in this book. For the Scottish wars before 1337, see Nicholson, *Edward III and the Scots*. For 1328–1342, see Déprez, *Les Préliminaires de la Guerre de Cent Ans* and Lucas, *The Low Countries and the Hundred Years War*. For the period 1328–1346, Sumption, *Trial by Battle*, is very useful. Kenneth Fowler, *The King's Lieutenant*, is particularly valuable for the period after 1344. Delachenal's *Histoire de Charles V* is indispensable for the last decade covered in this work. Some of these works are quite old, but they are thoroughly documented and grounded in the primary sources, which makes their value timeless.

Aberth, John. *Criminal Churchmen in the Age of Edward III : the Case of Bishop Thomas de Lisle.* University Park, Pa. : Pennsylvania State University Press, 1996.

Allmand, Christopher. *The Hundred Years War.* Cambridge: Cambridge U.P., 1988.

Allmand, C. T. "The War and the Non-Combatant." In Kenneth Fowler (ed.) *The Hundred Years War.* London: Macmillan, 1971.

Autrand, Françoise. "La déconfiture. La bataille de Poitiers (1356) à travers quelques textes français des XIVe et XVe siècles." In Philippe Contamine *et al.* (eds), *Guerre et société en France, en Angleterre et en Bourgogne. XIVe–XVe Siècle.* Lille: Centre d'histoire de la region du nord et de l'Europe du nord-ouest, 1991.

Ayton, Andrew. "Edward III and the English Aristocracy at the Beginning of the Hundred Years War." In Matthew Strickland (ed.), *Armies, Chivalry and Warfare in Medieval Britain and France.* Stamford: Paul Watkins Publishing, 1998.

Ayton, Andrew. "English Armies in the Fourteenth Century." In Anne Curry and Michael Hughes (eds), *Arms, Armies and Fortifications in the Hundred Years War.* Woodbridge: The Boydell Press, 1994. [Also reprinted in Rogers, *Wars of Edward III.*]

Ayton, Andrew. "The English Army and the Normandy Campaign of 1346." In D. Bates and A. Curry (eds), *England and Normandy in the Middle Ages.* London: Hambledon Press, 1987.

Ayton, Andrew. *Knights and Warhorses: Military Service and the English Aristocracy under Edward III.* Woodbridge: The Boydell Press, 1994.

Babinet, L. "Étude de la bataille de Poitiers-Maupertuis (19 septembre 1356)." *Bulletin de la Société des Antiquaires de l'Ouest,* 2nd ser., 3 (1883).

Baldwin, James F. "Early Records of the King's Council." *American Historical Review* 11 (1905), 1–15.

Balfour-Melville, E. W. M. *Edward III and David II.* London: George Philip & Son, 1954.

Barber, Richard. *Edward, Prince of Wales and Aquitane.* London: Allen Lane, 1978.

Barnes, Joshua. *The History of the Most Victorious Monarch Edward IIId etc.* Cambridge, 1688.

Barnie, John. *War in Medieval English Society: Social Values in the Hundred Years War 1337–99.* Ithaca, NY: Cornell U.P., 1974.

Barrow, Geoffrey W. S. *Robert Bruce and the Community of the Realm of Scotland,* Third Edition. Edinburgh: Edinburgh University Press, 1988.

Bean, J. M. W. "The Percies and their Estates in Scotland." *Archaeologia Aeliana,* 4th ser., 35 (1957).

Bean, R. "War and the Birth of the Nation State." *Journal of Economic History* 33 (1973).

Bennett, Matthew. "The Development of Battle Tactics in the Hundred Years War." In Anne Curry and Michael Hughes (eds), *Arms, Armies and Fortifications in the Hundred Years War.* Woodbridge: The Boydell Press, 1994.

Bertrand de la Grassière, Paul. *La chevalier au vert lion. Le maréchal de France Robert Bertrand, etc.* Paris: Promotion et Édition, 1969.

Borderie, A. le Moyne de la. *Histoire de Bretagne.* Rennes, 1905–1914.

Bossuat, R. *et al. Dictionnaire des Lettres Françaises. Le Moyen Âge,* revised edn. Paris: Fayard, 1992.

Boutruche, R. *La Crise d'une société: seigneurs et paysans du Bordelais pendant la Guerre de Cent Ans.* Paris: Publications de la Faculté des Lettres de l'Université de Strasbourg, 1947.

Boutruche, R. "The Devastation of Rural Areas During the Hundred Years War and the Agricultural Recovery of France." In P. S. Lewis (ed.), *The Recovery of France in the Fifteenth Century.* New York: Harper & Row, 1972.

Bradbury, Jim. *The Medieval Archer.* Woodbridge: The Boydell Press, 1985.

Bradbury, Jim. *The Medieval Siege.* Woodbridge: The Boydell Press, 1992.

Breuils, A. "Jean I, comte d'Armagnac." *Revue des questions historiques* 59 (1896).

Burne, Alfred H. *The Crecy War.* London: Eyre & Spottiswoode, 1955. Reprint, Greenhill Books, 1990.

Campbell, J. "England, Scotland and the Hundred Years' War in the Fourteenth Century." In J. R. Hale *et al.* (eds), *Europe in the Middle Ages.* London: Faber & Faber, 1965. [Also reprinted in Rogers, *Wars of Edward III.*]

Cazelles, R. *La Société politique et la crise de la royauté sous Philippe de Valois.* Paris: Librairie d'Argences, 1958.

Cheney, C. R. *Handbook of Dates for Students of British Chronology.* London: Royal Historical Society, 1991.

Clausewitz, Carl von. *Vom Kriege.* Reinbek bei Hamburg: Rowohlt, 1987.

Clausewitz, Carl von. *Vom Kriege.* Ed. W. Hahlweg. Bonn: Ferd. Dümmlers Verlag, 1952. [Citations are to this edition unless otherwise noted.]

Contamine, Philippe. *La France aux XIVe et XVe siècles. Hommes, mentalités, guerre et paix.* London: Valorium Reprints, 1981.

Contamine, Philippe. *Guerre, état et société à la fin du moyen âge. Études sur les armées des rois de France, 1337–1494.* Paris: Mouton, 1972.

Contamine, Philippe. *La guerre de Cent ans.* Paris: Presses Universitaires de France, 1972.

Contamine, Philippe *et al.* (eds) *Guerre et société en France, en Angleterre et en Bourgogne. XIVe–XVe Siècle.* Lille: Centre d'histoire de la région du nord et de l'Europe du nord-ouest, 1991.

Contamine, Philippe. *War in the Middle Ages*, tr. Michael Jones. Oxford: Basil Blackwell, 1987.

Curry, Anne and Michael Hughes. *Arms, Armies and Fortifications in the Hundred Years War.* Woodbridge: The Boydell Press, 1994.

Cuttino, G. P. *English Medieval Diplomatic Administration, 1259–1339*, 2nd edn. Oxford: Clarendon, 1971.

Cuttino, G. P. "Historical Revision: The Causes of the Hundred Years' War." *Speculum* 31 (1956).

Cuttino, G. P. "The Process of Agen." *Speculum* 19 (1944).

Daumet, G. *Étude sur l'alliance de la France et de la Castille aux XIVe et XVe siècles.* Paris: Bibliothèque de l'École des hautes études, 1898.

Delachenal, R. "Premières négociations de Charles le Mauvais avec les Anglais (1354–1355)." *Bibliothèque de l'École des chartes* 61 (1900).

Delachenal, Roland. *Histoire de Charles V.* Paris: Alphonse Picard & Fils, 1909 etc.

Denifle, Henri [Heinrich]. *La désolation des églises, monastères et hôpitaux en France pendant la guerre de Cent ans.* Paris, 1899.

Déprez, Eugène. "La Conférence d'Avignon (1344)." In A. G. Little and F. M. Powicke (eds), *Essays in Medieval History Presented to Thomas Frederick Tout.* Manchester: Manchester U.P., 1925.

Déprez, Eugène. *Les préliminaires de la guerre de Cent ans: La papauté, la France et l'Angleterre (1328–1342).* Paris, 1902. Reprint, Geneva: Slatkin, 1975.

DeVic, C. and J. Vaissette. *Histoire Générale de Languedoc*, vol. 9, with annotations by Auguste Molinier. Toulouse: Privat, 1885.

DeVries, Kelly R. "Contemporary Views of Edward III's Failure at the Siege of Tournai, 1340." *Nottingham Medieval Studies* 39 (1995).

DeVries, Kelly R. "Hunger, Flemish Participation and the Flight of Philip VI: Contemporary Accounts of the Siege of Calais, 1346–47." *Studies in Medieval and Renaissance History*, n.s. 12 (1991).

DeVries, Kelly R. *Infantry Warfare in the Early Fourteenth Century.* Woodbridge: The Boydell Press, 1996.

Duncan, A. A. M. "The War of the Scots, 1306–1323." *Transactions of the Royal Historical Society* 6th ser., 2 (1992).

Duncan, A. A. M. "*Honi soit qui mal y pense:* David II and Edward III, 1346–52." *Scottish Historical Review* 67 (1988).

Emerson, Barbara. *The Black Prince.* London: Weidenfeld and Nicolson, 1976.

Evans, D. L. "Some Notes on the Principality of Wales in the Time of the Black Prince, 1343–76." *Transactions of the Honourable Society of Cymmrodorion* (1925–6).

Favier, Jean. *La guerre de Cent ans.* Paris: Fayard, 1980.

Favreau, R. *La Ville de Poitiers à la fin du moyen âge: Une capitale régionale* (*Mémoires de la société des antiquaires de l'ouest*, 4th ser., 14). Poitiers: Société des antiquaires de l'Ouest, 1977–8.

Fournier, G. "La défense des populations rurales pendant la guerre de Cent ans en Basse-Auvergne." *Actes du quatre-vingt dixième congrès national des sociétés savantes (Nice, 1965), section d'archéologie.* Paris, 1966.

Fowler, Kenneth. *The Age of Plantagenet and Valois.* New York: Putnam, 1967.

Fowler, Kenneth (ed.) *The Hundred Years War.* London: Macmillan, 1971.

Fowler, Kenneth. *The King's Lieutenant: Henry of Grosmont, First Duke of Lancaster, 1310–1361.* London: Elek, 1969.

Fowler, Kenneth. "News from the Front: Letters and Despatches of the Fourteenth Century." In Philippe Contamine *et al.* (eds), *Guerre et société en France, en Angleterre et en Bourgogne. XIVe–XVe Siècle.* Lille: Centre d'histoire de la region du nord et de l'Europe du nord-ouest, 1991.

Fowler, Kenneth. "Truces." In Kenneth Fowler (ed.), *The Hundred Years War.* London: Macmillan, 1971.

Fryde, E. B. "Edward III's Wool Monopoly of 1337." *History* 37 (1952).

Fryde, E. B. "Parliament and the French War, 1336–40." In T. A. Sandquist and M. R. Powicke (eds), *Essays in Medieval History Presented to Bertie Wilkinson.* Toronto: University of Toronto Press, 1969.

Fryde, E. B. *William de la Pole. Merchant and King's Banker.* London: Hambledon Press, 1988.

Fryde, Natalie M. "Edward III's Removal of his Ministers and Judges, 1340–1341." *Bulletin of the Inst. of Historical Research* 48 (1975).

Fuller, J. F. C. *The Decisive Battles of the Western World*, ed. John Terraine. London: Granada, 1970.

Galbraith, V. H. "The Battle of Poitiers." *English Historical Review* 59 (1939).

Gillingham, John. "Richard I and the Science of War in the Middle Ages." In J. Gillingham and J. C. Holt (eds), *War and Government in the Middle Ages.* Woodbridge: The Boydell Press, 1984.

Given-Wilson, C. "The King and the Gentry in Fourteenth-Century England." *Transactions of the Royal Historical Society*, 5th ser., 37 (1987).

Greimas, A. J. *Dictionnaire de l'ancien Français*, 2nd edn. Paris: Larousse, 1982.

Haines, Roy M. "An English Archbishop and the Cerberus of War." In W. J. Sheils (ed.), *The Church and War.* London: Ecclesiastical History Society/Basil Blackwell, 1983.

Haines, Roy Martin. *Archbishop John Stratford: Political Revolutionary and Champion of the Liberties of the English Church, ca. 1275/80–1348.* Toronto: Pontifical Institute, 1986.

Hale, J. R. *War and Society in Renaissance Europe 1450–1620.* London: Fontana, 1985.

Hallam, Elizabeth M. *Capetian France, 987–1328.* New York: Longman, 1980.

Halle, Edward. *The Union of the Two Noble Families of Lancaster and York.* Reprint, Menston: Scolar Press, 1970.

Handbook of British Chronology, Third Edition, ed. E. B. Fryde *et al.* Cambridge: Cambridge U.P., 1996.

Hardy, Robert. "The Longbow." In Anne Curry and Michael Hughes (eds), *Arms, Armies and Fortifications the Hundred Years War.* Woodbridge: The Boydell Press, 1994.

Hardy, Robert. *Longbow: A Social and Military History.* Cambridge: Patrick Stephens, 1976.

Harriss, G. L. *King, Parliament and Public Finance in Medieval England to 1369.* Oxford: Clarendon, 1975.

Harriss, G. L. "The Formation of Parliament, 1272–1377." In R. G. Davies (ed.), *The English Parliament in the Middle Ages.* Manchester: Manchester U.P., 1981.

Harriss, G. L. "War and the Emergence of the English Parliament, 1297–1360." *Journal of Medieval History* 2 (1976). [Also reprinted in Rogers, *Wars of Edward III.*]

Hay, D. "Booty in Border Warfare." *Transactions of the Dumfriesshire and Galloway Natural History and Antiquarian Society*, 3rd ser., 31 (1954).

Hay, D. "The Divisions of the Spoils of War in Fourteenth Century England." *Transactions of the Royal Historical Society*, 5th ser., 4 (1953).

Henneman, J. B. *Royal Taxation in Fourteenth Century France: The captivity and ransom of John II.* Philadelphia: American Philosophical Society, 1976.

Hewitt, H. J. *The Black Prince's Expedition of 1355–1357.* Manchester: Manchester U.P., 1958.

Hewitt, H. J. "The Organisation of War." In Kenneth Fowler (ed.), *The Hundred Years War.* London: Macmillan, 1971. [Also reprinted in Rogers, *Wars of Edward III.*]

Hewitt, H. J. *The Organization of War Under Edward III 1338–62.* Manchester: Manchester U.P., 1966.

Hughes, D. *A Study of Social and Constitutional Tendencies in the Early Years of Edward III.* London: University of London Press, 1915.

Jeanjean, J. F. *La Guerre de Cent Ans en pays Audois. Incursion du Prince Noir en 1355.* Carcassonne: Imprimeries Gabelle, 1946.

Jones, Michael. "Edward III's Captains in Brittany." In W. M. Ormrod (ed.), *England in the Fourteenth Century: Proceedings of the Harlaxton Symposium.* Woodbridge: The Boydell Press, 1986.

Jones, Michael. "War and Fourteenth-Century France." In Anne Curry and Michael Hughes (eds), *Arms, Armies and Fortifications in the Hundred Years War.* Woodbridge: The Boydell Press, 1994. [Also reprinted in Rogers, *Wars of Edward III.*]

Jones, Michael C. "Les capitaines anglo-bretons et les marches entre la Bretagne et le Poitou de 1342 à 1373." In *La 'France Anglaise' au Moyen Age.* Paris: Editions du C.T.H.S., 1988.

Kaeuper, Richard W. *War, Justice and Public Order. England and France in the Later Middle Ages.* Oxford: Clarendon, 1988.

Keegan, John. *The Face of Battle.* New York: Penguin Books, 1984.

Keen, Maurice H. *Chivalry.* New Haven: Yale U.P., 1984.

Keen, Maurice H. *England in the Later Middle Ages.* London: Methuen, 1973.

Keen, Maurice H. *The Laws of War in the Late Middle Ages.* London: Routledge & Kegan Paul, 1965.

Labarge, Margaret Wade. *Gascony: England's First Colony, 1204–1453.* London: Hamish Hamilton, 1980.

Lampe, Karl. *Die Schlacht bei Maupertuis (19 September 1356).* Ph.D. dissertation, Friedrich-Wilhelms-Universität, 1908.

Larson, Alfred "English Embassies during the Hundred Years' War." *English Historical Review* 55 (1940).

Le Patourel, J. "Edward III and the Kingdom of France." *History* 43 (1958). [Also reprinted in Rogers, *Wars of Edward III.*]

Le Patourel, J. "The Origins of the War." In Kenneth Fowler (ed.), *The Hundred Years War.* London: Macmillan, 1971.

Le Patourel, J. "The Treaty of Bretigny, 1360." *Transactions of the Royal Historical Society*, 5th ser., 10 (1960).

Lewis, N. B. "The Organisation of Indentured Retinues in Fourteenth-Century England." *Transactions of the Royal Historical Society*, 4th ser., 27 (1944).

Liddell Hart, B. H. *Strategy* [revised edn]. New York: Praeger, 1954.

Lomas, Richard A. *North-East England in the Middle Ages.* Edinburgh: John Donald, 1992.

Lot, Ferdinand. *L'Art militarie et les armées au moyen âge.* Paris: Payot, 1946.

Louandre, F.-C. *L'histoire d'Abbeville et du comté de Ponthieu.* Abbeville & Paris, 1844.

Lucas, Henry S. "Edward III and the Poet Chronicler John Boendale." *Speculum* 12 (1937).

Lucas, Henry S. *The Low Countries and the Hundred Years War.* Ann Arbor: University of Michigan Press, 1929.

Lucas, Henry S. "The Machinery of Diplomatic Intercourse." In J. F. Willard *et al.* (eds), *The English Government at Work, 1327–1336.* New York: Medieval Academy of America, 1940.

Luce, Siméon. *La France pendant la Guerre de Cent Ans: épisodes historiques et vie privée.* Paris: Librarie Hachette, 1893.

Luce, Siméon. *Histoire de Bertrand du Guesclin et de son époque. La jeunesse de Bertrand, 1320–64.* Paris: Librairie Hachette, 1876.

Mas Latrie, L. de *Trésor de chronologie, d'histoire et de géographie pour l'étude et l'emploi des documents du moyen âge.* Paris: Victor Palmé, 1889.

McHardy, Alison K. "The English Clergy and the Hundred Years War." In W. J. Sheils (ed.), *The Church and War.* London: Ecclesiastical History Society/Basil Blackwell, 1983.

McKisack, May. *The Fourteenth Century, 1307–1399.* Oxford: Clarendon, 1959.

McNamee, Colm. *The Wars of the Bruces. Scotland, England and Ireland, 1306–1328.* East Linton: Tuckwell Press, 1997.

Ménard, L. *Histoire civile, ecclésiastique, et littéraire de la ville de Nîmes.* Nîmes, 1744–58.

Miller, Edward. *War in the North.* Hull: University of Hull Publications, 1960.

Mirot, L. and E. Déprez, "Les ambassades anglaises pendant la guerre de cent ans. Catalogue chronologique." *Bibliothèque de l'école des chartes,* 59 (1898), 60 (1899) [as corrected by Larson, "Embassies."]

Moisant, J. *Le Prince Noir en Aquitaine, 1355–6, 1362–70.* Paris: Picard, 1894.

Molinier, E. "Étude sur la vie d'Arnoul d'Audrehem, maréchal de France, 1300–1370." *Mémoires de la académie des inscriptions et belles-lettres,* 2nd ser., 6, part 1 (1883).

Mollat, G. "Innocent et les tentatives de paix entre la France et l'Angleterre (1353–1355)." *Revue d'histoire ecclésiastique* 10 (1909).

Moranvillé, H. "Le siège de Reims, 1359–60." *Bibliothèque de l'école des chartes* 56 (1895).

Morgan, Philip. *War and Society in Medieval Cheshire, 1277–1403.* Manchester: Chetham Society, 1987.

Morris, J. E. "Mounted Infantry in Medieval Warfare." *Transactions of the Royal Historical Society,* 3rd ser., 8 (1914).

Morris, John E. *The Welsh Wars of Edward I.* Oxford: Clarendon, 1901.

Mullot, Henry and Joseph Poux. "Nouvelles recherches sur l'itinéraire du Prince Noir à travers les pays de l'Aude." *Annales du Midi* 21 (1909).

Nicholson, Ranald. *Edward III and the Scots.* Oxford: Oxford U.P., 1965.

Nicholson, Ranald. *Scotland in the Later Middle Ages* (The Edinburgh History of Scotland, v. 2). Edinburgh: Oliver and Boyd, 1978.

Noël, R. P. R. "Town Defence in the French Midi during the Hundred Years War." Ph.D. dissertation, University of Edinburgh, 1977.

Offler, H. S. "England and Germany at the Beginning of the Hundred Years War." *English Historical Review* 54 (1939).

Oman, C. W. C. *A History of the Art of War in the Middle Ages.* London: Methuen, 1924.

Ormrod, W. M. "The Domestic Response to the Hundred Years War." In Anne Curry and Michael Hughes (eds), *Arms, Armies and Fortifications in the Hundred Years War.* Woodbridge: The Boydell Press, 1994.

Ormrod, W. M. "The Double Monarchy of Edward III." *Medieval History* 1 (1991).

Ormrod, W. M. "The Personal Religion of Edward III." *Speculum* 64 (1989).

Palmer, John. "The War Aims of the Protagonists and the Negotiations for Peace." In Kenneth Fowler (ed.), *The Hundred Years War.* London: Macmillan, 1971.

The Parliamentary or Constitutional History of England v.1. London: Printed for J. & R. Tonson & A. Millar, 1762.

Perroy, Edward. "France, England and Navarre from 1359–1364." *Bulletin of the Inst. of Historical Research* 13 (1935–6).

Perroy, Edouard. *The Hundred Years War,* tr. W.B. Wells. New York: Capricorn Books, 1965.

Plaisse, André. *À Travers le Cotentin. La Grande chevauchée guerrière d'Édouard III en 1346.* Cherbourg: Editions Isoète [December] 1994.

Prentout, Henri. *La Prise de Caen par Edouard III, 1346.* Caen: Henri Delesques, 1904. (Extrait des *Mémoires de l'Academie nationale des Sciences, Arts et Belles-Lettres de Caen,* 1904.)

Prestwich, Michael. *Armies and Warfare in the Middle Ages. The English Experience.* New Haven: Yale University Press, 1996.

Prestwich, Michael. "*Miles in Armis Strenuus:* The Knight at War." *Transactions of the Royal Historical Society,* 6th ser., 6 (1996).

Prestwich, Michael. *The Three Edwards: War and the State in England 1272–1377.* London: Weidenfeld and Nicholson, 1980.

Prince, A. E. "The Army and Navy." In J. F. Willard *et al.* (eds), *The English Government at Work, 1327–1336.* New York: Medieval Academy of America, 1940.

Prince, A. E. "The Importance of the Campaign of 1327." *English Historical Review* 50 (1935).

Prince, A. E. "The Indenture System under Edward III." In J. G. E. Edwards *et al.* (eds), *Historical Essays in Honour of James Tait.* Manchester: Printed for the subscribers, 1937.

Prince, A. E. "The Payment of Army Wages in Edward III's Reign." *Speculum* 19 (1944).

Prince, A. E. "The Strength of English Armies in the Reign of Edward III." *English Historical Review* 46 (1931).

Ramsay, Sir J. H. *Revenues of the Kings of England, 1066–1399. Volume II: Edward I–Richard II.* Oxford: Clarendon, 1925.

Reid, R. C. "Edward de Balliol." *Transactions of the Dumfriesshire and Galloway . . . Antiquarian Society,* 3rd ser., 35 (1956–7).

Rogers, Clifford J. "The Anglo-French Peace Negotiations, 1353–1360: A Reconsideration." In James Bothwell (ed.), *The Age of Edward III.* York: York Medieval Press, forthcoming 2001.

Rogers, Clifford J. "By Fire and Sword: *Bellum Hostile* and 'Civilians' in the Hundred Years War." In Mark Grimsley and Clifford J. Rogers (eds), *Civilians in the Path of War*. Lincoln: University of Nebraska Press, forthcoming.

Rogers, Clifford J. "Edward III and the Dialectics of Strategy, 1327–60." *Transactions of the Royal Historical Society*, 6th ser., 4 (1994). [Also reprinted in Rogers, *Wars of Edward III*.]

Rogers, Clifford J. "The Efficacy of the English Longbow: A Reply to Kelly DeVries." *War in History* 5 (1998).

Rogers, Clifford J. "The Military Revolutions of the Hundred Years' War." *The Journal of Military History* 57 (April 1993). Reprinted with revisions in C. J. Rogers (ed.), *The Military Revolution Debate*. Boulder: Westview, 1995. [References in the notes are to the latter.]

Rogers, Clifford J. "The Offensive/Defensive in Medieval Strategy." *From Crécy to Mohács: Warfare in the Late Middle Ages (1346–1526). Acta of the XXIInd Colloquium of the International Commission of Military History (Vienna, 1996)*. Vienna: Heeresgeschichtlichen Museum/Militärhistorisches Institut, 1997.

Rogers, Clifford J. "The Scottish Invasion of 1346." *Northern History* 34 (1998).

Rogers, Clifford J. (ed.) *The Wars of Edward III: Sources and Interpretations*. Woodbridge: Boydell & Brewer, 1999.

Roncière, Charles de la. *Histoire de la Marine Française. I. Les origines*. 2nd edn. Paris: Plon-Nourrit, 1909.

Rorschach, M. E. "Les Quatres Journées du Prince Noir dans la viguerie de Toulouse." *Académie des sciences, inscriptions et belles-lettres de Toulouse*, 10th ser., vol. 5 (1906).

Russell, F. H. *The Just War in the Middle Ages*. Cambridge: Cambridge U.P., 1975.

Scammell, J. "Robert I and the North of England." *English Historical Review* 73 (1958).

Scott, Ronald McNair. *Robert the Bruce*. New York: Peter Bedrick, 1989.

Smail, R. C. "Art of War." In A. L. Poole (ed.), *Medieval England*. Oxford: Clarendon Press, 1958.

Sumption, Jonathan. *The Hundred Years War, v. 1: Trial by Battle*. London: Faber and Faber, 1990.

TeBrake, William H. *A Plague of Insurrection*. Philadelphia: University of Pennsylvania Press, 1993.

Templeman, G. "Edward III and the beginnings of the Hundred Years War." *Transactions of the Royal Historical Society*, 5th ser., 2 (1952) [Also reprinted in Rogers, *Wars of Edward III*.]

Terry, S. *The Financing of the Hundred Years War, 1337–1350*. London: LSE, 1914.

Tierney, Brian, and Sidney Painter. *Western Europe in the Middle Ages, 300–1475*, 4th edn. New York: Knopf, 1983.

Tourneur-Aumont, J. M. *La Bataille de Poitiers (1356) et la construction de la France*. Paris: Presses Universitaires de France, 1940.

Tout, T. F. "Some Neglected Fights between Crécy and Poitiers." *English Historical Review* 20 (1905).

Trautz, Fritz. *Die Könige von England und das Reich, 1272–1377*. Heidelberg: Carl Winter, 1961.

Tuck, J. A. "War and Society in the Medieval North." *Northern History* 21 (1985).

Tyerman, C. J. *England and the Crusades, 1095–1588*. Chicago: University of Chicago Press, 1988.

Tyerman, C. J. "Philip VI and the Recovery of the Holy Land." *English Historical Review* 100 (1985).

Vale, J. *Edward III and Chivalry*. Woodbridge: The Boydell Press, 1982.

Vale, M. G. A. "The Anglo-French Wars, 1294–1340: Allies and Alliances." In Philippe Contamine *et al.* (eds), *Guerre et société en France, en Angleterre et en Bourgogne. XIVe–XVe Siècle.* Lille: Centre d'histoire de la region du nord et de l'Europe du nord-ouest, 1991.

Vale, M. G. A. *The Origins of the Hundred Years War. The Angevin Legacy, 1250–1340*, 2nd edn. Oxford: Clarendon, Paperbacks 1996.

Verbruggen, J. F. *The Art of Warfare in Western Europe During the Middle Ages. From the Eighth Century to 1340*, tr. S. Willard and R. W. Southern. 2nd edn. Woodbridge: The Boydell Press, 1997.

Viard, Jules. "La Campagne de juillet-août 1346 et la bataille de Crécy." *Moyen Âge* 2e. sér., 27 (1926).

Viard, J. "Itinéraire de Philippe VI de Valois." *Bibliothèque de l'école des chartes* 74 (1913), 84 (1923).

Viard, J. "Le siège de Calais: 4 septembre 1346–4 août 1347." *Moyen Âge* 2e sér., 30 (1929).

Waugh, Scott L. *England in the Reign of Edward III*. Cambridge: Cambridge U.P., 1991.

Willard, J. F. "The Scotch Raids and the Fourteenth-Century Taxation of Northern England." *University of Colorado Studies* 5 (1908).

Wright, N. "Ransoms of Non-combatants during the Hundred Years War." *Journal of Medieval History* 17 (1991).

INDEX

Abbeville   262–264, 403
Aberdeen   77, 118
Acheu   262
Agace, Gobin   263n
Agen   288n, 290, 292n, 305n, 329
   Process of   90, 95
Agenais   88–89, 92, 95, 105, 229, 288, 292n,
   294, 305, 353, 387–388, 419
Agnes, Countess of March ("Black Agnes")
   151
Aiguillon   220–225, 225n, 227, 242, 283,
   294, 305, 329
Airaines   262
Aisne   405–406
Albret, Bérard   159, 314n
Alençon, Charles of (Count of Alençon)
   29, 270, 284
Alfonso, King of Castile   140–141, 140n
Alquines   297
Alsace-Lorraine   419
Alzonne   312
Amblainville   395
Amboise   355
   Lord of   398
Ami, Guillaume   213
Amiens   254, 256n, 262, 297, 299, 393, 395,
   403
Angoulême, Angoumois   388, 419
Angus   83
Angus, Earls of see Umfraville, Gilbert
   (English, 1331–1381); Stewart, Thomas
   (Scottish, 1344–1368)
Anjou   291, 329, 388, 390, 398–399, 418
   Count of see Louis
Annan   57
Annan (River)   97n
Annandale   75, 112n
Antoing   188–189
Antwerp   151, 154, 159,210
Appatis (*patis*, ransoms of places, protection
   treaties)   11, 24, 25n, 288, 311–313, 313n,
   314n, 315n, 330, 407, 409, 411
Appleby-in-Westmorland   17
Aquitaine, Guienne   2, 29, 87–96, 123–124,
   127–130, 140–141, 159–160, 218, 280,
   291, 294, 305, 307n, 326, 329–330, 330,
   350, 355, 388, 388n, see also Gascony

not primary *causus belli*   77, 87–88,
   102–103, 113–114; *see also* Franco-
   Scottish Alliance *but see*   218
Arbroath   47
   Delcaration of   10, 10n, 54
Ardres   279n, 288, 297
Argency   342
Argentan   347n
Ariège   310
Arleux   131, 133
Armagnac   305–308
Armagnac, Jean Count of   164, 201–202, 247,
   290n, 291–292, 292n, 294, 305–310, 305n,
   312, 314, 317, 319–322, 321n, 330–331,
   352
Armentières   188
Arouille   307
Arpajon   393, 395
Arques   200, 202
Arras   204, 209, 332, 402–403
Array, Commissions of Array, Arrayed Troops
   82, 84, 85–86, 203n, 425n
Artevelde, Jacques van   179–183, 188–190,
   199, 210, 213–214, 226; *see also* Flanders
Artois   164, 200, 288
Artois, Robert of   77, 93n, 114, 114n,
   123–124, 124n, 125n, 130, 132n, 159, 175,
   200–202, 214, 226
Arundel, Earl of see FitzAlan.
Astarac   308
Athens, Duke of see Brienne, Gautier de
Athis-sur-Orgue, Treaty of (1305)   180n, 182,
   215
Atholl   83
Atholl, Earls of see Strathbogie, David
   (English); Campbell, John (Scottish, d. at
   Halidon, 1333); Douglas, William
   (Scottish, 1335–1342)
atte Woode, William   425
Attigny   406, 409
Aubenton   189
Auberchicourt, Eustache   406, 409–410
Auberoche   344
Aubian   316
Aubigny   355–356
Auch   322
Auchterarder   38